Dana

flying visits
FRANCE

CADOGANguides

Contents

About the authors

A huge fan of French cities, which seem to him light years ahead of British ones and serious rivals to their Italian counterparts, **Philippe Barbour** is delighted to see this new Cadogan guide published, featuring many of France's finest towns, now so much easier to reach. He is he author of several other guides for Cadogan, including their *Brittany* and *Loire*, and is co-author of the Cadogan *France* guide.

Dana Facaros and **Michael Pauls** have written over 30 books for Cadogan Guides, including all the Italy and Spain series, and the Cadogan Guides *Paris*, *South of France*, *Dordogne and the Lot*, and *Gascony and the Pyrenees*. They have lived all over Europe, but have recently settled in a farmhouse in the Lot Valley.

Acknowledgements

Philippe Barbour extends special thanks to **Norfolkline** for organizing a ferry trip at short notice, and to all the **tourist authorities** who helped complete this project so swiftly.

The publishers would like to thank **Jacqueline Chnéour** for consultancy, research, updating and French proofreading.

Cadogan Guides
165 The Broadway,
Wimbledon, London
SW19 1NE, UK
info.cadogan@virgin.net
www.cadoganguides.com

The Globe Pequot Press
246 Goose Lane, PO Box 480, Guilford,
Connecticut 06437–0480, USA

Copyright © Philippe Barbour, Dana Facaros
and Michael Pauls 2003

Cover design by Jodi Louw
Book design by Andrew Barker
Cover photographs by OLIVIA and John Miller
Maps © Cadogan Guides,
    drawn by Map Creation Ltd
Managing Editor: Christine Stroyan
Series Editor: Linda McQueen
Design: Sarah Gardner
Proofreading: Sheilagh Wilson and Jacqueline
    Chnéour
Indexing: Isobel McLean
Production: Navigator Guides Ltd

Printed in Italy by Legoprint
A catalogue record for this book is available
    from the British Library
ISBN 1-86011-895-X

Introduction
and Themes

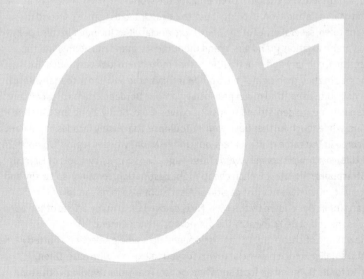

Suddenly, a host of new cheap flights to France has put a whole range of brilliant French cities just a stone's throw from Britain, ideal for a long weekend or a short break, a flying visit, if you like...or of course more, should you find that you've fallen for one of the destinations and decide to snap up a bargain French property.

Many people think automatically of France as a country of great countryside, of great villages, of great coastlines, of great resorts. But many people don't realize what a country of great cities it is. While foreign tourists flock to the towns of Italy, they've tended to bypass the splendid towns of France up until now. That's set to change. *Flying Visits France* is the new Cadogan guide to French destinations you can reach from Britain in just one journey, without any changes. We don't ignore the old Channel port favourites, but we also want to encourage you to appreciate the many French cities made so much easier to reach by the flowering of cheap flights from Buzz and Ryanair among others. They include many of France's regional capitals, absolutely bursting with civic pride, and far too little known.

Paris has hogged the limelight for too long among French cities, although we just didn't have the heart to leave it out here. However, many of France's finest provinicial towns feature alongside it in these pages. Do you realize, for example, that such cities as Marseille or Lyon, the two largest towns in France after Paris, are sensational places, with civilizations going back much further than that of the French capital? **Marseille**'s breathtaking hills rise dramatically above the glittering Mediterranean corniche, on a glorious bay that seduced the Phoenicians into settling some 2,600 years ago, creating the first-ever French city. In **Lyon**, Roman theatres peer down impe-riously from Fourvière hill on to the posh Presqu'île peninsula, recalling the fact that this city was far more important than little Lutetia on the Seine in Gaulish times. Out east lie the spacious Lyonnais quarters where, in the 19th century, the Lumière brothers brought about the birth of cinema for the world.

Beyond Marseille and Lyon, battling it out to be regarded as France's second most important town, several other of the French provincial cities included in this book have the grand location, grand airs, grand monuments, grand museums, and the grand cultural, culinary and café traditions that make them look very much like capital cities in their own right. Their grandeur may come as a shock to many British visitors not quite used to so much provincial glamour. **Bordeaux**'s amazing crescent of Ancien Régime, golden-stoned mansions curves majestically along the Garonne in Aquitaine, while much further upstream, in **Toulouse**, the stately façades in pink brick are reflected in the same river's waters, only in the Midi-Pyrénées region. Up north, in central **Lille**, vast towers soar skywards from huge civic squares, symbols of Flemish pride. **Strasbourg**, the latest French cheap-flight destination, certainly isn't a shy and retiring place, nowadays not just capital of Alsace, but also joint-capital of the European Union. Back down by the Med, **Nice**, beloved of so many artists of the 20th century, is the self-styled capital of the glamorous French Riviera.

The new range of cheap flights has also opened up a whole selection of utterly delightful smaller French provincial towns for you to explore with ease. **Dijon**, acclaimed for its Burgundian food and wine, boasts mansions dripping with stone fruit, while **Tours**, capital of the old province of Touraine, the Garden of France,

What to Go For...

	Art City	Architecture	Museums	Culture	Scenery	Beaches	Mountains	River Setting	Vineyards	Gastronomy	Shopping
Avignon	●	●	●	●				●	★	●	●
Bergerac		★	●		●			●	●	★	●
Biarritz				●		●					
Bordeaux	●	●	●	●	★	★			★	●	●
Brest			●		●	★					
Caen		●	●			★		★			
Calais						★					
Carcassonne		●	★		●		★				
Chambéry		●	●		●		★				
Cherbourg			●		●	★					
Dieppe						●					
Dijon	●	●	●						★	●	●
Dinard/St-Malo		●		●	●	●				●	●
Dunkerque						★					
Grenoble	●		●		●		★				
La Rochelle		●	●	●	●	★				●	●
Le Havre	●				●	●					
Lille	●	●	●	●						●	●
Limoges	●		●								●
Lyon	●	●	●	●	●			●	★	●	●
Marseille	●	●	●	●	●	●	★		★	●	●
Montpellier	●	★		●	★	★					
Nice	★		●	●	●	●					●
Nîmes	●	●	●			★					
Paris	●	●	●	●				●		●	●
Perpignan		●	●			★					
Poitiers			●	●							
Roscoff			●		●	●					
St-Etienne	●						★				
Strasbourg	●	●	●	●				●			
Toulon						★	●				
Toulouse	●	●	●	●				●		●	●
Tours	●	●	●	●	●			●		●	●

● In the gateway city itself   ★ Within easy reach of the gateway city

Culture = theatre, cinema, opera, etc. **Mountains** includes skiing **Beaches** includes watersports

lounges luxuriously by the Loire. **Poitiers**, home to Eleanor of Aquitaine's scandalous troubadour court, has preserved an extravagantly decorated medieval church to visit for every day of the week. Long-socialist **Limoges** looks attractively rugged in its tough granite, but its international reputation is, ironically, built on exquisite luxury goods, particularly enamels and porcelain.

Self-confident and very stylish **Montpellier**, by contrast, is capital of the vibrant modern Languedoc, but has to fight it out with near-neighbour **Nîmes** (sometimes honoured with the title of 'Rome of France' because of its classical legacy) for the title of most glamorous city of the region. **Grenoble** and **Chambéry**, both lively places too today, occupy spectacular Alpine locations. Chambéry played host for some time to an extraordinarily famous Christian shroud, until the dukes of Savoy had it moved it to Turin. **Avignon**, by contrast, found itself briefly elected the city of the popes instead of Rome in medieval times, and transformed at the same time into one of the most religious, but also one of the most notorious cities in Europe. If Avignon became the capital of the Catholic world for a time because of turbulent events in the 14th century, **La Rochelle** on France's Atlantic coast became the refuge and quasi-capital of the French Protestants, or Huguenots, as they suffered from terrible persecution from the second half of the 16th century on. They were brought to their knees by pitiless Cardinal Richelieu; but, thanks in good part to slave-trading, the merchant families became spectacularly wealthy once again, as the glorious arcaded town centre shows.

Of the other destinations we cover in the greater southwest, **Bergerac** and **Biarritz** have less troubled pasts, lying in delightful spots for a break, the one by the tranquil waters of the Dordogne river, close to tempting vineyards, the other by the bracing rollers of the Atlantic, beloved of surfers. As to **Carcassonne**, this most famous of fortified citadels is today besieged by nothing more offensive than tourists.

Four of the French cheap-flight destinations might be described as oddballs, sitting alongside such obviously appealing destinations. **Brest** and **Toulon** are France's two major naval ports, as such bombed to smithereens in the Second World War. But they both lie by sensational bays, and are great places from which to discover the Breton coast and the Côte d'Azur respectively. As to **Perpignan**, it stands close to the Med on the Spanish border and makes something of a song and dance of its bizarre connection with that weirdest of Iberian artists, Salvador Dali. **St-Etienne** may seem a bit lost on the edges of the Massif Central, but it could in fact serve as an easy gateway to the Rhône Valley and Provence, or to the sensational volcanic region of the Auvergne.

Back in more familiar waters, we cover the Channel ports that the British use in such huge numbers, from **Calais** and **Dunkerque** in the north, via the four Normandy ports, **Dieppe**, **Le Havre**, **Caen-Ouistreham** and **Cherbourg**, to the prettiest of the lot, the Breton destinations of **Roscoff** and **St-Malo**. The latter corsair city is paired with its wonderfully prim sister resort, **Dinard**.

We've divided all these various destinations into regional chapters, after Paris, working our way anticlockwise around France. For each destination, we've tried to evoke the spirit of the place, giving descriptions and explanations of the sights, monuments and museums, plus practical pages on where to stay, eat and shop. Then come suggestions for a **day trip** or two from the destination, or pehaps an **overnight stay**, with details on public transport for those without a car. Lastly, we've included a **five-day touring itinerary** for those of you who'd like to hire a car and spend a week exploring the area, gallivanting through the vineyards of Burgundy or Bordeaux, pottering round Provence or Languedoc, losing yourselves in peaceful Poitou or the Limousin, taking your time to visit war sites and cathedral cities in northern France and Normandy, or lounging on Basque or Breton beaches. We recommend many rather special hotels and restaurants on these itineraries, so we'd advise you try booking them some time in advance.

Travel and Practical A–Z

Travel

Getting There

By Air: the Lowdown on Low-cost Flights

Over the last few years the airline industry has undergone a revolution. Inspired by the success of Stelios Haji-Ioannou's 'upstart' easyJet company, many smaller airlines – Buzz, Ryanair, go, Bmibaby – flocked to join him in breaking all the conventions of air travel in a remarkable attempt to offer fares at rock-bottom prices. After September 11th, just when major carriers were hitting the ropes in a big way, these budget airlines experienced unprecedented sales and have responded by expanding their list of destinations throughout Europe; Buzz in particular has joined together with French regional tourist offices to promote its destinations as the latest place to holiday.

No Frills, No Thrills

The ways in which these low prices are achieved sometimes have a negative effect on the experience of the traveller, but sometimes can actually be a bonus. First, the airlines have made use of a range of **smaller regional airports**, where the landing-fees and tarmac-time charges to the airline are at a minimum: easyJet flies out of Luton and Liverpool as well as Gatwick; Ryanair, go and Buzz from Stansted (go from Bristol also); Bmibaby from East Midlands, and so on; and they land at France's smaller towns.

The **planes** are small and are all of the same type, which saves maintenance costs.

Fares are one-way – dispensing with the traditional need to stay over on a Saturday night to qualify for the lowest fares – and vary widely; easyJet sells each aircraft's seats in price blocks, for example, with the cheapest seats being sold first.

You will not be issued with a **ticket** when you book, and you will be encouraged, sometimes even by a price discount, to book on-line. Often you will not be issued with an **allocated seat** either, but will board on a first-come, first-served basis.

There are no 'air miles' schemes, no discounts on top of the low ticket price, and no formal **meal** will be served, though there will usually be snacks for sale on board. There are no refunds, though some of the companies will allow you to **change** your destination, date of travel or the named traveller for a fee of around £15. Note there are charges for **excess baggage**.

You may also notice that **staffing levels** are kept very low, at booking stage, in the air, and on the ground.

Airline Carriers
Air France, t 0845 0845 111, **f** (020) 8782 8115, *www.airfrance.co.uk.*
Bmibaby, t 0870 264 2229, *www.flybmi.com.* From East Midlands.
British Airways, t 0345 222 111, **f** (0161) 247 5707, *www.britishairways.com.*
British Midland, t 0870 6070 555, *www.british midland.com.*
Buzz, t 0870 240 7070, *www.buzzaway.com.* From Stansted.
easyJet, t 0870 600 0000, **f** (01582) 443355, *www.easyjet.com.* From Luton, Liverpool and Gatwick.
go, t 0845 605 4321, *www.easyjet.com.* From Stansted. Has merged with easyJet.
Ryanair, t 08701 569 569, *www.ryanair.com.* From Stansted and Glasgow.

What's the Worst that Can Happen?

From time to time the press ripples with stories of a 'holiday hell' caused by low-cost air travel, from people ending up a four-hour journey away from their destination, because of falsely advertised destinations (Malmö as Copenhagen, Brescia as Verona), to lost baggage with no one to look for it, to queues and cancellations and so many hidden extras – taxes, supplements, expensive food, travel to and from outlying airports – that it would have been cheaper to travel by private jet. There are no 'spare' planes, so if one breaks down, the day's schedules tend to collapse like a house of cards, although, surprisingly, the punctuality record of the budget airlines is no worse than that of major carriers.

Who Goes Where?

	page	Ryanair	Buzz	easyJet/go	bmiBaby	Brittany Ferries	Condor ferries	Hoverspeed	Norfolkline	P&O Portsmouth	P&O Stena	Transmanche	SeaFrance	Eurostar
Avignon	308													•
Bergerac	193		•											
Biarritz	212	•												
Bordeaux	200		•											
Brest	142		•											
Caen	100					•								
Calais	47							•			•		•	
Carcassonne	254	•												
Chambéry	338		•											
Cherbourg	110					•				•				
Dieppe	79							•				•		
Dijon	355		•											
Dinard	124	•												
Dunkerque	51								•					
Grenoble	346		•											
La Rochelle	174		•											
Le Havre	87									•				
Lille	66													•
Limoges	184		•											
Lyon	319			•										
Marseille	296		•											
Montpellier	242	•												
Nice	275			•	•									
Nîmes	235	•												
Paris	27		•	•	•									•
Perpignan	264	•												
Poitiers	166		•											
Roscoff	134					•								
St-Etienne	330	•												
St-Malo	119					•	•							
Strasbourg	364	•												
Toulon	288		•											
Toulouse	220		•		•									
Tours	153		•											

Getting to France cheaply from North America

US and Canadian citizens will be able to find flights direct to some of the larger French cities listed in this guide. But is also possible for North Americans to take advantage of the explosion of cheap inter-European flights, by taking a charter flight to London, and booking a London–France budget flight on the airline's website. This will need careful planning: you're looking at an 8hr flight followed by a 3hr journey across London and another 1½–2hr hop to France; it can be done, and you may be able to sleep on a night flight, but you may prefer to spend a night or two in London.

Direct to France

There are frequent flights to Paris, the gateway to France, on most of the major airlines. During off-peak periods (the winter months and fall) a scheduled economy flight from New York to Paris can be as little as around $370–$460, and a transfer to one of the regional airports (e.g. Bordeaux, Lyon, Marseille, Toulouse) an extra $100 or so. Delta flies regularly from New York to Nice, and in summer you may also be able to get non-stop charters to regional destinations.

Air France, 125 West 55th St, New York, NY 10019, t 800 237 2747, Canada t 800 667 2747, *www.airfrance.com*. Non-stop flights from New York to Lyon, daily flights to Paris from other US airports.

American Airlines, t 800 433 7300, *www.aa.com*.

British Airways, t 800 AIRWAYS, *www.britishairways.com*.

Continental, t 800 231 0856, Canada t 800 525 0280, *www.continental.com*.

Delta, t 800 241 4141, *www.delta.com*. Flights from Cincinnati and Atlanta to Paris, and regularly from New York to Nice.

Northwest Airlines, t 800 225 2525, *www.nwa.com*. Flights from Detroit to Paris.

Nouvelles Frontières, 6 East 46th St, New York, NY 10017, with branches on the West Coast and Canada, t 800 677 0720, t (212) 986 3343, *www.newfrontiers.com*. Discounted scheduled and charter flights on Corsair from LA, Oakland and New York to Paris, and non-stop to some French provincial cities.

TWA, t 800 892 4141, *www.twa.com*.
United Airlines, t 800 241 6522, *www.ual.com*.

Via London

Start by finding a cheap charter flight or discounted scheduled flight to London; check the Sunday paper travel sections for the latest deals, and if possible research your fare on some of the US cheap-flight websites: *www.priceline.com* (bid for tickets), *www.expedia.com*, *www.hotwire.com*, *www.bestfares.com*, *www.travelocity.com*, *www.eurovacations.com*, *www.cheaptrips.com*, *www.courier.com* (courier flights), *www.fool.com* (advice on booking over the net).

When you have the availablity and arrival times for possible London flights, match up a convenient flight time on the website of the budget airline that flies to your chosen French city (*see p.x*). *Be careful if using easyJet to opt for its flights from Luton, not Liverpool, and note also that Bmibaby's hub, East Midlands airport, is not near London and would be fairly impractical for a single day's journey.*

You will most likely be arriving at Heathrow terminals 3 or 4 (possibly Gatwick), and may be flying out from Stansted (Ryanair and Buzz), Luton (easyJet/go) or Gatwick (some easyJet flights), all of which are in different directions and will mean travelling through central London, so leaving enough time is essential. Add together the journey times and prices for Heathrow into central London and back out again to your departure airport. You could mix and match – the Tube to Victoria and the Gatwick Express, or a taxi from Heathrow to King's Cross Thameslink and a train to Luton – but don't even think of using a bus or taxi at rush hours (7–10am and 4–7pm); train and/or Underground (Tube) are the only sensible choices. Always add on waiting times and delays in London's notoriously creaky transport system; and finally, although the cheapest budget airline fares are early morning and late at night, make sure your chosen transport is still operating.

Airport to Airport Taxis

A taxi directly between airports might avoid central London but is an expensive option:
Heathrow–Gatwick: 1hr 30mins, £85–100.
Heathrow–Stansted: 2hrs 15mins, £140–160.
Heathrow–Luton: 1hr 15mins, £80–90.

Heathrow

Heathrow is about 15 miles west of the centre. **Airport information: t** 0870 0000 123.

By Tube: Heathrow is on the Piccadilly Line. Tube trains depart every 5–9 minutes from 6am to midnight and the journey time to the centre is 55 minutes. A single fare into the city centre costs £3.60.

By bus: The Airbus A2 (**t** 0870 575 7747) departs from all terminals every 30 minutes and makes several stops before terminating at King's Cross. Tickets cost £8 single. It's a long ride: at least 1hr 45mins.

By train: The Heathrow Express is the fastest option: trains every 15mins between 5.10am and 11.40pm to Paddington Station, which is on the Tube's Bakerloo, Circle and District Lines, taking 15mins. Tickets cost £13 single.

By taxi: There are taxi ranks at all terminals. Fares into central London are about £35–50.

Gatwick

Gatwick is about 20 miles south of London. There are two terminals, North and South, linked by a shuttle service. **Airport information: t** 0870 000 2468.

By train: The fastest service is the Gatwick Express (**t** 0870 530 1530), which runs from Victoria Station to the South Terminal to every 15 minutes and takes about 30mins. Tickets cost £11 for a single. There are two other slower train services: another from Victoria, and one from London Bridge.

By taxi: Fares from central London with a black cab are about £40–60.

Luton

30 miles north of London. **Airport information: t** (01582) 405 100.

By bus: Greenline bus 757 (**t** 0870 608 7261) runs roughly every half-hour between Luton Airport and stop 6 in Buckingham Palace Road, Victoria, via Marble Arch. Tickets cost £7 single. The journey takes 1hr 15mins.

By train: Between 8am and 10pm, Thameslink (**t** 0845 330 6333) run frequent trains from King's Cross Thameslink Station (10 mins' walk from the King's Cross Station), via Blackfriars, London Bridge and Farringdon, to Luton Airport Parkway. Tickets cost £10 single. At Luton a free shuttle bus takes you on to the airport; the journey takes 55mins.

By taxi: A black cab will cost you around £40–60 from central London.

Stansted

Stansted is the furthest from London, about 35 miles to the northeast. **Airport information: t** 0870 000 0303.

By bus: Airbus A6 and Jetlink coaches (**t** 0870 575 7747) run every 30mins from Victoria Station, Marble Arch and Hyde Park Corner, taking 1hr 40mins. There are less frequent services all night. Tickets cost £8 single.

By train: The Stansted Express (**t** 0870 530 1530) runs every 30mins (15mins during peak times) between 5am and 11pm to and from Liverpool Street Station, in the City, taking 45mins. Tickets cost £13 single.

By taxi: A black cab from central London will cost £45–65.

Waterloo Station (for the Eurostar)

By Tube: Waterloo is on the Jubilee, Bakerloo and Northern Underground lines (from Heathrow, change at Green Park, Piccadilly Circus or Leicester Square); the journey takes 55mins). The international Eurostar terminal is about a five-minute walk from the Tube platforms; just follow the signs.

By taxi: If you're taking a taxi to Waterloo from Heathrow (c. £50, allow 1hr 45mins), make sure to specify the international terminal.

Sample Journeys

Heathrow–Luton: get to Heathrow Express from terminal 15mins; wait for train 10mins; journey 15mins; go from Paddington Station down into Tube 10mins; Tube to Farringdon 15mins; go up and buy Thameslink ticket 10mins including queueing; train and shuttle to Luton 55mins. **Total journey time** 2hrs 10mins, plus 45mins for delays and hitches, so 3hrs would be safest.

Heathrow–Stansted: get to Tube station from terminal 10mins, wait for Tube 5mins, Piccadilly Line to King's Cross 1hr 10mins, change to Circle Line and continue to Liverpool Street Tube Station 15mins, up into main line station and buy Stansted Express ticket 10mins, wait for train 20mins, train journey 45mins. **Total journey time** 2hrs 55mins, plus 45mins for delays and hitches, so 3hrs 40mins would be safest.

Making it Work for You: 10 Tips to Remember

1 Whichever airline you are travelling with, the earlier you book, the cheaper the seats will be. EasyJet, for example, divides its planes into blocks, with the first 10% of seats sold at the lowest price.

2 Book on-line for the best prices, special offers, and often for a discount of between £2.50 and £5 per journey.

3 Be prepared to travel at less convenient times. Early morning and late evening flights will be the last to fill up. But ensure you check that there is a means of getting from your destination airport if you arrive in the evening, allowing for at least an hour's delay – will that force you to fork out for a taxi rather than a shuttle bus or local bus service, and does that eat up the saving you made by travelling late?

4 Think hard whether you want to book by credit card. You will have the consumer protection that offers, but there is likely to be a supplement of anything up to £5. Consider using a debit card instead.

5 Check whether airport taxes are included in the quoted price; they are usually extra.

6 If you intend to travel often and can go at short notice, sign up for the airlines' email mailing lists to hear news of special offers.

7 Check the baggage allowance and don't take any excess. If you can travel light, take hand baggage only because at some busier airports your airline will be low priority for the baggage handlers and this can cause a long wait.

8 Take your own food and drink (allowing for possible delays) if you want to avoid paying for overpriced airport food or unsatisfying snacks.

9 Make sure you take your booking reference and confirmation with you to check in. (This reference will have been emailed or posted to you.)

10 Never ignore the advised check-in times, which can vary from half an hour to two hours. Don't be tempted to cut it fine; if you arrive too late you won't be allowed on the plane even if it is visible on the tarmac, as cheap flights depend on the airline keeping boarding time short. If you care where you sit, or are travelling in a group, either check in even earlier (seats are often allocated at check-in), or go to the departure gate as early as possible to be ahead of the bunch.

Of course disasters can always happen, but an awareness of how the system works and exactly why the fares are cheap can go a long way to avoiding mishaps or being caught out – see the tips in the box above. And, while corners are cut in many ways, there is no evidence that these corners are anything to do with safety.

By Sea

The ferry is a good option if you're travelling by car or with young children from Britain (children of 4–14 get reduced rates; under-4s go free), if you want to nip across the Channel to do some shopping (it takes 35mins from Dover to Calais by seacat), or to visit the northern Normandy or Brittany coasts.

Fares can be expensive and do vary according to season and demand (these days, annoyingly, the brochures will only print a rough 'price guide'). The most expensive booking period runs from the first week of July to mid-August; other pricey times include Easter and the school holidays. You should try to book as far ahead as possible and keep your eyes peeled for special offers.

Some good-value five-day mini breaks for a car and up to nine people (Caen and Cherbourg from £65) and 10-day saver-breaks (Caen and Cherbourg from £88) are available. On many sailings, bicycles go free. You will have to pay extra to bring a motorcycle or a trailer.

Useful Numbers
Shopping information in Calais: t 08 39 40 15 77.
Weather forecast for France: t 08 91 57 55 77.

Ferry Operators

Brittany Ferries, The Brittany Centre, Wharf Road, Portsmouth PO2 8RU, t 08705 360 360, *www.brittanyferries.com*. Portsmouth to Caen (6hrs) and St-Malo, Poole to Cherbourg (4¼hrs), and Plymouth to Roscoff (6hrs).

Condor Ferries, The Quay, Weymouth, Dorset DT4 8DX, t (01305) 761551, *www.condor ferries.co.uk*. Weymouth and Poole to St-Malo.

Hoverspeed Ferries, Int'l Hoverport, Dover CT17 9TG, t 08705 240 241, f (01304) 240 088, *www.hoverspeed.co.uk*. Seacats Dover–Calais (35mins), Newhaven–Dieppe (2hrs).

Norfolkline, t (01304) 218 410, f (01304) 218 420, *www.norfolkline.com*. An alternative, often very good value option to consider between Dover and Dunkerque, but for cars only, not foot passengers.

P&O Portsmouth, Peninsular House, Wharf Rd, Portsmouth PO2 8TA, t 0870 242 4999, f (01705) 864 211, *www.poportsmouth.com*. Day and night sailings from Portsmouth to Le Havre (5½hrs) and Cherbourg.

P&O Stena Line, Channel House, Channel View Rd, Dover CT17 9TJ, t 0870 600 0600, f (01304) 863 464, *www.posl.com*. Ferry and superferry from Dover to Calais (45mins).

SeaFrance, Eastern Docks, Dover, Kent CT16 1JA, t 08705 711 711, f (01304) 240 033, *www.seafrance.com*. Sailings from Dover to Calais (1½hrs).

Transmanche Ferries, t 0800 917 1201, *www.transmancheferries.com*. A year-round ferry service to Dieppe from Newhaven; 3 crossings a day, journey time 4½–5hrs.

Taking Your Car to France

Eurotunnel and Beyond

Taking the **Eurotunnel** (t 0870 53 53 535, *www.eurotunnel.com*) shuttle service is the most convenient way to travel by car to France. It takes only 35 minutes from Folkestone to Calais. Shuttles through the Channel Tunnel in low season cost £169 for a standard return (much cheaper for a special day return) rising to around £200 at peak times, but can drop as low as £139 for a five-day mini-break.

If you're driving down through France from the tunnel, the various *autoroutes* will get you there the fastest but be prepared to pay high tolls. A fairly comfortable but costly option is to put your car on the train. Motorail accommodation is compulsory, in a 4-berth (1st class) or 6-berth (2nd class) carriage. Be warned that compartments are not segregated by sex. In the UK contact Rail Europe (*see above*) or **French Motorail**, t 08702 415 415. For help with insurance for travelling abroad, contact **Europ Assistance**, Sussex House, Perrymount Rd, Haywards Heath, West Sussex RH16 1DN, t (01444) 442211.

By Rail: Eurostar and TGV

Air prices and the frustrations of airports make travelling by high-speed train an attractive alternative. **Eurostar** (t 0990 186 186) trains leave from London Waterloo or Ashford International, in Kent, and there are direct connections to Paris (Gare du Nord; 3hrs; from £70) and Lille (2hrs; from £60). Eurostar also goes directly to Disneyland Paris (3hrs), and offers directly bookable connections to the French Alps and Avignon and many other destinations. Fares are cheaper if booked at least seven or fourteen days in advance and you include a Saturday night away. Check in 20mins before departure.

When they're not breaking world records, France's legendary TGVs (*trains à grande vitesse*) zip along at an average speed of 180mph. From Paris there are connections to many cities: the journey from Paris's Gare de Lyon to Marseille takes only 3hrs; to Dijon and Poitiers 3hrs; to Avignon 3hrs 35mins; to Montpellier 4hrs 25mins; to Nice 6hrs 30mins. Ticket prices from London range from £95 to Dijon, to £125 to Nice, Toulouse and Marseille.

Rail Europe (UK), 179 Piccadilly, London W1V 0BA, t 08705 848 848, *www.raileurope.co.uk*.

Rail Europe (USA), 226 Westchester Ave, White Plains, NY 10064, t 1 800 438 7245, *www.raileurope.com*. Take your passport.

Entry Formalities

Holders of full, valid EU, US and Canadian passports do not need a visa to enter France for stays of up to three months.

For longer stays a *carte de séjour* is a legal requirement, something EU citizens can easily get around as passports are rarely stamped. Non-EU citizens can apply for an extended visa before leaving home, a complicated procedure requiring proof of income, etc. You can't get a *carte de séjour* without the visa, and obtaining it is a trial run in the *ennuis* you'll undergo in applying for a *carte de séjour* at your local *mairie* in France.

Duty-free allowances have been abolished within the EU. For travellers from outside the EU, the duty-free limits are 1 litre of spirits or 2 litres of liquors (port, sherry or champagne), plus 2 litres of wine and 200 cigarettes.

Much larger quantities – up to 10 litres of spirits, 90 litres of wine, 110 litres of beer and 3,200 cigarettes – bought locally, can be taken through customs provided that you are travelling between EU countries, and can prove that they are for private consumption only.

For more information, US citizens can telephone the US Customs Service, **t** (202) 354 1000, or see the pamphlet *Know Before You Go* available from *www.customs.gov*. You're not allowed to take back absinthe or Cuban cigars to the USA.

Getting Around

By Train

The SNCF runs a decent and efficient network of trains through all the major cities. Prices have recently gone up but are still reasonable. The SNCF's France-wide information number is **t** 08 36 35 35 35, or check out *www.sncf.com* (you can book advance tickets from the USA or UK prior to departure on this website, and pay by credit card at an SNCF machine in France).

For ordinary trains (excluding TGVs and *couchettes*), the SNCF has divided the year into blue (off-peak) and white (peak) periods, based on demand: white periods run from Friday noon to midnight, from Sunday 3pm to Monday 10am, and during holidays (all stations give out little calendars).

Tickets must be stamped in the little orange machines by the entrance to the lines that say *Compostez votre billet* (this puts the date on the ticket, to keep you from using the same one over and over again). Any time you interrupt a journey until another day, you have to re-stamp your ticket.

Nearly every station has large computerized lockers (*consignes automatiques*). It takes about half an hour to puzzle them out the first time you use them, so plan accordingly.

By Bus

There is no national bus network. The network is just about adequate between major cities and towns, but can be limited in rural areas, fitting the school schedule.

Most towns have a *gare routière* (coach station), usually near the train station, though many lines start from any place that catches their fancy.

For details on **local bus services**, enquire at the local tourist office.

By Car

While virtually all the day trips we propose are acccessible by public transport, if you plan to follow the touring itineraries suggested in this guide and you haven't brought your own car to France, you may decide to hire one.

Hiring a Car

Car hire in France can be an expensive proposition; to save money, look into air and holiday package deals. Prices vary widely from firm to firm: beware the small print about service charges and taxes. It's often cheaper to book through car hire companies at home.

If you are taking a budget flight and decide to hire a car once there, local tourist offices can provide information on car hire agencies. Car hire firms are listed for the main destinations in this book, and there will usually be a branch of one of the large firms at the airport.

The minimum age for hiring a car in France is around 21–25, and the maximum around 70.

Driving in France

French roads are generally excellently maintained, but anything of lesser status than a departmental route (D road) may be uncomfortably narrow.

WH Smith
Bristol Airport

FLYING VISITS:FRANCE	11.99
TOTAL	11.99
Cash Payment	12.00
CHANGE	0.01

Notified Terms and Conditions Apply
Thank you for shopping at
WH Smith

08/09/03 11:39 Tn:912803 Op:0223 2530/29

Save as you spend with

WHSmith CLUBCARD

It's FREE to join - ask for more details.

www.whsmith.co.uk
Customer Relations 0870 444 6 444
WHSmith Limited Registered no. 237811 England
Registered Office: Greenbridge Road, Swindon, Wiltshire SN3 3RX
VAT Reg no. 238 5548 36

Conditions vary widely: in rural Languedoc you may catch up on your sleep while you drive; traffic in the Côte d'Azur, the 'California of Europe', can be diabolically Californian, and **parking** a nightmare. Many towns now have pricey guarded **car parks** underneath their very heart, spectacularly so in Nice. Blue '**P**' signs infallibly direct you to a village or town car park.

France used to have a rule of giving **priority to the right** at every intersection. This has to some extent disappeared, but there will still be many intersections, usually in towns, where it applies. Generally, as you'd expect, give priority to the main road, and to the right if you are at all unsure. Give priority to the left on roundabouts. If you are new to France, think of every intersection as a new and perilous experience. *Cédez le passage* means give way.

When you (inevitably) get lost in a town or city, the *Toutes directions* or *Autres directions*

signs are like 'Get Out of Jail Free' cards. Watch out for the tiny signs indicating which streets are meant for pedestrians only (with complicated schedules in even tinier print).

The French have one delightful custom: if oncoming drivers unaccountably flash their headlights at you, it means that the *gendarmes* are lurking just up the way.

Petrol stations keep shop hours (most close Sundays and/or Mondays) and are rare in rural areas, so consider your fuel supply while planning any forays – especially if you use unleaded. If you come across a garage with petrol-pump attendants, they will expect a tip for oil, windscreen-cleaning, or air.

Rules and Regulations

You will need your vehicle registration document, full driving licence and an up-to-date insurance certificate. Your home insurance will automatically provide third-party cover in the EU; you may wish to extend it to comprehensive cover. If you're coming from the UK or Ireland, you'll need headlight converters to adjust the dip of the headlights to the right. Carrying a warning triangle is mandatory if you don't have hazard lights, and advisable even if you do. In the mountains you may need to buy (or hire from a garage) snow chains. Drivers with a valid licence from an EU country, Canada, the USA or Australia do not need to have an international driving licence.

Speed limits are 130km/80mph (110kmph in wet weather) on the *autoroutes* (toll motorways); 110km/69mph on dual carriageways (divided highways and motorways without tolls); 90km/55mph on other roads; 50km/30mph in an 'urbanized area' (as soon as you pass a white sign with a town's name on it and until you pass another sign with the town's name barred). **Fines** for speeding, payable on the spot, begin at €200 and can be astronomical if you fail the breathalyser.

If you have an **accident**, the procedure is to fill out and sign a *constat amiable*. If your French isn't sufficient to deal with this, try to find someone to help.

If you have a **breakdown** and are a member of a motoring club affiliated to the Touring Club de France, ring the latter; if not, ring the police.

Car Hire

UK

Auto Europe, *www.autoeurope.com*.
Avis, **t** 08705 900 500, **f** 08705 6060 100, *www.avis.co.uk*.
Budget, **t** 08701 565 656, **f** (01442) 280 092, *www.budget-international.com/uk*.
Europcar, **t** 0870 607 5000, **f** (01132) 429 495, *www.europcar.com*.
Hertz, **t** 08705 996 699, **f** (020) 8679 0181, *www.hertz.co.uk*.
easyCar, *www.easyCar.com*.

USA and Canada

Auto Europe, **t** 800 223 5555, **t** (207) 842 2000, *www.autoeurope.com*.
Auto France, **t** 800 572 9655, **t** (201) 934 6994, **f** (201) 934 7501, *www.autofrance.com*.
Avis Rent a Car, **t** 800 331 1084, **t** (516) 222 3000, *www.avis.com*.
Europe by Car, New York, **t** 800 223 1516, **t** (212) 581 3040, **f** (212) 246 1458; California **t** 800 252 9401/**t** (213) 272 0424, **f** (310) 273 9247; *www.europebycar.com*.
Europcar, **t** 800 800 6000, **t** (918) 669 2823, **f** (918) 669 2821, *www.europcar.com*.
Hertz, **t** 800 654 3001, *www.hertz.com*.

Practical A–Z

Climate and When to Go

France has a full deck of climates. Continental cold winters and hot summers prevail in the east and centre; the north is as changeable as Britain, while the west is tempered and wettened by the Atlantic.

France is the world's top tourist destination, and avoiding the crowds can be a prime consideration. The Easter school break in April and the months of July and August are the busiest, but it's also the season of the great festivals. From December to March most of the tourists are skiing in the mountains; in February the mimosa and almonds bloom on the Côte d'Azur. By April and May you can sit outside at restaurants in most places and start to swim in the Med. June is usually warm and a relatively quiet month, and the beginning of the walking season in the mountains. In August, the cities are empty except for tourists; shops and restaurants close, and a room on the coast can be impossible to get.

Once French school holidays end in early September, prices and crowds decrease with the temperature. In October the weather is often mild on the coast, although torrential downpours and floods are not unknown; the first snows fall in the high Pyrenees and Alps. November is a bad month to visit: it rains, and many museums, hotels and restaurants close.

Crime and the Police

France is a safe and well policed country, but it's important to be aware that thieves target visitors, especially their cars. Leave anything you'd really miss at home, carry traveller's cheques, insure your property, and be especially careful in large cities or on the Côte d'Azur. Report thefts to the nearest *gendarmerie* or *police nationale* – the reward is the bit of paper you need for an insurance claim. If your passport is stolen, contact the police and your nearest consulate for emergency travel documents. Carry photocopies of your passport, driver's licence, etc.

Electricity

French electricity is all 220V. British and Irish appliances will need an adapter with two round prongs; North American appliances usually need a transformer as well.

Average Daily High Temperatures in °C (°F)

	Jan	Feb	Mar	April	May	June	July	Aug	Sept	Oct	Nov	Dec
Biarritz	13 (55)	14 (56)	16 (61)	18 (64)	21 (70)	25 (77)	28 (82)	27 (81)	26 (79)	24 (75)	19 (66)	13 (55)
Grenoble	3 (37)	3 (37)	8 (45)	14 (56)	16 (61)	22 (71)	27 (81)	26 (79)	22 (71)	16 (61)	11 (51)	6 (42)
La Rochelle	10 (50)	9 (48)	12 (54)	18 (64)	16 (61)	22 (71)	25 (77)	25 (77)	22 (71)	18 (64)	14 (56)	10 (50)
Lyon	7 (44)	6 (42)	11 (51)	16 (61)	17 (63)	25 (77)	27 (81)	27 (81)	24 (75)	17 (63)	10 (50)	8 (45)
Nice	12 (54)	12 (54)	14 (56)	18 (64)	21 (70)	26 (79)	27 (81)	28 (82)	25 (77)	22 (71)	16 (61)	14(56)
Paris	7 (44)	7 (44)	10 (50)	16 (61)	17 (63)	24 (75)	25 (77)	26 (79)	21 (70)	17 (63)	12 (54)	8 (45)
Bergerac	10 (50)	12 (54)	14 (56)	17 (63)	19 (66)	23 (73)	25 (77)	26 (79)	22 (71)	18 (64)	15 (59)	12 (54)
St-Malo	9 (48)	9 (48)	11 (51)	17 (63)	16 (61)	23 (73)	25 (77)	24 (75)	21 (70)	16 (61)	12 (54)	9 (48)

Email and Internet

The old saying that it doesn't pay to be first certainly applies to France with its national computer system, Minitel, which was distributed to every phone subscriber in the 1980s. Next to the Internet it seems a Neanderthal, but its presence considerably slowed French interest in the World Wide Web. This is changing fast: most cities and towns now have cybercafés, and most towns have a website for tourists.

Health and Insurance

Ambulance (SAMU) t 15
Police and ambulance t 17
Fire t 18

France has one of the best health-care systems in the world. Local hospitals are the place to go in an emergency (*urgence*).

Pharmacists are trained to administer first aid and dispense advice for minor problems. In rural areas there is always someone on duty if you ring the bell; in cities, pharmacies are open at night on a rota basis, posted in their windows and in the local newspaper.

Citizens of the EU who bring along their E111 forms are entitled to the same health services as French citizens. In France, whichever way you're insured, you pay up front for everything, unless it's an emergency, when you will be billed later. Doctors will give you a brown and white *feuille de soins* with your prescription; take both to the pharmacy and keep the *feuille*, the various medicine stickers (*vignettes*) and prescriptions for insurance purposes at home.

As an alternative, consider a travel insurance policy, covering theft and losses and offering a 100% medical refund; check to see if it covers your extra expenses in case you get bogged down in airport or train strikes, and be aware that accidents resulting from sports are rarely covered by ordinary insurance.

Money and Banks

The **euro** is the official currency in France and the official exchange rate was set at **1 euro=6.559F**. Francs were phased out completely in February 2002.

Euros come in denominations of €500, €200, €100, €50, €20, €10 and €5 (banknotes) and €2, €1, 50 cents, 20 cents, 10 cents, 5 cents, 2 cents and 1 cent (coins).

Traveller's cheques are the safest way of carrying money, but the wide acceptance of credit and debit cards and the presence of ATMs (*distributeurs de billets* – automatic cash dispensers), even in small villages, make cards a convenient alternative. Visa is the most readily accepted credit card; American Express is often not accepted, however. Smaller hotels and restaurants, and bed and breakfasts, may not accept cards at all. Some shops and supermarkets experience difficulties reading UK-style magnetic strips (French credit cards now contain a chip, or *puce*, containing ID information), so arm yourself with cash.

Under the Cirrus system, withdrawals in euros can be made from bank and post office ATMs, using your PIN. The specific cards accepted are marked on each machine, and most give instructions in English. Credit card companies charge a fee for cash advances, but their rates are often better than those charged by banks.

In the event of **lost or stolen credit cards**, call the following emergency numbers:
American Express, Paris, t 01 47 77 72 00
Barclaycard, t (00 44) 1604 230 230 (UK number)
Mastercard, t 0800 901 387.
Visa (Carte Bleue), Paris, t 01 42 77 11 90.

Opening Hours, Museums and National Holidays

Shops: In large cities shops are now open continuously Tues–Sat from 9 or 10am to 7 or 7.30pm, but in smaller towns they still close down for lunch from 12 or 12.30pm to 2 or 3pm (4pm in summer). Nearly everything shuts on Monday, except for grocers and *supermarchés* that open in the afternoon. In many towns, Sunday morning is a big shopping time. Markets (daily in the cities, weekly in villages) are usually open mornings only, although clothes, flea and antiques markets run into the afternoon.

Banks: Open 8.30am–12.30pm and 1.30–4pm. They close on Sundays, and most close either on Saturdays or Mondays as well.

National Holidays

1 January New Year's Day
Easter Sunday March or April
Easter Monday March or April
1 May Fête du Travail (Labour Day)
8 May VE Day, Armistice 1945
Ascension Day usually end of May
Pentecost (Whitsun and Monday) beginning
of June
14 July Bastille Day
15 August Assumption of the Virgin Mary
1 November All Saints' Day
11 November Remembrance Day (First World
War Armistice)
25 December Christmas Day

Post Offices: Open in the cities Monday–Friday
8am–7pm, and Saturdays 8am–noon. In
villages, offices may not open until 9am,
then break for lunch and close at 4.30pm.
Museums: Most museums close for lunch,
and often all day on Mondays or Tuesdays,
and sometimes for all of November or the
entire winter. Hours change with the season.
Most museums close on national holidays.
Most museums give discounts on admission
(which ranges from €1.5–4.5) if you have a
student ID card, or are an EU citizen aged
under 18 or over 65.
Churches: Churches are usually open all day, or
closed all day and open only for Mass.
Sometimes notes on the door direct you to
the *mairie* or priest's house (*presbytère*),
where you can pick up the key.

Post and Telephones

Known as La Poste, post offices are easily
discernible by a blue bird on a yellow background. Post boxes are yellow. You can buy
stamps (*timbres*) in *tabacs* and post offices.

Nearly all public telephones have switched
over from coins to *télécartes*, which you can
purchase at any post office or news-stand
for €6 for 50 *unités* or €14.5 for 120 *unités*.

The French have eliminated area codes,
giving everyone a 10-digit telephone number.
If **ringing France from abroad**, the international dialling code is 33, then drop the first
'0' of the number. For **international calls** from
France, dial 00, wait for the change in the dial
tone, then dial the country code (UK 44; US

and Canada 1; Ireland 353), and then the local
code (minus the 0) and number. For directory
enquiries, dial **t** 12.

Price Categories

The hotels and restaurants listed in this
guide have been assigned categories
reflecting a range of prices.

Bon Week-end en Villes (*www.bon-week-
end-en-villes.com*) is an interesting deal
whereby selected hotels in 42 French towns
offer two weekend nights for the price of one.

Restaurant categories are for set menus or a
two-course meal for one without wine.

Hotel prices are for a double room with
bath/shower in high season.

Restaurant Price Categories

luxury over €60
expensive €30–60
moderate €15–30
cheap under €15

Hotel Price Categories

luxury €230 and over
expensive €90–230
moderate €60–90
inexpensive €30–60
cheap under €30

Tipping

Almost all restaurants and cafés automatically add an extra 15 per cent to the bill (*service
compris*), and there's no need to leave any
more unless you care to. Taxi drivers will be
happy with 10 per cent.

Tourist Information

Every city and town, and most villages, have
a tourist information office, usually called a
Syndicat d'Initiative or an Office de Tourisme.
In smaller villages this service is provided by
the town hall (*mairie*). They distribute free
maps and town plans, and hotel, camping and
self-catering accommodation lists for their
area, and can inform you about sporting
events, leisure activities, wine estates open for
visits, and festivals.

Food and Drink

Eating Out in France

Food

French **restaurants** generally serve meals between noon and 2pm and, at night, from 7 to 10pm; **brasseries** in the cities often stay open continuously. Most offer a choice of set-price (*prix fixe*) menus. If you summon up the appetite to eat the biggest meal of the day at noon, you'll spend a lot less money, as many restaurants offer special **lunch menus** – an economical way to experience some of the finer gourmet temples. At the humbler end of the scale, bars and brasseries often serve a simple *plat du jour* (daily special) and the no-choice *formule*. Menus sometimes include the **house wine** (*vin compris*). If you choose a better wine, expect a big mark-up. If **service** is included it will say *service compris* or *s.c.*; if not, *service non-compris* or *s.n.c.*

Don't overlook hotel restaurants, some of which are absolutely top-notch, even if a certain red book refuses on some obscure principle to give them more than two stars. To avoid disappointment, call ahead in the morning to reserve a table.

Drink

You can order any kind of drink at any bar or café – except cocktails, unless the bar has a certain cosmopolitan flair. Cafés are also a home from home. Prices are listed on the *Tarif des Consommations*: note they are progressively more expensive depending on whether you're served at the bar (*comptoir*), at a table (*la salle*) or outside (*la terrasse*). French coffee is strong and black; if you order *un café* you'll get a small black espresso; if you want milk, order *un crème*. If you want more than a few drops of caffeine, ask them to make it *grand*. For decaffeinated, the word is *déca*. In the summer, try a *frappé* (iced coffee). The French only order *café au lait* when they drop in for breakfast, and, if what your hotel offers is expensive or boring, consider joining them. *Chocolat chaud* (hot chocolate) is usually good. If you order *thé* (tea), you'll get an ordinary bag. An *infusion* is a herbal tea – *camomille*, *menthe* (mint), *tilleul* (lime or linden blossom) or *verveine* (verbena).

Mineral water (*eau minérale*) comes either sparkling (*gazeuse* or *pétillante*) or still (*non-gazeuse* or *plate*). The usual international corporate soft drinks are available, and all kinds of bottled fruit juices (*jus de fruits*). Some bars also do fresh lemon and orange juices (*citron pressé* or *orange pressée*). The French are also fond of fruit syrups – red grenadine and ghastly green *diabolo menthe*.

Beer (*bière*) in most bars and cafés is run-of-the-mill big brands from Alsace, Germany and Belgium. Draft (*à la pression*) is cheaper than bottled beer.

One of the pleasures of travelling in France is drinking great **wines** for a fraction of the price you pay at home, and discovering new ones you've never seen in your local shop. Wines labelled AOC (*Appellation d'Origine Contrôlée*) come from a certain defined area, guaranteeing a standard of quality. *Cru* on the label means vintage; a *grand cru* is a great, noble vintage. Descending in the vinous hierarchy are those labelled VDQS (*Vin de Qualité Supérieure*), followed by *Vin de Pays* (guaranteed to originate in a certain region; some are excellent), with *Vin Ordinaire* (or *Vin de Table*) at the bottom.

Regional Specialities

Each region of France is proud of its local cuisine, or *cuisine de terroir*. Some of these are so popular that you'll find them throughout France, but it's always worth trying them in their place of origin.

The North (Around the Channel Ports and Lille)

All sorts of stews feature on northern French menus – the cuisine is warming and copious. Rabbit is popular, as are stews with mixed meats, known as *hochepot*, and stews with beer. Soups are another favourite, from vegetable soups to broths with tripe and frogs. *Maroilles* is much the best-known cheese; its origins date back to Maroilles abbey in the 10th century. There are a lot of similarities with Flemish or Belgian cuisine, including a delight in sweet things and chocolate in particular. In the autumn, hillocks of white sugar beet are gathered on the edge of fields. Beer is a popular local tipple, as well as chicory coffee and locally produced gin.

Normandy

An anathema to the cholesterol-conscious, Normandy cuisine is often heightened by a rich dollop of cream and a dash of cider or calvados (apple brandy). But it is best known for its cheeses. Normandy **cheeses** are soft and creamy; they start off smelly and get tastier and more pungent with age. Most come from the Pays d'Auge and the Pays de Bray; the latter has produced Neufchâtel since the time of William the Conqueror. Normandy also makes fine Isigny butter.

Normandy has excellent **seafood**: try mussels (with cream), oysters and scallops, and sole – *à la normande*, cooked with cider, butter and mussels, or *dieppoise*, with wine and cream. Local meat dishes might turn your stomach, but locals love *tripes à la mode de Caen*, black puddings from Mortagne-au-Perche, or *canetons* (ducklings) from Rouen, stuffed with liver and served up in a blood and cream sauce.

Normandy produces a quantity of **cider**, and apples feature large in regional dishes. **Calvados** (nicknamed *calva*) can be added to just about anything, and is renowned as one of France's most densely flavoured brandies. The *trou normand* – a pause in a meal – is when diners drink a drop of *calva* to help the digestion.

Brittany

The Breton **crêpe** (or the savoury *galette*) is considered the aristocrat of the pancake world these days. Delicate and thin, it comes with all sorts of fancy fillings and in Brittany crêperies are generally reliable and cheap places to eat.

Brittany is also known for its **fish** and **seafood**. Don't be surprised if shellfish is served in its shell, or if oysters and clams are served *cru* (raw). If you order a *plateau de fruits de mer* you will be faced with a sumptuous spread which will normally include certain types of crab, *langoustines* (Dublin Bay prawns), *crevettes* (shrimps), *palourdes* (clams), *coques* (cockles), *bigorneaux* (winkles) and *bulots* (whelks). Wash it down with a white Muscadet from the south of Brittany. *Cotriade* is the traditional Breton sailors' soup, made with a combination of whiting, cod, haddock, hake, mackerel, eel, and even mussels. The marshes of Guérande in southern Brittany produce highly regarded salt, the *fleur de sel*. Crunchy little sprigs of *salicornes* (samphire) are another speciality from the salt-pans, increasingly experimented with in Breton cuisine.

Brittany is known for its **pork**, as well as for *saucissons* (salamis), *andouilles* (chitterlings) and *boudins* (black pudding). *Kig-ar-farz* (meat-and-pudding in Breton) is a traditional dish, now back in fashion in Breton restaurants.

Gâteau Breton is a dense, dry Breton butter cake, while *kouign aman* is a cake that drips with butter. Various Breton towns, notably Pleyben and Pont-Aven, produce buttery biscuits known as *galettes*. *Far* is a heavy eggy pudding with dried fruit. Brittany, like neighbouring Normandy, is **apple** country, and makes good cider and delicious but relatively rare *lambig*, the Breton equivalent to Calvados.

The Loire, Poitou-Charentes and the Limousin

Signs signal **wine** estates and tastings (*dégustations*) at every turn in the greater Loire valley, home to a surprisingly wide variety of whites, reds and rosés. Among the fine white wines, Sancerre, Pouilly-Fumé, Vouvray and Montlouis count among the best, while the more popular Muscadet wine region spreads out from Nantes. The areas around Chinon, Bourgueil and Saumur produce the fruitiest reds, while Saumur also conjures up a creditable sparkling white. Tiny Anjou appellations produce the rare, deliciously dry Savennières and the sweet Bonnezeaux and Quarts-de-Chaume.

Today the common features of Loire Valley cuisine are freshwater fish, vegetables and orchard fruits, goats' cheeses in a variety of building-block shapes, and game in autumn. The Loire Valley fish is *sandre* (zander; often translated as pike-perch). Other fleshy freshwater fish include *brochet* (pike), *brème* (bream) and *alose* (shad). Meat dishes are often accompanied by regional wine sauces, or local fruit, for example pork served with apples, or better still, prunes. By French standards, Loire Valley restaurants are generous with their vegetables. The majority of French *champignons de Paris* (button mushrooms) are actually produced in the region's vast underground caves.

Along stretches of the Atlantic coastline enormous **oyster and mussel parks** emerge in the shallow waters as the tide goes out. The coast's other great culinary asset is **salt. Duck** and other fowl are traditionally hunted in the band of marshlands which lies just inland, while the **sheep** reared on the salt marshes yield a succulent salty meat. **Eels, frogs** and **snails** thrive in the region; eels (*anguilles*) turn up in *matelote* (stew), snails often feature on menus under the aliases of *lumas* and *cagouilles*.

Southwest France

Although it may not seem like it at first glance, the southwest diet, with an emphasis on duck and goose fat, garlic and red wine, is good for you; the native rate of heart disease is half that of the United States. Besides foie gras (studded with a black truffle) and various pâtés, look for succulent *maigrets* (fillet of duck breast) and *confits* (duck preserved in its own fat) or even duck sausage. In autumn mushrooms and truffles are prized ingredients in local omelettes and sauces. Around Bordeaux, look for beef steaks with shallots cooked over vine cuttings, oysters and other seafood, with stewed lamprey (*lamproie*) the region's favourite.

The sunny southwest produces more fine **wines** than any other region. Bordeaux, of course, holds pride of place, covering four regions, which together produce 500 million litres a year: the Libournais; the Entre-Deux-Mers; the Graves; and the Médoc. You can study the subject before leaving home at *www.vins-Bordeaux.fr*. The Haut Pays is the general term for all of the wine-producing region up river.

For the sweet-toothed, *brioche vendéenne* is a wonderfully light bread once made for special occasions and now often enjoyed at breakfast. *Tourteau fromagé* is another sweet bread-like speciality, made with *fromage blanc*.

Marseille has its *bouillabaisse*, but the Basques maintain that their version, *ttoro* (pronounced 'tioro'), is the king of them all; the cooks of St-Jean-de-Luz make the best ones. Another icon is the red pepper, the *piment d'Espelette*; some go into *piperade*, the relish that can accompany almost any Basque dish. Other treats include the sheep cheese from the Pyrenees, and the famous Bayonne ham, hung for over a year.

The region is famous for golden Jurançon, the Gascon version of Sauternes, which is often served with foie gras; Pacherenc, the wines of Tursan and Chalosse, and the inimitable Madiran, the most tannic wine in France, perfect with rich duck dishes, red meat and cheese. The Basques use mountain herbs to make Izarra liqueur.

Languedoc-Roussillon

Castelnaudary's beans, combined with pork, sausage and *confits*, go into *cassoulet*, the totem dish of Languedoc; in second place comes *brandade de morue*, a salt cod purée with garlic. In the old days that was about it in France's 'culinary desert'. Now arty influences from Provence and Catalan nouvelle cuisine, the rage in Barcelona, have met and collided in Languedoc, and you'll find no end of Mediterranean surprises. The biggest revolution of all has been in the wines: a fresh emphasis in quality rather than quantity has made the region one of the rising stars on the French wine charts: Corbières and Minervois are the two biggest regions, but don't neglect smaller regions like Fougères and La Clape, or Banyuls – France's answer to port.

The South of France

The sunny cuisine of the south, influenced by neighbouring Italy, is one of the most popular in France: olive oil, fresh vegetables and seafood are basic ingredients. *Ravioli* and *gnocchi* were invented in Nice, along with the world-famous ratatouille, *salade niçoise* and *soupe au pistou*, a hearty soup of vegetables and vermicelli, served with *pistou*, a sauce similar to pesto. Another favourite is *bourride*, a fish soup served with *aïoli*, a creamy garlic mayonnaise that is one of the great symbols of Provence, while Marseille's justly celebrated *bouillabaisse* is served with a *rouille*, a red pepper and garlic sauce. On the meat side, look for lamb dishes and *daubes*, beef stewed slowly in red wine; vegetarians can sink their teeth into stuffed vegetables or courgette flowers (*farcies*) or delicious snacks such as *socca*, a chickpea-flour pie, *tapenades* (olive paste, served on toast) and *pan-bagnat* (basically a *salade niçoise* sandwich).

The Greeks introduced the syrah grape to Provence, and it remains one of the chief varieties of Côtes du Rhône, the region's main wine area; this embraces the cele-brated vintages of Châteauneuf du Pape and Gigondas among the reds, rosé Tavel, and the sweet muscat Beaumes-de-Venise. Ancient small vineyards along the coast produce lovely wines: white Cassis (the best with bouillabaisse), Bandol, and rare Palette and Bellet.

The Rhône and the Alps

Peaches, nectarines, cherries, apricots and a host of other **fruit** and **vegetables** grow in profusion along parts of the Rhône Valley and in the Drôme. Chestnut purée is used to create many delicious desserts, and fruit tarts and flans are popular.

Lyon is renowned for the quality of its hearty cooking. Sausages or salami-like *saucissons* remain perennial favourites, along with pigs' trotters, pigs' brawn and tripe. A slice of truffle may be added here and there.

Le Puy-en-Velay has an international reputation for fine green lentils and is also known for herbal teas, notably *verveine* (verbena). Bottled water is another hugely successful export, Volvic the best known. The slopes of the extinct volcanoes present much more of a challenge for farmers, but in summer cattle graze the high pastures. Five of the region's **cheeses** have been awarded *Appellation d'Origine Contrôlée* (AOC) status. Look out for traditional makers of St-Nectaire and Cantal. Fourme d'Ambert is the best-known blue cheese, and cone-shaped Gaberon is flavoured with generous amounts of garlic. Salers is an exclusive cow's milk cheese. Further into the Jura, most people imagine devouring a rich **cheese** fondue after a long day's skiing when they think of this region: two of the best local cheeses are Comté, made in the Franche-Comté, and Beaufort, made in Savoy. St-Marcellin, a runny mixture of goats' and cows' milk cheeses, is another excellent regional speciality. The Reblochon from the Aravis range in Savoy is especially good in a *tartiflette* – served with layers of potatoes, garlic and herbs. But the best way of serving potatoes bears the name of one of the old regions – *gratin dauphinois*, slices of potatoes baked with eggs and milk.

Meats are often served in stews, or with rich, mushroom sauces. Game such as venison, wild boar, hare and woodcock is still hunted in these wooded mountainous regions and chefs will often seek out wild *champignons*. **Pork** *saucissons* and smoked hams traditionally lasted well through the long mountain winters. River and lake **fish** often appear on the menus, as do *écrevisses*, the much-prized crayfish.

Some distinctly surprising **wines** and some positively dangerous liqueurs are produced in the Jura and the Alps. **Absinthe**, made from wormwood macerated in brandy, was long banned for its mind-rotting effects, but has been making a come-back recently. **Chartreuse**, a dangerous green liqueur made to a secret recipe of the Carthusian monks, is made in the Chartreuse mountain range near Grenoble. Mountain berries taste delicious in tarts from the local *pâtisseries*, while walnuts put in an appearance in traditional desserts. *Gâteau de Savoie* is a traditional sponge cake.

Burgundy

The Burgundians are very proud of their culinary traditions, which often combine alcohol with food. *Bœuf bourguignon* and *coq au vin* are famed regional dishes, while wine sauces are a great favourite, with beef, chicken, pork or hare. *Œufs en meurette* is a delicious recipe in which wine is combined with eggs. Bacon, pork, onions and

French Menu Reader

Hors-d'œuvre et Soupes

assiette assortie plate of mixed cold *hors-d'œuvre*

bisque shellfish soup

bouillon broth

charcuterie mixed cold meats

consommé clear soup

crudités raw vegetable platter

potage thick vegetable soup

velouté thick smooth soup, often fish or chicken

Poissons et Coquillages (Crustacés) (Fish and Shellfish)

aiglefin little haddock

alose shad

anchois anchovies

anguille eel

bar sea bass

barbue brill

baudroie angler fish

belons flat oysters

bigorneau winkle

brème bream

brochet pike

bulot whelk

cabillaud cod

calmar squid

carrelet plaice

colin hake

congre conger eel

coques cockles

coquillages shellfish

coquilles St-Jacques scallops

crevettes grises/roses shrimp/prawns

daurade sea bream

écrevisse freshwater crayfish

éperlan smelt

escargots snails

espadon swordfish

esturgeon sturgeon

flétan halibut

gambas giant prawns

grondin red gurnard

hareng herring

homard Atlantic (Norway) lobster

huîtres oysters

lamproie lamprey

langouste spiny Mediterranean lobster

langoustines Norway lobster

limande lemon sole

lotte monkfish

loup (de mer) sea bass

louvine sea bass (in aquitaine)

maquereau mackerel

merlan whiting

morue salt cod

moules mussels

pagel sea bream

palourdes clams

praires small clams

raie skate

rascasse scorpion fish

rouget red mullet

saumon salmon

St-Pierre John Dory

sole (meunière) sole (with butter, lemon and parsley)

telline tiny clam

thon tuna

truite trout

truite saumonée salmon trout

Viandes et Volailles (Meat and Poultry)

agneau (de pré-salé) lamb (grazed in fields by the sea)

aloyau sirloin

andouillette chitterling (tripe) sausage

biftek beefsteak

blanquette stew of white meat, thickened with egg yolk

bœuf beef

boudin blanc sausage of white meat

boudin noir black pudding

brochette meat (or fish) on a skewer

caille quail

canard, caneton duck, duckling

cassoulet haricot bean stew with sausage, duck, goose, etc.

chapon capon

châteaubriand porterhouse steak

chevreau kid

civet meat (usually game) stew, in wine and blood sauce

mushrooms are often thrown into traditional Burgundian sauces. Mushrooms are still quite easy to find in season in the region's many woods. Snails too are a regular feature on local menus. White Charolais cattle graze across large parts of southern Burgundy. The flatlands of the Bresse produce the white-plumed blue-stockinged

cœur heart

confit meat cooked and preserved in its own fat

côte, côtelette chop, cutlet

cou d'oie farci goose neck stuffed with pork, foie gras and truffles

cuisse thigh or leg

dinde, dindon turkey

entrecôte ribsteak

estouffade a meat stew marinated, fried and then braised

faisan pheasant

faux-filet sirloin

foie liver

gigot leg of lamb

graisse or *gras* fat

grillade grilled meat, often a mixed grill

jambon ham

langue tongue

lapereau young rabbit

lapin rabbit

lard (lardons) bacon (diced bacon)

lièvre hare

maigret/magret, (de canard) breast (of duck)

manchons duck or goose wings

marcassin young wild boar

moelle bone marrow

mouton mutton

navarin lamb stew with root vegetables

noix de veau (agneau) topside of veal (lamb)

oie goose

perdreau (or perdrix) partridge

petit salé salt pork

pieds trotters

pintade guinea fowl

porc pork

poulet chicken

poussin baby chicken

quenelle poached dumplings made of fish, fowl or meat

queue de bœuf oxtail

ris (de veau) sweetbreads (veal)

rognons kidneys

rosbif roast beef

rôti roast

sanglier wild boar

saucisses sausages

saucisson dry sausage, like salami

selle (d'agneau) saddle (of lamb)

steak tartare raw minced beef, often topped with a raw egg yolk

tête (de veau) head (calf's), fatty and usually served with a mustardy vinaigrette

tournedos thick round slices of beef fillet

travers de porc spare ribs

tripes tripe

veau veal

venaison venison

Légumes, Herbes, etc. (Vegetables, herbs, etc.)

ail garlic

aïoli garlic mayonnaise

algue seaweed

artichaut artichoke

asperges asparagus

aubergine aubergine (eggplant)

avocat avocado

basilic basil

betterave beetroot

blette Swiss chard

bouquet garni mixed herbs in a little bag

cannelle cinnamon

céleri (-rave) celery (celeriac)

cèpes ceps, wild boletus mushrooms

champignons mushrooms

chanterelles wild yellow mushrooms

chicorée curly endive

chou cabbage

chou-fleur cauliflower

choucroute sauerkraut

choux de Bruxelles Brussels sprouts

citrouille pumpkin

concombre cucumber

cornichons gherkins

courgettes courgettes (zucchini)

cresson watercress

échalote shallot

endive chicory (endive)

épinards spinach

estragon tarragon

fenouil fennel

fèves broad (fava) beans

flageolets white beans

fleurs de courgette courgette blossoms

poulets de Bresse, chickens with a formidable culinary reputation. Dijon is of course famous for mustard, but also for its gingerbread and blackcurrants, which go into making the intense liqueur, Crème de Cassis. One of Burgundy's finest cheeses, Epoisses, is matured in a marc, or liqueur.

frites chips (French fries)
genièvre juniper
gingembre ginger
haricot verts green (French) beans
jardinière with diced garden vegetables
laitue lettuce
lentilles lentils
maïs (épis de) sweetcorn (on the cob)
menthe mint
mesclun salad of various leaves
morilles morel mushrooms
navet turnip
oignons onions
oseille sorrel
panais parsnip
persil parsley
petits pois peas
piment pimento
pissenlits dandelion greens
poireaux leeks
pois chiches chickpeas
pois mange-tout sugar peas or mangetout
poivron sweet pepper (capsicum)
pomme de terre potato
potiron pumpkin
primeurs young vegetables
radis radishes
riz rice
romarin rosemary
roquette rocket
safran saffron
salsifis salsify
sarriette savoury
sarrasin buckwheat
sauge sage
thym thyme
truffes truffles

Fruits et Noix (Fruit and Nuts)
abricot apricot
amandes almonds
ananas pineapple
bigarreau black cherries
brugnon nectarine
cacahouètes peanuts
cassis blackcurrant
cerise cherry
citron lemon

citron vert lime
coco (noix de) coconut
fraises (des bois) strawberries (wild)
framboises raspberries
fruit de la passion passion fruit
grenade pomegranate
groseilles redcurrants
mandarine tangerine
mangue mango
marrons chestnuts
mirabelles mirabelle plums
mûre (sauvage) mulberry, blackberry
myrtilles bilberries
noisette hazelnut
noix walnuts
noix de cajou cashews
pamplemousse grapefruit
pastèque watermelon
pêche (blanche) peach (white)
pignons pinenuts
pistache pistachio
poire pear
pomme apple
prune plum
pruneau prune
raisins (secs) grapes (raisins)
reine-claude greengage plums

Cooking Terms and Sauces
à point medium steak
bien cuit well-done steak
bleu very rare steak
à l'anglaise boiled
à la bordelaise cooked in wine and diced
    vegetables (usually)
à la châtelaine with chestnut purée and
    artichoke hearts
à la diable in spicy mustard sauce
à la grecque cooked in olive oil and lemon
à la jardinière with garden vegetables
à la périgourdine in truffle and foie gras sauce
à la provençale cooked with tomatoes, garlic
    and olive oil
au four baked
auvergnat with sausage, bacon and cabbage
beignets fritters
béarnaise sauce of egg yolks, shallots and
    white wine

Most Burgundy vineyards are found on the eastern side of the region, along the slopes of the Saône valley. Heading south from Dijon past Beaune, the Côte de Nuits and the Côte de Beaune combine to make the legendary Côte d'Or which produces the most famous wines of all. Continuing southwards beside the Saône, the

bordelaise red wine, bone marrow and shallot sauce
chaud hot
cru raw
cuit cooked
diable spicy mustard or green pepper sauce
émincé thinly sliced
en croûte cooked in a pastry crust
en papillote baked in buttered paper
épices spices
farci stuffed
feuilleté flaky pastry
flambé set aflame with alcohol
forestière with bacon and mushrooms
fourré stuffed
frit fried
fumé smoked
galette flaky pastry case or pancake
garni with vegetables
(au) gratin topped with browned cheese and breadcrumbs
grillé grilled
haché minced
marmite casserole
médaillon round piece
mijoté simmered
Mornay cheese sauce
pané breaded
pâte pastry, pasta
pâte brisée shortcrust pastry
pâte à chou choux pastry
pâte feuilletée flaky or puff pastry
paupiette rolled and filled thin slices
parmentier with potatoes
pavé slab
piquant spicy hot
poché poached
pommes allumettes thin chips (fries)
raclette melted cheese with potatoes, onions and pickles
sanglant rare steak
salé salted, spicy
sucré sweet
timbale pie cooked in a dome-shaped mould
tranche slice
à la vapeur steamed
Véronique grape, wine and cream sauce

Miscellaneous
addition bill (check)
beurre butter
carte non-set menu
confiture jam
couteau knife
cuillère spoon
formule à €12 €12 set menu
fourchette fork
lait milk
menu set menu
nouilles noodles
pain bread
œufs eggs
poivre pepper
sel salt
sucre sugar
vinaigre vinegar

Snacks
chips crisps
crêpe thin pancake
croque-monsieur/madame toasted ham and cheese sandwich/with fried egg
frites chips (French fries)
gaufre waffle
pissaladière a kind of pizza with onions
sandwich canapé open sandwich

Boissons (Drinks)
bière (pression) beer (draught)
bouteille (demi) bottle (half)
brut very dry
demi a third of a litre
doux sweet (wine)
eau (minérale, plate ou gazeuse) water (mineral, still or sparkling)
eau-de-vie brandy
eau potable drinking water
gazeuse sparkling
glaçons ice cubes
jus juice
lait milk
moelleux semi-dry
mousseux sparkling (wine)
pichet pitcher
sec dry
verre glass

Côte Chalonnaise and the Mâconnais also yield splendid wines. Then comes brash Beaujolais of the famous young fresh wines. Chablis, in the northwest of Burgundy, produces a popular white wine.

Paris

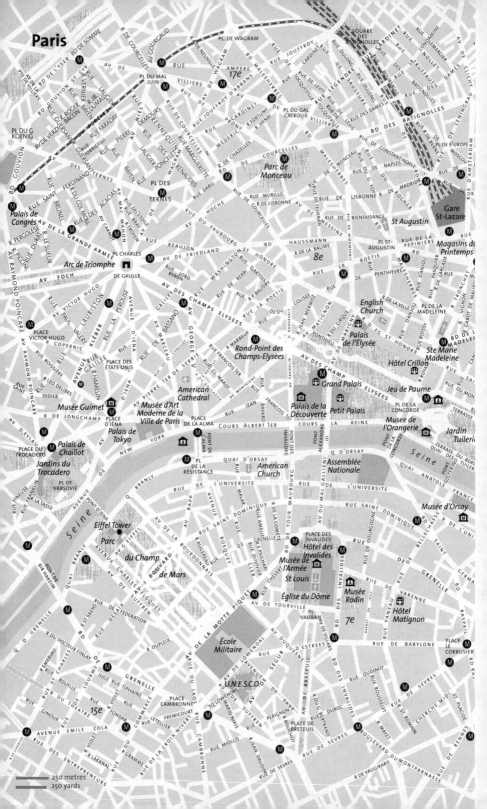

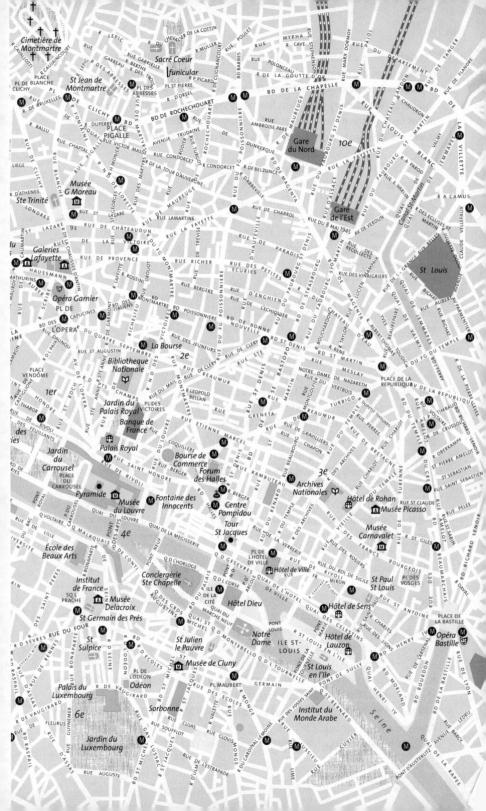

Paris has been a wonder for nearly a thousand years, from the time when masons came to learn the magic numbers of Gothic architecture to the present day. The Ville Lumière is France's collective dream, the vortex of all its vanity, its parasite and its showcase. But in many ways Paris has rarely been more delightful: *nouvelle cuisine* is out of fashion, the new museums are spectacular, the plonk in the cafés is better, the street markets are more seductive than ever; even rear-platform buses are back.

Ile de la Cité and Ile St-Louis

Paris made its début on the **Ile de la Cité** and the Parisians regard their river islet to this day as the centre of the city. Baron von Haussmann's mid-19th-century rebuilding of Paris banished 25,000 people who lived on a hundred colourful tiny streets and, like the City of London and Wall Street, the area is deserted at night. But two of the most luminous Gothic churches ever built are reason alone for visiting, and there are other delights – shady squares and *quais*, panoramic bridges, and the perfect symmetry of the **Ile St-Louis**, an island-village of the *haute bourgeoisie*, concocted by 17th-century speculators and architecturally little changed since, its narrow streets prettily lined with shops and cafés. A flower market on **Place Louis Lépine** (on Sundays a bird market) offers a haven of dewy green fragrances in the heart of the Cité.

The great cathedral of **Notre-Dame** (*open 8–6.45; part or all occasionally closed for services*) was destined to become the consummate work of the early Gothic, the measuring stick by which all other cathedrals are judged. During the Revolution, the Parisians first trashed Notre-Dame, wrecking most of its sculptures; then they decided to demolish it. The cathedral was saved, but little upkeep took place for centuries; serious restoration work began only in the 1840s, under Viollet-le-Duc. To see the façade as it was intended, remember that, as with the temples of ancient Greece, originally all the statues and reliefs of a Gothic church were painted in bright colours. We can only guess what the interior furnishings looked like in the days before the Revolution. Today, we must be content with the architecture and the remnants of the stained glass, with the three great rose windows, but they are more than enough.

At the beginning of Rue du Cloître signs beckon you to ascend the **Tours de Notre-Dame** for a Quasimodo's-eye view over Paris and a chance to eyeball the gargoyles at close quarters (*open daily 9.30–6.30; adm*).

At the **Sainte-Chapelle**, Cour du Mai, Palais de Justice, 4 Bd du Palais(*same opening hours as Conciergerie*), as at Notre-Dame, you will lose any notion you might have had about the Middle Ages being quaint and backward. Every inch declares a perfect mastery of mathematics and statistics, materials and stresses. The important part, the spectacular upper chapel, can only be entered from below; emerging from the narrow stair into the upper chapel is a startling, unforgettable experience. The other cliché in the books is that the Sainte-Chapelle is a 'jewel box' for St Louis' treasured relics; this too is entirely apt: awash in colour and light from the tall windows, the chapel glitters like the cave of the Forty Thieves.

At the tip of the Ile, the **Pont-Neuf** is the oldest bridge in Paris. By the late Middle Ages the ancient umbilical bridges tying the mother island to the banks of the Seine had become eternally jammed with traffic, and on 31 May 1578 the cornerstone for a

Getting There

You can still fly to Paris, arriving at Roissy airport a 20min RER ride from the centre, but by far the most convenient way is to take the **Eurostar** (*see* p.11) from London Waterloo, which speeds you right to the Gare du Nord in three hours and soon to be less.

Getting Around

By Métro and RER

The **Métro** is a godsend to disorientated visitors: quick and convenient for travelling, and its stations serve as easy reference points for finding addresses. To find the right train you'll need to look at the map and remember the name of the station at the *end of the line*. You can change Métro lines as often as you want on the same journey on the same ticket. There is a new automatic line, the *Météor*, Line 14, from Bibliothèque F. Mitterrand to the Gare St-Lazare, super efficient and hi-tech.

The Réseau Express Régional (**RER**) is Paris' suburban commuter-train system, and you can use métro tickets on it within the Paris boundaries. It can come in handy for getting across town fast or for visiting places like the Musée d'Orsay or the Jardin du Luxembourg, where it has the closest station. From almost all the other stations, you can easily change on to the Métro. The RER can also take you to Versailles or the airports.

Buy a **carnet** of 10 tickets for bus, Métro and RER, for €9.30.

By Bus

An unused Métro ticket is equally valid for the bus, but you'll need a fresh ticket with each bus you catch. Enter from the front of the bus and leave from the middle or the rear; press the *arrêt demandé* button just before your stop; you'll need to stamp (*oblitérer*) your ticket in the machine next to the driver.

The *Noctambus*, Paris' **night bus** network, can be useful; there are 16 lines, many converging at Place du Châtelet.

Route 29, through the Marais (from Gare St-Lazare to Gare de Lyon), features a modern version of the old Paris buses with open back platforms.

Sightseeing: *L'Open Tour*, a system of tourist buses with an open upper deck, follows a circular route of the principal sites with further loops out to Montmartre and to Bercy; *Montmartrobus* (route 64), another circular route, runs up, down and around Montmartre, get on or off anywhere, one ticket per journey.

By Taxi

There are 14,900 taxis in Paris. You can hail them in the street if their light is on.

By Boat

Bateaux-Mouches de Paris, t 01 42 25 96 10. From Pont de l'Alma, RER Pont de l'Alma (north side, 8e); night tours in summer and a fancy dinner cruise.

Canauxrama, t 01 42 39 15 00. Reserve for 3hr tours of Canal St-Martin.

Paris Canal, t 01 42 40 96 97. From the Musée d'Orsay up the Canal St-Martin to La Villette, passing through old locks.

Vedettes du Pont-Neuf, t 01 46 33 98 38. From Square du Vert-Galant, Ile de la Cité, 1er, Ⓜ Pont-Neuf.

Tourist Information

Paris: 127 Av des Champs-Elysées, 8e, **t** 08 36 68 31 12, near the Arc de Triomphe (*open daily 9am–8pm; low season same, but Sun 11–6*). A second office is at the Gare du Nord.

Weekly entertainment guides come out on Wednesdays: *Pariscope*, the similar *L'Officiel des Spectacles*, and *7 à Paris*. The Wednesday *Figaro* has weekly listings. FNAC has ticket offices all over the city and a general number, **t** 01 49 87 50 50; Virgin Megastore, 52 Av des Champs-Elysées, **t** 01 42 56 52 60, Ⓜ Georges V, is similar and open until midnight.

Shopping

You can tackle Paris' huge department stores, or there are endless little speciality shops tucked into nearly every *quartier*. Remember, most shops close on Sun and Mon.

The area around the **Opéra** is one of Paris' liveliest shopping districts, where the managers still send hucksters out on to the street to demonstrate vegetable choppers and dab cologne on the ladies.

Galeries Lafayette, 40 Bd Haussmann, 9e. A bit of Art Nouveau splendour with a wonderful glass dome. Ⓜ Chaussée d'Antin.

Printemps, 64 Bd Haussmann, 9e. A wee bit posher, stuffier and nearer the cutting edge of fashion. A good view from the café on the top floor. Ⓜ Havre-Caumartin.

The area around **Place de la Madeleine** is one of Paris' gourmet paradises, with famous restaurants such as Lucas Carton, and many of the city's finest food shops. There is also a small flower market (*daily exc Mon*).

Ladurée, 16 Rue Royale, 8e, Ⓜ Madeleine; 75 Av des Champs-Elysées, Ⓜ Franklin Roosevelt. Heavenly chocolates.

Au Nain Bleu, 408–10 Rue St-Honoré, 1er. Paris' most magical toy store. Ⓜ Concorde.

The **Champs-Elysées** is still the street to stroll, to see and be seen. The **Rue de Rivoli** is a long, busy street, lined with imposing, if not beautiful, buildings, and arcades.

WH Smith, 248 Rue de Rivoli, 1er, t 01 44 77 88 99. Especially good for their English-language magazines; fiction, children's and travel sections. Ⓜ Concorde.

Louvre des Antiquaires, next to the Louvre, 1er. The poshest, biggest antiques centre and a great place for browsing. Ⓜ Palais Royal.

Bazar de l'Hôtel de Ville (BHV), 52 Rue de Rivoli, 4e. BHV has been around since 1854 and lacks the pretensions of other department stores. A good bet for practical items. Ⓜ Hôtel de Ville.

La Samaritaine, 19 Rue de la Monnaie, 1er. The most beautiful department store in Paris, with its Art Nouveau façade, skylight and balconies (in the old building). The café on its 10th-floor terrace (*open April–Sept*) has one of the most gratifying views over Paris, across the Pont Neuf. Ⓜ Louvre-Rivoli.

The **Forum des Halles** is a subterranean labyrinthine 'new town' of shops and fast food outlets. The streets around are full of shops.

FNAC, Forum des Halles, Rue Pierre-Lescot. A Paris institution – the city's biggest and fullest book chain; also CDs, etc. Other outlets across the city. Ⓜ Châtelet-Les Halles.

Although you'll have to save up your pocket money just to be able to afford a *café au lait* in **St-Germain**, the bustling narrow streets,

legendary cafés and trendy bookshops invite you to explore and tempt you to spend. The **Latin Quarter** is the *quartier* of publishers and bookshops.

Le Bon Marché, 38 Rue de Sèvres, 7e. The only department store on the Left Bank, but the grandaddy of them all. Ⓜ Sèvres-Babylone.

Shakespeare & Co, 37 Rue de la Bûcherie, 5e, t 01 43 26 96 50. Just what a bookshop should be – a convivial treasure hunt. Ⓜ St-Michel.

The most ambitious restoration effort in Paris has spruced up the elegant streets and old palaces of the **Marais**, ready for your inspection; shops are exclusive and individual.

A short walk from Place de la Bastille down Rue de Lyon, or bus no.20, takes you to **Avenue Daumesnil**, where the old railway viaduct has been planted up into a charming *promenade plantée*, and below, every railway arch houses an *atelier* of a high-class specialized craft.

Markets

Les Puces de Saint-Ouen. The mother of all flea markets (*open Sat, Sun and Mon*). Ⓜ Porte de Clignancourt.

Puces de Montreuil. Great flea market (*open Sat, Sun and Mon*). Ⓜ Porte de Montreuil.

Marché aux Fleurs: Place de la Madeleine, 8e (*open daily exc Mon*); Place des Ternes, 8e (*open daily exc Mon*); and Place Lépine, 4e (*open Mon–Sat*).

Marché aux Vieux Papiers de St-Mandé, Av de Paris, 12e. Old books, postcards and prints (*open Wed*). Ⓜ Porte de St-Mandé Tourelle.

Place d'Aligre, 12e. Colourful food market, strongly North African. Ⓜ Ledru Rollin.

Buci, 6e. One of the liveliest, with a good selection; *best Sun am*. Ⓜ Mabillon.

Mouffetard, 5e. Lower end of Rue Mouffetard, with lots of character. Ⓜ Censier Daubenton.

Where to Stay

Advance bookings essential in June, and Sept/Oct when Paris is awash in conventions.

The annual hotel list for Paris available from the tourist office indicates all hotels with facilities for the **disabled**. **Postcodes** include the *arrondissement*, so an address with the postcode 75004 is in the 4th *arrondissement*.

★★★★**George V**, 31 Av George V, 75008, t 01 49 52 70 00, f 01 49 52 70 20, *par.reservations@ fourseasons.com, www.fourseasons.com* (*luxury*). Recently restored Art Deco hotel minutes from the shops of the Champs-Elysées, with 18th-century tapestries, a restaurant, bar and coffee lounge, health club, pool and spa, and some private terraces with fantastic views over Paris. Ⓜ George V.

★★★★**Jeu de Paume**, 54 Rue St-Louis-en-l'Ile, 75004, t 01 43 26 14 18, f 01 40 46 02 76, *www.hoteldujeudepaume.com* (*luxury–expensive*). Paris' last real-tennis venue is now the most enchanting little inn on the Seine, with a garden. Ⓜ Pont Marie.

★★★**Hôtel de l'Abbaye**, 10 Rue Cassette, 75006, t 01 45 44 38 11, f 01 45 48 07 86, *hotel.abbaye@wanadoo.fr, www.hotel-abbaye.com* (*luxury–expensive*). One of the swankiest small Left-Bank hotels – originally a monastery – and despite the traffic serenely quiet, especially if you get one of the rooms over the courtyard. Ⓜ St-Sulpice.

★★★**Tuileries**, 10 Rue St-Hyacinthe, 75001, t 01 42 61 04 17, f 01 49 27 91 56, *htuileri@ aol.com, www.members@aol.com/htuileri* (*expensive*). A quiet 18th-century *hôtel particulier* with antiques. Ⓜ Tuileries/Pyramides.

★★★**Hôtel de la Bretonnerie**, 22 Rue Ste-Croix-de-la-Bretonnerie, 75004, t 01 48 87 77 63, f 01 42 77 26 78, *hotel@bretonnerie.com* (*expensive*). A very popular small hotel with Louis XIII furnishings. Ⓜ Hôtel de Ville.

★★★**Le Colbert**, 7 Rue de l'Hôtel-Colbert, 75005, t 01 43 25 85 65, f 01 43 25 80 19 (*expensive*). Elegant, peaceful hotel with tearoom south of Place Maubert. Ⓜ Maubert-Mutualité, St-Michel.

★★**St-Louis Marais**, 1 Rue Charles V, 75004, t 01 48 87 87 04, f 01 48 87 33 26, *slmarais@cybercable.fr* (*expensive*). An 18th-century Celestine convent offering romantic if monk-sized rooms. Five floors, but no lift. Ⓜ Sully Morland/Bastille/St-Paul.

★★**Place des Vosges**, 12 Rue de Birague, 75004, t 01 42 72 60 46, f 01 42 72 02 64, *hotel.place.des.vosges@gofornet.com* (*expensive*). Well restored, and just a few steps from the *Place*. Ⓜ Bastille.

★★★**Grandes Ecoles**, 75 Rue du Cardinal Lemoine, 75005, t 01 43 26 79 23, f 01 43 25 28 15, *www.hotel-grandes-ecoles.com*

(*expensive–moderate*). One of the most amazing settings in Paris, a peaceful cream-coloured villa in a beautiful garden courtyard. Reserve weeks ahead. Ⓜ Cardinal Lemoine/Place Monge.

★★**'Hôtel de Charme' Ermitage**, 24 Rue Lamarck, 75018, t 01 42 64 79 22, f 01 42 64 10 33 (*moderate*). A charming little white hotel beneath the gardens around the Sacré-Cœur (no credit cards). Ⓜ Lamarck-Caulaincourt.

★★**Régyn's Montmartre**, 18 Place des Abbesses, 75018, t 01 42 54 45 21, f 01 42 23 76 69, *hotel@regynsmontmartre.com* (*moderate*). A simple but good address in the heart of Montmartre, with good views over Paris. Ⓜ Abbesses.

★★**Welcome**, 66 Rue de Seine, 75006, t 01 46 34 24 80, f 01 40 46 81 59 (*moderate*). Renovated, simple, soundproofed, and a warm welcome. Ⓜ Mabillon/Odéon.

★**Esmeralda**, 4 Rue St-Julien-le-Pauvre, 75005, t 01 43 54 19 20, f 01 40 51 00 68 (*moderate*). Endearing, romantic hotel in a 16th-century building with a *classé* stairway and 19th-century furnishings. Ⓜ St-Michel.

★★**Sévigné**, 2 Rue Malher, 75004, t 01 42 72 76 17, f 01 42 78 68 26 (*inexpensive*). Nice place right around the corner from the nosher's paradise of Rue des Rosiers. Ⓜ St-Paul.

★**La Vallée**, 84–6 Rue St-Denis, 75001, t 01 42 36 46 99, f 01 42 36 16 66, *hvallee@cybercable.fr, www.perso.cybercable.fr/hvallee* (*inexpensive*). Excellent bargain choice, between Les Halles and Beaubourg. Ⓜ Châtelet/Les Halles.

★**Le Central**, 6 Rue Descartes, 75005, t 01 46 33 57 93 (*inexpensive*). Family-run haven. Ⓜ Maubert-Mutualité/Cardinal Lemoine.

★**Hôtel des Académies**, 15 Rue de la Grande-Chaumière, 75006, t 01 43 26 66 44, f 01 43 26 03 72 (*inexpensive*). Simple, unpretentious, family hotel near the Luxembourg gardens. Ⓜ Vavin.

★**Henri IV**, 25 Pl Dauphine, 75001, t 01 43 54 44 53 (*inexpensive–cheap*). Four hundred years old, frumpy flowered wallpaper, and toilets and showers down the hall, but visitors book months in advance to stay in all simplicity in this most serendipitous square (no credit cards). Ⓜ Pont-Neuf/Cité.

Eating Out

Nearly all the restaurants listed below offer set-price menus; little adventures *à la carte* are liable to double prices. As anywhere in France, restaurants expect that most clients will order a *menu*, especially at lunch.

Jacques Cagna, 14 Rue des Grands Augustins, 6e, t 01 43 26 49 39 (*luxury*). One of Paris' most gracious institutions for an unforgettable culinary experience. Ⓜ Odéon.

Benoît, 20 Rue St-Martin, 4e, t 01 42 72 25 76 (*luxury–expensive*). Considered by many the most genuine Parisian *bistrot*, opened by current owner Michel Petit's grandfather, devoted to the most perfectly prepared dishes of *la grande cuisine bourgeoise française* with a wondrous *bœuf à la mode*. Ⓜ Châtelet.

Charlot Roi des Coquillages, 12 Place Clichy, 9e, t 01 53 20 48 00 (*luxury–expensive*). A 1930s brasserie; a fishy kitsch-palace. You would have to go to Marseille for better seafood. *Open daily until 1am.* Ⓜ Place Clichy.

L'Orangerie, 28 Rue St-Louis-en-l'Ile, 4e, t 01 46 33 93 98 (*expensive*). One of the most elegant and romantic dining rooms in Paris, founded by actor Jean-Claude Brialy as an after-theatre rendezvous for his colleagues; refined *cuisine bourgeoise*. *Dinner only; book.* Ⓜ Pont Marie.

Atelier de Maître Albert, 1 Rue Maître-Albert, 5e, t 01 46 33 13 78 (*expensive*). Stone walls, beams and an open fire create one of Paris' most medieval environments. *Closed Mon lunch, Sun.* Ⓜ Maubert-Mutualité.

Bofinger, 5 Rue de la Bastille, 4e, t 01 42 72 87 82 (*expensive*). One of the prettiest brasseries; wonderful seafood specialities. A great place. Also try cheaper **Le Petit Bofinger**, opposite. Ⓜ Bastille.

Tan Dinh, 60 Rue de Verneuil, 7e, t 01 45 44 04 84 (*expensive*). Excellent Vietnamese cooking – steamed crab, lobster triangles with ginkgo nuts. *Closed Sun.* Ⓜ Solférino.

Dominique, 19 Rue Bréa, 6e, t 01 43 27 08 80 (*expensive*). Restaurant, bar and deli; a favourite of Paris' Russians since the 1920s, with *chachlick caucasien* and Russian cheesecake. *Closed Sun and Mon.* Ⓜ Vavin.

Chez Paul, 13 Rue de Charonne, 11e, t 01 47 00 34 57 (*moderate*). Solid family cooking (rillettes, duckling with prunes) in an old Paris setting straight out of a Doisneau photo, complete with a pretty terrace. Ⓜ Bastille.

Caveau François Villon, 64 Rue de l'Arbre-Sec, 1er, t 01 42 36 10 92 (*moderate*). A *bistrot* in a 15th-century cellar, delicious fresh salmon with orange butter. *Closed Sun and Mon.* Ⓜ Louvre-Rivoli.

Le Roi du Pot au Feu, 34 Rue Vignon, 9e, t 01 47 42 37 10 (*moderate*). Entirely devoted to the most humble and traditional of all French dishes, but here raised to an art form. *Open 12 noon–10pm; closed Sun and end July to mid-Aug.* Ⓜ Madeleine.

La Ferme St-Hubert, 21 Rue Vignon, 8e, t 01 47 42 79 20 (*moderate*). The restaurant annexe to the famous *fromager*, serving a variety of delicious cheese dishes based on country recipes. *Closed Sun; open Aug.* Ⓜ Madeleine.

Le Montagnard, 102 Rue Lepic, 18e, t 01 42 58 06 22 (*moderate*). Good-quality traditional country cooking in an old Montmartre grill. Impressive attention to detail and excellent value. Ⓜ Abbesses.

Au Pied de Fouet, 45 Rue de Babylone, 7e, t 01 47 05 12 27 (*moderate*). Le Corbusier's favourite restaurant, shared table and long queues for its tasty and very affordable meals. *Closed Sat night, Sun and Aug.* Ⓜ Sèvres-Babylone.

Aux Charpentiers, 10 Rue Mabillon, 6e, t 01 43 26 30 05 (*moderate*). Located in the former carpenters' guild hall (with a little museum about it), serving excellent *pot-au-feu*, *boudin* and other everyday French basics; economical *plats du jour*. Ⓜ Mabillon.

Angelina, 226 Rue de Rivoli, 1er. A Viennese confection of a tearoom, vintage 1903 (when it was called Rumpelmayer), with a special rich African chocolate and the world's best *montblanc* (chestnut cream, meringue and chantilly). Ⓜ Tuileries.

Ladurée, 16 Rue Royale, 8e. Exquisite and precious *salon de thé*, famous for its macaroons. Bring your laciest great-aunt along for tea. Ⓜ Madeleine. Also at 75 Av des Champs-Elysées. Ⓜ Franklin-Roosevelt.

Berthillon, 31 Rue St-Louis-en-l'Ile, Ile St-Louis, 4e. Paris' best ice creams and sorbets; you can also enjoy them sitting down in most of the island's cafés. Ⓜ Pont Marie.

new bridge was laid by Henri III. Behind the equestrian statue of Henri IV, steps lead down to the **Square du Vert-Galant**, the leafy prow of the Ile de la Cité. From here you can embark on a tour of the Seine's other bridges on a *vedette du Pont-Neuf*.

The Marais and Bastille

One of the less frantic corners of old Paris, the Marais is the aristocratic quarter *par excellence*. The main attractions are the grand *hôtels particuliers* of the 16th–18th centuries and the museums they contain. In the area that has perhaps changed the least over the last 300 years, take time to look at details, like the 17th-century street signs or sculptural decoration on the scores of old *hôtels particuliers*.

When the Seine changed its present course, the old bed remained as low, marshy ground, especially at its eastern edge. Charles V enclosed the Marais within his new wall in the 1370s, and set the tone by moving in himself, and nobles and important clerics followed. What really made the Marais' fortune was Henri IV's construction of the striking **Place des Vosges** in 1605, today a favourite with tourists, Parisians and schoolchildren alike. During the Revolution most of the great *hôtels particuliers* were confiscated and divided up as homes for warehouses and clothing-makers. In the 1950s and '60s, Parisians finally rediscovered what had become a lost world. The old working population is long gone and the Marais has settled into a mixture of gay bars, hip boutiques, Hasidic Jews around Rue des Rosiers, and new immigrants from North Africa and the Middle East.

It is only fitting that the **Musée Carnavalet**, 23 Rue de Sévigné (*open Tues–Sun 10–5.40; closed Mon and public hols; adm*), the city museum of Paris, should be housed in the grandest of all the *hôtels particuliers*. The museum explores ancient and medieval Paris, with reproductions of rooms including the bedchamber of Marcel Proust, the ballroom of the Hôtel Wendel, the Fouquet jeweller's from Rue Royale, 1901, and a private room from the Café de Paris. Another section has paintings.

The **Musée Picasso**, 5 Rue de Thorigny (*open Wed and Fri–Mon 9.30–5, Thurs 9.30–8; closed Tues; adm*) is in the Hôtel Salé. There are few really famous pictures, but works can be seen from all Picasso's diverse styles. There is also a sculpture garden.

At **Place de la Bastille**, there's nothing to see of the famous fortress, of course. The square has been redesigned, with the outline of the fortress set into the pavement.

Les Halles and Beaubourg

For most of its life Les Halles was a vast colourful wholesale distribution market for all Paris, surrounded by slums. Today its bleak modern replacement, the **Forum des Halles**, is a subterranean labyrinthine 'new town' of failing shops, the park is as full of life as a cinder cemetery, and the streets are bleak un-spaces of plannerized compromise dominated by skateboarders and fast food outlets. Only the streets untouched by redevelopment are fun for ambling.

As soon as the **Centre Pompidou**, Place G. Pompidou and Rue St-Martin (*open Mon and Wed–Sun 11am–10pm, for guided visits call t 01 44 78 46 25; museum open 11am–9pm, last adm 8pm; adm; Atelier Brancusi open 1pm–9pm; closed Tues*) opened in 1977, Parisians and tourists voiced their opinion by making it overnight the most visited sight in the city. The 'Plateau' in front is filled with buskers and portrait-sketchers. Inside, you won't need a ticket for the escalator to the top, which runs along the outside, providing a spectacular view over Paris.

The major permanent feature of the centre is the newly reopened millennium-edition **Musée National d'Art Moderne**. This superlative collection of 20th-century art (*excellent audioguide available*) has been re-presented over two floors of open white space, punctuated at every turn with plate glass windows, alternating stunning views over Paris with flat, still lakes of water setting off stone and iron sculptures.

The Louvre

Open Thurs–Sun 9–6, Mon and Wed 9am–9.45pm; closed Tues; adm; free first Sun of month.

Here it is, the delicious, often indigestible 99-course feast that sooner or later all visitors to Paris must swallow. The Louvre was 350 years in the building, and the best parts are the oldest. Start on the eastern end, on Rue de l'Amiral de Coligny. The majestic **colonnade** (begun 1668) marks the beginning of the French classical style; its architect was Claude Perrault, brother of Charles, the famous writer of fairy-tales. The outer façades of the **north wing**, facing arcaded Rue de Rivoli, are contributions of Napoleon (right half, viewed from the street) and Napoleon III (left half); both lend much to the imperial dreariness of that street. As for the **south wing**, facing the Seine, the left half is the beginning of Catherine de' Medici's long extension. And then there's the **Pyramid** – for a simple geometric bagatelle, architect I. M. Pei's 1988 entrance to the Louvre has certainly generated a lot of ink.

Once through the door and down the long curving stairway, you are in the **Hall Napoléon**, where you can buy your ticket. From here you have a choice of three entrances into the labyrinth, up escalators marked **Denon**, **Sully** and **Richelieu**, the three sections into which the Louvre has been divided: Sully is the old Louvre, Denon the south wing, Richelieu the north wing. A free, colour-coded **orientation guide** is available at the front desk. Of course you will want to see the *Mona Lisa* (in the Salle des Etats), but make time for the Egyptian art, Etruscan and classical sculpture, French, Flemish, Dutch, German, Spanish and Italian painting, and the *objets d'art* in the Salle d'Apollon and on the first floor.

Opéra and Faubourg St-Honoré

This area was to the Paris of the early 1800s what the Champs-Elysées would be later in the century: the city's showcase and playground of the élite. It's still the home of all luxury; here you'll find the gilded fashion houses, department stores and jewellers whose names are known around the galaxy. Close to the Louvre and the *Grand Axe*, this corner of town attracted monumental projects from three of France's despots: Louis XIV's **Place Vendôme**, Napoleon's self-memorial that became the **Madeleine**, and Little Napoleon's incomparable Opéra.

The **Opéra** (*tours of the interior daily 10–4.30; guided tour at 1pm; museum open daily 10–4.30; separate adm for both; tours include the main hall on days when there is no*

performance; check beforehand, t 01 40 01 22 63, if you want to see Chagall's ceiling) is
the supreme monument of the Second Empire, conceived in 1858 by a fashionable
young architect named Charles Garnier. The inside is impressive, awash with gold
leaf, frescoes, mosaics and scores of different varieties of precious stone, from
Swedish marble to Algerian onyx. The highlight of the tour may be the hall itself, with
its **ceiling** (1964) painted by Marc Chagall; the nine scenes are inspired by the artist's
favourite operas and ballets.

Outside, the **Place de l'Opéra** was one of the status addresses of late 19th-century
Paris. To your left and right stretch the western **Grands Boulevards**. A century ago
these were the brightest promenades of Paris, home of all the famous cafés and
restaurants. Today the glamour has gone but the streets are popular just the same.

The Grand Axe

This is a part of Paris that every first-time visitor feels obliged to see. From the
Louvre to La Défense, the monuments line up like pearls on a string – some natural,
some cultured and some fake.

The first **Jardins des Tuileries** on this site were built at the same time as the Tuileries
palace, in the 1560s. It was Catherine de' Medici's idea; her new pleasure park,
designed by Philibert de l'Orme and others, was soon the wonder of Paris, symmet-
rical and neat. Accounts suggest it must have been much more beautiful, and more
fun, than the present incarnation. In the southwest corner, the **Musée National de
l'Orangerie** (*open daily exc Tues 9.45–5; adm*), offers a fine permanent collection,
complementary to the Musée d'Orsay, with a lower level devoted to Monet.

Without the cars the **Place de la Concorde** would be a treat, the most spacious
square and the finest architectural ensemble in Paris. Jacques-Ange Gabriel won the
competition for its design, breaking away completely from the enclosed, aristocratic
ethos of the other royal squares. A new exclamation mark along the Grand Axe, the
Egyptian **obelisk**, appeared in 1836. But in the meantime the Place had changed its
name six times, and had seen more trouble than any square deserves. In 1782 the spot
where the obelisk stands today held a guillotine, the venue for all the most important
executions under the Terror. On the western edge of the Place stands a pair of winged
horses to complement those on the Tuileries side, copies of the **Marly horses**.

The **Avenue des Champs-Elysées** was the second step in the creation of the Grand
Axe, the long radian that stretches, perfectly straight, from central Paris west to
La Défense. At first the Champs-Elysées was a less aristocratic promenade; all Paris
came on Sundays for a bit of fresh air, and in 1709 the pleasure promenade took its
present name, the 'Elysian Fields'. The upper Champs-Elysées, after decades of decline,
has been the subject of a major renovation which included everything from pavement surfaces to a second row of *platanes* (plane trees) on each side.

The **Arc de Triomphe** (*open Oct–Mar daily 10–5.30; April–Sept daily 9.30–6.30, Fri
9.30am–10pm; adm; pedestrian tunnel on right-hand side of Champs-Elysées*) is not a
tribute to Napoleon, although it certainly would have been if the Emperor had been
around to finish it; the arch commemorates the armies of the Revolution. It isn't
just its location and the historical connotations that make this such an important

landmark. It's also a rather splendid arch. Inside is a small museum of the arch – you can climb up to the roof for a remarkable view of the Grand Axe and the pie-slice blocks around the Etoile (recommended especially after dark).

Montmartre

From the Eiffel Tower, gleaming white Montmartre resembles an Italian hill town from Mars. A closer inspection reveals honky-tonk tourist Paris at its ripest, churning out francs from the fantasy-nostalgia mill for the good old days of Toulouse-Lautrec, can-can girls, Renoir and Picasso. On the other hand, get away from the Place du Tertre and the area holds some of Paris' last secret alleys and picturesque streets.

Many Parisians regard the **Sacré-Cœur** (*open daily 6.45am–11pm; free; dome and crypt open daily 9–6; adm*) with some embarrassment, with its preposterous Romano-Byzantine architecture. For a real descent into the abyss, visit the clammy crypt. The view from the dome isn't that much more spectacular than the view from the parvis, but you can look vertiginously down into the interior of the basilica.

Take a walk around the quiet streets of the hill. Part of the delight of little **Place des Abbesses** is Guimard's métro entrance, one of just two (the other is Porte-Dauphine) to survive with its glass roof intact. Leafy, asymmetrical **Place Emile Goudeau**, with its Wallace fountain, steps and benches, is the antithesis of the classic Parisian square down on the 'plain' below; note the curious perspective down **Rue Berthe**, which like many other streets up here, seems to lead to the end of the world. The last two of Montmartre's 30 windmills, **Moulin du Radet** (now an Italian restaurant) and to the left, **Moulin de la Galette**, built in 1640 and currently being restored, are on **Rue Lepic**.

The **Musée de Montmartre**, 12 Rue Cortot (*open Tues–Sun 11–6; closed Mon; adm*) is a genuine neighbourhood museum, set up and run by the people of Montmartre. Behind a pretty courtyard full of giant fuchsias, you'll see prints, pictures and souvenirs that tell the real Montmartre story.

Le Lapin Agile on Rue des Saules opened in 1860 as the Cabaret des Assassins, but in 1880 a painter named Gil painted the mural of a nimble rabbit avoiding the pot – a play on his name, the *lapin à Gil*. In 1903 Aristide Bruant purchased the place to save it from demolition and it enjoyed a second period of success. Artists could pay for their meals with paintings – as Picasso did with one of his *Harlequins*, now worth millions. Now, every evening, *animateurs* attempt to recapture that first peerless rapture. Opposite, **Montmartre's Vineyard** was planted by the Montmartrois in 1886 in memory of the vines that once covered the Butte.

The Latin Quarter

The area that houses the Sorbonne university and Grandes Ecoles can be good fun, especially at night. This is one of the rare corners of Paris to preserve the pre-Haussmann higgledy-piggledy. To see it all, wander the streets bordered by the Seine to the north and Boulevard St-Germain to the south, with Boulevard St-Michel to the west and the Ile de la Cité to the east.

Above the corner of Boulevards St-Michel and St-Germain rises the oldest surviving Roman monument in Paris, standing next to the Hôtel de Cluny, the Paris residence of the powerful abbots, and one of only two Gothic mansions in Paris. Appropriately, the two buildings contain one of the world's great collections of medieval art, the **Musée National du Moyen Age (Musée de Cluny)** (*open daily 9.15–5.45; closed Tues; adm*) a continuous trove of the rare and the beautiful in exquisite detail, including the six Aubusson tapestries of *La Dame à la Licorne*.

The **Panthéon** (*open daily Oct–Mar 10–6.15; April–Sept 9.30–6.30; adm*) stands on the summit of the Gallo-Roman Mont Leucotitius (Mont Lutèce), known since the Middle Ages as **Montagne Ste-Geneviève**. The church of **St-Etienne du Mont** (*open daily 7.45–12 and 2–7.30*) remains charming, asymmetrical and intact. This St-Etienne was begun in 1492, to squeeze in the great press of students. It retains a very fetching *jubé*, or rood screen, the only one left in Paris.

Mouffetard and Jussieu

This *quartier*, east of the medieval walls that cradled the Latin Quarter for most of its history, offers an unusual cocktail of sights and smells – gossipy village streets, a tropical garden and a Maghrebi mosque. Picturesque and piquant, the **Place de la Contrescarpe** (behind St-Etienne) dates only from 1852. For the next hundred years Paris' tramps flocked here, and now, even though most of the houses have been restored, it still has a bohemian atmosphere, particularly at weekends. Leading off Place de la Contrescarpe is **Rue Rollin**, a treeless street of blonde houses. Place de la Contrescarpe also stands at the top of **Rue Mouffetard**, one of the most ancient streets in Paris, following the path of the Roman road to Lyon. Since Roman times it has been lined with inns and taverns for the wayfarer. While strolling down the 'Mouff' and poking about in its capillary lanes and courtyards you can pick out a number of old signs, such as the carved oak at no.69 for the Vieux Chêne, which began as a Revolutionary club. Rue du Pot-de-Fer owes its name to the Fontaine du Pot-de-Fer, one of 14 fountains donated by Marie de' Medici. Further south, beyond Rue de l'Epée-de-Bois, begins Rue Mouffetard's **market** (*closed Mon*).

The **Grande Mosquée de Paris**, Rue Georges Desplas (*open for visits daily 9–12 and 2–6; closed Fri; adm*) was built between 1922 and 1926 in remembrance of the Muslim dead in the First World War and as a symbol of Franco-Moroccan friendship, and is nominally the central mosque for France's four million-plus faithful. Behind the mosque, at 41 Rue Geoffroy St-Hilaire, there's a Turkish **hammam** (*men Fri and Sun, women on other days 11–8; closed Tues*), with a quiet courtyard café serving mint tea.

The coolly elegant riverside **Institut du Monde Arabe**, 1 Rue des Fossés St-Bernard (*open Tues–Sun 10–6; closed Mon*), completed in 1987, is nearly everyone's favourite contemporary building in Paris. Its walls are covered with window panels inspired by ancient Islamic geometric patterns, but equipped with photo-electric cells that activate their dilation or contraction according to the amount of sunlight.

St-Germain

France is one country where brainy philosophers get respect, and St-Germain is their citadel. Since the 1960s it has cooled considerably, but St-Germain's essential conviviality remains intact. Its narrow streets, scarcely violated by the planners of the last two centuries, its art galleries and cafés (including on Bd St-Germain the **Café de Flore** and **Les Deux Magots**, haunted by the spirit of Sartre), its bookshops, and the elegant manicured **Jardin du Luxembourg** with its enticing metal chairs, all invite you to chat the day away.

If urbanity is St-Germain's middle name, it owes much to its parent, the abbey of **St-Germain-des-Prés**, one of the most important Benedictine monasteries in France and, until Dagobert (d. 639), the burial place of the Merovingian kings. Of this early church little has survived; the rest was rebuilt in 1193; architect Peter de Montreuil added a Lady Chapel, as beautiful as his Sainte-Chapelle. In 1840 Victor Hugo led a campaign for St-Germain's restoration, and for the next 20 years much of what the Revolutionaries missed fell victim to the hacks hired to save it. The marble shafts in the columns above the arcade are the only Merovingian work *in situ* in Paris.

Montparnasse

In the Middle Ages Montparnasse was where the flour was ground for the Left Bank's baguettes; in 1780 there were still 18 working windmills. The first houses date from the 17th century, when Louis XIV built the Observatoire. Land was still cheap enough in the early 1800s for Montparnasse to experience a first flash of fashion with its dance halls, *guingettes* and cabarets. After the Second World War the culture vultures retreated to St-Germain and the north side of Bd du Montparnasse, while the neighbourhood where Americans drank themselves silly was singled out for Paris' first experiment in American-style property development. Until the advent of London's Canary Wharf, the **Tour Montparnasse** (*viewing platforms open summer daily 9.30am–11.30pm; winter daily 9.30am–10pm; last ascent 30min before closing; adm*) was the tallest skyscraper in Europe, 656ft high and visible for miles around, perched at the top of Rue de Rennes. The 56th floor offers not only views but a bar, *Ciel de Paris*, and a film of aerial views over Paris; the 59th floor is an open terrace. On a clear day you can see for 25 miles. The submerged shopping mall in front overlooks Place du 18 Juin 1940, the date of de Gaulle's famous BBC speech. The streets around are filled with the everyday shops and bars of the real, non-touristy Paris of the Parisians.

Exhibition Paris

This isn't the cosy Paris of quaint *bistrots* and narrow streets; this is Paris, the national capital and showcase of France. Here at the self-designated centre of civilization both the buildings and the spaces between them are on an heroic scale, monuments baked through the centuries then iced by a succession of world fairs.

The Gare (now the **Musée) d'Orsay** at 1 Rue de la Légion d'Honneur (*www.musee-orsay.fr; open Tues, Wed, Fri, Sat 10–6, Sun and 20 June–20 Sept 9–6, Thurs 10–9.45pm; closed Mon; adm, half-price Sun*) is a monument born on the cusp of the 19th century: a daring work of iron weighing more than the Eiffel Tower. It opened as a museum in 1986. The core exhibits came from the former Jeu-de-Paume Museum and the 19th-century rooms of the Louvre. Here under one huge roof are gathered all the combative schools of painting and sculpture from 1848 to 1910, rounded out with a magnificent array of furniture, decorative arts, architecture and photography.

The Hôtel Biron (1731) at 77 Rue de Varenne is one of the most charming and best-preserved mansions in Paris from that period. When Auguste Rodin moved here in 1908, he was 68. The house is now the **Musée Rodin** (*open Tues–Sun 9.30–5.45; Oct–Mar Tues–Sun 9.30–4.45; closed Mon; adm; small fee for gardens only*). As well as his works, one room is dedicated to sculptor Camille Claudel, Rodin's mistress. Upstairs are paintings that Rodin owned and left to the state. Outside, amid the roses of the *Cour d'Honneur*, are *The Thinker* and other masterpieces in a delightful garden.

In 1670 Louis XIV's under-minister of war, Louvois, persuaded his warmongering king to provide a hospital for old soldiers, which could just incidentally double as a monument to the military glory of Louis himself. Set at the head of an enormous Esplanade stretching to the Seine, the **Invalides** has Siamese-twin churches, back to back, originally sharing the same altar and chancel: **St-Louis** (*open daily 10–6*) for the old soldiers and staff, and the Eglise-du-Dôme for royals. A large section of the **Musée de l'Armée** (*open daily 10–6; Oct–Mar daily 10–5; adm*) is devoted to Napoleon's life. Save your ticket for the **Eglise-du-Dôme**. The pointy dome is so impressive that the church is named after it, and so prominent on the skyline that it was freshly gilded with 27½ lbs of gold for the bicentennial of the Revolution. The big porphyry sarcophagus of **Napoleon's tomb** contains no fewer than six coffins fitted tightly together.

The incomparable souvenir of the 1889 Fair, the **Eiffel Tower** (*open winter daily 9.30am–11pm; summer daily 9am–midnight; adm exp*) was built to celebrate the Revolution's centenary and the resurrection of France after her defeat by Prussia in 1870. It was erected in two years, for less than 8 million francs, welded together with 2,500,000 rivets and built without a single fatal accident. Until 1930, when surpassed by the Chrysler Building in New York, it was the tallest structure in the world.

Over the river at the renovated **Palais de Tokyo** is an exciting new development in modern art presentation (*open noon–midnight*), breaking down traditional barriers.

Outside the Centre

Père-Lachaise Cemetery

Ⓜ *Père-Lachaise; 20ᵉ. Open Mon–Fri 7.30–6, Sat 8.30–6, Sun 9–6; 6 Nov–15 Mar daily 8–5.30.*

The 'most famous cemetery in the world', and the largest in Paris, Père-Lachaise has always been a favourite place for a stroll. In design, it is a cross between the traditional, urban French cemetery, with ponderous family mausolea in straight rows, and the modern, suburban-style model. At the main entrance you can buy a good map to all the famous stiffs. There are few signs to help you find the graves of the great and good, such as Héloïse and Abélard, Chopin, Balzac, Molière, Simone Signoret, Sarah Bernhardt, Proust, Isadora Duncan and Oscar Wilde.

Bois de Boulogne

After the Eiffel Tower, the Bois de Boulogne was not so long ago the most visited place in Paris. It owes its current appearance to Napoleon III, who spent his early years in London and gave it to the city as its own Hyde Park. Roads, riding and walking paths crisscross it, but for anyone with children in tow the biggest attraction is on the Neuilly side, to the north (Ⓜ *Les Sablons*) where the **Jardin d'Acclimatation** (*open daily 10–6; adm*) has nearly every possible activity for kids. The **Musée Marmottan**, 2 Rue Louis Boilly, Ⓜ La Muette (*open Tues–Sun 10–5.30; closed Mon; adm*) is on the edge of the Bois. The Marmottan family collected medieval miniatures, tapestries and Napoleonic art, but the Monets are the highlight.

The Catacombes

Ⓜ *Denfert-Rochereau; 14e. Open Tues–Fri 2–4; Sat and Sun 9–11 and 2–4; closed Mon and public hols; adm.*

Down, down the 90 steps of a spiral stair, and a tramp through damp and dreary tunnels to a vicious blue puddle called the *source de Léthé*, inhabited by little pale-eyed creatures who dine on bone moss. Then the doorway inscribed: 'Halt! This is the empire of the dead', beyond which is the main attraction: the last earthly remains of Mirabeau, Rabelais, Madame de Pompadour and five–six million other Parisians.

Day Trips from Paris

Versailles

*Château open April–Oct Tues–Sun 9–6.30; Nov–Mar Tues–Sun 9–5.30; closed hols; guided tours in English from 10am. You can visit, for various separate fees, the **Grands Appartements** (entrance A); the **Apartments of Louis XIV** and the **Apartments of the Dauphin and Dauphine** (entrance C); the **Opéra Royal**, a gem designed by Gabriel for Louis XV in 1768, which is all wood, painted as marble, but designed 'to resonate like a violin'. From April–mid-Oct the garden's **musical fountains** are turned on (all still using their original plumbing). A 'Passport' gives access to the **Château**, **Grand Trianon**, **Petit Trianon**, **Coach Museum** and the **Groves**.*

Versailles' name comes from the clods that the farmer turns over with his plough, referring to the clearing made for a royal hunting lodge. And so Versailles remained until the young Louis XIV saw Vaux-le-Vicomte and turned sour with envy. He would have something perhaps not better but certainly bigger, and he created for himself one of the world's masterpieces of megalomania. Versailles' 123 acres of rooms are strikingly devoid of art; the enormous façade of the château is as monotonous as it is tasteful, so as not to upstage the principal inhabitant. The object is not to think of the building, but of Louis XIV, and with that thought be awed; Versailles contributed greatly to the bankruptcy of France.

If there's no art in Versailles, there is certainly an extraordinary amount of skilful craftsmanship. Besides its main purpose as a stage for the Sun King (Versailles was open to anyone who was decently dressed, as long as they promised not to beg; anyone could watch the king attend Mass, or dine), the palace served as a giant public showroom for French products, especially luxury ones. As such it was a spectacular success, contributing greatly to the spread of French tastes and fashions throughout Europe. Today, Versailles' curators haunt the auction houses of the world, looking to replace as much of the original gear as possible – a bust here, a chair there. Even the gardens have been replanted with Baroque bowers.

The **Grands Appartements** are the public rooms open to all in Louis XIV's day. Then there are the **gardens**, last replanted by Napoleon III, with their 13 miles of box hedges to clip, and the 1,100 potted palms and oranges of the Orangerie. Not by accident, the sun sets straight into it on St Louis' day, 25 August, in a perfect alignment with the Hall of Mirrors. Louis kept a flotilla of gondolas on his Grand Canal, to take his courtiers for rides; today the gondoliers of Venice come to visit every September for the *Fêtes Vénitiennes*. The rest of the year you can hire a boat to paddle yourself about or a bike to pedal through the gardens, or even catch a little zoo train to a building far more interesting than the main palace, the **Grand Trianon** (*adm*). An elegant, airy Italianate palace of pink marble and porphyry with two wings linked by a peristyle, it was designed in 1687 for Louis XIV ('I built Versailles for the court, Marly for my friends, and Trianon for myself,' he said). After his divorce, Napoleon brought his new Empress Marie-Louise here.

The gardens in this area were laid out by Louis XV's architect, Jacques-Ange Gabriel, who also built the Rococo **Pavillon du Jardin des Français** and the refined **Petit Trianon** nearby (*adm*), intended for Louis XV's meetings with Mme de Pompadour. Louis XVI gave the Petit Trianon to Marie-Antoinette, who spent much of her time here. Beyond the Petit Trianon is the **Hameau de la Reine,** the delightful operetta farmhouse built for Marie-Antoinette, where she could play shepherdess. Nothing escaped Louis XIV's attention, and even his carrots and cabbages were planted in geometric rigidity in his immaculate vegetable garden, **Le Potager du Roi** (*entrance at 6 Rue Hardy, on the left side of Place des Armes, the square in front of the château; open April–Oct daily, guided tours Sat and Sun every hour 10–6; adm; book on t 01 39 24 62 62*).

Giverny

Monet's house and gardens, known as the **Fondation Claude Monet** (*open April–Oct Tues–Sun 10–6; closed Mon; adm*), may be one of the best-known sights in the whole of France, for British and American visitors, but be warned that it's only a small place, often infested with coachloads of tourists. Also be aware that you won't see any original Monet canvases here. Instead, wandering round the pretty pink-fronted house with its brightly coloured rooms you'll get a lesson in Japanese art, with virtually every inch of wall space hung with Japanese prints by Japanese masters, as arranged by the great French Impressionist himself. The links between the two styles don't jump straight out at you, but Monet's admiration is very clear.

Outside, you'll discover two separate gardens. The first, running down from the house, consists of the most densely planted rows of flowers you're ever likely to see, the colours and forms merging into a wonderful, unfocused blur. It's a bit like a poetic experience, such is this garden's brief, intense, mysterious impact.

Getting There

For **Versailles**, RER C or train from Gare Montparnasse or Gare St-Lazare to Versailles-Rive Droite, followed by a 15min walk.

For **Giverny**, take a **train** from Rouen to Vernon, then a **bus**, a **taxi** or a **bicycle** from the station. Most days, trains leave Rouen 7.58 and 10.08; the trip lasts about 40mins.

On Tues–Fri, **buses** from Vernon to Giverny go at 9.15 and 12.25. The last bus back leaves at 5.15 (Tues–Sat). For **taxis** in Vernon, pick one up at the station, or call **t** 02 32 21 37 50/06 09 31 08 99.

Tourist Information

Vernon ✉ **27201**: 36 Rue Carnot, **t** 02 32 51 39 60, **f** 02 32 51 86 55.

Eating Out

Versailles

Brasserie du Théatre, 15 Rue des Reservoirs, **t** 01 39 50 03 21 (*expensive*). Classic brasserie.

La Flotille, Parc du Château, near Grand Canal, **t** 01 39 51 41 58 (*moderate*). Some tables outside. Classic French cuisine, *sole meunière, etc.*

Giverny

Les Jardins de Giverny, t 02 32 21 60 80 (*moderate*). A rose garden surrounds the Belle Epoque house; the cooking is refined too. *Closed Sun pm and Mon.*

Musée-Hôtel Baudy, t 02 32 21 10 03 (*moderate*). For a more casual lunch with a bit of Impressionist history thrown in. *Closed Sun pm and Mon.*

An underground passageway leads visitors under the road to the second garden. It was from the railway line running along here that Monet first glimpsed the property of the Clos Normand which he would make his own. He lived here until his death in 1926, and the property was only sold by one of his sons in 1966. It had fallen into a state of disrepair, and a large amount of the money needed to restore it was donated by wealthy Americans. Nowadays, Monet's Japanese water garden looks immaculate, the big weeping willows dipping their fronds into the water, the Japanese bridge crossing it, and the waterlilies sitting ever so prettily on its surface. It makes a lovely photo, with the colourful splashes of tourists blurred in the background. But nothing can equal Monet's mystical transformations of his Nymphéas series, the crowning glory of his move towards a still more modern art form. Sadly, even his big, light-bathed studio has been turned into a mere souvenir shop selling poor reproductions of his works, imposed on all manner of objects. But if commerce has won out over art here, you'll at least leave with the reassuring certainty that art does beat commerce and reality hands down.

Along the main village street, the slick contemporary design of the **Musée d'Art Américain** (*open April–Nov Tues–Sun 10–6; closed Mon; adm*) calls for your attention, with its cool yet welcoming formal front garden, pool and café. As the name indicates, it displays works by American artists who came to France in the days when Monet was such an inspiration. The centre, you may have guessed, was paid for by wealthy American donors. The works are a mixed bag, not surprisingly, but pieces by Mary Cassat, for example, stand out. Theodore Butler, one American artist who came to worship the master, ended up marrying his stepdaughter. He and his fellow Americans started out by staying at the Hôtel Baudy, which is still thriving; as is a whole art industry – you can judge for yourselves what you make of the artists working here today.

Claude Monet and family are buried in the unfussy village church.

The Northern Channel Ports and Lille

Lille is a great surprise, a city where Parisian chic meets Belgian chocolate. Contrary to everyone's expectations of the capital of French Flanders and France's industrial north, its centre proves a very glamorous, grandiose place indeed. Striking buildings rise up around huge Flemish squares. You won't fail to be impressed by central Lille's grandeur. And it boasts several major cultural attractions, including the vast fine arts museum, plus a couple of superb modern art collections in the outskirts of the city. This is also the town which witnessed the birth of one Charles de Gaulle. Getting down to shopping, Lille has superb food and clothes boutiques that will definitely make your mouth water.

Lying like mirages in the far distance off the Kent coast on clear days of the year, the ports of Calais and Dunkerque are a rather different kettle of fish; as you approach them you'll soon make out the factories and smoking chimneys marking their skylines, while up close, functional post-war architecture dominates in their chaotic centres. But they have their particular attractions. Both of course have a war museum to recall their tormented 20th-century histories, helping to explain why they look the way they do. Of the two, Dunkerque has preserved or restored more of its historic buildings, in particular those soaring Flemish towers so greatly appreciated in these flatlands, and it has put together a fine maritime museum. Calais survives above all on its reputation for bargain shopping.

But you only have to go a short way out from either port to come to one of northern France's greatest tourist assets – big, broad, firm beaches backed by comfortably knobbly dunes whose foot-caressing soft white sands are held together by whispering grasses. Just inland lie fortified hill towns with much more historic atmosphere, plus the café life and delectable little shops that make France so very appealing to foreigners. Try St-Omer, Montreuil, or quieter Bergues. Then there's Boulogne, sadly deprived of its cross-Channel services recently, but holding its own with its lively historic upper town and its state-of the-art sea-life centre down below.

Around Lille, we suggest day trips to Douai and Arras. The former hosted the Parlement of French Flanders before the Revolution, while the latter was one of Flanders' wealthiest cities in medieval times, as you'll immediately see from the flamboyant display of scrolled Flemish gables. Through those times, this thin slice of border territory wasn't French at all, ruled over instead by the counts of Flanders, and then the dukes of Burgundy, before the Habsburgs acquired it for their Spanish Netherlands. With all its most un-French 'z's and 'q's in its place names, this portion of Flanders only became French after Louis XIV invaded it in the mid-17th century. French Flanders has suffered particularly appallingly in wars down the centuries, and especially in both world wars. Some of the towns bear the scars to this day, others, most notably Arras, have been brilliantly restored.

Calais and Dunkerque

Calais

Like Venice, Calais is best approached by sea. But it would take a drug-crazed advertising man to describe Calais as a Venice of the north. However ugly it may prove to be, Calais remains close to many an Englishman's heart – mainly, it has to be admitted, for cheap beer, wine and cigarettes these days. Its historic symbolism as an outpost of England hasn't been entirely forgotten, but Calais has been so fought over down the centuries that very little of its history remains visible. What is clear is that Calais' centre is now divided into two by a no man's land of bridges and roads.

Calais

Avant Port

Hoverport

Plage de Calais

Car Ferry Docks

Bassin Est

Capitainerie du Port

Camping

Cross-Channel Ferry Terminal

Calais-Maritime Train Station

DIGUE GASTON BERTHE

Arrière Port

RUE DU MARECHAL DU LATTRE DE TASSIGNY

RUE JEAN MOULIN

BD DU GENERAL DE GAULLE

Yacht Club

Bassin des Chasses

Darse des Yachts

Bassin Ouest

BD DE 8 MAI

BD DE LA RESISTANCE

BD DES ALLIES

PONT VETILLARD

Bassin Carnot

ROUTE DE QUAI DE LA LOIRE

RUE DU NORD

BD DE 8 MAI

Canal de la Citadelle

PLACE D'ARMES

Tour du Guet

RUE ROYALE

RUE CLEMENCEAU

RUE DU DUC DE GUISE

RUE DE BRUXELLES

RUE DE LONDRES

QUAI FOURNIER

RUE DE MOSCOU

AV PIERRE DE COUBERTIN

Musée des Beaux-Arts et de la Dentelle

Bassin de la Marne

Bassin de la Batellerie

Arrière Bassin

RUE MOLLIEN

Calais-Ville Train Station

Musée de la Guerre

Parc St-Pierre

Hôtel de Ville

Canal de Calais

Police Station

RUE DU PHALSBOURG

BD JACQUART

Monument des Bourgeois de Calais

RUE DE VERDUN

BOULEVARD LEON GAMBETTA

Bus Station

AVENUE LOUIS BLERIOT

RUE DE VILLARS

BD LA FAYETTE

600 metres

600 yards

PLACE CREVECOEUR

Hospital

To Channel Tunnel Terminals (4km) and Cité d'Europe

BD DE L'EGALITE

To A16-E40

N

Northern Central Calais

If you're visiting in holiday season, consider climbing to the top of the **lighthouse** (*open July–Aug and French school hols 2–6*) near the centre to get your bearings and to reassure yourself that there is life beyond Calais. Not far off, another tower rising hopefully out of town is that of the brick church of **Notre-Dame**. The crossing had to be rebuilt after the war, hence the different colour of the materials. Charles de Gaulle married his Calais bride here in 1921, between the wars which so devastated the city.

Before the German onslaught, Calais had been fought over by the French and the Spanish after the centuries-long dispute between English and French crowns. Now the tensions in town are likely to be between fellow Brits fighting over their place in a shopping queue. The big, shabby, post-war **Place d'Armes** close to the port is busy with bars and shops, and overseen from one corner by a grim 13th-century **watch tower** – a rare vestige of the old town, and about as friendly as a trained guard dog. **Rue Royale** heads south from here, the top part of the main shopping artery cutting through the two halves of the centre.

At the end of the Rue Royale, **gardens** stand either side; those of the **citadel**, remnant of a fort built by Louis XIV's military genius Vauban, are the more interesting of the two. But beside the other garden, **Parc Richelieu**, stands the brick and glass fine arts museum. Housed in its rather characterless 1960s building, this **Musée des Beaux-Arts et de la Dentelle** (*open Mon and Wed–Fri 10–12 and 2–5.30, Sat 10–12 and 2–6.30, Sun 2–6.30; closed Tues*) contains displays on the industrially produced but beautiful lace for which Calais was long renowned, plus an introduction to Flemish art. It also holds an interesting collection of sculptures. These works start with a provocative little equestrian statue of Napoleon, but the main focus of interest is Rodin's set of studies for his late 19th-century masterpiece, *The Burghers of Calais*.

Rodin's desperate, ragged figures, some still wearing their dignity, if little else, in their desolation, others utterly lost in their individual agony, were made to recall the terrible siege of Calais by King Edward III of England's troops from 1346 to 1347. After 11 months of terrible suffering, the governor of Calais announced to the English that the townspeople were prepared to surrender. Keen to humiliate them still further,

Getting to Calais

Hoverspeed Ferries (*see* p.11) operates the fastest cross-Channel service, on the Dover–Calais Seacat (35mins).

P&O Stena Line (*see* p.11) runs both a ferry and superferry service from Dover to Calais (45mins), while **SeaFrance** (*see* p.11) does the same trip in 1.5hrs.

Eurotunnel stops at Calais.

More detailed information about travelling by ferry and train is given in **Travel**, pp.10–11.

For **taxis** in Calais, call **t** 03 21 97 89 89/**t** 03 21 97 35 35/**t** 03 21 97 05 22/**t** 03 21 97 13 14.

Getting from the Port

The ferry and hovercraft services are on the eastern side of the town centre; the companies run cheap or complimentary buses into the centre for foot passengers. The Channel Tunnel terminal is a little way west of Calais, between Coquelles and Fréthun.

Car Hire

Several choices at the ferry terminals:

A.S. Location, t 03 21 96 25 26, **f** 03 21 97 71 00.
Citer, t 03 21 34 58 45.
Eurotogo Inglard, t 03 21 96 36 12.
Hertz, t 03 21 96 36 84.

Tourist Information

Calais: 12 Bd Clemenceau, **t** 03 21 96 62 40, **f** 03 21 96 01 92, *www.OT-calais.fr*, *ot@ot-calais.fr*.

Market Days

Place Crèvecœur and **Place d'Armes**: Wed, Thurs and Sat am.

Shopping

You can make huge savings on wine, beer and cigarettes by buying them in France rather than Britain, thanks to tax differences. But other products are far cheaper in France, especially in Calais' big stores and malls.

In the centre, **Place d'Armes** has a few interesting shops such as the lively Bar à Vins, a wine store as well as a bar, run by an impassioned connoisseur. There are also gift shops on the square. Down **Rue Royale** you can sniff out some appealing food stores. Crossing to **Boulevard Jacquard** and **Boulevard Lafayette**, you'll find big stores, plus Royal Dentelle selling Calais lace, especially for the table.

Just before the ferry port, off the Rocade Est (eastern ringroad), is **Zone Marcel Doret**, one zone of cheap wine, beer and other outlets.

West of town, by the Channel Tunnel (exit 12 or 14 from the A16 motorway), rises the vast **Cité Europe** mall (*open Mon–Thurs 10–8, Fri 10–9 and Sat 9–8*). It has around 150 shops, including a mass of clothes shops, gift and beauty boutiques, and food and wine outlets, plus a Tesco. The vast Carrefour hypermarket is open even longer hours than the rest, *Mon-Fri 9am–10pm and Sat 8.30am–10pm*.

The separate zone of **Parc La Française** just north of Cité Europe includes the likes of Auchan, Sainsbury's, and Nike Factory Store.

Edward III insisted that six of the town's leading merchants should come out barefoot, noosed and begging, to present him with the keys to Calais. The English king's wife, Queen Philippa of Hainaut, is said to have been so distressed by the scene that she entreated her husband to show mercy to the six sacrificial burghers. They were spared, as was the town of Calais on that occasion. Rodin's major work of art serves as an awful reminder of how English and French crowns fought over parts of France for so long. Famously, Calais remained the last piece of territory that the English monarchy held on to in France after the end of the Hundred Years' War, but that it lost when the powerful Duc de Guise arrived by surprise to win it back for the French in 1558. This supposedly led Mary Tudor to declare that she would die with Calais engraved upon her heart – with its loss, she saw the final destruction of all her dearest hopes to cement a lasting alliance between her Catholic England and the mighty Catholic Spain of her husband Philip.

Where to Stay

Calais ✉ 62100

Don't come to Calais expecting charming little French hotels just bursting with character; be prepared for mainly chain-hotel-type offerings. Our tip is to try one of the inexpensive hotels well located by the beaches on the western side of town.

***Holiday Inn, 6 Bd des Alliés, **t** 03 21 34 69 69, **f** 03 21 97 09 15, *www.holidayinn-calais.com* (*expensive*). In an unremarkable but usefully tall building between the port and the main shopping street, as it has rooms with sea views. (*Restaurant: basic French fare, closed weekend lunchtimes.*)

***George V, 36 Rue Royale, **t** 03 21 97 68 00, **f** 03 21 97 34 73, *www.GEORGEV-CALAIS.com* (*moderate*). Comfortable, and set in the thick of the action on the main shopping street. The restaurant (*expensive–moderate*) serves good fish and northern French classics. *Closed lunchtime Sat, and Sun.*

Kyriad Calais Plage, Digue Gaston Berthe, **t 03 21 34 64 64, **f** 03 21 34 35 39, *Kyriad.calais@libertysurf.fr* (*inexpensive*). Standard chain hotel, but in a good location very close to the beach on the western side of the port.

Hôtel du Golf, Digue Gaston Berthe, **t 03 21 96 88 89, **f** 03 21 34 75 48, *hoteldugolf.calais@libertysurf.fr* (*inexpensive*). Like its neighbour described immediately above.

Hôtel des Dunes, 48 Route Nationale, 62231 Blériot-Plage (west of town; if without a car, take bus line 3 from outside Calais' theatre), **t 03 21 34 54 30, **f** 03 21 97 17 63, *www.les-dunes.com* (*inexpensive*). A bit more individuality, as well as being very close to the beach. The restaurant (*moderate*) serves delicious fish dishes. *Closed Sun pm and Tues off-season.*

*Bristol, 13 Rue du Duc de Guise, **t/f** 03 21 34 53 24 (*cheap*). A cheap hotel with a cheerful front, well situated off Rue Royale.

Eating Out

L'Aquar'aile, Résidence Les Ridens, 255 Rue Jean Moulin, **t** 03 21 34 00 00, **f** 03 21 34 15 00 (*moderate*). One of the region's best seafood restaurants, perched high up in a modern block behind the western beach and looking out over the busy shipping lanes. *Closed Sun pm.*

Au Côte d'Argent, 1 Digue Gaston Berthe, **t** 03 21 34 68 07, **f** 03 21 96 42 10 (*moderate*). Another excellent seafood restaurant, in prime location by the beach. *Closed Sun pm and Mon.*

Le Channel, 3 Bd de la Résistance, **t** 03 21 34 42 30, **f** 03 21 97 42 43 (*moderate*). Popular for fish, with views over the marina.

La Sole Meunière, 1 Bd de la Résistance, **t** 03 21 34 43 01, **f** 03 21 97 65 62 (*moderate*). Neighbour of Le Channel, with similar features.

You can find many more restaurants around the Place d'Armes; fish is almost always the speciality.

Southern Central Calais

The finished group of Rodin's sculptures of the desperate burghers of Calais, erected in 1895, stands in the formal gardens below the soaring Flemish belfry of the rebuilt **town hall** that calls for your attention as you cross into the southern half of central Calais. This typical grand Flemish brick Hôtel de Ville reflects the pride of the Flemish merchants in their towns.

Well concealed in the unremarkable public park opposite the town hall lurks one of the most awesome Nazi bunkers you'll ever have the dubious pleasure of seeing, measuring almost 100 metres in length. Cleverly camouflaged by ruins when it was built, it survived all the Allied bombings and served as a Nazi naval headquarters. Now converted into the **Musée de la Seconde Guerre Mondiale** (*open May–Aug daily 10–6; April and Sept daily 11–5.30; Oct–mid-Nov daily exc Tues 12–5; mid-Feb–March daily exc Tues 11–5*), just one room is devoted to the First World War, when Calais was in British hands and had already received its first pasting from bombs. But the museum concentrates on the German occupation of Calais from May 1940 to autumn 1944. A clutter of cuttings, posters, uniforms, weapons and other war paraphernalia fills the claustrophobic spaces. At one point the Germans deliberately flooded the plain around Calais; for a long time afterwards the fields were so badly affected by the sea salt that nothing grew there.

Back with Calais' light relief – shopping – **Boulevard Jacquart** continues where Rue Royale left off. **Boulevard La Fayette** beyond also has major shops, while **Place Crèvecœur**, the large square just off it, hosts a major market.

Calais' Beaches

Long, sandy **beaches** stretch westwards from the port, first backed by cheap apartment blocks and rows of sometimes graffiti-covered white shacks that watch the ferries ploughing in and out of port, then with just a small line of dunes dividing the suburban string of houses from the comfortable sands. The name of **Blériot-Plage** and a monument there honour Louis Blériot, the Frenchman who succeeded in making the first-ever flight across the English Channel, in July 1909. God forbid you from thinking he might have been trying to escape from Calais.

Dunkerque (Dunkirk)

France's third-largest port after Marseille and Le Havre, with its 17 kilometres of industrial plant stretching along the coast, Dunkerque also has its own quite amusing sandy beach resort, Malo-les-Bains. It can prove hard to find the centre of Dunkerque, surrounded by such a mass of factories with their outsized chimneys, cranes and pylons, so look out carefully for the signs.

Dunkerque's Main Monuments

Dunkerque suffered appallingly in the Second World War, as everyone knows. Over 80 per cent of the city was destroyed. Despite this, in the centre, many more historic

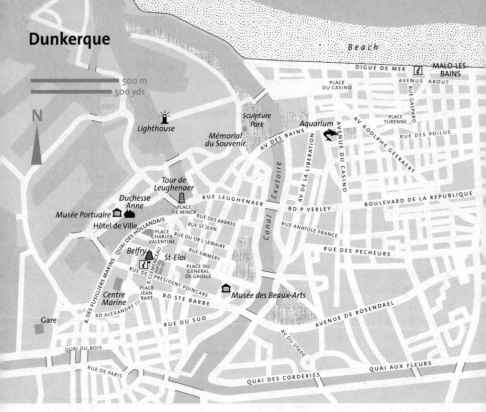

Dunkerque

Beach

DIGUE DE MER

MALO-LES-BAINS

PLACE DU CASINO · AVENUE ABOUT · RUE GASPARD

Lighthouse

Sculpture Park

Mémorial du Souvenir

Aquarium

PLACE TURENNE · AV ADOLPHE GEERAERT · RUE DES POILUS

AV DES BAINS · AVENUE DU CASINO · AV DE LA LIBERATION

Tour de Leughenaer

RUE LEUGHENAER · BD P VERLEY · BOULEVARD DE LA REPUBLIQUE

Duchesse Anne

Musée Portuaire · Hôtel de Ville

PLACE DE MINCK · RUE DES ARBRES · RUE ST JEAN · RUE DU DR L LEMAIRE · RUE ANATOLE FRANCE · RUE DES PECHEURS

PLACE CHARLES VALENTINE · RUE EMMERY

Belfry · St-Eloi

PLACE DU GENERAL DE GAULLE

QUAI DES HOLLANDAIS · RUE DE CLEMENCEAU · R. DE PRESIDENT POINCARE

Centre Marine · PLACE JEAN BART · BD STE BARBE · Musée des Beaux-Arts

R. DES FUSILLIERS MARINS · BD ALEXANDRE III · RUE DU SUD · AVENUE DE ROSENDAEL

Gare

QUAI DU BOIS · RUE DE PARIS · AV DU STADE · QUAI DES CORDERIES · QUAI AUX FLEURS

Canal Exutoire

monuments rise above the plain post-war brick and cement blocks than in Calais. The Flemish love their towers, and Dunkerque typically has a few major ones. The **Tour Leughenaer**, the town's oldest monument and a lone reminder of massive fortifications built in the 14th century when the mighty dukes of Burgundy ruled over Flanders, oversees the central harbour. Nearby rises the belfry of the mock-historic red-brick **town hall**. But the most impressive tower stands opposite the Gothic church of St-Eloi. At the base of this pale brick **belfry**, plaques honour the bravery of the soldiers who valiantly tried to defend Dunkerque against the Germans in the Second World War; its ground floor contains the tourist office. Climb to the top of this solid tower (*regular visits mid-June–mid-Sept; adm*), past an impressive collection of bells, to fathom out the structure of the port below and enjoy a splendid industrial panorama.

The **church of St-Eloi** to which the belfry was once attached is Dunkerque's most graceful building. The late Gothic façade stands out because of its pale white, pinnacle-covered stone and the stunning tracery of the rose window. The church is dedicated to a major French Merovingian bishop who was influential in consolidating Christianity in northern France under 7th-century King Dagobert. In fact, the port derives its name from a church (Kerque in Flemish) in the dunes. Dunkerque has a long history, therefore. But one single dashing figure dominates from the past – 17th-century corsair **Jean Bart**. The airy church interior with its gilded touches even contains his tombstone, plus others written in Flemish and Spanish as well as in French, an indication of the different influences brought to bear on the area.

Getting to Dunkerque

Norfolkline, t (01304) 218 410, f (01304) 218 420, *www.norfolkline.com*, runs a very good-value Dover–Dunkerque car-only service.

Getting from the Port
Ferries arrive at amusingly named but desolate-looking Loon-Plage, a fair way west of Dunkerque towards Calais.

Tourist Information

Dunkerque: Le Beffroi, Rue de l'Amiral Ronarc'h, t 03 28 66 79 21, f 03 28 63 38 34, *www.ot-dunkerque.fr.*

Market Days
Dunkerque: Place du Général de Gaulle, Wed and Sat all day.
Dunkerque-Malo: Place Turenne, Tues am.

Shopping

The main shopping streets lead off **Place Jean Bart**, notably **Boulevard Alexandre III** and **Rue Clemenceau**, for the big stores. **Rue du Président Poincaré** is good for food shops selling Flemish specialities, both meat dishes and beers; there's also a good cheese shop along this street. Short **Rue des Marines**, one of the most stylish shopping streets in Dunkerque, lined with silver birches and stone pillars, takes you from near Place Bart to the millennium-new **Centre Marine**, a pleasing glass cube of a shopping mall, fronted on one side by a grand arch, a rare remnant of Vauban's spectacular 17th-century defences for the city. The mall is good for clothes shopping in particular. Along **Rue des Marines** it's easy to spot the excellent pâtisserie. For fine wines, you could try Caves de la Transat, 25 Rue du Gouvernement, Quartier de la Citadelle, t 03 28 63 78 25,

Where to Stay

Dunkerque-Malo ✉ **59240**
It's nicer to stay in Dunkerque's beach resort, Malo-les-Bains, than in the old port.

★★Zanzibar Victoria Hotel, 5 Av de la Mer, t 03 28 28 28 11, f 03 28 20 77 11, *zanzibar.victoria@ wanadoo.fr* (*moderate*). Just 50m back from the seafront, rooms imaginatively decorated in warm wood furnishings and with amusing touches. Good ethnic restaurant (*moderate*).
★★Hôtel Eole, 77 Digue de la Mer, t 03 28 69 13 64, f 03 28 69 52 57 (*inexpensive*). Sandwiched between eccentric beachfront villas, with the great advantage of having the only rooms along the promenade looking out to sea. Basic restaurant (*cheap*).
B&B Croissant Lune, 59 Rue Louis Vanraet, t 03 28 63 73 48 (*inexpensive*). A decent B&B option in the midst of the resort.

Dunkerque ✉ **59140**
★★★Hôtel Borel, 6 Rue l'Hermitte, t 03 28 66 51 80, f 03 28 59 33 82, *www.hotelborel.fr* (*moderate*). Not exactly inspiring on the outside, but inside it's OK and has rooms overlooking the port in the centre of town.
★★★Welcome Hôtel, 37 Rue Poincaré, t 03 28 59 20 70, f 03 28 21 03 49 (*moderate*). Rooms recently redone, well located for the shops.

Eating Out

For excellent fish, try one of the rival gastronomic restaurants on the quay by the Musée Portuaire.
Le Corsaire, 6 Quai de la Citadelle, **t/f** 03 28 59 03 61 (*moderate*). Excellent spicy fish dishes, or such delights as seafood couscous.
L'Estouffade, 2 Quai de la Citadelle, **t/f** 03 28 63 92 78 (*moderate*). *Estouffades* are stews, the speciality here.

For meaty, beery Flemish specialities try:
Au Petit Pierre, 4 Rue Dampierre, t 03 28 66 28 36, (*moderate*). Warm Flemish food in warm Flemish restaurant in the centre.
Estaminet Flamand, 6 Rue des Fusilliers Marins, t 03 28 66 98 35 (*cheap*). Very Flemish decoration to accompany the dishes. Close to the Centre Marine.

Malo-les-Bains is crammed with basic seafront eateries.
Le Roi de la Moule, 129 Digue de Mer, t 03 28 69 25 37 (*cheap*). The most cheerful place to taste mussels on the seafront.

A grandiose 19th-century statue of Bart, once the scourge of the English navy, stands over the rather vacuous square nearby that is named after him. It may seem unsavoury for a corsair to have been elevated to such prominence, but, in the interminable wars between western European nations in the Ancien Régime, these daredevil men, backed by their states, were hailed as heroes – Louis XIV himself honoured Bart. Near Place Bart lies the main shopping district.

Dunkerque's Museums

Dunkerque's central harbour attracts plenty of yachts, but the tall ship, the *Duchesse Anne*, steals the show, making a great advertisement for the excellent **Musée Portuaire** (*open Wed–Mon 10–12.45 and 1.30–6; July–Aug 10–6; closed Tues; adm*), which tells the story of Dunkerque and its maritime past. First, go on board the *Duchesse Anne* to admire its decks. This splendid sailing ship was in fact built at the start of the 20th century as a German naval training boat. It seems a small compensation for Dunkerque to show off this vessel.

The spacious, shipshape museum itself is housed in a former tobacco warehouse. Different sections are devoted to Dunkerque's history, its fishing traditions of herring and cod, and the diverse trades exercised in such a massive port. You can take in some astonishing images of how the harbour looked after Vauban designed its defences under Louis XIV, as well as admiring a whole array of model ships. Homage is paid to the city's corsairs. Dunkerque changed hands so many times that it was even briefly English-owned, between 1658 and 1662, given to Cromwell for his help in fighting the Habsburgs. King Charles II sold it back to France for a hefty sum. The Musée Portuaire is a hive of activity in summer. It organizes boat tours of Dunkerque's **port** (*Tues–Sun; adm*) in July and August, when it also oversees the opening of the **Phare de Dunkerque** (*open weekends, 3–7; adm*), one of the tallest lighthouses in France.

Dunkerque's **Musée des Beaux-Arts** (*open Wed–Mon 10–12 and 1.45–6; closed Tues; adm*) lies in a serene grey-stoned building just east of the city centre. Inside, you can go for an interesting trawl through northern European art from the 16th century onwards. The collections include some fine Flemish still lifes, portraits by Pourbus and Reyn, and a noble head of a turbaned young black man by Rigaud, his neck collar a sign of his exploitation. Modern and contemporary artists are also represented.

Head up towards Dunkerque's resort of Malo-les-Bains, and you'll come to a contemporary outdoor **sculpture park** off Avenue des Bains. Tucked away behind it, the **Mémorial du Souvenir** (*open May–Sept 10–12 and 2–5.30*) is a small, traditional war museum set in the remnants of defensive bastions built to protect Dunkerque harbour and French border territory after France's humiliating defeat by Germany in the 1870 Franco-Prussian War. But the exhibits and stirring photographs inside recall Dunkerque's dreadful fate at the hands of the Germans at the start of the Second World War. The Nazis suddenly struck Holland on 10 May 1940. Five days later the Dutch surrendered. The Franco-British forces moved into Belgium to defend it, but, ill-prepared for the force of the German *Blitzkrieg*, they had to beat the hastiest, most desperate of retreats towards Dunkerque. It looked as though the French and British forces might be annihilated. In those harrowing days, the British put together

Operation Dynamo, a brave plan to rescue the soldiers caught in the Dunkerque pocket, using not just the navy's ships, but also a fleet of small private vessels. Between 27 May and 4 June, some 225,000 British, 125,000 French and 16,000 Belgians were saved by the skin of their teeth from the jaws of the Germans encirling Dunkerque. It's generally accepted that Operation Dynamo saved Britain from being beaten by the Nazis, although a common view long held by many French people was that the French troops were largely abandoned. Dunkerque, in the meantime, had been reduced to rubble, and the town suffered some 8,000 deaths in the appalling destruction. Just south of Dunkerque centre is a British war cemetery and memorial.

Malo-les-Bains

A bridge beyond the war museum leads to Dunkerque's resort of Malo-les Bains. A monument on its western end recalls some 250 boats lost in the Dunkerque evacuation as well as the airmen, seamen and soldiers who died. Malo can't exactly turn its back on industrial Dunkerque; the horizon to the west is so indelibly marked by the black silhouettes of massive factories and chimneys spilling out smoke. But lovely flat sands extend unbroken eastwards to the Belgian border. Malo's architecture is a mix of Belle Epoque follies and very dull modern blocks, while the hideous old brick casino has been upstaged by a modern glass one. A long, broad promenade leads to dunes in the east, while sand yachts share the beach with walkers and swimmers.

Day Trips and Overnighters from Calais and Dunkerque

Wissant, Cap Blanc-Nez and Cap Gris-Nez

To enjoy one of the most powdery-soft beaches in northern France, head for **Wissant** a short distance west of Calais, but hidden from its industry by Cap Blanc-Nez. The modest little resort is tucked behind an immense, 12km-long, curving beach and squeezed in by big pillowy dunes. In summer, you can lie on the generous soft white sands after which the resort is named, contemplating the harshness of the white cliffs of Dover across the Channel – Wissant has the best view you can get of Britain from France. Wissant is a sleepy, relaxing place, but before the sands smothered it with their stifling embrace, it served as a port. Caesar may have set off from here on his second invasion of Britain in 54 BC. Thomas à Becket apparently left French shores for the final time from here before he was murdered in Canterbury in 1170. The Nazis installed big bunkers on the dunes, some of which have toppled down on to the beach; nowadays lazing sunbathers lean against them in summer. If you're feeling energetic you can walk to either of the capes, each six kilometres from the resort.

Cap Blanc-Nez (Cape White Nose) has spectacular views not just of England but also of rural Artois. The ugly grey obelisk is a First World War memorial dedicated to the Dover Patrol which guarded the British Expeditionary Forces sent across the Channel to fight the Germans. Up on Mont d'Hubert, the hill behind the cape,

Getting There

If you're relying on public transport, there's a coastal bus service between Calais and Boulogne, run by Voyages Inglard, t 03 21 96 49 54, www.voyages-inglard.com, which stops at Wissant. Buses leave Calais Mon–Sat, from outside the theatre at 8.40 and 12.15 (or 4mins later from outside the railway station). The last bus back from Wissant goes at 5.25. Journey time *c*. 25mins.

Tourist Information

Wissant: Place de la Mairie, 62179 Wissant, t 03 21 82 48 00, f 03 21 85 39 64, www.ville-wissant.fr.

Market Day

Wissant: Wed am; plus July–Aug Fri eves.

Where to Stay and Eat

Wissant ✉ 62179

Auberge de l'Amiral Benbow, Rue Gambetta, t 03 21 35 90 07 (*moderate*). For a fine fish meal in a swish manor in the centre. *Closed Mon lunch and Wed lunch.*

★Le Vivier, t 03 21 35 93 61, f 03 21 82 10 99, www.levivier.com (*moderate*). Hotel with a welcoming maritime decor and a seafood restaurant that's often crowded with English visitors.

Hôtel de la Plage, Place Edouard Houssin, t 03 21 35 91 87, f 03 21 85 48 10 (*moderate*). A large, plain, rambling old-style French hotel, a bit misleadingly named as it's not right on the beach, but it's not far away, by a pond.

---

the **Musée du Transmanche** (*in the basement of the restaurant with a panoramic view – open April–Sept daily 10–6; adm*) catalogues great Channel crossings and celebrates all the attempts to dig a tunnel between France and England, beginning with Napoleon's.

Cap Gris-Nez (Cape Grey Nose) is as close as France comes to rubbing noses with Britain, just under 30km away. This headland has been colonized by tourists and the village of Framzelle, just set back from the point, has turned into aggressive B&B territory. The remnants of concrete bunkers recall how the Nazis could fire rockets at England from such close quarters. The shipping-flow into and out of the Channel is regulated from the cape, while millions of migrating birds apparently use the headland as a useful marker on their seasonal flights.

Boulogne

A heady perfume of fish suffuses the Boulogne air on many a day of the year. It probably has done ever since Roman times, when the town became the base for the Romans' British fleet – Caesar even set off from here on his first invasion of Britain in 55 BC. Boulogne today is the largest fishing port in France, and the largest port in northern Europe for preparing fish. No wonder it smells so fragrant. The harbours for industrial and craft fishing lie west of the Liane river, the shopping and tourist town to the east of it. Well known to the British as a day-trip destination since the war, Boulogne's ferry and Seacat services have come to a halt for the moment, eclipsed by Calais and the still closer Channel Tunnel. But the marina in the centre of town is expanding all the time, bringing in new visitors. The main tourist attractions are the slightly unfortunately named sea-life centre Nausicaa, by the beach, and the Ville Haute, the historic, ramparted upper town, with an imposing lanky-domed basilica

Getting There

Trains from Calais-Ville to Boulogne take 30–40mins, from Dunkerque to Boulogne 1hr 30mins. On weekdays, the last train back from Boulogne leaves c.6.40pm. Note that there are virtually no train services on this line at weekends. Contact the tourist office for details on **bus** services along the coast. For a **taxi service** in Boulogne, **t** 06 09 23 28 90.

Tourist Information

Boulogne: 24 Quai Gambetta, **t** 03 21 10 88 10, **f** 03 21 10 88 11, *www.tourisme-boulognesurmer.com*, *ot.boulogne@wanadoo.fr*.

Market Day

Place Dalton: Wed and Sat am. A feast!

Shopping

Rue Thiers in the commercial centre between port and Ville Haute has by far the best selection of clothes and food shops; **Philippe Olivier** runs one of the most illustrious cheese shops in northern France, a pongy paradise; nearby **Les Chocolats de Beussent** sells superlative locally made chocolates, while neighbouring **Comtesse du Barry** specializes in high-quality culinary products. There's also a range of big perfume shops on Rue Thiers. The **Grande Rue** leading to the Ville Haute also has some interesting shops, while up behind the ramparts, **Rue de Lille** has interesting gift shops.

Where to Stay

Boulogne ✉ 62203

★★★**Hôtel de la Matelote**, 70 Bd Ste-Beuve, **t** 03 21 30 33 33, **f** 03 21 30 87 40 (*expensive–moderate*). Smart new hotel by the beach and Nausicaa, recently opened by the people who run Boulogne's best restaurant next door (*see* below).

★★★**Métropole**, 51 Rue Thiers, **t** 03 21 31 54 30, **f** 03 21 30 45 72 (*moderate*). Very central, right on the best shopping street.

B&B Le Châtelet, 32 Rue de l'Oratoire, **t** 03 21 30 09 04 (*moderate*). Characterful rooms in part of a former convent in the Ville Haute, run by a Welsh woman and her French husband.

★★**Ibis Vieille Ville**, Rue Porte Neuve, **t** 03 21 31 21 01, **f** 03 21 31 48 25 (*inexpensive*). Well-located chain hotel just on the edge of the ramparts of the upper city.

Eating Out

For the highest quality seafood:

La Matelote, 80 Bd Ste-Beuve, **t** 03 21 30 17 97, (*luxury–moderate*). Acknowledged as the best seafood restaurant in town, in a lively location opposite Nausicaa, by the beach. *Closed Sun pm.*

La Plage, 124 Bd Ste-Beuve, **t** 03 21 99 90 90, (*moderate*). A high-quality alternative in the same quarter. *Closed Sun pm and Mon.*

If you're looking for a big, lively brasserie where the Boulonnais go:

Chez Jules, Place Dalton, **t** 03 21 31 54 12, **f** 03 21 33 85 47 (*expensive–moderate*). Welcoming, full of life, with a packed menu including fine fish, plus the best terrace in the commercial centre. *Closed Sun pm.*

Hamiot, 1 Rue Faidherbe, **t** 03 21 31 44 20, **f** 03 21 83 71 56 (*moderate*). Another lively, popular brasserie option in the commercial centre.

For something more intimate, with excellent cuisine, also in the commercial centre, try:

Le Doyen, 11 Rue du Doyen (nr Place Dalton), **t** 03 21 30 13 08 (*cheap*). Pretty, and a bargain. *Closed Sun.*

To eat with the fishermen and fish workers of Boulogne in a lively restaurant with fishermen's décor, head for:

Le Châtillon, 6 Rue Charles Tellier, **t** 03 21 31 43 95 (*cheap*). *Closed weekends.*

Up in the ramparted Ville Haute there's a very wide choice of pleasant touristy restaurants along Rue de Lille:

Le Vole Hole, 52 Rue de Lille, **t** 03 21 92 15 15 (*cheap*). A laid-back wine bar with an appealingly unkempt courtyard. *Closed Mon.*

rising high above its walls and the uninspiring modern blocks of post-war Boulogne. Between the quays and the ramparts, the sloping streets of commercial Boulogne offer good shopping.

Fish, and Shopping

The massive modern maritime centre of **Nausicaa** (*open daily exc 3 weeks in Jan, 9.30–6.30, July–Aug 9.30–8.30; adm*) sits just behind the sieved white sands of Boulogne's pretty beach, but somewhat unfortunately facing the grim black structures of an industrial plant on the other side of the harbour. Plunge into Nausicaa's darkened spaces to get away from this sight for a mind-altering underwater adventure. The highlights inside are the big aquaria, different ones being devoted to tuna (or at least a near relative), to tropical fish, to sharks and to sea lions. But it's a long, long trawl through the extensive tentacles of this state-of-the art building. A lot of information on the world's single, massive ocean (a point stressed from the start) lies under its surface. The pressure simply of reading all the panels in English will probably prove too much for most visitors – think of hiring the headset (*additional fee*) which offers English commentaries at some 40 locations.

Although Nausicaa looks dreadfully commercial in parts, with its plasticky boutiques and bars, it tries hard to transmit a serious ecological message: that the ocean is threatened by the explosion in the global population over the last century. So, after the preliminary areas explaining the formation of the ocean and the ocean's food chain, from plankton up to man, large numbers of the presentations are dedicated to the way man has exploited the seas. One large section, Tropical Village, looks specifically at the issues of sensible, sensitive tourism. High-tech temporary exhibitions are held in a separate area – that for 2003–4 will focus on climate. The name of Nausicaa has nothing to do with seasickness by the way; it refers to a heroine in Homer's *Odyssey* who comes to Ulysses' rescue after he's been shipwrecked.

Don't be fooled into thinking that the striking equestrian statue by the beach beyond Nausicaa might be yet another provocative French homage to Joan of Arc. It turns out to represent the South American independence fighter General José de San Martin. Having liberated Argentina from Spain in 1816, he went on to free Chile and Peru, before retiring to Boulogne, where he ended his days. Many South Americans come to visit his town house in Boulogne, preserved for posterity.

Boulogne's main **shopping area** is in the grid of streets that climb the slope to the Ville Haute, principally Rue Thiers. Rue Monsigny off it has a nice selection of café terraces. But the best place to sit and watch the Boulonnais go by is on **Place Dalton**, opposite the church of **St-Nicolas**, built in the Gothic era; different textured stone was used to give this edifice more style, but it has been much altered since; the original features stand out best in the choir.

The Ville Haute

The steep **Grande Rue** leads up to the Ville Haute, passing the **Musée Libertador San Martin** at No.113 (*open daily exc Wed, Thurs and public hols, 10–12 and 2–6; free*). You have to enter the Ville Haute by one of the four impressive gateways. Stairways up from these gates take you onto the **ramparts**. A pleasant walkway, sometimes shaded by trees, will take you all the way round, but the view of the sea is limited. Instead, you'll see how far modern Boulogne has expanded over the surrounding hillsides.

Up on the ramparts, you may spot the figures of the evangelists seated high up around the staggering dome of the **Basilique Notre-Dame**, in front of a ring of saints. Above these statues rise the two colonnaded levels holding up the vast, impressive cupola. The whole daunting church in honeyed stone was erected in the first half of the 19th century, a symbol of strength to replace its predecessor, the cathedral destroyed by fanatics at the French Revolution. Some find the church overblown, but it was certainly a hugely powerful response to the fearsome attack on the Catholic Church. Inside, the tall classical columns hold up an array of peeling oval ceilings. For a small fee, you can visit the maze of **crypts** (*open Tues–Sun 2–5; closed Mon*) down below. They contain colourful religious statuary collected from the area, with several representations of Notre-Dame de Boulogne, this version of the Virgin always shown carrying her baby in a boat. But the pride of this collection of religious finery is a royal reliquary piece, donated to Boulogne by King Philippe le Bel in the early 14th century, the green and blue circular box made to contain supposed drops of Christ's blood collected by Boulogne's crusading 'hero', Godefroi. He played a crucial part in the First Crusade and particularly in the triumphant, bloody taking of Jerusalem in 1099; in gratitude he was elected ruler of that city, only to die there in 1100, although he found the time to send the sacred droplets home to his mother before his sad demise, possibly by poisoning. His renown lives on in Boulogne.

The basilica isn't the only major monument in the upper town. Rising behind the town hall in its brick with stone trimmings is the solid old stone town belfry. The classical facade beyond is that of the 19th-century Palais de Justice, or law courts.

Separated by a moat from the rest of the Ville Haute's fortifications, the **château** is an impressively complete medieval castle of many sturdy towers, built, like the ramparts, in the 13th century for Philippe Hurepel, second son of King Philippe Auguste, the French monarch who kicked King John out of France. The château contains the superbly displayed collections of the **town museum** (*open Wed–Mon 10–12 and 2–5; closed Tues and Jan 1–14*). In the stunning circular walkway around the basement, you can see how the medieval masons built on the Roman foundations; among vestiges of Gallo-Roman Boulogne recently unearthed, the tantalizing Vierge Pudique stands out, one hand over her pudenda, the other across her breast. You can also admire stone carvings rescued from Boulogne's Gothic cathedral. Further rooms contain some exquisite carved heads, for example the rosy-cheeked Lady of Cambrai and a melancholic long-haired figure from Thoisy-le-Désert in Burgundy.

But the museum's most surprising collections come from far further afield. The place has an excellent array not just of Egyptian items, but also of antique pots, with some superb Greek vases depicting wrestling gods and men, plus such delights as Etruscan vases in the shapes of animals. The splendid Egyptian items are in part due to the great 19th-century Egyptologist from Boulogne, Auguste Mariette, who worked with the Egyptian authorities. Other Boulonnais explorers contributed the extensive ethnographic sections.

The château is so vast that the collections don't end there. The European fine arts of the Ancien Régime are covered too, albeit somewhat thinly, by the legacy of one generous art collector to his home town, including the odd intriguing Flemish piece and a couple of Boudin views of the northern coast. The ceramics section reveals the history of local as well as national production; the local styles were always quite coarse, if quite charming, unlike a typical piece of Sèvres depicting Marie-Antoinette in finest biscuit (twice-cooked) porcelain.

St-Omer

The very grandest buildings of St-Omer – the former cathedral, the churches, the town hall, the Musée Sandelin and the other very poshest mansions – stand out from the brick of the rest of the buildings of this historic, once ultra-religious little town, as they were made in fine pale stone.

An impressively solid square entrance tower, almost English in appearance, rises from the **Basilique Notre-Dame**, the former cathedral, the crowning glory of this now somewhat down-at-heel historic place. The building was erected between the 13th and 15th centuries. Wander all the way round the exterior, round the cobbled squares surrounding it, to enjoy the carvings perched up high and the late-Gothic flamboyant window tracery. The south entrance includes the Resurrection portal, the Virgin kneeling in admiring, hunch-shouldered prayer before a boldly upright Christ. An ecstatic Leviathan has its mouth crammed with the damned. The rarer good are gathered in God's cloth.

Inside, a Catholic extravaganza awaits you. The interior is crammed with statues and bas-reliefs, including the tomb of one Audomari, the 7th-century evangeliser of these parts, sent by King Dagobert to impose Christianity; the abbreviated, slightly altered name of this canonized figure gave the town its name of St-Omer. The side chapels are separated by elaborate marble and wood-carved screens from the aisles; peer through for views of the displays inside. The ambulatory wall around the choir has been turned into something of an art gallery, including Gothic panels. Nearby, a sober, seated Christ in stone in one of the transepts was recovered from the cathedral of nearby Thérouanne, traumatically destroyed in the mid-16th century by troops of Emperor Charles V – it was only after that time that St-Omer became the seat of a bishopric. There's so much to see inside the basilica that it's easy to miss things; but one unmissable piece is the vast wood-carved organ under the entrance tower, with extravagant figures playing gilded instruments.

Place Foch a short walk away is the main focus of the town, the archetypal central French square, with masses of café and brasserie terraces from which to watch the St-Omer world go by, all in the presence of the very grand, not to say pompous, 19th-century **town hall**. There's an excellent array of shops in the streets off this square. If the temptations prove too great, go and clear your head in the delightful **public gardens** just a stone's throw away from Place Foch, across the busy Boulevard Vauban; after Louis XIV had finally seized control of St-Omer for France in 1677, he had his beloved engineering marshal fortify the town with massive brick ramparts. A portion

Getting There

There's a reasonably regular train service between Calais-Ville and St-Omer, the last trains back from St-Omer leaving at 9.35pm and 11.09pm. The journey lasts just over half an hour. St-Omer's unbelievably grand station is down from the sloping historic town centre, beyond the abbey ruins.

Tourist Information

St-Omer: 4 Rue du Lion d'Or, **t** 03 21 98 08 51, **f** 03 21 98 08 07, *www.tourisme.fr/saint-omer, officetourisme.stomer@wanadoo.fr.*

Market Day
St-Omer: Saturdays.

Shopping

A truly splendid choice of shops lies in the streets off **Place Foch**; on this square itself, several very tempting pâtisseries compete for your attention, while the Caves du Vieux Chai wine cellars beckon you down on one corner. **Rue de Dunkerque** is the main shopping drag, with brand-name clothes stores and several big perfume and jewellery shops. **Rue des Clouteries** also has a particularly good selection.

Where to Stay

St-Omer ✉ **62500**

★★St-Louis, 25 Rue d'Arras, **t** 03 21 38 35 21, **f** 03 21 38 57 26, *www.hotel-saintlouis.com, contact@hotel-saintlouis.com* (*inexpensive*). Good, old-fashioned-style, slightly worn French hotel a short walk down from the centre, with a good restaurant.

★★Ibis, 2 Rue Henri Dupuis, **t** 03 21 93 11 11, **f** 03 21 88 80 20, *ho723@accor-hotels.com* (*inexpensive*). Exceptionally well-located between basilica and Place Foch, and very appealing for a chain hotel.

Eating Out

Le Cygne, 8 Rue Caventou, **t** 03 21 98 20 52 (*expensive–moderate*). An excellent, smart restaurant in a pleasant brick house at the top of a typical, central St-Omer square. *Closed Sun pm and Mon.*

La Belle Epoque, Place Paul Painlevé, **t** 03 21 38 22 93 (*cheap*). Admirably energetic chef Mme Dacheville serves comforting local dishes in this bright and popular restaurant just off Place Foch, with a small flowery terrace. *Closed Sun, Tues and bank hols.*

Les Trois Caves, 18 Place Foch, **t** 03 21 39 72 52 (*cheap*). On another corner of the great central square, a charming place offering tempting, simple menus.

---

of them remains, now in part balustraded, and the moat below has been transformed into formal French *parterres*, with a swimming pool fitted in one end. Beyond stretches a less formal *parc à l'anglaise*, the alleys shaded by magnificent trees.

Back in the historic centre, from the cathedral and Place Foch at the top of the town, many spectacular buildings stand out in the neat grid of streets and squares sloping gently down the hill. Almost all have seen better days. The one exception is the restored **Hôtel Sandelin**, with all the elegance you'd expect of the finest Ancien Régime town house in central Paris, the splendid white-stoned wings built around a large courtyard seemingly ready to receive gilded carriages. Unfortunately, the fine-arts museum inside is closed for renovations until at least 2004. The other town museum, the **Musée Henri Dupuis**, between the cathedral and Place Foch, is a much less interesting affair, a musty natural history museum containing a lot of stuffed birds, plus a fine Flemish kitchen. **Place Victor Hugo** nearby has plenty of life, though, in contrast to much quieter but almost equally stylish **Place Sithieu**.

Continuing down the hillside, if you're feeling charitable, you might quickly go and pay your respects to the grimy-stoned churches of **St-Sépulcre and St-Denis** standing rather neglected and forlorn in their side-squares. Near these, look out for the pilaster-fronted brick façades that clearly became a curious architectural fashion in this once wealthy little city. As to the **Chapelle Walloone**, it cries out for attention. A chapel built on the scale of a cathedral, its soaring scrolled façade is split into five levels like an extravagant Baroque cake in brick. The inside is sadly neglected, except for the large modern scale model of the town in the middle. But the buildings around its cloister have been converted into a fantastic high-tech **town library** which would be the envy of many a major British city. Go inside to marvel at the superb civic provisions, and head for the Salle du Patrimoine to inspect some of the medieval manuscripts saved from the region's abbeys. Walk down **Rue St-Bertin** and you'll pass intimidating buildings that once housed several of St-Omer's many religious communities, including one reserved for English Jesuits in the times when Catholics were terribly persecuted in England. Some way further down the slope, you come to the meagre ruins of the **abbey of St-Bertin**. It was around here that the original Dark Ages monastic foundation grew up which led to the creation of the whole town.

Bergues

Surrounded by moated ramparts, the quiet little town of Bergues makes a pleasant discovery so close to the massive industrial surrounds of Dunkerque. It developed around an abbey dedicated to St Winoc, a Breton who came to christianize these parts in the Dark Ages. On the **Groenberg**, the town's highest point, a couple of striking towers stand out, one sharply pointed, the other looking like a caricature of a giant in stone; they are virtually all that remains of the abbey, brought down at the Revolution. Below, the atmosphere of an old fortified town was well recreated after the war, curving streets leading off the interconnecting central squares. A proud Flemish **belfry** dominates here, decorated with bartizan towers, copper-meringue ornaments and 50 bells. The grandiose classical building distinguished by its balustraded roof and small obelisks is the **town hall**. A couple of busts pay homage to Alphonse Lamartine, generally considered France's greatest Romantic poet, but also a significant mid-19th-century political figure and member of parliament for Bergues in the 1830s. Several houses around the squares boast high-scrolled Flemish gables.

Head a short way from the centre for the massive, restored, severe brick church of **St-Martin**. Behind it, close to the war memorial for once showing a desperate soldier on his belly, rather than in triumphant pose, you'll spot the elaborated scrolled side of a grandiose Flemish almshouse turned **Musée Municipal** (*open daily exc Tues and Jan, 10–12 and 3–5; adm*). Its main claim to fame is a work by the Lorraine artist Georges de La Tour, *The Nightwatchman with a Dog*, but there's also an interesting array of Flemish painters on display.

Bergues' massive walls are still almost intact and you can walk along portions of the ramparts, although the views outwards aren't always worth seeking out. Rather, enjoy the delightful walk along the house-lined, serpenting waterway that cuts through the centre of town.

Getting There

Bergues is c.10mins from Dunkerque by train, Cassel c 25mins away, with regular services to and from both into the evening.

Tourist Information

Bergues ✉ 59380: Place de la République, t/f 03 28 68 71 06, *www.tourisme.bergues@ wanadoo.fr.*
Cassel ✉ 59670: Grand'Place, t 03 28 40 52 55, f 03 28 40 59 17, *www.ot-cassel.fr.*

Market Days

Bergues: Mon am.
Cassel: Thurs am.

Eating Out

Bergues

Au Cornet d'Or. 26 Rue Espagnole, t 03 28 68 66 27 (*expensive*). The poshest restaurant, close to the water, with décor of tapestries and beams, and grand cuisine to go with it. *Closed Sun pm and Mon.*

Le Berguenard, 1 Rue Faidherbe, t 03 28 68 65 00 (*moderate*). More discreet and cosy, tempting corner restaurant offering refined cuisine even if the menus are limited. *Closed Sun pm and Mon.*
Taverne Bruegel, 1 Marché aux Fromages, t 03 28 68 19 19 (*moderate*). A picturesque restaurant, an excellent spot by the water.
**Au Tonnelier, 4 Rue du Mont de Piété, t 03 28 68 70 05, f 03 28 68 21 87 (*inexpensive*). Quietly charming hotel set around a courtyard, with a good restaurant (*moderate*). *Closed Fri and Sun pm.*
**Le Commerce, Contour de l'Eglise, t 03 28 68 60 37, f 03 28 68 70 76 (*inexpensive*). Cheerful, cheap neighbour of the above.

Cassel

Estaminet T'Kasteel Hof, t 03 28 40 59 29 (*moderate*). Up at the top of the Mont Cassel, a slightly messy but charming restaurant with views, serving local Flemish dishes and speciality Flemish beers. *Open daily May–Aug, otherwise Thurs–Sun.*
La Taverne Flamande, t 03 28 42 42 59 (*moderate*). Flemish specialities with excellent views over the grandiose main square. *Closed Tues pm and Wed.*

Cassel

Cassel's hilltop may only reach 176m (under 600ft) in height, but it commands vast panoramas over the flat countryside around it, offering an excellent overview of French Flanders. Local legend has it that the hill was formed by a clod of earth that fell from the giant boots of Reuze Papa and Reuze Maman. Flanders is full of tales of such Gargantuan figures, effigies of whom are still brought out for local festivals. Real armies have fought over Cassel's strategic site for centuries, and it was even immortalized in a nursery rhyme: the Grand Old Duke of York led forces against the French Revolutionary army here, marching them up the hill and down again. During the First World War, General Foch, leader of the French army, had his headquarters at Cassel for some time, and he is remembered with an equestrian statue by the **windmill**, which still grinds flour, near the scruffy top of the hill.

Down below, the small town centre stretches around an outsized, sloping, cobbled main square. By far the grandest building, **La Châtellainie**, has been renovated and is used for temporary exhibitions. Many of the other buildings had to be rebuilt after the war. Just up from one end of the square, the brick **Collégiale de Notre-Dame** church stands out, a typical Flemish Hallekerque (a rectangular, rather than cross-shaped edifice in which the side aisles are as tall and wide as the central nave) with triangular gables.

Touring from Calais and Dunkerque

You'll find that the sights mentioned here are reliably open Easter–Oct, 10–12 and 2–5 at least, unless otherwise stated. Museums charge adm.

Day 1: Hitler's *Grands Projets*

Morning: Hidden in woods 12km north of St-Omer, by **Eperlecques** village, stands a vast, compellingly hideous bunker (*closed Dec–Feb*) built to fire V2 rockets at Britain.

Lunch: At nearby Houlle, **Au Rallye d'Artois**, t 03 21 93 12 82 (*moderate*), offers traditional French gastronomy and setting. *Closed Wed.* For a posher meal, eat in the delightfully converted outhouses of the ★★★★**Château de Tilques**, t 03 21 88 99 99 (*expensive*).

Afternoon: Hire a punt at **Tilques** to explore the tranquil, well-tended waterways of the Audomarois marshes. Then bypass St-Omer to reach **La Coupole**, another terrifying Nazi missile bunker, south of town, now a huge modern museum on war, rockets and space exploration. Pick up cut-price crystal at the huge Arc shop in nearby **Arques**.

Dinner: Either try our St-Omer suggestions (*see* p.61), or head southwest for hilltop **Montreuil**. All the delightful hotels listed below have good to excellent restaurants.

Sleeping: Luxurious ★★★★**Château de Montreuil**, t 03 21 81 53 04, f 03 21 81 36 43, *montreuil@relaischateaux.fr* (*expensive*) is really a big 19th-century manor set exclusively in the grounds of the town's historic citadel. ★★★**Les Hauts de Montreuil**, 21 Rue Pierre Ledent, t 03 21 81 95 92, f 03 21 86 28 83, *leshautsdemontreuil@wanadoo.fr* (*expensive–moderate*) has a wonderful old timberframe front to its quaint restaurant and comfortable rooms set around a restored courtyard. ★★**Le Clos des Capucins**, Place du Général de Gaulle, t 03 21 06 08 65, f 03 21 81 20 45 (*moderate*) makes a cheerful stop on the big main square.

Day 2: Culture before the Casinos

Morning: **Montreuil** used to be 'sur-Mer'; now you look out on to quiet countryside on a tour round its amazingly preserved ramparts. Covered with elaborate carvings on the outside, the Gothic churches in the centre are worth visiting inside too.

Lunch: Montreuil has an almost endless choice of fine restaurants. Smart brick **Le Cocquempot**, Place de la Poissonnerie, t 03 21 81 05 61 (*moderate*) looks the part for a hearty bourgeois meal; *closed Thurs*; while across the lovely little square, delightfully unkempt **Le Darnétal**, t 03 21 06 04 87 (*moderate*) serves good seafood.

Afternoon: The beach at **Le Touquet**, or, if it's rainy and cold and the kids want to swim, visit Aqualud behind the seafront. Or consider a round of golf. If you tire of Le Touquet, **Berck** to the south has a jollier seafront. Between the two, the Bagatelle theme park is popular with children.

Dinner: Le Touquet's premier restaurant is **Flavio**, 21 Av du Verger, t 03 21 05 10 22 (*expensive*) set back from the seafront. On the promenade, smart **Tante Isa**, t 03 21 05 22 55 (*moderate*) has a good reputation for seafood. Away from the cramped centre, the **Auberge de la Dune aux Loups**, t 03 21 05 42 54 (*moderate*) offers traditional cooking in a nice suburban wooded setting up by the Canche estuary.

Sleeping: At **Le Touquet**, ★★★★**Westminster**, 5 Av du Verger, t 03 21 05 48 48, f 03 21 05 45 45, *www.westminster.fr* (*expensive*) is palatial. ★★★**Le Bristol**, t 03 21 05 49 95, f 03 21 05 90 93 (*moderate*) is a swanky pink extravaganza just behind the seafront. ★★★**Novotel**, t 03 21 09 85 00, f 03 21 09 85 10 (*expensive*), and ★★**Ibis**, t 03 21 09 87 00, f 03 21 09 87 10 (*moderate*), offer seawater treatments. ★★**Le Chalet**, 15 Rue de la Paix, t 03 21 05 87 65, f 03 21 05 47 49 (*inexpensive*) is a cheaper option near the beach, but with mountain décor!

Day 3: Back in the Hundred Years' War

Morning: **Azincourt**, east, inland from Montreuil, is better known in English as Agincourt, where in 1415 the troops of King Henry V of England so famously destroyed a French army five times their size, taking a resounding lead at the start of the second half of the Hundred Years' War, as a small museum recalls. Then wander round delightful **Hesdin**'s picturesque streets, accompanied by the sounds of the river waters flowing through town.

Lunch: At Hesdin, **La Bretèche**, 19 Rue du Général Daullé, **t** 03 21 86 80 87 (*moderate*) is a solid address for traditional regional fare, while **L'Ecurie**, 17 Rue Jacquemont, **t** 03 21 86 86 86 (*moderate*), in swishly renovated stables, is a dash more experimental.

Afternoon: **Crécy-en-Ponthieu** tumbles down its hillside southwest of Hesdin. The battle site above the town was where King Edward III of England won a famous victory over the French at the start of the first half of the Hundred Years' War. Edward's warrior son, the Black Prince, won his spurs in this rout. To find natural majesty, and peace, head for the vast Somme estuary at **Le Crotoy** and **St-Valéry**, fantastic places for appreciating ornithology or sunsets.

Dinner and sleeping: Le Crotoy has an enchanting hotel overlooking the estuary, **Les Tourelles**, 2 Rue Guerlain, **t** 03 22 27 16 33, **f** 03 22 27 11 45 (*inexpensive*), with a lovely restaurant giving on to the garden. **Chez Mado, t** 03 22 27 81 22 (*expensive–moderate*), all decked out in wood, is another delightful restaurant on the estuary. Across in St-Valéry, **Le Relais Guillaume de Normandie**, **t** 03 22 60 82 36, **f** 03 22 60 81 82 (*inexpensive*) plays its part as a grand, slightly creaky 19th-century extravaganza, with an old-fashioned French restaurant.

Day 4: Amiens, Cathedral and Canals

Morning: Amiens' massive 13th-century cathedral overwhelms with its daunting architecture and the delicacy of its carved façade. For a wider cultural and historical view of Amiens and the Somme region, go to the overblown 19th-century Musée de Picardie (*closed Mon*).

Lunch: Down in the canalside quarter below the cathedral, **Les Marissons**, 68 Rue des Marissons, **t** 03 22 92 96 66 (*moderate*) stands out for its setting and refined cuisine. *Closed Sat lunch and Sun*. Otherwise, choose from the whole string of restaurants with tempting terraces along the waterside.

Afternoon: Wander round the canalside district of **St-Leu**. In good weather, go punting through the **Hortillonages**, the network of canals and gardens near the centre (**t** *03 22 92 12 18, April–Oct, to book an afternoon trip*). On a rainy day, expand your mind at the **Centre de Documentation Jules Verne** (*closed Mon*), in the house of that prolific 19th-century French pioneer of sci-fi.

Dinner: **La Couronne**, 64 Rue St-Leu, **t** 03 22 91 88 57 (*moderate*), for classic French cuisine in comfy surroundings. *Closed Sat*. Or try **Le Prieuré** listed below.

Sleeping: ***Grand Hôtel de l'Univers**, 2 Rue de Noyon, **t** 03 22 91 52 51, **f** 03 22 92 81 66 (*moderate*). In a lively shopping quarter near the centre (towards the station). ****Le Prieuré**, 17 Rue Porion, **t** 03 22 92 27 67, **f** 03 22 92 46 16 (*inexpensive*). Right by the cathedral, recently redone, with nice restaurant. ***Victor Hugo** , 2 Rue de l'Oratoire, **t** 03 22 91 57 91, **f** 03 22 92 74 02 (*inexpensive*). Gem of a simple hotel at the back of the cathedral.

Day 5: First World War Tour to Arras

Morning: East of Amiens, between Corbie and Villers-Bretonneux stands the **Australian National War Memorial**. Just north of grim Albert, at **Thiepval**, Lutyens' vast, lugubrious arch is inscribed with the names of countless British victims; nearby, the **Ulster memorial tower** is a copy of Helen's Tower at Clandeboyne near Belfast. The monuments around the cratered **Beaumont-Hamel Parc Terre-Neuvien** recall Scottish as well as Canadian fighters.

Lunch: The village of Authuille south of Thiepval has a good regional restaurant, the **Taverne du Cochon Salé**, **t** 03 22 75 46 14 (*moderate*). *Closed Sun pm and Mon*. Or try the good standard restaurant at Albert's ***Hôtel Royal Picardie**, Av du Général Leclerc, **t** 03 22 75 37 00, **f** 03 22 75 60 19. The place looks a bit like a monument itself, appropriately enough.

Afternoon: You won't find a more flamboyant show in French Flanders than in **Arras**, with its beautiful, vast squares. It also has subterranean surprises – *see* day trip to Arras, pp.72–4 for further details.

Dinner and sleeping: For Arras' excellent selection of restaurants *see* p.73. We'd just like to add here the most historic hotel to the choices, ***Les Trois Luppars**, 49 Grand-Place, **t** 03 21 07 41 41, **f** 03 21 24 24 80 (*inexpensive*), with its outstanding stepped gable, its comfortable rooms and its friendly welcome.

Lille

Hidden in layers of industry, the distinctly glamorous historic centre of Lille, with its huge squares, outrageous Flemish Baroque buildings, towering belfries and elegant shopping streets, used to be something of a secret to outsiders. The arrival of the Eurostar, and the tourists who pour out of it, is changing this, and Lille, centre of the fourth largest conurbation in France, seems all of a sudden to have the potential to grow into one of the most vibrant cities in France.

Lille survived its frequent changes of overlord, a bone of contention for much of its history as a market town and textile centre. By the time Charles de Gaulle was born here in 1890 it had developed into an industrial powerhouse. It was occupied by German forces in both World Wars; bombs rained down on the city in the Second World War, and after the war Lille's industrial base declined. Like its southern counterpart, Marseille, it suffered from a bad press, fuelled by images of gross industrialization and racism. Now a banking, administrative and university town, with some 100,000 students, Lille is an extremely lively place.

Vieux Lille

The very heart of Lille is split in two, Place du Théâtre to the right, Place du Général de Gaulle (also known as the Grand' Place) to the left, with the Vieille Bourse in between. Rue Faidherbe leads from the central Lille-Flandres station to Place du Théâtre. Hemmed in by houses off the Rue Faidherbe, the **Eglise St-Maurice** is a rare vestige of the city's medieval prosperity. In the form of a Flemish Hallekerque, the church has recently been scrubbed clean to reveal its white stone, but the interior still looks on the lugubrious side. The spacious five aisles look as if they're held up by a forest of columns; heavy 17th-century religious paintings line the walls.

Two outrageous buildings from the early 20th century flaunt themselves on **Place du Théâtre**. The sparklingly white **opera house** is crowned by the *Triumph of Apollo* by Hippolyte Lefebvre, a sculpture that's more than a match for the most ludicrous of opera plots. The architect was Louis-Marie Cordonnier, who was also responsible for the nearby **Palais de la Bourse** with its rocketing Flemish belfry on one corner.

The **Vieille Bourse**, although on a smaller scale, also smacks of excess, Baroque this time, with weighty, decadent garlands of fruit drooping from the caryatids and atlantes on the façades. Designed by Julien Destrée in the 1650s, its recently restored inner courtyard shelters market stalls. Plaques on the walls behind sing the praises of leading men of commerce and science. Above the colonnade, the stones have been squeezed and twisted like Plasticine to create grotesque animal faces.

In the centre of **Place du Général de Gaulle**, Lille's dominatrix of a **Déesse** (Goddess) holds court, a symbol of the city's success in repulsing the Austrian forces in 1792. The object in her hand, which looks like a whip from a distance, is described as a *boutefeu*, used to light cannons. This square has many grand façades, and looks predominantly Flemish, particularly the massive stepped gable of the *La Voix du Nord* building, headquarters of the largest newspaper in the region. The bronze figures on high stand for the historic provinces of Flanders, Hainaut and Artois.

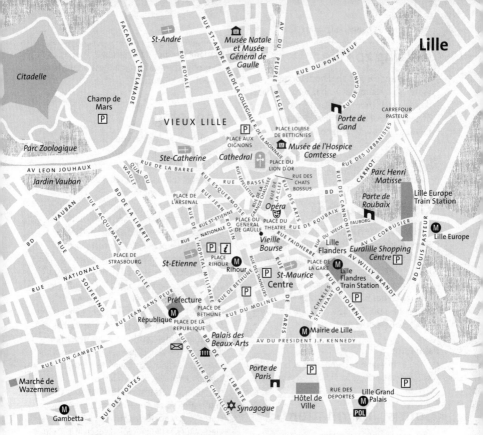

A third grand square connects with Place du Général de Gaulle, although **Place Rihour** has none of the architectural swagger of the other two: it's a bit of a 20th-century mess. A mausoleum-like war memorial dominates one corner. Behind it hides the tourist office, in the sorry remnants of the Palais Rihour, the Lille palace of the dukes of Burgundy. The Gothic chapel above the tourist office is used for exhibitions.

Just a little west of the Place Rihour, **St-Etienne**, on Rue de l'Hôpital Militaire, is one of several grand Baroque churches tucked into Lille's residential streets. **Rue Nationale** and **Rue de Béthune**, respectively north and south of Place Rihour, are major shopping arteries.

Place de la République, Palais des Beaux-Arts, and the Hôtel de Ville

The immense **Place de la République** at the end of Rue de Béthune looks overblown and vacuous at the same time. Two stupendously pompous buildings stare across at each other, both from the second half of the 19th century: the **Préfecture** and the **Palais des Beaux-Arts** (*open Mon 2–6, Wed–Sun 10–6; closed Tues; adm*).

Recently cleaned, and reopened by the French president in 1997, this is your most obvious cultural call in Lille. Don't miss the excellent medieval and Renaissance galleries of the first basement level, which include Donatello's bas-relief *Feast of Herod*. Still further down you can go in search of the excellent archaeological section and amazingly detailed large-scale 18th-century models of some of the fortified

Getting to Lille

Lille-Europe is just 2hrs from London-Waterloo by **Eurostar**, with 12 return services a day Mon–Sat (*from 6am*) and 8 return services on Sun (*from 8.30am*). The station has fantastic links with other parts of France and is only 10–15mins' walk from the city centre. More detailed information about travelling by Eurostar is given in **Travel**, p.11.

Getting Around

Note that Lille has two railway stations, Lille-Europe (see above), and Lille-Flandres, which is much more central and from which trains leave for local destinations. Lille has good public transport services, including a metro with two lines which meet at Lille-Flandres.

To book a **taxi** in Lille, **t** 03 20 06 06 06/ **t** 03 20 06 64 00/**t** 03 20 55 20 56.

Car Hire

You'll find car hire companies at both Lille railway stations.

Tourist Information

Lille: Palais Rihour, Place Rihour, **t** 03 20 21 94 21, **f** 03 20 21 94 20, *www.lilletourism.com*, *info@lilletourism.com*.

Market Days

Place du Concert (north of Hospice Comtesse): Wed, Fri and Sun 7am–2pm.
Place Sébastopol: Wed and Sat am.
Place de Wazemmes (some way south of Palais des Beaux-Arts; metro station Gambetta), Tues and Thurs am, plus great flea market Sun am.

Braderie de Lille The biggest flea market in Europe – two days of madness on the first weekend in Sept.

Shopping

Coming from Lille-Europe station, try not to be diverted by the vast **Euralille** shopping centre: it has about as much atmosphere as an airport terminal, though it does house Carrefour, excellent for basic French foodstuffs. Just 10mins' walk away, many of the same shopping names and many better ones besides are to be found along enchanting streets in **Vieux Lille**. The perfect starting point is the Grand' Place, surrounded by restaurants and cafés. **La Vieille Bourse** has ground-floor arcades, and a bustling flower and second-hand book market within its cloisters. Paul, one of Lille's two famous chains of *boulangeries-pâtisseries-chocolateries*, has its sensational main outlet at 8 Rue de Paris (opposite the Vieille Bourse). Meert, the other superlative chain, has a wonderful shop on Rue Esquermoise, in the maze of brilliant shopping streets just north of Place de Gaulle. In this area you'll find further excellent food stores (e.g. Madeleine Estienne, 8 Rue des Vieux Murs, selling regional specialities), plus fashion and household boutiques, and antiques specialists. The big stores are mainly on Rue Nationale and Rue de Béthune.

Where to Stay

Lille ✉ 59800
★★★★**Carlton**, 3 Rue de Paris, Lille 59026, **t** 03 20 13 33 13, **f** 03 20 51 48 17, *www. carltonlille.fr* (*luxury*). The plushest address in town, well located opposite the opulent

towns of northern France. In the sculpture gallery you'll find Rodin's extraordinary caramelized figure of *L'Ombre* (the Shadow), and pieces by Camille Claudel, Rodin's put-upon lover. Rubens' powerful depiction of the deposition of Christ opens proceedings among the paintings, superbly displayed on the first floor. Interiors by De Witte and De Hooch and landscapes by Van Ruysdael and Siberecht stand out.

Boudin and Sisley also feature, but perhaps the highlight of the 19th-century collection is Emile Bernard's cloisonné *Les Cueilleuses de pommes*. Born in Lille, Bernard was the man who, along with Gauguin in the 1880s, developed a challenging form of painting in big, bold bright blocks, moving art a stage closer to the abstract. There are

opera building. It has two restaurants and two bars, but the ugly Hippopotamus Grill beneath the hotel isn't connected.

****Alliance**, 17 Quai du Wault, Lille 59027, t 03 20 30 62 62, f 03 20 42 94 25 (*luxury*), *alliancelille@wanadoo.fr*. The other posh hotel in the centre, in a converted 17th-century convent. 80 rooms, with moderately priced restaurant.

***Grand Hôtel Bellevue**, 5 Rue Jean Roisin, t 03 20 57 45 64, f 03 20 40 07 93 (*expensive*). In the very heart of town. Insist on a room overlooking the Grand' Place.

***Hôtel de la Treille**, 7–9 Place Louise de Bettignies, t 03 20 55 45 46, f 03 20 51 51 69 (*moderate*). Appealingly located and comfortable.

***Brueghel**, 5 Parvis St-Maurice, t 03 20 06 06 69, f 03 20 63 25 27 (*inexpensive*). Well located and well run, overlooking the grand Eglise St-Maurice. It has an appealing lobby and tasteful corridors, a hilarious little lift and comfortable smallish rooms.

***Hôtel de la Paix**, 46 bis Rue de Paris, t 03 20 54 63 93, f 03 20 63 98 97 (*inexpensive*). Nearby and not quite as appealing, but the rooms are well kept.

***Ibis Opéra**, 21 Rue Lepelletier, t 03 20 06 21 95, f 03 20 74 91 30 (*inexpensive*). Centrally located chain hotel very handily located in the midst of luxury shopping streets.

Mister Bed, 57 Rue de Béthune, t 03 20 12 96 96, f 03 20 40 25 87 (*inexpensive*). A cheap chain option, in an excellent position in the most popular shopping street in the centre.

The cheapish hotels in the arc of buildings outside the Lille-Flandres railway station are close to the centre of town, and vie for your attention with their flashing neon signs.

****Flandre-Angleterre**, 13 Place de la Gare, t 03 20 06 04 12, f 03 20 06 37 76 (*inexpensive*). One of the best and one of the most expensive by this station.

Les Voyageurs, 10 Place de la Gare, t 03 20 06 43 14, f 03 20 74 19 01 (*cheap*). Amusing and cheap hotel.

Eating Out

A l'Huîtrière, 3 Rue des Chats Bossus, t 03 20 55 43 41 (*luxury–expensive*). Seafood heaven at the back of a sensational fish shop. *Closed Sun pm*.

Le Compostelle, 4 Rue St-Etienne, t 03 28 38 08 30 (*moderate*). The finest setting for a smart traditional Flanders dinner, in the only Renaissance mansion in Lille with a courtyard.

Le Porthos, 53 Rue de la Monnaie, t 03 20 06 44 06 (*moderate*). Opposite the Hospice Comtesse, filled with lively lawyers during the week .

Les Compagnons de la Grappe, 26 Rue Lepelletier, t 03 20 21 02 79 (*cheap*). Set back in its own gravelled courtyard off this prime shopping street, the interior has a striking modern art décor and the food and wine are as interesting as the setting. *Closed Sun*.

Bistrot de Pierrot, 6 Place de Béthune, t 03 20 57 14 09 (*cheap*). Down by the Palais des Beaux-Arts, this very well-known *bistrot* is run by a bit of a TV star, Pierrot. He's a big character, and although his *bistrot* is small it is packed with atmosphere.

Paul, 8 Rue de Paris, t 03 20 74 50 67 (*cheap*). Has a good-value restaurant, overlooking the Place de l'Opéra, above the wonderful *boulangerie*.

works by Picasso and Léger, but for other 20th-century art you must visit the museum at Villeneuve-d'Ascq, east of the town (*see* below).

The most talked-about works among the foreign collections are the typically disturbing fruits of Goya's imagination. *Le Temps, dit Les Vieilles* shows two caricatures of decrepit society women who look like coquettish grimacing cadavers dressed up for their walk. Matisse explained well the effect these extraordinarily characterful canvases had on him: 'Then I saw the Goyas at Lille. That was when I understood that painting could be a language. I thought that I could become a painter.' A separate room is devoted to drawings, notably Italian Old Masters.

A short walk southeast from the Musée des Beaux-Arts brings you to the **Porte de Paris**, the most imposing of Lille's surviving gates, now isolated by traffic. This homage to Louis XIV was designed by Simon Vollant and shows Victory crowning the Sun King. In a square to one side stands the **Hôtel de Ville**, completed in 1932. Another breathtaking Flemish **belfry** (open first Sun in April–last Sun in Sept, Sun–Fri; adm) blasts up over 300ft into the sky from here. The legendary giant founders of Lille, Phinaert and Lydéric, are portrayed on the belfry but totally dwarfed by it. You can climb up for views over the whole of Lille. At night, the belfry turns into a great lighthouse.

To the Musée de l'Hospice Comtesse and de Gaulle's Birthplace

Back up by the Grand' Place, **Rue Esquermoise**, **Rue de la Bourse**, **Rue Lepelletier** and the **Grande Chaussée**, just about the most glamorous shopping streets of Vieux Lille, strung with delightful little squares, head off north from the main central square. Pretty **Rue Esquermoise** is followed by **Rue de la Barre**, off which lies the neglected but beautiful old Gothic church, **Ste-Catherine**. **Rue Basse** takes you back to the end of the Grande Chaussée to **Rue des Chats Bossus** (the Hunchbacked Cats), which ends in the charming triangular **Place du Lion d'Or**. The vast, incomplete and hideous 19th-century **cathedral** lurks in this quarter, but thankfully it's surprisingly well hidden from views and vistas. Another excellent historic shopping street leads off Place du Lion d'Or, **Rue de la Monnaie**, along which you'll find Lille's second most important museum.

The **Musée de l'Hospice Comtesse** (open Mon 2–6, Wed–Fri 10–12.30 and 2–6, weekends 10–6; closed Tues; adm) contains Flemish collections set within what was formerly a hospital. Founded in 1237, and rebuilt in 1468 after a fire, it was much altered again after another fire in the 17th century. Its long medieval ward is used for temporary exhibitions. Beyond a screening wall at one end you can make out the ceiling of the chapel, adorned in the mid-19th century with 66 coats of arms representing the hospital's principal benefactors. The community building in the main courtyard contains fine Flemish art, ceramics and furniture, including a couple of rooms covered with Delft tiles showing windmills, men fishing in canals, and shepherds and shepherdesses among very typical Flemish scenes. Look out also for the paintings of Flemish interiors and urban scenes, including processions and the **Lille Braderie**, an annual great market that still exists as a massive antiques fair.

A demanding walk north from here, in a quietly prosperous corner of town, the **Maison Natale et Musée Général de Gaulle** (open Tues–Fri 2–5) is most easily reached by heading up Rue de la Collégiale and Rue St-André; it is signalled by the French flag waving above the door at 9 Rue Princesse. This is where Charles de Gaulle was born on 22 November 1890, in his grandmother's house – a bourgeois Lille property with a pretty little courtyard. Charles lived here only for the three months following his birth, but he visited his maternal grandmother regularly. Inside, the overwhelming feeling is of bourgeois piety preserved in aspic. A bust of the general stands in the small garden beyond the conservatory. In the former workshops, the general's life story is told in indigestible fashion with panels, texts and photos, the emphasis on the military writings which he penned throughout his extraordinary career.

West from the museum, beyond the massive, free Champ de Mars car park, lurks the Lille **citadel** (*open May–Aug; contact tourist office for Sun pm tours; adm*), concealed behind woods within the loop of the river Deule. The French army still owns this star-shaped fortification, a well-preserved example of Vauban's defensive architecture.

Two Extraordinary Art Museums Outside the Centre

Major roads speed round the **Musée d'Art Moderne** at **Villeneuve d'Ascq** (*open daily exc Tues 10–6; adm*), in Lille's eastern suburbs (*take metro to Pont de Bois, then bus 41, stopping at Parc Urbain*). The brick architecture makes the place look something like a 1960s university campus. Inside, however, the museum contains a really good collection by some of the great names of 20th-century art. Modigliani's elongated, almond-eyed portraits outshine a run-of-the-mill selection of Picassos. Braque, Rouault and Léger are well represented, as well as the intriguingly flattened forms of Henri Laurens' sculptures. The museum also puts on excellent temporary exhibitions.

Yes, **Roubaix**'s **La Piscine Musée d'Art et d'Industrie** (*open Tues–Thurs 11–6, Fri 11–8, weekends 1–6; closed Mon; adm*) is set in a former public swimming pool (*take metro to Gare-Roubaix and the museum is a short walk away*). On top of that, it's an inter-war extravaganza that was built in the shape of a Cistercian abbey! With its wonderful recent transformation, the vast, mosaic-bottomed pool has been turned into a sculpture garden, where fashion shows also take place. The Lille area has a long tradition of textile manufacturing, and remains the largest textile producer in France, so it's appropriate that, alongside the good art collections of the 19th and 20th centuries, fashion features large; the changing booths have even been turned into display cabinets. It's all rather weird and wonderful, a boost for this often much put-upon town glued on to the Lille conurbation, closer to the Belgian border.

Day Trips from Lille

Douai

Douai was once a much more important town, as a major religious and intellectual centre, than it is today. Its origins go back to Roman times. In the 16th century, it became a highly significant Catholic centre, combating the rise of Protestantism. Philip II of Spain endowed the town with a university in 1562, and its religious houses promoted the Counter-Reformation with zeal. Douai became a particularly important gathering place for English, Irish and Scottish Catholics hounded out of their home countries. A handful of institutions for English-speaking Catholics were even set up in town. William, later Cardinal, Allen, was active here, founding the English seminary in Douai in 1568. He organized the translation of the Bible into English – the so-called Douay Bible, published in town in 1610. Kennedy, the first Catholic president of the United States, took his presidential oath on the Douay Bible. A number of the English priests trained in Douai returned to preach in England, coming to a sticky end as Catholic martyrs. Through most of the 18th century the *Parlement* of French Flanders was based in Douai, taking over a former abbey on the banks of the River Scarpe.

Getting There

Trains from Lille-Flandres (the central station) take 20–30mins. Last trains from Douai depart Mon–Sat 7.43pm, Sun 8.08pm.

Tourist Information

Douai ✉ 59500: 70 Place d'Armes, **t** 03 27 88 26 79, **f** 03 27 99 38 78, *www.douai-ville.fr*.

Market Day

Place du Barlet: Sat am.

Eating Out

★★★★La Terrasse, 36 Terrasse St-Pierre, **t** 03 27 88 70 04, **f** 03 27 88 36 05 (*expensive*). Posh hotel-cum-restaurant, the entrance strangely located opposite public lavatories, but elegant within, the cuisine refined.

Romagnant, Place St-Amé, **t** 03 27 87 27 27. In one of the finest buildings in town, a grand 19th-century setting for a fine meal.

Le Bistrot de Gérard, 46 Rue St-Jacques, **t** 03 27 88 79 60. On the main street, nothing special on the outside, but a delight inside, with veranda and terrace too.

Douai no longer retains a cohesive historic core because of terrible war bombing, but several buildings have survived dull post-war reconstruction, including the wide Gothic arches of the *Parlement*. Heading for the showy restored Gothic **town hall**, you can climb the big fat medieval Flemish **belfry** to get a bird's-eye view over the town. Begun in the late 14th century, the tower contains what is claimed to be the largest collection of bells in Europe, 62 in all; on Saturday mornings you can hear them in full swing. The church of **St-Pierre** also stands out in the centre, its ends marked by eye-catching towers.

The main attraction over the river is the **Musée de la Chartreuse** (*open Wed–Sun 10–12 and 2–6; closed Mon and Tues; adm*). The brick and stone façades from the 16th and 17th centuries look inviting, and some of the art within is outstanding. In the first room, the quality of the Spanish nativity scene and marriage of the Virgin are immediately striking, as is the Flemish crucifixion painting. But the greatest discovery is that of the late 15th- and early 16th-century Douai artist Jean Bellegambe, very well represented here. The power of his altarpiece panels is overwhelming, and his *Polyptique d'Anchin* stands out as the most remarkable of his works, for the richly coloured main panels and the staggering grisaille work on the back. The other highlight is Veronese's *Portrait of a Venetian Woman*, an arrogant young thing in gorgeous autumnal brown velvet and pearls. The few 19th-century pieces include works by Boudin, Jongkind, Sisley, Renoir and Pissarro. Douai's postimpressionist Henri Edmond Cross puts on a good show too.

Arras

A pageant of scrolled Flemish gables line up to be admired around Arras' **Grand-Place**, the greatest of several staggering squares at the centre of the most glamorous city in French Flanders. Arras became one of the richest cities in medieval Europe with its dynamic merchants and its thriving international markets, held on its huge squares. One luxury produced in town was fine tapestries, exported across Europe – one even features as a celebrated, fatal stage prop in Shakespeare's *Hamlet*.

The Grand-Place isn't the only *grand place* in Arras. The misleadingly named adjoining **Petit-Place**, or **Place des Héros** is very grandiose too. The restored **town hall** dominates here, with an impressive array of dormer windows in its steep acres of roofing. Most startling is the **belfry** (*open May–Sept Mon–Sat 9–6.30, Sun 10–1 and 2.30–6.30; rest of year Mon–Sat 9–12 and 2–6.30, Sun 10–12.30 and 3–6.30; adm*) rocketing 75m (246ft) skywards. From the town hall, not only can you climb to the top (the lift helps) for panoramic views, but you can depart from the basement for a tour of subterranean Arras and its **Boves**, or tunnels (*open same times as belfry; adm*). France is so substantially made up of holey limestone that there's a whole exciting underground country to visit, bearing the traces of so many layers of civilization.

Arras' caves were used as far back as Gallo-Roman times, when a settlement developed here. Limestone was extracted for building over the centuries, creating elaborate galleries and caves. All these tunnels could be used for storage and for refuge. Catholics held secret masses in them in Revolutionary times; during the First World War, when Arras lay so close to the front line, British troops not only made use of the Arras underground tunnels, but also extended them, using them to move to the front, as well as setting up an underground hospital. The confusing labyrinth of the Boves proves fascinating.

Getting There

A good **train** service connects Lille-Flandres (the central Lille station) to Arras throughout the day, journey time 40mins–1hr. The last train back from Arras leaves Mon–Fri 8.27pm, Sat 7.54pm, Sun 9.25pm.

Tourist Information

Arras ✉ **62000**: Place des Héros, **t** 03 21 51 26 95, **f** 03 21 71 07 34, *www.ot-arras.fr*.

Market Days

Arras: Wed and Sat am.

Shopping

While **Rue Gambetta** has a wide selection of high-street names, seek out the tempting specialist stores around the big squares, notably Fromagerie Leclercq and Pâtisserie Delestrez on **Place des Héros**, and Charcuterie Briet just off it, Rue de la Housse. On **Place Vacquerie**, the Caudrons, who revived the traditional **blue Arras pottery** in the 1960s, have a lovely shop.

Eating Out

★★★L'Univers, 5 Place de Croix Rouge, **t** 03 21 71 34 01, **f** 03 21 71 41 42. Plush Ancien Régime hotel in a fomer monastery; with refined restaurant (*expensive*) to match.

La Faisanderie, 45 Grand-Place, **t** 03 21 48 20 76 (*expensive*). Has a splendid cave of a restaurant where the cooking reaches the highest culinary heights.

Le Victor Hugo, 11 Place Victor Hugo, **t** 03 21 71 84 00, **f** 03 21 71 84 00 (*expensive*). The other top restaurant in the centre, a posh address serving classic French cuisine.

La Rapière, 44 Grand-Place, **t** 03 21 55 09 92 (*moderate*). Great traditional location with modern decoration and cooking, and more reasonable value.

For appealing, very well-located, lively cheap cafés-cum-hotels on Place Vacquerie, try: **Le Beffroi**, **t** 03 21 23 13 78 or **OK Pub**, **t** 03 21 21 30 60.

For the buzzing brasserie experience, try: **Aux Grandes Arcades**, Grand-Place, **t** 03 21 23 30 89 (*moderate*). In a great location.

Back outside, behind the town hall, the more down-to-earth **Place Vacquerie** leads through to the most significant religious foundation left in Arras, the **abbey of St-Vaast**, named after the first bishop of the city. The abbey lives up to its namesake and the unintentional pun in English – it's enormous. The medieval institution was rebuilt during the Ancien Régime. The work may well have been ordered by one of the most outrageously ostentatious and corrupt bishops of 18th-century France, one of the cardinals of Rohan, who held numerous religious posts at the same time.

The abbey was certainly rebuilt on a palatial scale. It now contains the **Musée des Beaux-Arts** (*open April–Sept Wed–Mon 10–12 and 2–6; rest of year Wed–Mon 10–12 and 2–5; closed Tues; adm*). The artefacts take you as far back as the Gallo-Roman Cité. Sadly, virtually no medieval tapestries of Arras have survived beyond one adorable one showing St Vaast taming a bear, but some wonderful medieval carvings have found refuge here, which demonstrate the intensity Gothic carvers could convey. Some accomplished Flemish artists feature among the mass of painters, and 18th-century French artists are represented. A number of rooms concentrate on Arras' history, and you will also see how a regional tradition of pottery developed.

Arras' original cathedral, Notre-Dame de la Cité, was brought down by Revolutionary fanatics. The abbey's huge **church**, completed in the 19th century, took over the role. It's a neoclassical building of phenomenal power, a show of body-builder Christianity. Wall paintings inside tell the life of St Vaast, including that bear again, while more typical Christian images adorn other corners and chapels in the huge edifice.

Ironically supported by one of Arras' late-Ancien Régime bishops, perhaps Arras' most famous, or infamous, citizen became the most terrifying exponent of Revolutionary Terror – Maximilien Robespierre. Brought up in part in the city (his father was a barrister in Artois), Maximilien followed in his father's footsteps, practising in Arras before he moved on to Paris with such devastating effect. The Revolution was bloody and devastating in Arras too, you'll have gathered. **Robespierre's house** (*open April–Sept Tues–Sun 2–6.30, closed Mon; rest of year Tues and Thurs 2–5.30, weekends 3–6.30*) survives, near the abbey. It contains a few sad mementos of the Incorruptible One, plus a rather unrelated display on cycling to cheer you up. Which has been the greater force for good in French culture, you might ask, the guillotine or the bicycle? Rue Robespierre leads off **Place du Théâtre**, modest in scale by Arras' standards, but surrounded by delightful buildings, including the theatre itself. Arras' shopping street, **Rue Gambetta**, passes in front of the square.

Arras is a place of harrowing First World War memories, as we've indicated. On the outskirts of the centre, beyond the elegant if neglected Ancien Régime quarter around the striking octagonal **Place Victor Hugo**, you might go to pay your respects at the huge **British cemetery**; it contains over 2,500 graves, and the names of some 40,000 British soldiers who disappeared without trace in the carnage. **Vauban**'s 17th-century **citadel** nearby is a reminder of Louis XIV's wars to acquire Flanders; it still holds a regiment of the French army. The **Mur des Fusillés**, also in this neighbourhood, recalls the Resistance fighters shot here in the Second World War. War memories lie all around Arras, not just in the battlefields and cemeteries of the surrounding countryside, but also in the city itself.

Touring from Lille

You'll find that the sights are reliably open Easter–Oct, 10–12 and 2–5 at least, unless otherwise stated. Museums charge adm.

Day 1: Killing Fields and a Surprise Cathedral

Morning: Péronne's war museum (*closed Mon Oct–April*), set within the protective remaining walls of a medieval castle, provides one of the clearest and most stirring introductions to the First World War.

Lunch: ★★**Hostellerie des Remparts**, 23 Rue Beaubois, **t** 03 22 84 01 22 (*moderate*) is a pleasant place for lunch in Péronne. Or head north for Rancourt and ★★**Le Prieuré**, **t** 03 22 85 04 43.

Afternoon: **Noyon**, birthplace of that shattering Protestant, Calvin, has a museum to its troublesome son, but also a spectacular, little-known Gothic cathedral.

Dinner and sleeping: ★★**Le St-Eloi**, 81 Bd Carnot, **t** 03 44 44 01 49, occupies a timber-frame building towards Noyon station, and has a good traditional restaurant. ★★**Le Cèdre**, 8 Rue de l'Evêché, **t** 03 44 44 23 24 (*inexpensive*) may be in modern brick with standard modern rooms, but it's right by the cathedral and rather pleasant. **La Dame Journe**, 2 Bd Mony, **t** 03 44 44 01 33 (*moderate*) doesn't look anything special but serves respectable regional cuisine.

Day 2: Stunning Castles to Compiègne

Morning: **Blérancourt** (southeast of Noyon) has the clipped wings of a grandiose Ancien Régime château (*closed Tues*) bought by Anne Morgan (daughter of the mega-wealthy US banker), who set up an American women's humanitarian service here in 1917. Now the place houses the intriguing National Museum of Franco-American Friendship, especially as expressed through painting. The **Château de Pierrefonds** (towards Compiègne) is a famous picture-book restoration of a mighty, ruined medieval castle, the neo-Gothic masterpiece of 19th-century Viollet-le-Duc.

Lunch: **Aux Blés d'Or**, 8 Rue Michelet, **t** 03 44 42 85 91, is a very sweet inn by Pierrefonds' lake, with a pleasing restaurant (*moderate*). Slightly grander-looking, with its own

grounds, **Le Domaine des Thermes**, 8 Rue Sabatier, **t** 03 44 42 19 82 (*moderate*) has style and outdoor dining.

Afternoon: **Compiègne** wasn't only a royal town once; it became positively imperial under the Napoleons. Built for Louis XV, the enormous château (*closed Tues*) with its 1,000 rooms is almost on a scale to rival Versailles. Marie-Antoinette met the future Louis XVI here for the first time, in 1770, while in 1810 Marie-Louise of Austria was brought here to meet Napoleon I. She became his second wife and they had a child, François, who briefly became king of Rome and, for five days, Napoleon II. Napoleon III and his Empress Eugénie later entertained here on a lavish scale. The grounds are splendid too, as is Compiègne's historic centre close by. Head east into the forest to visit the copy of the carriage where the First World War's armistice was signed.

Dinner and sleeping: Compiègne's characterful, concave-fronted, timberframed ★★**Hôtel de France**, 17 Rue Eugène Floquet, **t** 03 44 40 02 74, **f** 03 44 40 48 37 (*inexpensive*), tucked away off the main square, is a delight, with traditional French restaurant (*moderate*). In a different, neoclassical style, ★★**Les Flandres**, 16 Quai de la République, **t** 03 44 83 24 40, **f** 03 44 90 02 75 (*inexpensive*) is another good option, with the lively **Bistrot des Flandres** (*moderate*) down below.

Day 3: From Religion to Rousseau via Châteaux

Morning: **Senlis** is a quietly spectacular historic city, its cobbled streets like onion rings encircling its splendidly fronted Gothic cathedral, all contained in the Gallo-Roman walls. Brilliant carvings from Roman to Gothic times feature in the main museum (*closed Tues, and Wed am*).

Lunch: Head on towards Chantilly for lunch. Nearby Gouvieux has very posh, *expensive* addresses: the ★★★★**Château de Montvillargenne**, **t** 03 44 62 37 37, and the ★★★**Château de la Tour**, **t** 03 44 62 38 38. For a nice, less pretentious lunch in central Chantilly, try **Rôtisserie du Connétable**, **t** 03 44 57 02 91, or **Le Goutillon**, **t** 03 44 58 01 00, both on Rue du Connétable.

Afternoon: **Chantilly** is best-known for its racecourse. You'd be forgiven for mistaking its stunning Ancien Régime stables, which contain a major museum on horses, for the castle. The château itself (*closed Tues*), reflected in a lake, houses a fabulous art collection. **Ermenonville** (southeast of Senlis) is renowned for its links with 18th-century philosopher Rousseau, who spent his last years here – a beautiful landscaped park with follies is dedicated to him.

Dinner and sleeping: Stunning, moated ★★★**Château d'Ermenonville**, t 03 44 54 00 26, f 03 44 54 01 00 (*expensive–moderate*) is the castle where Rousseau was so warmly received at the end of his days. It has a fine restaurant. At ★★**L'Hermitage**, 36 Rue Souville, t 03 44 54 00 25 (*inexpensive*), a peaceful, pretty little hotel, the dining room dominated by a big fireplace used for grilling meats. ★★**Auberge de la Croix d'Or**, 2 Rue Radziwill, t 03 44 54 00 04, f 03 44 45 05 44 (*inexpensive*), is full of rustic charm; its restaurant is open only at lunchtimes.

Day 4: From Desert Sands to Soissons

Morning: Just north of Ermenonville, the **Abbaye de Chaalis** and **La Mer de Sable** compete on opposite sides of the road, the first an elegant semi-ruined abbey containing the Musée Jacquemart-André, with its clutter of paintings, the rejects of the more famous Parisian museum of the same name, while the second (**t** 03 44 54 00 96 to check times) is a popular children's theme park set in a startling sandy landscape caused by 19th-century deforestation.

Lunch: Either try Ermenonville again, or head northeast past Villers-Cotterêts for the ★★**Hôtel de l'Abbaye**, t 03 23 96 02 44 (*inexpensive*) an old-style inn in the delightful village of Longpont with its ruined abbey.

Afternoon: **Soissons** suffered badly in the First World War, but the medieval abbey of St-Léger has been turned into a distinctive archaeological and fine arts museum (*closed Tues*). If the massive cathedral looks a bit grubby, surrounded by car parks, the outlying ruined abbey of St-Jean-les-Vignes won't disappoint. Before evening falls, follow the beautiful, tragic hilltop road of **Le Chemin des Dames** northeast from Soissons, lined with war cemeteries and memorials, in this, one of the worst areas of

First World War fighting for the French. The **Caverne du Dragon** (*closed Mon*) is an excellent subterranean museum devoted to the subject. Continue on to **Laon** for the night.

Dinner and sleeping: In Laon's historic upper town, ★★★**La Bannière de France**, 11 Rue Franklin Roosevelt, t 03 23 23 21 44, f 03 23 23 31 56 (*expensive*) is a good hotel in an old former coaching inn, plus plainer modern block. The restaurant (*expensive–moderate*) offers fine cuisine. ★★**Les Chevaliers**, 3 Rue Sérurier, t 03 23 27 17 50, f 03 23 23 40 71 (*inexpensive*) may be in a rather dull modern block, but it's very well located. **Des Chenizelles**, 1 Rue du Bourg, t 03 23 23 02 34, is a part 12th-century restaurant (*cheap*) with a good reputation and a terrace.

Day 5: Crowning Glories of Laon and Coucy

Morning: Crowned by one of the most remarkable Gothic cathedrals in France, hilltop **Laon** has a splendid historic centre packed with former religious buildings. Also, don't miss the delightful Romanesque Templars' chapel with a macabre surprise, in the garden of the fine arts museum (*closed Tues*).

Lunch: South of Laon (D967), at Martigny-Courpierre, the **Auberge du Moulin Bertrand**, t 03 23 24 71 73 (*moderate*) is a smart spot for a good lunch, possibly on the waterside. Cessières, west of Laon (D7), has a more old-fashioned country inn, **Le Rustique**, t 03 23 24 03 15 (*moderate*). *Closed Sun pm and Mon.*

Afternoon: **Coucy-le-Château's** hilltop is crowned by the finely preserved ramparts of one of the most impressive early medieval castles in France, built for the powerful Enguerrands. Although the Germans dynamited the place at the end of the First World War, it retains plenty of atmosphere.

Dinner and sleeping: At Coucy-le-Château, appealing ★★**Le Belle Vue**, t 03 23 52 69 70, f 03 23 52 69 79 (*inexpensive*), with its belvedere, is set in a characterful post-war house. The place has bright rooms with new wood flooring. The restaurant serves pleasant fare. Twelve km west, back at Blérancourt, the **Griffon**, t 03 23 39 23 39 (*inexpensive*) is a decent old-style option with good restaurant (*moderate*).

The Normandy Coast

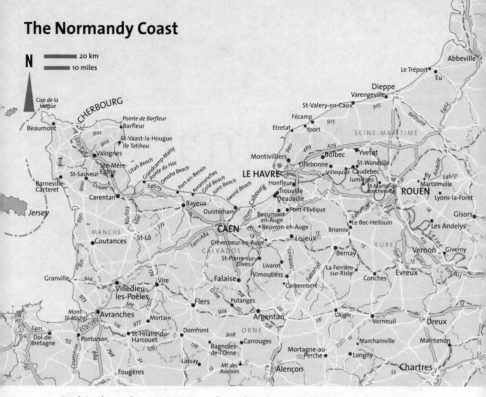

The Normandy Coast

Back in the 10th century, Rouen, that other great city on the Seine beyond Paris, became the capital of the powerful Norseman, Viking Wrolf. Threatening French royal authority, he accepted a dukedom, converted to Christianity, and became Rollo. One century later a still mightier descendant of his, Guillaume, or William, crossed the Channel with his army to conquer England, by force tying the futures of Normandy and Britain closely together. Once the centuries upon centuries of warring between French and English monarchs finally came to an end in the 19th century, the flow of people has tended to go the other way – vast numbers of British visitors landing in the Normandy ports featured here along with Rouen. Dieppe, set in a gap in the dramatic white cliffs of eastern Normandy, attracted great artists and Oscar Wilde. At Le Havre, looking over the leviathan mouth of the Seine estuary, several superlative French 19th-century artists were brought up, and one of them, Monet, painted a view of Le Havre's harbour which would give its title to a shocking new style of painting, called Impressionism.

Caen became the capital of western Normandy under William the Conqueror, who endowed it with major buildings. Cherbourg, at the end of the Cotentin peninsula sticking its long neck out into the Channel, boasts the largest man-made harbour in the world. Like Le Havre, famous ocean liners headed off from here to America.

All five of our Normandy destinations inevitably lost some of their historic character or Belle Epoque glamour in the Second World War. They suffered terribly (as did almost every town in the region) in the crucial Battle of Normandy of 1944 which led to the liberation of France from the Nazis. At the outset of the campaign, the beaches just west of Caen's ferry port of Ouistreham witnessed the arrival of surely the most famous fleet in modern history, startling the Germans on the morning of D-Day, 6 June 1944. But each of these towns still offers very varied attractions, somewhat surprisingly in architecture as well as art.

While the eastern Norman coast with Dieppe and Le Havre is made up of steep cliffs, west of the Seine estuary, broad long beaches stretch out in front of such famous resorts as Deauville and Trouville. Inland, you can follow the river valleys that meander to the sea. Normandy's lush green meadows, where cider-apple trees provide shade for dappled cows that produce the milk for all those splendidly creamy regional cheeses, always lie close at hand. Eastern Normandy has many famous tourist sights, such as Monet's garden at Giverny or Richard the Lionheart's Château-Gaillard, but the most remarkable of all Normandy's attractions are in the west – the Bayeux tapestry recording William the Conqueror's victory, the D-Day landing beaches, and the Mont St-Michel, an almost magical mirage of another world.

Dieppe

Behind its broad shingle beach, Dieppe may look a bit shabby nowadays, having suffered not just in the Second World War but also from poor property development afterwards. However, it still has a certain scruffy appeal. Its greatest attractions are its harbour and its main shopping street, rather than the seafront. However, this is the port that became France's first ever seaside resort, set in vogue by English tourists arriving after Napoleon's demise, and then by the visit of the ultra-royalist, briefly ultra-fashionable Duchesse de Berry in 1824, copying the English fashion for taking the healthy sea air and a dip in the chilly Channel waters.

A very grim medieval castle glowers down from its clifftop on to the shore. For a long time before Dieppe became a resort, it was one of France's most important ports, one with a very spicy history. It had the great advantage of its excellent natural harbour, tucked in behind the cliffs, its waters helpfully deep – yes, the name of the place comes from that old Viking word. Dieppe sailors were often involved in battles with the English through medieval times, although English pilgrims also stepped ashore here for their very long walk to Santiago de Compostela in northern Spain.

Dieppe's heyday came with the 16th-century exploration of the New World. A Dieppe sailor, Jean Cousin, is claimed as one of the discoverers of Brazil. The still more renowned Florentine explorer Verrazano worked for the most famous of all Dieppe's merchants, Jean Ango, who supplied him with the ship *La Dauphine* in which Verrazano became the first European to discover the bay of New York. Ango had many other irons in the fire – his fleet of privateers challenged the Portuguese and Spanish in Africa and the New World. Ango made a killing when one of his captains grabbed Cortés' treasure-filled fleet in 1522, and has been portrayed as a local hero ever since. Meanwhile, other Dieppois left France altogether, and were among the first to settle in Canada.

One Dieppe Protestant, Abraham Duquesne, played a crucial role in reviving the French navy for Louis XIV, even though the Sun King's anti-Protestant 1685 Revocation of the Edict of Nantes would cause many important Huguenot merchants and craftsmen of Dieppe to emigrate to England. Disaster then struck the town in the ensuing war, when in 1694 an Anglo-Dutch fleet under Admiral Berkeley came to bombard the place, reducing much of it to rubble. Eventually peace did come, in the 19th century, and Dieppe embarked on its new career as a tourist port; the first, steam-operated ferry landed in 1825. Artists and celebrities, and those fleeing the rigid morality of Victorian Britain, escaped here to enjoy a taste of more open French living, including Aubrey Beardsley and Walter Sickert. Much of Dieppe was destroyed once again, however, in the Second World War. Tragically, on 19 August 1942, the Allies sent a mainly Canadian force into the port on the disastrous Dieppe Raid.

Touring Dieppe

Dieppe's **harbour** is the centre of the tourist action, restaurants with conservatory fronts lining up behind the **Quai Henri IV** like a row of aquariums. Sailors moor their yachts in the Bassin Jehan Ango below this quay. The other grand harbourside row, arcaded **Quai Duquesne**, stands in front of the Bassin Duquesne, reserved for Dieppe's fishing fleet. These quays are also the centre of Dieppe nightlife, the façades along them well lit up after nightfall. High up on the cliff on the other side of the harbour, **Notre-Dame du Bon Secours**, a 19th-century sailors' chapel, stands out.

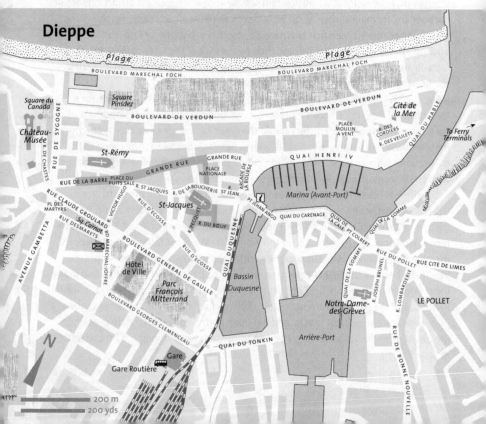

Getting to Dieppe

Transmanche Ferries, t (France) 0800 917 12 01, *www.transmancheferries.com*, have recently set up a new ferry service , providing crossings (4–4½hrs) all year round between Newhaven and Dieppe.

Hoverspeed Ferries, t 08705 240 241, **f** (01304) 240 088, *www.hoverspeed.co.uk*, operates a very fast Superseacat Newhaven–Dieppe service (2–2½hrs) through the summer. By the way, the extraordinary Vietnamese Communist leader Ho Chi Minh worked for a time as a pantry boy on the Newhaven–Dieppe ferries! Today, Transmanche offers the more upmarket dining experience of the two.

Getting from the Port

The ferries arrive on the eastern side of the harbour, not far from the centre, but a **shuttle bus** is provided for foot passengers.

Car Hire

Budget, 1 Av Norm. Sussex, **t** 02 35 84 32 28. **Europcar**, 33 Rue Thiers, **t** 02 35 04 97 10.

Tourist Information

Dieppe: Pont Jehan Ango, Quai du Carénage, **t** 02 32 14 40 60, **f** 02 32 14 40 61, *OFFICETOUR.DIEPPE@ wanadoo.fr*.

Market Day

Sat am, really bringing Dieppe to life.

Shopping

The **Grande Rue** has a wide range of shops, including tempting pâtisseries and LC Vins for wines. Sommelier is another popular wine merchant nearby, in **Rue des Maillots**.

On **Rue St-Jacques**, Olivier is a good delicatessen. The tourist office has a list of the many cheap **antiques shops** around town. You can even visit a Dieppe **ivory carver**, Ivoiriers Colette, Rue Ango, keeping up the centuries-old tradition, if that appeals.

Apart from the cafés, one place to take tea is in the delightful old-style elegance of Roussel, a pâtisserie-cum-tea-shop on the square facing St-Rémi church.

Where to Stay

Dieppe ✉ **76200**

★★★Présidence, 1 Bd de Verdun, **t** 02 35 84 31 31, **f** 02 35 84 86 70, *www.hotel-la-presidence. com* (*moderate*). Of the handful of hotels looking out to sea, this is the smartest, in a modern block below the castle.

★★★L'Aguado, 30 Bd de Verdun, **t** 02 35 84 27 00, **f** 02 35 06 17 61 (*moderate*). Close to the harbour, but with some rooms facing the Channel. Has tried to brighten up the otherwise uninspiring modern architecture.

★★Europe, 63 Bd de Verdun, **t** 02 32 90 19 19 (*moderate*). Run by the same people as L'Aguado, better value, with jazzy bar.

★★Les Arcades, 1–3 Arcades de la Bourse, **t** 02 35 84 14 12, **f** 02 35 40 22 29, *www.les-arcades.fr* (*moderate–inexpensive*). Some rooms overlook the pretty harbour.

Au Grand Duquesne, 15 Place St-Jacques, **t** 02 32 14 61 10, **f** 02 35 84 29 83, *www.augrandduquesne.fr* (*inexpensive*). By the best church, recently renovated, with a good restaurant (*moderate*).

Eating Out

Restaurant du Port, 99 Quai Henri IV, **t** 02 35 84 36 64 (*moderate*). Of the countless restaurants vying for attention on the quays, this is the most tempting, with good-quality cooking. *Closed Thurs.*

La Marmite Dieppoise, 8 Rue St-Jean, **t** 02 35 84 24 26 (*moderate*). Behind Quai Duquesne, an old-established favourite reputed for its fish stew. *Closed Sun pm and Mon.*

Les Ecamias, 129 Quai Henri IV, **t** 02 35 84 67 67 (*moderate–cheap*). Another quayside address with a touch more originality than the rest. *Closed Sun, Mon, and Tues pm.*

Bellevue, 70 Bd de Verdun, **t** 02 35 84 39 37 (*moderate–cheap*). Just round the corner, on the eastern end of the seafront, one of the rare options looking out to sea, offering classic French dining. *Closed Sun pm and Mon.*

Les Tourelles, 43 Rue du Commandant Fayolle, **t** 02 35 84 15 88 (*cheap*). A bargain, characterful, old-fashioned restaurant close to St-Rémi church. *Closed Sun pm and Mon.*

Heading into town from Quai Henri IV, the buildings immediately look more jaded. While so many other French towns have been scrubbed clean in the last few decades, Dieppe seems to have missed out so far on a thorough going-over. The main shopping street, the **Grande Rue** contains good shops, though. Along the side of the small triangular **Place du Puits Salé**, the substantial form of the **Café des Tribunaux** stands out, haunt of many of the 19th-century artists who visited Dieppe. It even puts in a claim to being the place where Oscar Wilde, a shattered man after serving his prison term for his harrowing public condemnation as a homosexual, wrote much of his moving *Ballad of Reading Gaol*, although the **Café Suisse**, still a lively venue by the port, maybe has the better claim. The English Impressionist Walter Sickert is said to have invited Wilde to Dieppe originally, and was one of the most loyal visitors to the resort, also frequented by such French art stars as Renoir, Gauguin and Degas.

From the square, you get a fine vista on to the flamboyant Gothic façade of the church of **St-Jacques** (James in English, recalling the Santiago pilgrimage route). Although many of its statues were hacked off in fanatical 16th-century times (the Protestant Huguenots were often much more destructive in the French provinces than the Revolutionaries), the church retains many interesting features, including three splendid rose windows. The interior is packed with ornate side chapels, the most exclusive by the choir made for Ango's private worship. The most curious decoration adorns the entrance to the sacristy – along with a riot of Renaissance motifs, a bizarre 16th-century carved frieze apparently depicts small South American ritual scenes, probably commissioned by Ango once again. Swashbuckling Abraham Duquesne presides over **Place Nationale**, the main market square to one side of St-Jacques.

Dieppe's other main church, **St-Rémi**, stands west off the Grande Rue. It's a colossal, bold Renaissance structure with a grand Renaissance rose window, although the builders couldn't resist touches of late Gothic in the howling gargoyles and the choir windows. The building, begun in 1522, was only completed in the 17th century because of the dreadful French Wars of Religion. The great organ in the vast interior has been restored, held up by huge tubular columns.

Nearby, Dieppe's **Petit Théâtre** has been converted into the temporary home of the new **Mémorial du 19 Août 1942** (*open daily 2–6.30; adm*), paying homage to the Allies who lost their lives in the daring attempt to blow up the Germans' installations in and around Dieppe. Although a few of the peripheral attacks were successful, for example on the Varengeville battery, the main attack on Dieppe proved catastrophic. Of around 6,000 Allied troops, 1,380 were killed (including 913 Canadians), 1,600 wounded and more than 2,000 captured. The Germans only lost 345 men, and shot down 107 RAF planes supporting the naval campaign. The tragedy is retold with period photographs, documents and objects.

From beside the ugly but popular **casino** nearby, head out to the beach from the severe turreted gateway, the **Porte des Tourelles**, sole remnant of Dieppe's 14th-century fortifications, built in layered patterns of brick and stone typical of grand old buildings in the area. Dieppe's **seafront** looks somewhat dismal on cloudy days. Most of the 19th-century villas have been kicked out by dull post-war apartment blocks. A wide, treeless expanse of lawn separates the front from the beach, although there's an excellent **outdoor heated pool** (*open daily June–early Sept*), with tennis courts and mini-golf; and on the eastern end stands the **Estran-Cité de la Mer** (*open daily 10–12 and 2–6; adm*), with aquaria and exhibits on sea life, from marine biology to coastal structures, plus displays on shipbuilding and fishing.

The brown shingle **beach** leads to cliffs in the west from which the castle peers down, like the Colditz of the eastern Normandy coast. It's a steep climb up to it from Square du Canada, commemorating not just the victims of the Dieppe Raid, but also 17th-century Jesuit missionaries killed by Indians none too overjoyed at attempts to convert them to European ways and cults.

Although Dieppe's **Château-musée** (*open June–Sept daily 10–12 and 2–6; rest of year daily exc Tues, 10–12 and 2–5; adm*) looks so uninviting, it's well worth a visit. From the Nazi *blockhauses* outside, you get splendid views down on to the Channel's gorgeous churning green and turquoise waters. Elaborate carved ivories, for centuries an especially prized local craft, greet you as you enter, as well as a variety of model ships. The good, regionally inspired painting sections include harrowing scenes at sea, as well as more comforting Impressionist works. The exquisitely carved ivory objects displayed in further rooms range from religious pieces, figurines of great Frenchmen and sewing and toiletry items, to men's tobacco-graters, to women baring their breasts – probably as close as the Dieppois came to coarse seaside humour before the days of the popular beach resort.

Day Trips from Dieppe

Varengeville

Varengeville is a wonderful sprawling village west of Dieppe, made up of delightful wooded, winding lanes strung with a whole variety of swish village houses in different Norman styles. The **Bois des Moutiers** (*open 15 Mar–15 Nov 10–12 and 2–6;*

Getting There

Buses (Mon–Sat) from Dieppe's *gare routière* take 25mins, arriving in front of the Auberge du Relais. The first bus leaves Dieppe at 8.20. The last bus back leaves at 6.50pm.

Tourist Information

Varengeville doesn't have a tourist office. Contact Pourville's, **t** 02 35 84 71 06. The village sprawls, so expect a good walk to the sights. The Bois des Moutiers and church are easier to get to than the Manoir d'Ango, *c.* 30mins walk inland on busy roads.

Eating Out

Auberge du Relais, **t** 02 35 85 11 33 (*moderate*). A pleasing, typical timberframe Norman village inn for a relaxed lunch in the middle of Varengeville. *Open lunchtime weekdays exc Wed, lunch and dinner Fri–Sun.*

Hôtel de la Terrasse, Route de Vastérival, **t 02 35 85 12 54 (*moderate*). A peaceful hotel by the beach at the Dieppe end of the village, with a restaurant serving refined Norman fare.

adm) offers the charms of a lush English-style country garden created by Gertrude Jekyll around a house designed by Edwin Lutyens. This pair counted among the most influential designers of the late 19th and early 20th centuries. The house was constructed in 1898, for Guillaume Mallet, an anglophile banker with an eye for British talent, and is still owned by the family. In conceiving the house, Lutyens included Norman features, but managed to combine historical respect with his own especially elegant brand of modernity.

Perhaps the best thing of all in Varengeville is the **church**, at the end of a lane leading to the cliffs. From the churchyard you get splendid views down towards Dieppe and the Channel, and at the right time you can see boats going in and out of the port. Enter the church by the side door and you're greeted by a vomiting voyager carved on one of the extraordinary columns inside. Striking stained glass adds colour to the interior, including a piece by Georges Braque, who spent the last 20 years of his life here and whose grave lies in the cemetery, one of those near-spiritual places where you almost feel it would be a joy to be buried.

Turning its back on the village, the Renaissance **Manoir d'Ango** (*open April–Sept daily 10–12.30 and 2–6.30; rest of year Sat pm, Sun and hols only; adm*) stands aloof, looking determinedly inland. By the time Jean d'Ango commissioned this summer residence in the 1530s and 1540s he had amassed enough money to pay for the finest craftsmen. Although parts were badly damaged during the Revolution, splendid elements remain, most notably a Florentine loggia with busts of French royals and of Ango and his wife. Inside, a few of the original features are still in place. Outside, the brick patterning of the dovecote, claimed to be the largest in France – invariably a sign of a man's massive wealth – looks wonderfully extravagant, while the hydrangea garden can also dazzle in season.

Eu and Le Tréport

A trip east up the coast from Dieppe takes you to Normandy's border with Picardy and the town of **Eu**, a modest *ville royale* set back from the sea around the Bresle river. As early as the 10th century, Duke Rollo had a fort built here, marking the northern-most point of his territory. William the Conqueror's controversial marriage to Matilda of Flanders took place here. The story goes that he dragged her round screaming by the hair before the event. Eu is also the place where William first received Harold, having rescued him from his captivity by Guy de Ponthieu across in Picardy.

Eu still has a château, a 16th-century one. But it was never completed and is eclipsed by the enormous medieval church to **Notre-Dame et St-Laurent** nearby. Its second dedication isn't to the well-known early Christian martyr grilled alive, but to a 12th-century Irishman, Laurence O'Toole, archbishop of Dublin; for a long time he was the only Irish saint officially accepted by the Church of Rome, unwilling to endorse Celtic holy men. Already an aged, ailing man, in 1180 Laurence crossed the Channel in slow pursuit of King Henry II Plantagenet, trying to plead the cause of Irish lords, following the first Anglo-Norman invasion of the Emerald Isle in 1169. But Laurence got no further than Eu before dying, and was quickly canonized by a pope who was at odds with Henry II. A vast church in his honour was begun as early as 1186, and was built throughout the 13th century. The choir end was reconstructed in Flamboyant Gothic style after a destructive lightning strike in the early 15th century.

Inside, the grandiose 17th-century organ distracts from the medieval forms. Head for the chapel of the Holy Sepulchre to admire a moving Entombment of Christ, an anonymous masterpiece. Down in the crypt, a 13th-century effigy of Laurence survived Revolutionary destruction, while the other, mutilated figures represent the aristocratic Artois family, rulers of the area up to 1472. Three years later, the paranoid French king Louis XI had most of the town of Eu burnt down, allegedly fearing that the English might capture it.

The modest **Château d'Eu** (*open 15 March–1 Nov daily Wed–Mon 10–12 and 2–6; closed Tues; free while being restored*) situated across a rather barren square from the church represents little more than one wing of a vast castle planned in the 1570s for the notorious, pious man-eater Catherine de Clèves, Countess of Eu, and her second husband, the feared fanatical Catholic Henri de Guise, 'Le Balafré', Scarface. His sensational assassination on the instructions of the cowardly King Henri III of France at the Château de Blois in 1588 didn't help with the completion of the ambitious project. In the 17th century, Louis XIV's awkward cousin, Mlle de Montpensier, 'La Grande Mademoiselle', spent part of her exile here, ordering the elegant terraced gardens.

In the 19th century, the restored French monarchy took hold of the castle. Louis-Philippe, Duc d'Orléans, was yet to be elected by the people to replace the much-loathed King Charles X when he inherited the place in the 1820s and began restoring it. In 1830 he was crowned king on a wave of popular support. He loved this spot, and had a more modest separate building, looking a little like stabling, made to

Getting There

Buses from Dieppe to Le Tréport and Eu are infrequent, so plan the journey carefully. Double-check times with the bus company, Cars Denis, **t** 02 35 06 86 86, **f** 02 35 84 40 70. Normally there's a bus leaving Dieppe Gare around midday, taking *c.* 50mins to Le Tréport and 1hr to Eu, but the timetable may differ July–Aug. The last bus back normally leaves Le Tréport *c.* 5.15, Eu 5.30. There are no services on Sundays.

Tourist Information

Eu ✉ 76260: B.P.82, 41 Rue P. Bignon, **t** 02 35 86 04 68, **f** 02 35 50 16 03, *www.ville-eu.fr.*
Le Tréport ✉ 76260: Quai Sadi Carnot, **t** 02 35 86 05 69, **f** 02 35 86 73 96.

Market Days

Eu: Fri am.
Le Tréport: Tues and Sat am.

Eating Out

Eu
Hôtel Maine, 20 Av de la Gare, **t** 02 35 86 16 64 (*moderate*). A real surprise awaits you in the dining room behind the unassuming brick façade attached to the old railway station. The décor will keep you entertained while you enjoy either the excellent Norman fish or meat menu. *Closed Sun pm.*
La Bragance, Parc du Château, **t** 02 35 50 20 01 (*moderate*). Another big surprise, in the garden lodge and ice-house of the château, a friendly restaurant serving light menus or salads. *Closed Mon pm and Tues.*

Le Tréport
The quayside is lined with tempting options.
Le Homard Bleu, **t** 02 35 86 15 89 (*expensive–moderate*). Has the finest reputation for seafood; its cheaper neighbour, **Le Comptoir de l'Océan**, **t** 02 35 86 24 92, is run by the same family.

accommodate his ministers while he stayed here, and had the Bresle river cleared so that he could take his yacht to and from the sea. In 1843, he invited Queen Victoria to the château, not long after she had succeeded to the British throne. This was a significant moment in relations between French and English monarchies, who had for centuries upon centuries dragged their populations into war over their territorial disputes. In fact, it was the first time an English royal had entered France since Henry VIII had met François I at the disastrously competitive Field of the Cloth of Gold in 1520. Louis-Philippe and Victoria enjoyed parades and concerts and picnics together, much merrier than making war. But France's so-called 'Citizen King' rapidly lost his popularity as his regime became less and less tolerant. An angered populace overthrew him in 1848 and he fled to England under the subtle pseudonym of Mr Smith. A frisky equestrian statue outside the château shows his eldest son, Ferdinand d'Orléans, who would never become king, because his father was France's last monarch. Louis-Philippe's descendant, the Comte de Paris, did receive his French estates back in the 1870s, at which time Viollet-le-Duc partly restored the interiors of the Château d'Eu. In 1964, the castle was sold to the town, and was left to languish until the current restoration. Its royal credentials will be polished up and brought to the fore. In the meantime, a temporary exhibition fills the gap, while the gardens remain open.

After most of the town was burnt down in 1475, its fortunes revived. From O'Toole's church, walk along the main shopping street, **Rue Paul Bignon**, which proves quite charming, with some half-timbered buildings among the mainly brick façades. Also seek out the **Chapelle des Jésuites**, one of the rare religious institutions founded under the widowed Catherine de Clèves to have survived the Revolution. The Anguier brothers, local scuptors, did a rather fine job of decorating the façade. Inside, Catherine's tomb remains in place. The Bresle valley is well known for its glass-making traditions, and across the river the **Musée Traditions Verrières** (*open April–Oct, Tues and weekends, 2.30–6; adm*), housed in former barracks, keeps the craft alive. As well as the usual dry textual explanations, you can see retired glass-workers at work. Scent bottles are one great speciality.

Le Tréport, up at the Bresle estuary, is Normandy's most northerly resort, facing Picardy's resort of Mers-les-Bains, backed by the vast, hideous St-Gobain glass-making factory. Avoid looking inland and these resorts retain some of their old-fashioned charm. Le Tréport was briefly fashionable, while Louis-Philippe and his entourage were close by. The railway line then brought mass tourism from Paris. Today it has a pretty strip of a fishing and yachting harbour, and all the typical old-fashioned seaside attractions and stalls. Behind the seafront, the church of **St-Jacques** dominates on the hillside. Mainly 16th-century in style, it contains extravagant pendant vaulting. The energetic might climb the hundreds of steps to the **Calvaire des Terrasses** to make out the sea, and Eu, from on high.

Mers-les-Bains has preserved its seafront better than Le Tréport, with a colourful array of villas with differently shaped slate roofs and brightly painted balconies, making a very cheerful sight.

Le Havre

A voracious ogre so often full up that it's forced to vomit out another fleet of ships was one way the great Normandy writer Maupassant described 19th-century Le Havre in his novel *Pierre et Jean*. Today France's second harbour after Marseille, Le Havre was planned for King François Ier as a replacement for silting-up Honfleur and Harfleur further up the Seine estuary, and even back then it was designed on a grid plan. It grew from strength to strength, trading with the Americas in particular: nearly 350 slaving vessels set out in the 18th century. Before the Second World War, Le Havre greeted the *beau monde* off the ocean liners, but also featured in anti-establishment classics such as André Gide's *La Porte étroite* and Jean-Paul Sartre's *La Nausée*. The city was such an important industrial base and port by the war that it was almost inevitable it should become one of the most bombed targets in France. For architectural historians at least, Le Havre's post-war reconstruction with its wide boulevards has become a concrete classic. Its functional grid holds a brilliant fine arts museum, and Brazilian architect Oscar Niemeyer's astonishing Volcano Centre, while its location, on the leviathan mouth of the Seine, is sensational.

Touring Le Havre

In the straight-lined centre, the rectangular **Bassin du Commerce** is crossed by an elegant footbridge, one of the few curves in town, but it's the colossal **Espace Niemeyer** that steals the show with its still greater swooping lines. One of Oscar Niemeyer's fabulous 1970s constructions takes the form of a ship's funnel, the other a volcano. Unfortunately, the sunken square below has suffered badly from Le Havre's depression in the 1990s and most of the shops have been abandoned, even if the cultural centre inside is still going. Between the Espace Niemeyer and the Bassin, a hefty monument records the names of Le Havre's civilian war dead. Find out more

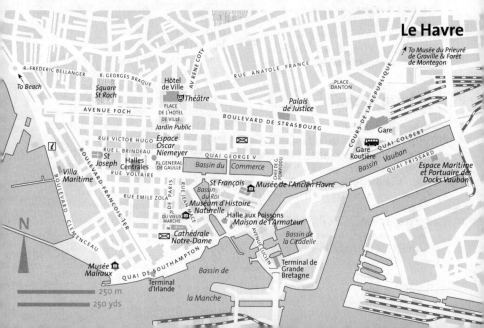

Getting to Le Havre

Le Havre is a key Channel port, and **P&O Portsmouth** (*see* p.11) run day and night sailings from Portsmouth (5½hrs).

Air France runs daily (not budget) **flights** to and from London City Airport and Le Havre (t 0845 0845 111, *www.airfrance.co.uk*).

Car Hire

There is a wide choice available, e.g. on central Av. Général Archinard (off northeast corner of Bassin du Commerce): **ADA, t** 02 35 22 94 31; **Hertz, t** 02 35 19 01 19, **f** 02 35 19 91 46; **Rent A Car, t** 02 35 41 76 76. Further east is **Avis**, Cours de la République, **t** 02 35 53 17 20;

Tourist Information

Le Havre: 186 Bd Clemenceau, **t** 02 32 74 04 04, **f** 02 35 42 38 39, *www.lehavretourisme.com*.

Market Days

Hôtel de Ville quarter: Mon, Wed and Fri.

Shopping

The main shopping quarter is along and west from arcaded **Rue de Paris**, with good clothes and gift shops.

The **Halles Centrales** is the place to aim for for food; the Comptoir des Arômes is an excellent delicatessen.

For quirky creations from Le Havre seadrift, seek out Bois d'Enfer, 64 Rue Paul Doumer, or Cyrille Plate, 30 Place du Vieux Marché.

Where to Stay

Le Havre ⊠ **76600**

★★★**Hôtel des Bains**, 3 Place Clemenceau, Ste-Adresse 76310, **t** 02 35 54 68 90, **f** 02 35 54 68 91, *lapetiterade@wanadoo.fr* (*expensive*). Best-located hotel in the area, with sea views, terrace and nice restaurant, **La Petite Rade** (*moderate*).

★★★**Vent d'Ouest**, 4 Rue Caligny, **t** 02 35 42 50 69, **f** 02 35 42 58 00, *www.ventdouest.fr*, *contact@ventdouest.fr* (*expensive–*

moderate). Rooms charmingly decked out in nautical style, making up for dull post-war architecture. In the shopping quarter.

★★★**Bordeaux**, 147 Rue Louis Brindeau, **t** 02 35 22 69 44, **f** 02 35 42 09 27, *www.bestwestern. com/fr/debordeaux, hotelbordeaux@ libertysurf.fr* (*moderate*). Comfortable hotel with rooms giving on to the dramatic Volcano Centre.

★★★**Marly**, 121 Rue de Paris, **t** 02 35 41 72 48, **f** 02 35 21 50 45, *www.hotellemarly.com*, *hotellemarly@libertysurf.fr* (*moderate*). Well located on the main arcaded shopping artery leading up to the town hall.

★★**Celtic**, 106 Rue Voltaire, **t** 02 35 42 39 77, **f** 02 35 21 67 65, *www.hotel-celtic.com, hotel-celtic@proximedia.fr* (*inexpensive*). Basic rooms, but views on the Volcano Centre.

★**Voltaire**, 14 Rue Voltaire, **t** 02 35 19 35 35, **f** 02 35 19 35 30 (*inexpensive–cheap*). Well-kept central option.

★**Le Séjour Fleuri**, 71 Rue Emile Zola, **t** 02 35 441 33 81, **f** 02 35 42 26 44 (*cheap*). For bargain-hunters, also well kept.

Eating Out

La Villa, 66 Bd Albert Ier, **t** 02 35 54 78 80, **f** 02 35 54 78 81 (*luxury–moderate*). The most luxurious restaurant in town, in a Belle Epoque villa beside the western beach, looking out to sea. Excellent French seasonal cooking. *Closed Sun pm, Mon and Wed pm.*

Le Grignot, 53 Rue Racine, **t** 02 35 43 62 07, (*moderate*). Favourite lively poster-decorated brasserie for the Havrais, by the Volcano Centre. *Closed Sun.*

Le Roi Léopold, 11 Place Clemenceau, Ste-Adresse, **t** 02 35 46 16 25 (*moderate*). Magnificent sea views to accompany excellent fish dishes, served in a modern décor.

Les Trois Pics, Sentier Alphonse Kerr, Ste-Adresse, **t** 02 35 48 20 60 (*moderate–cheap*). Closest to sea, and with a terrace, which makes it popular.

Le Lyonnais, 7 Rue de Bretagne, **t** 02 35 22 07 31 (*cheap*). Bargain meat dishes and seafood stews, south of Bassin de Commerce. *Closed Sun.*

about Le Havre's fiery and tragic history in the very old-fashioned and fragmentary **Musée de l'Ancien Havre** (*open Wed–Sun 10–12 and 2–6; adm*), set in an 18th-century mansion in a small pocket of grand pre-war houses just south of the Bassin that survived. Southwest of it, the Baroque **cathedral** stands out, its well-turned yellow stone contrasting strongly with the concrete arcades of the Rue de Paris, a main shopping street leading up to the town hall.

South along the shore, in the slick glass block of the ground-breaking 1960s **Musée Malraux** (*open Mon–Fri 11–6, Sat and Sun 11–7; closed Tues*) by Guy Lagneau and Raymond Audigier, slickly renovated at the end of the millennium, you can examine vibrant paintings of boats by Normandy's greatest artists, as real boats – tankers, tugs, ferries, yachts – slip silently by outside. You'll realize here how many great French modern artists were born, brought up in or inspired by Le Havre. Native Raoul Dufy's joyous, vibrant canvases so run with colour, it's as though he had poured seawater on them. Othon Friesz is another forceful contemporary from Le Havre. But the Impressionist collection will entice most visitors. Boudin taught Monet around here; the master is represented by some fine seascapes, but also by a huge wall of studies of cows and clouds, the subjects in which he remained unchallenged. Manet, Renoir, Pissarro, Sisley, Gauguin and Braque also put in memorable appearances.

By the Capitainerie opposite the museum, a **plaque** commemorates the 800 passengers and crew of the *Niobé* who died when the ship was sunk by the Germans on 11 June 1940. Walk north between the marina and the big seafront blocks to reach the central shingle **beach**, very lively in summer. Behind the wide strip of pebble beaches and car parks, a soaring tower marks Le Havre's skyline like a building escaped from New York, but the cross on top indicates that it's the post-war church of **St-Joseph**. Designed by Perret in his beloved (and cheap) concrete, the square-plan edifice looks grim on the outside, but walk inside on a bright day and you'll feel you've been caught in a kaleidoscope. East of the church, you come to the town's commercial centre leading down from the enormous square in front of the town hall. West of the church, the suburb of **Ste-Adresse** rises steeply up the slope, with fantastic views.

Day Trips and Overnighters from Le Havre

Etretat

In a break in the spectacular cliffs east of Le Havre, Etretat looks as though it's sold its soul to tourism. When you see the spectacular **beach**, you'll understand why. East along the beach, the two arches in the rock look, at low tide, like entrances to a mighty castle. The silhouette of a church perched high on the eastern cliffs adds to the drama. From this end of the beach you get the best view of the spectacular buttress arch in the cliff to the west of Etretat. Beyond that, the place's most famous symbol, the **Aiguille**, or Needle, points skywards; it actually looks more like a space shuttle in stone stuck awaiting lift-off. A coastal walk along the cliffs is a must.

Etretat's lively centre has a distinctive covered market that served as a British and American military hospital in the last war. To the French, Etretat is also the setting for

Getting There

Buses from Le Havre (*gare routière*) take 40mins–1hr to **Etretat** and 1hr 30mins for **Fécamp**. There's a good selection of buses every day, but fewer on Sun, t 02 35 26 67 23.

Tourist Information

Etretat ✉ 76790: Place Maurice Guillard, t 02 35 27 05 21, f 02 35 29 39 79, *www.etretat.net*.
Fécamp ✉ 76400: 113 Rue Alexandre le Grand, t 02 35 28 51 01, f 02 35 27 07 77, *www.fecamp.com*.

Market Day

Etretat: Thurs am.
Fécamp: Sat.

Eating Out

Etretat

★★★Le Donjon, Chemin de St-Clair, t 02 35 27 08 23, f 02 35 29 92 24 (*expensive*). On the hillside set back from the centre (15mins' walk away), a splendid neo-Gothic castle setting for a special lunch. *Closed Mon lunch and Thurs lunch*.

L'Huîtrière, t 02 35 27 02 82 (*moderate*). On the seafront, a smart seafood restaurant that makes the most of the sea views on account of its round shape.

Le Galion, Bd René Coty, t 02 35 29 48 74 (*moderate*). Very appealing Norman ingredients with its beams and fireplace, a setting in which to enjoy refined cuisine.

Fécamp

Le Martin, 18 Place St-Etienne, t 02 35 28 23 82 (*moderate*). Only has simple rooms, but does have a really appealing restaurant on the square, excellent for sampling Normandy classics. *Closed Sun pm and Mon*.

Le Maritime, 2 Place Nicolas Selles, t 02 35 28 21 71 (*moderate*). Vibrant quayside setting for seafood.

La Marée, 75 Quai Bérigny, t 02 35 29 39 15 (*moderate; closed Sun pm, all Mon, and Thurs pm*). Another good seafood option on the quays.

a much-loved children's detective story featuring Arsène Lupin, the creation of author Maurice Leblanc. Fans try solving the crimes of this gentleman burglar at **Clos Lupin** (*open June–Sept daily 9–7; rest of year weekends and hols 10–6; adm*), his old house.

Fécamp

Somewhat upstaged by the Mont St-Michel in the last 1,000 years, before the end of the first Christian millennium, Fécamp established itself as the premier pilgrimage centre in Normandy, claiming to hold a Phial of the Precious Blood of Christ. This little bottle had supposedly drifted ashore here after Joseph of Arimathea had placed it in a fig-tree trunk that he cast out to sea. One St Waninge founded a convent at Fécamp in 660. In the early 10th century, after the raiding Norsemen had settled and converted to Norman Christians, Duke William Longsword refounded the institution as a Benedictine monastery dedicated to the Holy Trinity, an angel having told him to do so, obviously. He also had a hall-fort built by the abbey. His successors appreciated the place. The abbey church even became the burial place for a couple of the Normandy dukes. In 1035, Duke Robert gathered his nobles in Fécamp to tell them that he was going off on pilgrimage to the Holy Land and that his seven-year-old illegitimate son William was to be his heir should he not return. He didn't, and William inherited Normandy. Some 30 years later, in 1067, he came back here for the greatest celebrations of his conquest of England. While the dukes then abandoned Fécamp, the abbey continued to flourish at various periods, maintaining strong links with Italy.

One Venetian monk brought a whole selection of herbs with him at the start of the 16th century and began the making of Benedictine liqueur, the town's speciality. While the monastery was shut at the Revolution, the recipe was revived and very successfully marketed in the 19th century by a local entrepreneur who built an outrageous home-cum-factory-cum-museum with his fortune, the Palais Bénédictine.

With such an extravagant history, today's Fécamp may appear a tad ordinary at first sight, a mainly workaday town spreading from a gap in the coastal cliffs down its flat-bottomed valley. Its fishing fleet has been decimated recently, but the place still has a couple of dramatic buildings connecting it with its more exciting past.

To the enormous **abbey church** first. Although it was given a jarring new façade in the 18th century, most of it dates from the late 12th to early 13th century, a fine example of the earliest period of Gothic architecture. It looks sober, in such contrast to its rival, the Palais Bénédictine. The fabulous phial is displayed on an Italian marble altar. But beyond its intriguing story, there are many more interesting religious items to admire in the church. The 12th-century relief panels of Christ's life on the sarcophagus beneath the gilded Louis XV high altar teem with action. The Lady Chapel contains vibrant medieval stained glass. Some beautiful late-Gothic pieces include screens and statuary, and a remarkable Entombment of the Virgin. The gorgeous ambulatory screens are Italian 16th-century. You shouldn't miss the giant 17th-century clock. Back outside, the principal parts of the monastery, rebuilt in the Ancien Régime, were turned into the town hall after the Revolution. A few ruins of the millennium ducal hall stand out nearby.

The heady, not to say sickly sweet Benedictine liqueur cooked up by the Venetian monk Bernardo Vincelli was supposed to have medicinal effects. After the Benedictines were kicked out of their monastery at the Revolution, a local wine merchant named Le Grand rescued many items from the abbey. A descendant, Alexandre le Grand, was leafing through some of the old documents when he came across the recipe and decided to revive it. Using canny advertising, playing on the pleasing history of the drink, he became a highly successful entrepreneur. He commissioned a mock-historic palace which you can still marvel at today, the **Palais Bénédictine** (open mid-July–Aug 9.30–6; April–mid-July and Sept 10–12 and 2–5.30; Feb–March 10–11.15 and 2–5; adm). Looking like an elaborate mix of Loire château, grand abbey and posh town hall, the building was the fruit of local architect Camille Albert's imagination. The museum inside contains a vast mixed bag of historic religious items from around France and further afield, which Alexandre le Grand collected avidly. Then you're treated to a tour of the distillery and cellars. Adults are offered a diluted taste of Benedictine in the stylish bar; the liqueur is now part of the Bacardi empire.

In the shopping centre of town, the **Musée des Arts et de l'Enfance** (open July–Aug daily 10–12 and 1.45–6.30; rest of year Wed–Mon 10–12 and 2–5.45, closed Tues) is the municipal museum, housed in a grand 18th-century house, the collections concentrating on regional painting, arts and crafts, with special collections of ceramics, maritime paintings and carved ivories, as well as the curiosity of children's bottles and other items from Roman times on.

The separate area of the **seafront** retains a few reminders of the 19th-century period when Fécamp became a popular resort with Parisians. But in one of the uninspiring-to-ugly modern blocks, the **Musée des Terre-Neuvas** (*open same times as the Musée des Arts*) effectively recalls the gruelling Newfoundland fishing expeditions from which much of the local community scraped a difficult living for so long.

Honfleur

Why would explorers ever have wished to leave for new worlds from as beautiful a place as Honfleur? But they did, most famously Samuel de Champlain at the beginning of the 17th century, whose voyages led to the founding of Quebec. Less trumpeted by the port is its trading and slaviery link with Africa; in the 18th century the shipping magnates of little Honfleur mounted well over 100 expeditions. They certainly built some spectacular homes on the proceeds. The fantastic quayside houses of Honfleur's **Vieux Bassin** date from this time. **Quai Ste-Catherine** has the most spectacular display of multi-storeyed houses, with slate and timber sides; they must have seemed the skyscrapers of their day. All sorts of touristy shops and restaurants do a roaring trade at ground level. At the end of Quai Ste-Catherine the painterly **Lieutenance** served as the well-located home of the governors of Honfleur. On one side stands a bust of Champlain, a plaque below recalling the various voyages he organized to Canada.

Behind Quai Ste-Catherine lies a delightful timberframe neighbourhood. A quirky belfry stands guard over 15th-century **Ste-Catherine**, probably the finest timberframe church in France. The hull of a roof was constructed by local shipbuilders. Some of the carving below has a definite touch of sailors' earthiness; the musicians along the organ gallery display an excess of shapely legs and unseemly bottoms.

A number of 19th-century artists from Honfleur appreciated the exceptional beauty of their home town and tried to render it in art, as you can see in the varied collection of works displayed in the substantial **Musée Boudin** (*open 15 Mar–Sept daily exc Tues 10–12 and 2–6; rest of year daily exc Tues 2.30–5, weekends also 10–12; adm*) in the neighbourhood. This fine arts museum is named after Eugène Boudin, born in Honfleur in 1824, the son of a sailor. Baudelaire came on holiday to the port in 1859 and was deeply moved by meeting Boudin and seeing some of his works with 'those horizons in mourning or streaming with molten metal, all those depths, all those splendours...'. They went to his brain 'like the eloquence of opium'. In the museum, along with those black horizons are studies of sunsets with touches of Turner, the wonderful *Route de Trouville* and some interesting still lifes. Another of the museum's highlights is Jongkind's silvery *Entrée du port d'Honfleur*. The paintings by Dubourg, disparaged by many critics, give a good notion of the 19th-century Normandy seaside, ladies wandering along the beach hemmed in by elaborate dresses and protected by parasols, vessels with great sails colouring the background. The museum also has views by 20th-century artists. Dufy is as irrepressible as ever, and Henri de St-Delis' naïve style is quite fun. Herbo stands apart in tackling the grittier, industrial side of the Seine estuary, and from the top of the museum you get a great view of the new Pont de Normandie crossing it.

Honfleur was also the birthplace in 1886 of maverick musician Erik Satie, and an experimental museum, the **Maison Satie** (*open July and Aug daily 10–7; rest of year daily 10.30–6; adm*) does him proud. Your senses are bombarded in this eccentric museum, quite in keeping with the enchanting quirkiness of Satie's music. The place is a riot, at times deliberately absurdist. On the way round you'll hear delightful extracts of Satie's music as well as learning about his life. Finish the tour riding on a basketball on the musical merry-go-round, for adults and children alike!

Back at the Vieux Bassin, cross to **Quai St-Etienne** to wander round the oldest part of the port, known as the Enclos. The adorable church of St-Etienne turned **Musée Maritime** (*open July and Aug daily 10–1 and 2–6.30; April–June and Sept daily exc Mon 10–12 and 2–6; 8 Feb–March and end Sept–mid-Nov daily exc Mon 2–5.30, weekends also 10–12; adm*) is hugged tightly by old houses. Inside the church, with the clutter of large-scale models of boats, wood carvings and pictures, it's hard to focus on anything. But fragments of Honfleur's history emerge. The plaques in the choir, for example, give a chronology of French expeditions to Canada. Near the entrance, large canvases depict 18th-century naval battles between the French and the British. The seafaring adventures of slave-trader Général Hamelin of Honfleur, en route to Australia in the early 19th century, also put in an appearance.

Tucked away to one side of the church, the Musée d'Ethnographie (*open same times as the Musée Maritime*) presents a fragrant picture of Normandy interiors, a very pretty, cleaned-up picture, except for the prison room. In the same quarter, the 17th-century salt lofts or **Greniers à Sel**, built to supply the Atlantic shipping fleets with the precious commodity needed to preserve cod, now house seasonal exhibitions. The tradition of painting, good and bad, flourishes around Honfleur to this day.

Getting There

There are regular **buses** from Le Havre (*gare routière*) to Honfleur (*gare routière* – close to the tourist office), starting around 8am. The journey takes 15–30mins. Check with Bus Verts, **t** 02 31 89 28 41.

Tourist Information

Honfleur ✉ 14600: Place A. Boudin, **t** 02 31 89 04 40, **f** 02 31 89 31 82.

Market Day

Wed am: organic market.
Sat am: traditional market.

Eating Out

***L'Absinthe**, 10 Quai de la Quarantaine, **t** 02 31 89 23 23, **f** 02 31 89 53 60 (*expensive–moderate*). Slate-covered and flint-patterned 16th-century hotel close to the Greniers à Sel, with appealing rooms as well as appealing, sophisticated, beamed **restaurant**, **t** 02 31 89 39 00 (*expensive*).
L'Assiette Gourmande, 2 Quai des Passagers, **t** 02 31 89 24 88, **f** 02 31 89 52 80 (*expensive*). If you want to splash out, this is Honfleur's most exclusive restaurant.
La Terrasse de l'Assiette, 8 Place Ste-Catherine, **t** 02 31 89 31 33, **f** 02 31 89 90 17 (*moderate*). The above's excellent little sister. *Closed Tues, and Wed out of season.*
La Lieutenance, 12 Place Ste-Catherine, **t** 02 31 89 07 52, **f** 02 31 89 07 52 (*moderate*). Has a nice terrace as well as a very smart dining room. Fine cooking served up too.
Au P'tit Mareyeur, 4 Rue Haute, **t** 02 31 98 84 23 (*moderate*). A favourite among Normandy foodies for its inventive cuisine, and it's yet again in a pretty setting. *Closed Tues.*

Rouen

You probably won't want to copy the most infamous tour made round Rouen: by Emma Bovary in Flaubert's famous novel committing adultery with her lover Léon as the horse-drawn cab bumps them round the cobbled streets. You certainly won't want to follow in the footsteps of Joan of Arc, whose visit to Rouen ended on the pyre. Close to the spot where the Pucelle was burnt stands a delicatessen called the Charcuterie Jeanne d'Arc which certainly deserves a prize for bad taste. Otherwise the city fairly ignores her, as it does Flaubert...and the other artistic geniuses born here or so closely associated with it; notably Corneille and Monet (although he and local boy Géricault are represented in the fine arts museum). Rouen even turns its back on the Seine to which it owes its existence and its success.

When the Viking leader Rollo was accepted as duke of Normandy in 911, Rouen became his capital. Under him, the Seine quays were developed for trade. William the Conqueror died in the great city, while two of his successors as kings of England, Richard and John, were crowned dukes of Normandy in Rouen cathedral; Richard's lion's heart was buried there. But with John the English lost Normandy to Philippe Auguste at the start of the 13th century. The French king had a massive new castle built in Rouen. The English king Henry V took back Rouen in 1418 after a long siege. It was during the ensuing decades of English occupation that Joan of Arc was tried here and burnt at the stake. When peace came at last, commerce changed the face of the city. Textiles and pottery then flourished, while the port grew. As a large industrial city it would suffered in the Second World War, but historic Rouen has been restored. This

Getting There and Around

A good **train** service links Rouen and Le Havre daily.

The railway station is just north of the centre and the main boulevards, on Place Bernard Tissot up Rue Jeanne d'Arc. For **taxis**, contact Radio-Taxis, **t** 02 35 88 50 50.

able shopping streets, explore the parallel **Rue du Gros Horloge**, **Rue St-Lô** and **Rue Ganterie**, plus perpendicular **Rue des Carmes**. Look out for Rouen ceramics, especially in shops around **Place du Vieux Marché** and on **Rue St-Romain**. South of the cathedral, **Rue du Général Leclerc** has more shops, as does the dullish **Halles aux Toiles**, the mall just off it.

Tourist Information

Rouen: 25 Place de la Cathédrale, **t** 02 32 08 32 40, **f** 02 32 08 32 44, *www.rouen.fr*, *tourisme@rouen.fr*.

Market Days

Place du Vieux Marché: Tues–Sun am.
Place St-Marc: Tues, Fri, and Sat, all day; Sun am flea market.

Shopping

For fine **food shops**, go to **Rue Rollon** off Place du Vieux Marché. For the most fashion-

Where to Stay

Rouen ✉ **76000**
★★★Le Dandy, 93 bis Rue Cauchoise, **t** 02 35 07 32 00, **f** 02 35 15 48 82, *www.hotels-rouen.net*, *contact@hotels-rouen-net* (*moderate*). Hotel with style and warm modern rooms, close to the big boulevards just northwest of the historic centre and the Place du Vieux Marché. No restaurant.
★★★Vieux-Marché, 15 Rue de la Pie, **t** 02 35 71 00 88, **f** 02 35 70 75 94, *www.hotelduvieux marche.com*, *hotelduvieuxmarche@ wanadoo.fr* (*moderate*). Excellent central

is by far the largest city in Normandy and still one of the largest ports in France, and every two years tall ships from around the world gather here.

Place du Vieux Marché and Around

Joan of Arc was burned at the stake on 30 May 1431 in the **Place du Vieux Marché**. The amazing fish-tailed, scaly-slated modern church of **Ste-Jeanne-d'Arc** twists round the spot, battling like a hooded stingray. The tormented design, by the Basque architect Arretche, was made to include space for the 16th-century stained glass saved from the church of St-Vincent, looking stunning lined up here. The **Musée Jeanne d'Arc** (*open May–10 Sept daily 9.30–7; rest of year daily 10–12 and 2–6.30; adm*), on the south side of the square, proves a measly, dismal thing hidden in the ugly basement of a touristy shop. Sadder still is the nearby **Musée Corneille** (*open daily exc Tues and Wed am 10–12 and 2–6; adm*) in Corneille's house, west along the Rue de la Pie. Flaubert too gets scant attention from his home town: the **Musée Flaubert et d'Histoire de la Médecine** (*open Tues–Sat 10–12 and 2–6; closed Sun and Mon; adm*) lies a long walk further west, attached to a hospital just outside the centre; more a medical museum than a literary one, this is a bizarre place.

Moving back to the centre, **Rue du Gros Horloge**, a major shopping street, links Place du Vieux Marché with the cathedral to the east, divided at one point by a spectacular gate and its elaborate **Gros Horloge**, a clock which dates back to the late 14th century. You can admire its mechanisms by climbing into the tower. North of the Rue du Gros Horloge, the **Palais de Justice** stands like an island of Flamboyant Gothic stone.

location just off Place du Vieux Marché, and stylish, recently renovated rooms.

★★Le Vieux Carré, 34 Rue Ganterie, **t** 02 35 71 67 70, **f** 02 35 71 19 17, *vieux-carre@mcom.fr* (*inexpensive*). Just north of the splendid Palais de Justice, set around a colourful renovated timberframe courtyard, a very central two-star restaurant (*cheap*), with simple food.

★★La Cathédrale, 12 Rue St-Romain, **t** 02 35 71 57 95, **f** 02 35 70 15 54, *www.hotel-de-la-cathedrale.fr*, *contact@hotel-de-cathedrale.fr* (*inexpensive*). Another of the best options in the very centre of town, set around a very pretty timberframe courtyard right by the cathedral. Some of the rooms are a bit worn, but they are good value.

★★Les Carmes, 33 Place des Carmes, **t** 02 35 71 92 31, **f** 02 35 71 76 96, *www.villederouen.fr/ hotels*, *hcarm@mcom.fr* (*inexpensive*). Well-maintained little hotel with bright rooms, a short walk north of the cathedral on a pleasant square presided over by a statue of Flaubert.

Eating Out

Many top Rouen restaurants have taken over splendid historic houses. There are plenty around Place du Vieux Marché. You'll find plenty of cheap and ethnic options between St-Maclou and St-Ouen.

Les Nymphéas, 7 Rue de la Pie, **t** 02 35 89 26 69 (*expensive*). Particularly beautiful restaurant, tucked away in a timberframe courtyard, serving superlative cuisine. *Closed Sun pm, Mon and Tues lunch.*

La Couronne, 31 Place du Vieux Marché, **t** 02 35 71 40 90 (*moderate*). Claims to be the oldest *auberge* still going in France, dating back to 1345. Luxurious interior, relatively light Norman cuisine.

Dufour, 67 Rue St-Nicolas, **t** 02 35 71 90 62 (*moderate*). Coloured glass panes stop hoi polloi peering inside this magnificent timberframe house. The food is as Norman as the décor. *Closed Sun pm and Mon.*

Brasserie Paul, 1 Place de la Cathédrale, **t** 02 35 71 86 07. For the terrace with the Monet view of the cathedral, plus lively French feel.

Rouen's Great Churches

Rouen **cathedral**'s exceptional fame stems in good part from Monet's gorgeous series of studies of the façade in changing lights. The famous west front lords it over a square which was largely wrecked by bombing during the war and the façade itself turns out to be something of a mess. The sober north tower, the **Tour St-Romain**, is, along with the crypt, a rare survivor of the Romanesque cathedral. The vast bulk is 13th-century Gothic, from the great period of northern French cathedral-building. The late 16th-century southern tower, the **Tour de Beurre**, was apparently paid for by wealthy townspeople to avoid having to give up such luxuries as butter during Lent.

Comparing a cathedral interior to a boudoir figures among Flaubert's more outrageous descriptions in *Madame Bovary*, but you may find a certain sensuous pleasure in the shapely Gothic arches. There is some wonderful bejewelled 13th-century stained glass in the choir. Art historians remain intrigued by the fact that the life of Joseph was actually signed, by one Clément de Chartres. Another famous window tells the Greek-like tragedy of St Julian the Hospitaller, who tried to avoid the prediction that he would murder his parents, a powerful story retold by Flaubert in one of his *Trois Contes*. Surprisingly little attention appears to be paid to Joan of Arc in the cathedral. One modern piece of stained glass portrays her – 'From the English in homage', it reads. The d'Amboise family made sure that they were better remembered: Georges II d'Amboise, relative of the great archbishop Georges d'Amboise, ordered the exquisite Renaissance tomb in the Lady Chapel, designed by Roulland Le Roux. The other, heavier Renaissance tomb was made for Louis de Brézé, seneschal of Normandy and husband of Diane de Poitiers, who pleased King Henri II of France more than his difficult wife Catherine de' Medici.

Do wander round the outside of the cathedral: the rows of triangular Gothic gables down the side create a fine effect. The north transept is a superb piece of Flamboyant Gothic, but the south transept portal is even finer. The crossing is topped by a late 19th-century cast-iron tower that rockets into the sky like Rouen's answer to the Eiffel Tower. Antiques shops and art galleries fill the streets of the cathedral quarter.

Two other churches, St-Maclou and St-Ouen, challenge the cathedral in their beauty. **St-Maclou**'s porch is a masterpiece of Flamboyant Gothic seduction, built between 1500 and 1514. The doors, affixed shortly before Georges II d'Amboise consecrated the church in 1521, represent Christ's circumcision and baptism and Old Testament figures. The beautiful relief work is also attributed to Jean Goujon. St-Maclou's square is full of charm, with timberframe houses and a little fountain of peeing figures. Close by, off Rue Martainville, the exquisitely morbid courtyard of the **Aître St-Maclou** served as a place of burial long before it became the School of Fine Arts; look at the carved beams from the 1520s and you'll see that each upright sports a skull and crossbones.

Handsome streets fill the space between here and the great Benedictine abbey church of **St-Ouen**, set by a pretty garden, timberframe houses, and the majestic town hall. The west front has been heavily restored, but the interior combines Gothic power with simple Gothic elegance from the 14th and 15th centuries. Enter through the south door, the Porte des Marmousets, named after the stone figures monkeying around on the portal. Inside, the nave is sober, dignified and airy, its multi-columned piers punctuated by elegant Gothic statue niches. The most impressive stained glass fills the strips of the choir chapels.

Rouen's Main Museums

Monet and Sisley are the stars in Rouen's **Musée des Beaux-Arts** (*open daily exc Tues 10–6; adm*), but there's plenty more in these handsome rooms, complete with descriptions in English. Several of the Flemish works are outstanding: Gérard David's *Virgin among the Virgins* is a serious pieced. Among the Italians, Caravaggio's *Flagellation of Christ* stands out. The Spanish school is represented by fewer pieces but holds its own with some ravishing still lifes and a chirpy Velázquez fool.

The substantial French collections feature superb portraits by Largillère, de Troy, and Vigée-le-Brun, busts and statues by Drouais, and a rare 16th-century Clouet of the goddess Diana. Of exceptional interest are a Poussin self-portrait, another attributed to Delacroix and a portrait by David. The views of historic Rouen are worth a good look, especially one by Paul Huet showing the pre-industrial city lying in shadow, dwarfed by the Seine valley and cloudy sky. Several artists born along the Seine in Normandy are recalled in the museum, most famously Théodore Géricault, born in Rouen in 1791. The short-lived prodigy gets a whole room, mainly of preparatory pieces for major works, including some amazing studies of horses. Normandy-born Boudin and Normandy-influenced Jongkind have fine contributions.

A Gothic church behind the Musée des Beaux-Arts houses the **Musée de la Ferronnerie Le Secq des Tournelles** (*open daily exc Tues 10–1 and 2–6; adm*), an eccentric and amusing collection of wrought-iron objects, from ornate gateways and inn signs to keys going back to the Dark Ages and even Gallo-Roman times. The more substantial **Musée de la Céramique** (*open daily exc Tues 10–1 and 2–6; adm*) tells the story of ceramics-making in Western Europe, in France and in Rouen. Masseot Abaquesne, in the mid-16th century, brought southern European techniques to Rouen, and production began on a major scale. All sorts of ceramic follies feature in the many rooms, including pottery busts, shoes, clocks, lions and even a violin.

The building housing the **Musée des Antiquités** (*open daily exc Tues 10–12.30 and 1.30–5.30, Sun 2–6; adm*), Rouen's collection of antiquities, has been in danger of falling into ruin, like some of its exhibits. Seek out the beautiful pointed helmet of Bernières d'Ailly (*c.* 900 BC) stands out among the pre-Roman exhibits, while the Gallo-Roman collections include two large and impressive mosaics showing Orpheus serenading wild animals and a nymph pursued by Poseidon. Some of the splendid medieval tapestries may have been made to celebrate French victory in the Hundred Years' War. Further pieces among the medieval treasures are very elaborate, such as a little book covered in enamels, a reliquary arm from the abbey of Saint-Saëns, and a whole array of Flemish retables.

Moving a little further out from the centre, you can learn a bit more about Rouen's history at the **Tour Jeanne d'Arc**, a solid but solitary remnant of the enormous castle Philippe Auguste built on Rouen's hillside, but little about Joan herself, who was a short-term inmate here. After she was burnt, her ashes were apparently thrown in the Seine, although it's said that her heart could not be consumed by fire.

Touring from Dieppe and Le Havre

You'll find sights open Easter–Oct, 10–12 and 2–5 unless otherwise stated, and charge adm. We start from Dieppe here; if you're starting from Le Havre, switch days 1 and 3.

Day 1: Small Delights around Dieppe

Morning: The vast dry moat at the ruined **Château d'Arques-la-Bataille** (*free*) just inland from Dieppe was dug for an uncle of the Conqueror foolish enough to take on his mighty nephew. The fortified hilltop played a major role in several wars. The **Château de Miromesnil** (*open pm only, and not Tues*) just west presents an elegant picture of 17th-century architecture. Guy de Maupassant, the sharpest of French short-story writers, was born here in 1850.

Lunch: **Offranville** with its twisted spire has a lovely old-fashioned timberframe restaurant, **Le Colombier, t** 02 35 85 48 50 (*moderate*), serving exciting modern cuisine. *Closed Sun pm and Mon.* On the way to the Phare d'Ailly lighthouse by **Varengeville**, **La Buissonnière, t** 02 35 83 17 13 (*moderate*) is a very stylish restaurant in a 1930s villa. *Closed Sun pm and Mon.*

Afternoon: Follow the **cliff-lined coast** west from Varengeville (its charms sung on p.83). Delightful surprises include **Sotteville's** stairway to the sea, and the sweet valley at **Veules-les-Roses**, the shortest river in France. **St-Valéry-en-Caux** presents a mix of historic and modern Norman harbour.

Dinner and sleeping: If the 18th-century **★★★Château de Sassetot** (west of St-Valéry), **t** 02 35 28 00 11, **f** 02 35 28 50 00, (*luxury–moderate*) was grand enough for Sissi, Empress of Austria, this magnificent place should do you. It has a posh restaurant (*expensive–moderate*). **Les Hêtres, t** 02 35 57 09 30, **f** 02 35 57 09 31, www.leshetres.com (*expensive–moderate*) at Ingouville-sur-Mer just south of St-Valéry contrasts in style, a typical Norman 17th-century farm – with a delicious restaurant (*expensive*).

Day 2: Clifftop Dramas

Morning: Set in a gentle gap in the cliffs of eastern Normandy, **Fécamp** has a couple of particularly extravagant buildings to visit (*see pp.90–92*). Or explore more coastal villages, like down-to-earth **Yport**, very posh **Vaucottes**, or delightful, rustic **Bénouville**.

Lunch: For hearty Norman country cooking, doubleback to the **Ferme-Auberge de la Côte d'Albâtre**, Criqueheuf-en-Caux near Fécamp, **t** 02 35 28 01 32 (*moderate; must book*). *Closed Wed pm and Sun pm.* Or lunch in style in one of our **Etretat** choices (*see p.90*)

Afternoon: The naturally sculpted cliffs are the highlight of **Etretat** (*see pp.89–90*). Go on a coastal walk from here, or explore the chinks in the cliffs to the west.

Dinner and sleeping: **Etretat** restaurants are served up on p.90, including that at the striking **★★★★Le Donjon** hotel. Other good places to stay in the centre would be **★★Le Corsaire, t** 02 35 10 38 90, **f** 02 35 28 89 74 (*moderate*), some rooms with splendid cliff views, or **★★L'Escale, t** 02 35 27 03 69, **f** 02 35 28 05 86 (*inexpensive*), with cosy cabins.

Day 3: Bridging the Seine Estuary

Morning: Three sensational **bridges**, the Pont de Normandie, the Pont de Tancarville, and the Pont de Brotonne, span the Seine to the east of Le Havre. They're all toll bridges, so it costs a bit to cross back and forth. **Caudebec**, by the last, although war-torn, has one of the most gorgeous late Gothic churches in France, plus a museum on Seine mariners (*open pm only, closed Tues*).

Lunch: Eat classic Norman cuisine on the banks of the Seine at Villequier's **Le Grand Sapin, t** 02 35 56 78 73 (*moderate–cheap*). *Closed Tues and Wed out of season.* For another uplifting setting and good Norman fare, try **Les Deux Couronnes, t** 02 35 96 11 44 (*moderate; closed Sun pm and Mon*), at St-Wandrille.

Afternoon: Just west of Caudebec, **Villequier** has a lovely bourgeois brick Seine-side house to visit, the Musée Victor-Hugo (*closed Tues and Sun am*), dedicated to the great author whose daughter lived here and died in a freak river accident. East of Caudebec, the grounds of the **abbey of St-Wandrille** (*guided tours daily at 3 and 4, or Sun 11.30 and 3.30*) include the ruins of major medieval church, plus later monastic buildings that a friendly monk will show you round. This was one of the most important Norman abbeys of the Dark Ages. Nature-lovers should enjoy a tour of the **Brotonne Forest** south of the Seine from Caudebec.

Dinner and sleeping: Close to thatched, timberframe heaven, ★★★★**Le Petit Coq aux Champs**, at Campigny south of Pont-Audemer, **t** 02 32 41 04 19, **f** 02 32 56 06 25 (*expensive*) has delectable rooms as well as a very pretty restaurant Also south of Pont-Audemer, ★★★**Les Cloches de Corneville**, **t** 02 32 57 01 04 (*expensive– moderate*) is an exuberant hotel, known for its bells, and decorated with surprising African pieces. The restaurant is equally interesting.

Day 4: Côte Fleurie; Forecast: Chic to Chichi

Morning: If you've already visited magical sight- and tourist-packed **Honfleur** (*see* pp.92–3), continue west, hugging the sensational coast road above the Seine estuary. With bustling **Trouville** descending to the Touques, you enter major tourist territory again. This was the most fashionable Norman resort until Deauville knocked it off the no.1 spot, but it has more old-fashioned character, a soft sandy beach, an aquarium, and a good little art museum (*open pm only, closed Tues*). Plus, it's a real fishing port.

Lunch: In Trouville, the top place to go is to Art Deco **Les Vapeurs** on the quays, **t** 02 31 88 15 24 (*moderate*). Locals as well as the stars frequent this brasserie. **Brasserie Le Central**, **t** 02 31 88 13 68, isn't a bad second-best next door. For a quieter atmosphere and lovingly prepared seasonal cuisine, try **La Petite Auberge**, 7 Rue Carnot, **t** 02 31 88 11 07 (*moderate*). *Closed Tues and Wed*.

Afternoon: Over to **Deauville**, to compare the beach and seafront, perhaps for an afternoon at the races, or celebrity-spotting in season. Proust devotees will head off to dunk a madeleine in their tea at **Cabourg**, a pleasant mix of historic and modern resort.

Dinner: If you're feeling flush, dine in the **Grand Hôtel** (*see* below). For a really cheerful restaurant, book at **Chez le Bougnat**, Dives-sur-Mer, **t** 02 31 91 06 13 (*cheap*), where meat is the speciality. *Closed Mon and Tues lunch*

Sleeping: Proust stayed at the ★★★★**Grand Hôtel**, **t** 02 31 91 01 79, **f** 02 31 24 03 20,

(*expensive*), the stylish-to-snooty white wedding cake on the promenade. Another good central options is ★★★**Le Cabourg**, 5 Av de la République, **t** 02 31 24 42 55, **f** 02 31 24 48 93 (*moderate*), in swish Napoleon III style.

Day 5: Cheesy Normandy Countryside

Morning: Even the countryside behind the Côte Fleurie is chic, white fencing separating one manicured stud farm from the next. The village of **Beuvron-en-Auge** is one of the prettiest, twee-est villages in Normandy. The splendid **Château de Crèvecœur** (*closed Tues and Oct, exc Sun*) a bit south looks a Norman cliché too, although it strangely contains a museum on oil exploration, and temporary exhibitions on Norman traditions.

Lunch: Eat in a superlative timberframe house in Beuvron-en-Auge, either at very refined **Pavé d'Auge**, **t** 02 31 79 26 71 (*expensive*), for cappuccino of langoustines and the like, or the **Auberge de la Boule d'Or**, **t** 02 31 79 78 78 (*moderate*) for more traditional fare. Or, to lose the crowds, and possibly yourselves, in the countryside, try to find the **Auberge de Laizon**, Cléville, **t** 02 31 23 64 67 (*moderate; always book*) for a country feast.

Afternoon: **St-Pierre** to the south is a historic small town with a splendid market hall and the messy remnants of a mutilated abbey. Although St-Pierre has closed its cheese museum, it all gets very *fromage*-y to the east: **Livarot** and **Vimoutiers** have cheese museums, although they can't compare with the delectable hillside village of **Camembert**, where the museums have been battling it out viciously.

Dinner: Head some way north for Pont-l'Evêque. In wonderful hilltop Beaumont-en-Auge, the **Auberge de l'Abbaye**, **t** 02 31 64 82 31 (*expensive*) is a joy. At Pierrefitte-en-Auge's **Auberge des Deux Tonneaux**, **t** 02 31 64 09 31 (*moderate*), the cooking is simpler, but the historic building splendid.

Sleeping: For a very agreeable final night close to the sea, try the **Auberge des Aulnettes**, **t** 02 31 28 00 28, **f** 02 31 28 07 21 (*inexpensive*), a timberframe delight, with nice restaurant, west of Villers-sur-Mer. Or for a sea view in pleasant Villers itself, try bright ★★★**L'Outremer**, **t** 02 31 87 04 64, **f** 02 31 87 48 90 (*moderate*).

Caen

Caen shot to greatness under William the Conqueror and his wife Matilda of Flanders. From a meagre village by the Orne, it grew into one of the main centres of the extraordinarily powerful Norman duchy. As well as getting ramparts and a castle thanks to William, it received, as a gift from him and his wife, two enormous Romanesque abbeys. The couple were forced into their acts of benevolence. William had married Matilda, a cousin, in the early 1050s, but she proved not to be a distant enough relation to avoid the wrath of the papacy, and they were excommunicated. William's powerful friend in the Church, Lanfranc, supposedly managed to have the punishment lifted in exchange for an expiatory abbey from each of the spouses.

The abbeys have survived, but much of Caen was devastated in the bombardments and fighting of the Battle of Normandy. General Montgomery pursued a deliberate policy around Caen of encouraging the Germans to concentrate their armoured units in the area. The Allies targeted the city relentlessly for a month as the Germans held on doggedly. The Allied troops suffered heavy losses. Canadian forces eventually managed to gain Caen west of the Orne on 10 July 1944, but the Germans remained ensconced on the opposite bank. They in turn shelled Caen ceaselessly for a further month. In fact, devastating fighting continued here until 20 August, at the very end of the Battle of Normandy. Seen from afar, today the town looks at first like a mass of postwar blocks dominated by a towering modern hospital, but in fact a great many historic buildings have survived or been rebuilt in the heart of Caen.

The Château and its Museums

In the centre, the mighty **castle walls** that remain standing today actually date from the time of Henry I, William's successor as duke of Normandy and king of England. The bailey walls hide a couple of good museums. The **Musée de Normandie** (*open daily exc Tues 9.30–12.30 and 2–6; adm*) contains particularly beautiful Gallo-Roman

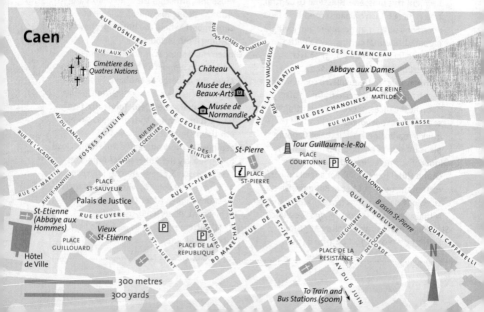

Caen

RUE BOSNIÈRES
RUE AUX JUIFS
Cimètiere des Quatres Nations
RUE DES FOSSES DE CHÂTEAU
AV GEORGES CLEMENCEAU
Château
Abbaye aux Dames
RUE DE LA VAUQUEUX
RUE DU LIBÉRATION
Musée des Beaux-Arts
PLACE REINE MATILDE
Musée de Normandie
RUE DES CHANOINES
RUE HAUTE
RUE BASSE
AV DU CANADA
RUE DE GEOLE
FOSSES ST-JULIEN
RUE ST-JULIEN
RUE DES CORDELIERS
CÉMARE
RUE PASTEUR
R. DES TEINTURIERS
St-Pierre
Tour Guillaume-le-Roi
PLACE COURTONNE
QUAI DE LA LONDE
RUE DE L'ACADÉMIE
RUE ST-MARTIN
RUE ST-MANVIEU
PLACE ST-SAUVEUR
PLACE ST-PIERRE
Bassin St-Pierre
QUAI VENDEUVRE
Palais de Justice
RUE ST-PIERRE
RUE DE STRASBOURG
RUE DE BERNIÈRES
RUE DE LA
QUAI CAFFARELLI
St-Etienne (Abbaye aux Hommes)
RUE ECUYÈRE
Vieux St-Etienne
BD MARÉCHAL LECLERC
RUE DE ST-JEAN
RUE GUILBERT
RUE MISÉRICORDE
RUE DES CARMES
PLACE GUILLOUARD
PLACE DE LA RÉPUBLIQUE
RUE ST-LAURENT
PLACE DE LA RÉSISTANCE
AV DU 6 JUIN
Hôtel de Ville

300 metres
300 yards
To Train and Bus Stations (500m)

Getting to Caen

Buzz (*see p.6*) flies from London-Stansted. Brittany Ferries (*see p.11*) runs a ferry service to and from Portsmouth (6hrs).

Getting from the Airport and Port

Caen-Carpiquet **airport**, **t** 02 31 71 20 10, *wwwcaen.cci.fr*, lies just west of town, off RN13 (Exit Carpiquet). There's a cheap **shuttle bus** once a day to and from the centre of town. The bus leaves the airport Mon–Sat at 1.05pm, and Sun at 2pm. It leaves the city centre Mon–Sat 11.25 and Sun 12.20. The journey costs €1 and takes *c*. 30mins.

The Caen **ferry terminal** is at Ouistreham, on the coast north of town. There's a local **bus** service to and from Ouistreham's Gare Maritime to central Caen (Place Courtonne) and Caen railway station.

Getting Around

The **train** station and main **bus** station lie some way south of the centre, down Avenue du 6 Juin and Rue de la Gare. For **taxis**, contact Taxis Abeilles, **t** 02 31 52 17 89, **f** 02 31 52 22 00.

Car Hire

There's a choice at the airport: **Avis, t** 02 31 84 73 80; **Budget, t** 02 31 83 70 47; **Europcar, t** 02 31 84 61 61; **Hertz, t** 02 31 84 64 50; **Lerat Location, t** 02 31 75 22 15; **National Citer, t** 02 31 82 66 10; **Rent a Car, t** 02 31 84 10 10.

Tourist Information

Caen: Place St-Pierre, **t** 02 31 27 14 14, **f** 02 31 27 14 18, *www.ville-caen.fr, tourisminfo@ville-caen.fr*.

Market Days

Place St-Sauveur: Fri am.
Port de Plaisance: Sun am.

Shopping

The main shopping quarter is below the castle close to the tourist office; you'll find both fine food shops and big department stores. The tourist office itself sells books on Norman history, from William the Conqueror to the Battle of Normandy. Down opposite the castle, Le Folklore has a good range of gifts.

Where to Stay and Eat

Caen ✉ 14300

★★★Le Dauphin, 29 Rue Gémare, **t** 02 31 86 22 26, **f** 02 31 86 35 14 (*moderate*). In a former priory, a comfortable, central hotel. The restaurant (*expensive–moderate*) has a good reputation for its Normandy cuisine.

★★Les Cordeliers, 4 Rue des Cordeliers, **t** 02 31 86 37 15, **f** 02 31 39 56 51 (*inexpensive*). Hotel with plenty of character, occupying one of the old town houses.

★Hôtel St-Etienne, 2 Rue de l'Académie, **t** 02 31 86 35 82, **f** 02 31 85 57 69 (*cheap*). Simple hotel in an old town house.

La Bourride, 15 Rue du Vaugueux, **t** 02 31 93 50 76 (*luxury–expensive*). Small, exclusive restaurant of the highest order, in an historic building. The chef's principal delight is in bringing Normandy cuisine up to date. *Closed Sun and Mon.*

L'Insolite, 16 Rue du Vaugueux, **t** 02 31 43 83 87 (*expensive–moderate*). With its stone walls and its beams, a stylish address in which to savour classic French cuisine, or fish dishes. *Closed Sun pm, and Mon out of season.*

Café Mancel, Le Château, **t** 02 31 86 63 64, *cafemancel@yahoo.fr* (*moderate*). Within the castle walls, a lively place to eat, appreciated by the locals. The cuisine is modern. Look out for jazz evenings and philosophical debates. *Closed Sun pm and Mon.*

L'Embroche, 17 Rue Porte au Berger, **t** 02 31 93 71 31 (*cheap*). Well-known because Edith Piaf's grandparents ran this place as a café at the start of the 20th century. *Closed Sat lunch, Sun, and Mon lunch.*

and Merovingian artefacts, but sadly little seems to have survived from the Viking period. Traditional crafts are well represented, and the separate Salle des Echiquiers, the great hall built for Henry I, provides a grand setting for temporary exhibitions.

The **Musée des Beaux-Arts** (*open daily exc Tues 10–6; adm*), located in a modern sunken bunker within the bailey, contains a colourful collection of paintings, surprisingly rich in Italian art. The two Veroneses are vibrant and dramatic; Perugino's famous *Marriage of the Virgin* directly inspired Raphael's even more famous one. Among the Flemish paintings highlights are a serene Van der Weyden *Virgin and Child*, a Breughel the Younger tax-collecting scene full of detail, and Rubens' bold, ruddy-faced *Abraham and Melchior*. Still lifes include an amazing goose hanging like a reflection of a crucified Christ by Frans Snyders. Robert Tournières, born in Caen in 1668, painted piercing portraits of his contemporaries, most notably that of the glistening-eyed engraver Andran. The museum also has an extensive collection of Old Master drawings. Among 19th-century highlights are a Courbet view of the sea and one of Monet's studies of waterlilies at Giverny.

The Historic City Below the Château

St-Pierre and its elaborate Gothic spire at the foot of the castle ramparts were rebuilt after the war. The stonework becomes lace-like in the choir with its kink. A short walk east beyond the lively café-surrounded **Place Courtonne**, overseen by the old **Tour Guillaume-le-Roi**, brings you to the **Bassin St-Pierre**, the broad marina in the centre of Caen, which is somewhat lacking in character.

Coyly distant from its twin, the **Abbaye aux Dames** was built for William the Conquerer's wife Matilda, east of the castle in what is now a quiet administrative quarter. More subdued than the church of the Abbaye aux Hommes, it is also more harmonious. Most of what you see dates from the start of the 12th century. The façade is sober. Inside, peace reigns. The decoration is limited to little heads and animals on the capitals and to the crinkly patterning around the arches. The false ambulatory in the apse gives the scrubbed interior added depth. A black marble slab in the choir marks Matilda's tomb.

Traffic races madly around the **Place Guillouard** in front of **St-Etienne**, the most famous and forceful church in Caen, attached to the **Abbaye aux Hommes**, in the grandiose western administrative quarter of town. Two towers rocket up above the stern Romanesque nave and the enormous wing added to the abbey in the 18th century. Lanfranc was the first abbot of St-Etienne, and the church was chosen to be William's burial place. His funeral in 1087 turned into a fiasco, with various factions causing mayhem during the ceremony, until his putrefying body broke up as it was being lowered into the tomb and the stench caused the mourners to flee. Architecturally, St-Etienne was a ground-breaking building. The sheer vertical wall of masonry of the façade is formidably daunting; inside, try not to let the greyness of the stone distract you from the power of the architecture. Although the choir was redone in Gothic style in the 13th century, the rest is the Romanesque original. The three different levels with the tribune and clerestory above the nave arches prefigure northern Gothic. An extraordinary lantern tower lets in light above the crossing. William the Conqueror's tomb was desecrated in the Wars of Religion.

The 18th-century abbey wing has been turned into the **town hall**, and some of the rooms are open to the public at certain hours. The other major buildings overlooking the Place Guillouard include the skeleton of the Gothic church of **Vieux St-Etienne** and the pompous Ancien Régime **Palais de Justice**. Not far away to the north, the triangular **Place St-Sauveur** has retained its grandeur too, with elegant houses looking on to a statue of Louis XIV in one of his favourite fancy-dress guises, as a Roman emperor.

On Caen's Outskirts

Caen's huge modern war (and peace) museum, the **Mémorial de la Paix** (*open June–Aug daily 9–9; rest of year daily 9–7; closed 2 weeks Jan; adm*), lies in a trendy new modern quarter of the city, just off the northern ring road (*exit 7; bus 17 from the centre*). The flags of countless nations wave outside the vast block. The presentations inside are slick, if somewhat chaotic. There's such a mass of information on offer, starting with the failure of the Versailles peace treaty after the First World War, that it's sometimes hard to know which way to turn, and there's a danger of the visit becoming rather superficial because it's so unfocused. Then you're herded into a series of auditoria showing three films on the Battle of Normandy. Although some of the images speak loudly of the terrible drama of the campaign, they pass too fast, and without commentary. The separate section on the Nobel Peace Prize proves disappointing. New sections are being prepared on the Cold War, and man-made threats to the future of the planet.

Day Trips and Overnighters from Caen

Bayeux

Capital of a small rich territory known as the Bessin, Bayeux was one of the very few cities in Normandy to be spared large-scale destruction in the war. So close to the D-Day landing beaches, it was the first town in France to be liberated, on D-Day +1. Thanks to this good fortune, many fine streets and houses survive, although restorers have sometimes been heavy-handed with the plaster.

The Bayeux Tapestry

Open May–Aug daily 9–7; 15 March–April and Sept–17 Oct daily 9–6.30; rest of year daily 9.30–12.30 and 2–6.

The most famous tapestry in the Western world isn't in fact a tapestry but an embroidery, and it probably wasn't made in Bayeux or Normandy, but in England. Although its exact origins remain a mystery, the most convincing story as to its creation runs something like this. Odo de Conteville, William the Conqueror's half-brother, bishop of Bayeux and a powerful Normandy landowner, seemingly commissioned the work, no doubt before 1082, when he was imprisoned by William. Odo, a battling bishop, took part in the conquest of England and he features a couple of times in the embroidery. After the conquest he acquired estates in southern England; similarities in style between the embroidery and certain Anglo-Saxon

Getting There

The **train** service from Caen is far preferable to the **bus** service, being faster (c. 20mins), cheaper and much more regular (last trains back around 9pm most days, but check).

Tourist Information

Bayeux: Pont St-Jean, **t** 02 31 51 28 28, **f** 02 31 51 28 29, *bayeux-tourisme@mail. cpod.fr.*

Where to Stay and Eat

Bayeux ✉ **14400**
★★★**Le Lion d'Or**, 71 Rue St-Jean, **t** 02 31 92 06 90, **f** 02 31 22 15 64 (*moderate*). Former posting inn right in the centre, which serves up good rooms and food for modern-day travellers.
★**Hôtel Notre-Dame**, 44 Rue des Cuisiniers, **t** 02 31 92 87 24, **f** 02 31 92 67 11 (*inexpensive*). A classic 19th-century building close to the cathedral, rather old-fashioned in style, but a cheerful place to stay and try classic Norman fare.
Le Pommier, 40 Rue des Cuisiniers, **t** 02 31 21 52 10 (*moderate*). Charming neighbour, popular with tourists, but maintaining local traditions.
Le Petit Bistrot, 2 Rue Bienvenu, **t** 02 31 51 85 40 (*moderate*). Great place for fish, a chic little address opposite the cathedral.
La Table du Terroir, 42 Rue St-Jean, **t** 02 31 92 05 53 (*moderate–cheap*). For meat-lovers, a convivial local favourite, run by a devoted local butcher.

manuscripts suggest to experts that it may have been made across the Channel. Some have even tried to pin it down to a nunnery either in Canterbury or Winchester. In France, however, it was long believed that William's wife Matilda had commissioned the work, and it is commonly referred to in French as the *Tapisserie de la Reine Matilde*. Many places in Normandy and neighbouring Brittany feature in it, depicted in stylized but still recognizable form, indicating that someone with a reasonable knowledge of northwest France played an important part in the conception. The crucial event, Harold's oath (it's presumed, promising the English throne to William, as the then king of England – Edward the Confessor – had stipulated) is reckoned to be shown taking place in Bayeux.

Visiting the embroidery begins with an in-depth introduction, although this hasn't kept up with recent scholarship. The copy of the embroidery and explanatory commentaries are, however, very helpful. Best of all are the accounts quoted from the contemporary chroniclers Guillaume de Poitiers and Guillaume de Jumièges. The film, though, peddles outdated, inaccurate stories. The embroidery, looking only mildly moth-eaten given its phenomenal age, has 55 'panels' in all, over half of which are devoted to the period before William's invasion; it explains the reasons for his actions, although the different episodes have been much disputed recently. It's even been claimed that it isn't Harold who's shown with an arrow in his eye.

The traditional interpretation is as follows. Edward the Confessor of England gives a mission to Harold, his most trusted earl, who sets sail for Normandy. But, blown off course, he's captured by Guy de Ponthieu (alias Wido) when he lands in France. The powerful William organizes Harold's release and invites him to his Norman court. They then go on an expedition together to put down the obstreperous Conan of Brittany to the west. The two friendly warriors William and Harold return to Bayeux where Harold appears to swear on holy reliquaries the crucial oath regarding the succession of the English crown. Harold then returns to England where King Edward is soon to die. Harold accepts the crown of England although he has promised that he will allow William to succeed.

Following the appearance of Halley's comet, considered a bad omen for Harold, William swings into action to assert his rights. Ships are prepared for the invasion and land at Pevensey in Sussex; the Norman troops set up camp and frighten the local population. The chaotic Battle of Hastings is where the embroidery ends, in the midst of fierce fighting. At one point it's rumoured that William has been killed, but he lifts his vizor to show that he's still alive. Harold is mortally wounded by an arrow in the eye. The very final scene shows the English army fleeing.

Artistically, the vibrant horses steal the show, while the Viking-prowed ships in stripy beach colours come a delightful second. The men, with their vague features and bonnets for hats, look rather comical; the spies in the first part of the story couldn't look more inept. Unlike the stallions, the soldiers seem sexless, emaciated creatures in chainmail mesh, rendered in fashionable pretty colours. The violent combat looks acrobatic rather than distressing, although the curious frieze of the dead below the battle scenes is a reminder that this was no circus.

The Cathedral Quarter

Bayeux's second trump card is its **cathedral**. Construction began under Odo's predecessor, but Odo's wealth no doubt helped the project to advance rapidly. It was consecrated in 1077, with all the major figures of the Norman court in attendance, including William the Conqueror and his Archbishop of Canterbury, Lanfranc. It's often said that the embroidery was originally made to hang in the cathedral, although this is now hotly disputed. A fire in 1105 destroyed important Romanesque sections, which helps explain the extravagant Gothic look of the exterior, although the soaring spires are Romanesque originals. Inside, the Gothic nave is superb, but the upper levels are supported on Romanesque arches, most decorated with crinkly patterns, one covered in devils' heads, their tongues sticking out over the edge. The carved panels between the arches have ornamental details influenced by Middle Eastern art.

The **Musée Baron Gérard** (*open June–15 Sept daily 9–7; 16 Sept–May daily 10–12.30 and 2–6; adm*) in the former bishops' palace displays the collections of the 19th-century baron: ceramics, archaeological artefacts and paintings, with local artists well represented. Lace is displayed here and in the **Hôtel du Doyen** (*open July–Aug daily 10–12.30 and 2–7; rest of year daily 10–12.30 and 2–6; adm*), which includes both a lace conservatory and a more specialist museum of religious art.

Although Bayeux escaped almost unscathed after D-Day, it does have the largest British **war cemetery** in Normandy. The substantial **Musée-Mémorial 1944, Bataille de Normandie** (*open May–mid-Sept daily 9.30–6.30; rest of year daily 10–12.30 and 2–6; adm*) stands opposite, the kind of war museum so crammed with artefacts, including uniforms and weaponry, that it's hard to know where to focus, while all the newspaper cuttings can seem overwhelming. Concentrate on small sections and the details that emerge become deeply moving.

The D-Day Beaches Along the Côte de Nacre

This is surely the most famous stretch of coastline in the Western World. The successful campaign by Allied American, British, Canadian and other troops to defeat Nazi Germany began with the massive military landings here in early June 1944.

From Caen to Arromanches

An almost unbroken line of seaside resorts have linked up from Ouistreham west to Courseulles to make the most of the sands code-named **Sword Beach** and **Juno Beach** for the D-Day operations, British and Canadian landing places respectively. At Courseulles the string of resorts comes to an end. The coast to Arromanches looks wilder, the strand below known as Gold Beach from the war, another British landing area.

On the heights just east of **Arromanches** you can look down on the remains of its Mulberry Harbour, the phenomenal portable port towed across the Channel just after D-Day to enable the huge ensuing Operation Overlord to take place, shifting a vast army of men and machines, and their supplies, to France. A modern cinema on the heights, **Arromanches 360** (*open June–Aug daily 9.10–6.40; May and Sept daily 10.10–5.40; Feb–April and Oct–Dec daily 10.10–4.40; showings start at 10 and 40 past the hour; adm*), presents a dramatic film about the D-Day landings on a 360° screen. The crude hype of the place promising '18 minutes of total emotion' could surely have been avoided, however. More soberly, a plain memorial by the dejected-looking white Virgin pays homage to the Sappers or Royal Engineers who played a key role in preparations for the D-Day landings. Some came across in midget submarines, canoeing to the beaches on their reconnaissance missions. Their specialist skills were crucial, and well over 6,000 died in daring actions between D-Day and VE Day.

Arromanches didn't see any landing craft on D-Day – it was important that the sea here shouldn't have any wrecks in the way to hamper the construction of the Mulberry Harbour. Allied tanks that had landed on Gold Beach made it to Arromanches by mid-afternoon on D-Day; the elements of the harbour arrived on D-Day +1. The main parts were five-storey-high concrete blocks, sunk on the rocks in front of Arromanches. By D-Day +9 the harbour was in operation. It survived the terrible storms of mid-June 1944, and by the end of that year, 220,000 men and around 39,000 vehicles had landed. The harbour stopped operating in mid-November. The Arromanches **Musée du Débarquement** (*open summer daily 9–6.30; winter exc Jan daily 9.30–5; adm*) tells the story well.

Beyond the power of the Second World War memories here, Arromanches is a rather cheerful-looking resort, the flat promenade and broad sands encouraging you to go walking by the sea.

From Omaha Beach to Utah Beach

West of Arromanches at **Longues** a row of concrete batteries, several with rusting guns still in place, gives an evocative picture of the Nazi defences along the coast. These guns weren't hit by the naval shelling early on 6 June and caused some difficulty for the Allies during that day.

Getting There

Ordinary local **buses** can take you to Sword Beach and Juno Beach. The local coach company, **Bus Verts du Calvados**, t (France) 0810 214 214, *www.busverts14.fr*, also runs a special D-Day service from Caen, and sells the good-value tickets from central Place Courtonne, or from the railway station. The bus leaves Place Courtonne *c.* 9.30, and stops at Arromanches, Longues, Omaha US cemetery and the Pointe du Hoc.

The **Mémorial de Caen**, t (France) 0825 06 06 44, *www.memorial-caen.fr/circuits*, organizes much more expensive 4hr guided tours of the beaches in vehicles taking up to 8 people.

Tourist Information

Ouistreham-Riva Bella: Jardins du Casino, t 02 31 97 18 63, f 02 31 96 87 33.

Arromanches: 4 Rue du Maréchal Joffre, t 02 31 22 36 45.
Vierville-sur-Mer and Omaha Beach: t 02 31 22 43 08.

Where to Stay and Eat

Arromanches ✉ 14117

★★**Hôtel Arromanches**, Rue du Maréchal Joffre, t 02 31 22 36 26 (*moderate*). On the pedestrian street just behind the seafront, the hotel has a couple of rooms with sea views, plus a bright restaurant, Papagall (*moderate*), serving good-quality Normandy cuisine.

★★**Hôtel de la Marine**, Quai du Canada, t 02 31 22 34 19, f 02 31 22 98 80 (*inexpensive*). Evocative views on to the Mulberry Harbour. The rooms are dull but comfortable; the restaurant (*moderate*) more exciting.

'This embattled shore, portal of freedom, is forever hallowed by the ideals, the valor and sacrifices of our fellow countrymen.' So reads one of the memorial sentences up at the **American cemetery** overlooking **Omaha Beach**. With its temple of a memorial, its long, long rows of pure white crosses on immaculately kept lawns and its evocative setting by the sea, this is a war cemetery that powerfully recalls the price paid for freedom in Western Europe. The large-scale maps at the memorial show the staggering size of the Reich in 1943 and speak more eloquently of the fight which the Americans crucially joined than the camp-looking loin-clothed figure of winged Victory. In the weeks leading up to D-Day, the German 352nd Panzer tank division was moved to guard Omaha Beach and inflicted terrible casualties on the American 1st Division as it landed. But only a minority of the 10,000 buried in the cemetery died on the beaches; most were brought here from other areas where the Americans fought in France and in Belgium. The **Musée Omaha** (*open July–Aug daily 9.30–7; Mar–June and Sept–Oct daily 9.30–12.30 and 2.30–6.30; adm*) is a modest affair, in particular featuring the meagre supplies with which the American soldiers landed, from toothbrushes to condoms. Down on the beach, even today it still seems a bit odd for people to be sand yachting on such symbolic terrain.

The mix of natural beauty and war horror makes the **Pointe du Hoc** just about the most moving Second World War location along the D-Day coast. Big chunks of Nazi cement bunkers still lie on their sides on the clifftop, the ground around them puckered with the big holes of heavy shelling. To either side you can see the beautiful pincers of cliffs which the Rangers tried desperately but vainly to scale and take on D-Day.

Touring from Caen

You'll find that the sights are reliably open Easter–Oct, 10–12 and 2–5 unless otherwise stated, and charge adm.

Day 1: D-Day in More Detail

Morning: The liberation of France in June 1944 began along the Orne's banks between Caen and Ouistreham with the securing of the river crossings, most famously that known as **Pegasus Bridge**, located at Bénouville. The Café Gondrée here is proudly maintained as a symbol of liberation, while the new Musée des Troupes Aéroportées displays the original bridge. From **Ouistreham** westwards you have a choice of resorts with sandy beaches and the odd reminder of the D-Day landings.

Lunch: Ouistreham has some refined restaurants, including that of the rather stylish **★★Le Normandie**, 71 Av Michel Cabieu, t 02 31 97 19 57 (*expensive–moderate*). The restaurant in the **★★★Thermes Marins**, Av du Commandant Kieffer, t 02 31 96 40 40 (*moderate*), an address offering seawater treatments, has sea views, and excellent food, even if the dining room is slightly clinical.

Afternoon: **Courseulles**, a lively, expanding estuary port, has a delightful maritime museum, the Musée de la Mer (*closed Mon, Sept–April*). A big shiny silver cross of Lorraine rises out of the dunes opposite, at **Graye-sur-Mer**, marking the place where De Gaulle finally made it back to France on 14 June 1944. West past Arromanches (for which, *see* p.106), **Port-en-Bessin** survives as a fishing community and contains the curious Musée des Epaves Sous-Marines (*open June–Sept only*), featuring a plethora of D-Day wreckage rescued from the sea, including an entire tank. Beyond Omaha cemetery (for which, *see* p.107), **Grandcamp-Maisy**, another fishing port, has a small Musée des Rangers (*closed Mon*), dedicated to the Pointe du Hoc tragedy.

Dinner and sleeping: The **★★★Château de Goville**, Le Breuil-en-Bessin (south of Colleville-sur-Mer), t 02 31 22 19 28, f 02 31 22 68 74 (*expensive*) is a charming family manor with restaurant (*moderate*). Or stay and eat in **Bayeux** and view the famous tapestry (*see* suggestions p.104).

Day 2: Back with the Classic

Morning: **Cerisy-la-Forêt**'s utterly daunting Romanesque abbey church reflects the power of Christianity in medieval Normandy. Across the forest, the **Château de Balleroy** was built in the best 17th-century taste, and restored by mega-rich American Malcolm Forbes. The stables contain a ballooning museum.

Lunch: The **Manoir de la Drôme**, t 02 31 21 60 94 (*expensive*) in Balleroy village goes well with the castle, a prettified, very sophisticated spot to eat. Southeast at Villers-Bocage, **Au Vieux Puits**, t 02 31 77 00 03 (*cheap*) has a down-to-earth, jolly restaurant.

Afternoon: Drive a good way south for **Mortain**, with gorgeous views over the patchwork fields below, and intriguing treasures in its church. Big, unkempt pear orchards beautify the countryside east to Domfront – follow the **Route de la Poire**. Old **Domfront** has a great location, perched on its rocky spur.

Dinner and sleeping: Bagnoles-sur-Orne is a surprisingly cheery spa town set in forests east of Domfront. The **★★★Manoir du Lys**, t 02 33 37 80 69, f 02 33 30 05 80 (*expensive–moderate*) is a very appealing place to stay, a modern timberframe manor by the golf course, with restaurant (*expensive*) to match. Right by the lake in the town centre, **★★La Potinière du Lac**, t 02 33 30 65 00, f 02 33 38 49 04 (*inexpensive*) has quirky architecture to raise a smile and provides regional fare.

Day 3: Into the Perche

Morning: The mammoth, moated, rough-brick bruiser of a fort, the **Château de Carrouges**, makes a substantial visit east of Bagnoles. Then visit the little city of **Sées** dominated by its cathedral.

Lunch: In Sées, **★★Le Dauphin**, t 02 33 80 80 70, has a pleasing restaurant (*moderate*) spilling on to the road in front. Outside town,

★★L'Ile de Sées, Macé, **t** 02 33 27 98 65 (*moderate*) is a characterful country stop.

Afternoon: The **Château d'O** (*outside July and Aug, open pm only, and closed Tues*) west of Sées, was built between the late 15th and late 16th century, and its long, slender roofs and turrets look irresistibly sexy. To the south, **Lassay-le-Château**'s granite fort gives a good lesson in medieval defence. East of here lies the distinctive area of the **Perche Normand**, with its ochre-walled manors. This is where the Trappist order of monks originated. There's also a big 19th-century pilgrimage church at **La Chapelle-Montligeon**.

Dinner and sleeping: Historic **Mortagne**, capital of the Perche Normand, has an adorable hotel-restaurant, **★★Le Tribunal**, **t** 02 33 25 04 77, **f** 02 33 83 60 83 (*inexpensive*), with traditional restaurant (*moderate*). Some way south, outside the old town of Bellême, the modern **★★★Hôtel du Golf**, Route du Mans, **t** 02 33 85 13 13, **f** 02 33 73 00 17 (*moderate*) occupies a pretty spot by the new golf course, with lovely views. It has a restaurant (*moderate*).

Day 4: Into Conqueror's Territory

Morning: Head some way north up the D932 from Mortagne, branching off for **Mont-Ormel**, a dramatic hilltop sight with the modern Mémorial Museum (*outside May–Sept, only open Wed and weekends*) telling the harrowing story of the Battle of the Falaise Gap below, in which the last German army in Normandy was trapped and largely wiped out in 1944. As an antidote to the horrors, visit the exquisitely beautiful stud farm, the **Haras National du Pin** (*in Oct, open afternoons only*), nearby.

Lunch: Treat yourselves to a stylish lunch at the timberframe manor of the **★★★Pavillon de Gouffern**, Silly-en-Gouffern (east of Argentan), **t** 02 33 36 64 26 (*expensive*). In another big timberframe building, west of Argentan, **★★Le Faisan Doré**, Fontenai-sur-Orne, **t** 02 33 67 18 11 (*moderate*) is another attractive option for lunch.

Afternoon: **Falaise** means cliff in French, and the massive medieval castle (*in Oct closed Wed*) of William the Conqueror's home town stands just above one. Much of the town was bombed in the Second World War, but it still retains several interesting historic buildings and a coherent feel.

Dinner and sleeping: **★★★Le Château du Tertre**, **t** 02 31 90 33 16 (*expensive*) at St-Martin-de-Mieux southwest of Falaise is a delightfully self-important little brick château with stylish rooms and cuisine. **★★La Poste**, **t** 02 31 90 13 14, **f** 02 31 90 01 81 (*moderate*) is a professionally run hotel-restaurant in the centre.

Day 5: Switzerland in Normandy?

Morning: West of Falaise there's a stretch of the Orne river encased by tall cliffs, known rather overgrandly as the **Suisse Normande**, but a delightful stretch to explore. Start at **Putanges** south of Falaise, where you might hire a boat for a river trip. Then head north along the quite dramatic valley road.

Lunch: At Pont-d'Ouilly, the **★★Auberge St-Christophe**, **t** 02 31 69 81 23 (*moderate*) is an appealing address for good regional cuisine. Or at charming Clécy, **★★★Le Moulin du Vey**, **t** 02 31 69 71 08 (*expensive–moderate*) is the most tempting place to eat, in a converted mill with terraces by the river.

Afternoon: **Clécy** is the lively stop in the centre of the Suisse Normande, with a sweet upper village, and boating down below. Explore the upper roads round and about with their fine views. Some of the highest 'peaks' of Normandy's little Switzerland rise around **Thury-Harcourt** at the northern end of the Orne gorges.

Dinner and sleeping: Northwest, at Villers-Bocage, the **★★Auberge Les Trois Rois**, **t** 02 31 77 00 32, **f** 02 31 77 93 25 (*inexpensive*), occupies a handsome stone house on the village square. It has well-looked-after rooms and a restaurant (*moderate*) serving quite elaborate dishes. At Noyers-Bocage (northeast), the simpler **★★Le Relais Normand**, **t** 02 31 77 97 37, **f** 02 31 77 94 41 (*inexpensive*) makes a peaceful stop, with thoughtful cooking (*moderate*).

Cherbourg

Long able to claim the largest man-made harbour in the world, the ferry port of Cherbourg may not look immediately appealing, but it has a dramatic natural setting and, beyond the chaotic jumble of its ports and the apartment blocks on the steep hill, it has some gripping stories to tell.

On the Waterfront

In the first half of the 20th century, before the advent of international flights, the great transatlantic lines plying their way between Europe and America often used to stop in Cherbourg on account of its huge harbour. These ships were taking many emigrants across the Big Pond, of course, not just glamorous tourists with a lot of time on their hands. Big cruise liners still sometimes stop in Cherbourg, making an

Getting to Cherbourg

P&O Portsmouth (*see* p.11) sails between Portsmouth and Cherbourg. **Brittany Ferries** (*see* p.11) runs ferries from Poole. The ferries arrive close to the centre; you just need to walk across the inner harbour, or Avant-Port. For **taxis**, call **t** 02 33 53 36 38, **t** 02 33 53 17 04, **t** 02 33 43 01 01, or **t** 02 33 08 46 46.

Car Hire

Ada, 10 Av de Paris, **t** 02 33 20 65 65.
Avis, 5 Rue de la Saline, **t** 02 33 88 66 99.
Europcar, 4 Rue des Tanneries, **t** 02 33 44 53 85.
Hertz, 43 Rue du Val de Saire, **t** 02 33 23 41 41.
National Citer, 25 Rue de Val de Saire, **t** 02 33 20 34 20.

Tourist Information

Cherbourg: 2 Quai Alexandre III, **t** 02 33 93 52 02, **f** 02 33 53 66 97, *www.ot-cherbourg-cotentin.fr*, *ot-cherbourg-cotentin@wanadoo.fr*. There's also an annexe right by the ferry terminal.

Market Days

Place de Gaulle: Tues.
Théâtre-Place Centrale: Thurs and Sat.

Shopping

The old shopping quarters, packed with shops and restaurants, surround the elaborate theatre and the glass and steel market.

Where to Stay and Eat

Cherbourg ✉ 50100
★★Régence, 42 Quai de Caligny, **t** 02 33 43 05 16, **f** 02 33 43 98 37, *www.logis-de-france.fr* (*inexpensive*). Rooms with sea views, and a traditional restaurant serving seafood.
★★Ambassadeur, 22 Quai de Caligny, **t** 02 33 43 10 00, **f** 02 33 43 10 01, *www.ambassadeur-hotel.com* (*inexpensive*). View of the port too, but no restaurant.
★★Chantereyne, Port de Plaisance, **t** 02 33 93 02 20, **f** 02 33 93 45 29, *www.hotel-chantereyne.com* (*inexpensive*). Comfortable, with views of the marina; no restaurant.
★★Croix de Malte, 5 Rue des Halles, **t** 02 33 43 19 16, **f** 02 33 43 65 66 (*inexpensive–cheap*). Comfortable, calm, cheap hotel in the heart of town, in a convenient location for restaurants.
Café de Paris, 40 Quai de Caligny, **t** 02 33 43 21 36 (*moderate*). Elegant 19th-century address where you can watch boats pass by as you eat the seafood.
La Ciboulette, 27 Rue de l'Abbaye, **t** 02 33 93 40 41 (*moderate*). A gourmet restaurant both for fresh fish and for traditional Normandy meat dishes.
Le Laurent, 59 Rue au Blé, **t** 02 33 93 07 07 (*moderate*). In the shopping centre, quite refined cooking in a rustic dining room.
Le Faitout, 25 Rue Tour Carrée, **t** 02 33 04 25 04 (*cheap*). Popular local restaurant near the marina, one room with a marine décor, the other in stone.

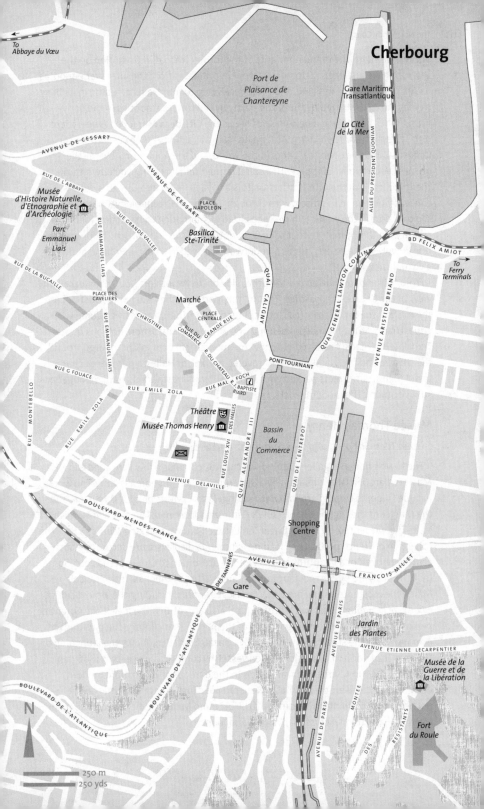

Cherbourg

To
Abbaye du Vœu

Port de
Plaisance de
Chantereyne

Gare Maritime
Transatlantique

La Cité
de la Mer

AVENUE DE CESSART

RUE DE L'ABBAYE

Musée
d'Histoire Naturelle,
d'Etnographie et
d'Archéologie

Parc
Emmanuel
Liais

RUE DE LA BUCAILLE

RUE EMMANUEL LIAIS

RUE GRANDE VALLÉE

AVENUE DE CESSART

PLACE
NAPOLÉON

Basilica
Ste-Trinité

QUAI CALIGNY

BD FÉLIX AMIOT

Allée du Président Quoniam

To
Ferry
Terminals

AVENUE ARISTIDE BRIAND

QUAI GÉNÉRAL LAWTON COLLIN

PLACE DES
CAVELIERS

RUE EMMANUEL LIAIS

RUE CHRISTINE

Marché

PLACE
CENTRALE

RUE DU
COMMERCE

GRANDE RUE

R. DU CHÂTEAU

RUE G FOUACE

RUE EMILE ZOLA

RUE EMILE ZOLA

RUE MONTEBELLO

RUE EMILE ZOLA

RUE MAL R. FOCH

J.-BAPTISTE
BIARD

PONT TOURNANT

Théâtre
Musée Thomas Henry

RUE LOUIS XVI

QUAI ALEXANDRE III

R. DES HALLES

AVENUE DELAVILLE

QUAI DE L'ENTREPÔT

Bassin
du
Commerce

BOULEVARD MENDES FRANCE

Shopping
Centre

AVENUE JEAN

RUE DES TANNERIES

AVENUE JEAN

FRANCOIS MILLET

Gare

BOULEVARD DE L'ATLANTIQUE

BOULEVARD DE L'ATLANTIQUE

AVENUE DE PARIS

Jardin
des Plantes

AVENUE ÉTIENNE LECARPENTIER

Musée de la
Guerre et de
la Libération

AVENUE DE PARIS

MONTÉE

DES

RESISTANTS

Fort
du Roule

N

250 m
250 yds

impressive sight. The grand remnants of the former transatlantic **station** on the seafront have just been restored and reopened. It dates from the inter-war period, as its Art Deco features indicate, and could receive up to four trains at a time in its busy heyday. Partly destroyed by the Nazis, partly by the town authorities in the early 1980s, it has been given a new lease of life as the **Cité de la Mer** (*open June–15 Sept 9.30–7; rest of year 10–6; adm*). Among its main attractions are *Le Redoutable*, the largest submarine open to visitors in the world, and the Aquarium Abyssal, the deepest aquarium in Europe, with a spiral ramp round it leading you down through the three levels of the Cité. It offers visitors a voyage down into the sea's depths, concentrating on man's discoveries through underwater technology; Cherbourg is the only port in the world to have specialized in submarine construction for over a century. On the 45-minute tour of *Le Redoutable*, you can learn about the preparations involved in a 70-day mission underwater, as well as trying your hand at driving a virtual submarine.

From the large **marina** across the other side of the Avant-Port, you get an excellent view of the Cherbourg coastline. The military port stretches westwards. Just behind the marina, the much-restored Gothic church of **La Trinité** stands by a square with an equestrian statue of Napoleon bearing one of the emperor's more dubious quotes. Translated, it reads: 'I resolved to renew the marvels of Egypt in Cherbourg.' Around the theatre and the glass- and steel-covered market, or **Halles**, a number of characterful pedestrian streets packed with shops, pubs and restaurants have managed to survive among the modern blocks.

Musée Thomas Henry

Open Tues–Sat 9–12 and 2–6, Sun 10–12 and 2–6; adm.

The town's fine-arts gallery, behind the theatre, contains a few very good Old Masters, part of a large donation by a discerning collector, Thomas Henry. The works include Filippino Lippi's *Entombment*, Fra Angelico's *Conversion of St Augustine* and the Master of the Legend of St Ursula's *Enthroned Madonna*. The range of Flemish styles is represented, including David Tenier's well-known mocking *Monkey's Ball*. The collection of French portraits by leading exponents displays more decorum. A 16th-century portrait of a beautiful coiffed woman attributed to Clouet stands out. Some (not the best) are by the most famous Cotentin artist of them all, Jean-François Millet; the most interesting are a few landscapes of his, including the almost cubist *Falaise de la Hague*. Other 19th-century local artists captured the feel of the Cotentin peninsula and revealed the importance of the port in that century; the paintings by Armand Fréret are striking. One canvas by Chazal, from 1840, shows the launching of the ship *The Friedland*, a classic wooden vessel; by contrast, a piece from 1896 depicts Tsar Nicholas II in town, the naval vessels in the harbour of much more modern design, engine-driven, even if masts were provided just in case. A plaque on the outside of the building pays homage to L'Hoste and Mangot, who in July 1886 made the first-ever Channel crossing by hot-air balloon.

Fort du Roule

High up above Cherbourg, reached by hairpin bends worthy of the Alps, stands the mid-19th-century **Fort du Roule**, which still bears the scars of shells from the vicious but remarkably short battle in June 1944 which liberated the town of Cherbourg. It very rapidly became a key port for the Allies; a vital oil pipeline from the Isle of Wight was already down and running by mid-August. Inside the fort you'll find just about the clearest Second World War museum in Normandy, the **Musée de la Libération** (*open April–Sept daily 10–6; rest of year daily exc Mon 9.30–12 and 2–5.30; adm*). The build-up to the D-Day landings and the taking of Cherbourg are presented with a rare and striking simplicity. The views from the fort over the harbour are spectacular, giving a good picture of the town's strategic importance. It was Louis XIV's genius of a military engineer, Vauban, who developed it into such a key French naval base.

Day Trips from Cherbourg

The coast of this peninsula, sticking its head into the Channel, is not unlike neighbouring Brittany with its tough but lovable granite edge and character. It is dotted with pretty ports and the up-and-coming resort of Granville; the nuclear power station of the Cap de la Hague is the one enormous blip along one of the most romantic stretches of French coastline.

St-Vaast-la-Hougue and the Ile Tatihou

St-Vaast-la-Hougue and Barfleur compete for the prize of prettiest port in western Normandy. **St-Vaast-la-Hougue** has a more eccentric character, with a confusion of low spits stretching into the sea around it. Forts to the south and on the island of Tatihou add a military twist to the horizon. They went up in 1694, after the Battle of La Hougue when much of the French fleet was set alight by the Anglo-Dutch enemy. Today St-Vaast's pretty port has been developed into a massively popular marina.

Getting There

From Cherbourg, the STN (**t** 02 33 44 32 22) **bus** service has a daily morning service leaving Cherbourg 10.50, via **Barfleur** 11.34, **St-Vaast** 11.48. The last bus back leaves St-Vaast 16.28.

Tourist Information

St-Vaast-la-Hougue ✉ 50550: 1 Place de Gaulle, **t** 02 33 23 19 32, **f** 02 33 54 41 37.

Eating Out

Hôtel de France et des Fuchsias, 18 Rue Mal Foch, **t 02 33 54 42 26, **f** 02 33 43 46 79 (*inexpensive*). For excellent seafood in particular, try this very pleasant restaurant (*moderate*) in a charming small hotel.

Le Débarcadère, Place de Gaulle, **t** 02 33 54 43 45 (*cheap*). Down-to-earth local with a terrace overlooking the harbour.

***La Granitière, 74 Rue Maréchal Foch, **t** 02 33 54 58 99, **f** 02 33 20 34 91 (*moderate–inexpensive; no restaurant*). Very pleasant little manor of a hotel with garden, in the village, in case you want to stay the night.

The Fort de La Hougue on the spit south of St-Vaast remains in military hands but you can visit the **island of Tatihou** in an amphibious craft (*book tickets in advance from Accueil Tatihou, Quai Vauban at St-Vaast, t 02 33 23 19 92*). The funny name derives from that of a Viking leader, Tati. It makes a delightful excursion, with a sea fort to visit as well as the former *lazare*, the quarantine hospital for crews struck by the plague or suspected of bringing home infectious diseases and, after the Revolution, when an extra ring of walls was added, for crews affected by cholera. Men and merchandise could be forced to stay on the island for between 8 and 40 days. Today, within its walls, there is an active ship repair yard, a **maritime museum** (*open Easter–Oct daily 10–5.30; rest of year weekends only 2–5.30*) and a walled maritime garden – Tatihou has a distinguished history of research into marine biology. It also hosts a summer festival of coastal music from around the world.

Ste-Mère-Eglise

Ste-Mère-Eglise has been immortalized on film, the most famous images from the D-Day film *The Longest Day* showing American parachutist John Steele coming down over the town and ending up stranded in midair, his parachute stuck to the church tower; Red Buttons memorably played the part in the film. As Steele dangled, Ste-Mère-Eglise became the first town liberated in France.

The **Musée des Troupes Aéroportées** (*open Feb–mid-Nov daily; mid-Nov–mid-Dec weekends; adm*), one of the most interesting war museums in Normandy, recalls the thousands of soldiers less fortunate than John Steele (who survived his ordeal) as well as explaining the D-Day airborne operations in detail. The two large rooms centre around spectacular exhibits – in one a US WACO glider, in the other a C47 Douglas, both vital to the Allied airborne operations. The two films in English, *Getting Ready* and *Mission Accomplished*, help to give you a fuller picture of the objectives and dangers of the parachute missions in which hundreds died. There's also the moving testimony of a Resistance fighter, and all sorts of related matter to pore over: rations, weapons, newspaper articles, photos, paintings...

Ste-Mère-Eglise's historic **church** interior has Gothic vaults in the Angevin style which look, appropriately enough, rather like parachutes in stone. A stained glass window pays homage to the paratroopers, while outside, the streets of Ste-Mère-Eglise bear the names of US soldiers.

Getting There

From Cherbourg, there's a limited **bus** service, leaving Mon–Fri at 12.30, arriving 13.15. There's a bus back Mon–Fri at 18.15.

Tourist Information

Ste-Mère-Eglise: t 02 33 21 00 33, f 02 33 21 53 91, *www.sainte-mere-eglise.info*, *ot.stemereeglise@wanadoo.fr*.

Eating Out

Auberge Le John Steele, Rue du Cap de Laine, t 02 33 41 41 16, f 02 33 41 89 89 (*rooms cheap; menus moderate*). This hotel-restaurant pays homage to the celebrated US parachutist in its name, but it's an old inn with old fireplaces and beams, serving traditional Norman fare. If you're staying, the rooms are simple.

Touring from Cherbourg

You'll find that sights are reliably open Easter–Oct 10–12 and 2–5, unless otherwise stated, and charge adm.

Day 1: Picturesque Cotentin Ports

Morning: Drive east from Cherbourg, enjoying the rocks and creeks along the coast road to **Barfleur**, a major Anglo-Norman port in medieval times, but nowadays a peaceful fishing village.

Lunch: Stay in Barfleur for a good-value seafood feast on oysters and lobster at the traditional old local **Hôtel Moderne**, 1 Place Charles de Gaulle, t 02 33 23 12 44, f 02 33 23 91 58 (*moderate–cheap*). Or head to St-Vaast-la-Hougue for a simple lunch at relaxed **Le Débarcadère**, Place de Gaulle, t 02 33 54 43 45 (*cheap*), with its terrace looking on to the port.

Afternoon: At **St-Vaast-la-Hougue**, with its delightful confusion of headlands, take the ferry out to the former quarantine **island of Tatihou** (*see* p.114; *book tickets in advance*).

Dinner and sleeping: In **St-Vaast-la-Hougue**, ★★★**La Granitière**, 74 Rue Maréchal Foch, t 02 33 54 58 99, f 02 33 20 34 91 (*moderate; no restaurant*), is a very pleasant little manor of a hotel in the midst of the village, with a garden. The ★★**Hôtel de France**, 18 Rue Maréchal Foch, t 02 33 54 42 26, f 02 33 43 46 79 (*moderate*), also has charm, and serves good seafood in its **Restaurant des Fuchsias** (*moderate*), much appreciated by British visitors. Just south down the coast at Quinéville, the ★★★**Château de Quinéville**, 18 Rue de l'Eglise, t 02 33 21 42 67, f 02 33 21 05 79 (*moderate*) is an elegant 18th-century home with comfortable rooms and a stylish restaurant (*moderate*).

Day 2: D-Day on the Cotentin

Morning: **Quinéville**'s rambling war museum, the Musée de la Liberté (*closed Dec–March*), offers a good, old-fashioned mass of information on the Second World War, plus a 50min film made for the 50th anniversary of D-Day. Afterwards, go for a walk on the low dunes of **Utah Beach**, cows grazing peacefully behind you. At the southern end is the modern Musée du Débarquement, devoted to the American D-Day landing there.

Lunch: The choice is limited in these parts. But **Le Roosevelt**, t 02 33 71 53 47 (*cheap*) is right on the dunes of Utah Beach and looks, appropriately, a bit like a diner as well as serving up souvenirs. For a rustic meal on a farm, try the **Chèvrerie de la Huberdière,** Liesville-sur-Douve (southwest of Ste-Mère-Eglise), t 02 33 71 01 60 (*moderate–cheap; must book at least 24hrs in advance*).

Afternoon: **Ste-Mère-Eglise** (*see* opposite) witnessed the most dramatic landing of American soldiers in the early hours of D-Day, as the classic film *The Longest Day* recalls; the Airborne Museum takes the subject more seriously. A typical, substantial local farm on the edge of town has been turned into a rural Musée de la Ferme (*closed Tues outside July and Aug*). In the Marais or marshlands to the south, you can go boating near **Carentan**, while the atmospheric village of **Graignes** conceals a tragic US D-Day story.

Dinner and sleeping: We suggest a B&B stop in these parts. You can stay in a delightful rustic room at the **Musée de la Ferme Ste-Mère-Eglise**, t 02 33 41 30 25, musee.sainte-mere@wanadoo.fr (*cheap, as museum visit included in price*), or, between Utah and Omaha beaches, in the **Manoir de la Rivière**, Géfosse-Fontenay, t 02 31 22 64 45, f 02 31 22 01 18 (*inexpensive*), where you can also book *table d'hôte* dinner (*cheap*) if staying. Or 6km northwest of St-Lô, the **Château de la Roque**, Hébécrévon, t 02 33 57 33 20, f 02 33 57 51 20 (*moderate*) makes for an atmospheric stop, *table d'hôte* also possible (*moderate*).

Day 3: The Southern Cotentin

Morning: **St-Lô** became known as the Capital of Ruins, it was so horrifically devastated in the Battle of Normandy, but it now has a splendid modern fine-arts museum. This Musée des Beaux-Arts (*closed Tues*) includes saucy Flemish tapestries and tranquil landscapes as well as war images.

Lunch: Head southwest for Villedieu-les-Poêles. Twelve km north lie the soaring ruins of the abbey of Hambye, with the **Auberge de l'Abbaye**, t 02 33 61 42 19 (*moderate*) close by, a fine country restaurant. *Closed Sun pm and Mon*. Or in Villedieu, try the traditional fare at the **Hôtel St-Pierre et St-Michel**, 12 Place de la République, **t** 02 33 61 00 11 (*moderate*).

Afternoon: Go on a tour of the truly peaceful **Abbaye de Hambye**, then potter about looking at the copper pots and pans even featured in **Villedieu**'s name.

Dinner and sleeping: Staying on Mont St-Michel is a magical experience, and ★★★**Mère Poularde**, **t** 02 33 60 14 01, **f** 02 33 48 52 31 (*expensive–moderate*) the classic address, both for board and lodging, at the entrance to the ramparts. ★★★**Auberge St-Pierre**, **t** 02 33 60 14 03, **f** 02 33 48 59 82 (*expensive*) is a little higher, tucked in behind the ramparts, with a nice restaurant (*moderate*). ★★**Hôtel du Mouton Blanc**, **t** 02 33 60 14 08, **f** 02 33 60 05 62 (*inexpensive*) is a cheaper option.

Day 4: Mesmerized by Mont St-Michel

Morning: To visit the **abbey** magically perched at the top of the mount (*see pp.128–30*), try to get there early. Down the touristy hill, children might like the modern introduction in the **Archéoscope**.

Lunch: At Courtils, east along the coast road, the 19th-century ★★★**Manoir de la Roche Torin**, **t** 02 33 70 96 55 (*moderate–expensive; book as sometimes closed at lunch*) stands in a splendid location overlooking the bay, a wonderful place for a leisurely Norman lunch. At nearby Servon, the ★★**Auberge du Terroir**, **t** 02 33 60 17 92, **f** 02 33 60 35 26 (*moderate*) offers a very peaceful place for lunch. *Sometimes closed Wed, and Sat lunch*.

Afternoon: A guided walk across the bay makes for a magical experience. Contact the **Maison de la Baie de Courtils**, **t** 02 33 89 66 00, **f** 02 33 89 66 09, in advance to see if one is possible. **Avranches** on its hill has an attractive historic centre as well as manu-scripts rescued from Mont St-Michel's abbey in its library, while the church of St-Gervais preserves the supposed skull of 8th-century Bishop Aubert – militant saint Michael is said to have made the hole in it, harrying him so insistently to build a great sanctuary to him.

Dinner and sleeping: ★★★**Le Gué du Holme**, St-Quentin-sur-le-Holme, **t** 02 33 60 63 76, **f** 02 33 60 06 77 (*moderate*) just southeast of Avranches has some views of the Mont St-Michel, refined rooms and fine cooking (*expensive–moderate*). *Closed Fri and Sat lunch*. Just slightly further south at Ducey, the riverside ★★**Auberge de la Sélune**, **t** 02 33 48 53 62, **f** 02 33 48 90 30 (*moderate*) has a wonderful garden and excellent cuisine.

Day 5: Gay Granville and the Western Cotentin

Morning: Hug the breathtaking coast road from Avranches to **Granville**. Its rocky promontory sticking out into the sea was first fortified by the English back in the 15th century. Even if the architecture within has been battered by time, the place has several attractions, including two good museums linked to two famous gay sons, the Musée Dior (*closed Mon*) for fashion, and the Musée Anacréon (*closed Tues*) for Fauves and a collection of other modern artists.

Lunch: In Granville, **Le Phare**, **t** 02 33 50 12 94 (*moderate*) by the fish market makes an obvious choice for seafood, a simple restau-rant with sea views. For slicker modern surrounds, book at the big modern ★★★**Le Grand Large** (*moderate*), also a seawater treatment centre. To appreciate a bright coastal villa out of town, head just north for ★★★**La Beaumonderie**, Bréville-sur-Mer, **t** 02 33 50 36 36, **f** 02 33 50 36 45 (*expensive*), Eisenhower's HQ for a time.

Afternoon: **Coutances**' cathedral rises majesti-cally above the small hilltown below it, sadly spoilt during the war. **Portbail**. a little port to the north, has preserved much of its historic atmosphere. Also well-protected from the sea, the neighbouring estuary resorts of **Barneville** and **Carteret** are popular.

Dinner and sleeping: At Barneville-Carteret the ★★★**Hôtel de la Marine**, **t** 02 33 53 83 31, **f** 02 33 53 39 60 (*moderate*) makes the most of its location down on the quays, its bright, excellent restaurant (*expensive*) spilling outside. **L'Hermitage**, **t** 02 33 04 96 29, **f** 02 33 04 78 87 (*inexpensive*) has a few nice rooms above a restaurant. ★★**Les Isles**, **t** 02 33 04 90 76 (*inexpensive*) is another good-value option.

The Brittany Coast

The North Brittany Coast

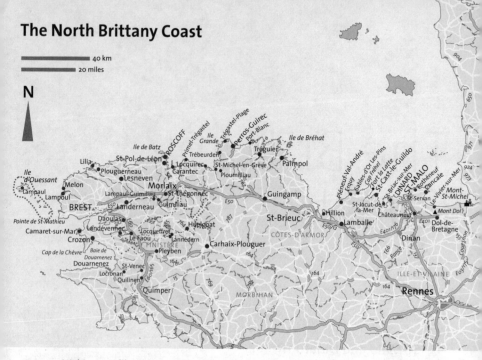

Sticking out like a dragon figurehead from the ship of Europe, on the map Brittany looks a vicious peninsula. Its tortured coastline of serrated cliffs, rocky islands, secretive inlets, huge bays and endlessly confusing peninsulas contrasts completely with France's long, straight Atlantic and Channel beaches. The region has a gritty, granite character all of its own. Its shores prove ceaselessly dramatic, the remnants of neolithic monuments, historic fortifications and Nazi *blockhauses* mingling with spectacular rocks, beaches, and ports along its whole length.

Our four Breton destinations all lie in spectacular locations on the north Breton coast. St-Malo and Roscoff, served by Channel ferries, have long and eventful seafaring traditions. St-Malo, its tall granite ramparts surrounded by the sea, became a quasi-independent medieval city state, although its notorious corsairs plagued English fleets on behalf of the French crown. Roscoff's links with Britain became much closer and more personal when its onion-sellers got on their bikes to sell their produce door-to-door in Britain, where they were dubbed the 'Breton Johnnies'.

Dinard and Brest have recently become cheap-flight destinations. The resort of Dinard right next door to St-Malo only grew up when British visitors colonized the sensational coast here in the mid-19th century. For a time it became one of the most glamorous holiday stops in Europe, its smart promenades overseen by the vast villas built for its wealthy visitors. Bombs rained down on naval Brest in the Second World War. The place was largely rebuilt along an American-style grid-plan, but it has fragments of a history going back to Roman times, plus a superb sea-life centre down by its huge, gorgeous bay so well protected from the Atlantic. And, as with all our Breton destinations, stunning beaches, coastal paths and islands lie close by, including in Brest's case the notorious windswept island of Ushant.

St-Malo and Dinard

St-Malo

St-Malo has one of the most spectacular, fiery and controversial histories of any French city. But in the Second World War, old St-Malo was reduced almost entirely to rubble by the Allied bombings of 1944; they destroyed 80 per cent of the buildings within the old ramparts. In June 1971, a stone cross was placed at the top of the cathedral of St-Vincent to symbolize the completion of St-Malo's long reconstruction.

The Walled City and its Ramparts

St-Malo's Ville Intra-Muros or walled city looks both noble and defensively aloof as you arrive. The many-storeyed mansion blocks in austere grey granite peer haughtily over the stupendous ramparts, while inviting golden-sand beaches spread out at their feet as the tide goes out. A Celtic and then a Gallo-Roman settlement grew up west of the present city, at Alet by the mouth of the river Rance, and the first cathedral was possibly built there around 380. With the arrival of immigrants from across the Channel the place thrived, and in the 6th century a man called Malo – or was it Maclou, or even Mac Low?– came from Britain to work miracles.

St Malo

250 metres
250 yards

Getting to St-Malo

Brittany Ferries (local t 02 99 40 64 41, f 02 99 40 64 42) runs services from Portsmouth, journey time 8–9hrs. Condor Ferries (local t 02 99 20 03 00, f 02 99 56 39 27) has a much faster ship, doing the trip from Poole in 4½hrs, but only late-May–Sept. See p.11. Ryanair (see p.6; France t 08 25 07 16 26) flies daily even faster from London Stansted to Dinard-Pleurtuit airport (t 02 99 46 18 46); a shuttle bus from there serves central St-Malo.

Getting Around

The railway station is a fair walk from the old centre, but a straight walk, down Avenue Martin from the Esplanade St-Vincent just outside the walled city. The *gare routière*, or bus station, is on Esplanade St-Vincent. For local bus information, call t 02 99 56 06 06. For local taxis, Allô Taxis Malouins, t 02 99 81 30 30, f 02 99 81 74 58, offers a 24hr service.

Car Hire

Avis, Gare Maritime du Naye, or train station, t 02 99 40 18 54, f 02 99 40 58 32.
Car'Go, 29 Bd des Talards (by train station), t 02 99 40 11 11, f 02 99 40 11 35.
Europcar, 16 Bd des Talards, t 02 99 56 75 17, f 02 99 56 86 74.
National Citer, 46 Bd de la République (by station), t 02 23 18 00 00, f 02 99 56 07 82.

Tourist Information

St-Malo: Esplanade St-Vincent, t 02 99 56 64 48, f 02 99 56 67 00, www.saint-malo-tourisme.com.

Market Days

St-Malo Intra-Muros: Tuesday and Friday.
Paramé: Wednesday and Saturday.
St-Servan: Tuesday and Friday.

Shopping

From café-lined Place St-Vincent, Rue St-Vincent heading towards the cathedral has a good choice of gift and clothes shops, including the Boutique St-James selling locally made Breton-style knitwear, while Aux Délices Malouins may entice you in with its chocolate specialities, such as its 'potatoes' and 'gulls' eggs'. The streets and squares off Rue St-Vincent offer a wide selection of shops – Armorlux on Rue Ste-Barbe is another specialist in stripy Breton jumpers. Rue Porcon de la Barbinais passes below the cathedral, with such temptations as Confiserie Guella making excellent local chocolates, and La Verrerie selling vibrant hand-made glass. Continuing through Place du Pilori, Rue Broussais and Rue de Dinan have lots of specifically Breton shops, for example La Trinitaine and Maison Taffin offering edible delights, Le Comptoir de Bretagne selling Breton music and books as well as gifts, and Vitrine de Bretagne specializing in Breton pottery and materials. Nearby, interesting wine shops include La Confiance, Rue Désilles, and Les Réserves de Surcouf, with historic cellars on Rue de Toulouse. Or try the Cave de l'Abbaye St-Jean on Rue des Cordiers by the Halle au Blé.

Where to Stay

St-Malo Intra-Muros ✉ 35400

★★★Hôtel Elizabeth, 2 Rue des Cordiers, t 02 99 56 24 98, f 02 99 56 39 24, www.st-malo-hotel-elizabeth.com (*expensive*). Small luxury hotels by the ramparts, with stylish rooms behind the 16th-century façade. No restaurant.

★★★Central, 6 Grande Rue, t 02 99 40 87 70, f 02 99 40 47 57, www.hotel-central-st-malo.com (*expensive–moderate*). Part of the reliable Best Western chain, with varied decoration in the rooms. Has restaurant.

★★★Hôtel des Abers, 10 Rue de la Corne de Cerf, t 02 99 40 85 60, f 02 99 40 94 09, (*expensive–moderate*). Flash rooms and a surprising Indonesian restaurant.

★★France Chateaubriand, Pl Chateaubriand, t 02 99 56 66 52, f 02 99 40 10 04, www.hotel-fr.chateaubriand.com (*high moderate*). Crowds spill around this characterful hotel at the heart of St-Malo, but it isn't cheap for a two-star.

★★Univers, Place Chateaubriand, t 02 99 40 89 52, f 02 99 40 07 27 (*moderate*). Also on the busiest square, with its own fair share of character, an excellent restaurant, and the well-known Bar de l'Univers below.

★★Hôtel Porte St-Pierre, 2 Place du Guet, t 02 99 40 91 27, f 02 99 56 06 94 (*inexpensive*). Popular, old-style hotel-cum-restaurant, on the pricey side.

★★Le Nautilus, 9 Rue de la Corne de Cerf, t 02 99 40 42 27, f 02 99 56 75 43, *www.lenautilus.com* (*inexpensive*). Cheerful little rooms above a loud, young bar.

★★Le Louvre, 2 Rue des Marins, t 02 99 40 86 62, f 02 99 40 86 93, *www.hoteldulouvre. fr* (*inexpensive*). Stylish family-run hotel.

★★Hôtel du Palais, 8 Rue Toullier, t 02 99 40 07 30, f 02 99 40 29 53, *www.hotels-st-malo.com/Palais* (*inexpensive*). Small and full of character, up the hill.

Towards Paramé and Rothéneuf

There are many excellent hotels looking on to the great arc of a beach leading east from the walled city of St-Malo.

★★★★Grand Hôtel des Thermes, 100 Bd Hébert, Courtoisville, t 02 99 40 75 75, f 02 99 40 76 00, *www.thalassosaintmalo.fr* (*luxury*). The poshest, on a grand scale, with a thalassotherapy centre as well as a swimming pool and gym. Very elaborate dishes are served up in its Art Deco dining room.

★★★La Villefromoy, 7 Bd Hébert, Rochebonne, t 02 99 40 92 20, f 02 99 56 79 49, *www. villefromoy.fr* (*expensive–moderate*). Much smaller-scale, many rooms with sea views either in a refined 19th-century town house, or in a very comfortable annexe by the garden.

★★★Le Beaufort, 25 Chaussée du Sillon, t 02 99 40 99 99, f 02 99 40 99 62, *www.hotel-beaufort.com* (*expensive–moderate*). Several of the modern-style rooms in this stylish old building have a terrace looking out to sea. The restaurant has a sea view too.

★★★Hôtel Alexandra, 138 Boulevard Hébert, Courtoisville, t 02 99 56 11 12, f 02 99 56 30 03, *www. hotelalexandra.com* (*expensive–moderate*). Another in the series of good villas on the beach; this one has many terraces.

★★★Hôtel Alba, 17 Rue des Dunes, Courtoisville, t 02 99 40 37 18, f 02 99 40 96 40, *www.hotelalba.com* (*moderate*). Yet another attractive seafront villa – a few rooms have sea-view terraces.

★Les Charmettes, 64 Bd Hébert, Courtoisville, t 02 99 56 07 31, f 02 99 56 85 96 (*inexpensive–cheap*). A good address with just a few rooms looking out to sea.

Le Neptune, 21 Rue de l'Industrie, t 02 99 56 82 15 (*cheap*). Bargain option for students.

Auberge de Jeunesse/Youth Hostel, 37 Avenue du R. P. Umbricht, B.P. 108, t 02 99 40 29 80, f 02 99 40 29 02 (*cheap*). South of Paramé.

Eating Out Intra-Muros

La Duchesse Anne, Place Guy La Chambre, t 02 99 40 85 33 (*expensive*). A classic, pricey Malouin restaurant set within the thick town ramparts. *Closed Wed, plus Sun pm and Mon lunch out of season.*

Delaunay, 6 Rue Ste-Barbe, t 02 99 40 92 46, (*expensive–moderate*). Fairly formal, with a good reputation for very fresh dishes, accompanied in season by fine local vegetables.

Le Chalut, 8 Rue de la Corne de Cerf, t 02 99 56 71 58 (*expensive–moderate*). A smart, good-looking restaurant, popular among fish aficionados, offering such delights as *poêlée de filet de Saint-Pierre* with chanterelle mushrooms and a light sauce pressed from langoustines. *Closed Sun and Mon.*

Le Chasse-Marée, 4 Rue du Grout St-Georges, t 02 99 40 85 10 (*moderate*). A real find, a little restaurant away from the crowds where you can taste refined seafood dishes. *Closed Sat lunch and Sun.*

Le Borgnefesse, 10 Rue du Puits aux Braies, t 02 99 40 05 05 (*moderate–cheap*). Atmospheric place serving traditional cuisine.

Crêperie Brigantine, 13 Rue de Dinan, t 02 99 56 82 82 (*cheap*). Its walls covered with photos of classic sailing ships, this is one of the most appealing crêperies in town. *Closed Tues pm and Wed out of season.*

Rue Jacques Cartier has a string of very touristy restaurants tucked in below the ramparts.

Perhaps prompted by the Viking raiders, the community transferred more and more to the near-island of rock to the north. As the remains of the now sanctified Malo were brought here, the centre became known as St-Malo-en-l'Isle. This city took off in the Middle Ages. In the 12th century, Bishop Jean de Chatillon saw to it that St-Malo was defended by solid ramparts and ordered the building of a much grander cathedral. St-Malo's fleet became active in both trade and war, and King Philippe Auguste used it to assist him in chasing the English out of Normandy. But the city cultivated its independent streak down the centuries: *'Ni Français, ni Breton: Malouin suis'* ('I'm neither French nor Breton, but Malouin'), ran a popular motto. The authorities built a massive castle in one corner of the island to try to oversee the tricky citizens.

The Malouin merchants prospered, in part from backing corsairs sent out to pillage English ships, in part through daring adventures of their own. Countless French explorers set out from St-Malo, most famously local boy Jacques Cartier, who claimed Canada for France in the 1530s. The Iles Malouines (the Falklands, or Las Malvinas) were put on the map by its adventurers. St-Malo grew glorious, and notorious. Merchants made fortunes from far-flung trade, including slavery.

On the splendid walk all the way round St-Malo's **ramparts**, you'll be rewarded with dramatic views of the islands strewn seawards, and of the beaches at the foot of the ramparts and those spreading shimmeringly to the east. You'll also pass dashing statues of some of St-Malo's most famous naval figures, not just Cartier, but corsairs like René Duguay-Trouin and Robert Surcouf. But the city's most famous son, France's greatest Romantic writer, was 19th-century François-René de Chateaubriand, who wrote of his childhood in St-Malo, 'companion of the waves and the wind', in his typically cheerily entitled autobiography, *Mémoires d'outre-tombe* (Memoirs from Beyond the Grave). In his lifetime, corsairs and slave-traders were driven off the scene. Codfishing took centre stage, and a radical change in Anglo-French relations brought a very different breed of invaders to St-Malo – tourists.

Down from the ramparts, the enclosed city streets can seem quite dark and overbearing. St-Malo was something of a high-rise city for the 18th century, given the height of the granite mansion blocks; the builders constructed short streets and used curves to break the force of the winds. Instead of vistas, you get the feeling that you're entering a disorientating labyrinth. Perhaps the most evocative way to imagine historic St-Malo is to think of the corsairs who brought such wild life to these streets in the Ancien Régime. Returning from successful raids, they would be greeted as heroes, and then they would often tour the town getting appallingly drunk.

Locked away in a grim part of the city's very stern château, the **Musée d'Histoire de la Ville et du Pays Malouin** (*open April–Sept daily 10–12 and 2–6; rest of year Tues–Sun 10–12 and 2–6; adm*) is a bit of a disappointment, a mainly dark and dismal, rambling place in need of modernization. It tells the story of St-Malo's maritime past in chaotic fashion. Perhaps the best of the museum's many rooms concentrates on the Malouin tradition of fishing in Newfoundland, with maps, icy paintings and models giving a good picture of the trade. One corner is devoted to St-Malo's destruction in the Second World War and its painstaking reconstruction. The top floor displays a mixed bag of paintings of the city, including an exceptionally cheering Signac.

The **Petit Aquarium d'Intra-Muros** (*open 15 June–Sept 9am–10pm; rest of period April–3 Dec, 10–6 but closed Mon am; adm*) occupies a dark corridor in the ramparts running west along Place Vauban. The setting is practical, although the tanks may be a bit high for youngsters. It is rather odd, however, to find yourself looking at tropical fish when you know the cold Channel waters are lapping at the other side of the wall.

Posterity has got its own back on France's most miserable romantic – **Place Chateaubriand** is now the most cheerful place in town, with plenty of cafés and bustle. Starting from here, you can follow a discreetly but well signposted, numbered **historical trail** through town. This route takes you almost immediately to the façade of the house where Chateaubriand was born in 1768, then past many other fine town houses, and up to the chapel at the highest point of the city.

The sharp spire of the **Cathédrale St-Vincent** rises far higher, a landmark in the centre of town for ships out to sea. Black and white photos in the side entrance show the extent of its devastation in the Second World War, although the nave, its vaulting and most of the 13th-century Gothic choir survived, and you can still make out Romanesque carvings high up on the columns' capitals. In this church God and the saints share the honours with Jacques Cartier: he features in the stained glass in one transept, and is buried in a chapel off the choir, while further plaques pay homage to him. The remains of another local 'hero', 18th-century corsair Duguay-Trouin, were returned here from Paris as recently as 1973. Around the cathedral you'll find the main **shopping quarters**, the streets sometimes giving on to little squares whose names, like the Place de la Poissonnerie, the Marché aux Légumes, or the Place aux Herbes, indicate that they were once occupied by specific traders.

To get the best picture of the life of the wealthy St-Malo merchants of the Ancien Régime, visit the **Demeure des Magon de la Lande** or **Maison Asfeld** (*open Mar–15 Nov, 10–12 and 2–6.30; adm*), one of the very few original 18th-century mansions in St-Malo to have survived the bombings intact. In this house, deals were struck, voyages planned, and exotic produce stored. Family life went on here too: François-Auguste Magon, the Malouin for whom this grand town house was built, had by the age of 45 amassed an immense fortune and constructed this home. The Magon family was one of the most successful of all St-Malo's trading dynasties. The 70-room building is now divided up into flats, but one of the tenants organizes guided tours round certain rooms inside. A couple of the reception rooms you pass through stand quite empty except when there is the odd amateur painting exhibition. But the guide brings the whole place wonderfully back to life, even sometimes handing round cutlass and impaler. There are hidden passageways behind the walls, and the visit ends in the cellars, now occupied by a wine merchant.

Paramé, Aleth and the Aquarium

Historic St-Malo has beaches right at its feet, as we've mentioned, but the city's seaside resort of **Paramé** stretches east from the old walled town, its glorious arc of beach backed by a mass of hotels. The manor of the great French 16th-century explorer Jacques Cartier stands further east, by Rothéneuf (*see* 'Touring', p.133).

On the other side of old St-Malo, the peninsula of **Aleth** has its own attractions, including a massive marina, a couple of beaches, and a memorial museum on St-Malo in the Second World War, set in a former Nazi *blockhaus* that is now part of a campsite. A little further round the coast, the imposing medieval **Tour Solidor** still guards the Rance estuary. The interior is occupied by old-fashioned displays on explorers round Cape Horn. Inland, in St-Malo's southern suburbs, the state-of-the-art **Grand Aquarium** (*bus 5 from Esplanade St-Vincent; open July 9.30am–8pm; Aug 9.30am– 10pm; rest of year 10–6*) on Avenue Patton, La Ville Jouan, is a major tourist attraction. Once you've got through the off-putting outer layers of mass commercialization, the big aquaria take you to a quite magical underworld. The most sensational room is the Anneau, with its large ring of an aquarium in which fish spin around you.

Walking Out to St-Malo's Islands

As the tide recedes, ant-trails of tourists head out from the ville intra-muros for the islands of Grand Bé and the Fort National. Looking back on the walled city, St-Malo looks stunning. Many French people go to the **Grand Bé** expressly to see **Chateaubriand's tomb**, a place of Byronic proportions to the French, even if the cross looking out to the Channel is simple. The **Fort National** (*open Easter–Sept at low tide during the day; adm*) is also splendidly situated, but its defences bring to mind brutal times. Walk out to its islet at low tide, picking your way through the rocks, to arrive at the sharp layers of the fortification. In such big forts it's always a bit of a disappointment to see the diminutive size of the building that lies at the heart of so many ramparts, the layers of fortified walls like diminishing Russian dolls. On the tour, though, you're taken down into atmospheric, dark underground chambers. No natural light can enter these sinister places, which were actually planned for storage, with ingenious zigzagging air vents to provide oxygen.

From the Grand Bé, you can catch a boat out to the **Petit Bé**, a little island occupied by a horseshoe-shaped **fort** (*open Easter–mid-Nov daily 10–6, plus French school hols; adm*). The views back to St-Malo are unbeatable. Inside are displays on the history of this exceptional fort and on the tides. When the tide is very low, you can actually walk out to this island as well. The **Ile de Cézembre** lies a boat ride away (*from Porte de Dinan, summer only*), a rocky island, harshly unshaded on a summer day. Breton monks retreated here from the 6th century. Legend has it that young women of St-Malo would come out to Cézembre on a pilgrimage to St Brendan's oratory. There they would pray for his help in finding a lizard with three tails, a sign that they would get married within the year. You're not supposed to wander from the blinding white sands these days, as German mines may still be lurking under the surface.

Dinard

We have one Mrs Faber to thank for Dinard. In the 1850s, she and a few other British and American families set the fashion for holidays in this beautiful location on the opposite bank of the Rance estuary from St-Malo. By the turn of the last century,

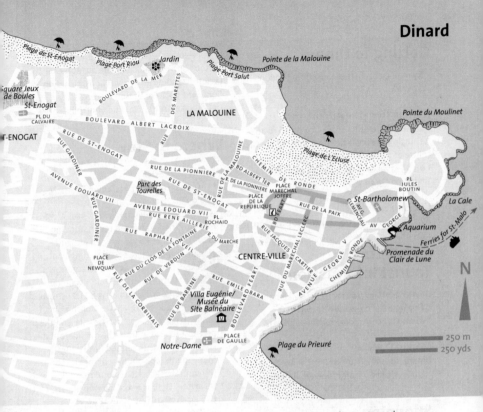

Dinard was one of the chic-est resorts in the world. European royalty swanned around town, as did the ultra-wealthy from many continents, together with the likes of the home-grown Cognac-Hennessey family. These massively rich visitors built palatial villas along the rocky cliffs, above the protected beaches of Dinard. The place attracted artists too, most notably Picasso; he spent two summers in the town and painted a few of his most wildly exuberant pictures here.

A Tour of Dinard

The central beach, backed by the main tourist promenade, is the **Plage de l'Ecluse**. While this may be the focal point of tourist Dinard, it isn't the finest part of the town. Several of the grand buildings that once lined the beach have sadly been destroyed or truncated. But there is action aplenty, with the casino, the swimming pools (indoor and outdoor), and of course the beach with its lines of changing-booths. In summer, fresh blue- and white-striped changing-tents are set up on the sands.

In the middle of the Plage de l'Ecluse, **Place Maréchal Joffre** is where everything collides. Hotels, restaurants and stalls cluster around the square. A statue pays homage to Alfred Hitchcock, shown standing on an egg, a bird on either shoulder – Dinard holds an annual festival of British cinema. In front of the square, towards the sea, you may spot a few panels reproducing provocative works by Picasso, perhaps in some small way inspired by this beach.

Getting to Dinard

Ryanair (*see* p.6) flies daily from London Stansted.

Getting from the Airport

Dinard-Pleurtuit airport, **t** 02 99 46 18 46. A **shuttle bus** serves flights, taking you to the centre of Dinard. For **taxis**, try Taxis Noslier, **t** 06 03 47 84 66, **f** 02 99 88 78 23, or Emeraude Taxis, **t** 02 99 46 75 75.

Car Hire

Avis, at the airport, **t** 02 99 46 25 20, **f** 02 99 46 95 08.

Tourist Information

Dinard: 2 Boulevard Féart, **t** 02 99 46 94 12, **f** 02 99 88 21 07, *www.ville-dinard.fr*, *dinard.office.de. tourisme@wanadoo.fr*.

Market Days

Dinard: Tuesday, Thurs and Sat, Place Crolard. Halles de la Concorde, open daily am.

Shopping

The shopping area is small. The main shopping streets lie behind Plage de l'Ecluse with its art galleries. **Rue Levasseur** has appealing shops, Douceurs de Bretagne for regional produce, Le Pressoir Nicolas for wine, other shops offering gifts. On parallel **Bd Wilson**, La Belle Iloise specializes in pre-prepared Breton fish. Perpendicular **Rue du Maréchal Leclerc** has some attractive shops, including Confiserie Batt. For Breton materials, try La Corbeille d'Argent on **Rue Churchill**.

Where to Stay

Dinard ✉ 35800

★★★★**Grand Hôtel Barrière**, 46 Av George V, **t** 02 99 88 26 26, **f** 02 99 88 26 27, *www.lucienbarriere.com* (*expensive*). Most distinguished address in town, standing aloof above the Rance promenade, with elegant rooms. There's a swimming pool and a cocktail bar as well as the restaurant.

★★★**Reine Hortense**, 19 Rue de la Malouine, **t** 02 99 46 54 31, **f** 02 99 88 15 88 (*expensive*). Another grand old Dinard establishment, but with far fewer rooms. The villa isn't the prettiest to look at from the outside, but it is stylish within, with refined furnishings. Many rooms look out to sea from just above the central beach. No restaurant.

★★★**Novotel Thalassa**, Av Château-Hébert, **t** 02 99 16 78 10, **f** 02 99 16 78 29, *H1114@accor-hotels.com* (*expensive*). A monster of a new luxury health hotel, above the rocks on the western end of St-Enogat beach; there's an indoor heated pool among the facilities at the sea-water treatments centre. The rooms have splendid sea views. The restaurant provides both diet and gastronomic meals.

From the Plage de l'Ecluse, you look out on to the splendid and eccentric neo-Gothic villas of the Pointe du Moulinet to the east and the Pointe de la Malouine to the west. Islands lie out to sea, notably the Ile de Cézembre. The **coastal paths** in both directions are fabulous. Head round the **Pointe du Moulinet** and St-Malo comes stunningly into view. Beyond the landing stage for the ferry service to St-Malo, you come to the **Promenade du Clair de Lune**. On summer nights the exotic plants along here are lit up in gaudy colours, and romantic recorded music is piped into the air. The coastal path then leads down to the well-protected **Plage du Prieuré**.

A steep climb from the Clair de Lune walk brings you up to Rue Faber and the neo-Gothic British-American church of **St-Bartholomew**. Its small palm garden makes a pretty little haven, while the church decoration, right down to the kneelers, takes you straight across the Channel. Set further back, the grand **Villa Eugénie** of 1868 carries

***Hôtel Roche Corneille**, 4 Rue Georges Clemenceau, t 02 99 46 14 47, f 02 99 46 40 80 (*expensive–moderate*). More reasonably priced, but the rooms don't look out on to the sea. However, they are elegant, set in a fine villa. The restaurant serves refined classics.

***Le Vieux Manoir**, 21 Rue Gardiner, t 02 99 46 14 69, f 02 99 46 87 87, *vieux.manoir@libertysurf.com* (*moderate*). Further back within town, a calm, good-value hotel with a garden, but no restaurant.

★★Printania, 5 Av George V, t 02 99 46 13 07, f 02 99 46 26 32, *PRINTANIA.DINARD@wanadoo.fr* (*moderate*). Stands out above the Rance, looking over to St-Malo, the rooms have fine views. The restaurant is slightly kitsch, with Breton furniture and waiters in Breton dress; not surprisingly, it serves traditional fare.

★★Eméraude Plage, 1 Bd Albert 1er, t 02 99 46 15 79, f 02 99 88 15 31, *htemeraude@aol.com* (*moderate*). Close to Dinard's central beach, this is a big hotel with welcoming staff well used to receiving English-speaking visitors. Has restaurant.

★★L'Améthyste, 2 Rue des Bains, in St-Enogat, t 02 99 46 61 81, f 02 99 46 96 91, *hotel-amethyste@wanadoo.fr* (*inexpensive*). A short walk from the beach, and comfortable, if a bit characterless.

★Hôtel du Prieuré, 1 Place du Général de Gaulle, t 02 99 46 13 74, f 02 99 46 81 90 (*inexpensive*). Its seven rooms and restaurant have superb views on to Dinard's eastern beach, the Plage du Prieuré. With restaurant.

★★Hôtel du Parc, 20 Av Edouard VII, t 02 99 46 11 39, f 02 99 88 10 58, *hotel.du.parc@infonie.fr* (*inexpensive–cheap*). Not glamorous, but good value, with a touch of old-fashioned charm. Has restaurant.

★Beauséjour, 2 Place du Calvaire, t 02 99 46 13 61, f 02 99 46 85 19 (*inexpensive–cheap*). Well-located in St-Enogat. Restaurant.

Les Mouettes, 64 Av George V, t 02 99 46 10 64, f 02 99 16 02 49 (*inexpensive–cheap*). Simple, good, family-run, and in the posh part of town. No restaurant.

Eating Out

Le George V, 46 Av George V, t 02 99 88 26 26 (*moderate*). Reputed, with some quite reasonably priced seafood menus allowing you to savour the atmosphere of the place without forking out too much.

La Salle à Manger, 25 Bd Féart, t 02 99 16 07 95 (*moderate*). Another well-regarded gastronomic restaurant; lobster from its own tank is a speciality.

Hôtel du Roy, 9 Bd Féart, t 02 99 46 10 57 (*cheap*). Popular, large, central crêperie. *Closed Tues.*

Le Dauphin, 5 Bd Féart, t 02 99 46 76 83 (*cheap*). Good-value crêperie. *Closed Mon.*

For more basic and bustling restaurants in Dinard, try the western end of the central Plage de l'Ecluse.

the name of Emperor Napoleon III's wife. Rumour had it that the imperial couple were coming to spend a summer in Dinard and officially inaugurate the resort. Apparently, however, they fell out over a dog which the empress wanted to bring but which the emperor couldn't abide. Eugénie flounced off to Biarritz solo, although the villa continues to carry her name. The place has served as town hall, then library, before becoming the town museum. Now, temporary exhibitions are held here.

Back at the main Plage de l'Ecluse, the coastal path leading west round the **Pointe de la Malouine** to St-Enogat makes for the most unforgettable of all Dinard's walks. The footpath takes you under rocks and grand villas to beautiful sandy beaches. The views out to sea, the waters strewn with reefs and sails, are superlative. The path may be narrow, hemmed in by cliff and sea, but the reward at the end is the beautiful beach of St-Enogat.

Day Trips and Overnighters from St-Malo and Dinard

Mont St-Michel

The mesmerizingly beautiful Mont St-Michel makes a truly glorious piece of Christian symbolism. Its triangular shape from afar can evoke the Holy Trinity, the narrow spit joining mainland to island the straight and narrow path to heaven, and the church steeple pointing fiercely to the skies acts as a sharp reminder for visitors to turn their gaze heavenwards. The needle is topped by a gilded statue of militant St Michael, weigher of souls at the Last Judgement. An early manuscript recounts the story of how Bishop Aubert of nearby Avranches was called upon by St Michael to build a shrine to him on the mysterious rock out in the bay below: in the year 708, the archangel swooped down into his dreams with his insistent message. Aubert dismissed this dream twice, but the third time the archangel gave him a vicious prod in the side of the head, prompting him into action. Aubert had a modest grotto built, modelled on Italy's Mount Gargano where St Michael had supposedly put in an earlier appearance. Monks were then sent across the Alps to fetch relics of St Michael, which would draw in vast numbers of pilgrims intent on saving their souls.

In 966 the mount became the site of the first Benedictine monastery in Western Normandy. These buildings were replaced by a more substantial Romanesque abbey, constructed in the 11th and 12th centuries. Donations of land from nobles and of money from pilgrims brought the abbey considerable wealth. It became a famed school of learning too, renowned for the production of illuminated manuscripts. Robert de Tombelaine and Anastase the Venetian counted among the most revered scholars of the 11th century, when a collection of stories of miracles connected with the holy mount was compiled. It was under the 12th-century abbot Robert de Torigni, however, that the abbey knew its greatest period. The number of monks reached its peak of 60, and this place of great learning became known as the 'City of Books'.

The Mont St-Michel became a strategic stronghold in the Middle Ages. In the 13th century Breton soldiers fighting for King Philippe Auguste caused a destructive fire in the abbey. The repentant monarch donated an enormous sum to build a magnificent new monastic wing. This *Merveille*, or Marvel, as it became known, counts as the greatest architectural achievement on the Mont St-Michel. The ramparts around the bottom of the mount date mainly from the 15th century, built to defend the rock from the English in the Hundred Years' War. The English allowed pilgrims to reach the abbey during the battles; but in the course of fighting, in 1421 the church choir collapsed. When the war was over, French pilgrims came to thank St Michael for delivering them from the English, contributing generously to the abbey's reconstruction.

French kings too came to Mont St-Michel on pilgrimage, but abbey life was radically altered in the early 16th century when the crown took control of the appointment of French abbots under the system of *commende*. Some of the *abbés commendataires* scarcely visited the mount, interested only in its revenue; it was inevitable that monastic life and scholarship would suffer dramatically. With the installation of the

Maurist Benedictine order in 1622, religious life revived somewhat, but the place lay in a precarious state. Only some 10 monks lived in the abbey before the Revolution, after which they were replaced by prisoners. The abbey served this demeaning purpose until 1863. Then the 19th-century restorers moved in in force. The neo-Gothic spire, built in 1897, was the work of Victor Petigrand, a pupil of Viollet-le-Duc. The sparkling gilded statue of St Michael was executed by Emmanuel Frémiet. Recently, monks have been allowed back into the abbey; there are only a handful, but they do receive people on religious retreats, keeping a small spiritual flame alive on the holy mount.

Unsurprisingly, the Mont St-Michel has been declared a UNESCO World Heritage Site. It is one of the most visited places in France, and in summer the crush can be hellish. The picturesque, steep, narrow **Grande Rue** up to the abbey panders to modern-day pilgrims, crammed with shops selling tat. Such a gem from a distance, the **abbey** turns out to be austere and forbidding close up, designed to incite awe and reflection. A daunting number of steps leads from the abbey entrance up to the level of the abbey church, but the reward is glorious, plunging views of both the abbey and the bay. A classical façade was tacked on to the church's plain Romanesque nave. Inside, even the luminous late-Gothic choir has little decorative detail. The church was an extraordinary work of engineering, however, its crossing placed on the very top of the rock, most of the rest of the edifice resting on four lower chapels or crypts.

The highlight of the tour is the brilliant three-storey **Merveille**, daringly built on the north side of the mount. On the top level the cloister garden stands open to the skies, while its galleries are held up on delicate double columns. Originally built as a peaceful retreat, nowadays it tends to be about as calm as Paris in the rush hour. The adjoining refectory is beautifully lit, but there are no direct views out; with typical Christian self-denying willpower (or perversity), many of the rooms in this magnificent site were deliberately deprived of views, given diagonal windows to let the light

Getting There

Buses leave from St-Malo's St-Vincent station, daily departures 10am and 11am, plus 9am Mon–Sat. The journey lasts 1hr 15mins. Last daily return 5.30pm.

Tourist Information

Mont St-Michel: t 02 33 60 14 30, f 02 33 60 06 75, OT.Mont.Saint.Michel @wanadoo.fr.

Where to Stay and Eat

Mont St-Michel ✉ 50116
★★★La Mère Poularde, t 02 33 60 14 01, f 02 33 89 68 69 (expensive–moderate). Famed in France. The rooms at the base of the mount are pretty, but the prices sky-high. The packed photogenic and photo-covered restaurant offers a wide range of choices.
★★★Hôtel St-Pierre, t 02 33 60 14 03, f 02 33 48 59 82 (expensive–moderate). Comfortable rooms and a welcoming if kitsch restaurant.
★★★La Croix Blanche, t 02 33 60 14 04, f 02 33 48 59 82 (expensive–moderate). Good rooms, and a restaurant in a similar price range.
★★Hôtel du Mouton Blanc, t 02 33 60 14 08, f 02 33 60 05 62 (expensive–moderate). The rooms are scattered in several houses, while there are two different restaurants, one in a 14th-century building.
La Vieille Auberge, t 02 33 60 14 34, f 02 33 70 87 04 (moderate–inexpensive). Boasts rooms with terrace and sea view, and has a brasserie.
La Sirène, t 02 33 60 08 60 (cheap). A good and popular option for crêpes.

in indirectly. On the middle level, the vast Salle des Hôtes was where noble and prestigious pilgrims were received. The neighbouring room may have served both as the chapterhouse and the scriptorium, where manuscripts were prepared. A copy of Frémiet's statue of St Michael is displayed in the massive cellar below, built to store mountains of provisions. Close up, God's *generalissimo* looks mean and militant, dressed in armour, sword raised for action above his spiky headgear, only the wings adding a slightly softer touch.

At night the abbey is gloriously lit. In August, you can even go on a **night tour** of the abbey, when it was filled with an eerie Gothic grandeur.

Other attractions on the mount lie along the Grande Rue. Tucked into the rock to one side of the street, the other serious religious stop besides the abbey is **St-Pierre**, a charming building from the 15th and 16th centuries. The **Archéoscope** (*open Feb–mid-Nov daily 9–6; adm*) almost opposite offers a lively, contemporary introduction to the abbey. Smoke, lights and videos bombard the senses and, although the commentary is in French, the splendid film footage (taken from a helicopter) and the special effects are easy for all to appreciate. By contrast, the **Musée Historique** (*open Feb–mid-Nov daily 9–6; adm*), back up close to the abbey entrance, is amusingly archaic. Waxworks and torture instruments remind you of the abbey's secondary use as a prison. The **Maison de Tiphaine** (*open June–15 Sept daily 9–7; rest of period Feb–mid-Nov daily 9–6; adm*) close by was built for the most famed Breton and French warrior of the Hundred Years' War, Bertrand du Guesclin, and his wife. At the bottom of the Grande Rue, the **Musée Maritime** (*open daily 9–6; closed Jan; adm*) clambers up four small floors filled with model ships and boats. A video on each level sensibly explains aspects of the bay and its natural habitat. With the bay silting up so fast in recent times, there are major plans to restore the natural tidal effects around this amazing holy island.

Dinan

A memorable winding street bordered by timberframe houses links the two halves of Dinan, the port down by the Rance river, and the splendidly fortified upper town. The views from the **Tour du Gouverneur** along the **ramparts** take in much of the three kilometres of medieval fortifications which still encircle upper Dinan. The **Château de Dinan** (*open June–15 Oct daily 10–5.45; March 16–May and Oct 16–Nov 15, 10–1 and 2–5.45; 16 Nov–15 Mar Wed–Mon 1.30–5; closed Jan; adm*) is a slightly misleading name for the soaring keep along the walls, built for Duke Jean IV of Brittany late in the 14th century. Exhibits on Dinan's history fill the different levels, while the dank basement of the neighbouring Tour de Coëtquen contains evocative medieval tombs.

In the centre of the historic town, the **Tour de l'Horloge**, Dinan's substantial belfry, was built as a major symbol of civic pride and mercantile success. In the nearby Gothic church of **St-Sauveur** on its adorable old square, look out for nearly kissing dromedaries among the stone decorations. The story goes that 12th-century Dinan crusader Riwallon le Roux made a vow that he would build a church if he got back alive from Arab imprisonment, which he evidently did, with some vivid memories. The heart of the most famous of all medieval Breton warriors, Bertrand du Guesclin, lies in

Getting There

There are **buses** from St-Malo to Dinan from 8am, except on Sun, when the first departure is much later. Note that the last bus back to St-Malo leaves 5pm, including Sun.

Tourist Information

Dinan ✉ **22100**: 9 Rue du Château, t 02 96 87 69 76, f 02 96 87 69 77, *www.dinan-tourisme.com*, *infos@dinan-tourisme.com*.

Market Days
Dinan: Thursday.

Eating Out

Chez La Mère Pourcel, 3 Place des Merciers, t 02 96 39 03 80 (*expensive–moderate*). Characterful, elegant restaurant in the historic centre. *Closed Sun pm and Mon out of season.*

Les Grands Fossés, 2 Place du Général Leclerc, t 02 96 39 21 50 (*expensive–moderate*). Another top restaurant in town, in a big bourgeois Breton stone house on a square just outside the ramparts. *Closed Thurs out of season.*

La Fleur de Sel, 7 Rue Ste-Claire, t 02 96 85 15 14 (*expensive–moderate*). Some powerful dishes on the menu in this tasteful restaurant. *Closed Tues and Wed out of season.*

La Courtine, 6 Rue de la Croix, t 02 96 39 74 41 (*moderate*). Excellent local cooking. *Closed Wed and Sun pm.*

Le Cantorbéry, 6 Rue Ste-Claire, t 02 96 39 02 52 (*moderate–cheap*). Cantorbéry is French for Canterbury, and this is a popular place with British visitors, offering some interesting dishes like spicy rabbit or potted fish. *Closed Sun pm and Mon out of season.*

Le St Louis, 9–11 Rue de Léhon, t 02 96 39 89 50 (*moderate–cheap*). Particularly popular for its buffet, with *charcuteries*, seafood and mixed salads. *Closed Sun pm, Mon lunch and Wed out of season.*

Relais des Corsaires, 3 Rue du Quai, t 02 96 39 40 17, f 02 96 39 34 75 (*moderate–cheap*). Down by the river, lies behind one of the prettiest old façades of lower Dinan; seafood particularly recommended.

Les Jardins du Jerzual, 15 Rue du Petit Four, t 02 96 85 28 75 (*cheap*). Hard to beat among Dinan's *crêperies*, opposite the Maison du Gouverneur. Eat either in the old house or on the shaded terrace with its Venus fountain. *Closed Mon out of season*

Crêperie Le Connétable, 1 Rue de l'Apport, t 02 96 39 06 74 (*cheap*). Another popular *crêperie* in splendid old town quarters.

a chest in the north transept. His famous joust with one Thomas of Canterbury in the terrible Breton war of ducal succession (a kind of secondary plot in the Hundred Years' War) took place in Dinan in 1357, as recalled in the triumphant early 20th-century equestrian statue of him by Emmanuel Frémiet on the large **Place du Guesclin**.

Down by the Rance, take a lovely walk along the towpath, or enjoy a boat trip on the river. Set in terraced gardens just above the yachting harbour, the **Maison d'Artiste de La Grande Vigne** (*open June–Sept 10–6.30; adm*) is too sweet for words; you feel a bit as though you're going to visit Miss Marple of Dinan when you arrive at the gate. This is the former home of the prolific painter Yvonne Jean-Haffen; and it also served as her studio from 1937 until the early 1990s. A student of Mathurin Méheut, an important recorder of daily Breton life through art, Jean-Haffen was introduced to Brittany by him. The two artists apparently became lovers in Méheut's later years, although Yvonne was married. Méheut's life is celebrated alongside hers here, but most of the works are by Jean-Haffen. Breton themes predominate.

In a separate part of town, the **Musée du Rail** (*open June–mid-Sept 2–6*) at Dinan's railway station has a large collection of model railways.

Touring from St-Malo and Dinard

You'll find that the sights are reliably open Easter–Oct, 10–12 and 2–5 at least, unless otherwise stated, and charge adm.

Day 1: The Colourful Côte d'Emeraude

Morning: Immerse yourselves in the confusion of beach-lined peninsula resorts west of Dinard, **St-Lunaire**, **St-Briac**, **Lancieux**, **St-Jacut-de-la-Mer** and **St-Cast-le-Guildo** all worthy rivals, with bright rocks that legend says were coloured by the blood of persecuted Celtic saints in the Dark Ages.

Lunch: South of St-Cast, **Le Biniou**, Plage de Pen Guen, t 02 96 41 94 53 (*moderate*), combines beach location and panoramic views with interesting seafood dishes. In St-Cast centre, try traditional Breton crêpes at holidaymakers' favourite, **Le Bretan'or**, 8 Place Anatole Le Braz, t 02 96 41 92 45 (*cheap*), or **L'Etoile de Mer**, Rue du Port, t 02 96 41 92 45 (*cheap*).

Afternoon: Perched on a wind-battered promontory, medieval **Fort La Latte** (*open June–Sept and Easter hols 10–12.30 and 2.30–6.30; rest of year weekends and public hols only 2.30–5.30*) is the most dramatic coastal castle in Brittany. At **Cap Fréhel**, walk along the coastal path or climb the lighthouse to appreciate this cliff-lined stretch.

Dinner: Erquy's restaurants serve fine seafood, **Le Relais** (*below*) by the port, **L'Escurial**, t 02 96 72 31 56, on the seafront, and **Le Nelumbo**, t 02 96 72 31 31, in the centre (*all moderate*).

Sleeping: ★★**Le Relais**, t 02 96 72 32 60, f 02 96 72 19 57 (*inexpensive*) has sweet rooms with sea views. ★★**Beauséjour**, t 02 96 72 30 39, f 02 96 72 16 30 (*inexpensive*) surveys the bay with its curious glassy eyeballs.

Day 2: Beautiful Greys on the Bay

Morning: It's a roller-coaster drive from Erquy to Hillion down the **Bay of St-Brieuc**. Stop in the creeks to admire the **Ile Verdelet**, the bay's answer to the Mont St-Michel, reserved for birds rather than monks or tourists – see it close up from the resort of **Pléneuf-Val-André**. Hillion's **Maison de la Baie** explains the environment of the bay. Set out from there for a sensational coastal walk.

Lunch: Pléneuf's **La Cotriade**, 1 Quai Célestin Bouglé, t 02 96 72 20 26 (*expensive*) serves superlative seafood and overlooks the bay, while **Au Biniou**, 121 Rue Clemenceau, t 02 96 72 24 35 (*moderate*) cooks up fish stews.

Afternoon: Inland, historic **Lamballe**, once capital of the powerful Breton region of Penthièvre, is now capital of the Breton horse. Admire these powerful steeds at the impressive *haras* or stud farm (*open daily 15 June–15 Sept; rest of year Wed and weekends; closed Jan–mid-Feb*) in the centre. Get an evocative picture of everyday life in Brittany in the first half of the 20th century in the Musée Mathurin Méheut, a fine house featuring drawings by this passionate artist.

Dinner and sleeping: Try traditional provincial French choices in Lamballe, with restaurants, at the ★★★**Hôtel d'Angleterre**, 29 Rue Jobert, t 02 96 31 00 16, f 02 96 31 91 54 (*moderate*), or ★★**La Tour d'Argent**, 2 Rue du Dr Lavergne, t 02 96 31 01 37, f 02 96 31 37 59 (*inexpensive*). For a good-value, historic B&B, book at **Le Teno**, 14 Rue Notre-Dame, t 02 96 31 00 41.

Day 3: A Tranquil Country Trip

Morning: Some 20km south of Lamballe, the heavily restored **abbey of Boquen** offers one of the most peaceful religious halts in the region. To the west, picture-postcard **Moncontour** looks like a village transferred here from southwest France.

Lunch: In Moncontour, the **Chaudron Magique**, t 02 96 73 40 34 (*inexpensive*) lays on ye olde touches a bit thick, but is fun. Crêperie **Au Coin du Feu**, t 02 96 73 40 34 (*cheap*) has character.

Afternoon: Follow the D792 northeast along Arguenon valley for **St-Esprit-des-Bois**, with La Ferme d'Antan, one of the best recreations in the region of a traditional farm; then go to admire the medieval ruins of neaby **Château de la Hunaudaye**. Before entering **Dinan** (*see* pp.130–31), pay your respects to the imposing abbey church in the delectable village of **Léhon** just south.

Dinner and sleeping: For Dinan dining, *see* p.131. ★★★**D'Avaugour**, 1 Place du Champ Clos, t 02 96 39 07 49, f 02 96 85 43 04 (*expensive–moderate*), has tasteful rooms in its 18th-century building and a delightful garden by the ramparts. Cheaper, but also by the ramparts, **★★La Porte St-Malo**, 35 Rue St-Malo, **t** 02 96 39 19 76, **f** 02 96 59 50 67 (*inexpensive*) has nice rooms. **L'Hostellerie du Vieux St-Sauveur**, 21 Place St-Sauveur, **t** 02 96 85 30 20 (*inexpensive*) is a bargain hotel above a bar, set in a cracking location.

Day 4: Châteaux to Mont St-Michel

Morning: East of Dinan, choose from a clutch of châteaux. **Bourbansais** (*outside May–Sept, open pm only*), a Renaissance delight in speckled schist, has a little zoo in its park. Some way south, **Caradeuc** boasts quite grandiose gardens to wander round, with comical statuary. Nearby **Bécherel** is an appealingly bookish old hilltop town, the Hay-on-Wye of Brittany.

Lunch: Push a bit east to Hédé for a good country lunch – gastronomic at **La Vieille Auberge**, **t** 02 99 45 46 25 (*expensive–moderate*), or more rustic at wood-side **Le Genty-Home**, **t** 02 99 45 46 07 (*moderate–cheap*). Or try amusing **★★Le Vieux Moulin**, **t** 02 99 45 45 70 (*moderate*).

Afternoon: Just west of Hédé, by the village of **Les Iffs** with its delightfully decorated church, the **Château de Montmuran** (*closed Sat*) offers a quirky tour and memories of Brittany's most awesome medieval warrior, Bertrand du Guesclin. **Combourg**'s fearsome medieval château (*closed Tues*) set above its lake was the chilling home of France's greatest Romantic, Chateaubriand. For something to cheer your spirits, rush east to hilltop **Bazouges-la-Pérouse**, at first sight a traditional Breton village, but in fact a wonderfully eccentric place colonized part of the year by cutting-edge artists and galleries. The adorable **Château La Ballue** close by continues the theme.

Dinner and sleeping: Dining and staying on the Mont St-Michel by night is magical, especially when the tourist hordes finally evaporate, but it's expensive to sleep in this divine place (*see pp.128–9*). For bargains with atmosphere, head west for the coastal *inexpensive* B&Bs of Cherrueix, for example **La Hamelinais**, **t** 02 99 48 95 26, **La Pichardière**, **t** 02 99 48 83 82, **Lair**, **t** 02 99 48 01 65, or **Les Trois Cheminées**, **t** 02 99 48 93 54.

Day 5: Dol, Cancale, Colette and Cartier

Morning: Moving west from the Mont St-Michel, an intimidating cathedral looms over one side of the historic small town of Dol; nearby, the Cathédralscope (*closed Jan*) presents a history of cathedrals in Europe and helpfully explains their symbolism. North of Dol, the **Mont-Dol** hill, where legend has it St Michael fought off Satan, offers spectacular views over the patchwork countryside leading to the bay of Mont St-Michel.

Lunch: In one of Dol's 16th-century timber-frame houses, **La Grabotais**, **t** 02 99 48 19 89 (*moderate*) is a characterful place to eat. **Le Plédran**, **t** 02 99 48 40 80 (*cheap*) serves great crêpes as well as grilled meats.

Afternoon: Follow the bay of the Mont St-Michel to the gorgeous oyster port of **Cancale**, where you can visit an oyster farm as well as lazing in the port-side cafés. Pioneering 20th-century writer Colette used to holiday in one of the string of bays to the west, while France's most celebrated explorer Jacques Cartier, 'discoverer' of Canada, lived in these parts. His modest manor (*not open weekends outside July and Aug, and with tours only at 3pm Oct–May*) lies not far back from the curious Rochers de Rothéneuf, cliffs carved with a whole series of cartoon-like figures representing local folk tales, the work of a frustrated 19th-century priest.

Dinner and sleeping: Cancale has some enchanting choices. One of the best hotels in Brittany, the **★★★★Maisons de Bricourt**, **t** 02 99 89 64 76, **f** 02 99 89 88 47 (*luxury–expensive*) is owned by one of the best chefs in northern France. The rooms are distributed between several delectable locations, while Olivier Roellinger oversees two restaurants, **Le Relais Gourmand** the luxury option, **Le Bistrot Marin** offering more reasonably priced fare. **★★L'Emeraude**, 7 Quai Thomas, **t** 02 99 89 61 76, **f** 02 99 89 88 21 (*moderate–inexpensive*) has stylish rooms and a restaurant. The **★★Hôtel de la Pointe du Grouin**, **t** 02 99 89 60 55, **f** 02 99 89 92 22 (*moderate*) has a location to die for, on a headland looking across the Bay of Mont St-Michel. It's a bit pricey, but rooms and restaurant have sensational views.

Roscoff

Once described as a 'buccaneers' hideout, a corsairs' den' by Breton poet Tristan Corbière, old Roscoff is a delightfully genteel resort today, even if the port can seem somewhat chaotic in summer. The silver sailing ships crossing blue waters depicted on Roscoff's coat of arms recall the times before yachts and ferries became the main shipping interest, when the local ship-owners, corsairs and smugglers were engaged in a centuries-long struggle with the English. On a more positive, diplomatic note, Roscoff is where Mary Queen of Scots landed in 1548, coming over as a child bride to join the French court. In 1746 Bonnie Prince Charlie, Young Pretender to the English throne, landed here, having escaped from England disguised as 'Betty Burke'.

One of the joys of Roscoff today is simply promenading up and down the quays. The protective sea walls stick out at odd angles into the bay, like unruly tentacles. The old port is always full of bustle with the boats for the island of Batz, the fishing fleet, and, in the holidays, yachts. Behind the quays, the merry steeple of the central **church of Notre-Dame de Croaz Batz** looks as if it's built out of stone bells. Below these graceful Renaissance lanterns, the rest of the church, completed in 1548, is in Flamboyant Gothic style. The shipowners of the period contributed considerable amounts to its building, which probably explains why carvings of sailing vessels were permitted in the stone. Around the church, the grand granite houses of the 16th and 17th centuries, often with stylish dormer windows, reflect the prosperity of some of Roscoff's most successful merchants. Roscoff's **Musée des Johnnies** (*open 15 June–15 Sept Wed–Sun 10–12 and 3–6; closed Tues; adm*), newly relocated to Rue Brizeux, tells the story of the more modest Breton onion-sellers who cycled forth to make a living selling their veg on British doorsteps. As this is a tale of Breton-British cooperation and neighbourliness, you'll find several elements in English at the museum.

The didactic if decrepit **aquarium** (*open July and Aug daily 10–12 and 1–7; Easter–June and Sept, daily 1–6; adm*) occupies an outmoded part of a marine biology research centre west along the shore. You can take a close look here at Breton fish, molluscs, algae and other marine life displayed in simple aquaria. West again, and another bay

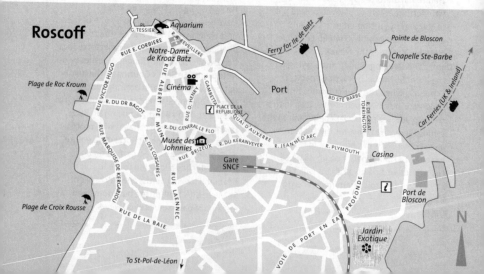

Getting to Roscoff

Brittany Ferries' ships (in France, **t** 0825 828 828 or **t** 02 98 29 28 00, *see* p.11) arrive at the Port de Bloscon, a 15–20min walk east of town.

Getting Around

For **taxis**, try: Allô Taxis Roscoff, **t** 02 98 69 74 38; Armor Taxi, **t/f** 02 98 69 70 67; Taxis Goarnisson, **t/f** 02 98 29 74 53; or Taxis Stéphane, **t** 02 98 61 25 06.

Three companies run **ferries** to the nearby island of Batz: Compagnie Maritime Armein, **t** 02 98 61 77 75, **f** 02 98 61 74 04; Compagnie Maritime Armor Excursion, **t** 02 98 61 79 66, **f** 02 98 61 74 07; and Compagnie Finistérienne-Vedettes de l'Ile de Batz, **t** 02 98 61 78 87, **f** 02 98 61 75 94. The walk across the spectacular footbridge to the embarkation point alone is worth the trip. The trip costs around €5–6 and takes 15mins.

Car Hire
Roscoff Automobiles, 69 Rue A. de Mun, **t** 02 98 69 72 09, **f** 02 98 69 76 94.

Tourist Information

Roscoff: 46 Rue Gambetta, **t** 02 98 61 12 13, **f** 02 98 69 75 75, *www.sb-roscoff.fr/Roscoff*,

tourisme.roscoff@wanadoo.fr. Ile de Batz: **t** 02 98 61 75 70.

Market Days
Roscoff: Wednesday.

Shopping

Algae is very big in northern Brittany, and Boutique Algoplus on Quai Charles de Gaulle specializes in algae products. **Rue Gambetta** parallel to this quay has several specialist shops, including La Belle Iloise selling Breton fish produce, and Bleu Marine specializing in regional pottery. Along **Rue Réveillère** are further interesting attractions, including local crafts and pâtisseries, plus Breton clothes at M.F.P. Tradition. A bit out of the centre, Usitex, Le Rhun, also sells Breton ware. Back with algae, *see* Thalado below.

Where to Stay and Eat

Roscoff ✉ 29680
★★★Le Brittany, 22 Bd Ste-Barbe, **t** 02 98 69 70 78, **f** 02 98 61 13 29, *www.hotel.brittany.com* (*expensive*). Great if you stay in the old part of the hotel, wonderfully located by the old port. The rooms in the annexe are less interesting. The cuisine at the Yachtman

opens out in front of you, the **Anse de l'Aber**, small beaches tucked into its eastern shore. Behind the **Plage de Roc Kroum** stands the smart modern **Institut Marin RockKroum** for seawater treatments (**t** 02 98 29 20 00, **f** 02 98 61 22 73). Also in this neighbourhood, you can visit **Thalado**, a centre devoted to algae. It takes its seaweedy subject seriously – after all, as it reminds us, we are in the area with the 'richest seaweed bed in the world'. It is quite mind-boggling to discover all the uses to which algae are now put, from cuisine to cosmetics. No prizes for guessing what the boutique Le Comptoir des Algues sells.

Moving east of the centre, the **Pointe de Bloscon**, with its tiny Chapelle Ste-Barbe, is whitewashed to serve as a seamark for boats. The seawater in the giant **tanks** (*visits possible working weekdays, 9.30–12 and 2–5; adm*) beyond the chapel is regularly replaced by the tide for the lobsters, crayfish and crabs reared here. Approaching the ferry terminal, **Algoplus**, a maker of algae products, opens its doors to visitors weekdays, and has another seaweed boutique here. The **Jardin Exotique de Roscoff** (*open Nov, Dec, Feb and March Wed–Sun and Mon 2–5pm; April–June and Sept–Oct daily 10.30–12.30 and 2–6; July and Aug daily 10–7; closed Jan; adm*) below the ferry restaurant is adventurous. The place has a heated, covered pool with jet streams.

★★★Talabardon, 27 Place Lacaze, **t** 02 98 61 24 95, **f** 02 98 61 10 54, *www.transtel.TO/Talabardon* (*expensive–moderate*). Comfortable hotel in an imposing 19th-century building, some rooms looking on to the sea, others on to the church square. The restaurant has panoramic views.

★★★Le Gulf Stream, 7 Rue Marquise de Kergariou, **t** 02 98 69 73 19, **f** 02 98 61 11 89, *www.hotel-roscoff.com* (*moderate*). A modern hotel with many attractions, including sea views, a heated swimming pool in the well-flowered garden extending down to the beach, and excellent seafood (*moderate*). The *institut marin* for seawater treatments is just a hundred metres away.

★★Les Alizés, Quai d'Auxerre, **t** 02 98 69 72 22, **f** 02 98 61 11 40 (*moderate*). Good-value option, some rooms overlooking the port. No restaurant.

★★Les Chardons Bleus, 4 Rue Réveillière, **t** 02 98 69 72 03, **f** 02 98 61 27 86 (*inexpensive*). Well-kept hotel in a Renaissance house in the centre of town, with tastefully decorated rooms and a restaurant.

★★Hôtel des Arcades, 15 Rue Réveillière, **t** 02 98 69 70 45, **f** 02 98 61 12 34, *www.acdev.com* (*inexpensive*). Good-value option, rooms recently redone, some with sea views. The dining room looks out on to the Channel.

★★Aux Tamaris, 49 Rue Edouard Corbière, **t** 02 98 61 22 99, **f** 02 98 69 74 36, *www.auxtamaris.com* (*inexpensive*). A welcoming address well located by the sea, with some bright rooms looking out to Batz. No restaurant.

Le Temps de Vivre, Place de l'Eglise, **t** 02 98 61 27 28, **f** 02 98 61 19 46 (*expensive*). Excellent restaurant in an old corsair's house. The cuisine is luxurious and inventive.

L'Ecume des Jours, Quai d'Auxerre, **t** 02 98 61 22 83 (*moderate*). Utterly delightful, set in a 16th-century house looking out to sea. Good value for fine cooking.

Le Surcouf, 14 Rue Réveillière, **t** 02 98 69 71 89 (*moderate*). Pretty good-value seafood menus.

Crêperie de la Poste, 12 Rue Gambetta, **t** 02 98 69 72 81. Appealing rustic décor.

Crêperie Ti Saozon, 30 Rue Gambetta, **t** 02 98 69 70 89. Only open in the evenings and very small, so reserve a place if you want to try crêpes a cut above the average, with interesting fillings such as artichoke hearts with cream of seaweed.

Ile de Batz ✉ 29253

Hotels **Roch Armor**, **t** 02 98 61 78 28 and the **Grand Hôtel**, **t** 02 98 61 78 06 (*both cheap*), are at the port, and have a restaurant. Further places to eat cluster around the harbour.

terminal looks out over the spectacular Bay of Morlaix. Palm trees, cacti and plants from the southern hemisphere prosper here, reflecting the surprisingly mild climate. In this quarter, you can also visit Roscoff's Second World War museum, or a couple more beaches.

Ile de Batz

As Breton islands go, Batz, lying very visibly just off the coast at Roscoff, has remained relatively agricultural and unspoilt. The whole island is under 4km long and around 1.5km wide, so you can walk around the coastal path in 3–4hrs if you apply yourself. The main **village** stretches round the large **Baie de Kernoc'h**. Plots of vegetables still manage to keep their place among the village houses. The 19th-century church contains a statue of Dark Ages saint Pol. History and legend are hard to disentangle from the Dark Ages. This Celtic saint came from Wales to Brittany in the 6th century, supposedly having spent some time at King Marc'h of Cornwall's court at Tintagel, his fiery lord deeply upset to see him go. Pol set up a monastery first on Ushant, and then one on Batz. Legend also credits him with many miracles, and with fighting off a dragon (for which you might read paganism) that was terrorizing Batz, devouring both livestock and people.

It's a pretty walk to the eastern tip of the island to find the **Jardin Delaselle** (*open April–Nov 2–6; adm*). After Georges Delaselle had fallen in love with the spot and decided to convert it into a garden in the late 1890s, he had an artificial string of dunes dug to protect the site. In the process, many mysterious old tombs were discovered. Then Delaselle imported all manner of exotic plants. Over 40 species of palms are nurtured here, the largest outdoor collection in Brittany. It does seem extraordinary that in such a windy, salty environment so many subtropical plants survive, but this part of the Brittany coast remains fairly mild all year round.

Batz's best-known **beaches**, the Grève Blanche and the Porz Mellok, lie nearby; the sand is sometimes likened to flour, such is its colour and texture. The ruins of the Chapelle Ste-Anne, also in the east, are the remains of a Romanesque building from around the 10th century, which may stand on the site of Pol's original monastery. Heading up to the **north side** of Batz, the wild reefs stick out sharply. The **western side** of the island is dominated by the imposing 19th-century **lighthouse**.

Day Trips from Roscoff

St-Pol-de-Léon

St-Pol-de-Léon was long the main religious centre for this area of Brittany, its history going back to the Welsh evangelizer Pol (*see* opposite). In the Middle Ages, the city became one of the major stops on the Tro Breizh, the pilgrimage route round Brittany. Only at the Revolution did the place lose its important religious status as the centre of a diocese. The city's dramatic religious architecture still dominates the flat fertile plain for miles around; the cathedral is eclipsed by the staggering spire of Notre-Dame du Kreisker, the tallest in Brittany, commissioned out of pride by Léonard merchants, not the Church. 'Of a worrying lightness' is the way the Breton art historian Victor-Henry Debidour described its steeple, the defiant arrow shooting over 75m (246ft) skywards. Not surprisingly, Notre-Dame du Kreisker looks rather top-heavy close up. Some of it was built in the 14th century, but the flamboyance of 15th-century Gothic triumphs. There are nearly 170 steps up to the viewing gallery.

Getting There

There are regular **buses** from Roscoff, taking about 10mins.

Tourist Information

St-Pol-de-Léon ✉ 29250: Place de l'Evêché, t 02 98 69 05 69, f 02 98 69 01 20.

Market Days
St-Pol-de-Léon: Tuesday.

Eating Out

La Pomme d'Api, 49 Rue Verderel, t 02 98 69 04 36 (*moderate*). Refined decor in an old Breton house, and excellent food.

Le Passiflore, 28 Rue Pen ar Pont, t 02 98 69 00 52. A cheap hotel, with bargain menus at the Routier workers' restaurant.

Crêperie Les Fromentines, 18 Rue Cadiou, t 02 98 69 23 52. Good crêpes, close to the Kreisker's soaring steeple.

The Gothic **cathedral** went up painfully slowly, building-work on the nave and aisles lasting through the 13th and 14th centuries, the side chapels and choir completed in the course of the 15th and 16th centuries. The long nave with its pointed Gothic arches and Gothic decoration has a sober simplicity. Surprisingly, the internal stone came from Caen in Normandy, in contrast to the Breton granite employed on the outside. Saint Pol's tomb lies by the main altar, his supposed skull in an aisle reliquary, as well as a miraculous bell which a fish is said to have taken from enraged King Marc'hs court. The great organ was the work of Robert Dallam, who also made the one in King's College, Cambridge.

The streets around these churches contain splendid houses from the 16th and 17th centuries, but the commercial bustle from whose proceeds they were built doesn't seem very apparent today, except on market days.

Morlaix

The historic port of Morlaix is tucked well out of sight of the sea, its estuary guarded by the spectacular 16th-century island fort of the Château du Taureau, built to protect the place after a surpise English raid in 1522. Through medieval times, Morlaix sailors had often been a thorn in the side of the English. Trade in Breton cloth flourished though, especially with Iberia, and may explain the town's distinctive *maisons à lanterne*, with features possibly adapted from the Spanish patio courtyard.

Start a tour of Morlaix in the shadow of the unmissable great 19th-century **viaduct** in the centre. Climb up either side of the valley and take the path leading through the viaduct's monumental arches. From there you can enjoy the drama of the architecture and the views. Come down on to **Rue Ange de Guernisac**, passing the Flamboyant Gothic church of **St-Melaine**. The slate-covered and timberframe sides of the houses give the street great appeal. Picturesque alleyways known as *venelles* lead up the slopes. Reaching Place des Viarmes, turn down Rue Carnot for the **Grand'Rue**, the main shopping street. Look upwards to see the old houses leaning in towards each other. For those interested in architecture, No.9, the Maison de Pondalez, is a 16th-century house open to visitors all year round.

Head for the **Eglise et Musée des Jacobins** (*open July and Aug daily 10–12.30 and 2–6.30; Easter–June, Sept and Oct daily 10–12 and 2–6; rest of year 10–12 and 2–5, but closed Tues and Sat am*). The 13th- and 14th-century monastic buildings have been much abused since the Revolution, when they were turned into stables. Before that, and of profound consequence for Breton culture, the monk Albert Le Grand studied here in the early 17th century. He wrote a book on the life of the Breton saints, *La Vie des saints en Bretagne*, which would be a Breton bestseller for centuries. Now the monastery is a history and arts museum. Inside, the Gothic arches are put to good use, providing elegant separations between the various collections, which range from items on the history of Morlaix, old paintings of the town and religious statuary from the town's lost religious establishments to modern art. The stained-glass rose window of the apse counts as one of the most beautiful and original exhibits.

The grandiose Breton lantern-house, the **Maison de la Duchesse Anne** (*open April–Sept Mon–Sat;* **t** *02 98 88 23 26 to check times; adm*), overlooks sizeable Place

Getting There

Morlaix is 30km from Roscoff and you can easily reach it by **train** or by **bus**.

Tourist Information

Morlaix ✉ **29600**: Place des Otages, 29600 Morlaix, **t** 02 98 62 14 94, **f** 02 98 63 84 87.

Market Days
Morlaix: Saturday.

Eating Out

Hôtel Europe, 1 Rue d'Aiguillon, **t 02 98 62 11 99, **f** 02 98 88 83 38 (*inexpensive*). The most stylish establishment in the centre, with excellent food (*moderate*) served in the extravagant dining room.

Brasserie de l'Orf next door, also owned by the Europe. Quite different to look at, it has a modern split-level design with a teak-tinted aesthetic for the bar downstairs. The cuisine is also modern, but is not particularly cheap.

La Marée Bleue, 3 Rampe St-Melaine, **t** 02 98 63 24 21 (*moderate*). Warm, cosy, and quite quiet, offering well-prepared seafood in refined surroundings displaying more than a hint of the marine.

Brocéliande, 5 Rue des Bouchers, **t** 02 98 88 73 78 (*moderate*). Looks a bit like a porcelain museum inside. The food as well as the décor is refined.

Les Bains Douches, 45 Allée du Poan Ben, **t** 02 98 63 83 83 (*moderate*). Set in the most eccentric of locations, having taken over a former public baths, décor 1900. You have to cross the water to the door via a footbridge. Inside it is large and pleasant with a (firmly redundant-looking) piano and leather *banquettes*. The food is typical French *bistrot* fare.

Le St-Melaine, 75 Rue Ange de Guernisac, **t** 02 98 88 08 79 (*cheap*). The closest to the viaduct, a friendly, family-run small hotel with good old-fashioned French food (*cheap*) served in the dining room.

Tempo, Quai de Tréguier, **t** 02 98 63 29 11 (*cheap*). The trendiest place in town at the moment, with a terrace overlooking the port. The food is basic.

Crêperie du Kiosque, 11 Place des Otages, **t** 02 98 88 41 40 (*cheap*). Quite sophisticated, very central and makes crêpes in the old-fashioned way.

L'Hermine, 35 Rue Ange de Guernisac, **t** 02 98 88 10 91 (*cheap*). More rustic and very pretty, the crêpes again traditionally made.

Allende. It may appear in a sadly grimy state on the outside, but the architecture and carvings provide entertaining surprises. The numerous figures on the façade include saints and archetypal Gothic figures. Inside, the cavernous central room stretches way up to the roof. This is really like a covered patio, just provided with a monumental fireplace, and is characteristic of Morlaix's *maisons à lanterne*. The inner courtyard was traditionally covered over by an opaque roofing from which a lantern was hung to give light to the silo-sized room, hence the name. Here, the most splendid feature is the elaborate spiral staircase, decorated with more rich carvings, from saints to a chained wolf. Nearby, the **Eglise St-Mathieu** also contains several intriguing carvings.

To finish a tour of Morlaix, wander back north in the direction of the viaduct, maybe stopping at a café to try Coreff, the locally brewed beer, a Breton bitter. Continue on to the **port** and quays, where you'll see the elegant 18th-century **Manufacture de Tabac** buildings, designed by the king's architect, Blondel. This splendid early factory manufactured cigars up to the end of the 20th century, but is now due to close. On the opposite bank, the **Feunten ar Saozon** (Fountain of the Saxons, i.e. the English) is said to have run red with blood when sailors on a raid across the Channel got drunk on alcohol they had pillaged, and were easily slaughtered on the spot.

Touring from Roscoff

You'll find that the sights are reliably open Easter–Oct, 10–12 and 2–5 at least, unless otherwise stated, and charge adm.

Day 1: Tourist and Prehistoric Man

Morning: Follow the coast road southeast to **Carantec**, an excellent introduction to Breton resorts, with its smart feel and fine beaches, plus a small maritime museum.

Lunch: Locquénolé, the charming next resort, has a couple of simple, appealing choices: **Le Bruly**, Route de Carantec, t 02 98 72 21 11 (*moderate*), looking down on Morlaix Bay, and the **Auberge du Vieux Chêne**, Place de la Liberté, t 02 98 72 24 27 (*moderate–cheap*) on a delightful village square.

Afternoon: Cross the river at **Morlaix** (*see* p.138) and follow the coast north to the **Cairn de Barnenez** (*guided tours only*), possibly the largest neolithic burial barrow in Europe, an awesome dual structure, the oldest part dating back to c.4500 BC, the whole lot rediscovered by accident in the 1950s. At the nearby unkempt resort of **Primel-Trégastel**, clamber round the headland fortified back in the Bronze Age.

Dinner and sleeping: Locquirec with its nine beaches is a delightful place to spend an evening. ★★★**Le Grand Hôtel des Bains**, t 02 98 67 41 02, f 02 98 67 44 60 (*expensive*) is a joy of a seaside hotel, with splendid balconied rooms, a fine restaurant, follies in the garden, and an indoor pool in case of bad weather. The **Hôtel du Port**, t 02 98 67 42 10 (*inexpensive*) is at the heart of the summer action by the port, its restaurant a great place to enjoy the bustle.

Day 2: A Legendary Coastline

Morning: The Irishman St Efflam left his wife Enora to come and Christianize the area around the superb long wood-backed **Grève de St-Michel** bay in the Dark Ages – all sorts of dragon-slaying supposedly went on here. In the church in nearby **Ploumilliau**, the statue of l'Ankou, the Grim Reaper of many Breton legends, stands out. On the coast, the **Pointe de Séhar** is an extraordinary spit of pebbles extending into the sea, the **Pointe du Dourven**, a beautiful high, pine-shaded promontory with a contemporary art centre.

Lunch: For a rustic lunch in a lovely location, try either a simple grill or crêpes at the **Auberge St-Erwan**, Trédrez, t 02 96 46 48 80, or ★★**Ar Vro**, t 02 96 46 48 80, in the beautiful hillside village of Le Yaudet with its traces of prehistoric ritual and its superstition-laden chapel.

Afternoon: Modern civlization comes as a shock round the corner, with an array of modern museums at **Pleumeur-Bodou**, including the high-tech centre on satellites in the Radôme, sitting like a giant golf ball on the horizon. **Trébeurden** brings you back to normal Breton seaside delights, with several beaches, the central ones dominated by Le Castel, a natural fort of rock.

Dinner and sleeping: For delightful rooms with sea views and maritime touches, plus a dining room like the interior of a ship, but serving the most refined cuisine, try the ★★★**Manoir de Lan Kérellec**, t 02 96 23 50 09, f 02 96 23 66 88 (*luxury–moderate*). Down the slope, but still in a great position for appreciating sunsets, ★★**Ker An Nod**, t 02 96 23 50 21, f 02 96 23 62 14 (*inexpensive*) has a great restaurant with sea views and neat little rooms.

Day 3: Outrageous Pink Rocks

Morning: L'Ile Grande has an interesting bird centre. But this pales somewhat compared with the fantastic rocks of **Trégastel**, for instance the Skull, the Die, or the Pile of Crêpes. The little aquarium is set among sensational huge boulders.

Lunch: Make the most of the rock views of Trégastel at ★★★**Armoric**, t 02 96 23 88 16 (*moderate*), with its reliable restaurant, or at ★★**Beau Séjour**, t 02 96 23 88 02 (*moderate*), with a good restaurant terrace.

Afternoon: Enjoy more absurd rock displays on your way to neighbouring **Perros-Guirec**. Here go on a boat trip to the **Sept-Iles bird reserve** (*book seats on t 02 96 23 22 47 or t 02 96 91 11 13*). Or simply enjoy a great seaside resort, with several big beaches to choose from.

Dinner and sleeping: The two smart places to stay and eat at in Perros are ★★★**Les Feux des Iles**, 53 Bd Clemenceau, **t** 02 96 23 22 94, **f** 02 96 91 07 30 (*expensive–moderate*), with wonderful views to the Sept-Iles, and ★★★**Le Manoir du Sphinx**, 67 Chemin de la Messe, **t** 02 96 23 25 42, **f** 02 96 91 26 13 (*moderate*), a typical Belle Epoque villa with great views. For a very Breton experience and meal, book at ★★**Ker Ys**, 12 Rue du Maréchal Foch, **t** 02 96 23 22 16, **f** 02 96 23 28 36 (*inexpensive*).

Day 4: Like a Meteorite Shower

Morning: Follow the otherworldly coast road east to **Port Blanc** and the coast above **Plougrescant**, places which look as if a shower of meteorites has rained down on them. The little city of **Tréguier** is more soberly attractive, its cathedral the highlight, wonderfully eccentric, and arguably the most appealing in Brittany. Inside, look out for the tombs of Duke Jean V of Brittany, and of 13th-century saint Yves, a local boy canonized by the papacy and revered by the region's poor for his fairness. Behind the lacy Gothic tracery of the cloister lies a kind of museum of medieval tomb effigies.

Lunch: Down at Tréguier's port, ★★★**Aigue-Marine**, **t** 02 96 92 97 00 (*moderate*), prepares a good lunch, as does **Le St-Bernard**, **t** 02 96 92 20 77 (*moderate*).

Afternoon: The peninsula east of Tréguier ends with an amazing tongue of pebbles, the **Sillon de Talbert**. You almost feel like you're walking on water as you walk along it. Or inland, **Pontrieux** has a quiet charm and craft shops. **Paimpol**, synonymous with the gruelling Breton fishing voyages to Newfoundland, appears a bit of a coward of a port, well-hidden from the sea.

Dinner: Dine in style in one of the few grand old quayside houses left in Paimpol, now the ★★★**Repaire de Kerroc'h**, **t** 02 96 20 50 13, **f** 02 96 22 07 46 (*moderate*); or the **Restaurant du Port**, **t** 02 96 20 83 18 (*moderate*) has a first-floor dining room overlooking the harbour, the obvious place for a good seafood platter.

Sleeping: To be in poll position for the ferry to Bréhat, stay either at ★★★**Le Barbu**, Pointe de l'Arcouest, **t** 02 96 55 86 98, **f** 02 96 55 73 87 (*expensive–moderate*) close to the landing stage, its rooms looking over to the archipelago, or at ★★**Le Grand Large**, Loguivy-de-la-Mer, **t** 02 96 20 90 18, **f** 02 96 20 87 10 (*inexpensive*), also in a superb coastal location.

Day 5: Outrageous Orange Rocks

Morning: The archipelago of **Bréhat** with its exquisite rock collection is surely the most beautiful in Brittany. Book well in advance for the ferry, **t** 02 96 55 86 99, **f** 02 96 55 73 96, as it's hugely popular. Leave the car on the mainland; you can go round Bréhat on foot or by bike.

Lunch: For a laid-back lunch of *moules-frites* or fresh seafood, **La Potinière** on Plage de Guerzido, **t** 02 96 20 00 29 (*moderate*) is the bright place to go. Or try one of the hotels listed for the evening.

Afternoon: Bréhat itself is really two islands joined by the smallest of bridges. The main settlements are on the south island. **Le Bourg** is quite attractive, centred around a cheerful circular square. Head up to the Chapelle St-Michel for fine views, although you can appreciate the archipelago from all round the island. There's also a very pretty 17th-century tidal mill you can visit. The **north island** is wilder, notably at the Phare du Paon lighthouse with its pink rocks and chasm.

Dinner and sleeping: The restaurant terraces of ★★**Hôtel Bellevue**, Port-Clos, **t** 02 96 20 00 05, **f** 02 96 20 06 06 (*moderate*) are invaded every time a tourist boat arrives, but this is a lovely place at which to stay on after the others have left, if you've managed to book early enough. It's pricey for what it is. So too is ★★**La Vieille Auberge**, Le Bourg, **t** 02 96 20 00 24, **f** 02 96 20 05 12 (*moderate–inexpensive*), the small hotel in the main village, with a restaurant. Otherwise, return to a hotel on the mainland.

For suggestions for touring Brittany west of Roscoff, see 'Touring from Brest', pp.149–50.

Brest

Brest overlooks one of the most beautiful bays in France, the huge Rade de Brest, a confusion of headlands stretching out into the sea. For centuries, being so well protected, it was France's main naval harbour, and it has a fascinating history, but in the Second World War it was turned into a major Nazi naval and submarine base, and was smashed to smithereens by Allied bombing. Brest's architecture is therefore mainly modern, an American-looking grid-plan of streets sloping down to the string of ports. The naval harbour now counts as only the second most important such base in France, after Toulon on the Mediterranean (*see* pp.288–93), but there are still thousands of sailors stationed here. Central Brest is roughly divided into two by the Penfeld river, the naval town stretching to the west, civilian and student Brest to the

Getting to Brest

Buzz (*see* p.6) flies from London Stansted.

Getting from the Airport

Brest-Guipavas airport (**t** 02 98 32 01 00) is around 10km northeast of the town centre. A bus shuttle service is planned, but for the present a **taxi** to the centre will cost €15.

Getting Around

The **bus station** is next to the SNCF **train station**, Place du 19ᵉ R.I. For **bus** service information, contact BIBUS, **t** 02 98 80 30 30, *www.bibus.fr*. For **taxis**, try Allô Taxis, **t** 02 98 42 11 11 or Radio Taxis Brestois, **t** 02 98 80 43 43 or **t** 02 98 80 18 01.

Car Hire

ABL, by the station, **t** 02 98 43 99 99, **f** 02 98 80 28 70.
ADA, at the airport, **t** 02 98 84 63 36.
Europcar, 45 Rue de Keranfurust, **t** 0820 820 448 or **t** 02 98 02 76 76, **f** 02 98 02 81 50.

Tourist Information

Brest: Pl de la Liberté, **t** 02 98 44 24 96, **f** 02 98 44 53 73, *Office.de.Tourisme.Brest@wanadoo.fr*.

Market Days

The **Marché de St-Martin**, Mon–Sat am, is interesting, while on Sunday morning make for the **Rue de Lyon** market.

Shopping

Rue de Siam is the place to start, with a wide range of shops. Les Lutins has one of the best choices of Breton gifts such as clothes and pottery, and Celtic-style jewellery.

On **Rue Ducouédic** at the bottom of Rue de Siam, A l'Elégant Marin does a good line in Breton clothes.

Up **Rue Jean Jaurès** behind the town hall you'll find big stores, including those in two malls, one of them, Espace Jaurès, just recently opened. At the **Port de Commerce**, Le Roi de Bretagne has an extensive choice of Breton specialities, including the culinary.

Where to Stay

Brest ✉ 29200
★★★Holiday Inn, 41 Rue Branda, **t** 02 98 80 84 00, **f** 02 98 80 84 84 (*expensive*). Spacious rooms in the centre of town.
★★★Océania, 82 Rue de Siam, **t** 02 98 80 66 66, **f** 02 98 80 65 50 (*expensive–moderate*). Spacious rooms on Brest's most famous street and some surprising decorative details within. The cuisine is good.
★★★La Corniche, 1 Rue Amiral Nicol, Porte Grande Rivière, **t** 02 98 45 12 42, **f** 02 98 49 01 53 (*moderate, menu for residents only*). Very comfortable rooms in an old Breton house outside the centre. There's a tennis court and a garden with terrace.
★★★Le Belvédère, Ste-Anne-du-Portzic (west of Brest), **t** 02 98 31 86 00, **f** 02 98 31 86 39

east. Océanopolis, the best aquarium in Brittany, lies east again, by the modern marina, where you can board boats round the Rade. But the grittier harbours to the west, and the centre of Brest, have their appeal too.

Central Brest and its Museums

The architecture of the **Château de Brest** has been greatly altered since the famed 14th-century chronicler Froissart claimed it to be one of the largest castles in the world, but this fort is still daunting. Most of the castle is occupied by the French maritime authorities, but the front section houses Brest's **Musée National de la Marine** (*open April–15 Sept daily 10–6.30; 16 Sept–15 Dec and Feb–March Wed–Mon 10–12 and 2–6*). This naval museum is devoted mainly to the great shipbuilding tradition in Brest. But certain major events in the history of the castle and the town are

(*moderate*). Also outside the centre, in a modern building with spectacular views over the Rade de Brest. Bright, comfortable rooms and reliable traditional cuisine.

**Abalys, 7 Av Clemenceau, t 02 98 44 21 86, f 02 98 43 68 32 (*inexpensive*). Good sea views and quite good value.

**Astoria, 9 Rue Traverse, t 02 98 80 19 10, f 02 98 80 52 41 (*inexpensive–cheap*). Near Rue de Siam, welcoming, and clean.

**Citôtel de la Gare, 4 Bd Gambetta, t 02 98 44 47 01, f 02 98 43 34 07 (*inexpensive*). Another good choice with sea views.

**B&B City, 45 Rue du Vieux St-Marc, t 02 98 42 62 62, f 02 98 42 62 00 (*inexpensive*). Rooms out east, close to the quay from which boats leave for tours of the Rade.

*Le Pasteur, 29 Rue Louis Pasteur, t 02 98 46 08 73, f 02 98 43 46 80 (*cheap*). Probably the best of the one-star hotels.

*St-Louis, 6 Rue d'Algésiras, t 02 98 44 23 91, f 02 98 46 07 94 (*cheap*). Central location.

Auberge de Jeunesse, 5 Rue de Kerbriant, t 02 98 41 90 41, f 02 98 41 82 66 (*cheap*). First-rate, in a park near the beach.

Eating Out

Le Nouveau Rossini, 22 Rue du Commandant Drogou, t 02 98 47 90 00 (*expensive*). In its own quiet grounds, this is one of the finest restaurants in Brest. *Closed Sun pm and Mon.*

Le Vatel, 23 Rue de Fautras, t 02 98 44 51 02, (*expensive–moderate*). Also top of the range. *Closed Sat lunch, Sun pm and Mon.*

La Fleur de Sel, 15 Bis, Rue de Lyon, t 02 98 44 38 65 (*moderate*). Near the centre, Art Deco feel and good reputation for refined cuisine. *Closed weekends.*

Le Ruffé, 1 bis Rue Yves Collet, t 02 98 46 07 70 (*moderate*). Pleasant, reliable. *Closed Sun pm.*

Crêperie Moderne, 34 Rue Algésiras, t 02 98 44 44 36 (*moderate*). Despite the name, oldest-established crêperie in the centre. *Closed Sun lunch.*

La Maison de l'Océan, 2 Quai de la Douane, t 02 98 80 44 84 (*moderate*). By the Port de Commerce, buzzing, popular fresh seafood restaurant with some outdoor tables.

Aux Patrouilleurs, 26 Quai de la Douane, t 02 98 44 10 25 (*moderate*). Another pleasant choice at the Port de Commerce.

Ma Petite Folie, t 02 98 42 44 42, f 02 98 41 43 68 (*moderate*). One of the most delightful restaurants in Brest, set in a former lobster-fishing boat at the Moulin Blanc marina, serving excellent seafood in appropriately eccentric surroundings. *Closed Sun.*

L'Amour de Pomme de Terre, 23 Rue des Halles St-Louis, t 02 98 43 48 51 (*moderate–cheap*). Devoted to the Breton-beloved potato.

La Chaumière, 25 Rue Zola, t 02 98 44 18 60 (*cheap*). Simpler, good-value central restaurant. *Closed Sat lunch and Sun.*

Blé Noir, Vallon du Stang Alar, at the northern end of the public gardens, t 02 98 41 84 66 (*cheap*). The best-located crêperie in Brest.

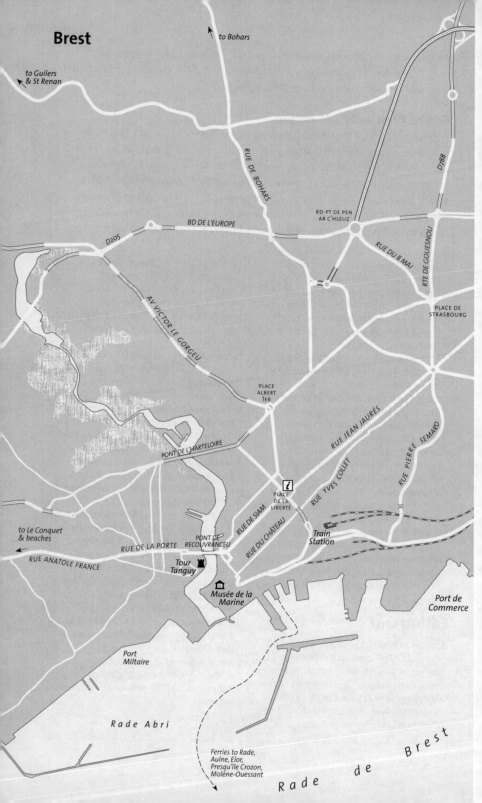

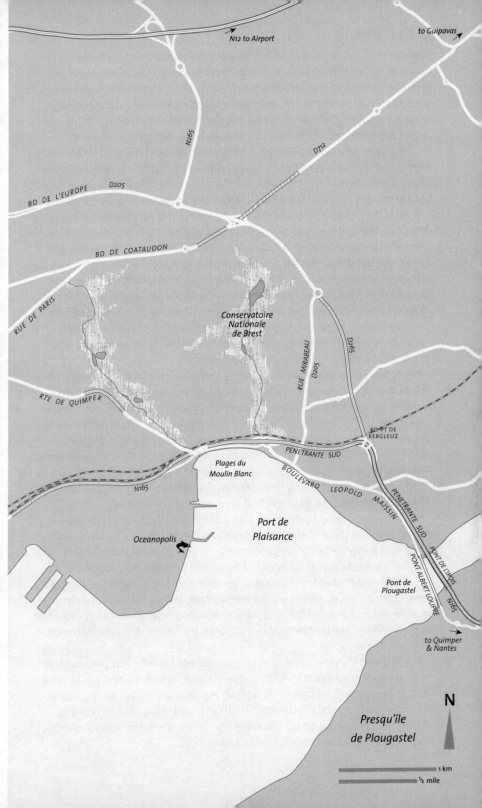

told along the way, as you wander from tower to tower and along the castle ramparts. Astonishingly, the bottom of the walls formed part of an impressive 3rd-century Roman fort, giving an indication of this harbour's credentials. Its great naval importance dates from the 17th century, when Cardinal Richelieu, and then Colbert, made it the largest naval port in France. The navy became referred to simply as La Royale. Prisoners were cruelly exploited to work on the vast vessels built here. Incidentally, in 1689, the deposed King James II of Britain left from Brest with a French fleet to invade Ireland as part of his campaign to regain the throne; he returned here after his defeat by William III at the Battle of the Boyne the following year, and lived out the rest of his days in France. The Stuart ex-king would never regain the throne.

Some of the fabulously detailed old-school paintings in Brest's **Musée des Beaux-Arts** (*open Mon and Wed–Sat 10–11.45 and 2–6, Sun and public hols 2–6; closed Tues; adm*) offer fine views of Brest in its Ancien Régime heyday. But this museum is best known for its postimpressionist collection, notably works by the Pont-Aven school; the lush green and yellow patches of Paul Sérusier's *Les Blés verts au Pouldu*, painted in 1890, make it one of his most appealing works. Emile Bernard's depiction of the pink rocks of St-Briac in typical *cloisonné* style is also outstanding. The painting adopted as the symbol of the museum is Georges Lacombe's view of nearby Camaret's cliffs, taking on vaguely human shapes against a bilious yellow sea. An engrossing collection of paintings depicts Breton religious processions.

Rue de Siam, Brest's most famous street, is now embellished with big modern black granite fountains streaming with water. In 1688 the thoroughfare witnessed the arrival of some of the earliest exotic Eastern foreign visitors to France: ambassadors sent by the King of Siam (now Thailand) to visit King Louis XIV's court landed in Brest and paraded up here, carrying with them the most precious of letters, engraved in gold. The name 'Rue de Siam' commemorates the visit. The way leads up to the **Place de la Liberté** with its town hall. Here you really feel as if you've arrived in 1950s urban America. Behind the Hôtel de Ville, the Rue Jean Jaurès leads up to the **Quartier St-Martin** where you can go in search of a few traces of pre-war Brest.

Cross the Penfeld river by the massive Pont de Recouvrance, long Europe's largest raising bridge, to take a look at the medieval **Tour Tanguy** (*open June–Sept daily 10–12 and 2–7; Oct–May Wed–Thurs 2–5, weekends 2–6*). It's been turned into a little museum on Brest's mainly vanished history. Further west, the shore is dominated by the military quarters and military boats. Schengen Agreement and British passport-holders can go on a guided tour of the **military Arsenal** (*open July–15 Sept daily 9–10.30 and 2–4*) on presentation of the non-offending proof of identity. Construction of France's latest and controversial aircraft carrier, the *Charles de Gaulle*, was recently completed here.

Heading east from the centre, Brestois enjoy the setting of the **Port de Commerce**, with its enormous docks, some of its vast berths built for supertankers. The portside bars and restaurants are popular on summer evenings, and in July and August, the free music concerts of the 'Jeudis du Port' attract crowds every Thursday evening. During the day, consider taking a **boat trip** from here to the military port and across the Rade with Vedettes Armoricaines, **t** 02 98 44 44 04.

Up behind the Port de Commerce lies a minute portion of US territory, 424 square metres to be precise. A pink granite tower of a US war memorial marks the spot. An earlier memorial, erected by the Brestois to commemorate the stopover here of US troops in the First World War, was destroyed in the Second. This area features in Jean Genet's infamous, fierily written novel about the underworld of the police and sailors, crime and homosexuality, *Querelle de Brest*.

Océanopolis and the Attractions of Eastern Brest

Further east, at the modern harbour by the Rade, **Océanopolis** (*open April–Aug daily 9–6; rest of year Tues–Sun 10–5; adm*) is both a centre for the study of the world's oceans and one of the best aquaria in France, gently encouraging visitors' understanding of marine life and clarifying Brittany's sometimes murky waters. Main themes include scientists' knowledge of the world's oceans and their latest research into them, navigation and security at sea, and the sea life of the Breton coasts. You're taken on a kind of tour of the world's water life via the Tropical Pavilion, the Temperate Pavilion, and the Polar Pavilion.

To get away from the hordes of Océanopolis, head for the peace of the **Conservatoire National de Brest** in the nearby **Vallon du Stang Alar** (*open summer 9–8; rest of year 9–6; greenhouses open July–15 Sept Sun–Thurs 2–5.30; rest of year Sun 2–4.30*), a gorgeous public garden, set apart from the town in its long, deep valley. A stream runs through it, supplying a whole chain of small lakes and ponds full of water lilies. Great clumps of elephant-eared gunnera and bamboos, clusters of palms and even of cacti and agaves make for an exotic atmosphere.

At the **marina of Moulin Blanc** by Océanopolis, you can choose between several different boats to go out on the waters of the Rade de Brest. Trips around the Rade in modern boats can be booked through the Société Maritime Azénor (**t** 02 98 41 46 23, **f** 02 98 41 46 50, *azenor.brest@wanadoo.fr*). La Recouvrance (**t** 02 98 33 95 40, **f** 02 98 33 95 50, *contact@larecouvrance.com*) is a schooner from the early 19th century, but it is pretty expensive for a day trip. *L'Escalenrade* (**t** 06 82 19 52 44) offers the option of a more conventional yacht for a tour. Or, towards the two huge bridges crossing the estuary of the Elorn river as it reaches the Rade de Brest, relax on Moulin Blanc's beach.

Day Trips from Brest

Ouessant or Ushant

The lethal rocks of Ouessant have long been notorious for causing shipwrecks. Tragedy has stalked the islanders too. Until recently it was the lot of many a Ouessant woman to become a widow before her time. Wile the men were away fishing or in the navy, the women were left to tend their tiny walled allotments. These have now been abandoned, but the other traditional mainstay – sheep – survive, even if the tiny blackish-brown Ouessant breed peculiar to the island is now very rare.

Getting There

Always book **ferry** tickets well in advance, especially during school holidays. Boats leave Brest's Port de Commerce daily at 8.30am, journey time 2hrs 30mins. The daily return boat leaves Ouessant at 5pm. Book via Compagnie Penn ar Bed, **t** 02 98 80 80 80, **f** 02 98 44 75 43, *www.pennarbed.fr*.

You can also **fly** from Brest-Guipavas to Ouessant using Finist'Air, **t** 02 98 84 64 87, **f** 02 98 84 64 60, *www.finistair.fr*.

Getting Around

The easiest way to travel around Ushant is by **taxi or minibus**. Hiring a **bike** is extremely popular, although **walking** is the only way to really appreciate the coast.

Tourist Information

Ouessant: Place de l'Eglise, Lampaul, **t** 02 98 48 85 83, **f** 02 98 48 87 09, *www.ot-ouessant.fr*.

Market Days

Ouessant: Tuesday, Thursday and Friday.

Eating Out

Lampaul

Most of the options are in the 'capital'.

**Le Fromveur, t 02 98 48 81 30 (*expensive*). The hotel restaurant has good Breton cuisine.

Roch Ar Mor, t 02 98 48 80 19 (*moderate*). Also offers traditional fare.

La Duchesse Anne, t 02 98 48 80 25 (*moderate*). Another hotel-restaurant that is worth a try.

Resto du Stiff, t 02 98 48 83 69 (*moderate*). Closer to the ferry terminal, on the main road to Lampaul, a new choice, 1km from the port.

Ty ar Dreuz, t 02 98 48 83 01, in Lampaul centre (*cheap*). Crêperie.

Crêperie du Stang, t 02 98 48 80 94, on the Route du Stiff as you leave Lampaul (*cheap*).

Ferries arrive in the **Baie du Stiff**, where a lighthouse, the enormous Phare du Stiff (the object of the odd English bawdy joke), marks the highest point on the island. Explore the sensational jagged north coast of the island by foot or by bike. Dragged around by the wind, you'll encounter the most formidable rock formations, assaulted by angry waves.

By contrast, bustling **Lampaul** (named after St Pol, *see* the island of Batz, p.137), the main settlement on Ouessant, in the west of the island, opens out on to a surprisingly friendly bay with small beaches lying around it. Two museums stand nearby: the **Maison du Niou Uhella Ecomusée** (*open June–Sept daily 10.30–6.30; April–May Tues–Sun 2–6.30; rest of year Tues–Sun 2–6; adm*) crams information on the island's history and life into two charmingly claustrophobic traditional cottages, every inch of space put to practical use, as in a ship's cabin; the unusual **Phare de Créac'h Lighthouses Museum** (*open June–Sept daily 10.30–6.30; April–May Tues–Sat 1–6.30, Sun 10.30–6.30, closed Mon; rest of year Tues–Sun 2–5, closed Mon; adm*) lies below the massive black and white Créac'h lighthouse. Lamps with some of the most powerful beams ever made on earth are displayed here; even if these aren't put on for you, the museum's explanations of lighthouses and other sea markers can blind you with science. Beyond the two museums, the bristling mounds of rocks of the **Pointe de Pern** mount up at Ouessant's most westerly point, curiously classified as a national monument. Certainly rocks are the pride of Ushant when it comes to tourists, but they have also been the cause of many of its woes down the centuries.

Touring from Brest

You'll find that the sights are reliably open Easter–Oct, 10–12 and 2–5 at least, unless otherwise stated, and charge adm.

Day 1: To the Pays des Abers

Morning: Head west from Brest for the **Pointe St-Mathieu**, a chillingly dramatic headland with a ruined abbey towering almost as high as the lighthouse, and with views of the archipelago ricocheting out to Ushant. Then head north for **Aber Ildut**, first of a series of deep inlets. The little harbours of **Lanildut** and **Melon** are typical, and with so many rocks around, seaweed-gathering is a major industry.

Lunch: Continue round the coast to St-Pabu's delightful **Crêperie de l'Aber Benoît, t** 02 98 89 86 26 (*cheap*), or to **Le Brennig, t** 02 98 04 81 12 (*moderate*), at St-Antoine on the Aber Wrac'h, an elegant restaurant with modern marine décor and inventive seafood cuisine.

Afternoon: North of Plouguerneau, **St-Michel** and **Lilia** have popular beaches with magical rockscapes, while the **Ile Vierge** out to sea has the tallest lighthouse in Europe to warn ships of the danger. The nearby church of **Tremenac'h** was long ago buried under the sands, its exceptional engraved tombstones only rediscovered in the 1960s.

Dinner and sleeping: By the rocks of Lilia, modern **★★Castel Ac'h, t** 02 98 04 70 11, **f** 02 98 04 58 43 (*inexpensive*) has rooms with sea views and serves excellent seafood, often with a touch of algae. Inland, by different waters near Plouvien, the **Moulin de Garéna, t** 02 98 04 01 37, **f** 02 98 04 49 74 (*inexpensive*) has rooms and stone dining rooms. Try the mead specialities.

Day 2: Colourful Country Chapels

Morning: Around the **Elorn valley** between Brest and Morlaix stand some of the most exuberant of all Breton chapels, several with extremely elaborate outdoor calvaries. Head for **Landerneau** first; its spectacular old Rohan bridge has houses built on it. **La Roche-Maurice** and **La Martyre** close by have interesting churches, but the most elaborately decorated are **Lampaul-Guimiliau** and **Guimiliau** further east.

Lunch: St-Thégonnec's spectacular church interior burned down recently, but the place still has character. Try refined cuisine at the **★★★Auberge St-Thégonnec, t** 02 98 79 61 18 (*moderate*), near the church.

Afternoon: Drive over the picturesque, bleak backbone of the **Monts d'Arrée** via the **Roch Trévézel** and **St-Michel-de-Braspart**. Down the southern slopes the countryside opens up joyously, especially around the unspoilt villages of **Lannédern** and **Loqueffret**, with their rustic churches. Still more remarkable is the country church of **St-Herbot**. **Huelgoat** with its big lake and boulder-strewn valley makes an atmospheric stop – try shifting a boulder or two before dinner.

Dinner and sleeping: Huelgoat's **★★Hôtel du Lac, t** 02 98 99 71 14, **f** 02 98 99 70 71 (*inexpensive*) looks over the lake and has a welcoming restaurant. You'll need to book well in advance to stay at the pretty **Ferme Auberge de Porz Kloz, t** 02 98 99 61 65, **f** 02 98 99 67 36 (*inexpensive*) near Trédudon in the countryside northwest of Huelgoat, *Table d'hôte* is possible most nights.

Day 3: Crozon's Awesome Cliffs

Morning: Head west for the **Crozon peninsula**, aiming for the timberframe town of **Le Faou**, a gateway to this spectacular area. Across the Aulne estuary stands **Landévennec abbey**, one of the most influential Christian centres in Brittany, with medieval ruins and a museum. The semi-legendary Dark Ages saint Guénolé is said to have founded the abbey, and to have gone on to save King Gradlon from drowning with his evil daughter Dahut (*see over*).

Lunch: Drive along the north side of the peninsula for lunch in **Camaret**, a well-hidden harbour. A row of hotel-restaurants looks on to decaying old boats, a Vauban tower, and a Gothic church. The **★★Hôtel de France, t** 02 98 27 93 06 (*moderate*) has a first floor dining room to enjoy the view, while **★★Le Styvel, t** 02 98 27 92 74 (*moderate*) has a good family restaurant.

Afternoon: Leaving protected Camaret, go and marvel at the most colourful and craggy cliffs in Brittany, on the peninsula's western side, made up of a series of dramatic headlands. It makes for a breathtaking afternoon.

Morgat, a popular resort, offers protection from the full force of the Atlantic.

Dinner: On Morgat's quays, **Les Echoppes**, **t** 02 98 26 12 63 (*moderate*) is a delightful little restaurant serving the freshest food; or for crêpes, try **La Flambée**, **t** 02 98 27 12 24 (*cheap*); its dining room has a view.

Sleeping: Morgat's Belle Epoque ★★★**Grand Hôtel de la Mer**, **t** 02 98 27 02 09, **f** 02 98 27 02 39 (*moderate*) is a smart option not far from the beach. ★★**La Ville d'Ys**, **t** 02 98 27 06 49, **f** 02 98 26 21 88 (*moderate*) has several rooms with balconies looking out to sea.

Day 4: The Bay of Douarnenez and Quimper

Morning:The dramatic road along the north side of the Bay of Douarnenez takes you to **Locronan**, one of the most picturesque villages in Brittany; it's very touristy, so arrive early. The historic wealth of its linen merchants still shows. Chateaubriand described the church as a 'masterpiece of humidity'. **Douarnenez**, by contrast, was a gritty working-class port, but it also stands in a mesmerizingly beautiful location. The Port-Rhu boat museum doesn't display model boats like most others, but the real things. Legend claims that the ruins of the churchless, godless Ville d'Ys, built by King Gradlon of Quimper for his evil daughter Dahut, lie somewhere under the waters of the bay.

Lunch: Douarnenez's Hôtel de France restaurant **Le Doyen**, **t** 02 98 92 00 02 (*expensive*) has a very solid reputation, while **La Criée**, **t** 02 98 92 13 55 (*moderate*), run by the same people, has the better views and prices. For crêpes, consider relaxing **Au Goûter Breton**, **t** 02 98 92 02 74 (*cheap*).

Afternoon:The twin spires of **Quimper** cathedral soar above the historic town by the Odet. A statue of downcast King Gradlon on horseback rides between them. Down beside the ramparts, the bishops' palace has been converted into the substantial regional Musée Départemental Breton. The excellent fine arts museum stands by the cathedral. Satisfy any taste for quaint Quimper pottery at the museum and factories of the Locmaria quarter across the Odet.

Dinner: Friendly **L'Ambroisie**, 49 Rue Elie Fréron, **t** 02 98 95 00 02 (*moderate*) offers inventive cuisine. **Le Jardin de l'Odet**, 39 Bd de Kerguélen, **t** 02 98 95 76 76 (*moderate*) has an amusing ocean-liner feel and tasty dishes.

Sleeping: ★★★**La Tour d'Auverge**, 13 Rue de Réguaires, **t** 02 98 95 08 70, **f** 02 98 95 17 31 (*moderate*) is a traditional French hotel with a posh restaurant. ★★**Le Dupleix**, 34 Bd Dupleix, **t** 02 98 90 53 35, **f** 02 98 52 05 31 (*moderate–inexpensive*) is modern, but has spacious rooms looking over the Odet.

Day 5: Curious Calvaries

Morning: Heading slowly north for Pleyben, take the D770 to pass the curious churches of **Quilinen** and **St-Vénec** with their rare little triangular calvaries and rustic Breton atmosphere. **Pleyben** boasts the grandest calvary of all Brittany outside its granite Renaissance church. The scenes of Christ's Passion are harder to make out than on most Breton calvaries as they're set on a grand triumphal arch, but the carving is of a high order by Breton standards.

Lunch: On Pleyben's main square, try reasonable **La Blanche Hermine**, **t** 02 98 26 61 29 (*moderate*) or the **Crêperie de l'Enclos**, **t** 02 98 26 38 68 (*cheap*).

Afternoon: Head northwest via Le Faou for **Daoulas**, a village packed with historic religious buildings, the former abbey buildings holding major international ethnographic exhibitions. Its Romanesque cloister is a small delight, with a medicinal herb garden next to it. At **Plougastel-Daoulas** the ornate calvary just about survived the war bombings. One of the most dramatic retellings in Brittany of Christ's Passion, it's covered with over 150 sculpted figures, the humans rather stilted, the donkeys and horses delightful. The lovely Plougastel peninsula is known for producing fine strawberries, and the town even has a strawberry museum.

Dinner and sleeping: In Plougastel, **Le Chevalier de Lauberlac'h**, 5 Rue Mathurin Thomas, **t** 02 98 40 54 56 (*moderate*) has charm, a little garden for an apéritif and refined cuisine. **La Belle Epoque**, 18 Rue de l'Eglise, **t** 02 98 40 23 14 (*moderate*) is a good, simpler second best.

The Loire Valley, Poitou-Charentes and the Limousin

08

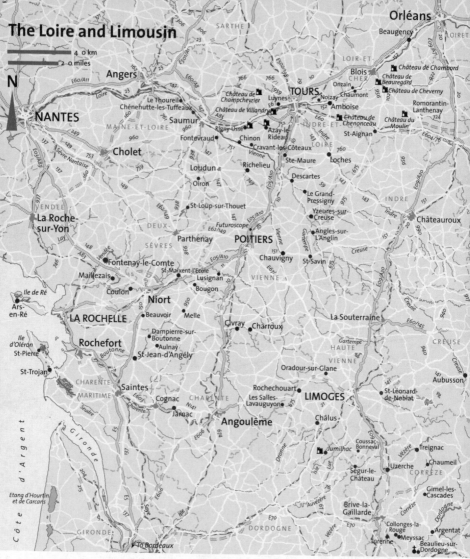

The Loire and Limousin

Between the Loire's châteaux and the Charente's Cognac, the four main destinations in this chapter prove both mellow and cultured. On the Loire itself, Tours is a sophisticated city, built in bright, light Loire limestone. It's a great base from which to visit châteaux and gorgeous Loire Valley towns and vineyards. In the city of St Martin – one of the greatest influences on the conversion of France to Christianity, back in the 4th century – timberframe Place Plumereau is the hip place to hang out.

Also rather cool and jazzy, La Rochelle on the Atlantic has been at the forefront of green city development in recent times. Its long-established wealth helps. The place's medieval prosperity remains highly visible around the harbour even today, while in the Ancien Régime its merchants made a killing from the slave trade, as the arcaded streets behind bear witness to so well. In between these periods, La Rochelle was briefly brought to its knees by Cardinal Richelieu crushing this major Protestant stronghold. Historic naval towns have languished beautifully down the coast, while splendid islands and beach resorts lie just a stone's throw away.

Poitiers, inland, was the third most important city in medieval France, long home to the dukes of Aquitaine, and the duchesses, including Eleanor. It still boasts a great medieval church to pray at for each day of the week. But it also has the liveliness of a university town, while just north of the city rises the wacky architecture of Planète Futuroscope, concealing the largest selection of extra-large cinema screens in Europe. Otherwise, Poitou is best known for the much quieter charms of Romanesque pilgrimage churches, often covered in carvings of violent scenes and weird creatures, demonstrating the medieval mind battling with its demons.

Limoges, further south and further inland, has an international reputation for its porcelain. In medieval times too, distinguished craftsmen thrived here, making the most gorgeous Christian reliquaries, exported across Europe. Capital of the Limousin, perhaps the quietest of all the modern French regions, Limoges turns out to feel quite lively. But in the countryside around, you'll have no trouble finding rural peace.

Tours

Tours, today a luminous, vibrant university city, has its roots in Roman times. Thanks to the great saint Martin's presence here in the early Christian era, it was a major pilgrimage site through medieval times; the city even briefly became capital of France, in the 15th century, under cunning, paranoid King Louis XI. Now, central Tours has two main quarters, the grand-to-haughty area around the ornate cathedral, and the more commercial, lively area around St Martin's church.

Touring Tours

The lantern tops of the **Cathédrale St-Gatien** stand out gracefully on the Tours skyline, while up close the façade reveals a mass of Flamboyant Gothic detail topped by Renaissance domes. Inside, the splendid choir contains truly superb stained glass. The most beautiful and moving work of art at ground level is a Renaissance tomb displaying the effigies of Charles-Orland and Charles, the two short-lived sons the ill-fated Anne de Bretagne had by King Charles VIII. Look out too for all sorts of visual references to St Martin's dividing his cloak in half for a poor beggar. The story goes that the Roman legionnaire had a dramatic conversion to Christianity after his encounter with this beggar in northern France. The following night, he had a dream in which Jesus appeared to him, holding the other half of his cloak – from then on, his mission was clear to him. Having helped found the first-ever monastery in France, outside Poitiers, he became bishop of Tours, where he was buried.

A triumphal arch by the cathedral leads into the grounds of the former archbishops' palace, now the **Musée des Beaux-Arts** (open Wed–Mon 9–12.45 and 2–6; closed Tues; adm). The main emphasis is on the 17th and 18th centuries, featuring fine statues, furniture and an impressive collection of paintings. Among the foreign highlights are a Rubens Ex-Voto and magnificent Mantegna panels. Rembrandt is represented by

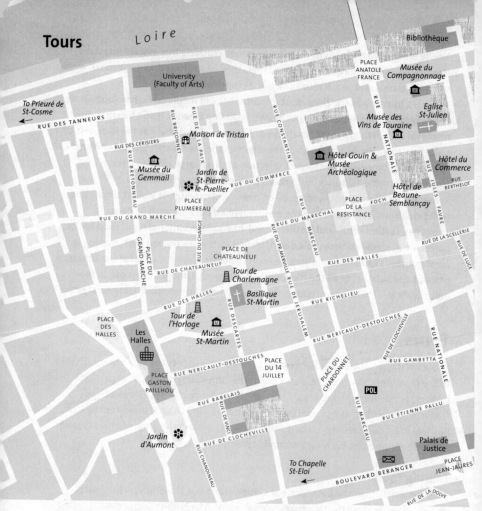

Tours

The Flight into Egypt. The most fascinating Tourangeau artist here is Abraham Bosse, a 17th-century engraver who depicted all walks of life under the reign of Louis XIII. Most famous perhaps of all the great figures Tours and Touraine have produced, Balzac stands in thoughtful pose in a study commissioned by his great love, Madame Hanska; he makes a further appearance in a copy of Rodin's sculpture of him.

The hushed, high-walled streets behind the cathedral are packed with former religious houses. One curving street in this quarter reflects the shape of a vanished Roman theatre, recalling that Tours was a lively trading centre back then. In the Logis du Gouverneur, part of the fragmentary **Château de Tours** nearer the Loire, the history of the city is portrayed by the **Atelier Histoire de Tours** (*open Wed and Sat only, 3–6.30; adm free*). West of the château and the cathedral, **Rue Colbert** is one of Tours' finest streets, with a fair number of timber-framed façades from the 15th and 16th centuries. More especially fine buildings line **Rue de la Scellerie**.

Behind the post-war precinct of Rue Nationale, the church of **St-Julien** looks grubby and neglected, yet for centuries it formed part of one of Tours' great monasteries;

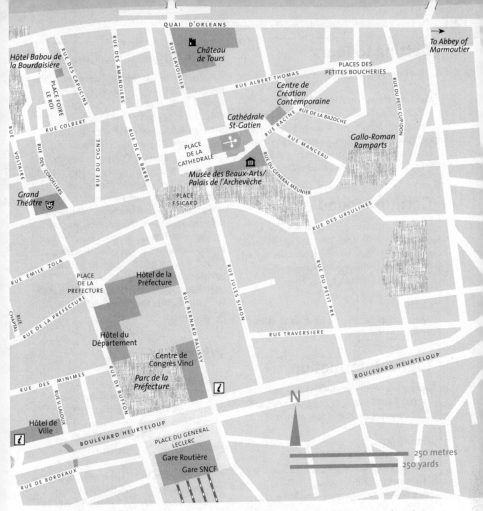

inside, you can appreciate its pure, uplifting Gothic style. In the 16th-century dormitory the eccentric, old-fashioned **Musée du Compagnonnage** (*open mid-June–mid-Sept daily 9–12.30 and 2–6, rest of year Wed–Mon 9–12.30 and 2–6; adm*) is crammed with a bizarre medley of craftsmen's *chefs-d'œuvre* from the 18th century to the present day. Most of the pieces are miniature examples of their craft, for example exquisite little wrought-iron gates or timberframe roofs, but perhaps the most astonishing objects are the elaborate *pâtisseries*, old cakes preserved for posterity. The **Musée du Vin** beneath has a disappointingly dusty old display on Touraine wines.

West of Rue Nationale, modern cafés line the way to the Hôtel Gouin. A riot of Renaissance detail has proliferated like brambles over its façade; it now houses the **Musée Archéologique** (*open daily 9.30–12.30 and 2–6.30; adm*), containing a fine collection of medieval and Renaissance pieces and a whole array of beautiful sculptures of saints. Rue du Commerce leads into the student quarter, an area packed with lively bars and restaurants heralding the superbly restored **Place Plumereau**. The streets around it, where many of King Louis XI's courtiers lived in the 15th century, are

Getting to Tours

Buzz (*see* p.6) flies from London Stansted.

Getting from the Airport

Tours Val de Loire airport (**t** 02 47 49 37 00) is 6km northeast of town. A cheap **bus service** will take you to the *gare routière* or the town bus station by the central railway station. **Taxis** to the centre cost around €16.

Getting Around

Tours has two main **train stations**. Don't confuse the central one with that of St-Pierre-des-Corps. The *gare routière* is near the central train station, on Place Jean Jaurès.

For a taxi, try **Taxis 13, t** 02 47 20 30 40.

Car Hire

Avis, t 02 47 20 53 27 or **t** 02 47 49 21 49, has an agent in the airport.

Tourist Information

Tours: 78–82 Rue Bernard Palissy, B.P.4201, 37042 Tours Cedex, **t** 02 47 70 37 37, **f** 02 47 61 14 22, *www.ligeris.com, info@ligeris.com*.

Market Days

Regular specialist markets include:

Place de la Résistance: *marché gourmand*, first Fri in every month, 4–10am.

Place de la Victoire: second-hand, Wed and Sat.

Boulevard Béranger: 4th Sun in month, plus flower market Wed and Sat.

Rue de Bordeaux: 1st and 3rd Fri of month.

Place des Halles: crafts, Sat.

Shopping

Rue Nationale has the big chain shops, while the streets to the west of it offer an excellent array of smaller boutiques selling clothes and gifts. East of Rue Nationale, along and between Rue Colbert and Rue de la Scellerie, lies the interesting antiques quarter.

Heading west of the Quartier St-Martin you'll come to the big modern covered market, Les Halles, a lively place for food shopping. Some particularly fine gastronomic shops scattered around town include: **Charcuterie Lebeau**, 34 Rue des Halles, for Touraine pork delicacies; **Parfums de Beurre**, 2 Rue Marceau, for Touraine goat's cheeses; **Le Calendos**, 11 Rue Colbert, another good *fromagerie*: **Pâtisserie Sabat** and **Pâtisserie Poirault** along Rue Nationale for cakes and chocolate, although you'll find further tempting *pâtisseries* in other quarters.

Where to Stay

Tours ✉ 37000

****Château Belmont Jean Bardet, 57 Rue Groison, **t** 02 47 41 41 11, **f** 02 47 51 68 72, *sophie@jeanbardet.com* (*expensive*). A name known across France for the highest standards of cuisine, but recently rocked by a scandal over misleading customers about wines. However, this is still a very chic to chi-chi restaurant and hotel. The substantial town house stands on the north bank of the Loire, east off Av de la Tranchée.

***Hôtel de l'Univers, 5 Bd Heurteloup, **t** 02 47 05 37 12, **f** 02 47 61 51 80 (*expensive*). At the heart of the town, a grand Belle Epoque

filled with beamed houses, the courtyards embellished with stair towers. Nearby, the **Musée du Gemmail** (*open weekends and public hols only, 10–12 and 2–6.30; adm*) celebrates a radiant 20th-century development in the art of stained glass.

Just south from Place Plumereau lies the old religious **Quartier St-Martin**, where two enormous towers give a clue to the vastness of the Romanesque church that once stood here. The beautiful remnants of the **cloister of St-Martin** lie just off the **Musée St-Martin** (*open mid-Mar–mid-Nov, Wed–Sun 9.30–12.30 and 2–5.30; adm*) on Rue Rapin, giving more details on the saint's life. St Martin's tomb, rediscovered during an archaeological dig in 1860, now lies in the crypt of the **Nouvelle Basilique St-Martin**, a self-important white whale of a building. Victor Laloux planned this

building where the famous automatically used to stay in Tours, as the portrait gallery on the ground floor proves. Churchill counted among the number to grace one of its soberly luxurious rooms. The restaurant isn't bad, the prices quite reasonable.

★★★**Le Grand Hôtel**, 9 Place du Général Leclerc, **t** 02 47 05 35 31, **f** 02 47 64 10 77 (*moderate*). Large and by the station, but has a certain charm and is quite reasonably priced.

★★**Hôtel du Cygne**, 6 Rue du Cygne, **t** 02 47 66 66 41, **f** 02 47 66 05 13, *hotelcygne.tours@wanadoo.fr* (*inexpensive*). There's a lovely old-fashioned character to this centrally located, good-value little hotel.

★★**Le Balzac**, 47 Rue de la Scellerie, **t** 02 47 05 40 87, **f** 02 47 05 67 93 (*inexpensive*). Another central small hotel with some charm, including a little inner courtyard where you can have breakfast in summer.

★**Mon Hôtel**, 40 Rue de la Préfecture, **t** 02 47 05 67 53, **f** 02 47 05 21 88 (*cheap*). Well located for such bargain prices, in one of the chicest parts of Tours, close to the railway station, but with most of the rooms you have to share the toilet and washing facilities.

La Rôtisserie Tourangelle, 23 Rue du Commerce, **t** 02 47 05 71 21 (*moderate*). Well-established restaurant with impeccable manners.

L'Atlantic, 59 Rue du Commerce, **t** 02 47 64 78 41 (*moderate*). High-quality seafood, plus eels in a Touraine wine sauce with prunes.

Le Petit Patrimoine, 58 Rue Colbert, **t** 02 47 66 05 81 (*cheap*). Lively narrow little restaurant, serving traditional Tourangeau dishes.

Chez Jean-Michel – Le Charolais, 123 Rue Colbert, **t** 02 47 20 80 20 (*cheap*). Friendly wine bar specializing in Loire *appellations*, and offering a simple selection of Touraine dishes.

Place Plumereau has been colonized by cafés with superb terraces, but best enjoy these for a drink rather than a meal. Most of the restaurants in the streets off the square cater for the tourist hordes. However, a couple of places in the secretive, ruin-surrounded **Place St-Pierre-le-Puellier** just north of the square prove enticing; or try Touraine's answer to *calzone* pizza, puffed-up dough balls with various fillings, at **Comme Autrefouée**, 11 Rue de la Monnaie, **t** 02 47 05 94 78 (*cheap*).

Eating Out

Jean Bardet, *see* 'Where to Stay', above.

Charles Barrier, 101 Av de la Tranchée, **t** 02 47 54 20 39 (*expensive*). The other really exceptional restaurant north of the Loire, in the same part of town as Jean Bardet; the place has been stylishly redecorated.

Les Tuffeaux, 21 Rue Lavoisier, **t** 02 47 47 19 89 (*moderate*). Opposite Tours' meagre château, this place offers beams, tufa walls, and warm traditional Touraine cooking.

Entertainment and Nightlife

Look out for *Tours Cultures*, the town's quarterly cultural magazine, listing events, or look at the cultural pages at *www.ville-tours.fr*.

For **bars** and **clubs**, the area around Place Plumereau is very lively and quite chic. Down Avenue Grammont are bigger, more popular places.

building, as well as the very grandiose town hall and railway station, worth a look at, along with Jean Nouvel's contemporary Vinci Centre, with its visor at the front.

Up by the Loire, you'll see how badly Tours was devastated by Second World War bombings, but the post-war university arts faculty and public library stand out with their unusual Moroccan-style pyramidal roofs. You can take a walk along the cobbled quays below them, a reminder of the days when the Loire was one of the great trading highways. The bridges may tempt you to cross on to one of the large islands in the midst of the Loire. If you go on a special tour with a tourist office guide, you can visit **Les Trois Tours** silk factory on the north bank of the river, the looms still clattering in the old-fashioned manner. It feels like stepping back into the 19th century.

Day Trips from Tours

Amboise

French towns don't come more royal than Amboise. Its **château** (*open July–Aug 9–7.30; April–June 9–6.30; Sept–Oct 9–6; Feb–March and Nov 9–12 and 2–5.30; Dec–Jan 9–12 and 2–5; adm*) was an important residence for a string of French monarchs and remains in would-be French royal hands today. Even though a large proportion of the vast complex has disappeared, it still makes a fine impression, flags flying from the battlements. A row of toadying riverside houses crouches under its massive ramparts.

The château was forfeited to the French king Charles VII in 1431 because of Louis d'Amboise's disloyal behaviour. Charles VII's son and successor King Louis XI installed his wife here, as well as creating the Order of St Michael to help bind the leading aristocrats to the crown, while his son Charles was groomed for kingship at the château. When he became King Charles VIII, the place became *the* favoured royal residence and this monarch ordered most of the building work above the ramparts. The jewel-box Chapelle St-Hubert is one glorious work of the late-Gothic period that survives, but Charles VIII's main legacy is the wing over the Loire, with its huge towers wide enough for carriages to drive up right into the upper courtyard. The man also loved magnificent furnishings and symbolic objects – Joan of Arc's suit of armour and Lancelot's supposed sword holding pride of place.

In the 1490s, Charles VIII embarked on a bold campaign in Italy to claim his inheritance rights there. The adventure almost ended in catastrophe, but in the end king and courtiers managed to return with a great deal of loot and several of Italy's finest artists and craftsmen in tow. So Italian tastes were imported to France, creating the French Renaissance, transforming noble architecture and ways of living. However, Charles VIII bumped his head on a door at the Château d'Amboise one day in 1498, and promptly died. For a while, up until the early 16th century, the centre of royal business moved upriver to Blois under his successor King Louis XII.

Meanwhile, another future French royal, François Ier, was being brought up at the Château d'Amboise under the watchful eye of his mother Louise de Savoie, who believed in a good education for him and his sister Marguerite d'Angoulême. Early in François' reign, he held fabulous entertainments in the castle, once even taking on a wild boar in the courtyard. But this insatiable monarch was interested in higher pursuits too, and famously invited Leonardo da Vinci to come and sit in attendance. Leonardo spent the final three years of his life at Amboise, and was buried at the château. François gradually moved the court closer to Paris, where his son and successor King Henri II was also based, having married the formidable Florentine Catherine de' Medici. But the couple had their many children (as well as some of the king's illegitimate offspring) brought up in the healthy atmosphere of Amboise, along with the young Mary Stuart, betrothed from a very early age to a sickly Valois prince, very briefly King François II of France – and king of Scotland – at the end of the 1550s.

This was near the start of the appalling French Wars of Religion, a religious and aristocratic conflict that turned into a country-wide civil war. François II and Mary were in the grip of the fanatical Catholic de Guises, on the lookout for Protestant Huguenot

Getting There

The **train** journey from Tours to Amboise takes under 20mins and services are frequent.

Tourist Information

Amboise ✉ 37400: B.P.233, Quai du Général de Gaulle, **t** 02 47 57 09 28, **f** 02 47 57 14 35, *tourisme.amboise@wanadoo.fr*.

Market Days
Amboise: Friday and Sunday morning.

Eating Out

★★★★**Le Choiseul**, 36 Quai Charles Guinot, **t** 02 47 30 45 45, **f** 02 47 30 46 10, *choiseul@wanadoo.fr* (*expensive*). This luxury hotel-restaurant is packed with interesting things and the cuisine is highly regarded. Its well-maintained gardens back onto the hillside which contains superb former grain stores, the **Greniers de César**, a sight in themselves. *Closed mid-Dec–Jan*.

Manoir St-Thomas, 1 Mail St-Thomas, **t** 02 47 57 22 52, **f** 02 47 30 44 71 (*expensive*). The fine house with its private grounds in the middle of town dates from the Renaissance and provides a splendid setting for a highly regarded restaurant. *Closed Sun pm and Mon, and Feb–mid-Mar*.

La Blason, 11 Place Richelieu, **t** 02 47 23 22 41 (*moderate*). This appealing half-timbered house on this large square offers reliably good food and has a pleasant courtyard.

L'Epicerie, 18 Rue Victor Hugo, **t** 02 47 57 08 94 (*moderate*). Set in a timberframe house close to the ramp up the side of the château, this restaurant serves classic Loire dishes. *16 Sept –14 June closed Mon pm and Tues*.

plots. The first major one, the Conspiration d'Amboise, was hatched at the nearby Château de Noizay in 1560. But the conspirators were caught in their feeble attack on the town and were then mercilessly killed, some hanged from the castle terrace, others from the town gates, yet more drowned in the Loire. Amboise's great royal days had come to an end.

After the French Wars of Religion, the château was abandoned by royalty, but in 1821 the future King Louis-Philippe regained possession and turned it into a royal summer residence. His Orléans successors, the Comtes de Paris, have owned the place since. In recent years, some of the interiors have been restored and embellished – the Gothic wing has some fine Gothic decoration and Renaissance-style furniture, while the Renaissance wing's rooms are given over to elegant 19th-century furnishings and Orléans family portraits.

Below the château, the **town of Amboise** grew fat and happy at the château's feet, supplying the court with its vast needs and picking up the crumbs from its table. Today, commercialization rules; Rue Victor Hugo and Rue Nationale are crammed with cafés, restaurants and shops.

Tourism is also rampant at Leonardo da Vinci's last home, the **Clos Lucé** (*open July–Aug 9am–8pm; late Mar–June and Sept–Oct 9–7; Feb–late Mar and Nov–Dec 9–6; Jan 10–5; adm*), a fairly long walk from the town centre. The house is rather fine, and the owners have tried to recreate a 16th-century atmosphere in many of the chambers, but you don't get any of Leonardo the artist other than cheap copies. Instead, you're treated to Leonardo the aphorist and Leonardo the arms-maker; the drawings show what a visionary engineer he was. In one outhouse, a video in French recalls his scientific genius. The delightful gardens have been transformed in an ambitious project to reflect the Tuscan genius' inventiveness through large-scale outdoor models.

Chinon

With medieval houses as close-knit as chain-mail fighting for space between the hillside and the Vienne river, Chinon is dominated by the ruins of its great Plantagenet castle. Distinctly provincial today, the place still retains more than a spark of courtly glory, however. Chinon's first great courtly age came with Henri Plantagenêt, who loved the castle and enlarged it to become the greatest fortress of its time in Europe. He died at Chinon in 1189 and his son Richard the Lionheart may have died here too after being mortally wounded at the Battle of Châlus quite far south, in the Limousin. In the second half of the Hundred Years' War, Chinon became home for a time to the would-be French king kicked out of Paris by the English, Charles VII. He received one of the most famous visitors in French history at the castle – Joan of Arc.

Looking up from the town below, the **Château de Chinon** (*open July–Aug 9–7; mid-March–June and Sept–Oct 9.30–6; rest of year 9.30–12 and 2–5; adm*) seems little more than a string of beautiful battered fortifications nowadays, but it still has wonderful views, a few rooms to visit and great ruins to clamber over. The remnants of King Charles VII's royal *logis* – where most of the exhibits are housed – were where Joan of Arc met the 'gentle dauphin' to convince him that she could help boot the English out of France. One tower is given over to Joan, showing in an old-fashioned but intelligent manner what a remarkable woman she was. To the west lies the better-preserved **Fort du Coudray**, from where Charles VII kept discreetly in touch with his mistress, Agnès Sorel.

If Chinon's castle is ruined and quiet now, the town below is often bustling. The few streets are crammed with splendid architecture, a great variety of especially beautiful stair towers standing out, some round, some square, some in timberframe and brick, others in local limestone. The wonderfully atmospheric main thoroughfare, along which you'll find the main churches, museums and squares, consists of Rue Haute St-Maurice, which turns into Rue Voltaire, then Rue Jean-Jacques Rousseau.

But first go and take a look at the quays by the Vienne river, where you may spot the odd riverboat on the waters. On the western end, in the very neatly cleaned up former abattoir, a rather noble building, the **Maison de la Rivière** (*open July–Aug Tues–Sun 10.30–12.30 and 2–6.30; April–June and Sept Tues–Fri 10–12 and 2–5, weekends 3–6; Feb–March and Oct Thurs–Sun 2–5; adm*) gives some notion of the importance of river life and trading here in times past. In high season you can take a boat trip from the quays outside. For the best views of historic Chinon topped by its castle, cross the river to take in the magnificent view from the south bank.

Back on the main thoroughfare in the centre of town, start with the medieval church of **St-Maurice**, its spire soaring skywards, squeezed between narrow side-streets on the western end of Rue Haute St-Maurice. The **Musée du Vieux Chinon** in the Maison des Etats Généraux (*open mid-April–mid-Oct 11–1 and 3–8; adm*) is sited in the house where it is claimed Richard the Lionheart died. Undoubtedly, the most moving exhibit inside is a mould of the Crucifixion taken from Chinon's church of St-Mexme, one of the most painfully emotional depictions of Christ's suffering from French medieval art, his face stretchmarked by agony. Among a further eclectic range of objects, the most exceptional is the so-called cope of St Mexme. This turns out to be a piece of 11th-century Arab silk, now thought to have been made for a horse!

Along Rue Voltaire the **Musée Animé du Vin et de la Tonnellerie** (*open April–Sept 10.30–12.30 and 2–7; adm*), contains displays on wine-making in the Chinonais, set in a former stone quarry. The street ends with the very pleasant 19th-century square of **Place du Général de Gaulle**, complete with the town hall and a crowd of cafés by a statue of Rabelais, the great 16th-century polymath, who was born here. A man of exceptional education, he followed careers as a monk, a lawyer and a doctor, and then went on to mock them all, and much more besides, in his brilliant satires of the Gargantua and Pantagruel series.

From the northern end of the square, Rue Jean-Jacques Rousseau takes you past the churches of **St-Etienne** and **St-Mexme**, the latter battered but deeply atmospheric still (*contact the tourist office for guided tours*). A path up the hillside to the east passes former cave dwellings before the curious remnants of the **Chapelle Ste-Radegonde** (*contact the tourist office for guided tours*), with its faded little wall paintings possibly depicting the Plantagenet royals out hunting. A quaintly cobwebby display of old-fashioned implements fills the caves next door, while a stairway leads down to one of the most mysterious little subterranean sights in the Loire Valley, an ancient underground well, once ascribed magical powers. In the Dark Ages, this is the place to which 6th-century Queen Radegonde is said to have fled from her violent husband Clotaire, to be offered sanctuary by the hermit Jean Le Reclus. She became an important early Christian figure in western France, going on to found a major nunnery at Poitiers. The hermitage was long a place of pilgrimage.

Getting There

Both **trains** and **buses** run between Tours and Chinon, but choice of times is limited.

At present, for a morning train, taking 40mins, you have to leave Tours at 7.35 on weekdays, while the weekday bus leaves at 9.15 and takes 1hr 10mins. The last services back leave around 7pm.

Check with the tourist office for weekend times.

The train and bus stations are about 1km east of the centre.

Tourist Information

Chinon ⊠ 37500: Place Hofheim, 37501 Chinon, t 02 47 93 17 85, f 02 47 93 93 05, *www.chinon.com*.

Market Day

Chinon: Thursday.

Eating Out

Au Plaisir Gourmand, Quai Charles VII, t 02 47 93 20 48, f 02 47 93 05 66 (*expensive*). The outstanding restaurant in town, discreetly set back from the river and with its own little garden. Jean-Claude Rigollet prepares mainly traditional French cuisine to perfection, such as oxtail in a deep, dark Chinon sauce, but also creates the odd more experimental dish. *Closed Sun pm and Mon, and Feb.*

L'Océanic, 13 Rue Rabelais, t 02 47 93 44 55, f 02 47 93 38 68 (*moderate*). For good seafood. *Closed Mon.*

La Maison Rouge, 38 Rue Voltaire, t 02 47 98 43 65, f 02 47 95 78 33 (*moderate*). Serves both as a fine food store and as a restaurant where you can sample regional specialities.

Touring: East from Tours

You'll find that the sights are reliably open Easter–Oct, 10–12 and 2–5, unless otherwise stated, and charge adm.

Day 1: Vouvray Vineyards to Chaumont

Morning: Vouvray's vineyards spread along the north bank of the Loire east of Tours, above beautiful white-stone villages. Stop for a gently tingling wine-tasting. Cross the Loire to visit the large **Aquarium de Touraine** near **Lussault**, presenting Loire fish alive, rather than on the plate.

Lunch: Back on the Loire's north bank, west of Amboise, the ★★★★**Château de Noizay**, **t** 02 47 52 11 01 (*expensive–moderate*) is a splendid historic little village castle in which to savour memorable Loire dishes. At the next village west, Vernou, ★★**Les Perce-Neige**, **t** 02 47 52 10 04 (*moderate*) has a lovely garden for summer dining.

Afternoon: For **Amboise**, *see* pp.158–9. South of town, the **Pagode de Chanteloup** is the charmingly melancholic remnant of a major 18th-century château, where you can play summer games. East along the Loire, the **Château de Chaumont** looks majestically down on the river. It has interesting 19th-century interiors and stables, plus a brilliant garden festival (*mid-June–mid-Oct*).

Dinner and sleeping: At Onzain just across the Loire from Chaumont, the ★★★★**Domaine des Hauts de Loire**, **t** 02 54 20 72 57, **f** 02 54 20 77 32 (*luxury–expensive*), a 19th-century hunting lodge disguised as a château, makes a luxury stop with an exceptionally refined restaurant (*expensive*). East of Chaumont at Candé-sur-Beuvron, ★★**La Caillière**, **t** 02 54 44 03 08, **f** 02 54 44 00 95 (*inexpensive*) has cosy rooms in an old inn, but puts a zest of modernity into its cooking (*moderate*).

Day 2: Blois and Forest Châteaux

Morning: The massive **Château de Blois** stands on a plateau above the Loire in the centre of this historic city. Briefly, in the 16th century, it served as the centre of the French kingdom. The castle presents an extraordinary fusion of contrasting architectural styles, haunting tales of royal shenanigans, and several museums, best of which is the fine-arts collection. A modern museum of magic also stands out on the plateau. The shopping streets down below are packed with interest.

Lunch: Down below the castle, **Au Rendez-Vous des Pêcheurs**, **t** 02 54 74 67 48 (*moderate*), set in a sweet little house, serves really excellent fish dishes and other fine cuisine. Cross the elegant Loire bridge for **Le Bistrot du Cuisinier**, **t** 02 54 78 06 70 (*moderate*), with views of the historic city to accompany rich regional food.

Afternoon: The forests south of the Loire from Blois teem with châteaux. The **Château de Beauregard** looks plain on the outside, but contains some extremely ornate rooms, including the portrait gallery, a lesson in European history. The **Château de Cheverny** is a rarity, a 17th-century Loire Valley castle, and arguably the most elegant of the lot, with gorgeously decorated interiors. For lesser-known castles, try Gothic **Château de Fougères**, with exhibitions on the craftsmen who built the Loire's châteaux, or charming little **Château de Villesavin**, a chip off the old block of massive Chambord.

Dinner: In Cellettes, a village just south of Beauregard, the **Château de Roselle**, **t** 02 54 70 31 27 (*moderate*) has a big, bright conservatory on the end of an 18th-century manor in which to enjoy elaborate French cuisine. **Le Grand Chancelier**, **t** 02 54 79 22 57 (*moderate*), in Cheverny, with its old-fashioned look, is good for tasty traditional cuisine.

Sleeping: The ★★★**Château du Breuil**, Route de Fougères, **t** 02 54 44 20 20, **f** 02 54 44 30 40 (*expensive*) is a dreamlike place set in a glade in its own woods outside Cheverny. At Mont-près-Chambord to the north, ★★**Le St-Florent**, **t** 02 54 70 81 00, **f** 02 54 70 78 53 (*inexpensive*) is pleasant, with light rooms, plus a reasonable restaurant (*moderate*).

Day 3: Chambord to Beaugency

Morning: Hidden in its massive walled forest, the **Château de Chambord** startles newcomers as the most awesome of all Loire Valley castles, a vast pile ordered by King François Ier in the first half of the 16th century. Its interiors are a bit vacuous, but the central spiral staircase, possibly designed by Leonardo da Vinci, and the roof-scapes, are magical.

Lunch: At Chambord, the **★★Hôtel St-Michel**, t 02 54 20 31 31 (*moderate*), in a very touristy position, has a solid reputation for its cooking, while **Le Chambourdin**, t 02 54 20 32 64 (*moderate–cheap*) is set a little away from the crowds. Up near St-Dyé-sur-Loire, the **★★Manoir de Bel Air**, t 02 54 81 60 10 (*moderate*) has a very pleasant large restaurant looking down on the river.

Afternoon: **Beaugency** to the east is a delightful riverside town, with the oldest bridge straddling the Loire, and impressive medieval monuments rising above its series of sloping squares. The Romanesque church is where King Louis VII and Eleanor of Aquitaine were separated, leaving the way open for Henri Plantagenêt (alias Henry II of England). The town hall contains superb embroideries. The museum in the heavily restored castle is a rambling affair.

Dinner and sleeping: Beaugency's **★★★Hôtel de l'Abbaye**, t 02 38 44 67 35, f 02 38 44 87 92 (*moderate*), set in a grandiose former abbey on the Loire's quays, has characterful rooms and a fine restaurant. The **★★Hôtel de la Sologne**, t 02 38 44 50 27, f 02 38 44 90 19 (*inexpensive*) is a charming little labyrinth of a hotel in the midst of the best monuments. **★★L'Ecu de Bretagne**, t 02 38 44 67 60 (*inexpensive*) has some rooms in an old inn, some in a modern annexe. The chef experiments with updating regional cuisine (*moderate*).

Day 4: Orléans and the Sologne

Morning: Historic **Orléans** is crowned by its cathedral. Next to it, the post-war fine arts museum (*closed Mon*) is the main cultural attraction. But the historic Hôtel Cabu archaeological museum (*closed Mon; outside May–Sept, only open weekends and Wed, 2–6*) amidst the best old shopping streets contains staggering Celtic sculptures.

Lunch: On different corners of central Orléans' main square, Place du Martroi (presided over by a statue of Joan of Arc, who liberated the city from the English), **La Chancellerie**, t 02 38 53 57 54 (*moderate*), is a stylish French brasserie, while popular **La Promenade**, t 02 38 81 12 12 (*moderate*) has a more contemporary look. Towards the river, **La Petite**

Marmite, 178 Rue de Bourgogne, t 02 38 81 12 12 (*moderate*) has an atmospheric setting.

Afternoon: The **Sologne forest** of silver birch, pine and heather lies south of the Loire from Orléans. Here brick buildings reign, the castle on the edge of **La Ferté St-Aubin** a wonderful run-down example. Follow the D922 through typical Sologne villages and forest interspersed with lakes for **Romorantin-Lanthenay**, built around branches of the river. Just west, the **Château du Moulin** is the most romantic of all the Sologne's brick châteaux.

Dinner and sleeping: Just north of the Cher river from St-Aignan, by Noyers, the **★★★Clos du Cher**, t 02 54 75 00 03, f 02 54 75 03 79 (*moderate*) hides coquettishly in its country garden. The rooms and restaurant (*expensive–moderate*) are stylish. In delightful St-Aignan, the **★★Grand Hôtel**, t 02 54 75 18 04, f 02 54 75 12 59 (*inexpensive*), a traditional French hotel, has large windows looking on to the river. Restaurant menus are moderately priced.

Day 5: Chenonceau and Loches

Morning: Head west along the picturesque **Cher valley**, making a small detour to look at the **Château du Gué-Péan** (*open July–Aug*) in the woods, or **Bourré** with its hillside caves. The exquisite **Château de Chenonceau**, crossing the Cher, needs no introduction.

Lunch: At **Chenonceaux** (the village is spelt with an 'x') the action is along Rue du Dr Bretonneau. Try one of the smart competing hotels' restaurants along here, or **Le Gâteau Breton**, t 02 47 23 90 14, for good-value Touraine specialities.

Afternoon: **Loches** is a beautiful medieval city south of Chenonceaux, on the Indre. Visit the citadel with its two castles, medieval church and little art museum. The D760 road east to **Montrésor** is one of the prettiest in the whole Loire Valley region.

Dinner and sleeping: Built almost over the river in Loches, the **★★★George Sand**, t 02 47 59 39 74, f 02 47 91 55 75 (*moderate*), is extremely attractive, with an excellent regional restaurant (*moderate*). Second best is the **★★Hôtel de France**, t 02 47 59 00 32, f 02 47 59 28 66 (*inexpensive*), in a smart town house, with reasonable restaurant.

Touring: West from Tours

You'll find that the sights are reliably open Easter–Oct, 10–12 and 2–5, unless otherwise stated, and charge adm.

Day 1: Stern Châteaux and Bourgueil Wines

Morning: Take the Loire's north bank west from Tours to visit a choice of severe-looking châteaux, which prove surprisingly bright inside. Knobbly **Château de Luynes** (*open April–Sept*) has sumptuous salons. The **Château de Langeais** intimidates its town, but colourful tapestries lighten the interiors.

Lunch: In Langeais, ★★★**Errard Harten, t** 02 47 96 82 12 (*moderate*) offers very fine dining in an elegant room. Cross the neo-Gothic bridge for ★★ **Le Castel de Bray et Monts, t** 02 47 96 70 47 (*moderate*), a charming country hotel with a good restaurant for freshwater fish, near Bréhémont. In that village, basic **La Clé d'Or, t** 02 47 96 70 26 (*cheap*) has a terrace over the water.

Afternoon: Back north of the Loire and Langeais, the **Château de Champchevrier** (*open July–Sept daily 11–6*) prides itself on its tapestries and its hunting pack. Hidden in forests north of Bourgueil, the huge **Château de Grizeux** (*open May–Sept; closed Sun am*) conceals amusing wall paintings of other châteaux. Finish the touring day with a red-wine-tasting in or around Bourgueil.

Dinner and sleeping: Cross the Loire and go west towards the beautiful hillside villages beyond the Loire and Vienne's confluence. In Turquant, the exquisite new little hotel, **Demeure de La Vignole, t** 02 41 53 67 00, **f** 02 41 53 67 09 (*moderate; meals on request*) stands between cliffsides and vines. In Monsoreau, ★★ **Hostellerie Le Bussy, t** 02 41 38 11 11, **f** 02 41 38 18 10 (*inexpensive; no restaurant*) occupies a charming house in the upper village. **Diane de Méridor, t** 02 41 51 71 76 (*moderate*) down on Monsoreau's quays is a warm place to eat. Cosier still is the **Auberge de la Route d'Or, t** 02 47 95 81 10 (*moderate*), by Candes St-Martin's church.

Day 2: Saumur's Sparkling Sights

Morning: At **Candes St-Martin**, pay homage to 4th-century saint Martin, who died here, by visiting the medieval pilgrimage church. Then potter past the startling semi-troglodyte dwellings along the Loire's south bank to **Saumur**. The dramatic castle (*closed Tues between Oct and March*) calls for the first visit, with collections of ceramics and equestrian items – Saumur is horse-mad.

Lunch: Up by the castle, sample extravagant cuisine in the refined **Délice du Château, t** 02 41 67 65 60 (*expensive*), or try the cheaper menus in adjoining **L'Orangerie, t** 02 41 67 12 88 (*moderate*). Down by the Loire, **Le Relais**, 31 Quai Mayaud, **t** 02 41 67 75 20 (*moderate*), makes a lovely stop.

Afternoon: Built in the brightest Loire stone, Saumur's streets and squares are a joy. The **Maison du Vin** offers an introduction to the area's wines. Three churches call for attention: St-Pierre in the centre, Notre-Dame-de-Nantilly and Notre-Dame-des-Ardilliers worth a trek further out. Drive east to adjoining St-Hilaire-St-Florent to visit one of the impressive cellars of the big Saumur sparkling wine producers, or head up the hill for the riding school, the Ecole Nationale d'Equitation (*open April–Sept 9.30–11 and 2–4; closed Mon am, Sat pm and all Sun*).

Dinner and sleeping: Saumur's ★★★ **Hôtel Anne d'Anjou**, 32 Quai Mayaud, **t** 02 41 67 30 30, **f** 02 41 67 51 00 (*expensive*) is a fabulous historic hotel between river and castle, with a wonderful restaurant. The ★★★ **Hôtel St-Pierre**, Rue Haute St-Pierre, **t** 02 41 50 33 00, **f** 02 41 50 38 68 (*moderate*) close by has loads of appeal too, but no restaurant. ★★**Central Hôtel**, 23 Rue Daillé, **t** 02 41 51 05 78, **f** 02 41 67 82 35 (*inexpensive*) is well kept as well as central. For a simple meal in a good location, try **Auberge St-Pierre**, 6 Place St-Pierre, **t** 02 41 51 26 25 (*cheap*).

Day 3: Magical Roads to Angers

Morning: The Loire looks at its most magical between Saumur and Angers. Follow the south bank through the memorable riverside villages of **Chênehutte, Trèves, Cunault** and **Gennes**.

Lunch: At Le Thoureil a little west, ★**Au Cabernet d'Anjou, t** 02 41 57 95 02 (*cheap*), a former mariner's bar, has a glorious terrace from which to watch the Loire. Further west, up the slope, at St-Saturnin-sur-Loire, the **Auberge La Caillotte**, t 02 41 54 63 74 (*moderate*) offers splendid views.

Afternoon: Angers is a majestic historic city lording it over the broad Maine river. You can't do the place justice in an afternoon, but competing attractions include the castle, with the greatest medieval tapestry cycle, the awesome early Gothic Cathédrale St-Maurice and, across the waters, the medieval Hôpital St-Jean (*closed Mon outside mid-June–mid-Sept*), in which the shocking modern Chant du Monde tapestries by Jean Lurçat contrast strongly with the medieval ones. In town, look out for local wines, Cointreau and pewter.

Dinner and sleeping: Take the breathtaking north bank of the Loire back towards Saumur and stay at Les Rosiers sur Loire. Here, ★★★**Auberge Jeanne de Laval**, t 02 41 51 80 17, f 02 41 38 04 18 (*moderate*) is the smart option, with a very refined restaurant (*expensive*). ★★**Au Val de Loire**, t 02 41 51 80 30, f 02 41 51 95 00 (*inexpensive*) is simpler but pleasant, with neat rooms and carefully prepared food (*moderate*).

Day 4: The Delights of the Chinonais

Morning: Cross south of the Loire at Saumur. The D93 leads to the massive hilltop **Château de Brézé** (*open May–Sept 10–6*), but its most astounding parts lie underground, off the cavernous dry moat. East, the great **abbey of Fontevraud** has been superbly restored. The church holds the tombs of the first Plantagenet kings of England.

Lunch: You can actually eat in one of the abbey's former cloisters, at the large conference-orientated ★★**Prieuré St-Lazare**, t 02 41 51 73 16 (*moderate*). Outside the walls, **La Licorne**, t 02 41 51 72 49 (*moderate*) has a fine reputation, and its own garden.

Afternoon: Chinon is described on pp.160–61. On this heady afternoon, take the country roads east through the **Chinon vineyards**. The D21 via **Cravant-les-Côteaux** is heavenly, leading to the secretive churches of the **Manse valley**. Head back for Chinon via the Vienne valley route, the villages of **L'Ile-Bouchard**, **Tavant** and **Rivière** containing moving fragments of medieval churches.

Dinner and sleeping: Chinon has lovely, unpretentious provincial hotels such as the ★★**Diderot**, 4 Rue Buffon, t 02 47 93 18 87, f 02 47 93 37 10 (*inexpensive*), set around a delightful courtyard, or ★★**Hostellerie Gargantua**, 73 Rue Voltaire, t 02 47 93 04 71, f 02 47 93 08 02 (*moderate*), occupying one of Chinon's finest historic houses. Or, on the quays, try delightful **Agnès Sorel**, t 02 47 93 04 37, f 02 47 93 06 37, or traditional **La Boule d'Or**, t 02 47 93 03 13, f 02 47 93 24 25, serving copious food (*moderate*). See also p.161.

Day 5: Gorging on More Châteaux

Morning: North of Chinon, the **Château d'Ussé**, backed by woods, is said to have inspired the original French tale of *Sleeping Beauty*. To the east, the bright little town of **Azay-le-Rideau** protectively shields another of the most famous Loire Valley castles, reflected in its river.

Lunch: Azay's ★★★**Le Grand Monarque**, t 02 47 45 40 08 (*moderate*) offers good food in this former posting inn. **L'Aigle d'Or**, t 02 47 45 24 58 (*moderate*) is a pleasant place to eat in summer. **Les Grottes**, t 02 47 45 21 04 (*moderate*), not far east of the centre, serves refined food in a cool cave.

Afternoon: On the troglodyte trail, on a weekend, visit the underground farm of **Les Goupillères** a short distance east. Or to the south, the valley village of **Villaines** specializes in wickerwork. But the main draw, to the north, is the formal garden of the **Château de Villandry**, where vegetable-growing is transformed into art. Nearby **Savonnières** is another sweet village.

Dinner and sleeping: For a taste of château life, head east to the delectable little ★★★**Château de Beaulieu**, t 02 47 53 20 26, f 02 47 53 84 20 (*expensive*), hidden in Tours' southern suburb of Joué-les-Tours (off the D207), with excellent restaurant. Close to Villandry, on the peaceful isthmus between the Cher and Loire rivers, at Berthenay, **La Grange aux Moines**, t 02 47 50 06 91 (*inexpensive*) offers very good B&B rooms, meals for guests, and a swimming pool. In Villandry itself, ★★**Le Cheval Rouge**, t 02 47 50 02 07, f 02 47 50 08 77 (*inexpensive*) has pleasant rooms near the château and startling décor in the dining room.

Poitiers

The provincial capital of Poitou has known successive periods of greatness, even if it has declined in size and importance since medieval times when it ranked as the third largest city in France, a golden period reflected in its superb Romanesque churches. The hill town still retains its historic atmosphere and, with its university, is fairly lively most of the time. The opening of the showy Futuroscope cinema park north of the city in the 1980s put Poitiers firmly back on the modern map.

Pottering Around Poitiers: the Upper City

The heart and soul of Poitiers, **Notre-Dame-la-Grande** has one of the most memorable and action-packed Romanesque façades in France. At the top of the great front, Christ sits in majesty, although, as with most of the other human figures on the façade, his face has been hacked off. Below his mandorla stand statues of the Apostles and St Hilaire (in the top left arch) and St Martin (with his shield in front of him in the right), who together founded the first-ever monastery in France at Ligugé just south of Poitiers, in 361. The best carving runs along above the ground floor arches. To the left you can make out Old Testament figures, from Adam trying to hide, via Nebuchadnezzar seated legs akimbo, to prophets holding scrolls as if they were advertisements. Then come New Testament scenes: the Annunciation, a Tree of Jesse, the Visitation and the Nativity, Mary in bed, exhausted, baby Jesus being bathed and Joseph meditating. A wealth of Romanesque creatures crammed in here and there adds to the medieval excitement. The interior has fared less well; according to Henry James, the geometrical patterns added in the 19th century were 'the most hideous decorative painting that was ever inflicted upon passive pillars and indifferent vaults'. He could be oversensitive. Cafés spill out over the large pedestrian square surrounding the church, and there's a busy covered market to one side.

The **Palais de Justice**, or law courts, now a confusing amalgam of buildings, has a core that dates back to the Plantagenets when this was the palace of Poitiers. Gothic alterations were made for the mega-rich, ruthless prince, Jean, Duc de Berry, and much later, after the buildings had been converted into courts, a grand classical façade was added on one side. You can enter via its majestic staircase to see the enormous early 13th-century Grande Salle or Salle des Pas Perdus. Measuring almost 160ft in length, and without any central columns to help hold up the ceiling, it's of impressive size even by today's standards. Jean, Duc de Berry had the splendid Gothic end done in grand style: angels hold coats of arms above the massive triple fireplace and, much higher up, four lords stand aloof, looking down on hoi polloi. These days, when the courts are in session, lawyers in black and white garb flit in and out of the doorways of the massive room as though engaged in some theatrical farce.

Head south along busy Rue Gambetta and its shops and pass **St-Porchaire**, with its Romanesque heads on the outside and its refined Gothic interior. The town hall presides over **Place du Maréchal Leclerc**, the second hub of the upper city. Wide Rue Victor Hugo leads off the square to the **Musée de Chièvres** (*open Tues–Fri 10–12 and 1–5, Sat and Sun 2–6; closed Mon; adm*), set in a grand town house, but backed by a

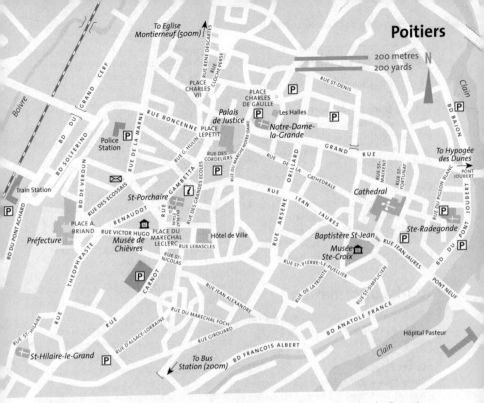

modern department store. Its varied art collections were left to the town by Rupert de Chièvres, a wealthy 19th-century traveller; some of the furniture is outstanding.

The Historic Quarter down the Hill

Take the **Grand-Rue**, with its old-style shops, down to Poitiers' even older historic quarter towards the Clain river, now containing a chaotic mishmash of buildings. The modern **Musée Ste-Croix** (*open Tues–Fri 10–12 and 1–5, Sat and Sun 2–6; closed Mon; adm*) conceals a substantial display of Poitou culture down the ages, including Gallo-Roman statues and funerary stelae, exquisite and weird Romanesque carvings, vestiges of the vanished 12th-century church of Ste-Croix, and beautiful pieces of medieval Limoges work. Most of the paintings date from the 19th and 20th centuries, with some small sculptural works by Rodin, Camille Claudel, Maillol and Max Ernst.

The nearby **Baptistère St-Jean** (*open April–Oct daily 10.30–12.30 and 3–6; rest of year daily exc Tues 2.30–4.30; adm*) conceals a rare remnant from early Christian Poitiers. As you enter, the jumble of sarcophagi resembles a junkyard for old tombs, but, as the details emerge, the place becomes quite fascinating. The tombs are Merovingian, covered with curious engravings. The sunken octagonal baptismal font is reckoned to date from the 4th or 5th century. Peer up to appreciate the fragments of Romanesque wall paintings. One particularly remarkable one depicts the Christ of the Ascension surrounded by the Apostles showing their wonder in exaggerated hand gestures, while angels float along almost waving the good news.

Getting to Poitiers

Buzz (*see* p.6) flies from London Stansted.

Getting from the Airport

You arrive at Poitiers-Biard airport (**t** 04 49 30 04 40), and you'll need to take a **taxi** to the centre. Try Compagnie des Radio-Taxis, **t** 05 49 88 12 34, for a 24hr service.

Car Hire

For the moment, there are no car hire companies at the airport, but the major operators have offices in town: **Avis**, **t** 05 49 58 13 00; **Budget**, **t** 05 49 58 28 14; **Europcar**, **t** 05 49 58 25 34; **Hertz**, **t** 05 49 58 24 24.

Tourist Information

Poitiers: 45 Place Charles de Gaulle, **t** 05 49 41 21 24, **f** 05 49 88 65 84, *www.ot-poitiers.fr*, *accueil-tourisme@interpc.fr*.

Market Days

Poitiers: Mon, Wed, Fri (including antiques), and Sat. The tempting covered food market is In an excellent location by **Notre-Dame-la-Grande** – go in the morning.

Shopping

The main shopping street is **Rue Gambetta**, with a wide choice of high-street names. For big stores, there's a Printemps on **Place du Maréchal Leclerc**, while the new **Cordeliers** mall nearby includes a Monoprix and FNAC. Two parallel roads going down to the cathedral, **Grand-Rue** and **Rue de la Cathédrale**, have a few interesting old-style shops, such as an umbrella-maker and a candle-maker. Along **Rue des Grandes Ecoles**, Le Dirigeable sells contemporary craft creations.

Where to Stay

Poitiers ✉ 86000

★★★Grand Hôtel, 28 Rue Carnot, **t** 05 49 60 90 60, **f** 05 49 62 81 89 (*moderate*). A slightly impersonal swish modern number with very comfortable rooms, discreetly positioned in a small modern precinct off one of the major old streets.

★★Hôtel de l'Europe, 39 Rue Carnot, **t** 05 49 88 12 00, **f** 05 49 88 97 30 (*moderate–inexpensive*). This larger hotel makes a grand impression set back in its own courtyard, and is quite swanky for a two-star.

★★Plat d'Etain, 7 Rue du Plat d'Etain, **t** 05 49 41 04 80, **f** 05 49 52 25 84 (*inexpensive*). Former posting inn tucked away in a great central position behind Place du Maréchal Leclerc.

★★Central, 35 Place du Maréchal Leclerc, **t** 05 49 01 79 79, **f** 05 49 60 27 56 (*inexpensive*). Which is indeed central, and a reasonable choice.

★★Chapon Fin, 11 Rue Lebascles, **t** 05 49 88 02 97, **f** 05 49 88 91 63 (*inexpensive*). Also well located.

Cheaper hotels crowd around the railway station down the hillside from the centre. One hotel stands out near Futuroscope: **★★★Le Clos de la Ribaudière**, Chasseneuil-du-Poitou, **t** 05 49 52 86 66, **f** 05 49 52 86 32. Rooms around a grand 19th-century castle, plus swanky restaurant serving excellent regional cuisine.

Eating Out

Le Maxime, 4 Rue St-Nicolas, **t** 05 49 41 09 55. Very fine restaurant (*moderate*) where the chef performs magic tricks with regional cuisine. *Closed Sat and Sun*.

Le St-Hilaire, 65 Rue Renaudot, **t** 05 49 41 15 45. Don't be put off by the entrance in a modern building: the restaurant itself (*moderate*) is hidden in 12th-century cellars. The chef uses spices to good effect. The waiters dress in medieval style. *Closed Sun and Mon lunch*.

Les Bons Enfants, 11 Bis Rue Cloche Perse, **t** 05 49 41 49 82 (*moderate*). An appealing tiny restaurant. *Closed Mon*.

Le Pavé de la Villette, 21 Rue Carnot, **t** 05 49 60 49 49 (*cheap*). Meats are the speciality, including garlicky local kid. *Closed Sun*.

Also look at the appealing terraces around Notre-Dame-la-Grande.

Although the city now somewhat ignores its **cathedral**, this massive, stern-faced building reflects the might of Poitiers in medieval times. On the main façade, the carved Day of Judgement stands out. Inside, the vast edifice, held up on Plantagenet-style vaults, contains many delightful decorative details. The carved kingly heads help recall that the future King Henry II of England married Eleanor of Aquitaine here in 1152, in one of the most significant weddings ever for Anglo-French relations; together, their lands would stretch from the Spanish to the Scottish borders. Other features to look out for include the odd panel of very old stained glass, the entertaining, awkwardly seated stone figures carved along the cornice, and the wood carvings on the 13th-century choir stalls, perhaps the oldest in France.

Don't miss the atmosphere-charged **Ste-Radegonde**, tucked out of sight below the cathedral. Radegonde, put-upon Dark Ages queen of violent Clotaire, founded the church here as a funerary chapel for the nuns of her abbey of Ste-Croix in the 6th century, and was herself buried here in 587. The entrance tower is Romanesque, as is the apse, but the main Gothic part very much resembles the cathedral, only on a more human scale. The superb rounded Romanesque apse is held up on chunky columns with chunky decoration. The wall paintings, added in the 13th century, were much restored in the 19th, but in the crypt, the sarcophagus of Ste Radegonde dates from the 8th or 9th century. The monument to a footstep is attached to the most outlandish story connected with Radegonde and this church: Christ appeared to Radegonde to announce her death and to tell her of the special place that awaited her in heaven – as he went off, he left an imprint of his right foot in the stone.

Ste-Radegonde lies close to the pretty banks of the Clain. Cross the river and climb the opposite hillside to find the **Hypogée des Dunes** (*open June–mid-Sept Tues–Fri 10–12 and 1–5, Sat and Sun 2–6; rest of year Tues–Sun 2–4; closed Mon; adm*), from where you get excellent views over the roofscape of Poitiers. The outer building is a 20th-century pastiche of a Gallo-Roman structure. It covers an underground chapel from around the 7th century, decorated with very rare pieces of Merovingian carvings.

Back in the historic centre, two further major churches grace either end of the old heart of town. **St-Hilaire-le-Grand** to the south is the more spectacular, another major Poitierian early medieval pilgrimage church on the route to Santiago de Compostela. The 19th-century restorers got carried away, though, ruining the façade in particular, but the series of Romanesque apses decorated with animal panels and other figures remains truly beautiful. Enter the church and you get a splendid view down to the raised choir with its thin Romanesque arcade. The nave is more striking still, and extraordinarily wide with its six side-aisles. Three curious octagonal cupolas hold up the main nave bays. In the choir, one capital shows St Hilaire being placed in his tomb, while some of the faded ochre wall paintings depict other dignified bishops of Poitiers, plus the story of St Martin. Beyond St-Hilaire, the picturesque public garden, the **Parc de Blossac**, has views down on to the Clain from its shaded walks behind the remaining portions of the city's ramparts. On the northern edge of the centre, severe **Mortierneuf** church stands in a neglected part of town, the most sidelined of the city's plethora of major churches, although it was consecrated in 1096.

On the western outskirts of town, close to the airport, the relatively small but beautiful stalagmite and stalagtite caves, the **Grottes de Norée**, long closed for restoration, should soon reopen to the public. Nearby, Les Saisons de la Norée is a very sweet little address at which to savour refined cuisine.

Day Trips from Poitiers

Planète Futuroscope Film Park

Springing up in the midst of the Poitou farmland north of Poitiers, Planète Futuroscope film park looks obscenely kitsch, but it offers the finest array of large screens anywhere in Europe, and possibly even the world. It's at the cutting edge of world cinema; entrance is expensive, but you're unlikely to regret it. It claims to offer the best large-scale screens anywhere in the world, and they deliver some unforgettable visuals, even if the contents of the films themselves are of varied quality and one or two look a bit jaded now.

Futuroscope was conceived and built by the Poitou-Charentes regional council, and three of the films are devoted to the region. **Le Pavillon de la Vienne** presents two: after you've sat quietly through the bureaucratic one, you're treated to a wild ride across Poitou-Charentes, shaken around violently in your seat – if you have a wobbly heart you should give it a miss. The new **Atlantis** building with its hemispheric screen showing 3D presentations also has alarmingly unstable seats. The vast **Imax** films are stunning, the **Kinémax** screen, the size of two tennis courts, is stupendous. Other screens have their good and bad points: the **circular screen** is liable to cause neckache; the **Tapis Magique** underfloor screen proves a bit awkward to appreciate – you feel as if you're trapped searching under your seat for something you've lost. There are a few simpler spaces with quieter interactive presentations and games geared towards younger children. Evenings end with a vulgar but vibrant fireworks show (*nightly in school hols; otherwise Sat night only*) around the artificial central lake with its shooting fountains.

Getting There

There's a **bus shuttle** service to Planète Futuroscope from Poitiers railway station, plus some direct services from the airport.

Tourist Information

For information and bookings in the UK, call t (020) 7499 8049; in France, t 05 49 49 30 00, *www.planete-futuroscope.com*. In high season (basically school holidays outside of 11 Nov–31 Mar), adults €30 per day, children €22. In low season, costs go down to €20 for adults, €16 for children. All Saturdays outside the main low season period are charged at high season rates. For English-speaking visitors, the Consigne by the main entrance provides free-dubbing earphones. Allow two days to see all the screens; *see p.168 for a hotel suggestion.*

Eating Out

On site, the restaurant **Kadélicescope** offers traditional French gastronomic cuisine or a buffet of specialties from around the world. There's also a crêperie, a brasserie, a pizzeria and fast food outlets to choose from.

Chauvigny

For such a small place, Chauvigny, east of Poitiers, has an amazingly sight-crammed medieval centre, with the remnants of five forts crammed into its upper village, all topped by the Romanesque church of **St-Pierre**. Inside, the columns are sculpted with memorably bold figures, some representing biblical characters, others monsters, including winged sphinxes wearing what look like jester's hats. Very rarely for medieval church carving, one is signed: '*Gofridus me fecit*'.

Chauvigny's main keep, the **Donjon de Gouzon** (*open 15 June–15 Sept Mon–Sat 10–12.30 and 2.30–6.30, Sun 11–6.30; 16 Sept–Oct weekends and public hols 2.30–6.30; rest of year daily 2–6; adm*) has been turned into a slick little museum. A funky lift takes you up to the terrace, with views over the rooftops of the town, and as far as the nuclear power station on the Vienne. In the floors below, the beautiful spaces are more impressive than the exhibits. One floor is dedicated to local pottery, from neolithic times to the present. Chauvigny still produces fine dinner services, several of which feature here, ordered for the Ritz, or embellished with scenes from Astérix and Obélix (available from La Boutique du Planty on Route de Montmorillon in town).

Chauvigny's biggest tourist draw takes place in another of the five castles, the massively walled **Château Baronnial**, which holds regular displays of **falconry** (*July–Aug, 4 displays daily 11.15, 2.30, 4 and 5.30; April–June weekends only 2.30 and 4; Oct–Nov weekends only 11.45 and 5.30; adm*). This château was built for the bishops of Poitiers in the early Middle Ages when they were lords of the land. The few remaining rooms in the courtyard of the neighbouring **Château d'Harcourt**, built a little later in the Middle Ages for the viscounts of Châtellerault, are devoted to seasonal displays by contemporary artists (*July–Aug only*). The remnants of the fifth château have been turned in part into a B&B. Lower Chauvigny has its own attractions, including a Romanesque church with more engrossing carvings, and a former bathhouse amusingly turned into a centre for contemporary art.

Getting There

The **bus** service between Poitiers railway station and Chauvigny is infrequent. On weekdays there's a 9am bus; a return bus departs Chauvigny at 6pm. At weekends the services are very limited. Check with Rapides du Poitou, t 05 49 46 27 45.

Tourist Information

Chauvigny ⊠ 86300: 5 Rue St-Pierre, t 05 49 46 39 01, *www.chauvigny.cg86.fr*.

Market Day

Chauvigny: Sat am is the main market, with smaller markets on Tues am and Thurs am.

Eating Out

**Le Lion d'Or, 8 Rue du Marché, t 05 49 46 30 28, f 05 49 47 74 28 (*inexpensive*). Traditional type of provincial French hotel restaurant in the lower village.

In the upper village you have a choice between two appealing crêperies.

La Bigorne, t 05 49 56 05 40 (*inexpensive*). A themed establishment where the waitresses serve you in medieval costume.

La Belle Epoque, t 05 49 46 55 23 (*inexpensive*). Provides tempting dishes of the day as well as crêpes.

Touring from Poitiers

You'll find that the sights are reliably open Easter–Oct 10–12 and 2–5 and charge adm, unless otherwise stated.

Day 1: Thouet Surprises

Morning: Head northwest for **Parthenay** with its ruined castle above a loop in the Thouet, its weeping willows by the river, and its monuments on the hillside.

Lunch: In Parthenay, gastronomes should make for **Le Fin Gourmet, t** 05 49 64 04 63 (*moderate*), by the covered market, to sample inventive-to-eccentric cuisine. *Closed Sun lunch and Mon.* For a meal in an atmospheric historic corner, opt for simpler food at **La Citadelle, t** 05 49 64 12 25 (*cheap*), serving regional fare at the foot of an impressive gateway. *Closed Sat lunch, Sun and Mon lunch.*

Afternoon: Continue north up the Thouet valley for **St-Loup**, with a delightful airy 17th-century château (*open May–Sept 2–7; rest of year weekends only*), whose grounds are being lovingly restored. Then make brief religious calls at the fort-like churches of **Airvault** and **St-Jouin**. The **Château d'Oiron** rises like a mirage out of the plain to the north. The interiors are a brilliant, energizing mix of Ancien Régime and contemporary decoration.

Dinner and sleeping: In Oiron village, **★Le Relais du Château, t** 05 49 96 54 96, **f** 05 49 54 45 (*cheap*) is a simple inn and serves hearty meals. East in Loudun, a town largely bypassed by the modern world, the coaching inn **★★Hostellerie de la Roue d'Or**, **t** 05 49 98 01 23, **f** 05 49 22 31 5 (*inexpensive*) fits the bill nicely enough, with generally old-style rooms and good country fare. Another pleasant place to stay is **★★Le Ricordeau, t** 05 49 22 67 27 (*cheap*), this 18th-century town house recently restored, the rooms spacious, the restaurant (*moderate–cheap*) with warm wood panelling.

Day 2: The Poitou-Touraine Border

Morning: Loudon may be historically associated with witchcraft, but it seems a very sweet, unspoilt country town now. **Richelieu** due east was built from scratch for the famed cardinal, a model of 17th-century town planning, scarcely disturbed, although the megalomaniac's huge castle has practically vanished.

Lunch: It's a bit of a trek northeast for Ste-Maure-de-Touraine, but this area, synonymous with tasty goat's cheese, offers the best choices. **★★★Les Hauts de Ste-Maure, t** 02 47 65 50 65 (*expensive–moderate*), another former coaching inn, has style, and the cuisine flair. *Closed Sun and Mon.* Or, a few km west at La Godinière, Noyant, **La Ciboulette, t** 02 47 65 84 64 (*moderate*) is a large establishment opposite the A10, exit 25, but with a pleasant country terrace.

Afternoon: After admiring **Ste-Maure**'s 17th-century covered market, continue southeast via dopey **Descartes**, where the 17th-century philosopher who so helped awaken the European world to modern thinking was first brought up. Then stop to tour the attractive fossil of a castle at **Le Grand-Pressigny**, its museum of prehistory recalling the thriving trade in this area's beautiful valleys in neolithic times.

Dinner and sleeping: To the south, at Yzeures-sur-Creuse, **★★★La Promenade, t** 02 47 91 49 00, **f** 02 47 94 46 12 (*inexpensive*) offers good-value, quite stylish rooms in yet another coaching inn, and a pleasant restaurant. **Dallais-La Promenade, t** 02 47 94 93 52 (*expensive–moderate*), at Le Petit Pressigny, is a sensational gourmet restaurant. *Closed Sun pm and Mon.* In the enchanting riverside village of Angles-sur-Anglin, **★★★Le Relais du Lyon d'Or, t** 05 49 98 32 53, **f** 05 49 84 02 28 (*inexpensive*) is the perfect inn for the place.

Day 3: Wonderful Angles on the Medieval

Morning: Wander up and down **Angles'** hillside, its ruined castle (*open July–Aug only; closed Tues*), and its upper chapel, the latter displaying fine local craftwork, both embroidery and cutlery. At nearby **Fontgombault** on the Creuse, admire the medieval abbey.

Lunch: For a peaceful lunch in a restored old country inn with a pretty terrace, try **★★Le Capucin Gourmand**, t 02 54 37 66 85 (*moderate*), to the north along the Creuse at Tournon-St-Martin. *Closed Mon lunch*. South along the Creuse, just south of Le Blanc, **★★★Domaine de l'Etape**, Rte de Belâbre, t 02 54 37 18 02 (*expensive–moderate*) has a sophisticated restaurant in its 19th-century manor surrounded by substantial grounds.

Afternoon: Head south of Angles for the village of **St-Savin**, whose church has what has been nicknamed the Sistine Chapel of Romanesque art, superb cartoon-like biblical scenes covering the tall barrel vault. This is a UNESCO World Heritage site.

Dinner and sleeping: Rather sleepy St-Savin has two simple but very pleasant choices near the abbey, **★★Hôtel du Midi**, t 05 49 48 00 40 (*inexpensive*), a former coaching inn, and **★La Grange** (*cheap*), a converted barn with basic rooms. Each has a restaurant.

Day 4: In Search of Relics

Morning: If you've already visited **Chauvigny**, its hilltop packed with castle ruins (*see* p.171), then head down to **St-Pierre-les-Eglises**, a gorgeously shaded church by the Vienne, and then to **Civaux**, with the most curious cemetery walls in France, made of boldly carved Dark Ages tombstones.

Lunch: Continue south along the Vienne river for old-style local favourite **★★Le Connétable Chandos** at Pont-de-Lussac, t 05 49 48 40 24 (*moderate*). *Closed Mon*. Or, some distance southwest in Charroux, **★★Hostellerie Charlemagne**, t 05 49 87 50 37 (*moderate*) was built from stones taken from the ruined abbey. Its restaurant serves up really tasty regional dishes. *Closed Mon*.

Afternoon: Christ's foreskin and Richard the Lionheart's brains and entrails – enticing relics for the abbey of St-Sauveur in **Charroux** to have bagged. Most of the abbey and its relics have long vanished, but the remnants tell several intriguing tales. Nearby **Civray** can boast one of the most startling Romanesque façades in Poitou.

Dinner and sleeping: West again, hilltop Melle makes a good small-town stop, particularly at **★★Les Glycines**, t 05 49 27 01 11, f 05 49 27 93 45 (*inexpensive*), a medieval house turned hotel, with quite refined restaurant. Just west at St-Martin-lès-Melle, **L'Argentière**, t 05 49 29 13 74, f 05 49 29 06 63 (*moderate*) comes second choice, a motel-style building on a main road, but with pleasant enough grounds. The restaurant with terrace isn't bad.

Day 5: Silver and Neolithic Discoveries

Morning: **Melle** has several remarkable churches, best of all that of St-Hilaire down in the valley, with the finest of Romanesque equestrian statues, plus shielded knights and curvaceous monsters. Out of town, the Mines d'Argent (*open June–Sept daily; rest of year weekends only 2–5*) recall the silver-mining that has long been important in these parts.

Lunch: At La Mothe-St-Héray due north of Melle, **★★Le Corneille**, t 05 49 05 17 08 (*moderate*) provides pleasant regional cooking. In Soudan, due north again, **★★L'Orangerie**, t 05 49 06 56 06 (*moderate*), offers local traditional cooking such as duck with apples, stuffed cabbage and eel in what looks like a pleasant modern family home.

Afternoon: A row of exceptional neolithic tombs stand among small oaks in the midst of large Poitevin fields outside **Bougon** a short way to the east, with a good museum (*open daily 10–6; Feb–Dec closed Wed am*) introducing the period. This is goat's cheese territory, so you could visit a specialist farm. Alternatively, **Lusignan** and **St-Maixent** prove pleasant provincial towns for an afternoon stroll.

Dinner and sleeping: **★★★Le Logis St-Martin**, t 05 49 05 58 68, f 05 49 76 19 93 (*expensive*), in the southeastern outskirts of St-Maixent is a very stylish old manor hotel, with excellent regional cuisine (*expensive–moderate*). The **Auberge du Port d'Aiript**, t 05 49 25 58 81, f 05 49 05 33 49 (*moderate*), 10km southwest (below the motorway) offers simpler traditional French hotel rooms and a popular local restaurant.

La Rochelle

The spectacular old port of La Rochelle owed its first time of good fortune partly to Eleanor of Aquitaine, and the importance of its harbour in medieval times is reflected in the three great towers still guarding the harbour. After the disastrous siege of 1627 to 1628 led by Cardinal Richelieu to suppress the independence of what had become a Protestant city-state within the Catholic state, the merchant families of La Rochelle soon recovered, building beautiful mansions along arcaded streets, in large part on the proceeds of slave-trading expeditions. La Rochelle is still a great nautical city, but most of the interest in seafaring these days is in yachts.

Round La Rochelle

All three striking medieval towers on the **Vieux Port** can be visited (*open July–Aug daily 10–7; 15 May–June and 1–15 Sept daily 10–1 and 2–6; rest of year Tues–Sun 10–12.30 and 2–5.30; adm*). The **Tour de la Lanterne**, by far the tallest, topped by a Gothic spire, served not just as a sea-marker for centuries, but also as a prison, and inside it is covered with centuries-old graffiti by desperate British and Dutch sailors. A cordon of trees below indicates elegant gardens running along where ramparts once stood. They end with La Concurrence beach, but this isn't an ideal spot for a swim.

At the narrow entrance to the inner harbour, the Tour St-Nicolas and Tour de la Chaîne stand guard opposite each other. A chain once used to be strung between them at night to stop illicit trafficking. The interior of the **Tour de la Chaîne** is a bit of a disappointment; inside, the panels in French recall the town's history. Heading round the Vieux Port, touristy restaurants with lovely terraces line the historic quay, the **Cours des Dames**, which leads to the chubby statue of Victor-Guy Duperré, twenty-second child of a Rochelais family, who grew up to become a scourge to the British on the high seas in the early 1800s. He wasn't popular with the Algerians either, commanding the fleet which captured Algiers in 1830, leading to the founding of France's North African colonies. Beyond Duperré's statue, the gateway through the mighty **Grosse Horloge tower** (*not open*) beckons. This impressive structure is another landmark of the Vieux Port. The building dates back to the 14th century, a rare vestige of the formidable medieval rampart. In the 18th century it was embellished with its elaborate top, including two great globes, terrestrial and celestial. Cross the Vieux Port to the **Tour St-Nicolas**, which was constructed in the 14th century as a residence for the port governors. Worn Gothic figures overlook the labyrinth of rooms inside.

Back on Quai Duperré, head for the grand **Place de l'Hôtel de Ville**. The statue in the centre represents a defiant Jean Guiton, mayor at the time of Richelieu's terrible siege. Although Guiton failed to withstand the cardinal's merciless campaign, he failed to live up to his promise to kill himself rather than surrender, and although he even went on to join the French royal navy, he has gone down in La Rochelle as a hero, a symbol of the city's proud defiance. Behind the crenellated Gothic walls of the **town hall** courtyard, a colourful ceramic statue of King Henri IV stands out under its canopy. This vital 16th–17th-century monarch spent time here as a Protestant child with his severe Huguenot mother Jeanne d'Albret, well before his famous conversion to

La Rochelle
200 metres
200 yards
N
Musée d'Histoire Naturelle
Jardin des Plantes
Rue Albert 1er
Rue Delayant
Rue Alcide d'Orbigny
Av des Cordeliers
Rue du Cordouan
Rue du Collège
Rue Rambaud
POL
Rue Chaudrier
Rue du Minage
Place des Cordeliers
Parc Charruyer
Place de Verdun
Musée des Beaux-Arts
Av du General Leclerc
Musée du Nouveau Monde
Rue Gargoulleau
Rue des Cloutiers
Place du Marche
Les Halles
Rue Gambetta
Rue St-Louis
Rue Fleuriau
Rue Thiers
Rue St-Come
Cathedral
Rue Bazoges
Rue St-Yon
Rue des Merciers
Rue Villeneuve
Musée d'Orbigny-Bernon
Rue Aufredy
Rue des Augustins
Rue Amelot
Place St-Michel
Rue de l'Abreuvoir
Maison Vennette
Rue Dupaty
Hôtel de Ville
Place Baptiste Marcet
Palais de Justice
Rue du Palais
Rue des Templiers
Rue des Gentilshommes
Place de l'Arsenal
Musée Protestant
Hôpital St-Louis
Bourse
Place de la Caille
Rue St-Sauveur
Quai Maubec
Quai Louis Durand
Delmas
Remparts
Rue Reaumur
Rue Admyrault
Rue du Temple
Rue Chef de Ville
Musée du Flacon à Parfum
Av Jean Guiton
Grosse Horloge
Place Barentin
Quai Duperre
Vieux Port
Rue Vieljeux
Rue du Duc
Rue St-Claude
Rue de Rempart St-Claude
Av Maurice
Chemin des Remparts
Musée Grevin
Rue des Sts-Peres
Rue des Carmes
Cour des Dames
Quai Carenage
Quai Valin
Rue St-Nicolas
Bassin de Retenue
Place Marechal Foch
Place de la Chaine
Tour St-Nicolas
Bassin à Flot
Rue de la Monnaie
Rue St-Jean du Perot
Le Gabut
Quai du Gabut
Rue de l'Ouvrage à Corne
Tour de la Lanterne
Rue sur les Murs
Tour de la Chaîne
Rue de l'Armide
Quai de la Georgette
Av du General de Gaulle
Plage de la Concurrence
Esplanade St-Jean d'Acre
Quai Georges Simenon
Bassin des Grands Yachts
Bd Joffre
Train Station
Av Marillac
Av du 123eme R.I.
Le Bout Blanc
Sennac de Meillan
Rue du Loup Marin
Quai Louis Prunier
Musée des Modèles Reduits
La Ville en Bois
Rue du Cerf Volant
Musée des Automates
Musée Maritime Neptunéa

Catholicism when he became king, an act carried out to help reunite France after the appalling trauma of the French Wars of Religion. Henri IV is remembered as a merry figure, not as a dour religious man, and here he sports caramel leggings and a purple top, in contrast to the staid statues of the Virtues on the Baroque façade.

Many of La Rochelle's superb arcaded streets lie around the town hall. Two great civic buildings, the former **Bourse** or exchange, with stone prows sticking out, and the **Palais de Justice**, stand side by side on Rue du Palais. One curiosity in this quarter is the **Musée du Flacon à Parfum** (*open Tues–Sat 10.30–12 and 2–7, Mon 3–7; closed Sun; adm*), along Rue du Temple, with its extensive collection of scent bottles.

The town's best museum, the **Musée du Nouveau Monde** (*open Mon and Wed–Sat 10.30–12.30 and 1.30–6, Sun 3–7; closed Tues; adm*) is one of the few in France to confront the subject of slavery, although many French Atlantic ports profited hugely from the triangular trade, not just La Rochelle. The story is told in good part by showing the luxuries purchased on the proceeds of the trade, including one of the sumptuous mansions which houses the museum. In the 18th century La Rochelle ships

Getting to La Rochelle

Buzz (*see* p.6) flies from London Stansted.

Getting from the Airport

There's a **shuttle bus** from the airport to central Place de Verdun, journey time 15–30mins. **For taxis:** Abeilles: t 05 46 41 22 22/ t 05 46 51 55 55 or Auto Plus t 05 46 34 02 22.

Getting Around

For local **bus** information contact RTCR: t 05 46 34 02 22.

Car Hire

ADA, 1 Av Général de Gaulle, t 05 46 41 02 17, f 05 46 50 67 75; **Avis**, 166 Bd Joffre, t 05 46 41 13 55; **Budget**, 11 Av Général de Gaulle, t 05 46 41 33 53, f 05 46 41 55 26; **RentaCar**, 29 Av Général de Gaulle, t 05 46 27 27 27.

Tourist Information

La Rochelle: Place de la Petite Sirène, t 05 46 41 14 68, f 05 46 41 99 85, *www.larochelle-tourisme.com*.

Market Days

Place du Marché: daily am; **Rue St-Nicolas**, flea market, mid-June–mid-Sept Thurs and Sat am, rest of year Sat am; **Minimes Marina**, Av du Lazaret, June–Aug Fri am.

Shopping

On the **quays**, as well as admiring the fish stalls, you can seek out a few themed shops among all the touristy restaurants, such as Bleu Marine, Cours des Dames, selling seafaring clothes and classic French stripy jumpers, Collection Philippe Godard, Cours des Dames, specializing in regional tipple, or Les Délices du Trinitain, Quai Duperré, with regional food. The streets heading inland from Quai Duperré are the best for shopping. Arcaded **Rue du Palais** and **Rue Chaudrier** form the main drag, with antiques shops and places offering household goods and gifts, La Boutique du Marin winning the prize for objects with a maritime theme, while the most delectable pâtisserie and ice cream shop is d'Jolly. The side streets are interesting too, especially pedestrian **Rue du Temple** one end, including tempting addresses like Le Tastevin with its wine cellar or Christian Lacaud for charcuteries. **Rue Gargoulleau** at the other end has La Boutique Landaise for regional culinary specialities and P. Bossuet, a Cognac and Pineau-maker. On the corner of Rue Chaudrier and **Place de Verdun**, the Café de la Paix boasts the most sumptuous décor of any brasserie in town. **Rue St-Yon/Pas de Minage** and **Rue des Dames** have more good shops, as does Rue Thiers. Down behind Quai Valin on the Vieux Port, **Rue St-Nicolas** is another lively corner.

Activities

Bikes are big in La Rochelle: for hire try **Autoplus Les Vélos Jaunes**, Place de Verdun, t 05 46 34 02 22; **Ecovélo**, 282 ter Av J. Guiton, t 05 46 00 90 00; **Vel'Ile**, Parking Le Belvédère, t 05 46 42 19 40; **Cyclo-Parc**, Plage de la Concurrence (*April–Sept*), t 05 46 41 02 24.

Taking a boat trip from La Rochelle is wonderful. Companies by the Vieux Port offering **mini-cruises** round the central islands of a couple of hours, half-day or day include: **Croisières Océanes**, Cours des Dames, t 05 46 50 68 44, f 05 46 44 52 69; **Croisières Inter-Iles**, Cours des Dames, t 05 46 50 51 88, f 05 46 41 16 96; **Ré-Croisières**, Cours des Dames, t 05 46 41 50 40, f 05 46 41 50 40; **Navipromer**, Tour de la Châine, t 05 46 01 52 96, f 05 46 01 52 96.

alone transported some 140,000 slaves from West Africa to the West Indies, principally to Haiti. Paintings and engravings offer an insight into the disturbing mentality of the period. Some of the revolutionary mementos of the anti-slavery movement are heartwarming. Napoleon reinstated slavery, but the trade declined after him.

Although the **Musée des Beaux-Arts** (*open daily exc Tues 2–7; adm*) is housed in another grand mansion, the collections have been shoved unceremoniously to the

For more exhilarating sea journeys, try: **Kapalouest**, 32 Av des Amériques, **t** 05 46 29 26 55, **f** 05 46 34 46 90, a mini-catamaran; **Notre-Dame des Flots**, **t/f** 05 45 32 17 63, *notredamedesflots@yahoo.fr*, to tour on an old-fashioned sailing boat; **Association Loisirs de la Mer**, at Les Minimes, **t/f** 05 49 52 97 80, to go sea-fishing.

Also at Les Minimes, **Cap' Mousse**, **t** 06 61 50 42 25, **Yacapartir**, **t** 06 87 04 02 71, and **Destination Océan**, **t** 05 46 45 17 29, organize yachting trips with skippers. To hire a yacht from Les Minimes, **Rivages**, **t** 05 46 44 70 93, **f** 05 46 45 47 99, or for a motor call **Aunis Motonautic**, **t** 05 46 44 23 66, **f** 05 46 44 52 67.

Where to Stay

La Rochelle ✉ 17000
★★★★**Résidence de France**, 43 Rue du Minage, **t** 05 46 28 06 00, **f** 05 46 28 06 03, *residence.de.france@wanadoo.fr* (*expensive*). The loveliest hotel in town in an old building further embellished with a new tower.
★★★**Hôtel de la Monnaie**, 3 Rue de la Monnaie, **t** 05 46 50 65 65, **f** 05 46 50 63 19 (*expensive–moderate*). Central hotel around an historic cobbled courtyard, with very comfortable, modern rooms.
★★★**Le St-Jean-d'Acre**, 4 Place de la Chaîne, **t** 05 46 41 73 33, **f** 05 46 41 10 01, *reservation@hotel-la-rochelle.com* (*moderate*). A characterful old building on the old port, in a great position for crowd-gazing.
★★★**France-Angleterre et Champlain**, 20 Rue Rambaud, **t** 05 46 41 23 99, **f** 05 46 41 15 19, *hotel@france-champlain.com* (*moderate*). Central, with plenty of charm, traditional furnishings and a garden.
★★**Trianon**, 6 Rue de la Monnaie, **t** 05 46 41 21 35, **f** 05 46 41 95 78 (*moderate*). Charming hotel close to the little town beach and town gardens, with restaurant.

★★**Hôtel du Commerce**, 6 Place de Verdun, **t** 05 46 41 08 22, **f** 05 46 41 74 85 (*inexpensive*). Slightly swanky hotel with some large if rather vacuous rooms on this large square, with restaurant (*moderate*).
★**Henri IV**, 31 Rue des Gentilshommes, **t** 05 46 41 25 79, **f** 05 46 41 78 64, *HENRI-IV@wanadoo.fr* (*inexpensive*). Right in the historic centre, by the Grosse Horloge.
★**Bordeaux**, 43 Rue St-Nicolas, **t** 05 46 41 31 22, **f** 05 46 41 24 43 (*inexpensive*). A very decent option, tucked away in a pretty quarter just behind the eastern side of the Vieux Port.

The hotel group **Ibis** has snapped up several historic buildings in the centre, turning them into two-star hotels: **t** 05 46 50 68 68, **t** 05 46 50 52 55, or **t** 05 46 41 60 22 (*inexpensive*).

Eating Out

La Rochelle is packed with restaurants. Indifferent ones stretch out across the pavements along the quays; they have great terraces, but head elsewhere for finer cuisine.

Richard Coutanceau, Plage de la Concurrence, **t** 05 46 41 48 19, **f** 05 46 41 99 45, *contact@coutanceaularochelle.com* (*expensive*). The chef is renowned for his seafood dishes. *Closed Sun.*
Les Flots, 1 Rue Chaîne, **t** 05 46 41 32 51, **f** 05 46 41 90 80, *contact@les-flots.com* (*expensive–moderate*). Richard Coutanceau's son cooks up inventive and refined dishes.
André, 5 Rue St-Jean du Pérot, **t** 05 46 41 28 24, **f** 05 46 41 64 22 (*moderate*). An institution in the centre of historic La Rochelle, with its long front resembling a ship.
A Côté de Chez Fred, 30 Rue St-Nicolas, **t** 02 46 41 65 76 (*moderate*). Surprising little fish restaurant attached to the adjoining fishmonger's. *Closed Sun and some Mons.*
Café du Nord. A good bet among the plethora of restaurants on the Vieux Port.

top of the building. At the entrance, the black and white representations of Christ's life by Rouault are striking, but they're followed by a chaotic display of cloying canvases. Bouguereau, born in La Rochelle, was a great salon favourite in the 19th century for his purist's titillating nudes, although now we might think his works would be more popular in saloons. But the local man comes out comparatively well in the company he keeps here, with a touching portrait of one Mme Deseilligny. There are also classic maritime scenes to compare with a vibrant Signac *pointilliste* view.

La Rochelle's **cathedral** occupies one corner of the massive, vacuous Place de Verdun. The church proves rather empty too behind its grand, wide, 18th-century classical façade, although it does contain some sickly 19th-century decoration, both in the stained glass and the paintings. Blame Bouguereau for the worst excesses in the choir. The sailors' ex-votos are more moving. The nearby **Musée d'Orbigny-Bernon** (*open Wed–Sat 10–12 and 2–6; Sun 2-6; closed Tues; adm*) turns out to have more charm than La Rochelle's fine arts museum. French ceramics are the forte, while engravings illustrate the siege of La Rochelle and the persecution of Protestants. Other sections are devoted to Oriental miscellany and to the Second World War.

If you're particularly interested in the history of Protestantism in France, make a special effort to see the little **Musée Protestant** (*open July–15 Sept daily exc Sun 2.30–6; adm*) back near the Vieux Port behind Quai Duperré. The museum stands next to the large Protestant church, with the wonkily arcaded **Cloître des Dames Blanches** an oasis of peace on the other side.

On the south side of the Vieux Port, quayside cafés and restaurants front the attractive modern village of the **Gabut** quarter. The impressive new **aquarium** (*open July–Aug 9am–11pm; April–June and Sept 9–8; rest of year 10–8; adm*) stands in this quarter, one of the best in France, with sensational lighting effects and a shark pool where you almost feel you're plunging in with the creatures. The major attractions at the substantial **Musée Maritime Neptunéa** (*open April–Sept daily 10–7.30; rest of year daily 2–6.30; adm*) are real ships, several of which you can board. The rest of this major educational museum on sea life occupies the former fish market. The **Musée des Automates** and **Musée des Modèles Réduits** (*open 15 June–Aug 9.30–7; Feb–May and Sept–Oct 10–12 and 2–6; Nov–Jan 2–6*) might amuse youngsters, the first with its animated figures, the second with some quite splendid model boats.

South again and you arrive at La Rochelle's massive modern marina, **Les Minimes** (*t 05 46 28 07 28*), full of fabulous real boats. This is one of the most prestigious sailors' addresses in France, with all the amenities alongside. A regular Bus de Mer boat service connects the Vieux Port and Les Minimes (*April–Sept, hourly 10–7, but not at 1pm; March–Oct weekends and public hols only*). Or consider cycling; La Rochelle is renowned as a green-friendly town, ecological policies pushed to the forefront by the much-respected long-time socialist mayor Michel Crépeau, who died in 1999, but whose legacy of progressive town planning continues.

Châtelaillon-Plage and Fouras – Beach Resorts South of La Rochelle

Buses from Place de Verdun (*Ligne 16 for Châtelaillon; for Fouras, use Océcars' regular services, t 05 46 00 95 15*) will take you to these appealing resorts. **Châtelaillon-Plage**, once capital of the medieval Aunis region around La Rochelle, is now a cheerful small, contemporary seaside town with a choice of modern hotels and restaurants lined up behind the mimosas of the promenade. **Fouras** by contrast has kept a strong historic atmosphere; a splendid medieval keep guarding the northern entrance to the Charente river rises from a high prow of land above the beaches and restaurants.

Day Trips and Overnighters from La Rochelle

The Ile de Ré

The island of Ré's similarity in name to the Egyptian sun god Ra doesn't do its image any harm as a highly prized destination for French sun-worshippers, who come to enjoy its special microclimate. The opening in 1988 of a road bridge (*expensive toll*) connecting Ré with the mainland has made the island somewhat less exclusive. **Rivedoux**, the closest village to the bridge, is too close to the industrial quarters of La Rochelle for comfort, but its sandy beach is popular. Heading along the southern side of Ré, **Ste-Marie-de-la-Mer**, though lacking a proper beach, has old streets full of charm, with shutters painted various shades of green. **Le Bois-Plage** is located close to long stretches of sand, and is also the island's wine centre. The southern road

Getting There

Régie d'Aunis-Saintonge, t 05 46 09 20 15, runs bus services all year from Place de Verdun. RTCR, t 05 46 34 02 22, puts on frequent buses July–Aug, plus Wed and weekends in June.

Tourist Information

Ile de Ré: 5 Rue de la Blanche, Le Bois-Plage-en-Ré, t 05 46 09 00 55, f 05 46 09 00 54.

Where to Stay and Eat

La Flotte-en-Ré ✉ 17630

★★★★Le Richelieu, 44 Av de la Plage, t 05 46 09 60 70, f 05 46 09 50 59 (*expensive*). The most exclusive address on Ré: a beautiful, luxurious hotel in this wonderful village, with a thalassotherapy centre and a fantastic restaurant, lobster the speciality.

St-Martin-en-Ré ✉ 17410

★★★La Jetée, 23 Quai Georges Clemenceau, t 05 46 09 36 36, f 05 46 09 36 06 (*moderate*). Exclusive hotel with 31 rooms.

★★Les Colonnes, 19 Quai Job Foran, t 05 46 09 21 58, f 05 46 09 21 49 (*inexpensive*). In the heart of the action with a bar spilling out below. Restaurant (*moderate*). *Closed Wed.*
★★Le Port, 29 Quai de la Poithevinière, t 05 46 09 21 21, f 05 46 09 06 85 (*inexpensive*). Simple hotel with spacious modern rooms.
★Le Sully, 19 Rue Jean Jaurès, t 05 46 09 26 94, f 05 46 09 06 85 (*inexpensive*). For a cheaper option, try this pleasant little hotel in the shopping streets up from the port.
La Baleine Bleue, Quai Launay Razilly, t 05 46 09 03 30, f 05 46 09 30 86 (*moderate*). Irresistible restaurant on the port's central island, attracting the smart set.

Ars-en-Ré ✉ 17580

Le Bistrot de Bernard, 1 Quai de la Criée, t 05 46 29 40 26, f 05 46 29 28 99 (*moderate*). Immediately eye-catching among the sweet restaurants at the port, and serving excellent seafood.

Bois-Plage ✉ 17580

★★L'Océan, 4 Rue St-Martin, t 05 46 09 23 07 (*moderate–inexpensive*). Delightful relaxing hotel in a relatively unspoilt part of the island, with a typical regional design and a maritime feel.

continues to **La Couarde**, a purpose-built resort, popular because of its good beaches. The road north from the toll bridge leads past the roofless Cistercian **Abbaye des Châteliers** and round **La Flotte**, a stylish village, home to Ré's new thalassotherapy centre and boasting a delightful strip of beach backed by pines which dwindles to nothing at high tide. **St-Martin-en-Ré** is Poitou-Charente's answer to St-Tropez. Even if the yachts are smaller here, its gorgeous circular harbour serves as a perfect stage for Côte d'Azur-style posing. Even St-Martin's penitentiary, set among the pointed Ancien Régime fortifications, looks almost picturesque.

Heading towards the western part of the island, a road branches north to **Loix**, past the isolated whitewashed building of the **Maison des Marais Salants**, which recalls the salt-making tradition of Ré, now much curtailed. Oyster-farming still counts as an important activity in these parts, though. The black and white spiky Gothic spire of the church of **Ars-en-Ré** serves a second purpose, as a sea-marker. North beyond **St-Clément-des-Baleines**, with its centre on Ré flora and fauna, the lighthouse, the **Phare des Baleines**, stands out, open to visitors for its great views across Ré and out to sea. The **Arche de Noé zoo** close by contains a collection of both living and stuffed animals. An enormous turtle that landed on Ré in 1978 is particularly honoured. **Les Portes-en-Ré**, tucked away in the least accessible corner of Ré, lies close to some of the best beaches, which suffer less from the receding tides.

Rochefort

Rochefort, an extremely handsome, muscular town, was born a child of war. In the 1660s it grew rapidly from a tiny thing into a square-shouldered worker to construct a fleet for the Sun King capable of taking on the great sea powers of the time, England and Holland. Rochefort was very well located: it lay up the Charente estuary, 15km from the sea, protected from the weather and easy to defend. A grand grid of streets up the slope from the river was constructed under Michel Bégon, the royal naval *intendant* at the end of the 17th century, now best known for giving his name to the begonia plant. Vast warships were put together here. Between 1690 and 1800, 300 vessels were launched from Rochefort. Lafayette sailed from here on his second expedition to America, on board the *Hermione*. But orders dried up by the start of the 20th century, and in 1944 the Nazis torched some of the old riverside buildings before leaving. Depressed, bruised and blackened, Rochefort waned. Things began to look up when the great film-maker Jacques Demy shot a successful musical here in the 1960s: *Les Demoiselles de Rochefort* starring Catherine Deneuve. Today, the grid town above the Charente has been scrubbed clean, some of its streets lined with palms.

Down by the Charente, the **Corderie Royale** is a stunning building, supported on one side by remarkable scrolled buttresses; the place goes on and on because it was made for ships' ropes to be twisted into shape inside. The interior now holds the **Centre International de la Mer** (*open summer daily 9–7; rest of year daily 9–6; adm*), with a permanent exhibition on rope-making, plus temporary exhibitions. Beyond one end of the Corderie Royale lies the provisions building which once churned out 20,000 kilos of bread a day lies Rochefort's yacht marina. Beyond the other end, a copy of Lafayette's **Hermione** (*guided tour only; open July–Aug daily 10–7; rest of year daily 10–1* *and 2–6; adm*) is being put together using old-fashioned techniques. In olden days, some 1,500 workers took around a year to complete such a vessel; the impressive new *Hermione* was started in 1997 and is due to be completed by 2007. Further splendid vessels are the glory of the **Musée de la Marine** (*open April–Sept daily 10–6; rest of year daily exc Tues 10–12 and 2–5; adm*), set in an elegant building just up from the *Hermione*, only this time the ships are beautiful scale models. Beyond the **Porte du Soleil** gateway, another elegant edifice serves as the covered market.

Grandiose **Place Colbert** is the centre of city life in the grid of streets beyond, the intimidating front of the classical church of **St-Louis** rising off one corner. Nearby, the **Maison Pierre Loti** (*guided tour only; open July–15 Sept daily 10–6, tours every half-hour; rest of year daily exc Tues and whole of Jan, tours at 11, 12, 2, 3 and 4; adm*) may not look much from the outside, but a riot of decoration awaits within, created by a man whose 'life was one long carnival,' according to one 19th-century admirer. Loti, born here in 1850, became a sailor and writer of exquisite romantic fiction. On his trips round the world he picked up a lot of exotica and half-digested ideas: hence the Arab room, the Turkish salon and the travesty of a mosque inside. But Loti was also a dedicated defender of many of the foreign peoples he visited. Although his novels are out of fashion, in 1891 he was elected to the Académie Française, beating one Emile Zola.

The **Musée d'Art et d'Histoire** (*open July–Aug daily exc public hols 1.30–7; rest of year daily exc Sun, Mon and public hols 1.30–5.30; adm*) close by contains a splendidly detailed scale model of 19th-century Rochefort and the town's art collections, while the **Musée des Commerces d'Autrefois** (*open 15 Mar–15 Nov daily 10–12 and 2–7; rest of year daily 10–12 and 2–6; adm*) pays homage to the shops of yesteryear. On the busy boulevard encircling Rochefort's centre, the grand 18th-century **Ancienne Ecole de Médecine Navale** (*open Feb–15 Nov, daily exc Mon; adm*) housed the first naval hospital in the world, and still contains a scientific cabinet of curiosities. Plant-lovers head half a mile out of the centre for the **Conservatoire du Bégonia** (*open for guided tours only, Tues–Sat at 2, 3 and 4pm; adm*). A further half-mile out of town takes you to the unmissable **Pont Transbordeur**, a huge transporter bridge over the Charente, still put into operation for tourists part of the year (*check times with tourist office; adm*).

Getting There

A good **rail** line links La Rochelle and Rochefort. A **bus** service by Océcars runs year-round, t 05 46 00 95 15.

Tourist Information

Rochefort ✉ 17300: Av Sadi Carnot, t 05 46 99 08 60, f 05 46 99 52 64, *www.tourisme.fr/rochefort*.

Market Day
Rochefort: Tues, Thurs and Sat, Av Charles de Gaulle, plus fish stalls in Les Halles.

Eating Out

*****La Corderie Royale**, Rue Audebert, t 05 46 99 35 35, f 05 46 99 78 72 (*expensive–moderate*). Occupies a wonderful 17th-century building by the Charente. The cuisine is of a high standard. *Closed Mon.*

****Le Paris**, 27–29 Rue La Fayette, t 05 46 99 33 11, f 05 46 99 77 34 (*inexpensive*). Hotel best known for its cheerful restaurant.

L'Escale de Bougainville, Quai de la Louisiane, t 05 46 99 54 99, f 05 46 99 54 99 (*moderate*). For reputed cuisine, opposite the marina. *Closed Sun eve and Mon.*

Try **Place Colbert** for other, cheaper options and cafés.

Touring from La Rochelle

You'll find that the sights are reliably open Easter–Oct 10–12 and 2–5 and charge adm, unless otherwise stated.

Day 1: France's Most Beautiful Marsh

Morning: The gorgeous poplar-lined waterways of the **Marais Poitevin** lie northeast of La Rochelle. Make for **Maillezais** (south of Fontenay-le-Comte) to visit the ruined abbey and to hire a punt nearby to go on the pea-soup waters.

Lunch: The staff at **Le Collibert, t** 02 51 87 25 07 (*moderate*), may go out of their way to tempt you with local specialities, from eels in wine and cabbage leaves to snails – go along with them! In Fontenay, you should get a warm welcome at **La Glycine, t** 02 51 69 17 24 (*moderate*), attached to the old coaching inn, Hôtel Fontarabie.

Afternoon: **Fontenay**'s arcaded streets, central church and local museum are worth a little look round. Then head for the capital of the Marais Poitevin, gorgeous **Coulon**, another excellent place to hire a punt, or walk round some of the waterways.

Dinner: Coulon has two utterly charming restaurants, **La Passerelle, t** 05 49 35 80 03 (*expensive*), on the quays, and **Le Central, t** 05 49 35 90 20 (*moderate*), nearby.

Sleeping: ***Au Marais, t** 05 49 35 90 43, **f** 05 49 35 81 98 (*moderate*) is bright and attractive, in pole position for Coulon's punting quays. Or return to Maillezais for a delightful French village B&B at **Mme Bonnet's, t** 02 51 87 23 00, **f** 02 51 00 72 44 (*inexpensive*).

Day 2: Seeking Out Weird Animals

Morning: Bustling **Niort** is the main town on the eastern edge of the Marais, with a very pleasant provincial atmosphere, pretty buildings and a serpent coiling down the main street. The two historic keeps in the centre are joined at the hip and contain one of the town's several modest museums.

Lunch: Enjoy lunch in Niort down by the river at **A La Belle Etoile, t** 05 49 73 31 29 (*expensive–moderate*), with its waterside

terrace and round dining room serving inventive local cuisine. *Closed Mon.* Or head some 20km south down the N150 to Beauvoir-sur-Niort and the smart, sprawling white manor-cum-château ***Domaine du Greffier, t** 05 49 32 62 62 (*moderate*).

Afternoon: Follow the N150 further south from Niort or Beauvoir and branch off for **Dampierre-sur-Boutonne**, with its charming run-down Renaissance château. Still cuter are the grungey Poitou donkeys at the **Maison de l'Ane** in the nearby countryside. **Aulnay** brings us to beasts and men in stone, brilliantly carved on one of Poitou's most famous Romanesque churches.

Dinner: Stop in sparklingly white St-Jean-d'Angély for creative cuisine in a contemporary setting at **Le Scorlion** (by the impressively vast central abbey), **t** 05 46 32 52 61 (*expensive–moderate*). *Closed Sun pm and Mon.* Or continue south towards Saintes for the adorable village of Taillebourg, and the **Auberge des Glycines, t** 05 46 91 81 40 (*moderate–inexpensive*), down by the river. *Closed Wed.*

Sleeping: For hotels, choose either our Saintes options (Day 4) or our Cognac town options (Day 3)

Day 3: Dipping into Cognac

Morning: Cognac is distilled from the grape of the *ugni blanc* vines planted in a wide radius around the town of **Cognac** on the Charente. The vineyards are divided up into six areas: the most famous, the Grande Champagne and the Petite Champagne, stretch south from the Charente valley below Cognac and Jarnac. If you're interested in the tipple you can take a cellar tour in Cognac-town, perhaps even an early tasting, at dominating Hennessy, at Otard in the former château, or at another competing famous name like Martell, Camus or Rémy Martin.

Lunch: For a gastronomic treat between Cognac and Jarnac, book at **Le Clos de la Ribaudière, t** 05 45 81 30 54 (*expensive*), renowned for refined regional and seafood cuisine, set by the river at Bourg-Charente. *Closed Sun pm and Tues.* In Jarnac's central square, the cheerful **Restaurant du Château**, 15 Place du Château, t 05 45 81 07 17, serves light, appealing cuisine.

Afternoon: Jarnac is the second-most important Cognac-making town. Courvoisier dominates the centre, but the likes of Louis Royer and upmarket Hine are also made here. Go on a Jarnac river cruise, and visit the amusingly excessive museum of presidential gifts (Mitterrand was born here). Or discover lovely Charente-side villages like **Bassac** with its quiet abbey.

Dinner and sleeping: In Cognac, **Les Pigeons Blancs**, 110 Rue Jules Brisson, t 05 45 82 16 36, f 05 45 82 29 29 (*moderate*) looks the part of a 17th-century posting inn and is an excellent place to stay and to eat. Set outside town in its own grounds, **★★Domaine du Breuil**, 104 Rue Robert Daugas, t 05 45 35 32 06, f 05 45 35 48 06 (*moderate*) is a grand two-star with a divine terrace for summer dining, even if the food is only average.

Day 4: Roman and Romanesque Saintes

Morning: A splendid provincial city, **Saintes** was named after the Celtic tribe of the Santons, and it grew into an extremely important Gallo-Roman city; with 30,000 inhabitants it was the capital for a time of the Roman province of Aquitaine. It has attractions on both sides of the Charente, including a Roman theatre, a little Roman museum, a major Romanesque abbey, a cathedral, and several small art museums. You'll be spoilt for choice.

Lunch: Despite the name, **La Rôtisserie**, 5 Rue André Lemoyne, t 05 46 94 15 01 (*moderate*), offers good fish dishes as well as succulent meats. *Closed Mon.* For a traditional French meal right by the river, **La Caravelle**, t 02 46 93 45 65 (*cheap*), is satisfying.

Afternoon: See more attractions in Saintes, and then perhaps retreat to the country and the balustraded gardens of the **Château de la Roche-Courbon**, a *Sleeping Beauty* dream of a castle.

Dinner and sleeping: Up on the outskirts of Saintes, **★★★★Le Relais du Bois St-Georges**, (off the Royan road), t 05 46 93 50 99, f 05 46

93 34 93 (*expensive*) is an extravagant hotel with lots of amenities and a posh restaurant. In the centre of town, at the gates to the women's abbey, **★★St-Pallais**, 1 Place St-Pallais, t 05 46 92 51 03, f 05 46 92 83 81 (*inexpensive*) has an atmospheric location and a restaurant.

Day 5: Sea, Sand and a Big Island

Morning: Before crossing the immense mirage of a viaduct to the island of **Oléron**, stop at **Brouage**, a ramparted port stuck in a time warp since the sea deserted it. Champlain, founder of Quebec, came from here. First stop on the island should be the fortified **Château-d'Oléron**.

Lunch: At Boyardville, looking on to the harbour, the **Hôtel l'Ecailler**, t 05 46 47 10 31 (*moderate*) has a very pleasant restaurant that would make a good stop. Inland at St-Pierre-d'Oléron, you'll find a good choice, **La Campagne**, t 05 46 47 25 42 (*moderate*), partcicularly agreeable. *Closed Mon.* Or eat at **Le Petit Coivre**, nearby on the D734, next to a restored mill, t 05 46 47 44 23 (*moderate*). *Closed Mon.*

Afternoon: The energetic might drive all the way round the island, or visit an oyster farm on the eastern side. For the lazy, the finest sandy beaches are in the northeast, above Boyardville, the village from which the workers set out to build TV-famed Fort Boyard out to sea.

Dinner and sleeping: On the southern end of Oléron island, St-Trojan-les-Bains makes a pretty place to stay among the pines. **★★L'Albatros**, 11 Bd du Dr Pineau, t 05 46 76 00 08, f 05 46 76 03 58 (*inexpensive*) has a wonderful unspoilt location on the coastal path, with a terrace right by the sea, a special place even if the rooms aren't that exciting. **★★La Forêt**, 16 Bd Pierre Wiehn, t 05 46 76 00 15, f 05 46 76 14 67 (*inexpensive*) is a big, pleasant, modern block shaded by tall trees, with some rooms and the restaurant looking out to the vast viaduct. **★★Le Homard Bleu**, 10 Bd Félix Faure, t 05 46 76 00 22, f 05 46 76 14 95 (*inexpensive*) is a diminutive option with a good seafood restaurant.

Limoges

Limoges has long been synonymous with luxury; even one of its 6th-century saints, Eloi, was a goldsmith. Through medieval times, the city was renowned for its exquisite *émaillerie champlevée*, first made in the abbey of St-Martial around 1185 and exported across Western Europe. Porcelain only took off after the discovery of kaolin in the 1760s at nearby St-Yrieix; Auguste Renoir, born in Limoges, began his artistic career as a porcelain-painter, like a number of other sons of the city.

These luxuries were produced by exploiting local labour, who occasionally rebelled. The butchers' guild, however, acquired a particular prominence in the city centre, and something of a stranglehold on power. Eventually, Limoges saw the founding of France's powerful trade union, the Confédération Générale du Travail, or CGT. And despite its reputation for delicate designer goods Limoges remains a militant and progressive force in a sleepy rural region.

The sturdy hilltop centre has a workmanlike authority to it. Its finest buildings are of timber-frame or granite – this tough stone characterizes the Limousin – but the odd show of flouncing Belle Epoque grandeur stands out.

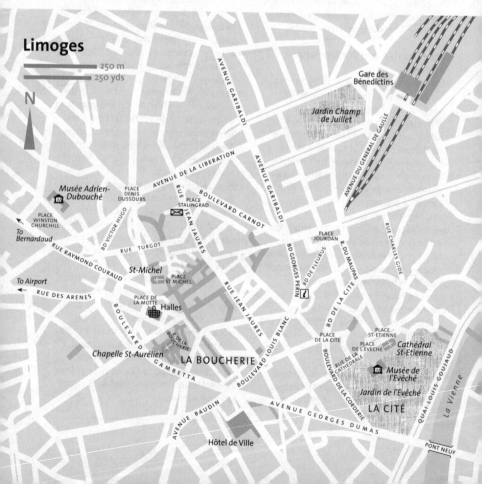

Limoges

Getting to Limoges

Buzz (*see* p.6) flies from London Stansted.

Getting from the Airport

Limoges Bellegarde **airport** (**t** 05 55 43 30 30, *www.aeroportlimoges.com*) is 15km from the city centre. There is currently no bus service. At least three **taxi** companies operate a 24hr service; expect to pay €17– 25 to the centre.

Getting Around

Local **bus** information: **t** 05 46 34 02 22. Local **taxi** companies include **Limoges Taxis**, **t** 05 55 38 38 38; **Taxis Verts**, **t** 05 55 37 81 81; **Transports du Haut-Limousin**, **t** 05 55 58 12 75.

Car Hire

Avis: airport, **t** 05 55 43 30 41; town centre, **t** 05 55 33 36 37.
Budget: airport, **t** 05 55 43 30 42; town centre, **t** 05 55 79 18 19.
Europcar: airport, **t** 05 55 43 30 44; town centre, **t** 05 55 77 64 52.
Hertz: airport **t** 05 55 43 30 45; town centre, **t** 05 55 79 44 65.

Tourist Information

Limoges: Bd de Fleurus, 87000 Limoges, **t** 05 55 34 46 87, **f** 05 55 34 19 12, *www.tourisme-limoges.com, info@tourismelimoges.com.*

Market Days

Place Marceau: Sat am. **Les Halles**, the delightful covered market in the centre, built in Belle Epoque style and decorated with ceramics of market produce, is open daily, including Sun, to 1pm. You can also find food stalls on **Place des Bancs** and **Place Haute-Vienne**, Tues–Sat.

Shopping

Fine Limoges porcelain at reasonable prices is the main aim for many visitors. The central selection of shops is on busy **Bd Louis Blanc**. The lovely large Lachainette store boasts the finest choice of classic and contemporary ranges. The smaller Atelier de la Porcelaine opposite has some tempting plates and dishes. Up the street, look out for a couple of addresses selling *porcelaine déclassée* or *démarquée* (seconds). You'll find a few more choices scattered around the centre, e.g. on **Bd Victor Hugo**, or if you're in a car head out to one of the factories selling direct, such as **Bernardaud**, northwest at Av Albert Thomas (*factory visits June–Sept daily 9–11 and 1–4*), or **Haviland**, 5mins from motorway exit 36, Limoges-Sud, with a splendid display of museum pieces too.

Enamelware is another Limoges speciality. This is a bit of an acquired taste, the designs tending towards the oversentimental or the overbright, but take a look along **Bd Louis Blanc** again, where Galerie Christel and L'Art Artisanal offer contemporary creations.

The main shopping streets slope away from big, central **Place de la Motte**, with the grand covered market and the Gorse porcelain shop. Timber-frame **Rue de la Boucherie** is lined with a mix of old-style boutiques selling antiques and more creative porcelain, enamelware and jewellery. On **Rue Darnet**, Au Palais du Café presents intriguing local produce (all

Lingering a While in Limoges

High above the Vienne river, the **Musée Municipal de l'Evêché** (*open July–Sept daily 10–11.45 and 2–6; rest of year daily exc Tues 10–11.45 and 2–5; adm*) has taken over the 18th-century bishops' palace. It throws up some surprises: fragments of Gallo-Roman frescoes depicting birds and wild cats, a figure of a decapitated Gaulish god holding a torque, and two plates with childlike graffiti that turn out to be very rare examples of Celtic writing. There are fine Romanesque capitals and tombs too, and two splendid heads with groomed moustaches and curled hair. Sadly, the museum's best early medieval enamels were stolen in the 1980s, but there are still a few good pieces and a

manner of chestnut specialities, Limousin mustard and pastis). The most interesting shopping street of all is **Rue Adrien Dubouché**, with a range of clothes, gift and gastronomic shops. Look out for Le Pré Gourmand and La Chocolaterie. The street ends at circular **Place Denis Dussoubs**, with its crescent of terraced bars including the Brasserie St-Michel, which brews beer on the spot, and sells it to take away. Also stroll down the streets descending from **Place des Bancs**, with clothes, antiques, interior decoration and more regional culinary specialtites on offer, including delicacies from *porcs cul noir* – black-bottomed pigs!

Where to Stay

Limoges ✉ 87000

★★★Le Richelieu, 40 Av Baudin, **t** 05 55 34 22 82, **f** 05 55 32 48 73, *www.hotel-richelieu.com* (*moderate*). Opposite the town hall just outside the main ring of boulevards, with good rooms and service.

★★★Royal Limousin, Place de la République, **t** 05 55 34 65 30, **f** 05 55 34 55 21, *www.royal-limousin.com* (*moderate*). A comfortable central modern hotel.

★★Ibis, 6 Bd Victor Hugo, **t** 05 55 79 03 30, **f** 05 55 79 31 50, *www.ibishotel.com* (*moderate*). A chain hotel, but located in a swish, central building, wrought-iron and all.

★★La Paix, 25 Place Jourdan, **t** 05 55 34 36 00, **f** 05 55 32 37 06 (*inexpensive*), by a pleasant green square just east of the centre; the owner has a passion for old gramophones, which gives this hotel its character. In fact, the breakfast room doubles as a museum.

★★Orléans Lion d'Or, 9–11 Cours Jourdan, **t** 05 55 77 49 71, **f** 05 55 77 33 41 (*inexpensive*). A good choice near the railway station.

★Beaux-Arts, 28 Bd Victor Hugo, **t** 05 55 79 42 20, **f** 05 55 79 29 13 (*cheap*). Central, if noisy, and most of the rooms are basic.

Eating Out

Philippe Redon, 3 Rue d'Aguesseau, **t** 05 55 34 66 22 (*moderate*). Refined dishes combining Limousin meats with seafood.

L'Amphitryon, 26 Rue de la Boucherie, **t** 05 55 33 36 39, **f** 05 55 32 98 50. An attractive timberframe front in the old butchers' quarter, with fine porcelain on the tables and refined cuisine – the best-known restaurant in Limoges.

Les Petits Ventres, 20 Rue de la Boucherie, **t** 05 55 34 22 90 (*moderate*). Behind its sweet timberframe façade, this little restaurant has extremely meaty options like *tartares* and *andouillettes*.

Le Gourmelin, 5 Rue de la Boucherie, **t** 05 55 33 58 23 (*moderate*). Another delightful timber-frame choice, with more local specialities.

Up around the Halles, try one of the more casual meaty bistrots, bursting at lunchtimes. **Chez Alphonse**, 5 Place de la Motte, **t** 05 55 34 34 14. For a lively, good-value lunch or à la carte dinner with pork specialities.

Rue Charles Michels, down from Place des Bancs, has a few ethnic restaurants.

Pont St-Etienne, Place Compostelle, **t** 05 55 30 52 54 (*moderate*), makes rather a lovely change; it is down beside the medieval pilgrim's bridge over the Vienne, on a pleasing square, and serving good fish as well as meat.

large collection of later, less original painted enamels inspired by German and Italian engravings. The paintings aren't up to much, beyond Renoir's *Portrait de Jean*. A separate building by the gardens is devoted to the Résistance; although Limoges of course honours its Résistance fighters, it is embarrassed that it celebrated Pétain's visit in 1941 rather too enthusiastically. It's then a steep drop down to the Vienne, its banks lined with walkways either side of the medieval St-Etienne bridge.

Back on high, enter the nearby **cathedral** via the enormous telescoping tower resembling an industrial chimney, or through the fine Flamboyant portal of St-Jean on the north side. The interior is splendid and simple, influenced by the Gothic of the north. An elaborate Renaissance roodscreen has been moved to the back of the church. In the choir, monumental tombs stand out, as does the 19th-century imitation medieval stained glass. The **Haute Cité** quarter surrounding the cathedral has grand houses but not a lot of life.

The nearby **Boulevard Louis Blanc**, by contrast, is rather too busy – a major artery for cars, and for porcelain and enamel shops. Head into the fine historic quarter sloping down around Place de la Motte and its dominating Halles. Two granite Gothic churches stand out in this area. Golden-stoned **St-Pierre-du-Queyroix**, with its soaring spire, conceals a striking series of gilded altars and a stained-glass window designed by Gustave Doré. At the top of the church's square, your gaze will inevitably be attracted to the joyous little tiled extravaganza, the **Pavillon Verdurier**, glistening green, blue and gold, built to be nothing more glamorous than a refrigerated warehouse in 1919, and now used for temporary exhibitions.

Standing discreetly back off the shopping street Rue Adrien Dubouché, **St-Michel-des-Lions** is the other grandiose church in the area. Inside, the slender Gothic pillars lean out under the strain of trying to hold up the three equally sized aisles. The place contains memories of Limoges' most famous saints, Martial and Valérie, and invites contemplation despite the distraction of some cloying 19th-century decoration. Before you leave, look out for the stone lions after which the church is named.

From Place de la Motte, head down **Rue de la Boucherie** for a richly patterned display of timberframe houses. The butchers of Limoges clearly amassed considerable power and wealth in times past, to build such substantial houses. These also served as their workshops, where the bloody business of preparing carcasses went on. One address has been turned into an **Ecomusée** showing how the butchers' families lived. The adorable tiny Gothic **Chapelle St-Aurélien** set back off the street was in fact saved from Revolutionary vandals by the butchers' fraternity, which still owns it. Its amusing bell-tower, clad in chestnut wood tiles typical of the Limousin, holds a collection of statues and furniture, plus the relics of the second bishop of Limoges.

You're unlikely to find more beautiful vases, pots and plates in one place than at the **Musée National de la Céramique Adrien-Dubouché** (*open July–Aug daily exc Tues 10–5.45; rest of year daily exc Tues 10–12.30 and 2–5.45; adm*), up on Place Wilson beyond the historic shopping centre and the pompous law courts that presided over Place d'Ainé. The building alone, a mishmash of Italianate, neo-Gothic and Arts and Crafts, is an arresting sight. A video explains the stages in making porcelain, using a mixture that includes kaolin, the secret of its translucent finesse discovered in China in the 8th or 9th century, but only worked out by Europeans in the 18th. Meissen in Saxony was the first to produce European porcelain in 1710; Limoges followed in the 1770s. The first European manufacturers obsessively made fake Chinese pieces, with silly, coarsely copied scenes of Chinese decoration. Funnier still are the pieces made in China during the Ancien Régime showing Europeans with long noses. Limoges is best known for its refined, elegantly bordered dinner services, but here too are some funkier modern creations.

Day Trips from Limoges

St-Léonard-de-Noblat

Grassy hills where Limousin brown cows graze surround the rustic hilltop town of St-Léonard-de-Noblat, while old houses with charming architectural details including religious statues encircle the intriguing pilgrimage church at the centre of town, dedicated to saint Léonard. Born into an aristocratic Frankish family in the 6th century, this holy man became a hermit in these parts, but one day saved the life of a queen who came into labour while out hunting with her husband. To thank Léonard, the king offered him a *noble lieu*, in this case, as much land as his donkey could walk round in 24 hours! Léonard founded a religious community on this territory, dedicated to reforming former captives and criminals through wholesome Christian labour.

An eccentric tower rises from the 11th-century church, built to receive pilgrims on one of the routes through France to Santiago de Compostela in Spain. Look out for some entertaining stone sculptures down below, including plump monsters, acrobats, and people doing battle. Inside, an extraordinary crowd of Gothic and Romanesque columns clusters round the choir. The bronze statue on one little square above the church represents Gay-Lussac, the great physicist and chemist born here in 1778. He made many ground-breaking discoveries in his fields at the start of the 19th century, several scientific laws being named after him, and also reached for the skies in 1804, making a record-breaking ascent to 7,000m, in hot-air balloon. A little museum is devoted to him. The town is also proud of its Limousin beef, and it traditional marzipan and candied prunes, available in the local *pâtisseries*. Train enthusiasts should head for Historail, a friendly railway museum, one room containing full-scale equipment, the second miniature railways. In summer, a real-life steam train runs between Limoges and St-Léonard.

Down the steep slope, by the Vienne river, a series of attractive timberframe buildings and former mills where flour, walnut oil and hides were once prepared, call for attention at **Le Pont-de-Noblat**, beside the 13th-century bridge. Porcelain manufacturers still operate in the valleys around.

Getting There

Trains and buses from Limoges take only 20–30mins, but are limited in frequency.

Tourist Information

St-Léonard-de-Noblat ✉ 87400: Place du Champ de Mars, t 05 55 56 25 06, f 05 55 56 36 97, *www.ville-saint-leonard.com*.

Market Day

St-Léonard-de-Noblat: Sat am.

Eating Out

Le Grand St-Léonard, 23 Av du Champ de Mars, t 05 55 56 18 18 (*expensive–moderate*). Excellent regional food makes this big updated posting inn worth a stop.

Le Gay-Lussac, 18 Bd Victor Hugo, t 05 55 56 98 45 (*moderate–cheap*). Popular country cooking.

Le Relais St-Jacques, 6 Bd Presseman, t 05 55 56 00 25 (*inexpensive–cheap*). Decent option.

Auberge Maître Pierre, t 05 55 56 29 73 (*moderate*). Charming location down by the Vienne.

Touring from Limoges

You'll find that the sights are reliably open Easter–Oct, 10–12 and 2–5 at least, unless otherwise stated, and charge adm.

Day 1: An Arty Lake and Ancient Tapestries

Morning: Get off to an early start to drive east via **St-Léonard-de-Noblat** (*see* opposite) to the wooded shores of the beautiful manmade **lake of Vassivière**. Walk across to the main island, with its exciting treasure hunt of outdoor contemporary art and excellent Centre d'Art Contemporain.

Lunch: Eat right by the western side of the lake at smart, modern ★★★**La Caravelle**, t 05 55 69 40 97 (*moderate*). Or head 7km west for pleasant ★★**Auberge du Bois de l'Etang**, t 05 55 69 40 19 (*moderate*), at Peyrat-le-Château.

Afternoon: On a warm afternoon you might like to go boating on the lake. Or head northeast for the appealing historic tapestry towns of **Felletin** and **Aubusson**, the latter with a good modern museum (*closed Tues exc in July–Sept*), devoted to the speciality.

Dinner and sleeping: Aubusson's central ★★**Hôtel de France**, 6 Rue des Déportés, t 05 55 66 10 22, f 05 55 66 88 64 (*inexpensive*) is the best option in town, with a restaurant. Or it's worth the 30km hike west along the N141 to St-Hilaire-le-Château's stylishly renovated inn, ★★**Hôtel du Thaurion**, t 05 55 64 50 12, f 05 55 64 90 92 (*inexpensive*), with charming rooms and excellent regional cuisine.

Day 2: Cascading down Rivers

Morning: From either hotel, it's a fairly long but pleasantly rural drive southwest on the D940 for **Treignac**, extending up the steep banks of the Vézère river, very popular with canoeists. The pudding-shaped hills of the **Monédières** stretch from here to the Corrèze valley, with gritty granite villages to explore such as **Chaumeil**.

Lunch: Seek out rustic *fermes-auberges* in the Monédières for cheap hearty meals (*booking ahead essential*), like **Le Malagnoux** at Gourdon-Murat (a little way east of Treignac), t 05 55 94 01 11 (*inexpensive*), or the **Ferme-Auberge Chauzeix** 4km from St-Augustin, west of Chaumeil, t 05 55 98 23 42 (*inexpensive*); or try the inns at Treignac or Chaumeil.

Afternoon: To the south, sleepy **Corrèze** and surprisingly lively **Gimel-les-Cascades**, the latter with spectacular waterfalls, are villages you could stop at. Then head for the banks of the less touristy stretch of the Dordogne, visiting cheerful **Argentat**, traditionally at the uppermost point of the river's navigability, and the well-named **Beaulieu-sur-Dordogne**, still full of medieval atmosphere around its abbey of St-Pierre.

Dinner and sleeping: In Beaulieu, turreted ★★**Le Turenne**, t 05 55 91 10 16, f 05 55 91 22 42 (*inexpensive*) keeps up the medieval theme and has a charming restaurant to match. Or head west for Collonges-la-Rouge's delightful ★★**Relais St-Jacques**, t 05 55 25 41 02, f 05 55 84 08 51 (*moderate*), with restaurant.

Day 3: Delightful Measled Villages, and Brive

Morning: Among a rash of supremely picturesque villages south of Brive, none is prettier than many-towered **Collonges-la-Rouge**, its stone so red it looks sunburnt; you can see the quirky Romanesque-Gothic church and a foie gras farm. Neighbouring **Meyssac** shares the startling look, but doesn't have as many intriguing little tourist sights to visit. **Curemonte**, southwest, is an enchanting place, with three castles crammed on to its ridge, and a darkly atmospheric church.

Lunch: In Collonges, **Le Prieuré**, Place de l'Eglise, t 05 55 25 41 00 (*moderate*), is particularly cute and cosy. West in neighbouring Turenne, try the deeply appealing **Maison des Chanoines**, Route de l'Eglise, t 05 55 85 93 43 (*moderate*), with its stone front covered in ivy and food served in a vaulted cellar.

Afternoon: In **Turenne**, climb the steep hillside to visit the grand church and ruined castle. Then move on to **Brive-la-Gaillarde**. The layers of this historic town are encased like onion rings within the bustling boulevards. The regional Musée Labenche (*closed Tues*) occupies one of the finest Renaissance houses, with portraits and tapestries.

Dinner and sleeping: Set back from Brive's boulvards at 22 Bd Anatole France, **★★★La Truffe Noire**, t 05 55 92 45 00, f 05 55 92 45 13 (*moderate*), is soberly comfortable and has a reputable restaurant. Or eat in the lively bistrot **Chez Francis**, 61 Av de Paris, t 05 55 74 41 72 (*moderate*) and then head back for a night in Turenne's **Maison des Chanoines** (*see* lunch).

Day 4: The Limousin Flirts with the Périgord

Morning: The motorway is free up to **Uzerche**, a many-towered dark historic town occupying a dramatic promontory above a hairpin bend in the Vézère river. Wander past the grandiose mansions to the church of St-Pierre, and maybe call in at the small local history centre.

Lunch: Uzerche has a few quite appealing old-style French hotel-restaurants, such as **★★Teyssier**, t 05 55 73 10 05 (*moderate*), with an outdoor terrace where copious helpings are served by friendly staff. Or head west for charming **Ségur-le-Château** to find a simple place to eat or picnic in the shaded curve of the river.

Afternoon: After pottering around **Ségur-le-Château**, its old castle in private hands, go on a proper turreted castle visit, either at little-known **Coussac** to the north, or at better-known **Jumilhac**, just in the Périgord, with its fantasia of towers. **Châlus**, north-west, boasts the keep on top of which Richard-the-Lionheart was mortally wounded; you can climb it for the same view as the king.

Dinner and sleeping: Back at Coussac, **★★Les Voyageurs**, t 05 55 75 20 24, f 05 55 75 28 90 (*inexpensive*), has decent rooms in a modern building and a restaurant in a charming old inn. At nearby St-Yreix (known for its pottery) the **★★Hostel de la Tour Blanche**, t 05 55 75 18 17, f 05 55 08 23 11 (*inexpensive*) has comfortable rooms, plus a restaurant serving hearty cuisine.

Day 5: Painful Memories

Morning: Many sights in **Rochechouart** are only open in the afternoons outside the main tourist summer season – call Rochechouart tourist office, t 05 55 03 72 73, to check. The Rochechouart area was struck by a vast meteorite back in the mists of time, as a fascinating little scientific centre in this pleasantly sleepy town recalls. The speckled château contains a surprising contemporary art museum. At **Les Salles-Lavaugugon** some way southwest, a startling and superb series of medieval wall paintings depicting gruesome martyrdoms has recently been discovered.

Lunch: East of Rochechouart, the **Auberge de la Vallée de la Gorre**, t 05 55 00 01 27 (*moderate–cheap; closed Sun pm, Mon, and Tues pm*) in the pretty village of St-Auvent is a delightful place for a country lunch. Or head for the relaxing provincial town of St-Junien north of Rochechouart, where **★★Le Relais de Comodoliac**, t 05 55 02 27 26 (*moderate*), has a good restaurant serving regional fare.

Afternoon: Savagely attacked by SS troops as the Allies landed in Normandy, its villagers massacred, the women and children burnt to death in the church, **Oradour-sur-Glane**'s ruins have been kept intact as one of the strongest reminders of Nazi atrocities in France. A major memorial museum has recently been opened beside the harrowing site to explain the history of this tragic event. Find comfort in the tranquil woods of the **Monts de Blond** just to the north, with a peculiarly Arthurian feel around their mysterious lakes.

Dinner and sleeping: For a luxurious final treat, book at **★★★★La Chapelle St-Martin**, near Nieul east of Oradour, around 10km northwest of Limoges up off the N147, t 05 55 75 80 17, f 05 55 75 89 50 (*expensive*), a wonderfully comfortable 19th-century bourgeois house with an excellent restaurant. At the other end of the scale, by the quaint covered market in Mortemart, the prettiest village in the Monts de Blond, stay and eat at simple **Le Relais**, t 05 55 68 12 09, f 05 55 68 12 09 (*inexpensive*).

Southwest France

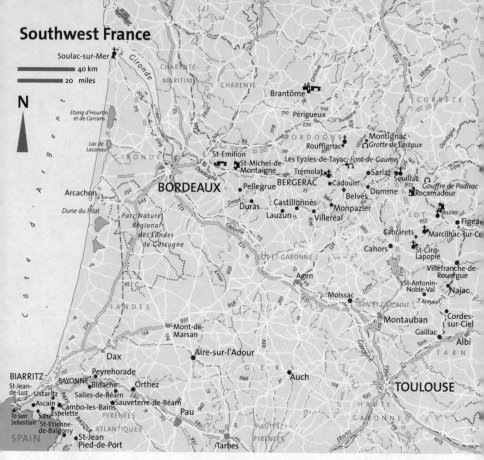

Southwest France

This part of France, with Bordeaux at one end and Toulouse at the other, is defined by rivers of exceptional beauty: the Dordogne, Lot, Aveyron and Tarn, all of which meander down through dramatic gorges into sunny valleys of vines and orchards to join the big one – the Garonne – and the Atlantic.

At the northern end of the region, the Dordogne passes through Périgord, the fat land of castles and foie gras that has been called the 'Tuscany of France'. In the south, the Gascons and Basques have created distinctive little regions for themselves between the Pyrenees and the beach playground of Biarritz.

Although battered by the Albigensian Crusade, the Hundred Years' War, and the Wars of Religion, much of the southwest has since kept clear of history (and what passes for progress), leaving it a remarkably intact architectural legacy of medieval châteaux, villages, 13th-century *bastides* (new towns) and Romanesque and Gothic churches, including some of the greatest, in Conques, Moissac, Albi and Toulouse. The southwest has other superlatives as well: the world's greatest concentration of Palaeolithic art, beginning with Lascaux; the wines of Bordeaux (and many others); the biggest sand dune in Europe by Arcachon; the immense subterranean fantasies of the Gouffre de Padirac and the Aven Armand; the breathtaking Gorges du Tarn, and pink Toulouse, the effervescent fourth city of France.

Bergerac

Bergerac, known far and wide as the name of a poetic cavalier with a big nose who never even set foot in the town, is a fine little city where swans swim in the Dordogne and a tidy cluster of medieval, half-timbered houses bask by the old river port. It has been christened 'Capital of Purple Périgord' in honour of *le vin*, but it might have been dubbed Nicotine-Brown Périgord: not only is it home to the national Institut du Tabac, it also boasts a unique museum devoted to the much-maligned weed.

Although Bergerac occupies both banks of the Dordogne, all the interesting points for visitors are concentrated in the pedestrian area on the north bank. Here, restoration work has uncovered a handsome set of buildings from the 14th–17th centuries. Some of the finest are in Place du Feu, a pretty square shaded by an enormous old tree, in particular the handsome turreted **Maison Peyrarède** (1604), now the **National**

Getting to Bergerac

Buzz (*see* p.6) flies from London Stansted.

Getting from the Airport

Bergerac's **airport**, Roumanières, t 05 53 22 25 25, lies 10km to the south. A Buzz **shuttle bus** takes you to the town centre for €5. A **taxi** costs approximately €9.

Getting Around

The **railway** station, north of the centre, is on the Bordeaux–Sarlat line. All the main town sights are within easy walking distance.

You can take a **river trip** with Périgord Gabares, leaving from Quai Salvette.

Car Hire

Avis, 26 Cours Alsace-Lorraine, t 05 53 57 69 83; **Budget**, 14 Av du 108e RI, t 05 53 74 20 00; **Cazes Location**, Rte de Bordeaux, t 05 53 74 44 46; **Hertz**, 15 Av du 108e RI (opposite train station), t 05 53 57 19 27.

Tourist Information

Bergerac: 97 Rue Neuve d'Argenson, t 05 53 57 03 11, f 05 53 61 11 04, *www.bergerac-tourisme.com*. Organizes guided town tours.

Market Days

Place Doublet: Tues am, organic food.

Sat mornings and Wed are the big shopping days, with stalls outside the covered market and around Notre-Dame church. A flea market takes place the first Sun of each month.

Shopping

The Maison des Vins down by the port is the most atmospheric place to buy wine. Up on **Grand-Rue**, L'Art et Le Vin sells wine gifts as well as bottles, and the Brûlene du Périgord sells chocolate. The main shopping thoroughfare is **Rue de la Résistance**, its outstanding shop the glittering gilded Confiserie Rosier Cartagna. There are three major *parfumeries* here, plus some clothes shops. Just off the *rue*, along pedestrian **Rue du Colonel de Chadois**, you'll come across a couple of gift shops selling pottery and glass. For traditional gifts look in the smaller shops in **Vieux Bergerac**.

Where to Stay

Bergerac ✉ 24100

★★★**Le Bordeaux**, 38 Place Gambetta, t 05 53 57 12 83, f 05 53 57 72 14 (*moderate*). This modern hotel offers a chance to relax in the centre of Bergerac, with its garden and pool; its restaurant serves unusual delicacies – the most upriver version of *lamproie à la bordelaise* and *aiguillettes de canard au miel*.

★★★**La Flambée**, 153 Av Pasteur, t 05 53 57 52 33, f 05 53 61 07 57 (*moderate*). Outside the centre on the Périgueux road, this is a welcoming family-run hotel noted for its kitchen's delicious southwest specialities;

Tobacco Museum (*open Tues–Fri 10–12 and 2–6; Sat 10–12 and 2–5, Sun 2.30–6.30; closed Mon; adm; no smoking!*). The museum is chock-full of curiosities on the weed, tracing it from its role as the sacred medicine of Aztec gods, through that of binder of peace agreements between North American tribes, to the 19th-century invention of the cigar and cigarette, which saw the masses awoken to the delights of smoking.

Behind the tobacco museum in Place du Dr-Cayla is Bergerac's 19th-century **Protestant Temple**, holding occasional services for the last die-hard Calvinists, while, just behind, on Quai Salvette, the picturesque 16th-century **Cloître des Récollets** has a wooden gallery and lone tree. The Récollets were a Franciscan order founded in Spain in the late 1400s, named, according to the *Catholic Dictionary*, 'from the detachment from creatures and a recollection in God which the founders aimed at'. The order was widespread in southwest France, and Louis XIII charged the Récollets with the task of bringing the burghers of Bergerac back to the Catholic fold; their methods of

work off that *filet de bœuf* in the pool or on the tennis court, or rambling about the panoramic park. *Closed Sun eve, Mon out of season, and Jan.*

★★★**Commerce**, 36 Place Gambetta, t 05 53 27 30 50, f 05 53 58 23 82 (*moderate*). A Logis hotel with comfortable, well-equipped rooms, but ask for one facing away from the square. The restaurant is standard (*cheap*).

★★★**France**, 18 Place Gambetta, t 05 53 57 11 61, f 05 53 61 25 70 (*moderate*). A similar hotel just up the way but perhaps with better sound-proofing; it can also boast a pool, but there is no restaurant.

★★★**Manoir Le Grand Vignoble**, St-Julien-de-Crempse (12.5km north of Bergerac), t 05 53 24 23 18, f 05 53 24 20 89 (*moderate*). A 17th-century building set amid woods, with a pool and tennis. *Closed mid-Nov–Feb.*

★★**Le Family**, 3 Rue du Dragon, near Place du Marché Couvert, t 05 53 57 80 90 (*inexpensive*). Central, simple and friendly. Parking is available in a nearby garage.

Eating Out

The picturesque old streets around the tobacco museum are the place to head for for Bergerac's most characterful restaurants.

La Tour des Vents, t 05 53 58 30 10 (*expensive*). Once the Moulin de Malfourat, as well as splendid views it offers well-prepared southwest favourites. *Closed mid-Jan–mid-Feb, Sun eve and Mon out of season.*

L'Imparfait, 8 Rue des Fontaines, t 05 53 57 47 92 (*expensive*). In the historic centre. Shares top billing with the aforementioned hotels with its fresh sunny cuisine. A warm, sticky dining room, but on summer evenings its very comfortable chairs and tables stretch across the whole narrow street outside. Choices are limited, but the cuisine is very refined and recherché for these rustic parts. *Closed Sun and Nov–mid-Jan.*

Le Sud, 19 Rue de l'Ancien Port, t 05 53 27 26 81 (*moderate*). Tasty Moroccan *tajines* and couscous. *Closed Sun, Mon, and early June.*

Le Poivre et Sel, 11 Rue de l'Ancien Port, t 05 53 27 02 30 (*moderate*). Old, timbered and elegant, in a narrow street, surrounded by plants. In summer, the place spills out over the best square in town, under the domineering gaze of the tobacco museum, beautifully lit at night. You can opt for a hearty traditional Périgord menu (foie gras, melon with Monbazillac, duck, walnut cake) or choose form a healthy range of salads. *Closed Mon in winter.*

Château de Monbazillac, t 05 53 58 38 93 (*moderate*). The restaurant in the former *chai* is a favourite of local wine barons for its fine classic cuisine, with a long and interesting wine list and summer dining from the terrace. *Closed Nov–start April.*

Café-Brasserie Le Perroquet, Place Pélissière (*inexpensive*). A popular spot with outside terrace and glazed dining room.

Le Dalacos, Place du Docteur Cayla (*inexpensive*). A characterful café in prime position in the historic centre. Simple menus.

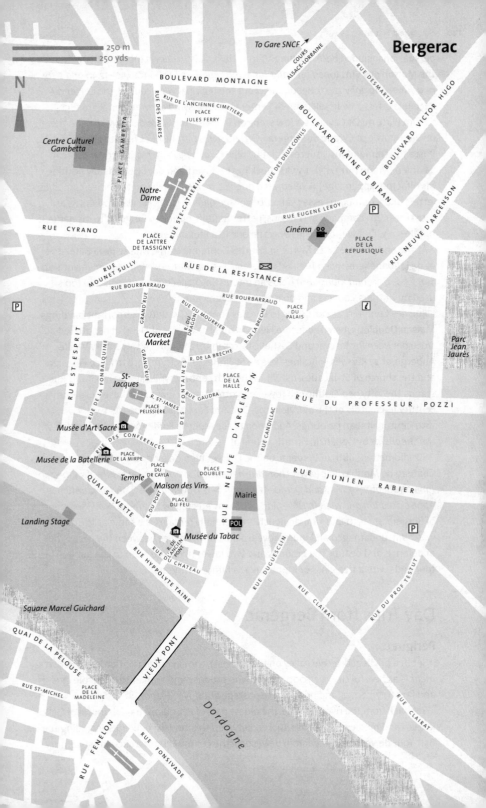

persuasion included book-burnings. Today their cloister serves more congenially as the **Maison des Vins** (*open Feb–mid-June and Sept–Dec Tues–Sat 10.30–12.30 and 2–6; mid-June–Aug daily 10–7*), headquarters of the regional wine council, the Cellier de Récollets offers a wide selection of Bergerac vintages and other regional products.

From Place du Dr-Cayla it's a few steps up to charming Place de La Myrpe and the revered statue of **Cyrano de Bergerac**. Cyrano owes his presence here to Edmond Rostand's tremendously successful 1897 play *Cyrano de Bergerac*, based on the real Savinien Cyrano (1619–55), a swashbuckling extrovert and poet (records say nothing of his olfactory appendage). A celebrated duellist, he also published tragedies, comedies, letters and a humorous essay called 'Le Voyage dans la Lune'. He was appointed as musketeer in a company of Gascons; better to fit in, he added Bergerac to his name. If not literally a native son, he'll always be one in a literary sense.

At the end of Place de La Myrpe in Rue des Conférences, the **Musée de la Batellerie et de la Tonnellerie** (*open Tues–Fri 10–12 and 2–5.30, Sat 10–12; mid-Mar–mid-Nov also Sun 2.30–6.30, and Mon; adm*) holds an interesting collection of models and tools used by vintners, coopers and boatmen in days of yore.

Rue des Conférences continues to Rue des Fontaines, with two important buildings: **Maison Doublet**, where the future Henri IV and the agents of Henri III negotiated a truce between Protestant and Catholic forces in 1577, and the 14th-century **Vieille Auberge**, at 27 Rue des Fontaines. Rue de St-James leads from here to Place Pélissière and the **church of St-Jacques**, rebuilt in the 17th century, while along the Grand-Rue stands the lofty neo-Gothic bell tower of **Notre-Dame**, created by those busy 19th-century re-creators of the old, Viollet-le-Duc and Paul Abadie. It boasts two 16th-century Italian paintings: *Adoration of the Magi* by Pordenone and *Adoration of the Shepherds* by Godenzio Ferrari, a pupil of da Vinci.

Six kilometres south of Bergerac on the D13, set high on a ridge, the four-square **Château de Monbazillac** (*www.chateau-monbazillac.com; open daily July–Aug 10–7.30, June and Sept 10–7, May and Oct 10–12.30 and 2–6, Nov–Mar 10–12 and 2–5, until 6 in April; closed Jan and Mon in Nov–Mar; adm*) was erected by Charles d'Aydie, Seigneur of Bergerac, in 1550 and – miraculously – essentially remains the same as the day it was built, undamaged and unimproved: a nice compromise between the necessities of defence, and beauty. The grounds and two lower floors are open to the public. The tour ends with a free glass of Monbazillac's famous wine.

Day Trips from Bergerac

Périgueux

Set in a privileged, fertile valley on the river Isle, the capital of the Dordogne *département* is a cheerful city of 35,000 people who produce and market truffles, foie gras and fat strawberries, and print all the postage stamps in France.

Set back from the river, the **Cité**, the oldest part of Périgueux, has a handful of Gallo-Roman and medieval souvenirs tucked between the modern buildings, including the 65ft **Tour de Vésone** in the Jardin de Vésone, the central *cella* of a circular 1st-century

Getting There

Périgueux's **train** station is in Rue Denis-Papin, but there aren't many trains a day.

Buses from Bergerac serve Périgueux three times a day, arriving at Place Francheville and the station (call CFD, **t** 05 53 08 43 13).

The biggest **car park** is at Place Montaigne, near the Musée du Périgord.

Tourist Information

Périgueux ✉ **24000**: Rond-Point de la Tour Mataguerre, 26 Place Francheville, **t** 05 53 53 10 63, **f** 05 53 09 02 50, *www.ville-perigueux.fr*. Guided tours in summer.

Market Days

Périgueux: Wed and Sat am, Places du Coderc and de la Clautre; same days mid-Nov–mid-Mar, *marché de gras*, Place St-Louis.

Eating Out

Le 8, 8 Rue de la Clarté, near to the cathedral, **t** 05 53 35 15 15 (*expensive–moderate*). Very good reputation. Serves imaginative regional dishes in its small and lively dining room. *Closed Sun and Mon; best to book.*

Aux Berges de l'Isle, 2 Rue Pierre Magne, **t** 05 53 09 51 50 (*moderate*). On a terrace overlooking the river and St-Front. *Closed Sun eve and Mon.*

Le Rocher de l'Arsault, 15 Rue de l'Arsault, **t** 05 53 53 54 06 (*moderate*). Regional delicacies in a Louis XIII dining room to the northeast of the centre. *Closed several weeks in summer.*

Hercule Poireau, 2 Rue de la Nation, **t** 05 53 08 90 76 (*moderate*). Book a table in their vaulted Renaissance cellar north of the cathedral for *Rossini de canard* and other treats at very reasonable prices. *Closed Sat lunch, Sun and most of Aug.*

AD Gallo-Roman temple. Just west are the ruins of the **Villa de Pompeïus**, from the same period (*guided tours run by the tourist office*), housing a deluxe set of heated Roman baths; frescoes and mosaics survive as well. Périgueux's oldest church, **St-Etienne**, was founded on the site of a Temple of Mars, but rebuilt in the 12th century. Its style became the prototype of the Périgourdin domed Romanesque church, with wide Byzantine cupolas not only over the crossing but cupping the length of the nave. The interior has a fine if incongruous 17th-century wooden retable and a 12th-century Easter calendar.

The compact quarter of **Puy-St-Front** has been beautifully restored; you can take a tour into some of the courtyards, and into the last remnant of Puy's walls, the **Tour Mataguerre** in Place Francheville. If St-Etienne was the prototype, the **Cathedral of St-Front**, looming above Place de la Clautre, was the ultimate expression of medieval Périgord's romance with domes. It is breathtaking from a distance, especially when floodlit; close up, it is harder to overlook the fact that most of it was rebuilt at the end of the 19th century, including the pinnacles on the domes. Inside, the lingering impression is one of vastness; in its minimal decoration it looks more like a mosque.

The north door of the cathedral opens on to **Place Daumesnil**, the centre of a fascinating web of 15th- and 16th-century pedestrian lanes. Steep, stepped streets descend to the river; houses in Rue du Plantier have terraced gardens, while medieval Rue du Port-de-Graule is lined with tiny boutiques.

Just to the north, the **Musée du Périgord**, 22 Cours de Tourny (*open weekdays April–Sept 11–6, Oct–Mar 10–5, weekends 1–6; closed Tues and hols; adm*) is a cut above average. Particularly impressive are its extensive **prehistoric section**, with three of the oldest skeletons ever found, and the **Gallo-Roman rooms**, filled with fascinating jewellery, frescoes, mosaics and an altar dating from the 2nd century BC.

Getting There

Bergerac to Brantôme is quite difficult by public transport; it has no train station, but you can get a **bus** via Périgueux.

Tourist Information

Brantôme ✉ **24310**: Pavillon Renaissance, **t** 05 53 05 80 52, **f** 05 53 05 80 52, *www.ville-brantome.fr*.

Market Days

Brantôme: Fri; also farmers' market Tues in July and Aug, and truffle market Fri Dec–Feb.

Eating Out

★★★Hôtel Chabrol, 57 Rue Gambetta, **t** 05 53 05 70 15, **f** 05 53 05 71 85 (*moderate*). In a handsome old white building right on the river Dronne, this excellent, elegant restaurant serves generous portions of favourites such as *millefeuille de ris de veau au foie de canard et truffe*, as well as desserts. *Closed Sun eve, Mon, 15 Nov–15 Dec and most of Feb.*

Au Fil de l'Eau, 21 Quai Bertin, **t** 05 53 05 73 65 (*moderate*). Across the Dronne, and you can eat outside. *Closed Mon eve and Tues out of season and two months in winter.*

Le Vieux Four, 7 Rue Pierre de Mareuil, **t** 05 53 05 74 16 (*moderate*). Set in a cave, they serve some of the best pizzas in Périgord.

Resto-Grill, 40 Rue Gambetta, **t** 05 53 05 86 25 (*moderate*). A stroll away from the tourist hub, offering quite simple meals in a pleasant, intimate atmosphere. You can eat on a shaded terrace.

Brantôme

Northeast of Bergerac lies Brantôme, a charming town of medieval and Renaissance houses built on an island in the river Dronne. A 16th-century dogleg bridge with a Renaissance pavilion crosses from the island town to the white pile of the **abbey** (*open Oct–June Wed–Mon 10–12 and 2–5; July and Aug 10–7; Sept 10–12.30 and 2–6, exc Tues; adm*) founded by Charlemagne in 769. The 11th-century church, after suffering a string of bad luck and reconstructions, was given the coup de grâce when it was handed over to the 19th-century architect-restorer Paul Abadie. Only the detached **bell tower** (the oldest in France), with its Merovingian base and complex tiers of windows and arches from the 11th century, attests to the abbey's former grandeur. A bas-relief of the *Massacre of the Innocents* under the porch and a carved capital, used as a font, survive from the original church. The best bits are the curious *grottes et fontaines sacrées* in the cliff behind the abbey, including a grotto where the 15th-century monks carved striking reliefs of the *Last Judgement* and the *Crucifixion*.

Among a long line of abbots, Pierre de Bourdeilles (1540–1614) stands out; never content as a simple churchman, he set to writing spicy accounts of the people of his time, all so true that he left instructions for his heirs to wait 50 years before publishing them. Known in French literature simply as Brantôme, he is remembered in town with a bust by the Fontaine Médicis.

Sarlat-la-Canéda

Cocooned in its clinking ring of 20th-century sprawl, this golden Renaissance town is architecturally the foie gras of southwest France. The most lavishly ornate town house is the **Hôtel de La Boétie**, birthplace in 1530 of Sarlat's most famous son,

Etienne de La Boétie, who is principally remembered as Montaigne's perfect pal in the latter's beautiful *Essay on Friendship*. The house was built in 1525 by Etienne's father, with richly ornamented mullioned windows squeezed between a vertiginously steep gable. The decoration reaches a curlicue frenzy in the dormer window, in frilly contrast to the sombre *lauzes* of the roof. Opposite the house stretch the flying buttresses and bulb-topped steeple of the **Cathédrale St-Sacerdos**, rebuilt in the dull 17th century and with little to distinguish it beside its spaciousness.

From Place du Peyrou, Passage Henri-de-Segogne leads to another of Sarlat's architectural gems, the **Hôtel de Maleville** (now the tourist office), with two Renaissance façades: one French, one Italian. The French one overlooks **Place de la Liberté**, Sarlat's favoured café stop; its northern extension is **Place du Marché**, one of the venues for Sarlat's prestigious summer theatre festival, starring Paris' Comédie Française. The **Rampe Magnanat**, to the right, is popular for filming duels before the brooding 16th-century Hôtel de Gisson. Among the magnificent *hôtels particuliers* on the narrow Rue des Consuls, the **Hôtel Selve de Plamon** (Nos.8–10) stands out: early Gothic on the ground floor; Flamboyant Gothic on the first and Renaissance on the second.

A 19th-century street, the **Traverse**, separates the wealthy Sarlat of splendid town houses from the steeper, more popular and piquant neighbourhood to the west, where some alleys are scarcely wide enough to walk arm-in-arm.

Getting There

Direct **trains** from Bergerac serve Sarlat's Av de la Gare; in July and Aug there are daily links from Bergerac, known as *Autorail Espérance* – a guided tour, with tastings of local products (tickets and information **t** 05 53 59 00 21).

Taxi: t 05 53 59 39 65 or **t** 05 53 59 02 43.

Bike hire from the station, or from Christian Chapoulie, 4 Av de Selves, **t** 05 53 59 06 11.

Tourist Information

Sarlat-la-Canéda ✉ 24200: Rue Tourny, **t** 05 53 31 45 45, **f** 05 53 59 19 44, *www.sarlat.com*.

Market Days

Sarlat-la-Canéda: Wed and Sat.

Eating Out

Le Présidial, near the Place de la Liberté, **t** 05 53 28 92 47 (*expensive–moderate*). Formerly the site of a royal court, with an elegant dining room and a large patio. There are extravagant regional dishes such as *suprême de pigeonneau en croûte sauce aux truffes*, with a choice of wines, particularly local ones.

Rossignol, near the Mairie at 15 Rue Fénelon, **t** 05 53 31 02 30 (*moderate*). Good-value, regional cuisine. *Closed Thurs*.

Criquettamu's, 5 Rue des Armes, **t** 05 53 59 48 10 (*moderate*). They do tasty things with foie gras, *magrets* and morel mushrooms. *Closed Mon, and Nov–Easter*.

★★★La Madeleine, 1 Place de la Petite Rigaudie, **t** 05 53 59 10 41, **f** 05 53 31 03 62 (*moderate*). Near the medieval centre, this hotel was converted from a 19th-century town house. Owned by a chef, the restaurant serves regional specialities: *civet d'oie* in *vin de Cahors* and such share the menu with lighter, more modern dishes. *Closed Mon lunch exc July, and Aug and Jan–mid-Feb*.

Le Relais de Poste, Impasse de la Vieille Poste, **t** 05 53 59 63 13 (*moderate–cheap*). Good menus, mostly focused on the regional, with a wide wine selection and a range of *eaux-de-vie*. There is a large secluded patio surrounded by walls with plenty of plants. *Closed Sun lunch in summer and Wed rest of the year*.

La Rapière, Place de la Cathédrale, **t** 05 53 59 03 13 (*cheap*). A wide choice of well-priced dishes. *Closed Sun out of season, and Jan–Feb*.

Bordeaux

Bordeaux is both terribly grand and terribly shabby and monotonous, a mercantile city that has lost its port, tinted in a thousand nuances of white. Most of what you see now was begun in the 18th century, when Bordeaux's *intendants* replaced its medieval streets with brand new squares, wide tree-lined *allées* and the first public gardens. By the Revolution, Bordeaux was the third city in France; these days 220,000 Bordelais can claim to take up more room per capita than any other city dwellers in France.

The South Side of Town: Ste-Croix and St-Michel

The main monuments in this genteelly dilapidated neighbourhood are in the vicinity of the former monastery church of **Ste-Croix**. Built in the 12th century, it was almost entirely rebuilt in 1860 by Paul Abadie, although the south tower, portal, figures of Avarice and Luxury and some carved capitals in the transept have survived his touch.

North of here, the grimy, Flamboyant Gothic church of **St-Michel** lies in what is now a lively Portuguese–North African neighbourhood. A morning flea market takes place under its 15th-century detached bell tower, the **Flêche** (377ft). The church was largely built by the city's guilds; the chapels they furnished contain the best art, mostly from the 15th century. The stained glass was blasted away by Allied bombers in the last war.

Central Bordeaux

Bordeaux's great Gothic **Cathédrale St-André** (*open 8–11.30am and 2–6.30pm*) was built under English rule between the 13th and 15th centuries. Like St-Michel, it has a lofty detached bell tower, the **Tour Pey-Berland** (*open June–Sept Tues–Sun 10–6.30; Oct–May 10–12.30 and 2–5.30, closed hols; adm*), affording superb views over Bordeaux. The cathedral itself is supported by an intricate web of buttresses; its west front is strikingly bare, but a fine 14th-century tympanum with the *Last Supper* crowns the north transept door. The nearby Porte Royale (used by visiting dignitaries) has another, with a rhythmic *Last Judgement*. As in the Middle Ages, the doors are usually left wide open, as a pedestrian shortcut; the single nave is nearly as long and wide as Notre-Dame.

Just north of the cathedral, the **Centre National Jean Moulin** (*open Tues–Fri 11–6, weekends 2–6*) contains a collection devoted to the Occupation, Resistance and Deportation, from posters to an ingenious folding motorcycle.

Southeast of the cathedral lies one of the most compelling museums in southwest France, the **Musée d'Aquitaine**, 20 Cours Pasteur (*open Tues–Sun 11–6; adm, free 1st Sun of each month*). Treating the history of Aquitaine, one of its first works is a mysterious 25,000-year-old bas-relief of the *Venus with a Horn* from Laussel in the Dordogne. The excellent Gallo-Roman section has coins, mosaics, sculptures and a fascinating set of reliefs from everyday life in ancient Burdigala. Further on is a legless but still impressive bronze Hercules, and a room dedicated to finds from a *mithraeum* discovered in 1982 in Cours Victor Hugo; in the 2nd and 3rd century Mithraism, an all-male, monotheistic religion from the east, posed serious competition to Christianity.

Most of the large and luxurious **Palais Rohan** (1770s), across from the cathedral, holds Bordeaux city hall (*guided tours Wed 2.30*), but one wing contains the **Musée**

des Beaux-Arts, 20 Cours d'Albret (*open daily 11–6 exc Tues and hols; adm; free 1st Sun of each month. Call ahead for the guided tour in English*), with paintings by artists rarely seen in French provincial museums: Titian, Perugino, Van Dyck, Rubens, Reynolds, Ruysdael, Chardin, Delacroix, Boudin, Magnasco, and Bordeaux native Odilon Redon (1840–1916). Two other native sons are also represented: Albert Marquet (1875–1947), a fellow student of Matisse and co-founder of Fauvism, and André Lhote (1885–1962), represented by his hallmark colourful, geometric compositions on various planes. There is also a selection of minor paintings by major 20th-century artists: Matisse, Bonnard, Renoir and Seurat.

Nearby the excellent **Musée des Arts Décoratifs,** 39 Rue Bouffard (*open Wed–Sun 2–6, free 1st Sun of each month; closed Tues; adm*) has a perfect home in a neoclassical *hôtel particulier* (1779), with fine furniture, wallpaper, ceramics, paintings, gold and silverwork, glass, jewellery and costumes.

Bordeaux's oldest church, **St-Seurin** (*open daily 8–12 and 2–6.30*) has often been remodelled, but it retains a 14th-century porch with lavish sculptures and also an 11th-century porch, hidden behind the undistinguished façade of 1828. Inside, there is a beautiful 15th-century alabaster retable in the Chapelle of Notre-Dame-de-la Rose and 14 alabaster panels in the choir. Note, too, the magnificent 15th-century episcopal throne, curiously made of stone imitating wood, and the sculpted choir stalls. The **crypt** (*you may have to ask the sacristan to open it*) holds a collection of 6th- and 7th-century treasures; excavations have revealed the 4th-century **Palaeo-Christian crypt** underneath, with sarcophogi and frescoes (*guided tours June–Sept daily 3–7; adm*).

From the 3rd to the 12th century, **Quartier St-Pierre** was a separate walled quarter outside Bordeaux. From the **Porte Cailhau** (*guided tours June–Sept daily 3–7; adm*), you can see the 18th-century **Grande Façade** project running from Cours du Chapeau Rouge to Porte de la Monnaie: a row of pale stone houses, with arcades and *mascarons*, topped by two floors of large windows and mansard roofs with dormers. The presence of the Parlement led to the construction of stately 18th-century *hôtels particuliers*, the best of which can be seen by walking straight through Porte Cailhau to Rue du Loup, crossing Rue Ste-Catherine, and turning right into Rue de Cheverus. Bordeaux's neoclassical showcase, the **Place de la Bourse**, lies alongside the river north of the Porte Cailhau. In the centre a fountain of the Three Graces (1864) holds court between the Palais de la Bourse (now the Chamber of Commerce) and the grandiose Hôtel des Douanes, now home to the **Musée des Douanes,** 1 Place de la Bourse (*open Tues–Sun 10–6; adm*), which traces the history of the French customs.

North of Cours de l'Intendance

Bordeaux's Golden Triangle of good taste and luxury shops is formed by Cours de l'Intendance, Cours Georges-Clemenceau and Allées de Tourny. The lavishly Baroque **Notre-Dame** (1684–1707) in Place du Chapelet sets the tone; behind it is the shopping mall, the **Marché des Grands-Hommes**, or *bouchon de carafe* (the 'carafe stopper'). The quarter's proudest showcase is the **Grand Théâtre,** designed by Victor Louis (1773) and resembling a Greek temple, fronted by mighty Corinthian columns and crowned with statues of goddesses and muses. If fairly restrained on the outside, all sumptuous hell

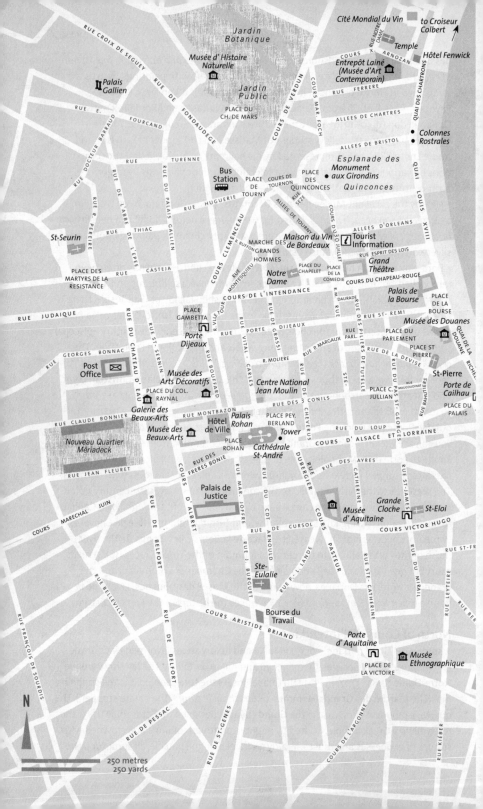

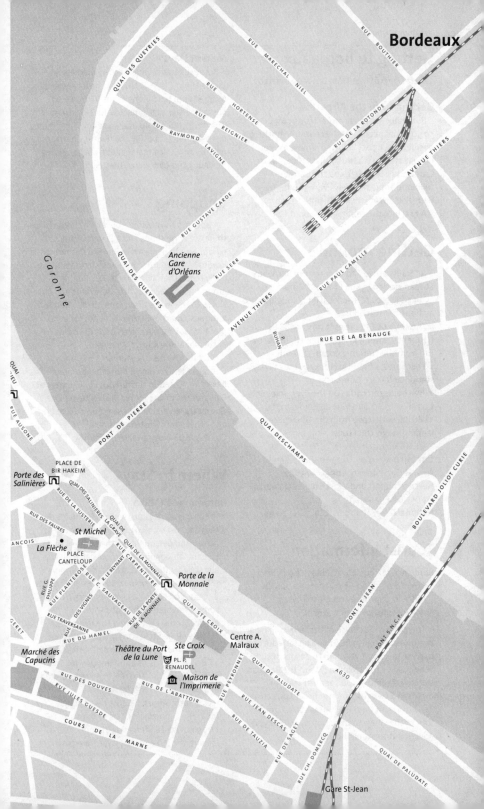

Getting to Bordeaux

Buzz (*see* p.6) flies from London Stansted.

Getting from the Airport

Bordeaux Mérignac **airport** (**t** 05 56 34 50 50), is 12km west of the centre. A **shuttle bus**, 'Jetbus', €5.80, links the airport to the railway station via the tourist office (Place Gambetta: stop M13), and the Barrière Judaïque approximately every 30mins from 6am, 8.45am at weekends, until 10.45pm.

A **taxi** into the centre costs about €25.

Getting Around

All trains arrive and depart from **Bordeaux St-Jean station** in Rue Charles Domerq, **t** 08 36 35 35 35. There are also local lines, roughly once an hour, to Arcachon.

The city's **CGFTE buses** (**t** 05 57 57 88 88) are frequent, convenient and huge. **Night buses** run from the station 9.30pm–12.30am.

There are 24-hour **taxi** ranks at the railway station and Place Gambetta.

Two **boats** offer trips on the river l'Aliénor, **t** 05 56 51 27 90, and Ville de Bordeaux, **t** 05 56 52 88 88; both leave from the Quinconces landing stage, Quai Louis XVIII.

Car Hire

Avis: at Gare St-Jean, **t** 05 56 34 38 22.
Hertz: at airport and 7 Rue Charles Domercq, **t** 05 56 34 59 59.
National Citer: at airport, **t** 05 56 34 20 68.

Tourist Information

Bordeaux: 12 Cours du 30-Juillet, **t** 05 56 00 66 00, **f** 05 56 00 66 01; there's a branch office in Gare St-Jean, **t** 05 56 91 64 70; *www.bordeaux-tourisme.com*.

There is a wide choice of themed walking or bus **tours** in English, including an introduction to wine tasting. If you plan to do lots of sightseeing, you can save money with the *Bordeaux Découverte* card. If you spend at least two nights in a two- to four-star hotel, you can also get a discount on the bill, as well as a guided tour of the vineyards. Book at least 10 days in advance at the tourist office.

Market Days

Bordeaux has several covered **markets**: at Victor-Hugo, Place de la Ferme de Richemont, Mon–Sat am (and along Cours Victor Hugo Sun am); Place des Capucins, Tues–Sun am; Chartrons, Rue Sicard, Tues–Sat am. There is an open-air market beside the river at Chartrons on Sun, and a flea market at St-Michel, Places Meynard and Canteloup, Tues–Sun.

Shopping

A bottle is the obvious souvenir of Bordeaux: there are **wine shops** and all kinds of vinous paraphernalia. Pedestrian **Rue Ste-Catherine** is Bordeaux's favourite shopping street, especially for clothes. Two streets, Rue Bouffard around the Musée des Arts Décoratifs and Rue Notre-Dame in the Chartrons, are devoted to **antiques**. **Quartier St-Pierre** is another good place to look for old things and curiosities, in particular along Rue de la Devise.

Not far from here is Saunion, 56 Cours Georges Clemenceau, a must for **chocolate**-lovers. You can find the famous *canalé* **cakes** at Baillardran, 90 Rue Porte Dijeaux, near Place Gambetta. If you want to stock up on **foie gras** and other southwest staples head for Comtesse du Barry, 2 Place de Tourny.

Where to Stay

Bordeaux ✉ 33000
★★★★Burdigala, 115 Rue Georges Bonnac, **t** 05 56 90 16 16, **f** 05 56 93 15 06 (*expensive*). For luxury and personality in the heart of town. Elegant, air-conditioned rooms all individually styled with wood, stone and marble.
★★★Ste Catherine, 27 Rue du Parlement, **t** 05 56 81 95 12, **f** 05 56 44 50 51 (*expensive*). A handsomely restored 18th-century *hôtel particulier* near the Grand Théâtre.
★★★Le Bayonne Etche-Ona, 4 Rue Martignac, on the corner of the Allées de Tourny, **t** 05 56 48 00 88, **f** 05 56 48 41 60 (*moderate*). The 18th-century building has been redecorated in a contemporary style.
★★Les Quatre Sœurs, 6 Cours du 30-Juillet (near the Quinconces), **t** 05 57 81 19 20, **f** 05 56 01 04 28 (*moderate*). Rooms, overlooking the street or courtyard, are cosy.

★★Le Continental, 10 Rue Montesquieu, **t** 05 56 52 66 00, **f** 05 56 52 77 97, *www.hotel-le-continental.com* (*moderate*). An elegant hotel on a pedestrianized street in the centre near the shopping centre.

★★Notre Dame, 36 Rue Notre Dame, **t** 05 56 52 88 24, **f** 05 56 79 12 67 (*inexpensive*). A pretty 19th-century building in Chartrons.

★★La Tour Intendance, 16 Rue Vieille Tour (off Cours de l'Intendance), **t** 05 56 81 46 27, **f** 05 56 81 60 90 (*inexpensive*). Simple and sweet.

★★Acanthe, 12–14 Rue St-Rémi, **t** 05 56 81 66 58, **f** 05 56 44 74 41, *www.acanthe-hotel-bordeaux.com* (*inexpensive*). A pretty sitting room and simply furnished but well-equipped bedrooms; the large family room is the most stylish. Probably most appropriate for those without a car.

Amboise, 22 Rue Vieille-Tour (near Place Gambetta), **t** 05 56 81 62 67 (*inexpensive*). Old-fashioned.

Eating Out

Pavillon des Boulevards, 120 Rue Croix-de-Seguey, **t** 05 56 81 51 02 (*luxury*). Near the Parc Bordelais, in a sophisticated, tastefully designed house with a veranda in the back garden. Here chef Denis Franc presents delicate, sophisticated dishes based on the absolutely best and freshest ingredients. *Closed Sat lunch and Sun.*

Le Chapon Fin, 5 Rue Montesquieu, **t** 05 56 79 10 10 (*luxury*). The oldest restaurant in Bordeaux is still one of the best. Its rococo décor and inner garden are a perfect match for the likes of the *marbès de ris de veau et foie gras, marmite* of fish and crustaceans with *pistou. Closed Sun and Mon.*

Jean Ramet, 7 Place Jean Jaurès, **t** 05 56 44 12 51 (*expensive*). One of Bordeaux's best and classiest, where chef Ramet prepares both old-fashioned food and original dishes. *Closed Sat lunch, Sun and mid-Aug.*

Le Vieux Bordeaux, 27 Rue Buhan, **t** 05 56 52 94 36 (*expensive*). Dine in their delightful closed court. Famous for the painstakingly high quality of every dish. *Closed Sat lunch, Sun, Mon lunch.*

Didier Gelineau, 26 Rue du Pas St-Georges, **t** 05 56 52 84 25 (*expensive*). A charming place offering *haute cuisine* at affordable prices: try the breaded lamb chops with truffles. *Closed Sat lunch and Sun.*

Dubern, 42–4 Allées de Tourny, **t** 05 56 79 07 70 (*moderate*). It seems quite a simple brasserie when you walk in but the upstairs opens into a plush green room with a chandelier. The menus are quite simple. *Closed Sun.*

Gravelier, 114 Cours Verdun, **t** 05 56 48 17 15 (*moderate*). This place in the Chartrons offers very toothsome cuisine, especially seafood, prepared with an exotic touch. *Closed Sat lunch and Sun and half of Aug.*

Chez Philippe, 1 Place du Parlement, **t** 05 56 81 83 15 (*moderate*). Fish-lovers come to worship here. *Closed Sun, Mon and Aug.*

Le Café Gourmand, 3 Rue Buffon, **t** 05 56 79 23 85 (*moderate*). An elegant bistro with a turn-of-the-century feel, the walls covered in old family photos. Menus for midday and evening, both good, including *aiguillettes de canard aux pêches* and *moussaka d'agneau à la coriande fraîche.* The desserts are yummy as well, so leave space. *Closed Sun.*

Le Bistro du Sommelier, 163 Rue Georges Bonnac, **t** 05 56 96 71 78 (*moderate*). Simple meals enhance its wide array of bottles. *Closed Sat lunch and Sun.*

Le Père Ouvrard, 12 Rue de Maréchal Joffre, **t** 05 56 44 11 58 (*moderate*). Lovely imaginative southwest food served in a laid-back atmosphere at kind prices. *Closed Sat lunch, Sun and Aug.*

Restaurant de Fromages Baud et Millet, 19 Rue Huguerie, **t** 05 56 79 05 77 (*moderate*). A paradise for anyone who loves cheese and wine, offering 950 wines from all around the world to go with its two hundred types of farm cheese and *raclettes. Closed Sun.*

Au Bonheur du Palais, 74 Rue Paul-Louis Lande, **t** 05 56 94 38 63 (*cheap*). Excellent, very serious Chinese food, with plenty of seafood. *Closed Sun and lunchtimes.*

Le Rital, 3 Rue des Faussets, **t** 05 56 48 16 69 (*cheap*). Delicious fresh pasta, made on the premises, and home-made desserts. *Closed weekends and the first two weeks in Sept.*

La Casa Pino, 40 Rue Traversanne (St-Michel), **t** 05 56 92 82 88. Considered the best Portugese eatery in the city. *Morue* (dried cod) features, of course. Excellent value. Full of regulars. *Closed Sun.*

breaks loose within. The vestibule columns support a magnificent coffered ceiling, lit by a 62ft cupola; the grand stair was copied for the Paris Opéra; the auditorium has golden columns and a massive crystal chandelier weighing 2,860lbs.

Just down Cours 30 Juillet rises the irresistibly overblown 19th-century **Monument aux Girondins**, a tall column crowned by Liberty over a fountain mobbed by Happiness, Eloquence, Security, a crowing cockerel and a host of other allegories. Stretching out endlessly from here is Europe's largest, and one of its least interesting, squares-cum-car parks, the **Place des Quinconces**. In contrast, the **Jardin Public** (*open till 9pm summer and 6pm winter*) makes for a delightful wander; it contains the **Jardin Botanique** (*open daily 8–6*) and the **Musée d'Histoire Naturelle** (*open 11–6, weekends 2–6; closed Tues; adm, free 1st Sun of each month*).

The old wine merchants' quarter of **Chartrons** has seen much development since the 1960s, now with plenty of hotels, shops and a conference centre, but maintains as much of its original wine trade as possible. The old trade is recalled in the **Musée des Chartrons,** 41 Rue Borie (*open Mon–Fri 2–6; adm*), while a new (and utterly sterile) **Cité Mondiale du Vin** stands on the Quai des Chartrons. Nearby, the vast Entrepôt Lainé hosts the giant installations of the **Musée d'Art Contemporain** (*open 11–6, until 8 on Wed, closed Mon and hols; adm, free 1st Sun of each month*), as well as a charming café.

Day Trips from Bordeaux

St-Emilion

Set in a natural amphitheatre surrounded by its famous vines, St-Emilion is a gem, a lovely town mellowed to the colour of old piano keys. The haunt of medieval kings and popes, it has been restored to much of its old elegance; its uneven lanes, called *tertres*, are so steep that handrails have been installed along them. The town's greatest secrets are underground; not only the ruby nectar in its cellars, but Europe's largest subterreanean church. Four of the principal sights can only be seen on the tourist office's **guided tour** (*see* box, opposite), but do take a wander on your own.

The ruined, partially overgrown Romanesque **Cloître des Cordeliers** (*open 10–12 and 2–6.30*), was built in 1383 by the Franciscans. In the adjacent chapel, note the carving of two snakes entering a jar, a symbol that goes back to the ancient Greeks; it must have been copied from the Eglise Monolithe, where it appears twice. Further up, Rue Gaudet runs into **Place du Marché**, a magnificent urbane stage set, its cafés shaded by a liberty tree from the Revolution of 1848. Built into the cliff is the strange **Eglise Monolithe**, started by the Benedictines in the 8th century and one of the highlights of the tour. When they had attained a cavity measuring 124ft by 66ft in the 11th century, they gave it up to construct the Collégiale. It is a primitive, sombre and uncanny place, its nave supported by 10 rough, ill-aligned pillars. The only remaining decorations are bas-reliefs: four winged angels, signs of the zodiac, and a dedicatory inscription. Bell ropes from the original bell tower hang through the hole in the ceiling.

Next door is the round **Chapelle de la Trinité**, built in the 13th century by Augustinian monks to the memory of St Emilion, with fascinating wall paintings

Getting There

St-Emilion's **railway** station is 2km away in the middle of the countryside, on the Bordeaux–Bergerac–Sarlat line. There are several Citram **buses** daily from Bordeaux (**t** 05 56 43 68 43). For a **taxi**, **t** 06 09 33 11 58.

The country lanes around St-Emilion make for a fun spin on a **bike**; hire one at the tourist office.

Tourist Information

St-Emilion ✉ **33330**: Place des Créneaux, **t** 05 57 55 28 28, **f** 05 57 55 28 29, *www.saint-emilion-tourisme.com*. The 45min tour of St-Emilion's subterranean monuments starts here (*daily 9.30–12.30 and 1.45–6, July and Aug 9.30–8*). Other tours are available, some in English.

Market Days

St-Emilion: Sun mornings at Place Bouqueyre.

Eating Out

In town you'll see signs for the traditional *Macarons de St-Emilion*, made at **Moulierac**, Tertre de la Tente, **Blanchez**, Rue Gaudet, and **Ertle**, Rue de la Grande Fontaine.

Le Tertre, Tertre de la Tente, **t** 05 57 74 46 33 (*expensive–moderate*). After briefly becoming a pizzeria Le Tertre has reverted to its former mission. Dine heartily on a broad range of good regional dishes. *Closed Tues in summer, Mon and Tues out of season.*

Francis Goullée, 27 Rue Guadet, **t** 05 57 24 70 49 (*moderate*). For food equal to the surroundings: taste-packed Rabelaisian cuisine. *Closed Sun eve, Mon and late Nov–mid-Dec.*

Le Clos du Roy, 12 Rue de la Petite Fontaine, **t** 05 57 74 41 55 (*moderate*). For dishes that harmonize well with the lifeblood of St-Emilion; try the breast of duck with Granny Smith apples. *Closed Tues, Wed and several weeks in Nov and Feb.*

Amelia Canta, Place de l'Eglise Monolithe, **t** 05 57 74 48 03 (*cheap*). A reliable brasserie, with a strategically located terrace. *Closed mid-Nov–start of Feb.*

L'Envers du Décor, Rue du Clocher, **t** 05 57 74 48 31 (*cheap*). Wine bar with a terrace, where you can try a wide variety of local labels by the glass, with a snack or light meal. *Closed weekends out of season.*

between the ribs of the apse. In the adjacent 8th-century **catacombs**, you can make out the engraved figures of three corpses with upraised arms, weird zombies symbolic of the Resurrection. Bones were deposited through the funnel-like cupola connecting the catacombs with the cemetery.

The **Grotte de l'Ermitage**, the cave where the hermit Emilion lived, was reshaped over the centuries into a chapel in the form of a Latin cross. The cave's natural spring has been worshipped since pagan times, renowned to be good for relieving afflictions of the eye; the story also goes that any young woman who can drop two hairpins into the water in the form of a cross will surely be married within the year.

St-Emilion's landmark 11th–15th-century **bell tower** rises up 173ft from Place des Créneaux; for a small fee you can climb the 198 steps for a superb view (*if it's closed, the tourist office has the key*). Here, too, is the entrance to the **Collégiale**, a hotchpotch of a church begun in 1110 – the period of its west portal, Byzantine cupolas, and frescoes on the right wall of the nave. The north portal is adorned with a *Last Judgement* from 1306; in the choir are 15th-century stalls and the treasure, where the relics of St Emilion are currently installed. From the nearby tourist office you can enter the pretty twin-columned Gothic **Cloître de la Collégiale** (*open summer 9.30–7; adm*). More views can be had from atop the austere Norman **Tour du Roi** (*open June–Sept 10.30–12.45 and 2.15–8.30; adm*), all that remains of the castle built by Henry III *c.* 1237.

Arcachon and the Dune du Pilat

Arcachon was a small fishing village until 1841, when a pair of brothers, Emile and Isaac Pereire, took over the railway from Bordeaux and laid out a new resort with winding lanes and four residential sections, each named after a season. Spring and Autumn never really caught on, but the sheltered **Ville d'Hiver**, always 3°C/37°F warmer than the rest of Arcachon, attained full fashion status by the 1860s – Gounod, Debussy, Alexandre Dumas and Napoleon III were all habitués of its lacy gingerbread villas. The **Ville d'Eté**, facing the Bassin and cooler in the summer, has most of Arcachon's tourist facilities, seaside promenades and sheltered sandy beaches. Its most notorious resident was Toulouse-Lautrec, who liked to swim in the nude, offending the sensibilities of his neighbours. To pacify them, he erected a fence between his house and the beach – then mischievously covered it with obscene drawings. The neighbours eventually banded together to buy the house and gleefully burned the fence, much to their descendants' chagrin. The **Musée-Aquarium** (*open mid-Feb–June and Sept–Oct 10–12.30 and 2–7; July–Aug 9.30–12.30 and 3–8; adm*) has a pretty collection of tropical fish, tortoises, seashells and shark skeletons.

Getting There

There are regional **trains** nearly every hour from Bordeaux to Arcachon. Several CITRAM **buses** a day from Bordeaux (from 8 Rue Corneille, **t** 05 56 43 68 43, or the station) serve Pyla-sur-Mer and Pyla-Plage for the dune.

For a **taxi**, **t** 05 56 83 88 88 or **t** 05 56 83 11 11. The *Union des Bateliers Arcachonnais* (**t** 05 57 72 28 28) run a Bateau Bus in season between Arcachon's Port de Pêche, Petit Port, Jetée d'Eyrac, Jetée Thiers and Le Moulleau.

You can hire **bikes** at Locabeach, 326 Bd de la Plage, **t** 05 56 83 39 64; and Dingo Vélo, Rue Grenier, **t** 05 56 83 44 09.

Tourist Information

Arcachon ✉ 33120: Esplanade Georges Pompidou, **t** 05 57 52 97 97, **f** 05 57 52 97 77, *www.arcachon.com*.

Market Days

Arcachon: daily in Place de Gracia.

Eating Out

L'Ombrière, 79 Cours Héricart-de-Thury, **t** 05 56 83 86 20 (*moderate*). Sample delicious seafood platters as well as duck and veal, and a good selection of wine on Arcachon's classiest terrace. *Closed Sun night and Wed.*

Le Patio, 10 Bd de la Plage, **t** 05 56 83 02 72 (*moderate*). Set amid trailing vines with a waterfall, this offers delicious lobster salad, oysters in flaky pastry, hot stuffed crab and *bouillabaisse océane*. *Closed Tues in winter.*

Restaurant l'Avenue, 196 Bd de la Plage, **t** 05 56 83 43 98 (*moderate*). Plain, simple and good value despite its prime location by the casino, with splendid seafood platters, rich *bouillabaisse* and paella.

Chez Yvette, 59 Bd Général Leclerc, **t** 05 56 83 05 11 (*moderate*). More formal, with an enviable reputation for fresh seafood, and a cellar of white Bordeaux wines. Choose *à la carte* or try the *Escale Gourmande*.

La Plancha, behind the market, 17 Rue Jéhenne, **t** 05 56 83 76 66 (*cheap*). Fill up on *gambas à la plancha* and other Spanish-style seafood treats at good prices. *Closed Sun in winter.*

La Marée, 21 Rue De Lattre-de-Tassigny, **t** 05 56 83 24 05 (*cheap*). For just a bit more, you can tuck into a satisfying fish soup, seafood platter and stuffed oysters at the best place of all – a fishmonger's. *Closed Mon out of season, and Nov–mid-Feb.*

Restaurant Le Chipiron, 69 Bd Chanzy, **t** 05 57 52 06 33 (*cheap*). An authentic Spanish bistro near the marina, serving tapas and other seafood with a good value lunch *menu*.

Eight kilometres south of Arcachon, the awesome **Dune du Pilat** rises up like Moby Dick between sand and sea. It began to form 8,000 years ago, and at 347ft it is the highest pile of sand in Europe, at 1.7 miles the longest, and at 550 yards the widest. Like all dunes, it is in a constant state of flux, every year it creeps up about 15 yards, consuming the pines and forcing campsites and cafés to move a bit further inland. A wooden stair with 190 steps helps you up to an unforgettable view; try it at sunset.

Soulac-sur-Mer

Legend has it that **Soulac-sur-Mer**, 'the Pearl of the Côte d'Argent', is the descendant of Noviomagus, the fabled ocean port of the Bituriges, which one cataclysmic day sank into the sea. In the 18th century, Soulac underwent a slower cataclysm, methodically swallowed up by sand, with the result that little remains of the medieval port except for the **Basilique de Notre-Dame de la Fin des Terres** (Our Lady at the End of the Earth), classed as a World Heritage site. Even this was buried twice by the voracious dunes; in 1859, it was exhumed again and now sits tidily in a sand-lined hollow. Apparently founded by St Veronica, it became a popular pilgrimage site and was always the first shrine that English pilgrims visited in France. It has a remarkable apse from the 13th century; inside, the polychrome wooden statue of the Virgin worshipped by the pilgrims is still in place; the carved capitals show Daniel in the lion's den, St Peter in prison, and the tomb and reliquary of St Veronica, who is said to have been buried here before her body was moved to Bordeaux. Three marble columns from the pre-Romanesque church survive in the apse; the stained glass dates from 1954.

Soulac also has a small **Musée d'Art et d'Archéologie**, Av El Burgo de Osma (*open July and Aug 3–7, June and Sept weekends only, 3–6*), with some interesting prehistoric and Gallo-Roman artefacts. On Boulevard du Front-du-Mer you can see the lighthouse of Cordouan, 8km away, or play the slots at the casino; just south is Soulac's small resort of **L'Amélie-sur-Mer**, named after a ship that was wrecked here decades ago. The big sand dune here is party of the coastal natural park.

Getting There

Frequent **trains** in the summer and less frequent but regular ones in the winter link Bordeaux St-Jean or Bordeaux St-Louis to Soulac-sur-Mer.

In summer, the little **PGV train** runs along the ocean from Soulac to Verdon and Pointe de Grave (*July and Aug daily, June and Sept weekends, call tourist offices for schedules*).

CITRAM **buses, t** 05 56 43 68 43, run several times a day in summer, less frequently in winter and on Sundays, from Bordeaux's *gare routière*.

Tourist Information

Soulac-sur-Mer ✉ 33780: 68 Rue de la Plage, t 05 56 09 86 61, f 05 56 73 63 76.

Market Days
Soulac: daily.

Eating Out

**Hôtel des Pins, t 05 56 73 27 27, f 05 56 73 60 39 (*moderate–cheap*). The restaurant at this simple Logis de France is one of the best in the area, serving good reliable food. *Closed mid-Jan–mid-Mar.*

Touring from Bergerac and Bordeaux

Day 1: St-Emilion

Morning: The N89 and D670 from Bordeaux through Libourne, or the D936 west from Bergerac, will bring you to **St-Emilion** (*see* pp.206–7), a beautiful wine town with early medieval monuments, including a unique rock-cut monastic church, the Eglise Monolithe (*guided tours of the town daily 9.30–12 and, 1.45–6, July and Aug 9.30–8*).

Lunch: Duck with apples, and everything else that goes well with rich St-Emilion wines, are on the bill at **Le Clos du Roy**, 12 Rue de la Petite Fontaine, **t** 05 57 74 41 55 (*expensive–moderate*). *Closed Tues and Wed, parts of Nov, Feb*. **Amelia Canta**, Place de l'Eglise Monolithe, **t** 05 57 74 48 03 (*inexpensive*) is a good brasserie with a terrace. *Closed mid-Nov–Feb*. Or else enjoy a light lunch and lots of St-Emilion at the wine bar **L'Envers du Décor**, Rue du Clocher. *Closed weekends out of season*.

Afternoon: From St-Emilion, head back towards Bergerac on the D670-936, and then north just before Lamothe-Montravel for **St-Michel-de-Montaigne**, and the famous tower of the Renaissance philosopher and essayist Montaigne (*open Wed–Sun 10–12 and 2–6.30; adm*). Then it's south on the D9, across the Dordogne for a tour through medieval *bastides*: **Gensac**, then the D16 to **Pellegrue** and the D15 to **Monségur**.

Dinner: Both the **Château de la Bûche** and the **Grand Hôtel** (*see* below) in Monségur have restaurants with good regional cooking at *moderate–inexpensive* rates.

Sleeping: Book ahead for the **Château de la Bûche**, Av de la Porte des Tours, **t** 05 56 61 80 22, **f** 05 56 61 85 99 (*inexpensive*), an 18th-century building with four guest rooms. On quiet Place Darniche is the **★★Grand Hôtel**, **t** 05 56 61 60 28, **f** 05 56 61 63 89 (*inexpensive*).

Day 2: Castles and *Bastides*

Morning: Just east on the D668, **Duras** will reveal one of the region's most imposing castles (*open daily June–Sept 10–7; rest of the year 10–12 and 2–6; adm*) as well as a working museum of parchment and

bookmaking. Continue through **Allemans-sur-Dropt**, with an interesting church; at Miramont-de-Guyenne, take the D1 through **Lauzun**, with the castle of a Renaissance rogue, and on to **Castillonès**.

Lunch: By the walls of this *bastide*, there is superb cooking on a pretty terrace at the **Hôtel des Remparts**, 26 Rue de la Paix, **t** 05 53 49 55 85 (*moderate*). *Closed Mon out of season*. A little further east at Villeréal, you can do just as well (but book ahead) at **Le Moulin de Labique**, at St-Vivien, **t** 05 53 01 63 90 (*moderate*).

Afternoon: From Castillonès, the road east (D2, then D104) carries on through two more attractive *bastides*, **Villeréal** and **Monpazier**. Between them lies the grandest of all Périgord castles, the **Château de Biron** (*open daily 10–12.30 and 2–5.30; July and Aug 10–7; closed Jan and Feb; adm*). From Monpazier, the scenic D53 winds north for **Belvès**, a picturesque town famous for walnuts.

Dinner: The best chef in the area works at the **Auberge de Nauze**, at Sagelat, **t** 05 53 28 44 81 (*expensive–moderate*). *Closed mid-Jan–mid-Feb*. There are also good meals with plenty of *cèpes* on offer at **Le Belvédère** (*moderate; see* below).

Sleeping: Belvès has the elegant, renovated **★★Le Belvédère**, Av Crampel, **t** 05 53 31 51 41, **f** 05 53 31 51 42 (*inexpensive*). *Closed Tues out of season, and Jan and Feb*. Or else move on to Cadouin (*see* below) for a restored farm with a garden, pool and a good restaurant: **★★La Salvetat**, on the D54 east of the village, **t** 05 53 63 42 79, **f** 05 53 61 72 05 (*inexpensive*). *Closed Wed, and Dec and Jan*.

Day 3: Les Eyzies and its Caves

Morning: Head west from Belvès on the D54 for the 12th-century **Abbey of Cadouin** (*open daily 10–12.30 and 2–6.30; closed Jan and Feb, and Tues Sept–April; adm*). From there the D28 will take you to the Dordogne, and across to charming **Trémolat**. From here, the D31 follows the river Vézère up to **Le Bugue**, where there are two caves to visit, a warm-up for the 'World Capital of Prehistory', just up the river: **Les-Eyzies-de-Tayac**.

Lunch: Among many choices in this popular spot, truffles and mushrooms and the best of Périgordin cuisine can be had at the attractive **Hôtel Cro-Magnon**, **t** 05 53 06

97 06 (*expensive*). *Closed Wed lunch, mid-Oct–April*. The **Moulin de la Beune**, in an old mill, t 05 53 06 94 33 (*moderate*) offers innovative twists on local cooking.

Afternoon: There are several painted caves around Les Eyzies, but you might start with a visit to the Musée National de Préhistoire (*open 9.30–12 and 2–5 or 6; July and Aug 9.30–7; adm*). The best of the Paleolithic art is in the cave of **Font-de-Gaume** (*ring ahead, t 05 53 06 86 00, for booking and information*). When you're done, follow the D706 up the valley of the Vézère to **Montignac**.

Dinner: **De la Grotte**, Rue 4 Septembre, Montignac, t 05 53 51 05 96 (*moderate–inexpensive*), is a good bargain restaurant on a riverside terrace, there's another excellent restaurant at the **Manoir de Hautegente** (*see* below).

Sleeping: Up in the hills on the D62 at Coly is the ★★★**Manoir de Hautegente**, t 05 53 51 68 03, f 05 53 50 38 52 (*moderate; book well ahead*): a 13th-century building, antique furnishings, heated pool. *Closed Nov–April*. In Montignac itself, ★★★**La Roseraie**, Place d'Armes, t 05 53 50 53 92, f 05 53 51 02 23 (*moderate*) occupies a charming 19th-century house. *Closed Oct–Mar*.

Day 4: Montignac, and More Caves

Morning: Montignac's centre has a scenographic ruined castle, though the main attraction here is the replica **Cave of Lascaux** (*open April–Sept daily 9–7, otherwise 10–12 and 2–6; adm; in May–Sept, tickets from the Montignac tourist office*). If there's time, visit the Renaissance **Château de Losse**, south off the D706 (*open mid-April–mid-Sept daily 10–12.30 and 1.30–6; June–Aug 10–7; adm*).

Lunch: Just south of the château at Sergeac, the usual Périgourdin treats and a rare vegetarian menu are available at the **Auberge de Castle-Merle**, t 05 53 50 70 08 (*moderate–inexpensive*). *Closed Mon and Nov–April*. The duck and foie gras are just as good, in a room with a view, at the nearby **Auberge du Peyrol**, t 05 53 50 72 91 (*moderate–inexpensive*). *Closed Mon and Nov–Mar*.

Afternoon: Backtrack a little more on the D706, and then head north on the D6 for **Rouffignac**, where there's yet another cave, full of painted mammoths and such, the Grotte de Rouffignac (*open April–Oct*

10–11.30 and 2–5, till 6 in July and Aug; adm), as well as the sinister Château de l'Herm (*April–mid-Sept 10–7, mid-Sept–Nov 11–6; adm*). Return on the D32 and D47 through Les Eyzies, and on east to **Sarlat-le-Caneda**.

Dinner: *Pigeonneau en croûte*, plenty of truffles and an expansive wine list await at **Le Présidial**, Place de la Liberté, t 05 53 28 92 47 (*expensive–moderate*). Good local cooking at more reasonable rates, on a garden patio, can be had at **Le Relais de la Poste**, t 05 53 59 63 13 (*inexpensive*). *Closed Wed out of season*.

Sleeping: The ★★★**Hôtel de Selves**, 93 Av de Selves, t 05 53 31 50 00, f 05 53 31 23 53 (*moderate*) is a classy modern place with a garden and pool. *Closed part of Jan and Feb.* For something a little more unusual, ★★**La Couleuvrine**, 1 Place de la Bouquerie, t 05 53 59 27 80, f 05 53 31 26 83 (*inexpensive*) offers antique-furnished rooms in a tower of the town walls. *Closed part of Jan*.

Day 5: Sarlat

Morning: Périgord's capital of foie gras, **Sarlat** (*see* pp.198–9) is also a beautiful city of golden stone, full of Renaissance mansions and churches. After a look around, the D46 will take you south to **Domme**, the 'Acropolis of Périgord'. In this charming *bastide* on its lofty height, you can visit another cave with an entrance right under the market building: the Grottes de Domme (*open Mar–Oct daily 9.30–12 and 2–6; July and Aug 9.30–7; Oct and Mar afternoons only; adm*).

Lunch: In Domme, the **Hôtel L'Esplanade**, t 05 53 28 31 41 (*expensive*) has one of the best restaurants in Périgord, where truffles figure prominently. *Closed Mon and Nov–Feb*. If you carry on to La Roque-Gageac, there's the wonderful **Le Pres Gaillardou**, t 05 53 59 67 89 (*moderate*); great food in a charming room furnished with antiques.

Afternoon: From Domme, the next step is **La Roque-Gageac**, back north over the Dordogne on the D703, a striking medieval village built into the face of the cliffs. The D703 continues along the river to the huge **Château de Beynac** (*open daily 10–6, June–Sept till 6.30; in winter until dusk; adm*). There are three more castles to explore around **Castelnaud**, just across the river, and when you've had enough the D703 will take you back to Bergerac and Bordeaux.

Biarritz and Bayonne

Biarritz

For their 1959 season, the designers at Cadillac came up with something special: a sleek and shiny convertible, nearly 25ft long, with the highest tail-fins in automotive history (22ins). They called it the *Biarritz*, a tribute to the Basque village that was chosen by fortune, for a few decades in the 19th century, to be the most glittering resort in Europe. Nowadays, freed from the burden of being the cynosure of fashion, the resort has become pleasantly laid-back.

In the 1860s, Biarritz was a simple fishing village with a great whaling past, when it began to make part of its living from a new phenomenon, the desire of northerners to spend a holiday beside the sea. It owes its present status to Empress Eugénie, who summered at Biarritz as a girl. As empress, she dragged Napoleon III down with her and established the summer court on the most prominent spot along the beach in 1854. Everybody who was anybody in Paris soon followed; the Belle Epoque brought grand hotels, the casino, a salt-water spa and acres of villas. The First World War started Biarritz's fall from fashion; in the 1920s everybody shifted to Nice and Cannes.

Biarritz has begun to shake off its dusty image with dramatic refurbishment of its hotels and fine buildings, including the splendid Casino Municipal on the Grande-Plage, with its entertainment centres and old-style grand café. Plenty of young people come, too – to surf.

The Atalaya

Here, on the tip of old Biarritz's little peninsula, the watch used to send up smoke signals when whales were sighted. To the right, the Port des Pêcheurs now holds only pleasure craft, while to the left lie the old fishing port and the **Rocher de la Vierge**. Napoleon III and Eugénie are responsible for this system of causeways and tunnels, connecting a number of crags and tiny islands into a memorable walk just above the pounding surf; the biggest rock carries a marble statue of the Virgin Mary.

Up on top of the Atalaya, the **Musée de la Mer**, (*open daily 9.30–12.30 and 2–6, plus evenings in summer, closed first week of Jan; adm; the seals are fed at 10.30 and 5*), in a clean Art Deco building, contains an imaginatively decorated old aquarium.

Descending eastwards from the Atalaya, the Boulevard Maréchal Leclerc takes you to the **church of Ste-Eugénie**, another modest contribution of the Empress; it faces the beautifully restored **Casino Bellevue**, now converted to residences and conference rooms. Not far away, on Rue Broquelis, the **Musée du Vieux Biarritz** (*open Fri–Sat and Mon–Wed 10–12 and 2.30–6; adm*) shows photos and mementos of the good old days.

Beaches and Villas

Below this, the shore straightens out into the luscious expanse of the **Grande Plage**, dominated by the magnificently restored casino. Farther up, behind wrought-iron fences, Biarritz's sumptuous **Hôtel du Palais** marks the spot where Eugénie built her palace, which was destroyed by fire in 1881. **Avenue Edouard VII** was *the* status

address of Belle Epoque Biarritz, lined with ornate hotels and residences; scores of wealthy villas still survive in the streets behind, in a crazy quilt of styles from Art Nouveau to neo-Moorish to Anglo-Norman.

At the end of Plage Miramar stands the landmark on this stretch of the coast, the 143ft **Phare St-Martin** (*open Sept–June Sat–Sun 3–7; July–Aug Tues–Sun 10–12 and 3–7*), a rare example of an old-fashioned lighthouse from 1834, and little changed since.

As for **beaches**, there is plenty of choice. At Biarritz's southern limits is the broad expanse of the Plage de la Milady, Plage Marbella and the Côte des Basques, a favourite of the surfing set. Under the old town is the tiny Plage du Port Vieux. The Grande Plage and Plage Miramar, the centre of the action, are lovely if often cramped, but further out, stretching miles along the northern coast, there are plenty more.

Bayonne

Bayonne is as attractive and lively an urban setting as you'll find in the southwest, with a remarkable history, a majestic cathedral and a delicious medieval centre full of brightly painted old half-timber buildings.

Grand Bayonne

Bayonne's delightful main street is a river, the little Nive, lined on both sides with busy quays and old tall houses in bright colours. The Nive also marks the division

Getting to Biarritz

Ryanair (*see* p.6) has daily flights to Biarritz from London Stansted (1hr55).

Getting from the Airport

Biarritz's airport, the Aérogare de Parme, **t** 05 59 43 83 83, is about 2 miles from Biarritz; it is served by a **shuttle bus** to the centre (€1.07). A **taxi** will cost €9–13.

Getting Around

Public transport in the Bayonne-Biarritz area is run by STAB (**Biarritz**, Av J Petit, **t** 05 59 24 26 53; **Bayonne**, Place du Général de Gaulle, **t** 05 59 59 04 61; Infobus has information on all local services, **t** 05 59 52 59 52). Regular **city buses** connect the two cities, from the Hôtel de Ville in Bayonne to the Hôtel de Ville in Biarritz – line 1 or 2, or, faster, the Express BAB. Biarritz's **train station** is 3km from the city centre; the no.2 bus goes there.

Car Hire

Biarritz: **Avis, t** 05 59 23 67 92, **Budget, t** 05 59 63 11 77, and **National Citer, t** 05 59 41 21 12, all at the airport.
Bayonne: **ADA Location**, 10bis Quai de Lesseps, **t** 05 59 50 37 10, or **Basque Automobile**, 59 Av des Allées Marines, **t** 05 59 58 59 07.

Tourist Information

Biarritz: Javalquinto, **t** 05 59 22 37 00, **f** 05 59 22 14 19, *www.ville-biarritz.fr*.
Bayonne: Place des Basques, **t** 05 59 46 01 46, **f** 05 59 59 37 55. Offers guided tours of town.

Market Days

In **Bayonne's Halles**: Mon–Sat mornings and all day on Fri.
Place des Gascons: Wed and Sat am.
Quais de la Nive: Tues, Thurs and Sat am.

Shopping

In Biarritz, buy Basque table linen, chocolate and espadrilles around **Place Clemenceau** and **Rue Mazagran**, and **Av Edouard VII**. EKI, 21 Av de Verdun, sells Basque music and crafts.

In Bayonne, try **Rue du Pont-Neuf**, **Rue des Arcades**, **Rue de la Salie** and **Rue Orce** for modern products, and within the old city walls for local crafts. Antiques shops congregate behind the cathedral.

Where to Stay

Biarritz ✉ 64200

★★★★Hôtel du Palais, 1 Av de l'Impératrice, **t** 05 59 41 64 00, **f** 05 59 41 67 99, *www.hotel-du-palais.com* (*luxury*). The most prestigious address, built in Biarritz's glory days on the site of Napoleon's villa by the beach. Old wrought-iron fences separate you from the rest of the world; some rooms are palatial, many with period furnishings. *Closed Feb.*

★★★★Miramar, 13 Rue Louison Bobet, **t** 05 59 41 30 00, **f** 05 59 24 77 20, *www.thalassa.com* (*luxury–expensive*). A younger, modern luxury contender, this may not have the panache of the Palais, but compensates with very high standards in every respect: one of Biarritz's best restaurants, a pool, sauna, and its own thalassotherapy centre.

★★★Plaza, 10 Av Edward VII, **t** 05 59 24 74 00, **f** 05 59 22 22 01 (*expensive–moderate*). Built in 1928, with restrained Art Deco elegance. It has retained much original decoration.

★★★Maison Garnier, 29 Rue Gambetta, **t** 05 59 01 60 70, **f** 05 59 01 60 80 (*expensive–moderate*). In a 19th-century Basque house, this has seven exquisitely restored rooms.

★★Hostellerie Victoria, 12 Av Reine Victoria, **t** 05 59 24 08 21 (*moderate–inexpensive*). Set in a delightful villa from the old days.

★★Palacito Hotel, 1 Rue Gambetta, **t** 05 59 24 04 89, **f** 05 59 24 33 43 (*inexpensive*). A traditional small hotel in the middle of town.

between the two old quarters of the walled town, Grand Bayonne and Petit Bayonne. The former is the business end, jammed with animated, pedestrian shopping streets.

Bayonne's landmark and symbol is the **Cathédrale Ste-Marie**, one of the finest examples of the northern Gothic in the southwest. Though begun in the 12th century, it wasn't finished until the 1800s so it is surprising how elegantly it all fits together.

Bayonne ✉ 64100

If you're not bothered about proximity to a beach, the animated streets of Bayonne might make a nice, cheaper alternative to Biarritz.

★★★Best Western Grand Hôtel, 21 Rue Thiers, **t** 05 59 59 62 00, **f** 05 59 59 62 01 (*expensive–moderate*). Bland but stately.

★Monbar, 24 Rue Pannecau, **t** 05 59 59 26 80 (*inexpensive*). Well-kept little hotel on a lively street in Petit Bayonne, across the Nive.

Eating Out

Biarritz

La Rotonde, Hôtel du Palais, **t** 05 59 41 64 00 (*luxury–expensive*). Perhaps the southwest's ultimate trip in luxurious dining: a magnificent domed room with its original decoration, and views over the sea. A new chef means the personality of the cuisine is yet unclear; only expect it to remain first-rate. There is a formidable wine list.

Café de Paris, 5 Place Bellevue, **t** 05 59 22 19 53 (*luxury–expensive*). Stylish brasserie and restaurant specializing in southwestern cuisine, with excellent crab and lobster. *Closed mid-Nov–mid-Feb.*

Le Relais, Miramar Hotel, **t** 05 59 41 30 00 (*expensive*). Without the ambience of the former, but you can eat as well for a bit less. Seafood is the attraction, cooked with delightful lightness.

Chez Albert, Port des Pêcheurs, **t** 05 59 24 43 84 (*moderate*). Popular with visitors and Biarrots alike for quality seafood, specializing in squid in ink. *Closed Wed.*

La Goulue, 3 Rue E. Ardouin, **t** 05 59 24 90 90 (*moderate*). A Belle Epoque-style restaurant with attentive service; classic local dishes; try baby squid or monkfish with bacon. *Closed Mon and Tues.*

Le Clos Basque, 12 Rue Louis Barthou, **t** 05 59 24 24 96 (*moderate*). An authentic *bistrot* with stone walls and Spanish tiles inside, and a charming terrace outside. Local specialities such as squid with peppers.

Bistrot des Halles, Rue du Centre, **t** 05 59 24 21 22 (*moderate*). Usually crowded for lunch and dinner. You won't go wrong looking around the market, and you won't do better than the daily special (grilled fish or steak).

The Players, Esplanade du Casino de Biarritz, **t** 05 59 24 19 60 (*moderate–cheap*). Can't be beaten for good seafood and vast pizzas. It's right next to the Grand-Plage, with views out to sea. *Closed Tues out of season.*

Bar Jean, 5 Rue des Halles, **t** 05 59 24 80 38 (*cheap*). A Biarritz classic for superb fresh tapas, oysters and a good choice of wines in a traditional Spanish tiled *bodega*.

Pâtisserie Miremont, Place Clemenceau (*cheap*). An essential part of the Biarritz experience is to drop in at 4pm for a coffee and a pastry too pretty to eat. It retains its original décor, and overlooks the sea.

Bayonne

Good inexpensive places in Petit Bayonne lie on the quays or in the streets behind them.

Le Cheval Blanc, Rue Bourg Neuf, **t** 05 59 59 01 33, **f** 05 59 59 52 26 (*expensive*). A long-established, family-run favourite, with innovative twists on traditional Basque fare: stuffed squid or *poulet basquaise* with *cèpes*. *Closed Sun eve and Mon.*

Miura, 24 Rue Marengo **t** 05 59 59 49 89 (*moderate*). A stylish fish restaurant with con-temporary furniture and paintings. *Closed Sun eve and Wed.*

Bayonnais, 38 Quai des Corsaires, **t** 05 59 25 61 19 (*moderate*). Traditional Basque restaurant in the old town, with décor dedicated to local sporting heroes. *Closed Sun eve and Mon.*

Le P'tit Chahut, Quai Galuperie, **t** 05 59 25 54 60 (*inexpensive*). Hole-in-the-wall offering fresh seafood. *Closed Sat lunch and Mon lunch.*

Best of all, amid these narrow streets and tightly packed tall buildings, its presence and verticality can make exactly the impression its designers intended. No church in the southwest, save the Jacobins in Toulouse (*see* p.221), can match its lofty interior, with its nave carried by slender pilasters. The **sacristy** shelters the 13th-century sculptures that survived the Revolution.

Petit Bayonne

The smaller but livelier side of Bayonne lies on the right bank of the Nive, its old, narrow back streets crowded with unspoiled neighbourhood bars and restaurants. Right in the middle, on the Quai des Corsaires, is the 16th-century **Musée Basque** (*open 1 Nov–31 Mar 10.30–12.30 and 2–6; 1 April–31 Oct 10–6.30; closed Mon and hols; adm*), the largest collection of objects on Basque culture and folk life anywhere.

Bayonne's own Léon Bonnat, one of the best-known salon painters of late 19th-century France, bequeathed his own collection of art to Bayonne, to form the nucleus of the **Musée Bonnat**, 5 Rue Jacques Laffitte (*open Wed–Sun 10–12 and 2.30–6.30pm, Fri until 8.30, closed Mon, Tues and hols; adm*). Besides works of *quattrocento* masters Domenico Veneziano and Maso di Banco, there are a number of highly stylized Catalan-Aragonese paintings from the same age. From the late Renaissance and Baroque there are good Flemish tapestries, two El Greco portraits, and a whole room devoted to Rubens. Almost all the great schools of 17th- and 18th-century painting are represented; prime exhibits include a Murillo, *Daniel in the Lions' Den*, Jan Bronkhorst's chilling military *General Octavio Piccolomini*, and a disturbing painting by Ribera of a distraught girl combing her hair, exuding a weird intensity that seems to prefigure Goya. There are several works by Ingres, Bonnat's fellow salon favourite, and 36 works by Antoine Barye, the most popular sculptor of his day. Nearby, the *cabinet des dessins* is a wonderful collection of almost 2,000 drawings and prints from the Renaissance up to the 20th century.

On the eastern edge of the walls, the **Château-Neuf** (*open Tues–Fri 2–6, Sat 9–1, closed Sun, Mon; adm free*) looms over the town, a stronghold begun in 1460 by the French to consolidate their control over the city. Adjacent, the formidable **Remparts de Mousserolles** have become an attractive park with a lagoon and open-air theatre.

Day Trips from Biarritz and Bayonne

St-Jean-de-Luz

Few seaside resort have that special, intangible quality that characterizes St-Jean-de-Luz. The name is perfect. Light and colour can be extraordinary here, illuminating an immaculately white Basque town and the acres of rose-silver seafood glistening in its restaurants. The beaches are fine, and, best of all, it hasn't entirely succumbed to the tourist tide; the fishermen on the quay still strut around as if they own the place. It's tuna and sardines they're after now, and tourists.

A casual visitor could walk around St-Jean all day and never notice its long, deep beach, tucked away on the northern side of town; being protected by a jetty, it's very safe for swimming. At its centre is the lavish **casino**, built in 1924.

St-Jean naturally turns its face to the port, lined with blue, red and green fishing boats, and a broad quay where the fishermen spread their nets. There will be boats offering excursions around the area, to the Spanish coast, or deep-sea fishing trips. Behind the port is the town hall and the adjacent **Maison de Louis XIV**, Place Louis XIV (*open June and Sept–mid-Oct Mon–Sat 10.30–12 and 2.30–6.30; July–Aug Mon–Sat*

Getting There

Don't bother with the train in this case. There is a convenient **bus** service down the coast run by the ATCRB line, t 05 59 26 06 99 – about a dozen a day from Bayonne and Biarritz to St-Jean de Luz and Hendaye.

Tourist Information

St-Jean-de-Luz ✉ 64500: Place Maréchal Foch, t 05 59 26 03 16, f 05 59 26 21 47, *www.saint-jean-de-luz.com*.

Market Days

St-Jean-de-Luz: Tues and Fri am.
Clothes market Fri, Place des Basques.

Eating Out

Everyone knows St-Jean as the capital of Basque cuisine in France, and there is a marvellous collection of restaurants around the centre. Rue de la République is almost entirely lined with seafood restaurants.
Chez Pantxua, Av du Ct Passicot, t 05 59 47 13 73 (*expensive*). A long-established favourite decorated with Basque paintings, serving *fruits de mer* and the catch of the day. *Closed Tues, also Mon out of season.*

Le Kaïku, 17 Rue de la République, t 05 59 26 13 20 (*expensive–moderate*). The oldest house in St-Jean (1540) rolls out one of the most sumptuous tables; no fixed menus, but you can negotiate your way to a fine repast. *Closed Tues, and Wed lunch..*

Bakea, 9 Place Camille Jullian, in Ciboure, t 05 59 47 34 40 (*moderate*). Has outside tables right on the port, this is a local favourite for *ttoro* and grills. *Closed Wed eve and Thurs out of season.*

Le Pasaka, 9 Rue de la République, t 05 59 26 05 17 (*moderate*). A cosy interior and two terraces, so you can feast on local grilled sardines, or *ttoro*, a satisfying fish soup. *Closed Mon and Tues out of season.*

La Vieille Auberge, 22 Rue Tourasse, t 05 59 26 19 61 (*moderate*). For a filling Basque meal. *Closed Tues lunch and Sat lunch, plus Tues eve and Wed out of season.*

Le Peita, Rue Tourasse, t 05 59 26 86 66 (*cheap*). Basque seafood favourites. *Closed Tues and Wed in summer.*

10.30–12.30 and 2.30–6.30; closed Sun and hols; adm), a typical Basque townhouse (1643) where the Roi Soleil stayed for his wedding.

From the port, the main stem, pedestrian Rue Gambetta, takes you to **St-Jean Baptiste**, largest and greatest of all Basque churches in France, where Louis XIV and Maria Teresa were married. Begun in the 1300s, it is a lesson in Basque subtlety, plain and bright outside, and plain and bright within. The aesthetic is in the detail, especially the wonderful wooden ceiling formed like the hull of a ship, and the three levels of wooden galleries around both sides of the nave, carved with all the art and sincerity the local artisans could manage. Another typically Basque feature is the ornate gilded altarpiece, dripping with Baroque detail. The main door of the church was sealed up after Louis and Maria Teresa passed through it on their wedding day.

Right across the port from St-Jean is the less touristy working town of **Ciboure**, over a little bridge, with a mirror-image of St-Jean's picturesque port, though this side is mostly used by pleasure boats. Behind the port, there are pretty streets of old Basque houses such as Rue de la Fontaine, and the simple **St-Vincent**, a 16th-century fortified church with an octagonal tower. On the northern end of town is the quarter of **Socoa** with its **castle**, begun by Henri IV and now housing a surfing and windsurfing school. Ciboure is also the home of Maurice Ravel, born at No.12 Quai Ravel, and who once started a concerto based on Basque themes and rhythms (called *Zaspiak Bat*), but never finished it.

Touring from Biarritz and Bayonne

Note that this itinerary is not suitable mid-Nov–Jan, except at Christmas, as most places are shut.

Day 1: A Dip into Spain

Morning: Hop on the A63 motorway in Biarritz, and in less than an hour you'll be in Spain's **San Sebastián**, one of most beautiful and endearing of all resort cities. Besides broad beaches, there's the fascinating Museum of San Telmo (*open daily exc Mon 10.30–1.30 and 5–8.30, Sun 10–2; adm*), an aquarium and a Naval Museum, all in the old town, *La Parte Vieja*, a walk up Mount Urgell for the view, and big-time shopping in the *Centro Romántico*.

Lunch: This being Spain, you can do yourself in with drinks and tapas; the Parte Vieja has more bars per square metre than anywhere in the world. For something more substantial, **Beti Jai**, C/Fermin Calbetón 22, in the Parte Vieja, t 94 342 77 37 (*moderate*) is a lively seafood restaurant. *Closed Mon, Tues.* For traditional Basque dishes, the **Bodegón Alejandro** is right down the street at C/Fermin Calbetón 4, t 94 342 77 37 (*moderate*).

Afternoon: San Sebastián has more than enough to keep you busy for a day, but if you want to get out, take the coastal road west to **Getaria**. This old fishing village has become a small, charming resort, as well as the production centre for *txakoli* wine; don't miss the eccentric church of San Salvador.

Dinner: The Basques' culinary capital, San Sebastián is the place for a splurge. **Casa Nicolasa**, Aldemar 4, t 94 342 17 62 (*expensive*) has been a shrine of Basque cooking since 1912; great desserts. *Closed Sun eve and Mon.* Another old favourite is **Casa Uruola**, C/Fermin Calbetón, t 94 342 11 75 (*moderate*), with a consistently good *menú del dia*.

Sleeping: San Sebastián has plenty of elegant Belle Epoque palaces; one of the more reasonable is ★★★**Niza**, C/Zubieta, t 94 342 66 63, f 94 344 66 63, right on the beach (*expensive*). Still elegant, though less dear, is the ★★**Pensión Donostiarra**, C/S. Martin 6, t 94 342 61 67, f 94 343 00 71 (*moderate*).

Day 2: Through the Labourdin

Morning: Head back into France on the A63 (A8 in Spain) and exit at Ciboure; the D918 will take you up into this green region of tidy, perfect Basque villages. First comes **Ascain**, from which you can ride an open tramway to the top of the Basques' holy mountain, La Rhune (*every 35mins from 9am, 8.30am in summer; closed mid- Nov–mid-Mar; adm*).

Lunch: In Ascain, there is a restaurant with a delightful garden terrace at the **Hôtel du Pont**, Route de St-Jean-de-Luz, t 05 59 54 00 40 (*moderate*). *Closed Nov–Feb.* **Achafla Baïta**, out in the countryside on the Chemin Mortzelay, t 05 59 54 00 30 (*moderate*) offers a wide variety of seafood and river fish.

Afternoon: From here, the next village is **Sare**, just south on the D4, full of traditional Basque houses and a wooden-balconied church. On the D306 to the south, some Paleolithic drawings survive in the Grottes de Sare (*hours vary, but always open from 2pm; adm*). From Sare, navigating the D4-D3-D918 brings you through **Espelette**, famous for its special red pepper (take some home!), to the genteel spa of **Cambo-les-Bains**.

Dinner: In the Basque country almost all the restaurants are in hotels. Cambo's ★★**Bellevue**, Rue des Terrasses, t 05 59 93 75 75 (*inexpensive*) is near the top of town. In tiny Itxassou just south, the *confits* and foie gras go down well at the **Fronton**, Place du Fronton, t 05 59 29 75 10 (*moderate*).

Sleeping: Besides the two good choices listed above, Cambo has ★★**Auberge Tante Ursule**, Bas Cambo, t 05 59 29 78 23, f 05 59 29 28 57 (*inexpensive*), which also has a fine restaurant. Up in the hills, the **Domaine Xixtaberri**, Quartier Hegala, t 05 59 29 22 66 (*moderate*), offers superb panoramas.

Day 3: St-Jean Pied-du-Port

Morning: Before heading south into the Pyrenees, you may want to detour for an even better cave, the **Grottes d'Ustaritz** at St-Esteben (take the D10 east to Hasparren; *open mid-Mar–mid-Nov 10–12 and 2–6;*

closed Mon and Tues mornings; adm) with delicate stalactites and prehistoric relics. Find your way back southwest to the valley of the River Nive and **Bidarray**.

Lunch: Bidarray's landmark is a graceful medieval bridge, which gives its name to the **Pont d'Enfer**, Rte Pont Olha, **t** 05 59 37 70 88 (*moderate*); here you can get a *ttoro* (Basque fish soup) from the sea or a trout from the Nive. If they're full press on south to St-Etienne-de Baïgorry and the **Hôtel Arcé**, Route du Col d'Ispéguy, **t** 05 59 37 40 14 (*moderate*), with a terrace overlooking the river.

Afternoon: Continuing down the D918, wine-lovers may detour south on the D948 for **St-Etienne-de-Baïgorry**, centre of the vine-yards of that good strong Iroleguy, the Basque lands' finest. The final destination, though, will be the rugged but welcoming medieval town of **St-Jean-Pied-de-Port**, gateway to the mountains.

Dinner: St-Jean has a wide choice, including one of the most renowned temples of Basque cuisine, **Des Pyrenées**, Place de Gaulle, **t** 05 59 73 01 01 (*expensive*). Many of the hotels have good restaurants, including the **★★Central**, Place de Gaulle, **t** 05 59 37 00 22, **f** 05 59 37 27 79 (*rooms and dinner both inexpensive*). *Closed Fri.*

Sleeping: St-Jean can be expensive, but there are some cheaper options, such as the **★★Hôtel des Remparts**, Place Floquet, **t** 05 59 37 13 79, **f** 05 59 37 33 44 (*inexpensive*), and the **★★Ramuntcho**, 1 Rue France, **t** 05 59 37 03 91, **f** 05 59 37 35 17 (*inexpensive*); here some rooms have balconies with a view.

Day 4: Béarn

Morning: From St-Jean, the D633 northeast will steer you out of the Basque lands into this equally individualistic old region. The first town is **Sauveterre-de-Béarn**, with its medieval walls and church; 9km east on the D27, **Laás** has a castle with a lovely garden and an interesting museum of antiques and historical curiosities (*open daily exc Tues 10–7; closed Nov–Mar; adm*)

Lunch: There's a good restaurant in Sauveterre's **★Hostellerie du Château**, Rue Bérard, **t** 05 59 38 95 11 (*moderate–*

inexpensive); or else continue to Salies-de-Béarn for *confits* and foie gras on a riverside terrace at **La Terrasse**, Rue Saley, **t** 05 59 38 09 83 (*moderate–inexpensive*).

Afternoon: A short hop north on the D933 brings you to **Salies-de-Béarn**, an old spa town where the lovely historic centre is laced with streams and canals. Continue on the D933 for **Orthez**, another stoutly medieval town with a perfectly preserved 14th-century bridge and a haunted tower.

Dinner: Orthez's favourite is the **Auberge St-Loup**, 20 Rue du Pont-Vieux, **t** 05 59 69 15 40; duck dishes in a pretty courtyard (*moderate*). There's also a good restaurant at **★★La Reine Jeanne**, Rue du Bourg-Vieux **t** 05 59 67 00 76 (*moderate*), which also has simple rooms.

Sleeping: Just west on the D933 at Berenxin is the **★★Auberge du Relais**, **t** 05 59 65 30 56 (*inexpensive*), in a rustic setting with a park, restaurant and pool. If you liked Salies, you can stay there at the good-value **★★Hôtel du Golf**, **t** 05 59 65 02 10, **f** 05 59 38 16 41 (*inexpensive*), with a golf course and a good restaurant. *Open July–Sept.*

Day 5: Back to the Coast

Morning: From Orthez or Salies, take the A64 motorway east to peaceful **Peyrehorade** with its ruined château, and from there the D27 south to **Sorde l'Abbaye**, where an unusual medieval monastery lies atop a Roman villa with some excellent mosaics.

Lunch: In Peyrehorade, the **Hôtel Central**, Place Aristide Briand, **t** 05 58 73 03 22 (*moderate*) offers some unpretentious good cooking, such as a *pot au feu* with foie gras. On the road to Bidache, there is the simple restau-rant-pizzeria **Restaurant des Pêcheurs**, **t** 05 58 73 02 40 (*inexpensive*).

Afternoon: The D19 leads south from Peyrehorade to **Bidache**, which has a roman-tically ruined castle and the Cité des Aigles, with trained eagles, kites and falcons (*open daily April–Nov, shows at 3.30 and 5; adm*). There isn't a lot else to see in these parts, but the motorway or the D936 from Bidache will take you back to the beaches and Biarritz, the best place to end the day and the week.

Toulouse

One thing that keeps southwest France from nodding off in its goose fat and wine is this big pink dynamo, *La Ville Rose*, built of millions of pink bricks. It should have been the rosy capital of a nation called Languedoc, but was knocked out of the big leagues in the 1220s by the popes and kings of France and their henchman Simon de Montfort. Nearly eight centuries later, it is finally getting its rhythm back. Home to Aérospatiale, the French space agency and the national weather service, Toulouse is now the fourth city in France, counting 650,000 lively inhabitants and 70 per cent of the industry in the Midi-Pyrénées region.

Place du Capitole and Around

Large **Place du Capitole** is the heart of Toulouse, emblazoned with the Cross of Languedoc, the arms devised in 1095 by Count Raymond IV, when he led the first Crusade. Rimmed with neoclassical brick façades, the square is dominated by the city hall, or **Capitole** (1750), named after the *capitouls*, who were first appointed by the Counts to run the city in the 12th century. Pedestrians cut through its Cour Henri IV to Square Charles de Gaulle, where the capitouls kept the city archives; it's now the city tourist office. Running north from Place du Capitole, narrow Rue de Taur commemorates the bull which dragged the body of Toulouse's first saint, Sernin, through the city streets to his death in c. 240. Completed in 1220, his basilica, the **Basilique St-Sernin**, is the largest surviving Romanesque church in the world. Its plan is identical to the basilica of St James at Compostela: a cross, ending in a semi-circular apse with five radiating chapels. Seen from Rue St-Bernard, this apse is a fascinating play of white stone and red brick, a crescendo culminating in the octagonal **bell tower** that is Toulouse's landmark, boasting five storeys of arcades for the sole purpose of upstaging the campanile of the Jacobins across town. The odd, asymmetrical **Porte Miège-ville** on the south side has a tympanum carved by the 11th-century master Bernard Gilduin, showing the *Ascension of Christ*, a rare scene in medieval art. On the brackets are figures of David and others riding on lions; the magnificent capitals tell the story of the Redemption. The eight capitals on the south transept door, the **Porte des Comtes**, also by Gilduin, show the torments of hell: a man having his testicles crushed and a woman whose breasts are being devoured by serpents.

Begun in 1969, the 'de-restoration' of the **interior** stripped the majestic brick and stone of Viollet-le-Duc's ham-fisted murals and fiddly neo-Gothic bits. In the process some 12th-century frescoes have been found; note the serene angel in the third bay of the north transept, which also has the best capitals. For a small fee you can enter the **ambulatory** (*open Mon–Sat 10–11.30 and 2.30–5, Sun 2.30–5; July–Sept daily 10–6; closed Sun am*) to see some 17th-century bas-reliefs and panels. Opposite the central chapel are seven marble bas-reliefs (1096) by Bernard Gilduin.

On the south side of Place St-Sernin are the rich archaeological collections of the **Musée St-Raymond** (*open daily 10–6; June–Aug daily 10–7*), while the surrounding neighbourhood has been the city's Latin Quarter since 1229 when the **University of Toulouse** was founded in Rue des Lois.

Les Jacobins

In 1215, the Spanish priest Domingo de Guzmán founded a preaching order in Toulouse west of Place du Capitole. The Dominicans soon became so popular that in 1230 they built **Les Jacobins** (*open daily 9–7; adm for the cloister*), the prototype for all Dominican churches. A masterpiece of southern French Gothic, it so impressed the popes that they sent it the relics of the greatest Dominican of them all, St Thomas Aquinas (d. 1274). Gargoyles are the only exterior sculpture, alternating with flamboyant windows; its octagonal bell tower is a landmark on the city skyline. The interior is breathtakingly light and spacious, consisting of twin naves, crisscrossed by a fantastic interweaving of ribs in the vault, reaching an epiphany in the flamboyant *palmier* in the apse.

Just south of Les Jacobins is one of the city's most splendid residences, the **Hôtel de Bernuy**, built in 1504, its Gothic exterior hiding an eclectic fantasy courtyard. Just west, off Rue de Metz, the elaborate **Hôtel d'Assézat** (1555) houses the **Fondation Bemberg** (*open Tues–Sun 10–12.30 and 1.30–6; closed Mon; night visits Thurs at 9pm; themed visits Thurs at 7pm; adm*), with a fine collection of Renaissance and modern French paintings, including over 30 by Bonnard. The 19th-century Rue de Metz continues to Toulouse's oldest bridge, the **Pont Neuf** (1544–1632), with its seven unequal arches.

Around the Cathedral of St-Etienne

In the mesh of quiet lanes between the old *parlement* and the cathedral are distinguished houses, all uniform pink brick, with grey shutters and wrought-iron balconies, such as the ornate **Hôtel du Vieux Raisin** (1515), 36 Rue du Languedoc. The **Musée Paul Dupuy** (*13 Rue de la Pleau; open daily 10–5; summer 10–6; closed Tues*) is named after the collector who bequeathed his watches, automata, fans, faïence and ivories.

The **cathedral of St-Etienne** was begun in the 11th century and only completed in the 17th, resulting in a church that seems a bit drunk. In the centre of the façade rises a massive brick bell tower with a clock, over the Romanesque base. To the right is a worn, asymmetrical stone Gothic façade, where the portal and rose window are off-centre; to the left extends the bulge of the chapel of Notre-Dame, a small church in itself stuck on the north end. It's even tipsier inside, but many of its best decorations are stowed away in the **Musée des Augustins** at the corner of Rue de Metz and Rue d'Alsace (*open daily 10–6, Wed 10–9; closed Tues and hols*). The museum, one of the oldest in France, is housed in a 14th-century Augustinian convent. Gothic sculptures occupy the flamboyant chapterhouse, and the church holds religious paintings by Van Dyck, Rubens and Murillo. Best of all are the Romanesque works from St-Etienne. The first floor has paintings by Guido Reni, Simon Vouet, Guardi, Delacroix, Ingres, Manet, Morisot, Vuillard, Maurice Denis and Toulouse-Lautrec.

South of the Place du Parlement, the Grand Rond at the end of Allée Jules-Guesde was planned as a garden in the midst of six wide radiating promenades: the old **Jardin Royal** and the 19th-century **Jardin des Plantes** are delightful refuges from the

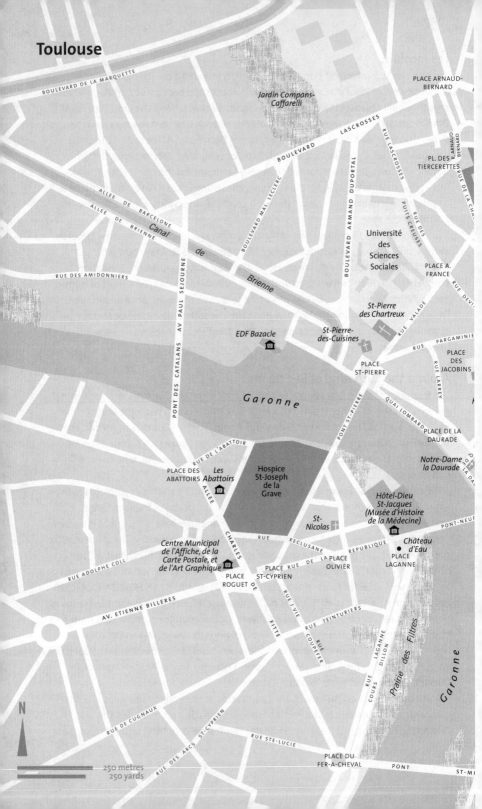

Toulouse

BOULEVARD DE LA MARQUETTE

PLACE ARNAUD-
BERNARD

Jardin Compans-
Caffarelli

LASCROSSES

PL. DES
TIERCERETTES

BOULEVARD

RUE LASCROSSES

ALLEE DE BARCELONE

Canal

ALLEE DE BRIENNE

de

BOULEVARD MAL-LECLERC

BOULEVARD ARMAND DUPORTAL

RUE DES PUITS CREUSES

RUE DE LA CHA...

R. ARNAUD BERNARD

Université
des
Sciences
Sociales

PLACE A.
FRANCE

RUE DES AMIDONNIERS

Brienne

AV PAUL SÉJOURNE

St-Pierre
des Chartreux

RUE DEVI...

EDF Bazacle

St-Pierre-
des-Cuisines

RUE VALADE

RUE PARGAMINIE

PLACE
DES
JACOBINS

PONT DES CATALANS

PLACE
ST-PIERRE

RUE LARREY

Garonne

PONT ST-PIERRE

QUAI LOMBARD

PLACE DE LA
DAURADE

RUE DE L'ABATTOIR

PLACE DES
ABATTOIRS

Les
Abattoirs

Hospice
St-Joseph
de la
Grave

Notre-Dame
la Daurade

ALLEE

CHARLES

Hôtel-Dieu
St-Jacques
(Musée d'Histoire
de la Médecine)

PONT-NEUF

St-
Nicolas

Centre Municipal
de l'Affiche, de la
Carte Postale, et
de l'Art Graphique

RUE

RECLUSANE

REPUBLIQUE

Château
d'Eau

PLACE
LAGANNE

PLACE
ROGUET

PLACE
ST-CYPRIEN

PLACE RUE DE LA PLACE
OLIVIER

RUE ADOLPHE COLL

RUE J-VIE

FITTE

RUE TEINTURIERS

RUE LAGANNE DILLON

RUE COUPEFER

Prairie des Filtres

AV. ETIENNE BILLERES

COURS DILLON

Garonne

N

RUE DE CUGNAUX

RUE DES ARCS ST-CYPRIEN

RUE STE-LUCIE

PLACE DU
FER-A-CHEVAL

PONT

ST-MI...

250 metres
250 yards

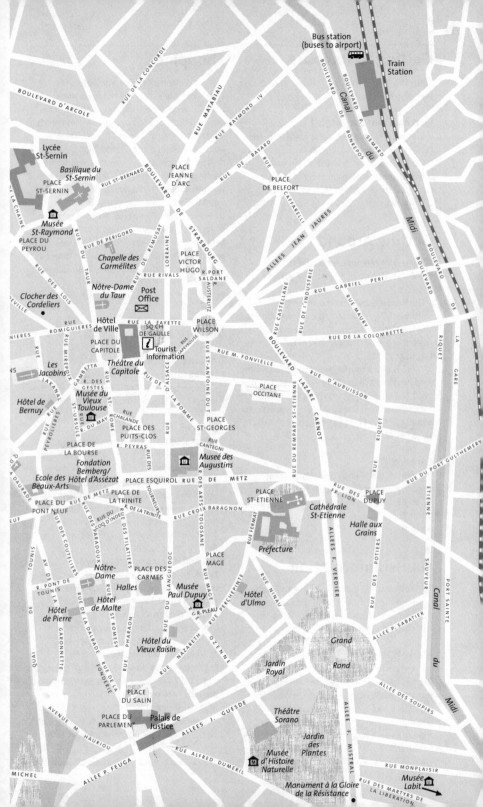

Getting to Toulouse

Buzz flies from London Stansted, and bmibaby from East Midlands (*see* p.6).

Getting from the Airport

Toulouse-Blagnac airport is 10km from the centre. The **airport bus, t** 05 34 60 64 00, travels back and forth to the *gare routière* (next to the train station) every 20mins or so from 5.20am to 8.20pm Mon–Fri for €4.

A **taxi** will cost €20, more like €26 at night.

Getting Around

Toulouse's *gare routière* is next to the **railway station** at 68 Bd Pierre Sémard, **t** 05 61 61 67 67.

The Toulouse *métro* line runs northeast to southwest from Joliment, the railway station and the Capitole to the Mirail. The *métro* and city buses are run by SEMVAT (7 Place Esquirol, **t** 05 61 41 70 70).

There is also a **tourist train** for the main sites (departs Place Wilson daily June–Sept, **t** 05 62 71 08 51), and a **tourist taxi** (**t** 05 34 250 250).

If you can't find one cruising the streets or at a **taxi** stand, try **t** 05 34 25 02 50 or **t** 05 61 42 38 38 (all 24 hours).

Car Hire

There are quite a few companies at the airport. **ADA, t** 05 61 30 04 77; **Avis, t** 05 34 60 46 50; **Budget, t** 05 61 71 85 80; **Citer, t** 05 61 30 00 01; **Europcar, t** 05 61 30 04 34; **Hertz, t** 08 25 80 10 31.

Tourist Information

Toulouse: Donjon du Capitole, Rue La Fayette, behind the Capitole, **t** 05 61 11 02 22, **f** 05 61 22 03 63; *www.ot-toulouse.fr*. Offers a range of themed **guided tours**.

Market Days

There are regular **markets** at Place des Carmes (*daily exc Mon 7–1*) and at Les Halles in Bd Victor Hugo (*Tues–Sun 6–1*). On Wed mornings, Place du Capitole has a lively food and flea market. Sun (and to a lesser extent Sat) morning sees a huge flea market around St-Sernin.

Shopping

With all the major French department stores, the Pink City is the shopping mecca of the southwest. Specifically local products are mostly **violet**, especially candied-violet **confits**, made since 1730 at Olivier, 20 Rue Lafayette; Maison Pillon, at 2 Rue Ozenne, also produces delicious **chocolates** which won the prize for the best in France in 1996. If you fancy some of the best **cheese** France has to offer, head for Betty, 2 Place Victor Hugo; you can smell it from fifty paces. There is also a good selection of southwest **wines**. The shop also has a stall in Marché Victor Hugo opposite. For fine **preserves** and French classics such as **olive oil** and very dark chocolate go to La Boutique des Saveurs at 1 Rue Ozenne, **t** 05 61 53 75 21, a delightful shop with tantalizing smells.

Where to Stay

Toulouse ✉ 31000

★★★★Grand Hôtel de l'Opéra, 1 Place du Capitole, **t** 05 61 21 82 66, **f** 05 61 23 41 04 (*expensive*). This, the most beautiful hotel in Toulouse, has 50 luxurious rooms and three suites set in a former convent, with sumptuous Italianate rooms, indoor pool, fitness room and a magnificent restaurant.

★★★★Des Capitouls, 22 Descente de la Halle aux Poissons, **t** 05 34 31 94 80, **f** 05 34 31 94 81 (*expensive–moderate*). Stylish boutique hotel with 14 rooms, located in former fish warehouse in now-trendy historic Toulouse. Sumptuous meals offered in proprietors' **Restaurant Le 19**, opposite.

★★★Grand Hôtel Capoul, 13 Place Wilson, **t** 05 61 10 70 70, **f** 05 61 21 96 70 (*expensive–moderate*). Large, light, air-conditioned rooms, a Jacuzzi, and an excellent *bistrot*.

★★★Hôtel des Beaux Arts, 1 Place Pont-Neuf, **t** 05 34 45 42 42, **f** 05 34 45 42 43 (*expensive–moderate*). In an 18th-century *hôtel particulier*, this is warm and welcoming.

★★★Brienne, 20 Bd du Maréchal Leclerc, **t** 05 61 23 60 60, **f** 05 61 23 18 94 (*moderate*). Ultramodern, with well-equipped rooms, many with balconies.

★★★Mermoz, 50 Rue Matabiau, **t** 05 61 63 04 04, **f** 05 61 63 15 64 (*moderate*). Near the station, with delightful air-conditioned rooms overlooking inner courtyards, and perhaps the best breakfast in Toulouse.

**Grand Hôtel d'Orléans, 72 Rue de Bayard, t 05 61 62 98 47, f 05 61 62 78 24 (*inexpensive*). Near the station. Plenty of character, with its interior galleries and garden.

**Park Hotel, 2 Rue Porte-Sardane, t 05 61 21 25 97, f 05 61 23 96 27 (*inexpensive*). Within easy walking distance of the Capitole; modern rooms with most creature comforts, including a sauna and Jacuzzi.

**Hôtel du Grand Balcon, 8 Rue Romiguières, t 05 61 21 48 08 (*inexpensive*). At the corner of Place du Capitole, this is one of Toulouse's best-loved institutions. The phrase *grand balcon* is how early French pilots used to describe the view from the cockpit, and this is where St-Exupéry and friends stayed when on the ground. The current owners have carefully preserved the rooms as they were, along with a fascinating collection of photos and memorabilia from France's early days of aviation. *Closed for Christmas and three weeks in Aug.*

**Castellane, 17 Rue Castellane, t 05 61 62 18 82, f 05 61 62 58 04 (*inexpensive*). Down a quiet side street off Bd Carnot; light and spacious rooms. The breakfast area is pleasant and it's next to a good restaurant, L'Edelweiss (*see below*).

*Anatole France, 46 Place Anatole France, t 05 61 23 19 96 (*cheap*). Near the Capitole, with some of the nicest cheap rooms in Toulouse.

Eating Out

Toulouse claims to make a *cassoulet* to beat all others, enhanced by a foot or two of the renowned *saucisse de Toulouse*.

Les Jardins de l'Opéra, 1 Place du Capitole, t 05 61 23 07 76 (*expensive*). Toulouse's finest gastronomic experience is also one of the most beautiful restaurants in the southwest. It manages to stay light years away from the hubbub just outside the door. The food matches the setting. *Closed Sun, Mon and end of July.*

Michel Sarran, 21 Bd Armand Duportal, t 05 61 12 32 32 (*expensive*). A wonderful synthesis of sun-soaked southwest and Provençal cuisines. Superb food in an elegant town

house, and charming service too. *Closed Sat, Sun and Aug.*

Le Pastel, 237 Rue St-Simon, in a villa at Mirail, t 05 62 87 84 30 (*expensive*). Make the extra effort to book for some of the finest, most imaginative gourmet food in Toulouse at some of the best prices; the lunch menu is exquisite. *Closed Sun and Mon.*

Chez Emile, 13 Place St-Georges, t 05 61 21 05 56 (*moderate*). A city institution, preparing some of the finest seafood in Toulouse or a *confit de canard* or meat. *Closed Sun and Mon, open Mon eve in summer.*

Le Bibent, 5 Place du Capitole, t 05 61 23 89 03 (*moderate*). One of the most beautiful brasseries in Toulouse, strategically located, with a grand dining room last remodelled in the Roaring Twenties, and a terrace; excellent shellfish selection and southwest favourites.

Le Colombier, 14 Rue Bayard, t 05 61 62 40 05 (*moderate*). One of the chief contestants in the 'best cassoulet in Toulouse' contest. *Closed Sat lunch, Sun, Aug and Christmas.*

L'Edelweiss, 19 Rue Castellane, t 05 61 62 34 70 (*moderate*). Behind the concrete is a refined restaurant producing lovely meals, some of it classic southwest. *Closed Sun, Mon and most of Aug.*

Les Caves de la Maréchale, 3 Rue Jules Chalande, t 05 61 23 89 88 (*inexpensive*). Set in the immense cellar of a 13th-century Dominican priory off Rue St-Rome. *Closed Sun and Mon lunch.*

Grand Café de l'Opéra, 1 Place du Capitole, t 05 61 21 37 03 (*inexpensive*). Excellent versions of seafood classics in a cosy brasserie atmosphere.

Benjamin, 7 Rue des Gestes (off Rue St-Rome), t 05 61 22 92 66 (*inexpensive*). In the centre of old Toulouse, serving up the likes of fennel and courgette terrine and steak with *cèpes* for some of the friendliest prices in town.

La Daurade, Quai de la Daurade, t 05 61 22 10 33 (*inexpensive*). Dine on a barge (*péniche*) anchored in a magnificent setting. *Closed Sat lunch and Sun; book.*

A la Truffe du Quercy, 17 Rue Croix-Baragnon, t 05 61 53 34 24 (*cheap*). The same family has been dishing out southwest home cooking for three generations. *Closed Sun and hols.*

big city. If you're fond of oriental art, don't miss the **Musée Georges Labit**, 43 Rue des Martyrs-de-la-Libération (*open daily 10–5; summer daily 10–6; closed Tues and hols*) – considered the best museum of its kind in France after the Musée Guimet in Paris.

Toulouse's Left Bank

Just over the Pont Neuf, the round brick tower of a pumping station, built in 1817 to provide drinking water to the city, has found a new use as the **Galerie Municipale du Château-d'Eau** (*open daily 1–7; closed Tues and hols; adm*). The hydraulic machinery is still intact, while upstairs you can visit one of Europe's top photographic galleries; an annexe has been installed in an arch of the Pont Neuf.

Day Trips from Toulouse

Moissac

There's only one reason to make the trip to Moissac, but it's a solid five-star reason: the Romanesque **Abbaye de St-Pierre**, founded by Clovis in 506 and one of the crown jewels of medieval French sculpture. The town, washed clean of most of its character in a flood in 1930, now busies itself growing pale golden *chasselas de Moissac*, France's finest dessert grapes.

Sheltered by a 12th-century tower, the sublime porch is one of the most powerful and beautiful works of the Middle Ages. The **tympanum** rests on a lintel recycled from a Gallo-Roman building, decorated with eight large thistle flowers and enclosed in a cable or vine, spat out by a monster at one end and swallowed by another monster at the other. The main scene represents Christ sitting in the Judgement of Nations, with the Book of Life in his hand. You might notice that this Christ has three arms, one on the book, one raised in blessing, and another on his heart; no one knows why. The four

Getting There

Moissac is on the slow **railway** line from Toulouse-Matabio station. There are up to six trains a day and the journey takes 1hr.

No **buses** travel this route.

An old barge, Le Grain d'Or, offers **cruises** of 2hrs or more of the Canal Latéral and the river Tarn, t 05 63 04 48 28.

Taxis: t 05 63 04 03 88 and t 05 63 04 08 82.

Tourist Information

Moissac ✉ 82200: 6 Pl Durand-de-Bredon, t 05 63 04 01 85, f 05 63 04 27 10, *www.frenchcom.com/moissac*. *Open Jan–Mar and Oct–Dec 10–12 and 2–5; April and May 9–12.30 and 2–6; June and Sept 9–6; July and Aug 9–7.*

Market Days

Moissac: Farmers' market, Sat and Sun am.

Eating Out

★★Le Pont Napoléon, 2 Allées Montebello, t 05 63 04 01 55 (*moderate*). Named after the bridge commissioned by Bonaparte in 1808, this hotel overlooks the Tarn; having been purchased by master chef Michel Dussau, its reputation of serving the best food in Moissac on its lovely terrace will only increase. *Closed Wed, Sun eve and Mon lunch.*

Bar de Paris, across from the market on Place des Récollets, t 05 63 04 00 61 (*cheap*). Pizzas and brasserie-style dishes, including a fine plate of frogs' legs. *Open till 1am.*

symbols of the Evangelists twist to surround him, and two seraphim, carrying scrolls, are squeezed under the rainbow. The rest of the tympanum is occupied by the 24 Elders, no two alike, each gazing up from their thrones at Christ. The whole wonderfully rhythmic composition could be an old-timers' band raising their glasses in a toast to a stern but respected and beloved bandleader.

But that's not all. The central pillar of the door, the *trumeau*, is sculpted with three pairs of lions in the form of Xs symbolically guarding the church. On either side are Peter, Isaiah, Paul and Jeremiah, elongated, supple figures that sway and nearly dance. To the right are scenes from the life of the Virgin; to the left, poor Lazarus' soul is taken into the bosom of Abraham, while, below, the soul of the rich, feasting Dives is carried off in the other direction.

Inside the porch, the vaulted square of the **narthex** has some excellent Romanesque capitals, carved with voluptuous vegetation playfully metamorphosed into animals. The **interior** had to be rebuilt in 1430 and can't begin to compete with the fireworks on the portal; just one chapel has managed to retain its 15th-century geometrical murals, which inspired the restoration on the other walls. Some of the church's excellent polychrome sculpture survives, especially a 12th-century *Christ* and, from the 15th century, the *Flight into Egypt* with a serious-minded burro.

Behind the church is the abbey's serenely magnificent **cloister** (*t 05 63 04 01 85; open same hours as the tourist office, where tickets are bought; adm*), with 76 magnificent 11th-century capitals, set on alternating paired and single slender columns; they are the oldest *in situ* in France. They also mark a major artistic turning point, towards fluid, stylized poses with a sense of movement, exquisite modelling, and a play of light and shadow hitherto unknown in Romanesque sculpture. The capitals are carved with foliage of luxuriant virtuosity; others are intricately intertwined with birds and animals. Some 46 capitals tell the lives of the saints – don't miss the dynamic martyrdoms: St Lawrence on the grill; St Martin dividing his cloak with the beggar; St John the Baptist and the feast of Herod; St Stephen being stoned. Other scenes are rare: the city of Jerusalem versus unholy Babylon, the story of Nebuchadnezzar, and Shadrach, Meshach and Abednego in the furnace. At the corners and in the centre of each gallery are square pillars, covered with recycled tops of Roman sarcophagi; the corners are carved with bas-reliefs of eight apostles, the 'pillars of the Church'.

South of the abbey is Moissac's market square, **Place des Récollets**. From here **Rue des Arts** leads past the deconsecrated church of St-Jacques to the Canal Latéral à la Garonne, spanned by the **Pont St-Jacques**. Upstream, under an impressive 1,168ft **Pont Canal**, the charming **Pavillon Uvarium** (1933; *open May–Sept*), offers glasses of *chasselas* grape juice in September.

Auch

Auch, with its elegant core of squares above the river Gers, has all the ingredients of a lovely little town, but aspires to be little more than an overgrown farmers' market. So, visitors must be content to settle for two of the greatest artistic achievements

Getting There

Auch is 1½–2½hrs away from Toulouse by **rail**. You can also go by **bus** (**t** 05 61 61 67 67) from the *gare routière* several times a day in summer only.

Tourist Information

Auch ✉ 32200: 1 Rue Dessoles, **t** 05 62 05 22 89, **f** 05 62 05 92 04.

Market Days

Auch:Sat and Thurs.

Eating Out

Jardin des Saveurs, in Hôtel de France, Place de la Libération, **t** 05 62 61 71 84 (*expensive*). This famous hotel also claims the highest-rated restaurant of the *département*, with an accomplished new chef. They lay it on thick:

the very best foie gras, perhaps with a hint of truffles. Some dishes are traditional favourites, others inspired flights of fancy. To accompany them, they have probably the best cellar in the southwest.

Claude Lafitte, Rue Desoules, **t** 05 62 05 04 18 (*expensive–moderate*). Here is a champion of regional cooking and fresh local ingredients. For a small price you will get *charcuterie* and a Gascon favourite such as Henri IV's *poule au pot*; there are also formidable menus which are not to be entered into lightly.

★★**Relais de Gascogne**, 5 Av de la Marne, **t** 05 62 05 26 81 (*moderate*). This hotel-restaurant delivers good local cuisine: *daube à l'armagnac*, cassoulet, duck and fish.

Le Chouan, Rue Mazagran, **t** 05 62 05 08 47 (*inexpensive*). This choice offers a *plat du jour* and *menus* which often include seafood.

Café Gascon, Rue Lamartine, **t** 05 62 61 88 05 (*inexpensive*). After visiting the cathedral nearby, a good light lunch can be had here. *Closed Wed and Sun out of season.*

France has ever produced: Arnaut de Moles' spectacular stained-glass windows, and a set of choir stalls that have to be seen to be believed. Both are in the cathedral.

At first sight, the **Cathédrale Ste-Marie** is a bit disconcerting. There isn't another façade quite like this anywhere in the south of France; the French would call it *classique*, being lots of bits and pieces from Italian Renaissance style books pasted together every which way, though they go together harmoniously enough. Auch began its cathedral in the 14th century on the Gothic model, but it was in the 1500s, when Renaissance ideas and styles really took root, that the most important features of the interior were begun: the choir stalls and the **stained glass**.

Nobody knows much about Arnaut de Moles, except that he came from St-Sever in the Landes, and that he started work here in 1507. In all, Arnaut's work, in which he engraved details on the glass with acid, is an art that seems much closer to painting, born of an age obsessed with all the tricks of light, colour and composition. The 18 windows in the ambulatory chapels make a complete account of the Christian story. Old and New Testament figures are mixed together according to the medieval idea of typology, in which everything in the Old Testament prefigures something in the New. Their complex symbolism makes a progression from Genesis, through the Crucifixion, to the Resurrection.

The **choir** is an unusual feature, completely enclosed as in a Spanish cathedral. It is usually locked, but someone is sure to be around with the key. The entire space is filled with a set of 113 choir stalls. The oak was soaked and hardened to permit carving of the tiniest of details, and this ensemble is one of the masterpieces of Renaissance woodcarving. It is also one of its most ambitious projects; two centuries ago, a monk of Auch tried to count all the figures and came up with over 1,500.

An eccentric but glorious example of that Renaissance innovation, these choir stalls took over fifty years to make, and many hands assisted in the work, which would explain the wide range of styles and subject matter. There is no grand scheme here; rather, within limits each artist seems to have done as he pleased. Some works mirror the figures in the stained glass, which was under way at the same time; others represent other biblical personages or vignettes. Mythology is represented; others are pure flights of fancy. Unfortunately, none of the artists added much to their works that would clear up exactly who all these figures really are. The same monk who tried to count all the figures also attempted to identify them all. You can get a brochure with his guesses from the caretaker. At any rate, the main panels, above the seats, echo a motif of the windows, with pairs of male and female figures, beginning with Adam and Eve and continuing through sibyls, saints and Old Testament figures.

The vast majority of the figures, however, are concealed among the magnificent carved Gothic traceries; on the arms or under the seats you'll find something beautiful, surprising or amusing, making for one of the best treasure hunts imaginable. A different generation of woodcarvers, Parisians this time, contributed the cabinet for the great **organ**, a work of architecture in itself (1694).

Leading down from the cathedral apse, a **monumental stair** from the 1860s takes you to the river, its 370 steps punctuated by landings and a **statue of d'Artagnan**. Also behind the cathedral you can see the striking 14th-century tower called the **Tour d'Armagnac**, one of the landmarks of the city and a proud monument for all Gascons. South of the stair and the cathedral is one of the oldest neighbourhoods of Auch, the **Quartier du Caillou**, a forbidding tangle of narrow hillside alleys.

There's more life on the streets north of the cathedral. Find your way to Rue Daumesnil/Place Louis-Blanc, where a 17th-century monastery holds the **Musée des Jacobins** (*open Tues–Sun 10–12 and 2–6; closes at 5pm Oct–April; adm*), one of the best-run provincial museums in France. Among the displays are 1st-century frescoes from a Roman villa, medieval tombs, some beautiful musical instruments and large collection devoted to traditional Gascon crafts, but the best and most surprising is saved for last: a collection of pre-Colombian and colonial **Latin-American Art**, with pottery, figures and fabrics from Mexico, Peru and the Caribbean.

Albi

'Red Albi', the brick capital of the Tarn, has often been compared to a Tuscan hill-town piled under the extraordinary **Cathédrale Ste-Cécile**, a huge red fortress. This show of ecclesiastical force was begun in 1280 in the purest southern Gothic style, with a single nave 100ft high and as long as a football pitch. It was no sooner consecrated in 1480 than an arty string of bishops began embellishing it, giving it an exotic 256ft bell tower. The finely carved stone porch at the top of the stairs is a preview of the richness of the **interior** (*open daily 9–12 and 2.30–6.30; June–Sept daily 8.30–7*), which positively glows with colour, the vaults completely covered with 16th-century frescoes by painters from Bologna. On the west wall, an enormous, harrowing 15th-century fresco of the *Last Judgment,* by an unknown French or Flemish painter, was mutilated to provide an entrance to the tower chapel; now a magnificent

Getting There

Albi's **train** station is a 10-minute walk from the centre in Place Stalingrad and is linked frequently by train with Toulouse.

The **bus** station is in Place Jean Jaurès, **t** 05 63 54 58 61. Buses from Toulouse *gare routière* go several times a day all year and take 1hr.

Tourist Information

Albi ✉ 81000: Place Ste-Cécile, **t** 05 63 49 48 80, **f** 05 63 49 48 98, *www.tourisme.fr/albi*.

Market Day

Albi: Halle du Marché Couvert: Tues–Sun am.
Halle du Castelviel: Sat am flea market.

Eating Out

Moulin de la Mothe, Rue de Lamothe, **t** 05 63 60 38 15 (*moderate*). Wonderful, refined regional cuisine by chef Michel Pellaprat on the banks of the Tarn in a charming brick-walled garden or indoors by the fire. *Closed Sun eve, Wed, and Nov.*

★★**Vieil Alby**, 23 Rue Toulouse-Lautrec, **t** 05 63 54 14 69, **f** 05 63 54 96 75 (*inexpensive*). In the historic centre, this friendly hotel restaurant features well-prepared *cuisine de terroir*, with plenty of lamb and duck dishes. *Demi-pension obligatory in July and Aug.*

Auberge Rabelaisienne, 22 Av du Colonel Teyssier, **t** 05 63 47 97 19 (*inexpensive*). Cosy bourgeoise house specializing in classics like foie gras, free-range pigeon, and *gigot de lotte*. *Closed Sun eve, Mon lunch*. They have a few pleasantly old fashioned rooms.

Le Tournesol, Rue de l'Ort-en-Salvy (off Place du Vigan), **t** 05 63 38 44 60 (*inexpensive*). Best vegetarian restaurant in the Tarn, with apple crumble for the homesick and organic beer. *Open Tues–Sat for lunch, and Fri and Sat eve.*

18th-century organ replaces the central figure of Christ the Judge. The flamboyant *jubé* or choir screen is a masterpiece of delicate tracery in stone, in spite of being deprived of its many figures in the Revolution. Behind, the choir itself (*adm*) is decorated with a full quorum of biblical figures and saints, very human figures sculpted at the tail end of Gothic, including a lovely sensuous Cecilia and charming child angels.

The **Musée Toulouse-Lautrec** (*open June–Sept daily 9–12 and 2–6; April and May from 10; other times daily 10–12 and 2–5; closed Tues; adm*) is next door in the Palais de la Berbie, or bishop's palace, housing the world's largest collection of works by Henri de Toulouse-Lautrec (born in Albi in 1864). Here are his first childhood efforts and pictures of his aristocratic family before he left aged 18 for Montmartre, where he charted the depths and exhilaration of the other side of life with a keen eye, compassion and superb draughtsmanship. One of the rare paintings is the famous *Au Salon de la rue des Moulins* (1894). Most of the other works are drawings, including remarkable portraits and caricatures, as well as the famous posters. There are other paintings, including fine ones by Matisse and the Fauves.

You can easily spend a day poking around the rest of Albi; the tourist office has set up three different walks, marked with explanatory panels. The old quarter below the Cathedral, **Vieil Alby**, has handsome *hôtels particuliers*, including the artist's birthplace (14 Rue de Toulouse-Lautrec); also look for the charming, decrepit 11th–13th-century **Collégiale St-Salvy** and its cloister.

The centre of life in modern Albi is **Place du Vigan**; from here the Lices Pompidou (named after the president, who as a young man taught in Albi) leads to the river and its two bridges; from the Pont du 22-Août there are fine views of the city, its mills and the 13th-century **Pont-Vieux**.

Touring from Toulouse

Day 1: Through the Aveyron to St-Cirq

Morning: Take the A68 motorway towards Albi as far as Gaillac, and then the D922 north for **Cordes-sur-Ciel**, a lovely medieval *bastide* with a fine museum and a unique park called the Jardin des Paradis. A scenic drive follows, up the D600 and west on the D958 along the Gorges of the Aveyron to another elegant medieval town, **St-Antonin-Noble Val**.

Lunch: In St-Antonin, there's a filling *ferme-auberge* on the way to Caylus (D926), the **Bés de Quercy, t** 05 63 31 97 61 (*moderate*). Or else stay in Cordes and try **Le Vieux Cordes**, Rue St-Michel, **t** 05 63 63 79 20 (*moderate*), where an award-winning chef does wonderful things with seafood and duck.

Afternoon: From St-Antonin, head east on the D115; from Cordes north on the D922. Either way, you'll find the little D106 near Laguepie for another beautiful stretch of the Aveyron gorges, and the dramatically sited village of **Najac**, with its castle atop a volcanic cone. Follow the back roads north along the river to **Villefranche-de-Rouergue**, another medieval town with an arcaded square and interesting churches. From there, the D911 winds west across the lonely Causse de Limogne, but the reward at the end of the trip is the picture-postcard village of **St-Cirq-Lapopie**, north on the D40.

Dinner: **Lou Bolat, t** 05 65 30 29 04 (*moderate*) is a café-restaurant-crêperie on a terrace with a view. The restaurant at the **Sombral** (*moderate; see below*) offers a delicious *gratin aux cèpes* and trout in Cahors wine. *Closed Nov–Mar.*

Sleeping: St-Cirq has two attractive accommodations in medieval houses, **★★★La Pélissaria, t** 05 65 31 25 14, **f** 05 65 30 25 52 (*moderate*), hanging over the cliffside; and the **★★Auberge du Sombral, t** 05 65 31 26 08 (*inexpensive*). *Closed Nov–Mar.*

Day 2: Pech-Merle and Figeac

Morning: We promise we won't make you drive nearly as far today. From St-Cirq, cross the River Lot, and the D41 will take you right to Cabrerets and the **Grotte du Pech-Merle**,

the finest prehistoric painted cave anywhere that is open to the public (*open mid-April–Oct 9.30–12 and 1.30–5; adm*). Also at Cabrerets, on the D41, a local eccentric artist has created his **Petit Musée de l'Insolite** (*open April–Sept 9–1 and 2–8*).

Lunch: You can have lunch in Cabrarets at **Hôtel des Grottes, t** 05 65 31 27 02 (*inexpensive*), or else carry on through the afternoon itinerary to Boussac and a wonderful *ferme auberge*, the **Domaine des Villedieu, t** 05 65 40 06 03 (*moderate; book ahead*).

Afternoon: From Cabrerets, follow the pretty D41 along the banks of the Célé to **Marcilhac-sur-Célé**, with a stalactite cave, the Grotte de Bellevue, and on through Boussac to **Figeac**, a town with fine historic buildings and churches, and Egyptian art in the **Musée Champollion** (*open 10–12 and 2.30–6.30; closed Mon exc July and Aug; Nov–Feb 2–6 only; adm*) dedicated to the local boy who deciphered the Rosetta Stone.

Dinner: The hotels listed below both have exceptional restaurants, or else you might like to try the innovative cooking at **La Cuisine du Marché**, 15 Rue Clermont, **t** 05 65 50 18 55 (*moderate*), under the arches of a restored wine cellar.

Sleeping: For a treat, there's the **★★★★ Château du Viguier du Roi**, Rue Droite, **t** 05 65 50 05 05, **f** 05 65 50 06 06 (*expensive*), filling several historic buildings; antique furnishings and a pool. *Closed Nov–early April.* More modestly, there's the stylish **★★ Hostellerie de l'Europe**, 51 Allées Victor Hugo, **t** 05 65 34 10 16, **f** 05 65 50 04 57 (*inexpensive*).

Day 3: Rocamadour

Morning: Leave Figeac northwest on the N140; a short detour on the D653 will give you a look at the remarkable Renaissance **Château d'Assier** (*open daily exc Tues 9.30–12.15 and 2–6.15; adm*). Further up the N140, turn right at Gramat for another cave – no paintings this time, but a spectacular underground boat trip through the stalactites at the **Gouffre de Padirac** (*open April–mid-Oct 9–12 and 2–6; adm*).

Lunch: There are choices around the cave, including duck kebabs at the **Auberge de Mathieu, t** 05 65 33 64 68 (*inexpensive*).

Closed mid-Nov–mid-Feb. Or else carry on to Rocamadour and **Jehan de Valon**, Rue LePreux, **t** 05 65 33 63 08 (*moderate*), a great place to try the area's famous *cabecou*. *Closed mid-Nov–mid-Feb.*

Afternoon: From Padirac, the D673 heads west to **Rocamadour**, a medieval pilgrimage town on a dramatic site. The village is full of attractions; beyond the picturesque village and religious monuments, there are museums of everything from model trains to apiculture, as well as eagles and Barbary apes – but eventually carry on down the D673 and north on the N20 for **Souillac**.

Dinner: **La Vieille Auberge**, 1 Rue de la Recège, **t** 05 65 32 79 43 (*expensive–moderate*) bases its dishes on recipes of a century ago. *Closed out of season; ring first.* The **Grand Hôtel** (*see* below) has a busy and popular restaurant (*moderate*).

Sleeping: Ask for a room with a balcony at the charmingly old-fashioned ★★★★**Grand Hôtel**, 1 Allée du Verninac, **t** 05 65 32 78 30, **f** 05 65 32 66 34 (*moderate*). *Closed Nov–Mar.* On the D703 towards Sarlat, ★★★**Les Granges Vieilles**, **t** 05 65 37 80 92, **f** 05 65 37 08 18 (*moderate*) has rooms in a shady park with a pool and a good restaurant.

Day 4: Souillac to Cahors

Morning: Souillac's attractions are the great Romanesque sculpture in the church of Ste-Marie and a museum of mechanical dolls, the Musée de l'Automate (*hours vary; ring* **t** 05 65 37 07 07). Before lunch, take the N20 or the new A20 motorway south, and in less than an hour you'll be in **Cahors**.

Lunch: Along the way, you might stop to get to know the local Quercy cuisine at **La Bergerie**, on the N20 at St-Pierre-Lafeuille, 8km before Cahors, **t** 05 65 36 82 82 (*moderate*). *Closed mid-Jan–mid-Feb, and Mon except July and Aug.* There's more of the same, with such dishes as duck with *cèpes*, 5km before Cahors on the N20 at St-Henri: **La Garenne**, **t** 05 65 35 40 67 (*moderate*). *Closed Feb–Mar, and Wed.*

Afternoon: The highlights of this refined and very medieval city are the perfectly preserved 14th-century **Pont Valentre**, and a Romanesque-Gothic **cathedral**. Walking its

ancient but lively streets is a delight, or you can drive up Mt St-Cyr for a great view over the town.

Dinner: Everybody knows Cahors' finest is **Le Balandre**, in the Hôtel Terminus, **t** 05 65 53 32 00 (*luxury*): Quercy *haute cuisine* and fine Cahors wines in an elegant room from 1910. *Closed Sun and Mon exc July and Aug.* For a modest dinner in a memorable setting, there's **Au Fil des Douceurs**, on an old river-boat in the Lot, Quai Verrerie, **t** 05 65 22 13 04 (*moderate–inexpensive*). *Closed Sun eve and Mon.*

Sleeping: ★★★**Le Terminus**, 5 Av Charles de Freycinet, **t** 05 65 53 32 00, **f** 05 65 53 32 26 (*moderate*) is the best choice, a charming, retro, ivy-covered establishment across from the station. Down by the river, there's the more modern ★★★**La Chartreuse**, St-Georges, **t** 05 65 35 17 37, **f** 05 65 22 30 03 (*moderate*), with a pool and restaurant.

Day 5: Medieval Montauban

Morning: Cahors' old medieval rival, **Montauban** waits just half an hour south on the A20. Completely different in atmosphere, a brick 'pink city' like Toulouse, Montauban shows off the paintings of its favourite son at the Musée Ingres (*open daily 10–12 and 2–6; closed Sun morning and Mon in winter; adm*).

Lunch: In a pleasant spot by the river, there's more duck and other local favourites at **Au Fil de l'Eau**, 14 Quai Dr Lafforgue, **t** 05 63 66 11 85 (*moderate*). *Closed Mon, Sun.* Near the Pont-Neuf, more of the same, and some seafood, are on the bill at **Au Chapon Fin**, Place St-Orens, **t** 05 63 63 12 10 (*moderate*). *Closed Fri eve and Sat, and early Aug .*

Afternoon: Montauban has a few other attractions, including the arcaded Place Nationale, and an interesting Musée du Terroir. You might spend the afternoon on a trip to **Moissac** (*see* pp.226–7), with some of France's finest medieval art, if you haven't already; it lies just to the west on the D958, by way of the medieval *bastide* of **Castelsarrasin**. From either Montauban or Moissac, the A68 will take you back to Toulouse to catch your flight home.

Languedoc-Roussillon

10

Languedoc-Roussillon is France's 'other' Mediterranean province, with rugged sun-baked scenery, long sandy beaches, and more vineyards producing more tons of wine than any other region in France. It flourished under the Romans – *see* Nîmes, opposite, and the Pont du Gard, p.239 – and under the counts of Toulouse, until the 13th-century Albigensian Crusaders destroyed its civilization (the name Languedoc comes from its language, Occitan, where '*oc*' meant 'yes'). When the region began to revive in the 16th century, it embraced Protestantism. The subsequent Wars of Religion and Revocation of the Edict of Nantes were tremendous setbacks; and later, in the 19th century, phylloxera destroyed the local wine industry and brought economic ruin.

In 1959, Leo Larguier of the Académie Goncourt wrote of Languedoc, 'Talent has never flowered again, and the genius is forever dead.' His obituary now seems premature: the dawn of the 21st century finds Montpellier one of the most dynamic and progressive cities in France, with Nîmes nipping at its heels. As Provence begins to seem all full up (and expensive), Languedoc-Roussillon is gaining a reputation as the great alternative.

Nîmes

Built of stone the colour of old piano keys, Nîmes disputes with Arles the honour of being the 'Rome of France' – the Rome of the Caesars, of course, not of the popes: the the Church has never gone down well in this mercantile, Protestant town. The textile trade was important; its heavy-duty blue *serge de Nîmes* was reduced to the more familiar 'denim' in 1695, in London, and exported; some of it found its way to California and the rest is history.

After the passions of the Wars of Religion, Nîmes fell into a doze that lasted for centuries. Travellers in the 19th century found it the quintessential dusty southern city; they came to marvel at the city's famous Maison Carrée, the best-preserved

Getting to Nîmes

Air France has four flights a day (three on Saturday) from Paris-Orly Ouest to Nîmes-Garons airport. **Ryanair** (*see* p.6) flies from London Stansted to Nîmes once a day.

Getting from the Airport

Nîmes-Garons **airport** is 8km from Nîmes along Rte de St-Gilles (A54). *Navettes* (**t** 04 66 70 06 88) run regularly into Nîmes (Palais de Justice), costing €4.30. A **taxi** costs €20.

Getting Around

Nîmes' **train** station is at the south end of Av Feuchères on Bd Sgt. Triaire. There are direct trains to Carcassonne, Montpellier, Arles and Marseille; and TGVs to Paris and Lille.

The *gare routière* is just behind the train station in Rue Ste-Felicité, **t** 04 66 29 52 00.

Car Hire

Budget, 2000 Av Maréchal Juin, **t** 04 66 70 49 42; **Europcar**, 1bis Rue de la République, **t** 04 66 21 31 35; **National Citer**, 14 Av Carnot, **t** 04 66 21 03 62.

Tourist Information

Nîmes: 6 Rue Auguste, near the Maison Carrée, **t** 04 66 58 38 00, **f** 04 66 58 38 01, *www.ot-nimes.fr*. There's also a booth in the station, which has a hotel booking service.

Market Days

Tues and Fri am, Av Jean Jaurès, organic /farmers' market; Monday, Av Jean Jaurès,

flower market; Sunday am, Av Jean Jaurès, flea market. On Thursday nights in summer, the city puts on *marchés du soir* until 10pm, around the squares of the *centre ville*.

Festivals

24-hour info line on **t** 04 66 58 38 00.

There are usually a couple of bullfights each month in the summer, but to see the best *toreros* come for the *ferias* at **Carnival** time in February or the third week of September, and especially the 10-day **Feria de Pentecôte** (Whitsun). A recent addition to the town's calendar is the **Mosaïques Gitanes**, a festival of Gypsy music and dance in mid-July, right before the **Jazz Festival**.

Shopping

Shopping is concentrated around **Rues de l'Aspic, de la Madeleine, Général Perrier, du Chapître** and **Régale**, and in the **Centre Commercial Coupole des Halles**.

The city is proud of its *croquants Villaret*, almond biscuits cooked by the same family in the same oven since 1775, available at Raymond Villaret, 13 Rue de la Madeleine.

Where to Stay

Nîmes ✉ 30000

Reservations are essential during the *ferias*.
★★★★**Hôtel Impérator Concorde**, Quai de la Fontaine, **t** 04 66 21 90 30, **f** 04 66 67 70 25, *www.hotel-imperator.com* (*expensive*). A 19th-century dowager with a recent facelift,

Roman temple in the world. Today, with its new Carré d'Art designed by Sir Norman Foster, the city vies for avant-garde cultural supremacy in this corner of France with Montpellier. But what really makes the juices flow in Nîmes is not modern architecture but bulls; Nîmes is passionate about its *ferias*, featuring top matadors.

Les Arènes and the Maison Carrée

Twentieth in size, but the best-preserved of the 70 surviving amphitheatres of the Roman world, the **arena** at Nîmes (late 1st century AD) is just a bit smaller than its twin at Arles (*open 9–6.30; winter 9–12 and 2–5; Oct–April free guided tours; closed public hols and days of concerts; adm*). When new, the arena could accommodate 24,000 people, who could reach or leave their seats in only a few minutes thanks to

a lovely garden, TVs, air-conditioning, and Nîmes' top restaurant to boot.

***New Hotel La Baume, 21 Rue Nationale, **t** 04 66 76 28 42, **f** 04 66 76 28 45, *www.new-hotel.com* (*expensive*). Stylish modern rooms in a 17th-century mansion with a garden terrace.

***L'Orangerie, 755 Rue de la Tour de l'Evêque, **t** 04 66 84 50 57, **f** 04 66 29 44 55, *www.orangerie.com* (*moderate*). Just outside the centre; garden, small pool and restaurant.

Royal, 3 Bd Alphonse Daudet, **t 04 66 58 28 27, **f** 04 66 58 28 28 (*inexpensive*). A delightful Art Deco hotel with artistic rooms and a palm-fronded lobby.

Kyriad, 10 Rue Roussy, **t 04 66 76 16 20, **f** 04 66 67 65 99 (*inexpensive*). An old house (with a private garage) converted into an air-conditioned hotel with retro furnishings.

Hôtel de L'Amphithéâtre, 4 Rue des Arènes, **t 04 66 67 28 51, **f** 04 66 67 07 79, *hotel.amphitheatre@wanadoo.fr* (*inexpensive*). Sweetly restored 18th-century building in the old town, with antique furniture and nice big bathrooms.

Hôtel de la Mairie, 11 Rue des Greffes, **t 04 66 67 65 91, **f** 04 66 76 07 92 (*inexpensive*). Rugged, simple and in the historic centre.

Central, 2 Place du Château, **t 04 66 67 27 75, **f** 04 66 21 77 79, *www.hotel-central.org* (*inexpensive*). Rugged, simple and in the historic centre.

Eating Out

Nîmes isn't exactly famous for its restaurants, but it has some delicious specialities:

brandade de morue (pounded cod mixed with fine olive oil), a recipe said to date back to Roman times, and *tapenade d'olives*, an appetizer made of olives, anchovies and herbs.

L'Enclos de la Fontaine, Hôtel Impérator (*see above*), **t** 04 66 21 90 30 (*expensive*). *Escalope de foie gras* is often on the menu at one of Nîmes' top restaurants.

Magister, 5 Rue Nationale, **t** 04 66 76 11 00 (*expensive*). A smart Nîmes restaurant with good service and highly professional cooking, as well as a good local wine list. *Closed Mon lunch, Sat, Sun, and 2 weeks Feb.*

Aux Plaisirs des Halles, 4 Rue Littré, **t** 04 66 36 01 02 (*moderate*). Cosy little *bistrot* near the market for *aïoli* with vegetables or *brandade* with truffles and black olives. *Closed Sun and Mon, and Feb.*

Jardin d'Hadrien, 11 Rue de l'Enclos Rey, **t** 04 66 21 86 65 (*moderate*). A current favourite, with its beamed dining room and verandah; try the cod with olive oil. *July and Aug closed Wed lunch, Sun and Mon; Sept–June closed Sun lunch and Wed.*

Nicolas, Rue Poise (off Bd Amiral Courbet), **t** 04 66 67 50 47 (*moderate–cheap*). One of the more affordable fine restaurants.

La Fontaine du Temple, 22 Rue de la Curaterie, **t** 04 66 21 21 13 (*moderate–cheap*). Friendly bar and restaurant; try bull's meat (*taureau*). *Closed Jan, Feb and Sun.*

Au Flan Coco, 31 Rue du Mûrier d'Espagne, **t** 04 66 21 84 81 (*cheap*). A delightful tiny restaurant run by two *traiteurs* alongside their shop. *Closed Sun, and Mon–Fri eves, and mid–end Aug.*

an ingenious system of five concentric galleries and 126 stairways. Near the top are holes pierced in the stone for the supports of the awning that sheltered the spectators from sun and rain. Like the Maison Carrée, it escaped being cannibalized for its stone by being put to constant use – as a castle for the Visigoths and the knightly militia of the Frankish viscounts, then, after union with France, as a slum, housing some 2,000 people. The event that has packed the crowds in since 1853 is the *corrida*.

To the north stands Nîmes' ragamuffin **Cathédrale Notre-Dame-et-St-Castor**, which was consecrated in 1096 but flattened by rampaging Huguenots, who spared only the campanile to use as a watchtower. Across the façade runs a vigorous frieze of Old Testament scenes. There's another good Romanesque frieze nearby, in Place aux Herbes, this time adorning a rare, well-preserved 12th-century house (**Maison Romane**).

Then there's the best-preserved Roman temple anywhere, the graceful little 1st-century BC **Maison Carrée** just off the Via Domitia (*open summer 9–6.30; winter 9–5*). Built by the great General Agrippa, who also built the Pantheon in Rome, the temple was dedicated to the imperial cult of Augustus' grandsons, Caius and Lucius. Known as 'Carrée' or square, because of its right angles and 'long' square shape (85 by 50ft), its *cella* (cult sanctuary) and the Corinthian columns of the porch are perfectly intact. It now houses a museum.

The Maison Carrée is overlooked by Sir Norman Foster's **Carré d'Art** (*open 10–6; closed Mon; adm; the museum also offers guided tours Mon–Fri at 4.30, weekends and holidays 3 and 4.30*). Inaugurated in May 1993, this palace of glass and steel houses a modern art museum (the Musée d'Art Contemporain), audiovisual centre and library. The ancient columns of the Maison Carrée are reflected in Sir Norman's own slender columns of steel; the walls and even the stairways are of glass.

The Jardin de la Fontaine and the Tour Magne

A short stroll to the west down Quai de la Fontaine is the great spring that originates in the karst caverns of the *garrigue* to gush out at the foot of Mont Cavalier. It was domesticated in the 18th century as the lovely **Jardin de la Fontaine**, a kind of neo-Roman nymphaeum. Paths wind up Mont Cavalier to the oldest Roman monument in Gaul, the octagonal 106ft **Tour Magne** (*open summer 9–7, winter 9–5; adm*). No record of its origin has survived.

Museum-crawling

Two museums share the former Jesuit college at 13 bis Boulevard Amiral Courbet: the **Musée Archéologique**, with a striking Celtic lintel found at Nages, with a frieze of galloping horses and human heads, and the old-fashioned **Musée d'Histoire Naturelle et de Préhistoire**, home to a collection of two-headed lambs and so on, and those mysterious menhirs-with-personality, the statue-steles (*both open 10–6, closed Mon; joint adm*).

For the **Musée du Vieux Nîmes** (*open 11–7, closed Mon; adm*), with its exceptional collection of 19th-century textiles and 500 print designs from Nîmes' wool and silk industries, follow Grand' Rue behind the museums, north to Rue Lacroix. The worthy **Musée des Beaux-Arts** is in Rue Cité-Foulc (*open 10–6, closed Mon; adm*).

Day Trips from Nîmes

The Pont du Gard

By 19 BC, the spring of Nemausus could no longer slake Nîmes' thirst and a search was on for a new source. The Romans were obsessed with the quality of their water, and when they found a spring near Uzès, the fact that it was 50km away hardly mattered to antiquity's star engineers. The resulting aqueduct, built under Augustus's son-in-law Agrippa, was like a giant needle hemming the landscape, piercing tunnels through hills and looping its arches over the open spaces of the *garrigues*, all measured precisely to allow a slope of .07 centimetres per metre.

No matter how many photos you've seen before, the Pont du Gard's three tiers of arches of golden stone without mortar makes a brave and lovely sight. What the photos never show are the two million people who come to pay it homage every year, and you may well find it more evocative if you arrive very early in the morning or about an hour before sunset. As you walk over it, note how it's slightly curved (the better to stand up to floods) and how the Roman engineers left cavities and protruding stones to support future scaffolding. In the 18th century, the bottom tier was expanded to take a road, now fortunately limited to pedestrians.

Uzès, the First Duchy of France

'O little town of Uzès', wrote André Gide. 'Were you in Umbria, the Parisians would flock to visit you!' Now they do, more or less. Houses tumbling into ruin have been repaired, creating the perfect stage for films like *Cyrano de Bergerac*.

Uzès' café life engulfs most available space around Place Albert 1er, just under the **Duché** or duke's residence (*daily guided tours July–mid-Sept 10–1 and 2–7, mid-Sept–June 10–12 and 2–6; adm exp*). The oldest section, the rectangular donjon called

Getting There

STDG (t 04 66 29 27 29) **buses** from Nîmes and Uzès and Avignon pass within a kilometre of the **Pont du Gard** eight or nine times a day. Note that you can no longer drive over the Pont du Gard, but will have to leave your car in one of the pay car parks on either side.

Uzès is linked by frequent **buses** to Nîmes, Avignon, Alès and the Pont du Gard, t 04 66 22 00 58 or STD Gard, t 04 66 29 27 29.

Tourist Information

Pont du Gard: Summer-only tourist office 200 yards from the aqueduct on the Remoulins side of the Pont du Gard, t 04 66 37 50 99.
Uzès ✉ **30700**: Chapelle des Capucins, Place Albert 1er, t 04 66 22 68 88, f 04 66 22 95 19.

Eating Out

Uzès

Les Jardins de Castille, t 04 66 22 32 68 (*expensive*). An elegant hotel-restaurant, with a classy lunch menu.
**Hotel La Taverne, 7 Rue Sigalon, t 04 66 22 13 10 (*moderate*). In the centre, with a pretty terrace and garden.
Hotel de l'Ancienne Gare, outside Uzès on the Remoulins road, t 04 66 03 19 15 (*moderate–cheap*). Opened in summer 1999 in a former train station; the delicious, refined cooking has kept it full of happy customers. Be sure to book. *Closed Sat lunch and all of Mon.*
La Boulangerie Uzèsienne, Place des Herbes (*cheap*). The best bakery in town, famous for the local speciality, *fougasse*.

the **Tour Bermonde** was built over a Roman tower in the 10th or 11th century. The Renaissance façade in the central courtyard was built in 1550 and bears the dukes' motto: *Ferro non auro* ('iron, not gold' – i.e. they were warriors, not financiers).

Uzès is a lot smaller than it seems, and a short wander will soon bring you to the delightfully irregular, arcaded **Place aux Herbes**, for centuries the centre of public life. Set apart from the rest of the old town on a terrace, the **Ancien Palais Episcopal** (1671) was the seat of the powerful bishops of Uzès (64 bishops reigned here between the 5th century and the Revolution). A restoration attempt in the 1970s caused the interior to cave in, although the right wing is in good enough nick to hold the eclectic collections of the **Musée Municipal** (*open 3–7; closed Mon and Jan*) with its fossils, ceramics, paintings, and memorabilia of the Gide family. Behind stretches the pleasant **Promenade des Marronniers**, while adjacent is the **Cathédrale St-Théodorit**, built in 1663. The quaint neo-Romanesque façade was tacked on in 1875, with the idea of making a better partner to the stunning 12th-century **Tour Fenestrelle**, spared by the Protestants only because they found it useful as a watchtower. Unique in France, the 137ft tower is encircled by six storeys of double-lit windows, inspired by the Romanesque campaniles of Ravenna and Lombardy. The cathedral's interior was severely damaged during the Revolution, when it was converted into a Temple of Reason, leaving only the peculiar upper gallery with its wrought-iron railing and the cathedral's pride and joy – a splendid **organ** of 1670, the only one in France to have retained its original painted shutters.

Arles

Modern Arles, sitting amidst its Roman ruins, is still somehow charming, in spite of a general scruffiness that seems more intentional than natural. When Vincent Van Gogh arrived in Arles in 1888 he found a shabby, ugly town. But he decided to stay, and painted the Arles he saw around him. Van Gogh's output in Arles was prodigious but not a single painting remains in the city today.

As enormous as it is, the Roman arena, **Les Arènes** (*open 9–12.30 and 2–5*), 10ft wider than its rival at Nîmes, originally stood another arcade higher, and was clad in marble. From the Middle Ages on it sheltered a poor, crime-ridden neighbourhood with two churches and 200 houses, built from stones prised off the amphitheatre's third storey. These were cleared away in 1825, leaving the amphitheatre free for bullfights, and able to pack in 12,000 spectators. South of the nearby **Théâtre Antique** runs the plane-tree-lined **Boulevard des Lices** ('of the lists'), the favourite promenade of the Arlésiens since the 17th century.

From Boulevard des Lices, Rue Jean Jaurès (the Roman *cardo*) leads to the harmonious **Place de la République**, an attractive square on the Roman model. Overlooking it is the Romanesque **cathedral of St-Trophime**, and around the corner in Rue du Cloître is the entrance to St-Trophime's **cloister** (*same hours as the Arènes*). No other cloister in Provence is as richly and harmoniously sculpted as this. Sharing Place de la République with St-Trophime is Arles' palatial **Hôtel de Ville**, built in 1675 after plans by Hardouin-Mansart. Just around the corner on Rue Balze is the cryptoporticus of the forum, the **Cryptoportiques** (*same hours as Arènes; adm*).

Getting There

Trains run regularly from Nîmes and Montpellier. Arles' train station is on the northern edge of town, on Av Paulin Talabot.

Six **buses** a day run from Nîmes' *gare routière* to that of Arles (**t** 04 90 49 38 01), opposite the train station.

Tourist Information

Arles ✉ **13200**: Esplanade Charles de Gaulle, **t** 04 90 18 41 20, **f** 04 90 18 41 29, *www.arles. org*, and in the train station, **t** 04 90 49 36 90. If you intend to see more than two of Arles' monuments and museums, stop here to purchase the global ticket (also available at any museum). The tourist office also sells tickets for the two-hour Van Gogh tours

(departing every Tues and Fri at 5pm, July–Sept, in French only).

Eating Out

Lou Marquès, in Hôtel Jules César, Bd des Lices, **t** 04 90 52 92 32, **f** 04 90 93 33 47 (*expensive*). Arles' elegant citadel of traditional *haute cuisine*, in a former Dominican monastery, features dishes such as *croustillant de St-Pierre* and *carré d'agneau* with artichokes, and an excellent wine cellar.

Le Jardin de Manon, 14 Av des Alyscamps, **t** 04 90 93 38 68 (*moderate*). *Cuisine provençale* on a pretty terrace at the rear.

Vitamine, 16 Rue du Docteur Fanton, **t** 04 90 93 77 36 (*cheap*). For a light lunch in the centre, with 50 different salads. *Closed Sun, exc July.*

In 1904 the indefatigable Frédéric Mistral – poet and founder of the Félibrige literary school – set up the **Muséon Arlaten**, 29 Rue de la République (*open daily 9.30– 12.30 and 2–5; June–Aug daily 9.30–1 and 2–6.30; Oct–June closed Mon; adm*). Mistral's aim was to record the details of everyday life in Provence for future generations. The evolution of the traditional Arlésienne costume was one of his obsessions. A **statue of Mistral**, looking uncommonly like Buffalo Bill, stands on Place du Forum.

After the Revolution an academic painter named Jacques Réattu purchased the Priory of the Knights of Malta, and his daughter made it into the **Musée Réattu**, Rue du Grand Prieuré (*same hours as Arènes; adm*). Besides Réattu's own contributions, there are works by Théodore Rousseau and followers of Lorrain and Salvator Rosa. In 1972, the museum was jolted awake with a donation of 57 drawings from Picasso, in gratitude for the many bullfights he enjoyed in Arles.

Arles' newest museum, the **Musée de l'Arles Antique** (*open Mar–Oct daily 9–7; Nov–Feb daily 10–5; adm*), at Presqu'île du Cirque Romain, Avenue de la 1ère DFL, is situated in an eerie wasteland slightly out of town (*follow the Boulevard des Lices to its western end, and pass under the motorway*) and contains the contents of several of Arles' old museums. Brilliant architectural models bring the Roman city back to life. Amongst the other exhibits are the pagan statues and sarcophagi of the former Musée d'Art Païen; nearly everything here was made in the Arles region.

Because of the legend of St Trophime, who was said to be a disciple of St Paul himself, the **Alyscamps** (*follow Rue E. Fassin from the Bd des Lices, east, a 10min walk from the centre; same hours as Arènes; adm*) was one of the most prestigious necropolises of the Middle Ages. Burial here was so desirable that bodies sealed in barrels with their burial fee attached were floated down the Rhône. At its greatest extent the necropolis stretched for 2.5km and contained several thousand tombs. Now, only one romantic, melancholy lane lined with empty, mostly plain sarcophagi remains.

Montpellier

Montpellier's reputation as a centre of medicine began in the 13th century with the formation of a *Universitas Medicorum*, and later a *studium* of law. In 1349 the Catalan Kings of Majorca sold Montpellier, which they had acquired in the 12th century as part of a dowry, back to France for 120,000 golden écus. A period of relative peace and prosperity followed until the 1560s, when the university academics and tradesmen embraced the Reformation. For the next 70 years much of what Montpellier had achieved was wiped out. In 1622 Louis XIII came in person to besiege the city and reassert royal authority. Putting its merchant republic days behind it, Montpellier settled down to the life of a university town and regional capital of a wine region. The Revolution passed without kicking up much dust; a far bigger crisis for Montpellier occurred in the 1890s, when phylloxera knocked out the vineyards. Until 1977 and the election of Mayor Georges Frêche, Montpellier was a sleepy university backwater of fawn-coloured stone. With his Paris-sized projects, notably the monumental new quarter called Antigone, Frêche has made Montpellier a European model for innovative city government. Now trumpeted as 'Capital of Southern Europe' and 'the Rome of Tomorrow', this is one live-wire of a city, progressive, fun and friendly.

A Place Named Comédie

The various personalities of Montpellier all come together in the lively, café-lined **Place de la Comédie**, locally known as *l'Œuf*, or the Egg, owing to the shape it had in the 18th century. Its ornaments include a *doppelgänger* of the Paris Opera, and various 19th-century larded bourgeois buildings with domes reminiscent of bathyspheres, while opposite looms a modern glass-and-steel semi-ziggurat, the **Polygone**, a shopping mall and town hall complex. To the north of Place de la Comédie extends the **Esplanade Charles de Gaulle**, replacing the city walls demolished by Louis XIII after the siege of 1622. In the 18th century the Esplanade was planted with rows of trees and became Montpellier's chief promenade; along here is a rare survival of 1908, the **Cinématographe Pathé**, a little palace from the magical early days of cinema (now the Rabelais Cultural Centre; it often shows foreign films). The north end of the Esplanade is flanked by **CORUM**, 'the House of Innovation' designed by Claude Vasconi, one of Georges Frêche's showcases.

Antigone

East of Place de la Comédie (go through Polygone mall and out the back door of Galeries Lafayette) lies another Frêche initiative: **Antigone**, a moderate-income quarter with housing for 10,000 people, shops and restaurants, all designed by Barcelona architect Ricardo Bofill in 1979 and spread along a huge formal axis down to the river Lez. Bofill understood just what a Rome of Tomorrow needs: Mannerist neo-Roman arches, cornices, pilasters, and columns as big as California redwoods. On a bad day, Antigone looks like the surreal background to a De Chirico painting; on a good day, it seems like a delightful place to live, especially for kids, who can play football in the monumental Place du Millennium and still hear their parents call them in for lunch.

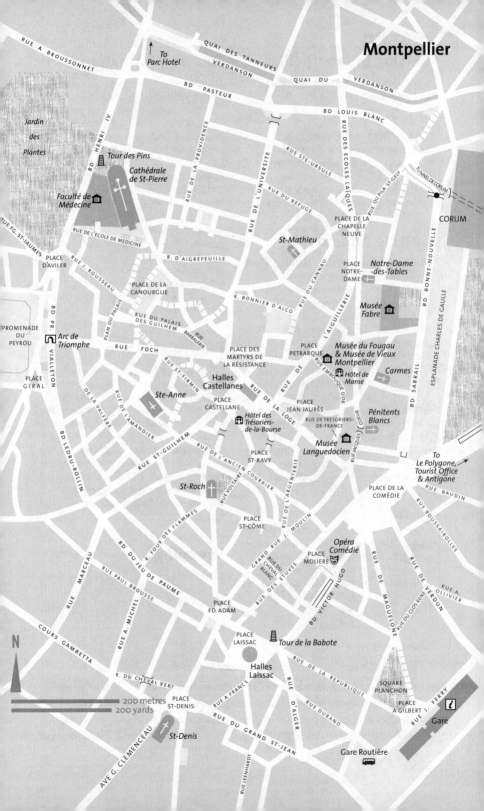

Getting to Montpellier

Ryanair (see p.6) flies from London Stansted. British Airways (t 0802 802 902) also flies direct from London daily.

Getting from the Airport

The airport, Montpellier-Méditerranée, is 8km southeast of the centre on the D21 (t 04 67 20 85 00). There is a regular airport shuttle bus to the gare routière; it takes 15mins and costs €4.55. A taxi will cost around €25.

Getting Around

The train station is in Place Auguste Gilbert, just south of the Ecusson. You can catch direct trains to Avignon, Nîmes, Marseille, Nice, Perpignan, Béziers, Narbonne, Agde, Lunel, Sète and Carcassonne.

The station is linked by an escalator to the gare routière in nearby Rue du Grand St-Jean (t 04 67 92 01 48), which has buses to Nîmes, La Grande Motte, Béziers, Aigues-Mortes, etc. Every 20mins bus no.17 trundles down to the sea at Palavas. In town the little Petibus vans can take you around the pedestrian zones of the Ecusson and Antigone.

In summer 2000, Montpellier opened the first stage of its tram project. The first line crosses the city centre from southwest to northeast. Information from TAM, t 04 67 22 87 87, or the tourist office.

Car Hire

Big-name car hire firms are at the airport, or try Avis at 900 Av Prés d'Arènes (south of the centre), t 04 67 92 51 92, or Hertz France, 18 Rue Jules Ferry, t 04 67 58 65 18 (outside the station). You can also hire a less expensive used car from A.D.A., 58 bis Av Clemenceau, t 04 67 58 34 35.

Tourist Information

Montpellier: 30 Allée Jean de Latte de Tassigny, t 04 67 60 60 60, f 04 67 60 60 61, www.ot-montpellier.fr, contact@ot-montpellier.fr. There are also offices in the station, t 04 67 22 08 80, and at Antigone, at the motorway exit, t 04 67 22 06 16, f 04 67 22 38 10.

Market Days

At Espace Mosson (La Paillade), there is a flower market on Tuesday and a flea market on Sunday morning; free buses go every 20mins from Square Planchon. Daily food markets take place in Place J. Jaurès, Halles Castellanes, Halles Laissac, Plan Cabannes and La Comédie; on Tuesday and Saturday there's an organic market at Aux Arceaux, by Rue Mariogé; and at Antigone a market of farmers' produce every Sunday.

Festivals

The city hosts four annual festivals: theatre in mid-June–beginning of July, during the Printemps des Comédiens at Château d'O, t 04 67 63 66 66; dance performances of all kinds at the Festival International Montpellier Danse, t 04 67 60 07 40, also June and July; and music to suit every taste during late July through August at the Festival de Radio-France et de Montpellier, t 04 67 02 02 01, and at the end of October, the Festival International du Cinéma Méditerranéen, t 04 99 13 73 73.

Shopping

The tourist office has a large display of wine, confits and other regional products; antiques shops cluster around Place de la Canourgue.

Musée Fabre

Open 9–5.30, until 5pm Sat and Sun, closed Mon; adm.

On Boulevard Sarrail, between the Cinématographe and CORUM, in the fastness of a former Jesuit college, the Musée Fabre was long the main reason for visiting Montpellier, with one of the most important collections of art in provincial France. François Xavier Fabre (1766–1837), a pupil of David, was in Florence at the outbreak of

Steve Davis' Bookshop, 4 Rue de l'Université, t 04 67 66 09 08. A good selection of reasonably priced English books and videos, and the latest lowdown on Montpellier.

Caves Notre-Dame, 1348 Av de la Mer, on the other side of the river, t 04 67 64 48 00. An excellent source of local wines and information, including tastings. *Closed Sun and Mon.*

Maison Régionale des Vins et des Produits du Terroir, 34 Rue St-Guilhem, t 04 67 60 40 41. A good range of local wines and food products from olive oil to caviar. *Closed Sun.*

Where to Stay

Montpellier ⊠ 30400

Le Jardin des Sens, 11 Av St-Lazare (off the N113 towards Nîmes; bus no.4), t 04 99 58 38 38, *www.jardin-des-sens.com* (*luxury–expensive*). See 'Eating Out'. Very modern rooms.

****Holiday Inn Métropole, 2 Rue du Clos-René, t 04 67 12 32 32, f 04 67 92 13 02 (*expensive*). Top of the line: antique-furnished, with a quiet garden courtyard and air-con, between the train station and Place de la Comédie.

***Demeure des Brousses, Rte des Vauguières (4km east of town on the D24 and D127E towards the Château de la Mogère), t 04 67 65 77 66, f 04 67 22 22 17, *www.demeure-des-brousses.com* (*moderate*). If you have a car, the most charming place to stay is this 18th-century ivy-covered *mas* in a vast park of shady trees, a few minutes from the city or the sea. Furnished with antiques; excellent restaurant (*expensive*).

***La Maison Blanche, 1796 Av de la Pompignane (off the route to Carnon), t 04 99 58 20 70, f 04 67 79 53 39 (*moderate*). Another gem requiring your own transport: 38 rooms in a big, balconied house that

looks as if it has escaped from the French quarter of New Orleans.

**Parc, 8 Rue Achille Bège, t 04 67 41 16 49, f 04 67 54 10 05 (*inexpensive*). An 18th-century *hôtel particulier* equipped with air-conditioning, TV, etc.

**Palais, 3 Rue du Palais (just off Rue Foch), t 04 67 60 47 38, f 04 67 60 40 23 (*inexpensive*). Comfortable rooms in a recently restored building.

**Nice, 14 Rue Boussairolles, t 04 67 58 42 54 (*inexpensive*). Very pretty and flowery, on a dull street near the station.

*Les Arceaux, 35 Bd Arceaux, t 04 67 92 03 03, f 04 67 92 05 09 (*inexpensive*). Clean and comfortable, with small garden and terrace.

*Les Fauvettes, 8 Rue Bonnard, t 04 67 63 17 60, f 04 67 63 09 09 (*cheap*). Good value for money near the Jardin des Plantes, with quiet rooms overlooking interior courtyards. *Closed 20 Dec–3 Jan and 20 July–10 Aug.*

Eating Out

Le Jardin des Sens, 11 Av St-Lazare (off the N113 towards Nîmes; bus no.4), t 04 99 58 38 38 (*luxury*). Montpellier, not renowned for its cuisine, is now home to one of the most celebrated restaurants in the southwest. It is run by local twins Jacques and Laurent Pourcel, who are devoted to the cuisine of Languedoc and the Med. Try the squid stuffed with ratatouille and crayfish tails, *bourride* soup, and traditional *oreillette* pastries. The restaurant has an exquisite garden, and now has its own vineyard, above Valmagne abbey. A few rooms are also available. *Closed Mon and Wed lunch, and Sun.*

Cellier Morel, 27 Rue de l'Aiguillerie, t 04 67 66 46 36 (*expensive*). Serves local produce in a 13th-century vaulted dining

the French Revolution; there he became a close friend of the countess of Albany, the merry widow of Bonnie Prince Charlie, and her lover, the Italian dramatist Vittore Alfieri. When Alfieri died in 1805, he left the countess his library and paintings. Fabre in turn inherited the countess' affections, and when she died in 1824, she left everything to her young man from Montpellier.

The museum has six levels, with floors devoted to 17th-century painting, ceramics and painters from Montpellier. The superb collection on **Floor 5** was donated by the

room, and sells it in the adjoining shop. *Closed Sun, and Mon and Wed lunch.*

Le Chandelier, 39 Place Zeus, t 04 67 15 34 38 (*expensive–moderate*). Another established temple of fine cooking (complete with columns), featuring well-polished versions of the classic French repertoire. *Closed Mon lunch and Sun.*

Le Petit Jardin, 20 Rue J-J Rousseau, t 04 67 60 78 78, f 04 67 66 16 79 (*moderate*). Remarkably quiet restaurant in the centre of town, with a delightful large shady garden with a view of the cathedral. Good local fish, salads and fresh pasta with vegetables. *Closed Mon.*

L'Ollivier, 12 Rue Aristide Ollivier, t 04 67 92 86 28 (*moderate*). A popular restaurant bang on the new tramway; Art Deco style, smooth service, classic cuisine and local wine. *Closed Mon and Aug.*

Le Vieil Ecu, 1 Place de la Chapelle Neuve, t 04 67 66 39 44, f 04 67 72 71 01 (*moderate*). Good French food, served in the old chapel or on the terrace. *Closed Sun and Mon.*

Lively Rue des Ecoles Laïques and Place de la Chapelle Neuve make up Montpellier's Latin Quarter, with Turkish, Greek, Spanish and Tunisian restaurants.

Pizzeria du Palais, 22 Rue du Palais des Guilhem, t 04 67 60 67 97 (*moderate–cheap*). Here you may safely break the Languedoc-Roussillon pizza rule (never order a pizza): it's Italian-run, with a wide choice of pizzas and other Italian dishes, and always crowded. *Closed Sun and Mon.*

Tripti-Kulai, 20 Rue Jacques Cœur, t 04 67 66 30 51 (*cheap*). A vegetarian restaurant and tearoom near the Musée Languedocien that offers some exotic dishes: a good spot for a light lunch. *Closed Sun.*

Café Bibal, 4 Rue Jacques Cœur. The place to stop for a coffee.

Nightlife

Listings can be found in the city weekly *La Gazette*. FNAC, in the Polygone, has tickets for most events.

CORUM, t 04 67 61 67 61. Home of the Orchestre Philharmonique de Montpellier and Montpellier Danse.

Opéra Comédie, t 04 67 60 19 99. Opera and theatrical performances.

In a city where a quarter of the population is students, nightlife is never going to be dull. Most bars and clubs do not heat up until after 11pm, and the clubs rock until dawn.

Mimi la Sardine, out of the centre at 131 Av de Toulouse, t 04 67 99 69 77. One of the most lively clubs in Montpellier.

Le Rockstore, down from Place de la Comédie on Rue de Verdun, t 04 67 58 70 10. Entry is usually free on dance nights and drinks are inexpensive.

At weekends and often on weekdays there's live jazz, blues or world music at:

Sax'Aphone, 24 Rue Ernest Michel, t 04 67 58 80 90.

L'Antrouille, 12 Rue Anatole France, t 04 67 58 75 28.

Le Fil, 16 Rue du Pila St-Gély, t 04 67 66 20 67.

Cotton Pub, 9 Place Laissac, t 04 67 92 21 60. *Closes at 8pm.*

The latest thing in Montpellier is 'philosophy cafés', where certain nights are appointed for discussions on anything from astrology to theology. Try the following places and check the local press or *La Gazette*:

Brasserie Le Dome, 2 Av Clemenceau, t 04 67 92 66 70.

Le César, Place du Nombre d'Or, t 04 67 64 87 87.

museum's other great benefactor, Alfred Bruyas (1821–77). Born into a Montpellier banking family, Bruyas resolved the frustration of his inability to paint by befriending many of the artists of his day and asking them to paint him – there are 24 portraits of the red-bearded patron in this museum alone, lined up one after another, including examples by Delacroix and Alexandre Cabanel of Montpellier (1823–89). Four are by Gustave Courbet (1819–77), who became Bruyas' friend, and whose works are the highlight of the museum.

Floor 6 is dedicated to painters from Montpellier: Eugène Castelneau (1827–94), Alexandre Cabanel (1823–89), and early Impressionist Frédéric Bazille (1841–70).

Into the Ecusson

There is nothing as compelling as the Musée Fabre in Montpellier's historic centre, the Ecusson; much was lost in the Wars of Religion, and even the many 17th- and 18th-century *hôtels particuliers*, as stuccoed and ornate as many of them are inside, show mostly blank walls to the street. But few cities in the south of France manage to be as pleasant and lively. The entire Ecusson is a pedestrian zone, and it's a delightful place for walking. One of the major crossroads of the Ecusson is Place Notre-Dame, under the cool gaze of the neoclassical **Notre-Dame-des-Tables** (1748). At the Hôtel de Varennes in Place Pétrarque there's a pair of small museums devoted to the good old days: the **Musée du Fougau** ('the Foyer', *open Wed and Thurs 3–6*) preserves the arts and traditions of old Montpellier; the **Musée de Vieux Montpellier** (*open Tues–Sat 9.30–12 and 1.30–5; adm*) exhibits portraits of notables, and plans and views of the city from the 1500s on. At 7 Rue Jacques Cœur is the **Musée Languedocien** (*open daily exc Sun 2–5; guided tours on request; adm*), with Greek vases and prehistoric finds from the Hérault; an excellent collection of Romanesque sculpture; three 12th-century Islamic funeral steles, and to round things off a major collection of 16th- to 18th-century faïence made in Montpellier.

Western Quarters: Rue Foch and the Promenade du Peyrou

From the centre of the Ecusson, **Rue Foch** was sliced out in the 18th century as a grand formal boulevard, just missing a rare Jewish ritual bath, or **Mikveh**, at 1 Rue Barralerie (*to visit, contact the tourist office*). Dating from *c.* 1200, it was part of the synagogue in the midst of what was then a large, active Jewish quarter. Since the late 17th century the lofty west edge of Montpellier has been devoted to tons of mouldy fol-de-rol glorifying Louis XIV, beginning with an **Arc de Triomphe** (his triumphs include digging a canal, wrestling the English lion to the ground and conquering heresy with the bigoted Revocation of the Edict of Nantes). Beyond stretches the **Promenade du Peyrou**, a nice park spoiled by an equestrian statue of his megalomaniac majesty as big as the Trojan Horse. At the edge of the promontory stands the far more elegant **Château d'Eau**, a neoclassical temple designed to disguise the reservoir of the **Aqueduc St-Clément** (1771).

The waters feed the unicorn fountain in the nearby **Place de la Canourgue**, a charming 17th-century square. It looks down on the medieval monastery college of St-Benoît, built by papal architects from Avignon. Since 1795 it has been used as the Faculté de Médecine. Adjacent, the former monastic chapel has been Montpellier's **Cathédrale St-Pierre** ever since the see was transferred here in 1563, although its status didn't spare it the usual depredations in the Wars of Religion and the Revolution. The cathedral's distinction is its unusual porch, supported by two conical turrets. Beyond lies the lovely **Jardin des Plantes** (*open summer 12 noon–8pm; winter 12–6; closed Mon*). The oldest botanical garden in France, founded by a decree of Henri IV in 1593, it has several magnificent 400-year-old trees.

Day Trips from Montpellier

St-Guilhem-le-Désert

'Desert', in French or English, originally meant *deserted*, and this is still as lonely a region as it was when the hermit St Guilhem came here, in the reign of Charlemagne. The little village northwest of Montpellier is stretched on the edge of a ravine and has changed little since medieval times. The abbey **church** (*www.saint-guilhem-le-desert.com; open Mon–Sat 8–12 and 2–5.30, to 6.30 in summer; Sun 11–4, closed for Mass*) is a remarkably grand and lovely specimen of Lombard architecture. The interior, lofty and dark, has lost almost all of its decoration. Some fragments of frescoes survive in the side chapels, and niches in the pillars around the choir once held the relics of St-Guilhem and a bit of the True Cross, a gift from Charlemagne. The cloister is ruined, and most of its capitals have ended up at the Cloisters Museum in New York.

Aigues-Mortes

Every French history or geography textbook has a photo of Aigues-Mortes in it, and every Frenchman, most likely, carries in his mind the haunting picture – the great walls of the port where St-Louis sailed off to the Crusades, now marooned in the muck of the advancing Rhône delta. In 1241 the Camargue was the only stretch of Mediterranean coast held by France. To solidify this precarious strip, Louis IX (St Louis) began construction of a new port and a town, laid out in an irregular grid. His successor, Philip III, finished Aigues-Mortes and built its great walls. Being the only French Mediterranean port, by the late 13th century it was booming.

Aigues-Mortes means 'dead waters', and it proved to be a prophetic name. The sea deserted Aigues and, despite efforts to keep the harbour dredged, the port went into decline after 1350. Attempts to revive it in the 1830s failed, ensuring Aigues' demise, but allowing the works of Louis and Philip to survive undisturbed. Forgotten and nearly empty a century ago, Aigues now makes its living from tourists, and from salt; half of France's supply is collected here, at the enormous **Salins-du-Midi** pans south of town in the Petite Camargue (*call t 04 66 53 85 20 for organized visits in July and Aug*).

Aigues-Mortes' **walls** are over a mile in length, streamlined and almost perfectly rectangular. The impressive **Tour de Constance** (*entry inside the walls on Rue E. Zola; open daily 9.30–7 in summer; 10–5 in winter, last admission 4pm; adm*) is a huge cylindrical defence tower that guarded the northeastern land approach to the town. After

Getting There

Several **buses** daily travel from Montpellier's *gare routière* to the entrance to St-Guilhem village. They take about an hour.

Tourist Information

St-Guilhem-le-Désert ✉ 34150: At the *mairie*, Rue Font de Portal, t/f 04 67 57 44 33.

Eating Out

Auberge sur le Chemin, 38 Rue Font de Portal, t 04 67 57 75 05 (*moderate*). A medieval inn; tasty regional food.

★★Hostellerie St-Benoit, Aniane, t 04 67 57 71 63, f 04 67 57 47 10 (*inexpensive*). A comfortable motel with a pool and a good restaurant (*moderate*) specializing in trout and crayfish. *Closed mid-Dec–Feb.*

Getting There

Buses run daily to Aigues-Mortes from Montpellier's *gare routière* on Rue du Grand St-Jean. You can only get by **train** from Nîmes.

Tourist Information

Aigues-Mortes ✉ 30220: Porte de la Gardette, **t** 04 66 53 73 00, **f** 04 66 53 65 94, *www.ot-aiguesmortes.fr*. They offer historical tours of the town, all year round.

Eating Out

★★★St-Louis, 10 Rue de l'Amiral Courbet, **t** 04 66 53 72 68, **f** 04 66 53 75 92 (*moderate*). Gracious and welcoming, in a distinguished and beautifully furnished 18th-century building just off Place St-Louis. *Closed Jan–15 Mar*. Its popular restaurant, **L'Archère**

(*moderate*), is the best in town for steaks and seafood.

Les Arcades, 6 Bd Gambetta, **t** 04 66 53 81 13, **f** 04 66 53 75 46 (*moderate*). With nine attractive *chambres d'hôte*, and a good restaurant (*moderate*): *viande de taureau* and other local favourites.

La Camargue, 19 Rue République, **t** 04 66 53 86 88 (*moderate*). The Gypsy Kings got their start here, but even in their absence this is the liveliest and most popular place in town, with flamenco guitars strumming in the background; try to eat in the garden.

Maguelone, 38 Rue de la République, **t** 04 66 53 74 60 (*moderate*). With a menu based on local ingredients: *matelote d'anguilles*, *bourride de lotte* and a *St-Marcel au chocolat croustillant aux coings*. *Closed two weeks Jan*.

★La Tour de Constance, 1 Bd Diderot, **t** 04 66 53 83 50 (*cheap*). A good choice for food, outside the northern wall. *Closed Nov–Mar*.

the Crusades, the tower became a prison for Templars and later for Protestants. One of them, Marie Durand, spent 38 years here in unspeakable conditions. On her release in 1768, she left her credo, *register* ('resist' in Provençal), chiselled into the wall where it can still be seen. The tower to the south was used as a temporary mortuary in 1431, during the Hundred Years' War, when the Bourguignons, who held the city, were suddenly attacked and decimated by their arch-enemies, the Armagnacs. There were so many gruesome bodies that the Armagnacs simply stacked them in the tower, covering each with a layer of salt: hence 'the Tower of the Salted Bourguignons'.

Sète

Gritty, salty, workaday Sète (the 'Venice of Languedoc') is an attractive town, laced with canals, and livelier and more colourful than any place on the coast, save only Marseille. France's biggest Mediterranean fishing port, it also claims the Bassin de Thau, one of the largest lagoons along the Mediterranean, where there are salt-pans, and now huge oyster and mussel farms. Businesslike freighters from Sète carry French sunflower and rapeseed oil to every corner of the globe.

The bustling centre of Sète is its 'Grand Canal', the **Canal de Sète**, lined with quays where the ambience ranges from boat-yards and ship's chandlers to banks and boutiques. At the southern end of the canal, the **Vieux Port** handles most of the fishing fleet, as well as offering tourist fishing boats and excursions around the Thau lagoon. From the Vieux Port it's a bit of a climb up to the **Cimetière Marin**, where the Sètois poet Paul Valéry was buried in 1945. The adjacent **Musée Paul Valéry** (*open Wed–Mon, 10–12 and 2–6; closed Tues; adm*) contains exhibits on the poet, and on the history of Sète. Sète's other contribution to French culture, modern troubadour Georges Brassens (died 1981), is buried in the **Cimetière de Py**, under the Pierres

Getting There

Trains from Montpellier run directly to Sète; there are also buses (journey 1hr) from the gare routière.

Tourist Information

Sète ✉ 34200: 60 Grand-Rue Mario Roustan, t 04 67 74 71 71, f 04 67 46 17 54, www.ville-sete.fr.

Eating Out

***Grand Hôtel**, 17 Quai De Lattre de Tassigny, t 04 67 74 71 77, f 04 67 74 29 27 (moderate). Right on Sète's 'Grand Canal', it almost deserves its name, with plenty of the original décor from the 1920s. If you can't swing the Danieli in Venice, this will do fine. The hotel's **Rotonde** restaurant (t 04 67 74 86 14 (moderate) is refined and rewarding.

La Palangrotte, Rampe Paul Valéry, t 04 67 74 80 35. Quality seafood on the lower end of the Canal de Sète (expensive–moderate): grilled fish, and several styles of fish stew, including bourride sètoise. Closed Sun eve and Mon, except in July and Aug.

Terrasses du Lido, Rond-Point de Europe, along the Corniche road, t 04 67 51 39 60 (expensive–moderate). A pretty Provençal-style villa serving authentic Sètoise dishes from bourride to bouillabaisse. Closed Sun eve and Mon.

Le Chalut, 38 Quai Maximin Licciardi, t 04 67 74 81 52 (moderate). The seafood, including many sètois specialities, is as tasty as the décor. Closed Wed, and Jan.

Blanches, overlooking the Etang de Thau; the nearby **Espace Georges Brassens**, 67 Bd Camille Blanc (open 10–12 and 2–6, to 7pm July and Aug, closed Mon Oct–May; adm), has photos and exhibits relating to his life.

Agde, the 'Black Pearl of Languedoc'

If Sète is a brash young upstart, Agde, a lovely grey town, built almost entirely of volcanic basalt from nearby Mont St-Loup, has been watching the Hérault flow down to the sea for some 2,500 years. Founded by Greeks from Phocis, in medieval times it was an important port, despite occasional visits by Arab sea-raiders. The stern basalt **Cathédrale St-Etienne** was begun about 1150. Its fortress-like appearance is no accident; Agde's battling bishops used it as their citadel. From the quay along the Hérault, Rue Chassefière leads into the bourg, or medieval addition. On Rue de la Fraternité, the **Musée Agathois** (open Wed–Mon 10–12 and 2–7; closed Tues; adm) is the best of the south's town museums, encapsulating Agde's history in a few well-arranged rooms.

Getting There

Trains from Montpellier run directly to Agde.

Tourist Information

Agde ✉ 34300: Place Molière, t 04 67 94 29 68, f 04 67 94 03 50, ot-agde@wanadoo.fr.

Eating Out

La Galiote, 5 Place Jean Jaurès, t 04 67 94 45 58, f 04 67 94 41 33 (inexpensive). Some rooms in this old bishop's palace overlook the river; there's a bar full of English beer, and an excellent restaurant (moderate): seafood or lamb with thyme, and alcoholic ices between courses. Closed Nov and Feb.

***La Tamarissière**, 21 Quai Théophile Cornu (D32E), t 04 67 94 20 87, f 04 67 21 38 40 (expensive). A real charmer amid century-old parasol pines and roses, 4km down the Hérault, with quiet, stylish, well-equipped rooms, a pool, and the best restaurant in the area (expensive–moderate): fresh, colourful dishes such as saint-pierre baked with stuffed baby courgettes and saffron.

Behind the museum, Agde's market shares Place Gambetta with the church of **St André**, where important Church councils were held in the days of the Visigoths; however, of the present building, the oldest part is the 12th-century tower.

Cap d'Agde, 4km away, is the biggest beach playground in all Languedoc. One surprising attraction is a fine, small archaeological collection at the **Musée de l'Ephèbe** (*open Wed–Sat 9–12 and 2–6.30; Sun 2–6.30; closed Tues; adm*), the star of which is the *Ephèbe d'Agde*, a Hellenistic bronze of a boy, discovered in 1964.

Pézenas

If Carcassonne (*see* p.254) is Languedoc's medieval movie-set, Pézenas has often been used for costume dramas set in the time of Richelieu or Louis XIV. Few cities have a better ensemble of buildings from what the French used to call the 'Golden Age'. Roman *Piscenae* was known for wool, the best in Gaul. In the 1200s, it became a possession of the French crown. Later, the troubles of Béziers and Narbonne in the Albigensian Crusade and the Hundred Years' War would prove lucky for Pézenas, and the town replaced Narbonne as seat of the Estates-General of Languedoc after 1456. The royal governors of the region followed, bringing in their wake a whole wave of wealthy nobles, clerics and jurists, who rebuilt Pézenas in their own image, with new churches, convents, government buildings and scores of refined *hôtels particuliers*.

The tourist information office offers a brochure with a detailed **walking tour** of the town and its 70-odd listed historical buildings. From the Renaissance through to the 1700s, Pézenas really did develop and maintain a distinctive architectural manner; this can best be seen in the *hôtels particuliers*, with their lovely arcaded courtyards and external staircases. West of Place Gambetta are some of the best streets for peeking inside their courtyards: Rue Sabatini, Rue F. Oustrin, Rue de Montmorency and especially Rue de la Foire, *the* address of the time. The broad Cours Jean Jaurès, site of the market, also has its palaces.

Molière spent some seasons in Pézenas in the 1650s, when his troupe was employed by the governor, the Prince de Conti. On Rue Alliès, the **Musée de Vuillod-St-Germain** contains memorabilia of the playwright, along with collections of tapestries, faïence and paintings (*open 10–12 and 3–7, closed Sun am and Mon out of season; adm*).

Getting There

Frequent **buses** make the 1hr journey from Montpellier's *gare routière* to the town centre.

Tourist Information

Pézenas ✉ 34120: Place Gambetta, t 04 67 98 36 40, f 04 67 98 96 80.

Eating Out

Le Pré Saint-Jean, 18 Av du Maréchal Leclerc, t 04 67 98 15 31 (*moderate*). Has a pretty terrace and serves classics like stuffed squid and *carré d'agneau en croûte*. Closed Sun eve and Mon.

Côté Sud, Place 14 Juillet, t 04 67 09 41 74 (*cheap*). For a shellfish feast this place comes up with the goods. *Closed Mon and Dec.*

Maison Alary, 9 Rue St-Jean. Pézenas' spool-shaped *petits pâtés* take French visitors by surprise ('what is this, half-sweet and half-mutton?'). The recipe was introduced in 1770 by the Indian chef of Lord Clive, Governor of India, who spent a holiday in Pézenas, and they still make them here; eat them warm.

Touring from Nîmes and Montpellier

Day 1: Aigues-Mortes and Sommières

Morning: From Nîmes, take the A9 motorway to the exit at Gallargues-le-Montlieu and continue south on D979 for **Aigues-Mortes** (from Montpellier, get there via the D21 to Carnon-Plage, then the D62). This perfectly preserved walled medieval town (*see* pp.248–9), now miles from the sea, was the port from which the French under Saint Louis set off for the Crusades.

Lunch: Guitars, grills and seafood share the spotlight at **La Camargue**, 19 Rue de la République, t 04 66 53 86 88 (*moderate*), where the Gypsy Kings got their start. More seafood, cooked in the local style, can be had at **Maguelone**, 38 Rue de la République, t 04 66 53 74 60 (*moderate*). *Closed two weeks in Jan*.

Afternoon: From Aigues-Mortes, take the D979 north and then the D34 at Marsillargues for **Sommières**, a delightful village built around a Roman bridge. Here you can visit the medieval-Renaissance Château de Villevieille (*open June–Sept daily 2.30–7, rest of the year Sun only; adm*), or inspect the ruins of a Celtic *oppidum* at **Nages**, off the N40 towards Nîmes.

Dinner: In town, **L'Evasion** has outside tables on the marketplace, 6 Rue Capmal, t 04 66 77 74 64 (*inexpensive*), *closed Sun*; or else try **L'Olivette**, 11 Rue Abbé Fabre, t 04 66 80 97 71 (*moderate*), a favourite for regional cuisine. *Closed Tues and Wed*. The **Auberge du Pont Romain**, below, is also an excellent place to eat dinner.

Sleeping: Sommières has two very attractive choices: the ★★★**Auberge du Pont Romain**, by the river at 2 Av E. Jamais, t 04 66 80 00 58, f 04 66 80 31 52 (*moderate*), with a pool and a good restaurant, *closed mid Jan–mid-Mar*; and the ★★**Hôtel d'Orange**, Chemin du Château Fort, t 04 66 77 79 94, f 04 66 80 44 87 (*moderate*); six rooms in a 17th-century building with a pool.

Day 2: Into the Garrigue

Morning: Much of the eastern Hérault consists of this romantically empty lime-stone plateau of holly oaks and *maquis*; head westwards on the D1 from Sommières; at St-Bauzille you can choose to head north-wards for **Claret**, with a number of artisan glassmakers – they've been at it for centuries; the nearby village of **Ferrières** has a restored Renaissance glassworks. If you continue straight at St-Bauzille, you'll pass scenic **Pic St-Loup**, with signs along the way for vineyards and a *dégustation* of Côteaux de Languedoc wines.

Lunch: Whichever way you go, wind up in **St-Martin-de-Londres** for lunch. Cêpes and seafood are usually on the menu at **La Pastourelle**, 350 Chemin de la Prairie, t 04 67 55 72 78 (*moderate*). *Closed Tue eve and Wed*.

Afternoon: However tiny, St-Martin is a gorgeous medieval village with a fine Romanesque church; just to the south at **Cambous**, you can visit a fascinating recon-struction of a Neolithic village 5,000 years old (*open July–Sept 2–6, rest of the year weekends only 2–6; closed Mon and Thurs; adm*)

Dinner: For a treat, take on the formidable gourmet menus and the best of the local wines at **Les Muscardins**, 19 Route des Cévennes, t 04 67 55 75 90 (*expensive*). *Closed Mon, Tues lunch and mid-Feb–mid-March*. Otherwise, the two accommodations below also have good restaurants.

Sleeping: Book ahead for the three elegant rooms at the ★★★**Hostellerie Le Vieux Chêne**, Causse de la Selle, west of Frouzet on the D122, t 04 67 73 11 00, f 04 67 73 10 54 (*inex-pensive*). *Closed mid Nov–Feb*. Just south of St Martin at Argelliers, the **Auberge du Saugras**, t 04 67 55 08 71, f 04 67 55 04 65 (*cheap*) has several rooms in a stone *mas* (traditional farmhouse). *Must book*.

Day 3: Ganges and the Cirque de Navacelles

Morning: North from St-Martin, the D986 will take you to the edge of the Cévennes moun-tains. Five km before you reach the peculiar old Protestant town of **Ganges**, you'll see signs for the Grotte des Demoiselles (*open daily summer 9–12 and 2–6.30, July and Aug 9–6, winter 9.30–12 and 2–5; adm*), one of France's most spectacular caves, visited by an underground funicular.

Lunch: In Ganges' old town, **Joselyn Mélodie** is an intimate place with dining on the terrace; Place Fabre d'Olivet, t 04 67 73 66 02 (*inexpensive*). *Closed Wed*.

Afternoon: Ganges is the gateway to an area of outstanding natural beauty. An afternoon excursion down the D25 west will take you into the long **Gorges de la Vis**, which ends in the colossal, crater-like formation called the **Cirque de Navacelles**.

Dinner: Back in Ganges, the **Domaine de Blancardy**, 7km east of town on the D999 at Moules-et-Baucels, t 04 67 73 94 94 (*inexpensive*), is a real *ferme-auberge* where they make their own *confits de canard* and pâté.

Sleeping: Gorniès, on the edge of the Gorges, has the luxury choice in this area: the ★★★★**Château de Madières**, t 04 67 73 84 03, f 04 67 73 55 71 (*expensive*), with park, pool, and rooms in a 14th-century castle. *Closed Nov–Mar*. In Ganges, there is the simple and welcoming ★★**Hôtel de la Poste**, t 04 67 73 83 79 (*inexpensive*).

Day 4: St-Guilhem-le-Désert

Morning: From Ganges, take the lonely D4 southwards, following the Hérault river. In a landscape made for saints and hermits, it will lead you to **St-Guilhem-le-Désert**, with its remarkable 11th-century abbey church (*see p.248; open daily 8–12 and 2–5.30, till 6 in summer; Sun 8–11 and 2.30–5.30*).

Lunch: Dining in St-Guilhem tends to be simple: try the **Taverne de l'Escuelle**, Place de la Liberté, t 04 67 57 72 05 (*inexpensive*), or the **Auberge sur le Chemin**, 38 Rue Fond du Portail, t 04 67 57 75 05 (*inexpensive*).

Afternoon: Spend a few hours touring the villages of this unique corner of the Hérault: just south of St-Guilhem on the D4, there's another beautiful cave to explore, the **Grotte de Clamouse** (*open daily 10–5, till 7 in summer; adm*). **Aniane**, another village with a monastic past, retains a sumptuous Baroque church, while some of the villages, like **St-Saturnin**, seem to have changed little since the Middle Ages. Finish the tour in **Clermont-l'Hérault**.

Dinner: In Clermont's medieval centre, **L'Arlequin**, Place St-Paul, t 04 67 96 37 47 (*moderate–inexpensive*) is good for *confits*

and smoked trout. *Closed Sat lunch and Sun eve*. There's another filling farm restaurant on the D8 west of town, the **Ferme-Auberge Vallée du Salagou**, t 04 67 88 13 39 (*inexpensive*). *Closed Tues eve*.

Sleeping: Clermont-l'Hérault offers the widest choices. ★★**La Source**, at Villeneuvette 4km southwest, t 04 67 96 05 07, f 04 67 96 90 09 (*inexpensive*) is a rural retreat with pool and tennis. *Closed mid-Nov–5 Mar*. South of town is the *Logis de France* ★★ Sarac, Rte de Nebian, t 04 67 96 06 81, f 04 67 88 07 30 (*inexpensive*). *Closed mid Nov–Mar*.

Day 5: Back to the Mediterranean

Morning: From Clermont l'Hérault, the N9 and N113 will bring you back, with a possible detour at **Montagnac** for another fine medieval church, the **Abbaye de Valmagne**, now France's fanciest wine cellar. The road meets the sea at **Mèze**, a fishing village with a Gallo-Roman villa to explore.

Lunch: At Bouzigues, just east of Mèze, the **Côte Bleue**, Av Louis Tudesc, t 04 67 78 30 87 (*moderate*) is a great place to look over the Bassin de Thau while you sample its shellfish and langoustines. *Closed Tues eve, Wed, and Feb*.

Afternoon: You may dedicate the afternoon to the beaches, around **Frontignan**, or further up the coastal N112 at the lively resort of **Palavas-les-Flots** or the quieter **Maguelone**. Wind it up, east of Montpellier, at the bizarre, futuristic resort called **La Grande Motte**, full of space-age 1960s buildings.

Dinner: La Grande Motte has more than its fair share of seafood palaces; one of the finest is the **Alexandre**, Esplanade de la Capitainerie, t 04 67 56 63 63 (*expensive*). *Closed Jan, Feb, Sun eve and Mon*. For less, you can do well at a local favourite, **La Cuisine du Marché**, 89 Rue Casino, t 04 67 29 90 11 (*moderate*). *Closed Mon and Tues*.

Sleeping: This popular resort can be pricey; right on the waterfront is the ★★★★**Grand M'Hôtel**, Quartier Point Zéro, t 04 67 29 13 13, f 04 67 29 14 74 (*expensive*), with a thalassotherapy centre. A more modest choice is ★★★ **Le Quetzal**, Allée des Jardins, t 04 67 56 61 10, f 04 67 56 86 34 (*moderate*).

Carcassonne

It was market day, and rustic villeins in coarse wool tunics were offering hung pheasants and great round cheeses from their wooden carts. Geese honked from cages made of twigs and rushes, while pigs and hounds poked about in the cobbled gutters. Then the director and his entourage appeared over the drawbridge. 'Lovely, everyone, but we'll want more sheep; lots more sheep!'

Plenty of obscure costume dramas have been shot here, drawn by Viollet-le-Duc's 19th-century romantic restoration. Even without pigs, Carcassonne is the Middle Ages come to life. The people of the city do their best to heighten the atmosphere every August for the two-week festival called the *Médiévales*, with costume, music and even jousts under the walls. Reality intrudes in the history of the place. Today a dour manufacturing town, Carcassonne was once the strategic key to the Midi; the castle built here by Saint Louis was a barrier greater than the Pyrenees to invaders.

Getting to Carcassonne

Ryanair (*see* p.6) flies directly from London Stansted.

Getting from the Airport

There is a regular **shuttle bus** to the centre of town and the train station, costing €0.90. A **taxi** costs approximately €10.

Getting Around

The **train** station is on Av du Maréchal Joffre at the northern edge of the Ville Basse. The *gare routière* is a few streets south of the station, on Bd de Varsovie (t 04 68 25 13 74).

To get up to the Cité from the lower town, take the no.4 city bus (every 30 minutes) from the train station or from Place Gambetta, near the tourist office.

Car Hire

Budget, 5 Bd Omer Sarrault, t 04 68 72 31 31. Cars are banned in the Cité during the day. **Europcar**, 7 Bd Omer Sarraut, t 04 68 25 05 09.

Tourist Information

Carcassonne: 15 Bd Camille Pelletan, opposite Place Gambetta, in the centre of the Ville Basse, t 04 68 10 24 30, f 04 68 10 24 38, *www.carcassonne-tourisme.com*. Also in the Porte Narbonnaise in the Cité (*summer only*), t 04 68 10 24 35, f 04 68 10 24 37.

Market Days

Place Carnot: Tues, Thurs and Sat.

Shopping

The main modern shopping areas are in the **Ville Basse**, around **Place Carnot** and **Rue Courtejaire**. Crafts and local produce are more readily available in the **Cité**, where shops tend to stay open until 9pm in summer.

Where to Stay

Carcassonne ✉ 11000

Stay in the more expensive Cité if you can.

****Hôtel de la Cité, Place St-Nazaire, t 04 68 71 98 71, f 04 68 71 50 15 (*luxury*). In a pretty garden right under the walls of the Cité, this hotel occupies the former episcopal palace, grandly restored in 1909, with marble baths, pool, restaurant (*expensive*). *Closed Dec.*

***Bristol, 7 Av Foch, t 04 68 25 07 24, f 04 68 25 71 89 (*moderate*). A grand 19th-century hotel near the station, with rooms overlooking the Canal du Midi. Restaurant. *Closed Dec–April.*

***Hôtel du Donjon, Rue du Comte Roger, t 04 68 11 23 00, f 04 68 25 06 60, *www.hotel.donjon.fr* (*moderate*). In a charming old mansion of the Cité, with a small garden and a fine restaurant.

***Trois Couronnes, 2 Rue des 3 Couronnes, t 04 68 25 36 10, f 04 68 25 92 92 (*moderate*).

After running north down from the Pyrenees, the river Aude makes a sharp right turn for the sea, providing not only an easy natural route into the mountains, but also one across the 'French isthmus', between the Mediterranean and the Atlantic. The river's angle is an obvious site for a fortress; there seems to have been one nearby since the 8th century BC. From 1084 to 1209 Carcassonne enjoyed a glorious period of wealth and culture under the Trencavels, a family who were also viscounts of Béziers and Nîmes, and very sympathetic to the Cathars. Under them the cathedral and the Château Comtal were begun. Simon de Montfort, realizing the importance of the town, made it one of his first stops in the Crusade of 1209. The last Viscount Trencavel was captured and probably poisoned by Montfort, who declared himself viscount.

When France gobbled up the province of Roussillon in 1659, this mighty bastion no longer had any military purpose and the Cité gradually decayed into a half-abandoned slum. It was the writer Prosper Mérimée, France's Inspector-General of Historic Monuments in the 1830s, who called attention to this sad state of affairs. Viollet-le-

A modern hotel by the river in the lower town, which makes up for its unprepossessing appearance with a stupendous view of the Cité, and a very good restaurant.

★★★**Auberge du Château de Cavanac**, Cavanac, 4km south on the Rte St-Hilaire, **t** 04 68 79 61 04, **f** 04 68 79 79 67 (*moderate*). A big old farmhouse in a quiet garden, with an excellent restaurant in the former stables which serves a unique five-course menu with wine. *Closed mid-Jan–mid-Feb, and Mon; restaurant only open eves, closed Sun.*

★★**Terminus**, 2 Av Maréchal Joffre, **t** 04 68 25 25 00, **f** 04 68 72 53 09 (*moderate*). For a touch of class; it's been used as a set in French films. Try to get one of the rooms that have not been 'renovated'. *Closed Dec–Mar.*

★★**Hôtel du Pont-Vieux**, 32 Rue Trivalle, **t** 04 68 25 24 99, **f** 04 68 47 62 71 (*inexpensive*). One of the closest hotels to the Cité, and one of the best. No restaurant.

★**Astoria**, 18 Rue Tourtel, **t** 04 68 25 31 38, **f** 04 68 71 34 14 (*cheap*). A friendly, family-run place, with a comfy *décor à l'anglaise*.

★★**Central**, 27 Bd Jean Jaurès, **t** 04 68 25 03 84, **f** 04 68 72 46 41 (*cheap*). One of the cheapest, but quite nice.

Eating Out

Le Languedoc, 32 Allée Iéna, **t** 04 68 25 22 17 (*expensive–moderate*). A popular restaurant with a patio, serving regional cuisine but particularly famed for its cassoulet with *confit de canard* and salad of foie gras. *Closed Sun eve and Mon.*

Château St-Martin Trencavel, Montredon (take Bd Jean Jaurès to Rue A. Marty and follow the signs), **t** 04 68 71 09 53 (*expensive–moderate*). If you have a car, this is situated in a handsome *gentilhommière* with a huge terrace over a park, offering a choice of traditional dishes and very seasonal fresh market cuisine; delicious seafood salad. *Closed Wed.*

Brasserie le Donjon, Hôtel du Donjon (*see above*), **t** 04 68 25 95 72 (*moderate*). Dedicates itself to the best of Languedoc cooking – *cassoulet* reaches new heights. *Closed Sun eve and Nov–Mar.*

Jardins de la Tour, 11 Rue Porte d'Aude, **t** 04 68 25 71 24 (*moderate*). A pretty, idiosyncratic restaurant with garden dining and authentic regional dishes and fish. *Booking advised in high season. Closed Sun, Mon and Nov–mid-Dec.*

Dame Carcas, 3 Place du Château, **t** 04 68 71 23 23 (*moderate*). Delicious wood-fired food (*eves only*). *Closed Jan–mid-Feb, and Mon.*

L'Œil, 32 Rue de Lorraine, **t** 04 68 25 64 81 (*moderate*). Down in the Ville Basse, you can feast on smoked duck *magret* and southwest fare. *Closed Sat lunch and Sun, and 1–15 Aug.*

In most of Carcassonne's pâtisseries you can sample the local favourite, *boulets de Carcassonne*, with peanuts and honey.

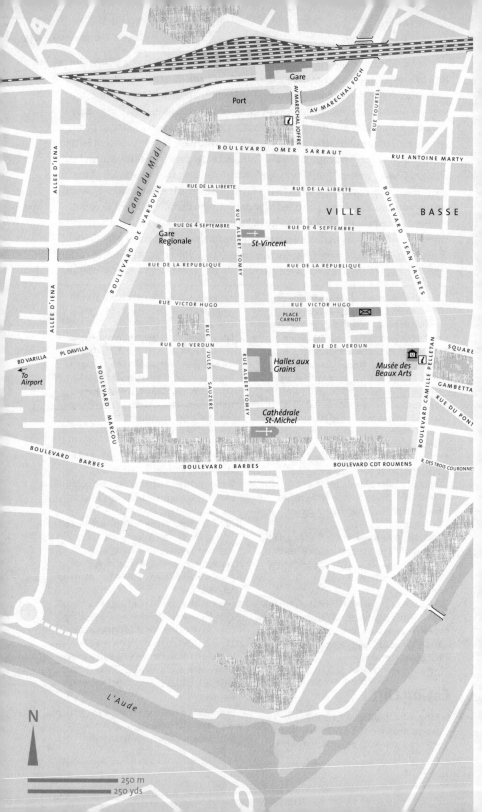

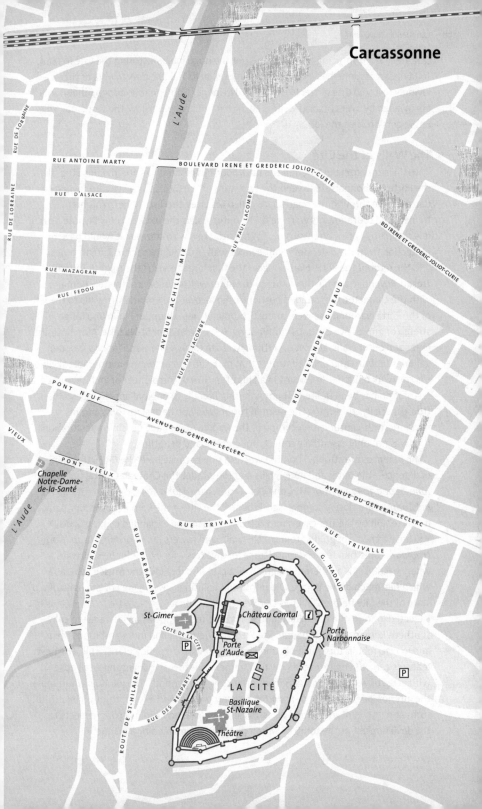

Duc, fresh from sprucing up Narbonne, got the huge job of restoring the Cité in 1844. Today's Carcassonne has a split personality: up on its hill, the pink towers of the lovingly restored Cité glitter like a dream. No longer impregnable, its 750 inhabitants are invaded by over 200,000 visitors each year, while down below, the workaday Ville Basse gets on with the job.

The Walls of the Cité

Most visitors come in through the back door, by the car parks and the bus stop, at the **Porte Narbonnaise**. Between the two walls of the Cité, you can circumnavigate Carcassonne through the open space called **Les Lices**, the 'lists', where knights trained, and tournaments were held. The **outer wall** is the work of Louis IX; note how it is completely open on the inside, so that attackers who stormed it would have no protection from the defenders on the **inner wall** – parts date back to Roman times.

To the right of the Porte Narbonnaise, the first large tower is the mighty **Tour du Trésau**. Beyond it, the northern side of the inner wall is almost completely Roman, with the characteristic rounded bastions used all over the Empire. The walls to the left of the Porte Narbonnaise were almost completely rebuilt under Philip III, a long stretch of impressive bastions culminating in the great **Tour St-Nazaire**. Atop both the inner and outer walls, almost everything you see today – the crenellations, wooden galleries (*hourds*) and pointed turrets that make up Carcassonne's memorable skyline – is the work of Viollet-le-Duc. As in all his other works, the pioneer of architectural restoration has been faulted for not adhering literally to original appearances. This is true, especially concerning the pointed turrets and northern slate roofs, but his romantic, 19th-century appreciation of the Middle Ages made possible a restoration that was not only essentially correct, but creative and beautiful.

The defences are strongest on the western side because here, the Cité's three lines of defence – the outer and inner walls and the citadel, the **Château Comtal** (*open June–Sept 9.30–7.30; April, May and Oct 9.30–6; Nov–Mar 9.30–5; closed most public hols; adm*) – are closely compressed. Probably the site of the Roman governors' palace, it was rebuilt by the Trencavels for their own palace, and expanded by King Louis IX . You have a choice of **guided tours** of the walls and towers (*40 or 90mins, usually on the hour*). Louis' builders laid many traps for invaders – for example the stairways where each riser is a different height. Your ticket also includes the **Musée Lapidaire**, which fills much of the palace. Old prints and paintings give an idea of the half-ruined state of the Cité before Viollet-le-Duc went to work on it.

Erected in 1096, the Cité's **Basilique St-Nazaire** took shape as an austere, typically southern Romanesque cathedral. The French conquerors had more ambitious plans, and in 1270 rebuilt the transepts and choir in glorious, perpendicular Gothic. The best features can be seen from outside: two tremendous rose windows and a tall apse with acres of windows and gargoyles projecting like cannons. The windows illuminate the interior (*open summer 9–12 and 2–7, winter 9.30–12 and 2–5.30*) through beautiful 16th- and 17th-century stained glass. In the right aisle, you can pay your respects to the devil himself, at the **tomb of Simon de Montfort**, marked by a plaque.

The Ville Basse

Before Louis IX, the Cité was surrounded by long-established suburbs. In 1240 these were occupied by Raymond Trencavel, son of the last viscount. With the help of the townspeople, he besieged the Cité and nearly took it back. Louis pardoned the rebels, but did find it necessary to knock their houses down, to deprive any future attackers of cover. To replace the old *bourg*, he laid out a new town across the river, in the strict (and here, rather drab) grid pattern of a *bastide* (*see* below). This medieval new town, one of hundreds constructed by the French and English rulers during the Hundred Years' War, has gradually replaced the Cité as the centre of modern Carcassonne.

Descending from the Cité through the Porte d'Aude, you'll pass some streets of houses that managed to creep back despite the royal decree. Rue Trivalle, with a pair of elegant Renaissance *hôtels particuliers*, leads down to the long, 14th-century **Pont-Vieux**. At the far end, there once was a sort of triumphal arch. Now there remains only the **chapel of Notre-Dame-de-la-Santé**, built in 1538. The Ville Basse proper begins two streets further down, with a circle of boulevards that replaced the old walls. In 1355, during the Hundred Years' War, the walls failed to keep out the Black Prince, who burned the *bastide* to the ground. Only the street plan survived and, at the north and south ends, two huge Gothic churches: **St-Vincent** and **St-Michel**.

A *bastide* was always built around a central market square (here, **Place Carnot**), while one street over, off Rue Verdun, you can see the handsome 18th-century **Halles aux Grains**. You can learn all about the famous heretics at the Centre for Cathar Studies in the **Maison des Mémoires**, 53 Rue de Verdun (*open Tues–Sat 9–12 and 2–6*); this was the home of Carcassonne's contribution to Surrealism, Joë Bousquet, and there's a display about him, and another organization dedicated to the study of folk traditions in the Aude. At 1 Rue du Verdun, the 17th-century Présidial houses the **Musée des Beaux-Arts** (*open mid-Sept–mid-June Tues–Sat 10–12 and 2–6; rest of year Wed-Sun 10–12 and 2–6*), with paintings and decorative arts.

Day Trips from Carcassonne

Narbonne

The Roman colony of *Colonia Narbo Martius*, a good site for a trading port along the newly built Via Domitia, was founded in 118 BC. It rapidly became the most important city of southern Gaul, renowned for its beauty and wealth. In the 12th century, Narbonne entered its second golden age, which lasted until the 14th century when wars, plagues and the harbour's silting-up led to its ruin. By the end of the century, the city had shrunk to a mere market town. Now Languedoc's capital, Narbonne has a local economy largely fuelled on wine. With its impressive medieval monuments, boulevards and lively streets, it is quite a happy and contented place, with an excellent museum, and the best cathedral in the south.

Take Rue Jean Jaurès from near the train and bus stations and you'll be following the **Canal de la Robine** into the centre of the city, lined with a delightful park called the **Jardin Entre Deux Villes**. Narbonne's centre is the busy **Place de l'Hôtel de Ville**. Facing

Getting There

There are regular **train** connections from Carcassonne (11 a day). The railway station is just north of the centre, on Bd Frédéric Mistral. **Buses** also run Mon–Fri from Carcassonne's *gare routière* to the one in Narbonne.

Tourist Information

Narbonne ✉ 11100: Place Roger Salengro, t 04 68 65 15 60, f 04 68 65 59 12.

Market Day

Narbonne: Outdoor market, Thurs.

Eating Out

Table St Crescent, Rte de Perpignan, t 04 68 41 37 37 (*expensive*). One of Narbonne's top restaurants is outside town at the Palais du Vin. A vine-covered terrace shelters a modern stylish establishment specializing in the best regional wines and dishes. *Closed Sun eve and Mon.*

Alsace, 2 Av Pierre Sémard, t 04 68 65 10 24 (*expensive–moderate*). This friendly brasserie with a verandah is a good source of fresh seafood.

Le Petit Comptoir, 4 Bd du Maréchal Joffre, t 04 68 42 30 35 (*moderate*). For more adventurous dishes. *Closed Sun and Mon in winter, Sun in summer.*

Le Billot, 22 Rue de l'Ancienne Porte de Béziers, t 04 68 32 70 88 (*moderate*). East of the centre, near a delightful park called the Place Thérèse et Léon Blum, specializes in meat. *Closed Mon, Tues lunch, and Aug.*

Restaurant de la Gare, 5 Av Pierre Sémard, t 04 68 32 66 02 (*moderate*). Grilled fish, oysters and seafood *brochettes*. *Closed Wed.*

the square, the twin façades of the **Palais des Archevêques** were blessed with a romantic Gothic restoration by the master himself, Viollet-le-Duc, in the 1840s. The passage between the two buildings (the Palais Neuf on the left, and the Palais Vieux on the right) leads to a small courtyard, and the entrances to Narbonne's two excellent museums, the **Musée d'Art et d'Histoire** and the **Musée Archéologique** (*both open Oct–Mar Tues–Sun 10–12 and 2–5; April–Sept daily 9.30–12.15 and 2–6*). The Musée d'Art et d'Histoire's Grande Galerie contains an intense *St Jerome* by Salvator Rosa, a Canaletto and, among many Dutch and Flemish pictures, a *Wedding Dance* by Pieter Breughel the Younger. In the Salle des Faïences are 18th-century ceramics. It is only luck that made Nîmes the 'French Rome', while only one of Narbonne's monuments from the same period has survived. There is, however, no shortage of remaining bits and pieces, and the best of them have been assembled in the Musée Archéologique.

Narbonne's one Roman monument is a warehouse or **Horreum**, on Rue Rouget de Lisle (*open 9–12.15 and 2–6, closed Mon Oct–mid-May; adm*). Typical of the state-run warehouses of any Roman city, this is the only complete one anywhere.

Narbonne's magnificent **Cathédrale St-Just** can be entered through the fine 14th-century cloister, a Gothic quadrangle with leering gargoyles. A better way, though, is to circumnavigate the huge bulk of the cathedral and palace complex towards the west front, and the Cour St-Eutrope, a spacious square that occupies the unfinished two-thirds of the cathedral itself. Inside, the best features are in the ambulatory and its chapels. Near the altar, facing the chapels, are two remarkable archiepiscopal tombs. The Tomb of Cardinal Briçonnet (1514) has a mix of Renaissance refinement and ghoulish, grinning skeletons, typical of that age. The other, the Tomb of Cardinal Pierre de Jugie, is an exquisite Gothic work of 1376. The ambulatory chapels are illuminated by lovely 14th-century glass; and the central Chapelle de la Vierge has something really special, unique polychrome reliefs of the late 1300s. Ruined and covered in a Baroque remodelling of 1732, these were rediscovered in the last century, and are currently being restored.

Across the river (now across the canal) is Narbonne's medieval extension, the **Bourg**. Behind the city's popular covered **market**, the deconsecrated 13th-century church of Notre-Dame-de-Lamourguier now houses the **Musée Lapidaire**, a large collection of architectural fragments from ancient Narbonne, displayed at random (*open July and Aug 9.30–12.15 and 2–6; adm*). The **Basilique St-Paul-Serge** was first built in the 5th century and dedicated to the first bishop of Narbonne. The present building was begun in 1229, one of the first in the south to adopt the new Gothic architecture.

Limoux

Even before you notice the vineyards, the civilized landscapes suggest wine. Limoux, the capital, is an attractive town, with a medieval bridge across the Aude, the **Pont-Neuf**; this meets the apse and steeple of **St-Martin**, a good piece of Gothic, if anachronistic – although the church was begun in the 14th century, most of the work is from three centuries later. The centre is the arcaded **Place de la République**. Like Carcassonne's Ville Basse, Limoux was a *bastide*, and this was its market square; the streets of the old town around it make a pleasant stroll. Rue Blanquerie, named for the tanneries that once were Limoux's main business, is one of the streets with 15th- and 16th-century houses, like the 1549 **Hôtel de Clercy**, with a lovely and unusual courtyard of interlocking arches.

On the Promenade du Tivoli, a broad boulevard that replaced the town walls, the tourist office shares the home of the Petiet family with the **Musée Petiet** (*open July and Aug daily 9–7; rest of year Tues–Sun 10–12 and 2–5; adm*). It contains a collection of 19th-century paintings, and canvases by the museum's founder, Marie Petiet, a talented, neglected artist of the 1880s. A woman painter, and a woman's painter, her work brings a touch of magic to very domestic subjects, nowhere better than in the serene, luminous composition called *Les Blanchisseuses* (The Washerwomen). Limoux's other attraction sounds like something P. T. Barnum would think up: **Catharama** (*47 Av F. d'Eglantine; open Easter–1 Nov 10.30–12 and 2–6, July–Aug continuously 10.30–7; adm*), a 30-minute audiovisual spectacular on the history of the Cathars.

Getting There

4–5 **trains** run daily from Carcassonne; or take a **bus** from the *gare routière* to Limoux's Promenade des Marronniers, journey ½hr.

Tourist Information

Limoux ✉ 11300: Promenade Tivoli, **t** 04 68 31 11 82, **f** 04 68 31 87 14.

Market Day

Limoux: Friday.

Eating Out

★★★**Grand Hôtel Moderne et Pigeon**, Place Général Leclerc, **t** 04 68 31 00 25. The restaurant (*expensive–moderate*) is good, appropriately serving *magret de pigeon*. *Restaurant closed Sat lunch and Mon.*

Maison de la Blanquette, 46 Promenade Tivoli, **t** 04 68 31 01 63 (*moderate*). Offers wine sampling and home cooking, with an emphasis on the local specialities, from Limoux's charcuterie to *confits. Closed Wed.*

Touring from Carcassonne

Day 1: The Montagne Noire

Morning: This wild, brooding little massif was for a long time almost inaccessible, and it remains quite unspoiled. Enter it on the D201-101, where you'll encounter its landmark, the four ruined castles called the **Châteaux de Lastours**. Continue on through the pretty half-timbered village of **Mas Cabardès**, and westwards to **Brousses-et-Villaret**, where you can visit an old local craft in action: papermaking, in an 18th-century mill (*tours at 11, 3, 4, and 5 in season; adm*).

Lunch: Mountain trout are popular here, and especially good at **La Cascade** in Brousses-et-Villaret, **t** 04 68 26 66 71 (*inexpensive*). Just to the south in Montolieu, there's more local cooking under the trees at **Le Floréal**, by the church, **t** 04 68 24 82 09 (*inexpensive*).

Afternoon: Retrace your route through Mas-Cabardès, and continue on the D9 eastwards past the top of the massif, the Pic de Nore. Then go down the D112, through the scenic Gorges de la Clamoux; along the way it passes an uncanny abyss, the **Gouffre Géant de Cabrespine** (*open Mar–Nov 2–6, continuously in summer; adm*) At the end of the road, the D620 and D11 will take you to **Rieux-Minervois**.

Dinner: Most of the restaurants in this little-visited region are in the hotels, and two of the best bets here are in the hotels listed below.

Sleeping: Rieux has the ★★ **Logis de Merinville**, Av Georges Clémenceau, **t** 04 68 78 12 49 (*inexpensive*), an atmospheric stone inn in the village centre. *Closed Feb–Mar*. Just west in Peyriac-Minervois, ★★★**Château de Violet**, Route de Pepieux, **t** 04 68 78 10 42, **f** 04 68 78 30 01 (*expensive–moderate*) is a lovely restored farmhouse with a pool, gardens and restaurant. Book.

Day 2: The Minervois and the Canal du Midi

Morning: Before you start off, be sure to inspect Rieux's attraction, a unique seven-sided church built with a touch of medieval mysticism. The Minervois is another ruggedly beautiful *pays*, with a wine that

has been growing steadily in reputation. From Peyriac, take the D35 and D168 northeast past the **Chapelle de Centeilles**, with medieval frescoes, to the region's tiny, charming capital, **Minerve**, whose dramatically sited medieval castle relic has become a peaceful, unambitious tourist attraction, set among its medieval alleys.

Lunch: In Minerve, the **Relais Chantovent**, 17 Grand Rue, **t** 04 68 91 14 18 (*moderate*) offers truffles and cêpes on a terrace overlooking the gorge. *Closed mid-Nov–mid Mar, Sun and Mon*. Just to the south in Beaufort, grilled meats and fish are the speciality at the **Auberge de St-Martin**, **t** 04 68 91 16 18 (*moderate*). *Closed Mon*.

Afternoon: From Minerve, the D10 leads through the heart of the wine region, south to **Olonzac**. From here you can follow the delightful, tree-lined **Canal du Midi** (you'll need a local map) and its sleepy villages: **Argens-Minervois**, **Le Somail** with a museum of hats, **Quarante** with a fine Romanesque church, **Capestang** and **Poilhes**. After that come the ruins of a pre-Roman town with a fascinating museum, the **Oppidum d'Ensérune** (*open daily 9–12 and 2–6, Nov–Mar 10–12 and 2–4, July–Aug 9.30–7; adm*)

Dinner: Nearby Poilhes has the excellent **La Tour Sarrasine**, Bd du Canal, **t** 04 67 93 41 31 (*expensive–moderate*). *Closed Sun eve out of season and Mon*.

Sleeping: Close to the oppidum in Nissan-lez-Ensérune, there's the antiquated charm of the ★★ **Résidence**, 35 Av de la Cave, **t** 04 67 37 00 63 (*inexpensive*). *Closed mid-Dec–mid-Feb*. Just to the north in Colombiers is the more modern ★★**Via Domitia**, **t** 04 687 35 62 63, **f** 04 67 35 62 00 (*inexpensive*).

Day 3: Béziers and Beaches

Morning: Just a few miles down the N113, **Béziers'** landmark, the striking hilltop Gothic cathedral, is visible from almost anywhere on the coastal plain. This city also has three interesting museums, including some fine painting in the Musée Fabreget behind the cathedral on Place de la Révolution (*open Tues–Sun 9–12 and 2–5; July and Aug Tues–Sun 9–12 and 2–6; adm*).

Lunch: Choices in the centre range from the popular **Bistrot des Halles**, Place de la Madeleine, **t** 04 67 28 30 46 (*moderate–inexpensive*), *closed Sun and Mon*, to the imaginative Mediterranean cooking at **Le Framboisier**, 12 Rue Boieldieu, **t** 04 67 49 90 00 (*expensive*). *Closed Sun and Mon.*

Afternoon: From Béziers, a quick hop south down the A9 motorway (Narbonne exit) takes you to the **Montagne de la Clape**, once an island and now a lovely little hideaway for the Narbonnais, complete with its own tiny AOC wine area . Have a look at the sailors' church of Notre-Dame-des-Auzils, off the D32, or just pass through to the broad beaches at **Narbonne-Plage** or **Gruissan**, an old fishing village set in concentric rings around a ruined 13th-century castle, surrounded by lagoons and salt pans, and a famous colony of beach houses on stilts, setting for the film *Betty Blue*.

Dinner: There's no shortage of seafood in these parts. In Gruissan, the restaurant of the **Hôtel Corail** (*see* below) is known for its *bouillabaisse* (*moderate–inexpensive*); or else try **L'Estagnol**, **t** 04 68 49 01 27 (*expensive–moderate*), in a converted fisherman's cottage. *Closed Oct–Mar.*

Sleeping: Gruissan has a number of choices, including the ★★**Corail** at the port, Quai Ponant, **t** 04 69 49 04 43, **f** 04 68 49 62 89 (*inexpensive*). *Closed Nov–Jan*. For something special, stay at a working wine estate with a group of small museums, the **Domaine d'Hospitalet**, on the D168 in the Montagne de la Clape, **t** 04 68 45 34 47, **f** 04 68 45 23 49 (*expensive–moderate*). *Closed Jan–Feb.*

Day 4: Across the Corbières

Morning: From Gruissan head west to Narbonne, and then for once we'll give you a choice of attractions. South on the N9 is the zoo and safari-park **Réserve Africaine** at Sigean (*open daily in summer 9–6.30, winter 9–4; adm*); or else, west on the N113 and D613, you can visit the medieval Cistercian **Abbaye de Fontfroide** (*guided tours every half-hour from 10–5, 9.30–5 in July–Aug; adm*). Whichever you choose, find the D611 and follow it southwards into the heart of this starkly beautiful region; after you pass

the impressive castle of **Aguilar**, turn west down the D14 for **Cucugnan**.

Lunch: There's not much choice in these wild spaces, but Cucugnan's **Auberge du Vigneron**, **t** 04 68 45 03 00 (*moderate*) is a treat, with a restaurant in a former wine cellar. *Closed Mon, and mid-Dec–mid-Feb.*

Afternoon: The Corbières is jam-packed with cloud-top castles, and Cucugnan sits between the two most spectacular: the Cathar stronghold of **Quéribus** (*open daily 10–6; winter weekends only; adm*) and **Peyrepertuse** (*open daily 10–7, July and Aug 9–8; adm*). Continue west on the D14, then the D7, D117 and D109 – a route through two wild and beautiful gorges, the Gorges de Galamus and the Défilé de Pierre-Lys, to **Quillan**.

Dinner and sleeping: Quillan has two modest but comfortable hotels: ★★★**La Chaumière**, 25 Bd Charles de Gaulle, **t** 04 68 20 17 90, **f** 04 68 20 13 55 (*inexpensive*), with cosy rooms and gratifying mountain cooking, *closed Dec–Feb*; and the more modern, quiet ★★**Pierre Lys**, Av de Carcassonne, **t** 04 68 20 08 65 (*inexpensive*), also with a good restaurant. *Closed mid Nov–mid Dec.*

Day 5: Along the Aude

Morning: From Quillan, the D118 follows the Aude River northwards; it will take you through **Espéraza**, with a dinosaur museum (*daily 10–12 and 2–6, July and Aug 10–7; adm*) and hat museum (*open same hours; adm*), and **Couiza**, from where you can digress up a steep mountain road to France's vortex of occult weirdness, where Cathars, Templars and God only knows what else come together, **Rennes-le-Château**.

Lunch: Back down in Couiza, the **Château des Ducs de Joyeuse** on the D118, **t** 04 68 74 23 50 (*moderate*) has some of the best cooking around in an elegant 16th-century manor. *Closed Sun night and Mon in winter.*

Afternoon: Carrying on northwards, the Aude and the D118 pass **Alet-les-Bains**, a medieval village with a ruined Benedictine abbey that is also a genteel spa, with baths and a casino. Beyond that is **Limoux** (*see* p.261). Don't worry about dinner or a hotel – Carcassonne is just 24km up the road.

Perpignan

PERPIGNAN DEAD CITY is the slogan the local anarchists write on the walls, and if that's slightly premature, you can't help wondering about a town named after a reactionary murderer (Perperna, a lieutenant in the Roman army who murdered his boss, the great 1st-century BC populist general, Quintus Sertorius); a town that has let its most beautiful Gothic monument become a hamburger franchise, and which highlights its tourist brochure with a photo of its trucking terminal. And how can any self-respecting city of 105,000 support 23 foxtrot academies?

The city enjoyed its most brilliant period in the 13th century when Jaime I, king of Aragon and conqueror of Majorca, created the Kingdom of Majorca and County of

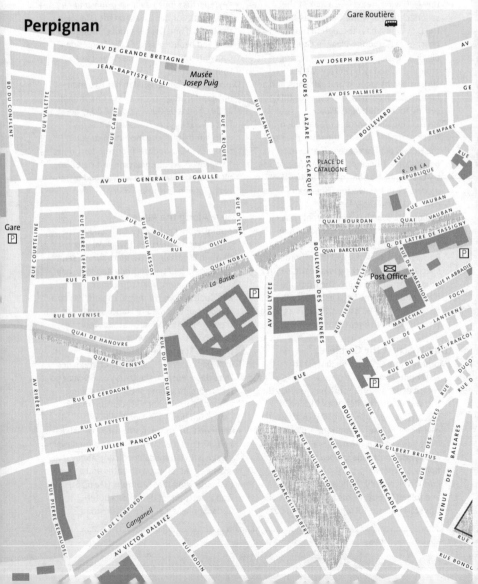

Roussillon for his younger son Jaime II. This little kingdom was absorbed by the Catalan kings of Aragon in the 14th century, but continued to prosper until 1463, when Louis XI's army came to claim Perpignan as payment for mercenaries sent to Aragon. Besieged, the Perpignanais ate rats rather than become French, until the king of Aragon himself ordered them to surrender. In 1493 Charles VIII, more interested in Italian conquests, gave Perpignan back to Spain. But in the 1640s, Richelieu pounced on the first available chance to grab it back, and, ever since, the forces of French centralization have suppressed the natural Catalan exuberance of *Perpinyà* (as its residents call it). While grateful for the croissants, not a few Perpignanais hope that as Europe's frontiers melt away, the electricity of Barcelona over the border may once again galvanize it along with the rest of greater Catalunya.

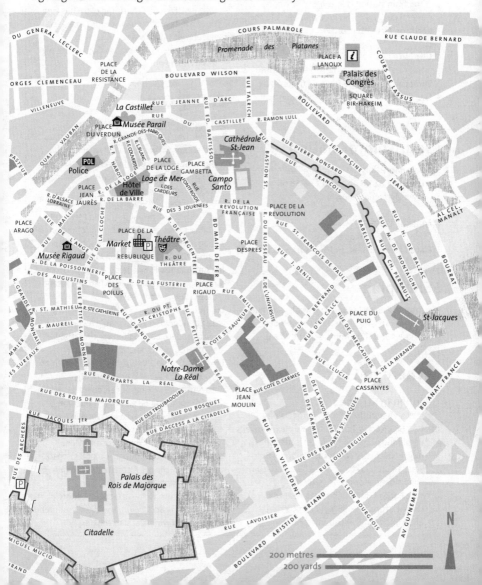

Getting There

Ryanair (*see* p.6) has a daily flight to Perpignan from London Stansted.

Getting from the Airport

Perpignan's **airport** is 7km northwest of the city and linked by **shuttle bus** to the station and the centre of town, €4.50. A **taxi** costs €15.

Getting Around

The **train station** is at the end of Av du Général de Gaulle. The *gare routière* is to the north, on Av du Gén. Leclerc, t 04 68 35 29 02.

Car Hire

You can hire a car at the airport, or from **Europcar**, 28 Av de Gaulle, t 04 68 34 65 03, f 04 68 34 02 60, or **Avis**, 13 Bd du Conflent, t 04 68 34 26 71.

Tourist Information

Perpignan: Palais des Congrès, Place Armand Lanoux, t 04 68 66 30 30, f 04 68 66 30 26, *www.perpignantourisme.com*.

Market Days

Place de la République: daily
Place Cassanyes: Sat and Sun am.

Shopping

Around **Rue de la Loge**, **Rue Mailly** and **Rue de l'Ange**; and, for crafts, **Rue Grande-des-Fabriques** and the **Jardins de Sant Vicens**.

Where to Stay

Perpignan ✉ 66000

★★★★La Villa Duflot, 109 Av Victor Dalbiez, t 04 68 56 67 67, f 04 68 56 54 05 (*expensive*). Perpignan's only luxury hotel is near the motorway exit, in an industrial zone! But you can pretend to be elsewhere in the air-conditioned rooms and garden.
★★★Le Park, 18 Bd Jean Bourrat, near the tourist office, t 04 68 35 14 14, f 04 68 35 48 18 (*moderate*). Plush, air-conditioned, soundproof rooms with an old Spanish feel and flair.
★★Hôtel de la Loge, 1 Rue Fabriques-Nabot, t 04 68 34 41 02, f 04 68 34 25 13 (*inexpensive*). The nicest in the centre, in a 16th-century building, this has pretty rooms and a lovely inner courtyard.
★★Le Maillol, 14 Impasse des Cardeurs, t 04 68 51 10 20, f 04 68 51 20 29 (*inexpensive*). In a 17th-century building: not too noisy, and convenient for the sights.
★★La Poste et Perdix, 6 Rue des Fabriques-Nabot, t 04 68 34 42 53, f 04 68 34 58 20 (*inexpensive*). This charming place has kept much of its original 1832 décor. *Closed Feb; restaurant closed Mon.*
★Le Berry, 6 Av du Général de Gaulle, t 04 68 34 59 02 (*cheap*).

Eating Out

Le Chapon Fin, Park Hôtel (*see* above, *expensive*). This has been Perpignan's finest restaurant for years, as well as one of the prettiest with its Catalan ceramics. *Closed Sun and first two weeks in Jan.*
Côté Théâtre, 7 Rue du Théâtre, t 04 68 34 60 00 (*expensive–moderate*). Elegantly converted restaurant in the old town, celebrated for its refined treatment of regional food; the squid and artichoke salad is sensational. *Closed Sun, and Mon lunch.*
Les Antiquaires, Pl Desprès, t 04 68 34 06 58 (*moderate*). A classy French fish restaurant. *Closed Sun eve and Mon.*
Les Trois Sœurs, 2 Rue Fontfroide, t 04 68 51 22 33 (*moderate*). Fashionable restaurant with modern bar and terrace on cathedral square. Catalan cooking with a twist.
Brasserie l'Arago, Place Arago, t 04 68 51 81 96 (*moderate*). Packed day and night; pizza.
Casa Sansa, 3 Rue Fabriques-Couvertes, near Le Castillet, t 04 68 34 21 84 (*moderate–cheap*). Lively, with excellent food in a 14th-century cellar – from Catalan *escargots* to rabbit with *aïoli*. *Closed Sun and Mon.*
Le Vauban, 29 Quai Vauban, t 04 68 51 05 10 (*moderate–cheap*). A sure bet, with well-prepared *plats du jour*. *Closed Sun.*
Les Expéditeurs, 19 Av du Général Leclerc, t 04 68 35 15 80 (*cheap*). The classic set menu lunch with wine; Catalan cooking.

The king of kookiness himself, Salvador Dalí, set off the first sparks when he passed Perpignan's train station in a taxi, and 'it all became clear in a flash: there, right before me, was the centre of the universe!' The otherwise ordinary Gare SNCF has been a hot destination for Surrealist pilgrims ever since, and the street leading to the station, Avenue du Général de Gaulle, has undergone a *traitement dalinien*, which included the installation of benches shaped like Mae West's lips and a Dalinien railway carriage suspended in front of the station.

Le Castillet and Around

When most of Perpignan's walls were destroyed in 1904, its easy-going river-cum-moat, La Basse, was planted with lawns, flower-beds, mimosas and Art Nouveau cafés. Only the fat brick towers and crenellated gate of **Le Castillet** were left upright; built in 1368 by Aragon to keep out the French, it became a prison once the French got in. In 1946 a mason broke through a sealed wall and found the body of a child, which on contact with the air dissolved into dust. From the surviving clothing fragments the corpse was dated to the end of the 18th century, and ever since, people have wondered: could it have been Marie-Antoinette's son, the dauphin Louis XVII?

Le Castillet now houses a cosy museum of Catalan art and traditions, the **Musée Pairal** (*open May–Sept Wed–Mon 10–7; Oct–April Wed–Mon 11–5.30; closed Tues; adm*), with items from casts of Pau (Pablo) Casals' hands to a kitchen from a Catalan *mas*. Place de Verdun, by Le Castillet, is one of Perpignan's liveliest squares, while, just outside the gate, the **Promenade des Platanes** is lined with magnificent plane trees.

Loge de Mer to the Musée Rigaud

In Place de la Loge stands Perpignan's most beautiful building, the Gothic **Loge de Mer**, or Llotja, built in 1397 by the king of Aragon to house the exchange and the *Consolat de Mar*, a branch of the Barcelona council founded by Jaime I to resolve trade and maritime disputes. This proud and noble building of ochre stone, with its Venetian arches and loggia and ship-shaped weathercock, fell on hard times – but Perpignan takes good care of its monuments. The city rented the Llotja to a fast-food chain, and now it looks very much the beggared pasha, flipping out Quick Burgers.

The neighbouring 13th-century **Hôtel de Ville** has been spared the Llotja's humiliation, probably because it still serves its original purpose. To the right, the **Palais de la Députation Provinciale** (1447) is a masterpiece of Catalan Renaissance, formerly the seat of Roussillon's parliament and now housing dismal municipal offices. South of the Députation, in Rue de l'Ange the **Musée Rigaud** (*open daily exc Tues 12–7; adm*) is named after Perpignan native Hyacinthe Rigaud (1659–1743), portrait painter to Louis XIV. Hyacinthe, master of raising the mediocre and unworthy to virtuoso heights of rosy-cheeked, debonair charm and sophistication, is well represented, as are works by Picasso, Dufy, Maillol and Miró.

Cathédrale St-Jean, the Dévôt Christ and the Quartier St-Jacques

Just east of Place de la Loge unfolds Place Gambetta, site of Perpignan's pebble-and-brick **cathedral**, topped by a lacy 19th-century wrought-iron campanile. Begun in 1324 but not ready for use until 1509, the interior is a success because the builders stuck to the design provided in the 1400s by Guillem Sagrera, architect of the great cathedral of Palma de Majorca. Typical of Catalan Gothic, it has a single nave, 157ft long, striking for its spacious width rather than its soaring height. The chapels, wedged between the huge piers, hold some unique treasures, the oldest of which is a marble **baptismal font** (first chapel on the left). The cathedral is proudest of its exquisite retables: on the high altar, the marble *Retable de St-Jean*, carved in a late Renaissance style in 1621 by Claude Perret; at the end of the left crossing, the *Retable des Stes-Eulalie et Julie* (1670s); in the apsidal chapels, the painted wood *Retable de St-Pierre* (mid-1500s), and to the right, the lovely, luminous *Notre-Dame de la Mangrana* (1500). A door in the right aisle leads out to a 16th-century chapel constructed especially to house the extraordinary **Dévôt Christ**. Carved in the Cologne region in 1307, this wasted Christ, whose contorted bones, sinews and torn flesh are carved with a rare anatomical realism, is stretched to the limits of agony on the Cross.

The piquant neighbourhood south of the cathedral, built on the slopes of Puig des Lépreux (Lepers' Hill), was once the *aljama*, or **Jewish quarter** of Perpignan. In its happiest days, in the 13th century, it produced a remarkable body of literature – especially from the pen of the mathematician and Talmudic scholar Gerson ben Salomon – as well as rare manuscripts and calligraphy, all now in Paris. After the Jews were exiled, the quarter was renamed St-Jacques, and inhabited by working men's families and Romanies, and most recently by Algerians. The 12th–14th-century church of **St-Jacques** is opulent and rich inside: there's a 'Cross of Insults', a statue of St James in Compostela pilgrimage gear (1450) and more fine retables. As in Seville, the confraternity reaches a wider audience during Holy Week, when it dons spooky Ku Klux Klan-like hoods and bears a procession of holy floats (the *misteri*) while singers wail dirges from the crowd.

The Palace of the Kings of Majorca

Enclosed in a vast extent of walls, originally medieval and later enlarged by Vauban, the Palais des Rois de Majorque (*entrance in Rue des Archers; open daily May–Sept 10–6, winter 9–5; adm*) is the oldest royal palace in France, begun in the 1270s by Jaime the Conqueror and occupied by his son Jaime II after 1283. Yet for all its grandeur, only three kings of Majorca were to reign here before Roussillon, Montpellier, the Cerdagne and the Balearic Islands were reabsorbed by Aragon in 1349. The scale of magnificence to which they intended to become accustomed survives, but not much else.

A rectangular building erected around a mastodontic but elegant Romanesque-Gothic courtyard, the palace is now a favourite venue for events, exhibitions and dancing the *sardana*, the Catalan national dance. The **Salle de Majorque**, or throne room, with its three vast fireplaces, and the double-decker chapels in the **Donjon**, with the queen's chapel on the bottom and the king's on top, both offer hints at the exotic splendour of the Majorcan court. The narrow grid of streets below the palace, around the church of **St-Mathieu**, were designed by the Templar tutors of Jaime the Conqueror, although most of the buildings date from the 18th century.

Day Trips from Perpignan

Elne and its Cloister

Set a little way inland on top of a steep hill, the citadel of Elne has guarded the Roussillon plain for at least 2,700 years. Through the Middle Ages, and until the 16th century, Elne remained the most important city in Roussillon and seat of the archbishops. Its **cathedral**, a fortified church begun in 1069, has a wonderful stage presence, with its crenellated roofline and stout, arcaded tower. Inside, in a chapel on the right is an Italianate 14th-century altarpiece of St Michael and there are some fine tombs, especially that of Ramon de Costa (1310). The **cloister** (*open daily, except during services, April–May 9.30–6, June–Sept 9.30–7, Oct–Mar 9.30–12 and 2–5; adm*) is perhaps the best in the Midi, and also the best preserved. Capitals and pillars are decorated with imaginative, exquisite arabesques and floral patterns. The four sides were completed in different periods, in roughly 50-year intervals; the one closest to the cathedral is the earliest, dating from the 12th century. The little history **museum** tells the sad tale of the cloister's lost upper gallery, dismantled in 1827 and sold off at

Getting There

There are frequent **train** services from Perpignan to Elne, and then on to Collioure. There are also frequent **bus** services from Perpignan's *gare routière*, arriving opposite the post office in Collioure and taking ¾hr.

Tourist Information

Elne ✉ **66201**: 2 Rue Docteur Bolte, t 04 68 22 05 07, f 04 68 37 95 05, *www.ot-elne.fr*.
Collioure ✉ **66190**: Place du 18-Juin, t 04 68 82 15 47, f 04 68 82 46 29, *www.collioure.com*.

Market Days

Elne: Monday, Wednesday and Friday.
Collioure: Thursday.

Eating Out

Elne

**Le Weekend, 29 Av Paul Roig, t 04 68 22 06 68, f 04 68 22 17 16 (*inexpensive*). Only eight rooms and a garden terrace far from the crowds; good home cooking, too (*moderate*). *Closed Nov–mid-Feb*.

Collioure

***La Frégate, Av Camille Pelletan, t 04 68 82 06 05, f 04 68 82 55 00 (*inexpensive*). This pink and jolly place is on the busiest corner of Collioure; it has a good restaurant, decorated with *azulejos* (seafood; *moderate*).

**Les Templiers, Quai de l'Amirauté, t 04 68 98 31 10, f 04 68 98 01 24 (*inexpensive*). Picasso, Matisse, Dufy and Dalí all stayed here, and original works cover the walls of this unique hotel. The bar is a trendy local hang-out, and the restaurant (*moderate*) is excellent, with a people-watching terrace and imaginative, good-value dishes like lamb on the bone with cinnamon scented onion *confit*, or cod with aïoli and pine nuts. *Closed Jan*.

Neptune, Rte Port-Vendres, t 04 68 82 02 27 (*expensive–moderate*). One of the best restaurants in town, with wonderful canopied sea views and the full *nouvelle* Catalan cuisine. Ravishing desserts include poached figs and rosemary sorbet. *Closed Tues, Wed and Feb*.

La Moulerie, Rte Port-Vendres (*cheap*). If Neptune's too pretentious, this place next door serves up simple mussels on wooden tables, but you still get the sea views.

La Marinade, Place du 18-Juin, t 04 68 82 09 76 (*moderate*). Delectable seafood from simple sardines *en papillote* to an elaborate Catalan *bouillabaisse*. *Closed Dec–Jan*.

Pica Pica, 10 Rue de la République, just back from the port, t 04 68 82 32 78 (*moderate*). A small Spanish place offering *tapas* and tasty seafood.

an auction in 1960; Elne, sadly, couldn't bid high enough. Admission to the cloister includes the chance to climb the steps up to the tower and admission to the new **Musée Terrus** across the square (*open daily, Nov–Mar 10–12 and 2–7; April–May 10–6; June–Sept 10–7; Oct 10–12.30 and 2–6*); the painter Terrus was a friend of Matisse and Derain and the museum contains mainly his works.

Collioure

If the tourists would only leave it in peace, Collioure would be quite happy to make its living in the old way, filling up barrels with anchovies. As it is, the town bears their presence as gracefully as possible. In a way, Collioure is unspoiled, but you'll still find every other requisite for a civilized Mediterranean resort: a castle, a pretty church by the sea, three small beaches, and a shady market square with cafés.

It's hard to believe, looking at the map, but in the Middle Ages this village was the port for Perpignan; with no good harbours on the dismal and (then) unhealthy coast to the north, Perpignan's fabrics and other goods had to come to the Pyrenees to go to sea. In the 14th century, Collioure was one of the biggest trading centres of Aragon, but nearly the whole town was demolished by the French after they took possession in 1659. In 1905 Collioure was discovered by Matisse and Derain. Many other artists followed, including Picasso, but these two were the most inspired by the place. The village has created the *Chemin du fauvisme*, placing copies of Matisse and Derain's works on the spots where the two set up their easels. There is also the **Musée d'Art Moderne** (*t 04 68 82 10 19; open daily June–Sept 10–12 and 2–6; Oct–May closed Tues; adm*), in a peaceful villa on the south edge of town, with a lovely terraced olive grove, which has good examples of works by lesser-known artists in the style of the Fauves, as well as an intriguing collection of Moorish ceramics.

Collioure is a thoroughly Catalan town, and the red and yellow striped Catalan flag waves proudly over the **Château Royal** (*t 04 68 82 06 43; open daily summer 10–6, winter 9–5; adm*), which dominates the harbour. First built by the Templars in the 13th century, it was expanded by various Aragonese kings. The outer fortifications, low walls and broad banks of earth, were state-of-the-art in 1669.

From the castle, cross the small stream called the Douy (usually dry and used as a car park) into the **Mouré**, the old quarter that is now the centre of Collioure. There is an amiable shorefront, with a small beach from which a few anchovy fishermen still ply their trade; several brightly painted fishing smacks are usually pulled up to complete the effect. At the far end you'll see Collioure's landmark, painted by Matisse and many others: the church of **Notre-Dame-des-Anges**. The best thing about the church is that you can hear the waves of the sea from inside, a profound *basso continuo* that makes the celebration of Mass here a unique experience. The next best are the retables, five of them, by Joseph Sunyer and others.

The second of Collioure's beaches lies right behind the church; really an old sand-bar that has become part of dry land, it connects the town with a former islet, the **Ilôt St-Vincent**, crowned with a tiny medieval chapel. A scenic footpath called the Sentier de la Moulade leads from near the church along the rocky shore north of Collioure. Above, you'll see **Fort Miradoux**, King Philip II's addition to Collioure's defences.

Touring from Perpignan

Day 1: Corbières and Castles

Morning: Leave Perpignan on the N9 north. This day is going to be full of castles, and first on the list is the **Forteresse de Salses**, the last word in advanced Renaissance military architecture, built by King Ferdinand of Spain (*guided tours on the hour from 9.30, 10 in winter; adm*). From there the D5b-D5 will take you inland through the strange little **Plateau d'Opoul**, where the French army does its desert training; then join the D9 at Perillos for **Tautavel**, where a little museum records the finds of France's oldest inhabitants, 430,000 years ago.

Lunch: If not for the bones, Tautavel merits a stop for **Le Petit Gris**, Route d'Estagel, t 04 68 29 42 42 (*moderate–inexpensive*), a very popular place with Catalan grills done at your table.

Afternoon: From here, follow the D59 and D611 north into the Corbières; turn left at the D14 for **Cucugnan**, set between two of the most spectacular mountaintop castles in France, **Quéribus** (*open daily 10–6, winter weekends only; adm*) and **Peyrepertuse** (*open daily 10–7, Jul and Aug 9–8; adm*). A little further west on the D14, you can cross back over into Roussillon by the scenic **Gorges de Galamus**.

Dinner: At the southern end of the Gorges de Galamus is **St-Paul-de-Fenouillet**, where you can dine at the restaurant of **Le Châtelet** (*moderate; see below*), or head a bit down the D619 to Caramany, for *confit de canard* and Catalan desserts on a terrace with a view, at the **Auberge du Grand Rocher**, t 04 68 84 51 58 (*moderate–inexpensive*) – do ring ahead to make sure they're open.

Sleeping: St-Paul-de-Fenouillet has two comfortable *Logis de France* hotels: **★★Le Châtelet**, Route des Caudies, t 04 68 59 01 20, f 04 68 59 01 29 (*inexpensive*); and the **★Relais des Corbières**, 10 Av Jean Moulin, t 04 68 59 23 89 (*inexpensive*).

Day 2: Across the Fenouillèdes

Morning: From St-Paul, the D619 south will take you into the heart of this lovely, little-visited forest region. At **Ansignan**, you can see its own version of the famous Pont du Gard, a 500ft Roman aqueduct that is still in use. Continue down the D619, through **Sournia** and over the pass of Roque-Jalère; before lunchtime you'll be in **Prades**.

Lunch: Some of the best places are in the hills, around St-Michel-de-Cuxa: the **Mas Lluganas** just outside Mosset, t 04 68 05 00 37 (*moderate*) uses its own farm produce. *Closed Oct–Mar*. In Prades, Catalan dishes are featured at the **Jardin d'Aymeric**, 3 Av de Gaulle, t 04 68 96 53 38 (*moderate*).

Afternoon: Prades is an interesting town, the home of Pablo Casals, with a little museum to honour him. The real attraction, however, is in the hills to the south: the medieval Catalan abbey of **St-Michel-de-Cuxa** (*open daily 9.30–11.50, 2–6, till 5 in winter; closed Sun morning; adm*)

Dinner: Both the hotels in **Molitg-les-Bains**, (*see* below) have excellent restaurants, and in Prades, besides the two listed above, there is the **Hostal de Nogarols**, Chemin Nogarols on the way to St-Michel, t 04 68 96 24 57 (*moderate*), offering pizza and Catalan cuisine.

Sleeping: The most exciting choices are up above Prades in the Belle Epoque spa of Molitg-les-Bains: the truly grand **★★★★Château de Riell**, t 04 68 05 04 40, f 04 68 05 04 37 (*expensive*), with all the amenities including a rooftop pool, *closed Nov–Mar*; and the less pricey but still impressive **★★★Grand Hôtel Thermal**, t 04 68 05 00 50 (*moderate*). *Closed Dec–Mar*.

Day 3: Villefranche to Mont-Louis

Morning: Heading further west into the mountains on the N116, you pass under the walls of **Villefranche-de-Conflent**, a fortress town built by the famous military architect Vauban; almost perfectly preserved, it is now full of potters and other craftsmen. Up in the hills to the south is another imposing medieval abbey, **St-Martin-de-Canigou** (*t 04 68 05 50 03; tours daily at 10, 11.45, 2, 3, 4 and 5; closed Tues in winter; call to confirm times; adm*).

Lunch: Morel mushrooms and a *filet mignon* of boar are among the delights of the **Auberge St-Paul**, Place de l'Eglise in Villefranche, t 04 68 96 30 95 (*expensive*).

Closed Mon in summer, Mon and Tues in winter. If that sounds too formidable there's **Au Grill**, 81 Rue St-Jean, t 04 68 96 17 65 (*inexpensive*). *Closed Tues eve and Wed.*

Afternoon: Continuing up the N116, you can soak in natural hot springs at **Fontpédrouse** – even in winter (*open 10–7, till 9 in summer; adm*). Further on you can tour a giant solar furnace and another Vauban fort at **Mont-Louis**, the highest in France.

Dinner: Almost all of the restaurants here are in the hotels. The **Planes** (*see below*), with its big open fire, is especially nice. In Mont-Louis, the family-run **Lou Roubaillou**, Rue des Ecoles-Laïques, t 04 68 04 23 26 (*moderate*), specializes in dishes with wild mushrooms. *Closed May, Nov and Dec.*

Sleeping: Ask for a room with a view at the cliffside **★★ Le Clos Cerdan** in Mont Louis, t 04 68 04 23 29 (*inexpensive*). *Closed Nov–Dec.* Or else carry on down the N116 to the **★★Planes** in Saillagousse, t 04 68 04 72 08, f 04 68 04 75 93 (*inexpensive*) , a country inn from the 1890s. *Closed mid Oct–Dec.*

Day 4: Exploring the Cerdagne

Morning: Tour this lovely region on a circular route along the D618 and N116. Along the way is the big ski centre of **Font-Romeu**, marvellous scenery, and plenty of *villages perchés* with Romanesque churches and medieval art (at Planes, Dorres, Angoustrine and Hix, among others). The meadows around **Eyne** are famous for wildflowers in spring.

Lunch: If lunchtime finds you around Angoustrine, try **Cal Xandera**, t 04 68 04 61 67 (*inexpensive*), with traditional cuisine in an 18th-century farmhouse. In Font-Romeu, the Cerdagne's biggest town, there's a good restaurant in the **Hôtel Clair Soleil**, t 04 68 30 13 65 (*expensive–moderate*). *Closed Nov, Dec.*

Afternoon: In the middle of the circle is the pretty village of **Llivia**, an enclave of Spain completely surrounded by France. Llivia has an interesting municipal museum (*open daily 10–1 and 3–7, Sun 10–2; closed Mon; adm*). If you want to see more Spain, the resort town of **Puigcerdà** waits just over the border, connected to Llivia by the N152.

Dinner: For dining on the Spanish side, you can't do better than the *modernista* hotel **Torre del Remei**, at Bolvir de Cerdanya, Cami Reial, t 972 14 01 82 (*expensive*). Back over in France, there's an excellent restaurant at the Auberge de Atalaya (*expensive, see* below)

Sleeping: At Llo, off the N116, the **★★★ Auberge de Atalaya**, t 04 68 04 70 04, f 04 68 04 01 29 (*expensive*) is a mountain inn in a tranquil setting. *Closed mid Nov–mid Dec.*

Day 5: The Vallespir

Morning: Get up early; in this blind valley there's nothing to be done but retrace your steps east on the N116, back past Prades. Turn right on the D618 at Bouleternère; this scenic road skirts the edges of Mt Canigou down to the next valley, the Vallespir, passing along the way the remarkable medieval sculpture at the **Prieuré de Serrabonne** (*open daily 10–6; adm*).

Lunch: The D618 ends at **Amélie-les Bains**, where there's a fine restaurant at the hotel **Castel Emeraude**, t 04 68 39 02 83 (*expensive–moderate*). *Closed mid-Nov–mid-Mar.* Just up the road in Arles-sur-Tech, **Les Glycines**, t 04 68 39 83 02 (*moderate*) offers some of the best Catalan cooking around, especially the seafood *panaché*. *Closed mid-Nov–mid-Feb.*

Afternoon: The Vallespir isn't a long valley, and can be easily explored in an afternoon. West of Amélie is **Arles-sur-Tech**, a craft-weaving town where you can also visit the narrow Gorges de la Fou and its waterfalls (*open April–Nov daily 10–6; adm*). To the east lies **Céret**, famous for cherries and as the retreat of many notable painters, represented in its Musée d'Art Moderne (*open daily 10–6, till 7 in summer; closed Tues in winter; adm*)

Dinner: in Céret, **Les Feuillants**, 1 Bd Lafayette, t 04 68 87 37 88 (*expensive*) offers ambitious Catalan cuisine in 1930s décor; there's also a cheaper brasserie. *Closed Sun eve and Mon.*

Sleeping: Le Mas Trilles, just west of Céret at Pont de Reynes, t 04 68 87 38 37, f 04 68 87 42 62 (*expensive*) is a restored farmhouse with a heated pool and charming garden. In town, there's **★★Les Arcades**, 1 Place Picasso, t 04 68 87 12 30 (*inexpensive*), with balconies overlooking the market square.

The South of France

11

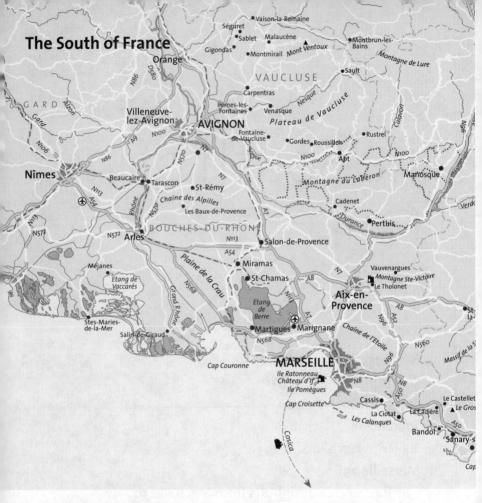

First settled by the ancient Greeks, Provence was the beloved Provincia of the Romans. Even the medieval popes and cardinals in Avignon fell prey to its sensuous *dolce vita*; the voluptuous Mediterranean light inspired Van Gogh, Cézanne, Renoir, Matisse, and the Fauves. After a century of hosting the consumptive and the wealthy in the winter, the Roaring Twenties introduced a new fad for turning brown by the sea. The French invented paid summer holidays for everyone in 1936, and the rest is history.

Today, after Paris, Provence and the Côte d'Azur – the French Riviera – are the most visited regions in France. Endowed with a sunny climate, naturally air-conditioned by the mistral wind, replete with dramatic scenery and beaches, fascinating Roman and medieval ruins, top-notch art museums, fantastic restaurants and hotels, this 'California of Europe' has its downsides as well: too many holiday villas, too many people, high prices, and too many shops selling lavender soap or *santons*, the omnipresent Provençal crèche figurines. Pick and choose carefully, though, and come on the cusp of the season, and you'll better understand what started all the fuss in the first place.

Nice

The capital of the *département* of Alpes-Maritimes and France's fifth largest town (pop. 400,000), Nice is France's most visited city after Paris. Agreeably named and superbly set on nothing less than the Bay of Angels, it has a gleam and sparkle in its eye like no other city in France: only a sourpuss could resist its lively old town squeezed between promontory and sea, its markets blazing with colour, and the famous voluptuous curve of the beach and the palm-lined Promenade des Anglais.

Vieux Nice

A dangerous slum in the 1970s, Nice's Vieille Ville, a piquant quarter east of Place Masséna, is fast becoming the trendiest part of the city as well as a rich treasure-trove of little shops and cafés. Old here means Genoese seaside Baroque – tall, steep *palazzi*, many with opulent 17th- and 18th-century portals and windows.

At its eastern end, the Vieille Ville is closed by the **Colline du Château**, the ancient acropolis of Nikaïa and site of the 10th- to 12th-century town and the cathedral of

Nice

To Prieuré du Vieux Logis & Villa Arson

To Musée Matisse, Musée Archéologique & Musée Franciscain

BOULEVARD DE CESSOLE

BOULEVARD AUGUSTE RAYNAUD

AVENUE BORRIGLIONE

BOULEVARD DE CIMIEZ

Eglise Ste-Jeanne d'Arc

RUE MICHEL ANGE

AV ST-LAMBERT

AVENUE PESSICART

BD JOSEPH GARNIER

PLACE GENERAL DE GAULLE

AVENUE MALAUSSENA

AV DR MENARD

Musée Marc Chagall

AV AIRES

BOULEVARD

Gare du Sud

RUE ALFRED BINET

RUE DE DION

RUE MARCEAU

AVENUE EMILE BIECKERT

AV GAY

GAMBETTA

AV PAUL ARÈNE

RUE VERNIER

RUE TRACHEL

BD RAIMBALDI

RUE ASSALIT

BD DE CIMIEZ

Gare Nice Ville

RUE DE PARIS

Cathédrale Russe

THIERS

RUE D'ALSACE LORRAINE

AV NOTRE-DAME

BD DU TZAREWITCH

DURANTE

RUE DE LA RUSSIE

AVENUE JEAN

RUE BISCCARA

PLACE SASSERNO

DUBOUCHAGE

RUE P DEVOLUY

BD F. GROSSO

URBAINE SUD

AVENUE

AVENUE

GEORGES

CLEMENCEAU

Centre Nice Etoile

BOULEVARD

RUE PASTORELLI

PLACE WILSON

AUTOROUTE

BOULEVARD

RUE ROSSINI

AVENUE AUBER

RUE PAUL DEROULEDE

MEDECIN

RUE DE L'HOTEL DES POSTES

AV DES BAUMETTES

RUE F. PASSY

GAMBETTA

RUE VERDI

Eglise Luthérienne

RUE GIOFFREDO

BOULEVARD

AV DES FLEURS

BOULEVARD VICTOR HUGO

RUE DE RIVOLI

RUE DU MARECHAL JOFFRE

RUE DALPOZZO

RUE DU CONGRES

PLACE GRIMALDI

MASSENA

AVENUE FELIX FAURE

RUE DES POTIERS

RUE DE FRANCE

RUE MEYERBEER

RUE Buffa

Eglise Anglicane

PLACE MASSENA

FRANCOIS

RUE DANTE

AV DE SUEDE

Jardin Albert 1er

AVE DES PHOCEENS

Opéra

GROSSO

Palais Masséna

Théâtre de Verdure

QUAI DES ETATS-UNIS

Musée des Beaux-Arts

PROMENADE DES ANGLAIS

RUE LOUIS DE COPPET

ESPACE MAGNAN

RUE DE FRANCE

To Musée d'Art Naïf Anatole Jakovsky & Airport

Baie des Anges

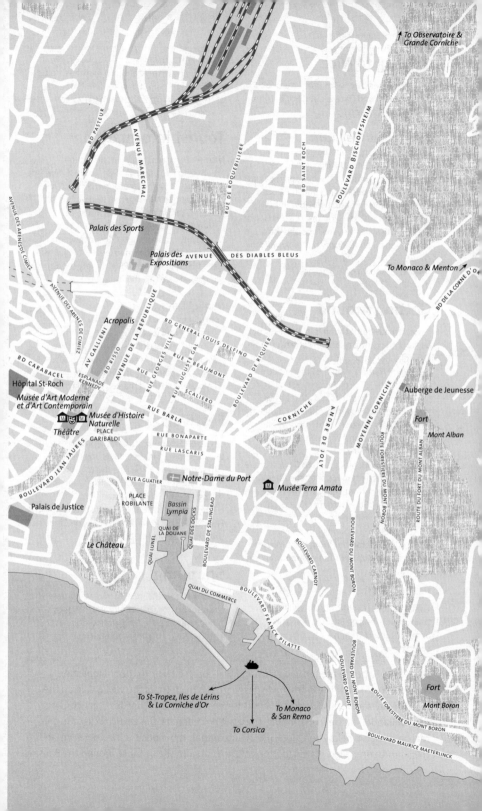

Getting to Nice

Nice is served by **easyJet** from Liverpool, London Luton and Gatwick, and **bmibaby** from East Midlands (*see* p.6).

Getting from the Airport

Buses run every 12mins between the modern **Aéroport Nice-Côte d'Azur** and the *gare routière* in the centre of town, stopping along the Promenade des Anglais and at Place Masséna, while bus no.23 provides links with the train station every 30mins. The bus ticket to town will also give you a free onward connection on another city bus (*only valid for 1 hour*).

A **taxi** into town costs €25–30.

Getting Around

Nice's **main train station** is in Av Thiers, not far from the centre of town. Métrazur trains run right along the coast.

The *gare routière* is on the Promenade du Paillon, on the edge of Vieux Nice, **t** 04 93 85 61 81. There are frequent and inexpensive buses to Aix-en-Provence, Antibes, Cagnes, Cannes, Grasse, Marseille, Menton, Monte-Carlo, St-Raphaël and Vence. Bus no.17 links the coach and train stations.

For **town buses**, pick up a free *Guide Horaire du Réseau Bus* with maps and schedules at the tourist office or from Sunbus, 10 Av Félix Faure, **t** 04 93 13 53 13. Several tourist tickets, called 'Sun Pass', are available from the Sunbus office. Buses stop around 9pm, and are replaced by **Noctambus**, from Place Masséna.

You cannot stop **taxis** in the street. Call **t** 04 93 13 78 78.

Car Hire

International car hire giant **Avis** is at the train station, **t** 04 93 87 90 11, **f** 04 93 87 32 82, or at the airport Terminal 1, **t** 04 93 21 36 33, **f** 04 93 21 45 13.

Among the cheapest car-hire places is **Rent-a-Car**, opposite the station on Av Thiers, **t** 04 93 88 69 69, **f** 04 93 88 43 36, or in the centre of town, **t** 04 93 37 42 22, **f** 04 93 37 42 20.

Tourist Information

Nice: Av Thiers, next to the train station, **t** 0892 707 407, **f** 04 93 16 85 16, *www.nicecoteazur.org*, *info@nicetourisme.com*. Open *June–Sept daily 8–8; rest of year daily 8–7.*

Museum card: A 1/3/7-day Carte Musées Côte d'Azur can be obtained for €8/15/25 from any museum ticket desk or the tourist office, or FNAC bookshop (Nice Etoile). On the first and third Sunday of every month, museums are free (but busy!).

Market Days

Cours Saleya: Food and flower market daily 6am–5.30pm except Mon; afternoon only on Sun. Old books, clothes and bric-a-brac on Monday. Arts and crafts, Wednesday afternoon and paintings on Sunday afternoons. **Av Malausséna**: food market, weekday am.

Festivals

Nice is famous for its **Carnival** in the two weeks before Lent, with floats and frivolity.

In spring there is the **Fête des Mai**, probably Nice's oldest festival, with stalls around town selling lily-of-the-valley, a traditional gift.

The third week of July sees the excellent **Festival de Jazz** in the Jardin Public de Cimiez (*mlprod@club-internet.fr*).

Shopping

Vieux Nice is the most attractive place to shop, for art, local souvenirs and Provençal fabric, cheap clothes and glorious food at the outdoor markets and local shops.

Ste-Marie. To get to the top you can either walk up the steps to the château, take a mini-train (€6) from the Promenade des Anglais (which tours the Vieille Ville on the way), or pay a few sous to take the lift at the east end of the Quai des Etats-Unis near **Tour Bellanda**. The view is stunning: from the belvedere by the artificial cascade, the real boats down below don't look much bigger than the models in the museum, and the shimmering, tiled, glazed rooftops of Nice curl into the distance around the Baie

The **pedestrian zone around Place Masséna** has scores of designer clothes shops (mainly on Avenue Félix Faure) and cheap boutiques (mainly on Rue Masséna), plus the wonderful Pâtisserie Vogade right on the square, while on **Av Jean Médecin** you'll find Nice's biggest department store, Galeries Lafayette, as well as Nice Etoile, a shopping centre with useful shops like the bookshop/ticket agency FNAC.

Where to Stay

Nice ✉ 06000

If you arrive without a reservation, the tourist office next to the station will book rooms for a €1.50 charge.

★★★★Negresco, 37 Promenade des Anglais, **t** 04 93 16 64 00, **f** 04 93 88 35 68, *reservations@hotel-negresco-nice.com* (*luxury*). Nice has luxury grand hotels galore, but for panache none can top the fabulous green-domed Negresco. The one hotel in Nice where a Grand Duke would still feel at home, and the last independent luxury hotel on the coast, its 150 rooms and apartments have Edwardian furnishings and paintings by the likes of Picasso and Léger.

★★★★Beau Rivage, 22–24 Rue St-François-de-Paule, **t** 04 92 47 82 82, **f** 04 92 47 82 83, *www.new-hotelcom, nicebeaurivage@new-hotel.com* (*luxury*). If hobnobbing with the rich and famous in the Negresco is not your style, there's this elegant Art Deco hotel, on a pedestrian street in Vieux Nice overlooking the sea. Private beach.

★★★★Château des Ollières, 39 Av des Baumettes, **t** 04 92 15 77 99, **f** 04 92 15 77 98, *www.chateaudesollieres.com, info@chateaudesollieres.com*. A flamboyant pink, orange and yellow crenellated folly which once belonged to a Russian prince. Now it has only eight heavenly rooms, including a suite in the tower, with antique furnishings, eccentric stained glass and four-poster beds.

★★★★Hôtel Grimaldi, 15 Rue Grimaldi, **t** 04 93 16 00 24, **f** 04 93 87 00 24, *zedde@le-grimaldi.com* (*expensive*). A delightful little hotel, with an excellent location, personal service and an agreeable charge of Provençal colour. *Closed 10–30 Jan.*

★★★Windsor, 11 Rue Dalpozzo, between the station and Promenade des Anglais, **t** 04 93 88 59 35, **f** 04 93 88 94 57, *contact@hotelwindsornice.com* (*expensive*). In the middle of a tropical garden, featuring a pool, an English-style pub, a Turkish-style hammam, a Thai-style sitting room and frescoes in the rooms.

★★Nouvel Hôtel, 19 bis Bd Victor Hugo, **t** 04 93 87 15 00, **f** 04 93 16 00 67, *www.nouvel-hotel.com, info@nouvel-hotel.com*, (*moderate*). More reasonable than some of the above, with bland, comfortable rooms, is this handsome Belle Epoque-style hotel.

★★Hôtel Trianon, 15 Av Auber, **t** 04 93 88 30 69, **f** 04 93 88 11 35 (*inexpensive*). Overlooking the Place Mozart in the musicians' quarter; a white grand piano serves as a reception desk, and the sweeping white staircase and little lift with a wrought-iron grille give it a comfortably old-fashioned feel.

★★Floride, 52 Bd de Cimiez, **t** 04 93 53 11 02, **f** 04 93 81 57 46. In quiet Cimiez, this hotel has lost some of its former charm, but is still an attractive old villa with a shady garden; each room has a TV and bath. The restaurant (*moderate*) only serves lunch.

★ La Belle Meunière, 21 Av Durante, **t** 04 93 88 66 15, **f** 04 93 82 51 76 (*inexpensive*). A stone's throw from the station, this friendly place is a long-time favourite of budget travellers in Nice – it even has parking and a little garden for breakfast. *Closed Dec–Jan.*

Les Orangeurs, 10 bis Av Durante, **t** 04 93 87 51 41, **f** 04 93 82 51 82 (*cheap*). A slightly downmarket, though comfortable alternative down the street from the Belle Meunière. Most rooms have balconies.

des Anges. If you descend by way of the Montée Eberlé and Rue Catherine Ségurane, you'll end up in the wide, yellow, arcaded 18th-century **Place Garibaldi**, named for Nice's most famous native son, who was born here when it was still called Nizza.

South of Place Garibaldi off Rue Neuve is the old parish church, **St-Martin-St-Augustin**, where a monk named Martin Luther said a Mass during his momentous pilgrimage to Rome in 1514. The dim interior was 'Baroqued' in the 17th century; its

Eating Out

The best restaurant-hunting territory is Vieux Nice and, especially for fresh fish, around Place Garibaldi and the port.

Chantecler, 37 Promenade des Anglais, t 04 93 16 64 00, f 04 93 88 35 68 (*luxury*). Gastronomic Nice is dominated by the Belle Epoque magnificence of this restaurant, which snuggles into the opulent arms of the Négresco. *Closed mid-Nov–mid-Dec.*

Don Camillo, 5 Rue des Ponchettes, t 04 93 85 67 95, f 04 93 13 97 43, *vianostephane@ wanadoo.fr* (*expensive*). Opened by a former pupil of Maximin and Paul Ducasse, and already celebrated for its home-made *ravioli* filled with Swiss chard *en daube,* and its desserts. *Closed Sun and Mon lunchtime.*

La Mérenda, 4 Rue de la Terrasse, near the Opera House and the Cours Saleya (*moderate*). Join the glitterati enjoying Dominique le Stanc's celebrated Niçois cuisine at this tiny bistro. *Closed weekends and school holidays. No credit cards.*

Le Safari, 1 Cours Saleya, t 04 93 80 18 44 (*moderate*). Enjoying a privileged spot overlooking the market, this is one of the few restaurants on this square where the waiters don't need to entice passers-by. With terrace and wood-fired oven.

Villa d'Este, 6 Rue Masséna, t 04 93 82 47 77, *infos@boccaccio-nice.com* (*moderate*). The best Italian restaurant in Nice, over three floors with *trompe-l'œil* Italianate décor in pretty pastel colours, attentive service and top-notch pasta. The plate of *antipasti* is a gastronomic feast.

Terres de Truffes, 11 Rue St-François-de-Paule, t 04 93 62 07 68. Tiny *bistrot* and shop, serving lots of truffle-flavoured dishes.

René Socca, 2 Rue Miralheti, t 04 93 92 05 73 (*cheap*). A self-service café offering *socca, pissaladière,* pizza by the slice and much more. *Closed Mon and Nov.*

Grand-Café de Turin, Place Garibaldi (*cheap*). Try this 19th-century café for a drink or a snack, or a platter of unidentifiable seafood.

M. Jo L'Ecailler, 5 Place Garibaldi, t 04 93 62 66 29 (*cheap*). This place serves up some of the best and cheapest oysters in town, and other shellfish. *Open until 11pm in summer.*

Fenocchio, Place Rossetti. It's hard to beat the 99 varieties of ice cream here: lavender cream, jasmine sorbet and the bitterest chocolate imaginable.

Entertainment

You can find out what's happening in Nice in the daily *Nice-Matin*

Rialto, 4 Rue de Rivoli, t 08 36 68 08 41. For films in their original language.

Opéra de Nice, 4–6 Rue St-François-de-Paule, information t 04 93 13 98 53, reservations t 04 92 17 40 00. Puts on operas, concerts and recitals at various locations.

Musée d'Art Moderne et d'Art Contemporain, t 04 93 62 61 62. Music, from ancient to avant-garde, and art videos.

CEDAC de Cimiez, 49 Av de la Marne, t 04 93 53 85 95. Big-league musicians and dancers, and jazz musicians.

Forum Nice Nord, 10 Bd Comte-de-Falicon, just off the A8 at Nice-Nord, t 04 93 84 24 37. A major venue for modern dance in July, and world music.

Clubs and Bars

Nice's nightlife is divided between expensive clubs, bland hotel piano bars and the livelier bars and clubs of Vieux Nice, which come and go like ships in the night.

De Klomp, 6 Rue Mascoïnat, near Place Rossetti, t 04 93 92 42 85, . A Dutch joint with live jazz and a hedonistic atmosphere (not for teetotallers or anti-smokers).

Bodéguita del Havana, 14 Rue Chauvain, t 04 93 92 67 24. Hopping salsa and Latin bar.

treasures include a fine *Pietà* (*c.* 1500) attributed to Ludovico Bréa, and a tatty photocopy of Garibaldi's baptismal certificate. Nearby, the **Palais Lascaris** at 15 Rue Droite (*open daily 10–12 and 2–6; closed Tues, hols and mid-Nov–mid-Dec*) is a grand 1648 mansion. The ground floor contains a reconstructed pharmacy of 1738; a fantastically opulent staircase leads up to the *étage noble*, saturated with elaborate Genoese *quadratura* (architectural trompe-l'œil) frescoes, Flemish tapestries, ornate wood-work, and a 1578 Italian precursor of the pianoforte.

Take Rue Rossetti west to the cafés of pretty Place Rossetti, dominated by Nice's 17th-century **Cathédrale Ste-Réparate**, designed by Jean-André Guibert and crowned with a joyful dome and lantern of glazed tiles in emerald bands.

Towards the sea in the heart of the Vieille Ville, **Cours Saleya** is an elongated little gem of urban planning, where bars and restaurants line up along the famous outdoor **market** and the **Chapelle de la Miséricorde**, designed in 1740 by Bernardo Vittone, a disciple of Turin's extraordinary Baroque architects Guarino Guarini and Juvarra; it has a superb interior (ask at the tourist office about your chances of getting in).

Around the Port

Overlooking the picturesque old port is the **Musée de Terra Amata**, 25 Bd Carnot (*buses 32 and 1 from central Nice; open daily 10–12 and 2–6; closed Mon and hols*), which incorporates a cave holding one of the world's oldest 'households', a pebble-walled wind-shelter discovered in 1966, built by elephant-hunters 400 millennia ago. Models, bones and tools evoke life in Nice at the dawn of time.

Up the Paillon: Modern Nice

In the old days Nice's laundresses plied their trade in the torrential waters of the Paillon, until the often dangerous river began to vanish under the pavements in the 1830s. Nearest the sea, **Jardin Albert Ier** is the site of the open-air **Théâtre de Verdure**, while upstream, as it were, vast terracotta-coloured **Place Masséna** is generously endowed with flower-beds and wisteria-shaded benches. Further up loom a pair of dreadnoughts erected by ex-mayor Jacques Médecin; the first of these is the 282-million-franc **Théâtre de Nice** and the marble-coated **Musée d'Art Moderne et d'Art Contemporain** (*open 10–6; closed Mon and hols; adm*). The building – four concrete towers, linked by glass walkways that seem to smile and frown and afford pleasant views over the city – is an admirable setting for the works of Christo, Niki de Saint-Phalle, Warhol, Dine, Oldenburg, Rauschenberg, Ben and other influential and irreverent figures of the 1960s and '70s. The view up the Paillon is blocked by the **Acropolis**, Médecin's 1985 megalithic congress and art centre and *cinémathèque*.

West of Place Masséna and the Promenade des Anglais

Important streets fan out from Place Masséna and the adjacent Jardin Albert Ier. Nice's main shopping street, **Avenue Jean Médecin**, leads up to the train station; **Rue Masséna** is the centre of a lively pedestrian-only restaurant and shopping zone; and the fabled, palm-lined sweep of the **Promenade des Anglais** around the Baie des Anges is still aglitter through the fumes of the traffic. The long pebble beach is crowded day and night in the summer. Visitors from the top end of the economic spectrum check into the fabled Belle Epoque **Hôtel Negresco** (No.37), vintage 1906. Next to it is the garden of the **Palais Masséna** (*closed for restoration, to reopen 2004*), now a *musée d'art et d'histoire*.

Fine Arts, and a Russian Cathedral

From the Masséna museum, a brisk 10-minute walk or bus 22 leads to the handsome 1876 villa that is home to the **Musée des Beaux-Arts**, 33 Av des Baumettes (*open daily 10–12 and 2–6; closed Mon; adm*), devoted to the 'old masters of the 19th century'. A room dedicated to Kees Van Dongen includes his entertaining 1927 *Tango of the Archangel,* which evokes the Roaring Twenties on the Riviera. Picasso also gets a look-in in this room with a small collection of ceramic pieces, while the cheerful Raoul Dufy's early Fauve works are his finest. One room is devoted to Jules Chéret.

In 1865, the young Tsarevich Nicholas was brought to Nice, and, like so many consumptives who arrived in search of health, he quickly declined. The luxurious villa where he died was demolished to construct the **Cathédrale Orthodoxe Russe St-Nicolas**, located a few blocks west of the train station at Av Nicolas II, just off Bd Gambetta (*bus 7 and 15; open daily, exc Sun am and services, 9.15–12 and 2.30–5; no shorts or sleeveless shirts; adm*). Paid for by Tsar Nicholas II and completed just before the Bolshevik Revolution, its onion domes glow with colourful glazed Niçois tiles; inside are frescoes, woodwork and icons.

Cimiez: Chagall, Matisse and Roman Ruins

On the low hills west of the Paillon, where wealthy Romans lived the good life in Cemenelum, modern Niçois do the same in Cimiez, a luxurious 19th-century suburb dotted with grand hotels, now genteel apartment buildings. Bus 15 from the Gare SNCF will take you to the main attractions, beginning with the **Musée National Message Biblique Marc Chagall** on Av du Docteur Ménard (*open Oct–June 10–5; July–Sept 10–6; closed Tues; adm*), built to house Chagall's cycle of 17 paintings based on stories from the Old Testament. They have been hung, as Chagall requested, chromatically rather than chronologically and are paired to complement each other's rich, glowing emeralds, cobalts and magentas. They leap with Chagall's idiosyncratic symbolism – tumbling flowers, fish, angels and rabbits.

Henri Matisse died in Cimiez in 1954 and left the city his works, now displayed in the **Musée Matisse**, set in the olive-studded Parc des Arènes (*take bus 15, 17, 20 or 22 from the Promenade des Anglais or Av Jean Médecin; open April–Sept 10–6; Oct–Mar 10–5; closed Tues and some hols; adm*). Matisse's last work, the gargantuan paper cut-out *Flowers and Fruit* (1952–3), dominates one whole side of the entrance hall. The main collection begins with some of his early bronze sculptures. There is also a lyrical series of back studies (*Dos*). Adjacent to the Matisse Museum is the new **Musée Archéologique** (*open April–Sept 10–12 and 2–6; Oct–Mar daily 10–1 and 2–5; closed Mon and some hols; adm*), entered through the excavations of Roman Cemenelum. These include the baths, a marble swimming pool, and the amphitheatre, with seating for 4,000. The museum houses vases, coins, statues, jewels, and models.

From here, walk back past the Matisse museum and across the park to the **Musée Franciscain, Eglise et Monastère de Cimiez** (*open daily 10–12 and 3–6; closed Sun and hols*). The Franciscans have been here since the 1500s; their church was heavily restored in 1850, although it still has two beautiful altarpieces by Ludovico Bréa, the *Vierge de Piété* and a *Crucifixion*.

Day Trips from Nice

Antibes

The old fishing port of Antibes belongs to the young – both locals who scoot, bike and skate to college, and visitors who frequent the mega-white boats mooored shoulder-to-shoulder in the harbour. Serious frolicking has moved to nearby Juan-les-Pins, but Antibes still retains an authentic vivacity all of its own.

A relic of Antibes' earlier incarnation as France's bulwark against Savoyard Nice are its sea-walls, especially the massive 16th-century **Fort Carré**. The handsome 17th- and 18th-century houses of Vieil Antibes look over their neighbours' shoulders towards the sea, obscuring it from **Cours Masséna**, the main street of Greek Antipolis, with its morning market selling cheese, olives and flowers, and café-filled **Place Nationale**.

The best sea views are monopolized by the **Château Grimaldi** – a seaside castle built by the same family who ran most of this coast at one time or another, including Antibes from 1385 to 1608. For six months in 1946, the owner, Romuald Dor, let Picasso use the second floor as a studio. Picasso, glad to have space to work in, quickly filled it up in a few months, only later discovering to his annoyance that all along Dor had intended to make his efforts into the **Musée Picasso** (*open summer 10–6 and Fridays 10am–10pm; winter 10–12 and 2–6; closed Mon and hols; adm*). Owing to the post-war lack of canvases and oil paint, Picasso used mostly fibro-cement and boat paint. You can't help but feel that he was exuberantly happy, inspired by the end of the war, his love of the time, Françoise Gillot, and the mytho-logical roots of the Mediterranean, expressed in *La Joie de vivre*, *Ulysse et ses sirènes* and 220 other works. Among the other artists represented, note the eight striking works on the top floor that Nicolas de Staël painted in Antibes.

Getting There

There are frequent Métrazur and TGV **trains** from Nice. Antibes' train station is at Place P. Sémard, about a 10min walk from the centre.

Buses from Nice's *gare routière* arrive at Place de Gaulle.

Tourist Information

Antibes ✉ 06600: 11 Place de Gaulle, t 04 92 90 53 00, f 04 92 90 53 01. *Open daily 9–7 in summer; winter Mon–Sat 9–12.30 and 1.30–6.*

Festivals

Europe's largest harbour, the Port Vauban in Antibes, fills up in July for the **Antibes Cup**, and there is more sporting fervour in October for the **Antibes Rally**.

Eating Out

Les Vieux Murs, Promenade Amiral-de-Grasse, t 04 93 34 06 73 (*expensive*). Cool and spacious, with wooden décor, and serving well-presented modern traditional food.

Le Sucrier, 6 Rue des Bains, t 04 93 34 85 40 (*moderate*). The chef is proud to be the great-great-nephew of Guy de Maupassant and spirits up traditional French classics with an exotic twist in a cavernous stone setting. *Closed Tues and Jan.*

Au Pied dans le Plat, 6 Rue Thuret, t 04 93 34 37 23 (*moderate*). The brave can try the house speciality, *tête de veau*, otherwise there's the sublimely simple fish soup. *Closed Mon.*

L'Oursin, 16 Rue de la République, t 04 93 34 13 46 (*moderate*). L'Oursin is famous for fresh fish and does particularly fine things with shellfish. *Closed Sun eve, and Mon.*

At the end of Promenade Amiral-de-Grasse, the Bastion St-André houses the **Musée d'Histoire et d'Archéologie** (*open June–Sept Tues–Sun 10–6, Fri till 10, guided tour Fri 3pm; Oct–May Tues–Sun 10–12 and 2–6; adm*), where Greek and Etruscan amphorae, monies and jewels dredged up from the sea and soil trace the history of Antibes.

Eze

Between Monaco and Nice, the highlight of the Moyenne Corniche has long been the extraordinary village of Eze, the most perched, perhaps, of any *village perché* in France, squeezed on to a cone of a hill 1,400ft over the sea.

Eze, they say, is named after a temple to Isis that the Phoenicians built on this hill. It then passed to the Romans, to the Saracens, and so on, although rarely did Eze change hands by force. Even if an enemy penetrated its 14th-century gate and walls, the tight little maze of stairs and alleys would confuse the attackers, the better to ambush them or spill boiling oil on their heads.

These days, if intruders reached far enough to assault what remains of the castle they would run into the needles of the South American cacti in the **Jardin Exotique** (*open Sept–June 9–12 and 2–6; July and Aug 9–8; adm*), a spiky paradise with a great view down to the sea. Eze's other non-commercial attraction, the cream and yellow

Getting There

Métrazur **trains** and all the frequent **buses** on the Nice–Menton route stop at Eze Bord-de-Mer on the Corniche Inférieure; in summer only, a minibus (*navette*) will shuttle you up to the village, but otherwise it's a long, steep 1½hr climb. There are 7 **buses** a day (no.112) from Nice directly for Eze-Village.

Tourist Information

Eze-Village ✉ 06360: Place Général de Gaulle, t 04 93 41 26 00, f 04 93 41 04 80, *www.eze-riviera.com*, *eze@webstore.fr*. Walkers can pick up an excellent little guide to walks in the area here. *Open April–Oct Mon–Sat 9–7, Sun 10–1 and 2–7; Nov–Mar Mon–Sat 9.30–6.30, Sun 9.30–1 and 2–6.30.*

Eating Out

★★★★**Château Eza**, Rue de la Pise, t 04 93 41 12 24, f 04 93 41 16 64, *www.slh.com/chatueza* (*luxury*). This former prince's residence is actually a collection of medieval houses linked together to form an eagle's nest, all sharing an extraordinary perched terrace restaurant (*luxury–expensive*), with aromatic

Niçois and other Provençal specialities to match. *Hotel closed Nov–Mar, restaurant closed Nov–Christmas.*

★★★★**La Chèvre d'Or**, Rue du Barri, t 04 92 10 66 66, f 04 93 41 06 72, *reservations@ chevredor.com, www.chevredor.com* (*luxury*). Chef Jean-Marc Delacourt creates refined, light versions of the French classics. *Reserve well in advance. Closed Dec–Feb.*

Mas Provençal, Av de Verdun, t 04 93 41 19 53 (*expensive*). Just outside the tangle of medieval streets, this *mas* is covered in flowers and ivy, and ensconced in the 19th century. Sink into plush red velvet chairs (with antimacassars) and dine on milk-fed pig roasted on a spit, or *risotto aux cèpes*, before ordering the carriage home. *Closed Sun in winter.*

Le Troubadour, 4 Rue du Brec, t 04 93 41 19 03 (*expensive–moderate*). Turbot or *filet de bœuf aux cèpes* go down nicely here, and the price is nice too. *Closed Sun and Mon lunch and mid-Nov–mid-Dec.*

Le Nid d'Aigle, Rue du Château, t 04 93 41 19 08 (*moderate*). Head to this place on the summit of the rock, next door to the Jardin Exotique, for lofty fish (*daurade au pistou*, salmon) and all kinds of Provençal staples, including *lapin à la provençale. Closed Tues eve and Wed eve.*

Chapelle des Pénitents Blancs, built in 1766, has gathered an eccentric collection of scraps.

A steep, winding scenic path descending to Eze-Bord-de-Mer is called the **Sentier Frédéric Nietzsche** after the philosopher. (It starts at the entrance to the old village, down a narrow, almost hidden, path on the left, which also leads to a small observation spot.) Nietzsche, however, walked up instead of down, an arduous trek that made his head spin and inspired the third part of his *Thus Spake Zarathustra*.

Entrevaux

High up the Var valley, under the sweeping twist of its cliffs, **Entrevaux** has had a fort of some kind since Roman times. Its present incarnation is particularly impressive – the work of Louis XIV's celebrated engineer Vauban – high above the village, complete with Second World War additions. At the time it was built, the French-Piedmontese border was only a few miles away (it is now the departmental boundary between Var and Alpes-Maritimes). The entrance is a fortified bridge, rebuilt by Vauban on medieval foundations. Around the village, vestiges of its old garrison days can be seen: barracks and powder-houses, and an ancient drawbridge, still in working order, behind the 17th-century cathedral.

There's a honeycomb of buildings and narrow alleys where people live; if you wander through the smelly damp alleys there are flowers high up in the windows, duvets thrown over the sills in the mornings. The serious part of the fort is a hard 15-minute climb if you're fit; take water, a sunhat, some historical imagination and some coins for the turnstile and you're on your own to explore the derelict tunnels and dungeons – once deliciously dangerous, now undergoing restoration to make them safe. The landscape below, with the little *Train des Pignes*, is as unlikely as an alpine train set. Try to get up there before 9am, when the first of the coaches are beginning to fit themselves in below. Harley fans will enjoy Entrevaux's **Musée de la Moto** (*open April–Sept 10–12 and 2–7*), a collection of motorcycles from 1901 to 1967.

Getting There

The scenic, recently modernized, narrow-gauge Chemin de Fer de Provence **rail line** travels from Nice to Digne. It leaves Nice every two hours from the **Gare du Sud**, 4 bis Rue Alfred-Binet, **t** 04 93 82 10 17, and follows the Var, stopping at Entrevaux.

Tourist Information

Entrevaux ☒ 04320: at the Porte Royale du Pont Levis, **t** 04 93 05 46 73, **f** 04 93 05 40 71, *www.netprovence.com/sivomentrevaux*, *sivomentrevaux@wanadoo.fr*. Open *Feb–June 9–12 and 1–5.30 (Feb–April Mon–Fri, April–June daily); July–Aug daily 9–7;* Sept–Nov 9–12 and 1.30–6 (Oct–Nov until 5.30).

Eating Out

Vauban, **t** 04 93 05 42 40, **f** 04 93 05 48 38 (*inexpensive; restaurant moderate*). Surprisingly, the only hotel in Entrevaux. *Closed Jan; restaurant closed Mon.*
L'Echauguette, Place de la Mairie, **t** 04 93 05 49 60 (*moderate*). Outside tables, and menus including some seafood and, for starters, a salad served with the local speciality, a beef sausage called *secca*.
Le Pont Levis, Place Louis Moreau, **t** 04 93 05 40 12 (*moderate*). Good cuisine; great view of fort, village and valley. *Closed Fri.*

Touring from Nice

You'll find that the sights are reliably open 10–12 and 2–5 and charge adm, unless stated.

Day 1: Shopping and Glamour

Morning: Take the N7 west from Nice and turn right just before Antibes on to the D4 for **Biot**. Visit the bubble-glass factories at the bottom of the hill, then go up to the village for pottery and pottering.

Lunch: Under the shady arcades in the charming central square at **Arcade**, 16 Place des Arcades, **t** 04 93 65 01 04 (*moderate*), for a salad or simple *soupe au pistou*.

Afternoon: Back down to the N7 and through Antibes, then right again onto the D145 for a quick stop in the ceramic *ateliers* of **Vallauris** (*Av G. Clemenceau*) and the decorated chapel that is the Musée National Picasso (*Place de la Libération; closed Tues*). Then head for the shops of **Cannes** and a late-afternoon stroll along the Croisette and up into the Vieux Port and lanes of Le Suquet.

Dinner: Push the boat out at **La Belle Otero**, on the 7th floor of the Carlton, 58 La Croisette, **t** 04 92 99 51 10 (*luxury*). The seventh heaven of gastronomy; it has two Michelin stars. *Closed June, and Sun, Mon, and Tues lunch out of season.* For affordable seafood and fine views of its original habitat, try **Lou Souléou**, 16 Bd Jean Hibert, **t** 04 93 39 85 55 (*moderate*). *Closed Mon and Nov.*

Sleeping: ★★★**Bleu Rivage**, 61 La Croisette, **t** 04 93 94 24 25, **f** 04 93 43 74 92, *www.cannes-hotels.com* (*expensive*). Or, if you aren't in Cannes on an MGM expense account, try ★**Le Chanteclair**, 12 Rue Forville, **t/f** 04 93 39 68 88 (*moderate*). *Closed Nov.*

Day 2: Grasse and the Gorges du Loup

Morning: Head north from Cannes on the N85 for perfumed **Grasse**. See the morning market in Place aux Aires, then follow your nose to the Parfumerie Fragonard (*20 Bd Fragonard*), for a free tour, and the 17th-century Villa Fragonard at no.23 (*closed Nov*).

Lunch: For a Tuscan feast *al fresco*, try chef Jacques Chibois' sumptuous creations at **Bastide Saint Antoine**, 48 Rue Henri Dunant, **t** 04 93 70 94 94 (*luxury*). **Les Arcades**, Place aux Aires, **t** 04 93 36 00 95 (*moderate*) offers an elegant lunch underneath the arches.

Afternoon: Take the D2085 and the D3 to **Gourdon** and its 13th-century château (*open summer 11–1 and 2–7, winter 2–7, closed Tues*). Then drive north, cross the river at Bramafan and drive south down the D6 along the fantastical cliffs and waterfalls of the spectacular **Gorges du Loup**. At **Pont du Loup** is the Confiserie Florian, where glacé fruits are made. From here the D2210 leads to **Tourrettes-sur-Loup**, in summer a veritable souk of handmade fabrics and crafts, where the 15th-century village church has a triptych by the school of Ludovico Bréa. From here it is only a short way on to the medieval *ville fortifiée* of **Vence** for dinner.

Dinner: Elegant and traditional French fare at **Les Templiers**, 39 Av Joffre, **t** 04 93 58 06 05 (*expensive*); rustic Provençal surroundings and warm service. *Closed Mon.* **La Farigoule**, 15 Av Henri Isnard, **t** 04 93 58 01 27 (*moderate*) has Provençal cuisine and good fresh fish. *Closed Tues, and Wed lunch.*

Sleeping: ★★★**Villa La Roseraie**, 14 Av H. Giraud, **t** 04 93 58 02 20, **f** 04 93 58 99 31 (*expensive*) offers a garden and enormous home-made breakfasts beside an impeccable pool. *Closed mid-Nov–mid-Feb.* ★★★**Diana**, Av des Poilus, **t** 04 93 58 28 56, **f** 04 93 24 64 06, *www.hotel.diana-vence.com* (*moderate*) has very reasonable single and double rooms in the historic centre of Vence.

Day 3: Art in Vence and St-Paul

Morning: Explore Vence: the solid walls and gates of the Vieille Ville, the old Roman forum and modern marketplace of Place du Peyra, and the little treasures of the rococo cathedral. Then follow Avenue des Poilus to the route for St-Jeannet or in summer take the mini-tourist train from the main square to the serene Chapelle du Rosaire (*open Tues and Thurs 10–11.30 and 2–5.30, Mon, Wed and Sat 2–5.30; closed Nov; adm*), built and designed by Matisse for the Dominican nuns and glowing with bright colour.

Lunch: **Le Pigeonnier**, Place du Peyra, **t** 04 93 58 03 00 (*moderate*), in the Vieille Ville, makes its own pasta and *ravioli*. *Closed Fri, Sat lunch and Nov–Mar.* Or try one of 500 combinations of pizza toppings at **Le Pêcheur du Soleil**, Place Godeau (behind the church).

Afternoon: Just south of Vence is **St-Paul-de-Vence**, another fortified hill town that has been a mecca for artists ever since the first owner of the Colombe d'Or restaurant began accepting paintings in exchange for hospitality. Its pretty little cobbled lanes are now packed with visitors and trinkets. A short woody uphill walk or shorter drive from St-Paul (*well signposted*) is the shady Fondation Maeght, a vibrant centre for contemporary art set in a sculpture garden populated by bronze Giacometti figures, mosaic fish and whimsical fountains.

Dinner: Le Sainte Claire, Espace Ste-Claire, t 04 93 32 02 02 (*moderate*) has sturdy Provençal décor to match the cuisine, served on its panoramic terrace a couple of minutes by car from St-Paul. *Closed Tues in summer.* Or eat at Les Remparts, below.

Sleeping: One of the loveliest hotels in the area is ★★★Le Hameau, 528 Rte de La Colle, t 04 93 32 80 24, f 04 93 32 55 75 (*expensive*), with wide views over the orange groves, and a small pool. *Closed mid-Nov–21 Dec and 7 Jan–mid-Feb.* Cheaper is ★★Hostellerie Les Remparts, 72 Rue Grande, t 04 93 32 09 88, f 04 93 32 06 91 (*inexpensive*), with medieval nooks and antiques; there's also a good, affordable restaurant.

Day 4: Hill Villages and Lemons
Morning: Set off early back down to Nice and take the D2204 towards Sospel. Just after Drap, turn right onto the D21 for a tour of the hill villages of **Peillon**, with its Chapelle des Pénitents Blancs, and the isolated **Peille**.

Lunch: Eat early in Peillon at the ★★★Auberge de la Madone, t 04 93 79 91 17 (*expensive*), just outside the walled village. *Closed Jan, 20 Oct–20 Dec and Wed.* Or try **Hostellerie Sérôme**, 20 Rue de Cessole, t 04 92 41 51 51 (*moderate*) for simple but delicious food.

Afternoon: Take the dramatic D22 Col de la Madone over the mountain to busier **Ste-Agnès**, a maze of shady passages and arches with a fort on the hillside above. Then drive down the D22 to smart, tidy **Menton** and visit the 17th-century harbour bastion that is now the Musée Cocteau (*closed Tues*), and the Salle des Mariages in the Hôtel de Ville (*weekdays only*), decorated by Jean Cocteau on the themes of love and lemons.

Dinner: La Coquille d'Or, on the corner of Quai Bonaparte, t 04 93 35 80 67 (*moderate*) packs in crowds of locals for the *bouillabaisse* and

paella. *Closed Wed.* **Le Nautic**, 27 Quai de Monléon, t 04 93 35 78 74 (*moderate*). Opposite the Musée Cocteau, this bright blue eatery serves fish. *Closed Mon and Sept–June.* All along Rue St-Michel, masses of restaurants vie for your attention.

Sleeping: ★★★Royal Westminster, 28 Av Félix Faure, t 04 93 28 69 69, f 04 92 10 12 30, westminster@wanadoo.fr (*expensive*). Part of a hotel chain on the seafront, with quiet rooms furnished in cool sea colours. *Closed Nov.* On the flowery, clipped Jardin Biovès is ★★Claridge's, 39 Av de Verdun, t 04 93 35 72 53, f 04 93 35 42 90 (*inexpensive*), a slightly old-fashioned, quiet hotel.

Day 5: Monte-Carlo or Bust
Morning: Head west along the coast for a quick wonder at the tall buildings and designer stores of **Monte-Carlo**. Then keep going on the N98 to **Beaulieu-sur-Mer** and the Villa Kerylos (*open Feb–Oct 10.30–6; Nov–Jan Mon–Fri 2–6, Sat and Sun 10–6; adm*), a striking reproduction of a 5th-century BC Athenian house.

Lunch: In summer, in the conservatory restaurant of the Villa Ephrussi, *see below*.

Afternoon: On the road to **St-Jean-Cap-Ferrat** is another fantastic repro-retro fantasy, the Villa Ephrussi de Rothschild (*open Feb–Oct 10–6, Nov–Jan 2–6*), a pink 18th-century-style house full of art and an eclectic set of little stylised gardens on the Cap Ferrat isthmus overlooking two bays. Then head for **Villefranche**, only half an hour from Nice, for a late-afternoon swim in the shallow bay as the buildings piled up above the quay turn golden in the setting sun.

Dinner: Le Carpaccio, Plage des Marinières, t 04 93 01 72 97 (*expensive*). Long a favourite of the Rolls-Royce crowd from Monaco, yet affordable for a night-time splurge or a pizza. Or, uphill from the sea, you pass **La Belle Epoque**, Place de la Paix, t 04 93 01 96 22 (*cheap*), with outside terrace.

Sleeping: Just beside the port at the ★★★Welcome, Quai Amiral Courbet, t 04 93 76 27 62, f 04 93 76 27 66, www.welcome-hotel.fr (*expensive*); rooms on the 5th floor are ravishing (*half board*). Or try the unpretentious ★★Provençal, 4 Av du Maréchal Joffre, t 04 93 01 71 42, f 04 93 76 96 00, provencal@riviera.fr (*moderate*).

Toulon

To the Provençal, the south's two great ports, Toulon and Marseille, are dangerous, salty cities, populated by untrustworthy strangers and prostitutes. But while Marseille is essentially a city of merchants and trade, Toulon has always been the creature of the French navy, and whatever piquant charms its old port and quarter once had were bombed into oblivion in the Second World War.

Central Toulon

From the train station, Av Vauban descends to Av du Maréchal Leclerc. On the right at No.113 is the grandly gloomy municipal museum and library; inside are the **Musée**

Getting to Toulon

Buzz (see p.6) flies to Toulon directly from London Stansted.

Getting from the Airport

Toulon's airport is out near Hyères. **Shuttle buses** take you the 40min journey into town at Bd Toesca, opposite the train station, costing €9.50. **Taxis** are a whopping €38 before 7pm and €53 after 7pm.

Getting Around

The **train** station is on the northern side of Toulon in Place Albert 1er, and has frequent services up and down the coast.

For St-Tropez and the coast between Hyères and St-Raphaël, catch an (expensive) SODETRAV bus from the *gare routière* (next to the train station), t 04 94 18 93 40.

From Quai Cronstadt, pleasant and very reasonably priced **sea-buses** go to La Seyne, Les Sablettes and St-Mandrier. **City bus** and sea-bus info can be obtained from Allô Bus on t 04 94 03 87 03. **Boat** companies departing from Quai Cronstadt offer tours of Toulon's anchorages and the surrounding coasts and islands, including Trans-med 2000, t 04 94 92 96 82, for tours to the Ile de Porquerolles.

Car Hire

Taxi firms congregate at the train station:
Avis, t 04 94 89 14 38.
Citer, t 04 94 92 52 29.
Europcar, t 04 94 92 52 92.
Hertz, t 04 94 22 02 88.

Tourist Information

Toulon: Place Raimu, t 04 94 18 53 00, f 04 94 18 53 09, *toulon.tourisme@wanadoo.fr*, *www.toulontourisme.com*. Open Mon–Sat 9.30–5.30, Sun 10–12.

Market Days

On **Cours Lafayette** every morning except Monday – don't miss it; big flea markets on the eastern (industrial zone) outskirts of the city on Sunday morning.

Shopping

Most of Toulon's hops, both modern and traditional, can be found around **Rue d'Alger**, **Rue Hoche**, **Rue Jean Jaurès** and **Rue Henri Seillon**; and the **Maillol** shopping centre is worth a visit also.

Where to Stay

Toulon ✉ 83000
***La Corniche**, 17 Littoral F. Mistral, Mourillon, t 04 94 41 35 12, f 04 94 41 24 58, *www.cornichehotel.com, info@cornichehotel.com* (expensive). A cleverly designed modern Provençal hotel, air-conditioned and near the beach. It has a restaurant built around the trunks of three maritime pines. *Restaurant closed Sun eve and Mon.*
La Résidence de Cap Brun, 192 Chemin de l'Aviateur Gayraud, off Corniche Gén. de Gaulle, t 04 94 41 29 46, f 04 94 63 16 16, *info@gaudefroy-receptions.com* (expensive–moderate). A magical old white villa set

d'Histoire Naturelle (*open Mon–Fri 9.30–12 and 2–6, Sat and Sun 1–6*), and the **Musée d'Art** (*open daily 1–6.30, closed hols*). The natural history museum has stuffed birds and beasts; and the art museum contains an above-average collection of paintings and sculptures, including a Fragonard and some sculptures by Vernet and France's great Baroque sculptor and architect, Pierre Puget. There's also a strong contemporary collection upstairs. Next door is the quiet, spacious **Jardin Alexandre I**er, with lovely magnolias and cedar trees, and, in the centre, an indomitable bust of Puget and a monument to the soldiers of the First World War. The Toulonnais do pretty well for local free museums; across the road, heading towards the centre of the town, the **Hôtel des Arts**, at 236 Av du Maréchal Leclerc, is a lofty, elegant building devoted to modern art which, again, usually puts the spotlight on the work of local artists.

on a clifftop beyond the beaches of Mourillon. Surrounded by pine and plane trees and a world away from the urban hubbub of Toulon, it has a small swimming pool and a steep stone path down to the shore. *No restaurant. Closed Nov–Mar.*

★★Grand Hôtel du Dauphiné, 10 Rue Berthelot, **t** 04 94 92 20 28, **f** 04 94 62 16 69, *www. grandhoteldauphine.com, contact@ grandhoteldauphine.fr* (*inexpensive*). In the pedestrian zone, not far from the opera, this is a comfortable, friendly older hotel, air-conditioned, with discounted parking.

★Le Jaurès, 11 Rue Jean Jaurès, **t** 04 94 92 83 04, **f** 04 94 62 16 74 (*inexpensive–cheap*). The top bargain choice; the rooms all have baths.

Eating Out

Le Lingousto, Rte de Pierrefeu, Cuers, **t** 04 94 28 69 10 (*expensive*). Toulonnais in search of a special meal drive 20km northeast to Cuers to eat here in an old *bastide*, where the freshest of fresh local ingredients are transformed into imaginative works of art. *Closed Sun eve and Mon, and Jan–Feb.*

Le Jardin du Sommelier, 20 Allées Amiral Courbet, **t** 04 94 62 03 27 (*expensive*). Gastronomic Provençal cuisine with wines to match in a small, intimate dining room, perfect for 'un tête-à-tête en amoureux'. *Closed Sat lunchtime and Sun.*

Le Lido, Littoral Frédéric Mistral, **t** 04 94 03 38 18 (*moderate*). A restaurant with nice, nautical décor and a window on to the kitchen. *Closed Sun eve and Mon in winter.*

La Chamade, 25 Rue de la Comédie, **t** 04 94 92 28 58 (*moderate*). Another local favourite which offers a very serious fixed three-course menu prepared by chef Francis Bonneau. *Closed Sun and first three weeks Aug.*

Le Cellier, 52 Rue Jean Jaurès, **t** 04 94 92 64 35 (*moderate*). Jovial and friendly, with good menus. *Closed Sat and Sun.*

Le Jardin d'Any, 115 Cours Lafayette, **t** 04 94 41 01 22 (*cheap*). Armenian cuisine. *Closed evenings.*

Entertainment

Pick up a paper or copy of *La Gazette* to tell you what's really going on. In July, there's also the **Jazz is Toulon** festival, **t** 04 94 09 71 00.

Opéra, Place Victor Hugo, **t** 04 94 92 70 78. Stages opera and inane comedies in winter.

Zenith-Oméga concert hall, Place des Lices, **t** 04 94 22 66 77. Rapidly becoming the number one rock venue in the south.

Bar à Thym, 32 Bd Cunéo, **t** 04 94 41 90 10. Live rock on a smaller, more relaxed scale.

Pathé Liberté, 4 Place de la Liberté, **t** 04 36 68 22 88. Six screens and comfortable seats.

Pathé Grand Ciel, opposite the university at La Garde, **t** 04 36 68 22 88. Twelve screens and films in their original language (*v.o.*).

Bars and Clubs

There is no lack of **bars**, both straight and gay, especially around Rue Pierre Sémard, but in general they're not places where you'll feel comfortable alone. Toulon society prefers the bars along Littoral Frédéric Mistral on Mourillon beach.

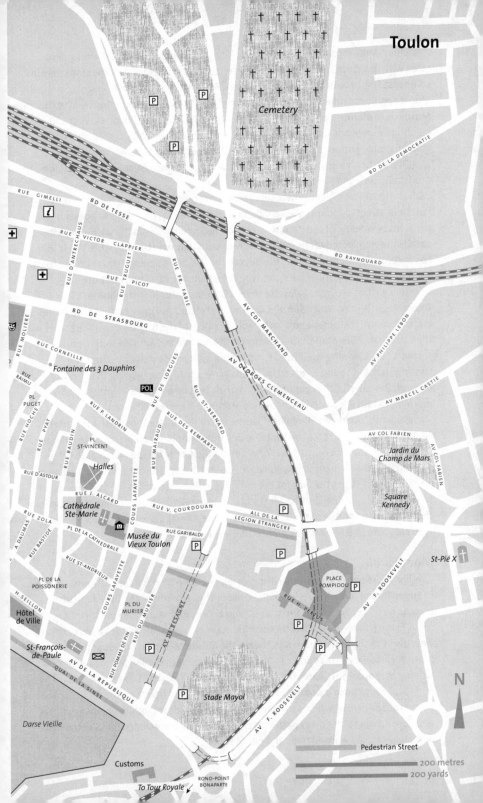

Toulon

Cemetery

RUE GIMELLI
BD DE TESSE
BD DE LA DEMOCRATIE
BD RAYNOUARD
RUE D'ANTRECHAUS
RUE VICTOR CLAPPIER
RUE TRUGUET
RUE PICOT
RUE FR. FABIE
BD DE STRASBOURG
AV CDT MARCHAND
AV PHILIPPE LEBON
RUE MOLIERE
RUE CORNEILLE
Fontaine des 3 Dauphins
AV GEORGES CLEMENCEAU
AV MARCEL CASTIE
RUE RAIMU
POL
RUE DE LORGUES
AV COL FABIEN
AV COL FABIEN
PL PUGET
RUE P. LANDRIN
RUE ST-BERNARD
Jardin du Champ de Mars
RUE HOCHE
RUE PYAT
RUE BAUDIN
PL ST-VINCENT
RUE MAIRAUD
RUE DES REMPARTS
Square Kennedy
RUE D'ASTOUR
Halles
COURS LAFAYETTE
RUE J. ALCARD
RUE V. COURDOUAN
ALL DE LA LEGION ETRANGERE
RUE ZOLA
Cathédrale Ste-Marie
PL DE LA CATHEDRALE
RUE GARIBALDI
St-Pié X
RUE DAUMAS
RUE BASTIDE
Musée du Vieux Toulon
PLACE POMPIDOU
AV F. ROOSEVELT
RUE ST-ANDRIEUX
PL DE LA POISSONERIE
COURS LAFAYETTE
PL DU MURIER
RUE H. PERTUS
Hôtel de Ville
RUE POMME DE PIN
RUE DU MURIER
AV DE BESAGNE
H. SEILLON
St-François-de-Paule
AV DE LA REPUBLIQUE
QUAI DE LA SINSE
Stade Mayol
AV F. ROOSEVELT
Darse Vieille
Customs
To Tour Royale
ROND-POINT BONAPARTE

Pedestrian Street
200 metres
200 yards

N

Avenue J. Moulin continues down to the large bleak square of **Place d'Armes**, decorated with ordnance from the adjacent arsenal, one of the biggest single employers in southeast France with some 10,000 workers. Alongside the arsenal in Place Monsenergue are miniature versions of the ships that it once made, displayed in the **Musée de la Marine** (*open daily 2–6; adm*). Puget started out in Toulon carving and painting figureheads for the ships, and the museum has works by his followers. The grand Baroque entrance to the building itself is the original Louis XIV arsenal gate of 1738. The best surviving works of Puget in Toulon are the two **Atlantes** (1657) on Quai Cronstadt, *Force* and *Fatigue*.

Off the Quai, Rue d'Alger, now a popular evening promenade, used to be the most notorious street in Toulon's **Vieille Ville**, or *'le petit Chicago'*, the pungent pocket of the pre-war town. Some of the narrow streets off here are still distinctly unsavoury after dark. However, blocked off from the sea by rows of ugly new buildings, the Vieille Ville has become almost respectable; the days of the last bit of genuine sleaze on the coast are numbered as the shifty bars give way to fashionable cafés and boutiques.

Further east, at 69 Cours Lafayette there's the dingy **Musée Historique du Vieux Toulon** (*open 2–5.45, closed Sun and hols*), with sketches by Puget, historical odds and ends, Provençal costumes and a 19th-century model of the town. Around the corner is the cathedral of **Ste-Marie**, 17th-century on the outside and Romanesque-Gothic within. Cours Lafayette itself used to be known as *'le pavé d'amour'*, a favourite trysting spot, but young lovers today would have a hard time fighting their way through the babel of the colourful daily market that now runs its length. Come in the morning to take it in, along with the fish market in Place de la Poissonnerie.

In attractive, café-lined Place Puget, at the top of the adjacent pedestrian quarter, is Toulon's prettiest fountain, the **Fontaine des Trois Dauphins**, sculpted by two young Toulonnais in the 18th century and now almost hidden by foliage. North of the three dolphins is Toulon's main street, Boulevard de Strasbourg, site of the **Opéra** (*t 04 94 92 70 78; open Oct–May*), the biggest opera-house in Provence, noted for its acoustics, with an interior inspired by Charles Garnier. In Place Victor Hugo, in front of the Opéra, there is a wistful statue of the actor Jules Muraire, affectionately known as 'Raimu', who was born at 6 Rue Anatole France, off the Place des Armes, in 1883.

Mont Faron

Toulon looks better seen from a distance. Bus no.40 will take you to Bd Amiral Vence in **Super-Toulon** (bus stop *Téléphérique*), site of the terminus of the little **funicular** (*t 04 94 92 68 25; open Tues–Sun 9.30–12 and 2–6; adm*) that runs to the top of 1,755ft Mont Faron (which means 'lighthouse mountain' in Provençal). Besides a tremendous view over the city and its harbours, there's the **Musée Mémorial du Débarquement** (*open Tues–Sun 9.45–11.45 and 1.45–4.30; adm*), devoted to the August 1944 Allied landing in Provence. It shares the summit with a **zoo** (*t 04 94 88 07 89; open daily May–Sept 10–7, closed mornings in winter; adm; combined tickets for the funicular and the zoo are available*), which specializes in breeding wildcats, including jaguars, tigers and lions. In 1997 a 'discovery path' was created among the wooded parks of the peak, with well-marked walking trails and picnic spots.

Around the Harbour

Buses 3 and 13 from in front of the station or on Av du Maréchal Leclerc will take you to the **Plage du Mourillon**, Toulon's largest beach and site of the city's oldest fort, Louis XII's 1514 Grosse Tour or **Tour Royale**, which once guarded the eastern approaches to Toulon with its rounded 16–24ft-thick walls. In later years the lower part, excavated out of the rock, was used as a prison and now contains an annexe of the **Musée Naval** (*open April–Sept daily 10–6.30; closed Tues; adm*), with more figureheads in a baleful setting. Two beautiful coastal paths – the Sentier des Douaniers and the gentler Promenade Henri Fabre – leave from the Plage du Mourillon, and offer glimpses of hidden coves shaded by umbrella pines.

Day Trips from Toulon

St-Mandrier-sur-Mer

Beyond the fine sands of **Les Sablettes** beach, the hilly St-Mandrier peninsula closes off the west end of the Grande Rade, which was an island until the mid-17th century. The quiet and unassuming fishing village and marina of **St-Mandrier-sur-Mer** is easily accessible by sea bus (28M) from Quai Cronstadt in Toulon and has a little sandy beach by the port and a wonderful, wild (if pebbly) beach, **Plage de la Cadoulière**, on the opposite side of the isthmus, popular with windsurfers and without a beach concession in sight. **Coastal paths** (*sentiers littoraux*), which are marked with yellow painted signs, leave from here to the equally unravaged Plage de Cavalas and the more sophisticated Plage de St-Asile, a favourite with families.

Hyères and Porquerolles

Hyères claims to be the original resort of the Côte d'Azur, with a pedigree that goes back to Charles IX and Catherine de' Medici, who wintered here in 1564. In the early 19th century, people like Empress Josephine, Pauline Borghese, Victor Hugo, Tolstoy and Robert Louis Stevenson built villas here, before it faded genteelly from fashion in the 1880s. For despite its mild climate and lush gardens (for which it has recently won prizes), Hyères was, unforgivably, three miles from the newly popular seaside.

Take a brief wander into the **Vieille Ville**, beyond Place Massillon. Here stands the Tour des Templiers, a remnant from a Templar's lodge, and, on top of a monumental stair, the church of St-Paul (1599) with 400 ex-votos dating back to the 1600s and a set of *santons* too large to move. The Renaissance house next to St-Paul doubles as a city gate, through which you can walk up to Parc St-Bernard. At the upper part of the park, the **Villa de Noailles** was designed as a *château cubiste* for art patron Vicomte Charles de Noailles. The Noailles' garden has been recently linked to that of Edith Wharton, author of *The Age of Innocence*, who lived on the same slope in a former convent of Ste-Claire, spread over 28 terraces (*open daily 8–7; free*). Further up the hill are the hollow walls and towers of the **Vieux Château** with an overview of Hyères' peninsula (originally the island of Giens, it has been anchored to the continent by two sand-bars whose arms embrace a salt marsh).

Getting There

Hyères–Toulon **airport** is served by **Buzz** (*see* p.6). If you're setting off from Toulon, the **train** is best. Hyères is a dead end, linked to Toulon but nowhere else; the station is 1.5km south of town, but there are buses into the centre.

SODETRAV, 47 Av Alphonse Denis, **t** 04 94 12 55 00, runs **buses** from Toulon's *gare routière*.

City buses (from the *gare routière* in the town centre) link Hyères to Hyères-Plage.

Boats for all three of Hyères' islands – Porquerolles, Port-Cros and Le Levant – depart at least twice a day, year-round, from **Port d'Hyères** (**t** 04 94 12 54 40), with additional sailings in the summer. There are more frequent connections from **La Tour-Fondue**, at the tip of the Giens peninsula, to Porquerolles (**t** 04 94 58 21 81). In summer boats also sail from Toulon to **Porquerolles**.

Tourist Information

Hyères ✉ 83400: 3 Av Ambroise Thomas, **t** 04 94 01 84 50, **f** 04 94 01 84 51, *www.ot-hyeres.fr. Open daily 8–8 in summer; Mon–Fri 9–6, Sat 10–4 in winter.*

Eating Out

Hyères
Le Bistrot de Marius, 1 Place Massillon, **t** 04 94 35 88 38 (*moderate*). A tiny stone establishment with big platefuls of Provençal favourites, a very jolly host and tables out on the main square in summer. *Closed Dec and Jan.*

La Colombe, Impasse Vieille, La Bayorre, **t** 04 94 35 35 16 (*moderate*). For a more elaborate dinner, try the delicious *turbot au beurre d'herbe tendre. Closed Sun eve and Mon.*

Les Jardins de Bacchus, 32 Av Gambetta, **t** 04 94 65 77 63 (*moderate*). Pulls out all the stops with its rich, flavoursome Provençal dishes and quietly elegant surroundings. *Closed Sun eve and Mon in winter; Sun lunch and Mon in summer.*

Ile de Porquerolles
Il Pescatore, **t** 04 94 58 30 61 (*moderate*). For all things fish: not just the predictable *bouillabaisse*, but *carpaccio* and *sashimi*. Eat on the restful terrace overlooking the boats bobbing in the port. *Closed Nov–Feb.*

Hyères' three islands, the **Iles d'Hyères**, are voluptuous little greenhouses that have seen more than their share of trouble. In the Middle Ages they belonged to St-Honorat by Cannes, and attracted pirates like moths to a flame; in 1160, after the Saracens carried off the entire population, the monks gave up and just let the pirates have the islands. In the late 19th century, they were used to quarantine veterans of the colonial wars and as Dickensian orphanages. Largest of the islands, **Porquerolles** stretches 7km by 3km and has the largest population, which in the summer explodes to 10,000. Its main village, also called Porquerolles, was founded in 1820 as a retirement village for Napoleon's finest soldiers and invalids. It still has a colonial air, especially around the central pine-planted Place d'Armes, the address of most of Porquerolles' restaurants, hotels and bicycle hire shops. Although the cliffs to the south are steep and dangerous, there are gentle beaches on either side of the village.

St-Tropez

In 1956 Brigitte Bardot came down here to star in Roger Vadim's *Et Dieu créa la femme* and incidentally made this lovely fishing village into the national showcase of free-spirited fun, sun and sex. Pre-BB, St-Tropez was discovered by painters in the early 1900s. Writers, most famously Colette, joined the artists' 'Montparnasse on the Mediterranean' in the 1920s. The third wave of even more conspicuous invaders,

Parisian existentialists and glitterati came in the 1950s, when Françoise '*Bonjour Tristesse*' Sagan and Bardot made St-Trop the pinnacle of chic.

If everything about St-Tropez fills you with dismay, let the **Musée de l'Annonciade** (*open Oct–May 10–12 and 2–6, June–Sept 10–12 and 3–7, closed Tues, holidays and Nov; adm*) be your reason to visit. It concentrates on works by painters in Paul Signac's St-Tropez circle, post-Impressionists and Fauves – colour-saturated paintings that take on a life of their own with Vlaminck (*Le Pont de Chatou*) and Derain (*Westminster Palace* and *Waterloo Bridge*), along with works by Braque, Matisse, Vuillard, Bonnard, Van Dongen and Dufy. Just outside the museum, the **port** is edged with the colourful pastel houses that inspired the Fauves. The view is especially good from the Môle Jean Réveille, the narrow pier that encloses the yacht-filled port.

Seek out **Place de l'Ormeau**, **Rue de la Ponche** and **Place aux Herbes**, poetic corners of old St-Tropez that have refused to shift into top gear. The rambling little **Quartier de la Ponche**, with several chic restaurants and bars, folds itself around the shore and the tower of the now defunct Château de Suffren. The narrow Rue de la Ponche leads out to a point surmounted by the Old Tower, with a little beach which is very nice for a quick dip. Another essential ingredient of St-Tropez is the charming Place Carnot, better known by its old name of **Place des Lices**, an archetypal slice of Provence with its plane trees, Tuesday and Saturday markets, cafés and eternal games of *pétanque*.

Although the **beaches** begin even before you enter St-Tropez, those famous sandy strands where girls first dared to bathe topless (circumventing local indecency laws by placing Coke bottle tops over their nipples) skirt the outer rim of the peninsula. In the summer minibuses link them with Place Carnot.

Getting There

There is no **train** station in St-Tropez. The nearest TGV stop is at Les Arcs, from where shuttle buses take travellers into St-Tropez. Call SODETRAV on **t** 04 94 97 88 51 for timetable information.

There's a regular **bus** in season linking Toulon to St-Tropez (contact SODETRAV in Toulon, **t** 04 94 18 93 40).

Tourist Information

St-Tropez ✉ 83990: Quai Jean Jaurès, **t** 04 94 97 45 21, **f** 04 94 97 82 66, *www.st-tropez.st, tourisme@st-tropez.st. Open daily July and Aug 9.30–1.30 and 3.30–10, rest of year 9.30–12 and 2–6.*

Maison du Tourisme du Golfe de St-Tropez/ Pays des Maures, **t** 04 94 55 22 00, **f** 04 94 55 22 01, *tourisme@golfe-infos.com*, at the N98/D559 junction just before the traffic gridlock, is a tourist's godsend.

Eating Out

Leï Mouscardins, Tour du Portalet, **t** 04 94 97 29 00 (*luxury*). For pure atmosphere and the best creative food in town, book a table overlooking the harbour at Leï Mouscardins; Laurent Tarridec's remarkable cuisine may be one of the high points of your holiday. *Closed Tues and Wed exc in summer; June–Sept closed lunch.*

Club 55, Plage de la Pampelonne, **t** 04 94 79 80 14 (*expensive*). One of the oldest and best-known beach restaurants. *Closed Feb.*

Chez Maggi, 5 Rue Sibille, **t** 04 94 97 16 12 (*moderate*). A busy, fashionable gay bar/restaurant serving up good and inexpensive Franco-Italian cuisine, such as delicious *petits farcis provençaux*, to a youthful clientele in a small room adjoining the raucous bar area. *Closed lunch in winter.*

Plage des Jumeaux, **t** 04 94 79 84 21 (*moderate*). If you want to eat right on the beach, head here for a lunchtime menu. *Closed Tues and Wed in season.*

Marseille

Founded by Greek colonists in 600 BC, Massalia (Marseille) boomed from the start. Conquered by Caesar for siding with Pompey, Marseille nearly went out of business. However, in the 11th century, when the Crusaders showed up looking for transport to the Holy Land, Marseille grew fat on the proceeds. It was Europe's greatest port in the 18th century, when its workers did their share in upholding the Revolution: as 500 volunteers set off in July 1792, someone suggested singing the new battle song of the Army of the Rhine. By the time they reached Paris, the 'song of the Marseillais' was perfected and became the the hit tune of the Revolution, and subsequently the most rousing and bloodcurdling of national anthems.

Today, amid Provence's carefully nurtured image of lavender fields, rosé wine and *pétanque*, Marseille is the great anomaly, the second city of France and the world's eighth largest port. Like New York, it has been the gateway to a new world for hundreds of thousands of new arrivals – especially Corsicans, Armenians, Jews, Greeks, Turks, Italians, Spaniards and Algerians. On the down-side, Marseille suffers from disproportionately high unemployment and the National Front has generally picked up about a third of the vote here. On the up side, the city is undergoing a vast renovation programme of 3,000 historic buildings, and has a new sparkle.

The Vieux Port and Le Panier

Marseille's Vieux Port is now a huge pleasure port with over 10,000 berths; its cafés have fine views of the sunset, though in the morning the action and smells centre around the Quai des Belges and its boat-side **fish market**. From the Quai des Belges *vedettes* sail to the Château d'If and Frioul islands, past the two bristling fortresses that still defend the harbour: to the north **St-Jean**, and to the south **St-Nicolas**.

Marseille concealed its age until this century, when excavations for the glitzy shopping mall, the Centre Bourse, revealed the eastern ramparts and gate of Massalia, dating back to the 3rd century BC, now enclosed in the Jardin des Vestiges. On the ground floor of the Centre Bourse, the **Musée d'Histoire de Marseille** (*open Mon–Sat 12–7; adm*) displays models, everyday items from ancient times, mosaics and a 3rd-century BC wreck of a Roman ship, discovered in 1974. Elaborate antique models of later ships that sailed into the Vieux Port and items relating to Marseille's trading history are the main focus of the **Musée de la Marine**, in the nearby Bourse, the palatial 19th-century exchange (*open daily 10–6; adm*).

The quarter rising up behind the north end of the Vieux Port is known rather oddly as the **Panier** or 'Basket' after a popular 17th-century cabaret, although its irregular weave of winding narrow streets and stairs dates from the ancient Greeks. During the war this warren of secret alleyways absorbed hundreds of Jews and other refugees from the Nazis hoping to escape to America. In January 1943, Hitler cottoned on and, in collusion with the French police and local property speculators, ordered the dynamiting of the lower Panier. Two buildings were protected: the 17th-century **Hôtel de Ville** on the quay, and behind it, in Rue de la Prison, the **Maison Diamantée**, Marseille's 16th-century Mannerist masterpiece, named after the pyramidical points of its

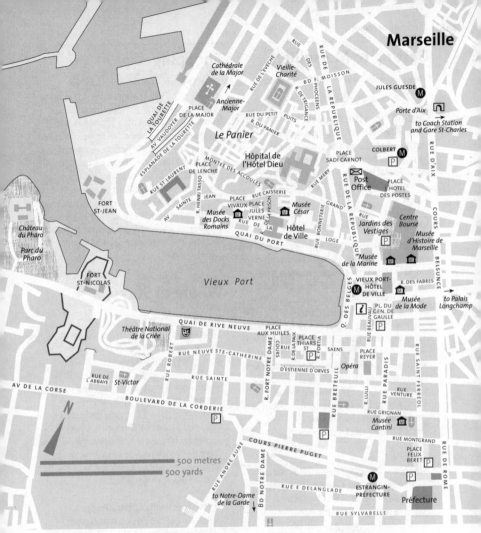

façade. It holds the **Musée du Vieux Marseille** (*open for guided tours only, ask at tourist office*), a delightful attic where the city stashes its odds and ends.

The Panier retains its original crusty character atop the well-worn steps of **Montée des Accoules** and around **Place de Lenche**, once the market or *agora* of the Greeks. Signs point the way through the maze to the top of Rue du Petit-Puits and the elegant **Vieille-Charité**, designed by Pierre Puget, a student of Bernini and court architect to Louis XIV – and a native of the Panier. Built by the city fathers between 1671 and 1745 to take in homeless migrants from the countryside, this is one of the world's most palatial workhouses, overlooking a court with a sumptuous elliptical chapel crowned by an oval dome. It has now been restored as a cultural centre. The Charité's middle gallery houses the excellent **Musée d'Archéologie Méditerranéenne** (*open winter 10–5; summer 11–6; adm*), featuring a remarkable collection of Egyptian art (second in France, after the Louvre) and beautiful works from ancient Cyprus, Susa, Mesopotamia, Greece and pre-Roman and Roman Italy.

Getting to Marseille

Buzz (*see* p.6) flies directly from London Stansted.

Getting from the Airport

Marseille's **airport** (**t** 04 42 14 14 14) is to the northwest at Marignane. A **bus** (**t** 04 91 50 59 34), every 20mins 6.30am–8.50pm, goes to the train station, takes 25mins and costs €8. A **taxi** will set you back €20–25.

Getting Around

Gare St-Charles, **t** 08 36 67 68 69, is the main **train** station. There are connections with most towns in the south. The *gare routière*, **t** 04 91 08 16 40, is behind the station at 3 Pl Victor Hugo; it has connections to Aix, Cassis, Nice, Arles, Avignon, Toulon and Cannes.

You can take the pedestrian-only '**ferryboat**' across the Vieux Port, immortalized by Marcel Pagnol and captained by Marseille characters.

Marseille runs an efficient **bus** network and two **métro** lines. Tickets are €1.40, valid for an hour, and transferable between bus and métro. At night, buses (Fluobus) run from La Canebière across town.

For a **taxi**, call **t** 04 91 02 20 20.

Car Hire

There are some car hire firms in the Gare St-Charles, including **Avis**, **t** 04 91 64 71 00. Others are **Hertz**, at 16 Bd Charles Nédelec (1er), **t** 04 91 14 04 24, and **Thrifty**, Place des Marseillaises (1er), **t** 04 91 95 00 00.

Tourist Information

Marseille: 4 La Canebière (1er), Vieux Port, **t** 04 91 13 89 00, **f** 04 91 13 89 20, *accueil@marseille-tourisme.com*, *www.marseille-tourisme.com*. Open July–Sept Mon–Sat 9–7.30, Sun 10–6; Oct–June Mon–Sat 9–7, Sun 10–5. Also at the station, **t** 04 91 50 59 18.

Market Days

Daily old book, postcard and record market in Place A. et F. Carli (1er), near the Noailles métro; every other Sunday am, flea market in Cours Julien (6e; **Ⓜ** Notre-Dame du Mont).

Shopping

Rue St-Ferréol, home of the Galeries Lafayette and Virgin Megastore, is the centre of the city's shopping district; parallel Rue Paradis has the upmarket boutiques, and Rue de Rome is a good place to look for fake leopardskin. Marseille holds a market of clay Christmas crib figures, the *Foire aux Santons*, from end Nov to Jan; at other times, you can find *santons* at **Marcel Carbonel**, near St-Victor at 47 Rue Neuve Ste-Catherine (7e), and even see them being made (**t** 04 91 54 26 58; *workshops open Tues and Thurs 2.30pm, closed Aug and Christmas; museum open all year Mon–Sat 9.30–12.30 and 2–7*).

Where to Stay

Marseille ✉ 13000

Marseille's top-notch hotels are the bastion of expense-account businessmen and women, while its downmarket numbers attract working girls of a different kind. Be sure to book if you come in mid-September.

★★★★**Le Petit Nice Passédat**, Anse de Maldormé (7e), off Corniche Kennedy, **t** 04 91 59 25 92, **f** 04 91 59 28 08, *hotel@petitnice-passedat.com,www.petitnice-passedat.com* (*luxury*). Marseille's most exclusive hotel is a former villa over the Anse de Maldormé, with a fine restaurant (*closed Sun and Mon*).

★★★**Mercure Beauvau Vieux Port**, 4 Rue Beauvau (1er), **t** 04 91 54 91 00, **f** 04 91 54 15 76, *H1293@accor-hotels.com* (*expensive*). Overlooking the Vieux Port and where Chopin and George Sand canoodled; wood-panelled and comfortable, with quiet, air-conditioned rooms (*no restaurant*).

★★★**Le Corbusier**, 280 Bd Michelet (8e), **t** 04 91 16 78 00, **f** 04 91 16 78 28, *hotelcorbusier@wanadoo.fr* (*inexpensive*). A slightly worn and dusty treat for students of architecture is this hotel-restaurant incorporated into the Unité d'Habitation; reserve one of its 22 rooms as early as possible.

★★**Azur**, 24 Cours Roosevelt (1er), **Ⓜ** Réformés, **t** 04 91 42 74 38, **f** 04 91 47 27 91, *www.azurhotel.fr* (*inexpensive*). Average rooms; frills such as colour TV and garden views.

**Le Richelieu, 52 Corniche Kennedy (7ᵉ), t 04 91 31 01 92, f 04 91 59 38 09, *hotelmer@club-internet.fr* (*inexpensive*). Breakfast terrace overlooks the sea.

*Little Palace, 37–9 Bd d'Athènes (1ᵉʳ), t 04 91 90 12 93, f 04 91 90 72 03 (*inexpensive*). The most benign choice near the Gare St-Charles, at the foot of the grand stair.

**Moderne, 11 Bd de la Libération (6ᵉ), t 04 91 62 28 66, f 04 91 50 90 22 (*cheap*). Nice rooms with showers and TV.

*Montgrand, 50 Rue Montgrand (6ᵉ), t 04 91 00 35 20, f 04 91 33 75 89 (*cheap*). Another palatable budget choice.

Eating Out

The Marseillais claim an ancient Greek – even divine – origin for their ballyhooed *bouillabaisse*: Aphrodite invented it to beguile her husband Hephaestos to sleep so that she could dally with her lover Ares – seafood and saffron being a legendary soporific. Good chefs prepare it just as seriously, and display like a doctor's diploma their *Charte de la Bouillabaisse* guaranteeing that their formula more or less subscribes to tradition: a saffron-and garlic-flavoured soup cooked on a low boil (hence its name). On menus you'll usually find three degrees of *bouillabaisse*: simple or *du pêcheur*, made from the day's catch with a few shellfish thrown in; *royale*, with half a lobster included; and, most expensive of all, *royale marseillaise*, the real McCoy, with all the right fish. When served, the fish is cut up before you and presented on a side dish of *aïoli* or *rouille*.

Restaurant Michel, 6 Rue des Catalans (7ᵉ), t 04 91 52 30 63 (*luxury*). The best and certainly the swankiest *bouillabaisse* is served at this snooty joint: you'll be mixing with politicians and showbiz people. *Open daily, year round.*

Le Passédat, Le Petit Nice Passédat hotel (*see* opposite), t 04 91 59 25 92 (*luxury*). Ravishing food in an exotic garden.

Les Mets de Provence Chez Maurice Brun, Second Floor, 18 Quai de Rive Neuve (7ᵉ), t 04 91 33 35 38 (*expensive*). For a genuine Provençal spread try this 50-year-old restaurant; it has a grand three-course lunch menu with wine. *Closed Sat, Sun, and Mon lunch.*

Chez Fonfon, Vallon des Auffes, t 04 91 52 14 38 (*expensive*). On the fishing port overlooking the Château d'If and Frioul islands you can feast on *bouillabaisse* from this charter member, which prides itself on the freshness of its fish. *Closed Sun, Mon lunch and Jan.*

L'Epuisette, Vallon des Auffes, t 04 91 52 17 82 (*expensive*). A Marseille institution for its seafood. *Closed Sat, Sun eve and Mon lunch.*

Les Arcenaulx, 25 Cours Honoré d'Estienne d'Orves (1ᵉʳ), t 04 91 59 80 30 (*moderate*). Serves fresh market fare in a busy square next to an art bookshop. *Closed Sun.*

Oscar, Quai du Port (2ᵉ), t 04 91 90 26 86 (*moderate*). Extremely popular and tasty *bouillabaisse*. *Closed Sun.*

Au Roi du Couscous, 63 Rue de la République (2ᵉ), t 04 91 91 45 46 (*moderate*). The best couscous in town. *Closed Mon.*

La Grotte, 1 Rue Pebrons, t 04 91 73 17 79 (*moderate*). A favourite for pizza by the sea.

Entertainment

You can find out what's happening in *Taktik* or *Atout Marseille*, distributed free by the tourist office, or in the pages of *La Marseillaise*, *Le Provençal* or the Wednesday edition of *Le Méridional*.

Théâtre National de la Criée, 32 Quai de Rive Neuve (7ᵉ), t 04 91 54 70 54. Since 1981, director Marcel Maréchal has put on performances to wide critical acclaim.

Cinéma Alhambra, 2 Rue du Cinéma (16ᵉ), t 04 91 03 84 66. Old movies and art films in their original language (*v.o.*).

Les Variétés, 37 Rue Vincent Scotto (1ᵉʳ), t 04 96 11 61 61. Swish cinema with pretty neon, a wine bar and first-run films in *v.o.*

Nightlife in Marseille is concentrated in several zones. Place Jean Jaurès/Cours Julien and around are perhaps the trendiest places.

Chocolat Théâtre, 59 Cours Julien (6ᵉ), t 04 91 42 19 29. Music, along with chocolates and *plats du jour* (*moderate*). *Closed Sun.*

Espace Julien, 39 Cours Julien (6ᵉ), t 04 96 12 23 40. Jazz, rock and reggae are all on offer; there's also a café with live music.

There are also bars and Latin clubs along the sea at Plage de Borély (8ᵉ); there are a number of new places at Escale Borély.

South of the Vieux Port: Quai de Rive Neuve and St-Victor

At 19 Rue Grignan, an *hôtel particulier* houses the modern art collection of the **Musée Cantini** (*open Sept–May 10–5; June–mid-Sept 11–6; adm*). Permanent displays include Paul Signac's shimmering *Port de Marseille*, and the first Cubist views of L'Estaque that Dufy painted with Braque in 1908; most of the Cantini's post-1960 works have been moved into the new Musée d'Art Contemporain (*see* opposite).

On **Quai de Rive Neuve** you'll find ship chandlers' shops, restaurants, and the national theatre, **La Criée**, installed in a former fish auction house. Further along the *quai*, steps lead up to battlemented walls and towers good enough for a Hollywood castle, defending one of the oldest Christian shrines in Provence, the **Abbaye St-Victor**. Below St-Victor is Louis XIV's **Fort St-Nicolas**, and beyond that, the **Château du Pharo** (*bus no.83 from the Vieux Port*), built by Napoleon III. The prize 360° city view is from Marseille's watchtower hill – a limestone outcrop, crowned by **Notre-Dame de la Garde** (*bus no.60, from Place aux Huiles on Quai de Rive Neuve*).

La Canebière

They used to make rope here, and the hemp they used has given its name to Marseille's most famous boulevard. This was the high street of French *dolce far niente*, which could swagger and boast that 'the Champs-Elysées is the Canebière of Paris'. In its day La Canebière sported grand cafés, fancy shops and hotels where travellers of yore had their first thrills before sailing off to exotic lands, but these days the street has suffered the same fate as the Champs-Elysées: banks, airline offices and heavy traffic, plus kebab and pizza stands.

Palais Longchamp and Environs

In 1834 Marseille suffered a drought so severe that it dug a canal to bring in water from the Durance. This feat of aquatic engineering ends with a heroic splash at the **Palais Longchamp**, a delightfully overblown nymphaeum and cascade (Ⓜ *Longchamp-Cinq-Avenues; bus no.80 from La Canebière*). In the right wing of the palace, some of the same creatures are embalmed in the **Musée d'Histoire Naturelle** (*open winter 10–5; summer 11–6; closed Mon; adm*). The left wing of the Palais Longchamp houses the **Musée des Beaux-Arts** (*open winter 10–5; summer 11–6; closed Mon; adm*). Local talent is represented by Baroque sculptor, architect and painter Pierre Puget (1671–1745); Françoise Duparc, a follower of Chardin (1726–76), who worked most of her life in England; and the satirist Honoré Daumier (1808–97), who went to prison for his caricatures. Behind the palace stretch the prettiest public gardens in Marseille.

Heading South: Le Corbusier

To pay your respects to Modular Man, take bus no.21 from the Bourse down dreary Bd Michelet to the Corbusier stop. In 1945, at the height of Marseille's housing crisis, the French government commissioned Le Corbusier to build an experimental **Unité d'Habitation**, derived from his 1935 theory of 'La Cité Radieuse'. Le Corbusier thought the solution to urban *anomie* and transport and housing problems was to put living-space, schools, shops and recreational facilities all under one roof, balanced on concrete *pilotis*, or stilts. Le Corbusier, who guessed the future starring role of cars, intended that the ground level should be for parking. Of the original extras, only the school, the top-floor gym and the hotel for residents' guests have survived.

Marseille's Corniche and Parc Borély

From the Vieux Port, you can catch bus no.83, and pass the Parc du Pharo to **Corniche Kennedy**, a dramatic road overlooking a dramatic coast – now improved with artificial beaches, bars, restaurants, villas and nightclubs. From the bus stop Vallon des Auffes you can walk down to the fishing village of **Anse des Auffes** ('of the ropemakers'), isolated from the *corniche* until after the Second World War and still determinedly intact. As soon as the *corniche* was built, the wealthy families of Marseille planted grand villas along it. The *corniche* then descends to the artificial **Plage Gaston Deferre**, where a copy of Michelangelo's *David* holds court at the corner of Av du Prado. Beyond him opens the cool green expanse of **Parc Borély**, with a botanical garden, duck ponds and the **Château Borély**, an 18th-century palace built according to the strictest classical proportions for a wealthy merchant. Behind it, Av de Hambourg leads into Ste-Anne, another former village, where César's Giant Thumb emerges at the Av d'Haïfa, signalling the vast new **Musée d'Art Contemporain** at No.69 (*open winter Tues–Sun 10–5; summer Tues–Sun 11–6; adm*), with a large collection of post-war art (New Realists, Arte Povera, 'individual mythologies' and more).

The *Calanques* and Grotte Cosquer

To continue along the coast from Parc Borély, you'll need to change to bus no.19, which goes past another beach and the **Musée de la Faïence**, 157 Av de Montredon (*open winter Tues–Sun 10–5; summer Tues–Sun 11–6; adm*). More *calanques* follow until the road gives out and the GR98 coastal path to Cassis begins. In 1991, the beautiful jagged **Calanque de Sormiou** made national headlines when local diver Henri Cosquer discovered a subterranean cave above sea level, covered with paintings of running bison, horses, deer and the ancestors of the modern penguin. The **Grotte Cosquer** (named in honour of its discoverer) is now recognized by prehistorians as a contemporary of Lascaux (*c.* 27,000 BC). To protect the art, the cave has been walled up, but reproductions are on display at the Exposition Grotte Henri Cosquer.

The Château d'If

If in French means yew, a tree associated with death, and an appropriately sinister name for this gloomy precursor of Alcatraz built in 1524 (*open daily 9.30–6.30 exc in rough seas; boats, t 04 91 55 50 09, from the Quai des Belges; departures hourly 9–5*). Even when Alexandre Dumas was still alive, people wanted to see the cell of the Count of Monte-Cristo, and a cell, complete with escape hole, was obligingly constructed to show to visitors. Real-life inmates included a Monsieur de Niozelles, condemned to six years in solitary confinement for not taking his hat off in front of Louis XIV; and, after the revocation of the Edict of Nantes, thousands of Protestants.

Day Trips and Overnighters from Marseille

Aix-en-Provence

Elegant and honey-hued, the old capital of Provence is splashed by a score of fountains, a charming reminder that its very name comes from its waters, *Aquae Sextiae*.
If tumultuous Marseille is in many ways the great anti-Paris, Aix-en-Provence is the
stalwart anti-Marseille – bourgeois, cultured, aristocratic, urbane, slow-paced,
convivial, and famous for its university and for France's most élite festival of music
and opera (*last three weeks of July*).

Aix was chosen as the capital of Provence by the counts of Provence in the early 13th
century. In 1409 Louis II d'Anjou founded the university; and in the 1450s Aix was the
setting for the refined court of Good King René, fondly remembered, not for the way
he squeezed every possible sou from his subjects, but for the artists he patronized,
such as Francesco Laurana, Nicolas Froment and the Maître de l'Annonciation d'Aix;
and for the popular festivities he founded, especially the masquerades of the Fête-
Dieu. When René died in 1486, France absorbed his realm but maintained Aix's status
as the capital of Provence, seat of the unpopular king-appointed Parlement. In 1789,
the tumultuous Count Mirabeau became a popular hero in Aix when he eloquently
championed the people and condemned Provence's Parlement as unrepresentative; in
1800, Provence's government was unceremoniously packed off to Marseille.

Canopied by its soaring plane trees, decked with fountains and flanked by cafés,
banks, pâtisseries, and *hôtels particuliers* of the 17th and 18th centuries, **Cours
Mirabeau** is the centre stage for Aixois society. Laid out in 1649, it begins in Place du
Général de Gaulle, and at the far end is the **Fontaine du Roi René**, with a statue of the
good monarch holding up a bunch of the muscat grapes he introduced to Provence.

South of Cours Mirabeau, the **Musée Granet** (*open daily 10–12 and 2–6; closed Tues;
adm*) houses Aix's art and antiquities. Downstairs are eerie relics of the Celto-Ligurian
decapitation cult from the *oppidum* of Entremont, 3km north of Aix. Holding court
upstairs is *Jupiter and Thetis* (1811), arguably Ingres' most objectionable canvas. There
are 17th-century portraits of Aixois nobility; Dutch and Flemish masters; and the
Italians. But what of Cézanne, who took his first drawing-classes in this very building?
For years he was represented by three measly watercolours, until 1984 when the
French government deposited eight small canvases here.

North of Cours Mirabeau, the narrow lanes and squares of **Vieil Aix** concentrate
some of Provence's finest architecture and shopping, especially off the elegant
cobbled and fountained Place d'Albertas. In the adjacent Place des Prêcheurs stands
the church of **Ste-Marie-Madeleine**, which has a pleasant Second Empire façade and
paintings by Rubens and Van Loo, although the show-stopper is the central panel of
the *Triptych of the Annunciation*, a luminous esoteric work of 1445, attributed to
Barthélémy d'Eyck. Aix's flower market lends an intoxicating perfume to Place de la
Mairie, a lovely square framed by the stately, perfectly proportioned **Hôtel de Ville**
(1671) and the flamboyant **Tour de l'Horloge** (1510), with clocks telling the phase of the
moon and wooden statues that change with the season.

Getting There

Aix's **train station** is on Rue G. Desplaces, at the end of Av Victor-Hugo; there are hourly connections from Marseille, and less frequently from Toulon. The network of local buses is good. The hectic *gare routière* is in Av de l'Europe, **t** 04 42 91 26 80, with **buses** every 20–30mins from Marseille and direct to the airport, and others to Avignon, Cannes, Nice and Arles. For a **taxi**, go to Av de l'Europe, **t** 04 42 27 71 11.

Car Hire

You can rent a car at **Rent a Car**, 35 Rue de la Molle, **t** 04 42 38 58 29, and **ADA Location**, Av Henry Mouret, **t** 04 42 52 36 36, as well as the big multinational companies.

Tourist Information

Aix-en-Provence: Place du Général de Gaulle, **t** 04 42 16 11 61, **f** 04 42 16 11 62, *info@aixenprovencetourism.com, www. aixenprovencetourism.com*. Without doubt, one of the most pleasant tourist offices in the south of France. *Open daily Mon–Sat 8.30-7, Sun 10–1 and 2–6.*

Market Days

There's local produce every morning in **Place Richelme**, but Tuesdays, Thursdays and Saturdays are the days to come, when the centre of Aix overflows with good things: food in **Place des Prêcheurs** and **Place de la Madeleine**, flowers in **Place de la Mairie**, antiques and fleamarket bits in **Place de Verdun**, and clothes, fabrics and accessories along **Rue Riflerafle**; on Saturday nights in the summer the stands stay open late, all bustling and brightly lit, while the birds squawk indignantly in the trees above.

Shopping

The traditional souvenirs of Aix are its almond and glazed melon sweets, *calissons*, which have been made here since 1473; buy them at:

Béchard, 12 Cours Mirabeau, **t** 04 42 26 06 78.
Confiserie Brémond, 16 Rue d'Italie, **t** 04 42 27 36 25.
Terre de Provence, 6 bis Rue Aude, **t** 04 42 93 04 54. Local, world-renowned pottery.

Where to Stay

Aix-en-Provence ✉ 13100

If you come in the summer during the festivals, you can't book early enough; Aix's less pricey hotels fill up especially fast.

★★★★Villa Gallici, Av de la Violette, **t** 04 42 23 29 23, **f** 04 42 96 30 45, *gallici@ relaischateaux.fr* (*luxury*). A member of the Relais & Châteaux group, just north of the centre, with all the warm atmosphere of an old Provençal *bastide*, charming rooms, garden, parking and pool.

★★★★Le Pigonnet, 5 Av du Pigonnet, **t** 04 42 59 02 90, **f** 04 42 59 49 77, *reservation@ hotelpigonnet.com* (*expensive*). A romantic

From here, Rue Gaston de Saporta leads to the **Musée du Vieil Aix** at No.17 (*open winter 10–12 and 2–5; summer 10–12 and 2.30–6; closed Tues; adm*). It stores some quaint paintings on velvet, a bevy of *santons* in a 'talking Christmas Crib' and 19th-century marionettes.

Rue Gaston de Saporta continues north to Place de l'Université, once part of the forum of Roman Aix, and the **Cathédrale St-Sauveur**, a dignified patchwork of periods and styles. The interior has naves for every taste: from right to left, Romanesque, Gothic and Baroque. The cathedral's most famous treasure, Nicolas Froment's *Triptyque du Buisson Ardent* (1476), is under restoration, though a copy is available to view in the foyer. On the lateral panels are portraits of a well-fed King René, who commissioned the work, and his second wife, while the central scene depicts the vision of a monk of St-Victor of Marseille, who saw the Virgin and Child appear amidst the miraculous burning bush vouchsafed to Moses.

old *bastide* on the outskirts, with rose arbours, pool, lovely rooms furnished with antiques, an excellent restaurant and views out over the Aix countryside.

★★★**Mercure Paul Cézanne**, 40 Av Victor Hugo, **t** 04 42 91 11 11, **f** 04 42 91 11 10, *mercure.paulcezanne@free.fr* (*expensive*). An exceptional little hotel two blocks from the train station, furnished with antiques.

★★★**Hôtel des Augustins**, 3 Rue de la Masse, just off Cours Mirabeau, **t** 04 42 27 28 59, **f** 04 42 26 74 87 (*expensive*). A 12th-century convent with soundproof rooms.

★★★**Grand Hôtel Nègre-Coste**, 33 Cours Mirabeau, **t** 04 42 27 74 22, **f** 04 42 26 80 93 (*expensive–moderate*). A renovated, elegant 18th-century hotel which still hoists guests in its original elevator (*no restaurant*).

★★★**Le Manoir**, 8 Rue d'Entrecasteaux, **t** 04 42 26 27 20, **f** 04 42 27 17 97, *Hr@hotelmanoir. com* (*moderate–inexpensive*). Built around a 14th-century cloister. *Closed 2 weeks Jan.*

★★**Hôtel dee France**, 63 Rue Espariat, **t** 04 42 27 90 15, **f** 04 42 26 11 47 (*moderate–inexpensive*). Cheaper, old-fashioned and in town.

★**Paul**, 10 Av Pasteur, **t** 04 42 23 23 89, **f** 04 42 63 17 80, *hotel.paul@wanadoo.fr* (*inexpensive*). Old-fashioned hotel with garden near the cathedral.

Eating Out

Le Clos de la Violette, 10 Rue de la Violette, **t** 04 42 23 30 71 (*expensive*). Under the masterful touch of Jean-Marc Banzo, who does wonderful things with seafood and Provençal herbs, this lovely restaurant has long been considered the best in Aix. *Closed Sun and Mon lunch.*

Le Bistro Latin, 18 Rue de la Couronne, **t** 04 42 38 22 88 (*moderate*). Features imaginative variations on local themes, such as lentil and sausage terrine, at refreshingly reasonable prices. *Closed Sun and Mon lunch.*

Chez Maxime, 12 Place Ramus, **t** 04 42 26 28 51 (*moderate*). Choose the shady terrace or cosy fireside for delicious meat or fish dishes, accompanied by a list of 500 wines. *Closed Sun and Mon lunch.*

Trattoria Chez Antoine, 3 Rue Clemenceau, **t** 04 42 38 27 10 (*moderate*). For fresh pasta and other Italian and Provençal dishes in an intimate, laid-back atmosphere.

Le Petit Verdot, 7 Rue d'Entrecasteaux, **t** 04 42 27 30 12 (*moderate*). More serious drinkers should head for this authentic evening *bistrot*, where red wines by the glass are accompanied by ancient jazz records and simple dishes or *charcuterie*. *Open eves only. Closed Sun.*

La Vieille Auberge, 63 Rue Espariat, **t** 04 42 27 17 41 (*moderate–inexpensive*). A cosy, popular place serving tasty gourmet Provençal dishes at great prices by an award-winning chef.

L'Hacienda, 7 Rue Mérindol (near Place des Cardeurs), **t** 04 42 27 00 35 (*cheap*). Least expensive of all, L'Hacienda is eternally popular. *Closed Sun and Mon.*

At the back of the cathedral, the 17th–18th-century residence of Aix's archbishops, the **Archevêché**, is the setting for the festival's operas. It also houses the **Musée des Tapisseries** (*open daily 10–11.45 and 2–5.45; closed Tues; adm*), with three sets of light-hearted Beauvais tapestries, hidden under the roof from the Revolution till the 1840s.

Around Aix: Cézanne and the Montagne Ste-Victoire

Paul Cézanne spent an idyllic childhood roaming Aix's countryside with his best friend, Emile Zola, and as an adult painted those same landscapes in a way landscapes had never been painted before. The **Atelier Cézanne**, 9 Av Paul Cézanne (*open winter 10–12 and 2–5; spring 10–12 and 2.30–6; mid-June–Sept closed Mon; adm*), the studio he built in 1897, has been rather grudgingly maintained as it was when the master died in 1906, with a few drawings, unfinished canvases, his smock, palette, pipe and some of the bottles and skulls used in his still lifes.

The rolling countryside around Aix is the quintessence of Provence for those who love Cézanne: the ochre soil, the dusty green cypresses, the simple geometry of the old *bastides* and villages and the pyramidal prow of the blueish limestone **Montagne Ste-Victoire**. This is encircled by the striking 60km **Route Cézanne** (D17), beginning along the south flank in the wooded park and Italianate château of **Le Tholonet** (*3km from Aix; take the bus from La Rotonde*). Here Cézanne often painted the view towards the mountain, which haunts at least 60 of his canvases. The ascent of the Montagne Ste-Victoire takes about two hours (bring sturdy shoes, a hat and water) and there's a 17th-century stone refuge with water and a fireplace. Crowning the precipitous west face, the 55ft **Croix de Provence** (which Cézanne never painted) has been here, in one form or another, since the 1500s. Northerly approaches to the summit of Ste-Victoire begin at Les Cabassols or **Vauvenargues**. The 14th-century Château de Vauvenargues was purchased by Picasso, and he is buried here.

Cassis

The old coral-fishing village of **Cassis**, with its fish-hook port, white cliffs, beaches and quaint houses spilling down steep alleyways, was a natural favourite of the Fauve painters. In the summer so many tourists descend on the now chic little port that it's often elbow-room only here and on the pebbly **Plage de Bestouan**. The sheer limestone cliffs that stand between Cassis and Marseille are pierced by startling tongues of lapis lazuli – mini-fjords known as *calanques*, or creeks. The nearest *calanque*, **Port-Miou**, is accessible by car or foot (*a 30min walk*): here the hard, white stone was cut for the Suez Canal. Another mile's hike will take you to **Port-Pin**, with a pretty beach, and another hour to **En-Vau**, the most beautiful of them all (you can also reach En-Vau with less toil from a car park on the Col de la Gardiole). Take a picnic and plenty of water. Note, however, that after being ravaged by forest fires in 1990 the paths to the *calanques* are strictly off limits from the beginning of July to the second Saturday in September, when the only way to visit is by motor boat from Cassis port.

Getting There

The **train** station for Cassis is quite far from the centre; to get from Marseille, take one of the frequent **buses** from the *gare routière*, which drop you off at Bd Anatole France.

Tourist Information

Cassis ✉ 13260: Oustau Calendal, Quai des Moulins, **t** 04 42 01 71 17, **f** 04 42 01 28 31, omt-cassis@enprovence.com, www.cassis.fr. *Open summer Mon–Fri 9–7, Sat and Sun 9–1 and 3–7; spring Mon–Fri 9.30–6, Sat 10–12 and 2–5, Sun 10–12; autumn and winter Mon–Fri 9.30–12.30 and 2–5, Sat 10–12 and 2–5, Sun 10–12.*

Market Days

Cassis: Wednesday and Friday mornings.

Eating Out

Cassis ✉ 13260

Chez César, 21 Quai des Baux, **t** 04 42 01 72 36. Fresh seafood served in Marcel Pagnol décor. The local, rosy-pink sea urchins (*oursins*), often crop up on the menu. *Closed Tues eve and Wed.*

Nino, 1 Quai Barthélémy, **t** 04 42 01 74 32 (*moderate*). Tasty fish soup and grilled prawns on a summery seaside terrace. *Closed Sun eve and Mon.*

Touring from Toulon and Marseille

Day 1: A Taste of the Côte d'Azur

Morning: From either Marseille or Toulon, take the A50 motorway to the exit for **Le Castellet** and **La Cadière d'Azur**. Both are lovely hill villages; Le Castellet, with its more dramatic site, has often seen duty as a film set. The country roads around both will take you to vineyards where you can sample fine AOC Bandol wines.

Lunch: La Cadière has one of the most acclaimed tables of the region, in a beautiful setting at the **Hostellerie Bérard**, Rue Gabriel Péri, t 04 94 90 11 43 (*expensive*). *Closed Mon and Sat*. Almost as good, and with panoramic views, is **Le Castel Lumière** in Le Castellet, t 04 94 32 62 20 (*expensive*). *Closed Mon, Sun eve and Jan*.

Afternoon: Back on the A50, the next exit towards Toulon takes you to the swanky resort of **Bandol**, offering tropical gardens and a zoo at the Jardin Exotique de Sanary-Bandol on the D559 east (*daily except Sun 8–12 and 2–7, adm*), or a short boat trip to Paul Ricard's Ile de Bendor.

Dinner: In Bandol you can splurge on a *bouillabaisse* at the **Auberge du Port**, 9 Allée Jean Moulin, t 04 94 29 42 63 (*expensive*) or try a Provençal salad with *tapenade* at **Le Jérôme**, t 04 94 32 55 85 (*cheap*), a local favourite pizzeria on the waterfront.

Sleeping: Bandol's best is ★★★**Master Ker Mocotte**, t 04 94 29 46 53, f 04 94 32 53 54 (*expensive*), with a seaside garden, private beach and pool. More modestly, ★★**L'Oasis**, t 04 94 29 41 69, f 04 94 29 44 80 (*inexpensive*), is just a short walk from the beach.

Day 2: Holy Relics and Crazy Curios

Morning: From Bandol, take the motorway (A50, then A501) to Auriol; from there, the N560 carries on around the back of the Massif de Sainte-Baume to **St-Maximin-la-Ste-Baume**, home of the finest Gothic building in Provence, the Basilica Ste-Marie-Madeleine, resting place of Mary Magdalen.

Lunch: St-Maximin's best affordable choice is **Du Côté de Chez Nous**, in the centre on Place Malesherbes, t 04 94 86 52 40 (*moderate*).

Afternoon: A few minutes east, down the A8 from St-Maximin, is the unprepossessing mining town of **Brignoles** – worth a stop for the incredible clutter in the Musée du Pays Brignolais (*daily except Mon and Tues, 9–12 and 2.30–5; adm*), with everything from France's oldest Christian art to a concrete canoe.

Dinner: Six km north of Brignoles in Montfort-sur-Argens (take the D554 to Le Val, then the D562), is the small and intimate **Relais des Templiers**, t 04 94 59 55 06 (*moderate*). *Closed Tues and Nov*. The other choice is east of Brignoles, **La Grillade au Feu de Bois**, t 04 94 69 71 20 (*moderate*), 12km out on the N7 at Flassans-sur-Issole.

Sleeping: The only interesting choices are outside Brignoles: 3km south on the D405 at La Celle, the ★★★**Abbaye de la Celle**, Place Hôtel de Ville, t 04 94 05 14 14, f 04 94 05 14 15, has luxurious rooms in a restored monastery with a beautiful garden (*expensive*). There are also 16 rooms in the gracious converted farmhouse at ★★**La Grillade** (*see above*), t 04 94 69 71 20, f 04 94 59 66 11 (*moderate*).

Day 3: Villages of Deepest Provence

Morning: The D24 passes over the dam at the Lac du Carces, then take the D13 and D79 to the austere, Cistercian **Abbaye du Thoronet**, one of the grandest medieval monuments of Provence. Backtrack to the Lac de Carces and follow the D13 north to **Cotignac**, a delightful village of flowers and ancient tufa caves (now used for wine); from here the D22 continues to **Sillans-la-Cascade**.

Lunch: In Sillans, the **Hôtel-Restaurant des Pins**, on the D32, t 04 94 04 63 26 (*moderate*) offers country cooking in an old stone house. *Closed Wed eve and Thurs out of season*. If it's full, the tiny village of Fox-Amphoux, just east on the D32, has a sweet village inn, the **Auberge du Vieux Fox**, Place de l'Eglise, t 04 94 80 71 69 (*moderate*).

Afternoon: Sillans has a 135ft waterfall just outside the village (don't bother in summer, when there's no water). From here, the D560 passes more picturesque villages; make the short detour for **Villecroze** and **Tourtour**, or carry on straight to **Lorgues**, with its 18th-century ensemble of fountains and plane trees, and of all things a Russian Orthodox monastery.

Dinner: There are two excellent possibilities for a memorable dinner: in Lorgues, **Chez Bruno**, Le Plan, t 04 94 85 93 93 (*expensive*), *closed Sun eve and Mon*, and, just east in Les Arcs, down the D10, the **Logis du Guetteur**, Place du Château, t 04 94 99 51 10 (*expensive*). *Closed mid-Jan–Feb.*

Sleeping: In Lorgues, the venerable ★★**Hôtel du Parc**, 25 Bd Clemenceau, t 04 94 73 70 01, (*inexpensive*). *Closed Nov.* There are also rooms at the ★★★**Logis du Guetteur** in Les Arcs (*see above*), t 04 94 99 51 10 (*expensive*) – in a restored castle with garden and pool. *Closed mid Jan–Feb.*

Day 4: Into the Massif des Maures

Morning: The D97 from Les Arcs will take you southwards, straight to **Gonfaron**, where according to old pious legend donkeys can fly. There is a donkey sanctuary (call t 04 94 78 26 41), a village museum dedicated to the old art of cork production (*open 2–6, closed Sat and Sun; adm*) a wine centre, and another sanctuary dedicated to France's only land tortoises, the Village des Tortues (*open 9–7; closed Dec–Feb; adm*). From here, take the D75 and then the D558 into the heart of the Massif des Maures for **La Garde-Freinet**.

Lunch: Lunch in La Garde-Freinet means a simple but filling meal at **La Sarrazine**, t 04 94 43 65 98 (*moderate*), on the Route Nationale. *Closed Wed.*

Afternoon: La Garde-Freinet, with its ruined Saracen castle, may detain you for a while, but continue along the D558 for **Grimaud**, one of the most beautiful *villages perchés* on the Côte d'Azur; if there's time, take a side trip out on the D14 to the romantic ruined monastery called the **Chartreuse de la Verne** (*open 11–6, 11–5 in winter, closed Tues and Jan; adm*).

Dinner: Grimaud is a popular spot, and there are plenty of choices: lobster salad in arch-Provençal surroundings at **Les Santons**, on the Route Nationale, t 04 94 43 21 02 (*expensive*), *closed Wed*; or a thyme-scented *selle d'agneau* at the **Hostellerie du Coteau Fleuri**, t 04 94 43 20 17 (*moderate*). *Closed Tues.*

Sleeping: The ★★★**Hostellerie du Coteau Fleuri**, in an old stone inn, also makes a comfortable place to stay, t 04 94 43 20 17, f 04 94 43 33 42 (*moderate*). *Closed mid-Nov–mid-Dec.* Just outside town on the Rte de Collobrières, ★★★**La Boulangerie**, t 04 94 43 23 16, f 04 94 43 38 27 (*expensive*), offers a pool, tennis and a restaurant, along with views over the mountains. *Closed Oct–Easter.*

Day 5: Along the Corniche to Le Lavandou

Morning: From Grimaud, get back to the coast on the D14 and D559, which eventually opens into the dramatic 'Corniche des Maures'. The first resort along the way, **Cavalaire-sur-Mer**, has broad beaches and exotic gardens at the Domaine du Rayol (*open 9.30–12.30 and 2.30–6.30, later in summer; by apt only Nov–Jan; adm*). Carry on down the Corniche, and if time permits have a look at medieval **Bormes-les-Mimosas**, where that lovely flower, now a symbol of the Côte, was first grown in France.

Lunch: If lunchtime finds you in Cavalaire, go for seafood at **Le Mistral**, in the Hôtel Raymond, Av des Alliés, t 04 94 64 07 32 (*moderate*) *closed Oct–April*. If you're in Bormes-les-Mimosas, **La Tonnelle des Délices**, Place Gambetta, t 04 94 71 34 84 (*moderate*), offers refined cooking under a vine-covered terrace. *Closed Wed.*

Afternoon: Its been a long five days, and you can rest up at the end on any of the twelve beaches of **Le Lavandou**, all connected by a '*petit train*'. This resort houses the official summer residence of the president of France, and it's a good spot for shopping.

Dinner: Back on the coast means a seafood orgy won't be far; **Les Tamaris de Saint-Clair**, Plage St-Clair, t 04 94 71 02 70 (*expensive*) has the *bouillabaisse*, the grills, and all the rest. *Closed late Dec and Jan.* If you're out of money but still need a fish, try **Au Vieux Port**, Quai G. Péri, t 04 94 71 00 21 (*cheap*).

Sleeping: For airy rooms and sea views, there's ★★★**Auberge de la Calanque**, 62 Av de Gaulle, t 09 94 71 05 96, f 04 94 71 20 12 (*expensive*). *Closed Nov–Mar.* The more modest pick is the small and cosy ★★ **L'Escapade**, 1 Chemin du Vannier, t 04 94 71 11 52 (*inexpensive*). *Closed Dec–Jan.*

Avignon

Avignon has known more passions and art and power than any town in Provence; the 14th-century papal court, a vortex of mischief that ruled Avignon for centuries, trailed violence, corruption and debauchery in its wake. Avignon today, however, is international, ebullient and fun, and in 1946 actor Jean Vilar founded the Avignon Festival, the liveliest and most popular event on the entire Provençal calendar.

The Famous Half-Bridge

From the Rhône, Avignon is a brave two-tiered sight: in front rise the sheer cliffs of the Rocher des Doms, inhabited since Neolithic times, and behind it the sheer man-made cliffs of the Palais des Papes. The ensemble includes the walls that the popes wrapped around Avignon. From the walls, four arches of a bridge leapfrog into the Rhône, sidle up to a waterbound two-storey Romanesque chapel and then stop abruptly mid-river. This is the famous **Pont St-Bénézet**, or simply the Pont d'Avignon, begun in 1185 (*open April–June and Oct daily 9–7; July–Sept 9–8, Nov–Mar 9–5.45; adm*).

The Palais des Papes

t 04 90 27 50 74, www.palais-des-papes.com; open daily April–Oct 9–7, July–Sept 9–8; Nov–Mar 9.30–5.45; adm.

Once crowded with houses, the traffic-free **Place du Palais** was cleared by antipope Benedict XIII to emphasize the message of the palace's vertical, impregnable walls: 'you would think it was an Asiatic tyrant's citadel rather than the abode of the vicar of the God of peace', wrote Prosper Mérimée. But the life of a 14th-century pope justified paranoia. What is less obvious is that the life of a 14th-century pope and his cardinals, courtiers, mistresses and toadies was also extremely luxurious. The palace was spared destruction in the Revolution only to end up serving as a prison and a barracks, and until 1920 its bored residents amused themselves by chipping off frescoes to sell to tourists. The **entrance** is up the steps, in the centre of Clement VI's façade.

After crossing the Cour d'Honneur, the great courtyard dividing Benedict XII's stern Cistercian Palais Vieux (1334–42) and Clement VI's flamboyant Palais Neuf (1342–52), the tour begins in the Jesus Hall, decorated with monograms of Christ. The rest of the tour takes in the Consistory, where the cardinals met and received ambassadors, and the Chapelle St-Jean, then continues to the first floor and the huge banqueting hall, or Grand Tinel, with its adjacent upper kitchen and Chapelle St-Martial. You then visit the pope's antechamber and bedroom, which leads directly into the New Palace and the most delightful room in the entire palace, the Chambre du Cerf, Clement VI's study. The arrows direct you next to the Sacristy, crowded with statues of kings, queens and bishops, followed by Clement VI's Great Chapel. A grand stair leads down to the flamboyant Great Audience Hall.

Around the Palace

To the left of the palace is Avignon's cathedral, **Notre-Dame-des-Doms**, built in 1150, its landmark square bell tower ridiculously dwarfed by a gilt statue of the Virgin added in 1859, in an attempt to make the church stand out next to the papal pile. Next to the cathedral, ramps lead up to the oasis of the **Rocher des Doms**, once a *citadela* and now a garden with panoramic views of the Rhône and Mont Ventoux.

At the end of Place des Papes, the Petit Palais once housed the cardinal legate and now holds Avignon's medieval art in the **Musée du Petit Palais** (*open daily 9.30–1 and 2–5.30; closed Tues; June–Sept daily 10–1 and 2–6; adm*). There are fascinating fragments of the 35ft, 8-storey Tomb of Cardinal Jean de Lagrange (1389), and six rooms glowing with the golden 14th- and early 15th-century Italian Madonnas; Sienese artists, with their more elegant, stylized line and richer colours, were favoured by the popes. The museum's best-known work, Botticelli's *Virgin and Child*, is a tender, lyrical painting of his youth. Rooms 17–19 are devoted to works by French artists in Avignon.

Just below the Place du Palais, an antique carousel spins gaily in the lively centre of old Avignon, **Place de l'Horloge**, site of the old Roman forum. The windows on the east side are filled with *trompe-l'œil* paintings of historic local personages.

Southwest Avignon

Behind the Hôtel de Ville lies the **Quartier des Fusteries**, named after the wood merchants and carpenters who had their workshops here in the Middle Ages, though they were replaced in the 18th century with *hôtels particuliers*. From the Quartier des Fusteries, the steep picturesque lanes of the **Quartier de la Balance** wind back up to the Place du Palais. Off Place de l'Horloge, Rue St-Agricol is named after the Gothic church of **St-Agricol** (1326); its treasure is the *Doni Retable*, a rare Provençal work from the Renaissance. At the end of Rue St-Agricol curves Rue Joseph Vernet, lined with 18th-century *hôtels particuliers*, antique shops, pricey restaurants and cafés. The overly ornate, spindly furniture, porcelains and knick-knacks that originally filled these mansions are on display nearby in Rue Victor Hugo's **Musée Louis Vouland** (*open May–Oct Mon–Sat 10–12 and 2–6, Sun and Nov–April 2–6; adm*). At 65 Rue Joseph Vernet, a fancy *hôtel particulier* houses the **Musée Calvet** (*open 10–1 and 2–6; closed Tues; adm*), which offers something for every taste: 6,000 pieces of wrought iron, Greek sculpture, 18th-century seascapes by Avignon native Joseph Vernet, mummies, tapestries, prehistoric statue-steles, dizzy kitsch paintings of nude men, and an excellent collection of 19th- and 20th-century paintings. At 27 Rue de la République, in the chilly 17th-century Jesuit chapel, are the sculptures of the **Musée Lapidaire** (*open daily exc Tues 10–1 and 2–6; adm*). It's worth popping in for the 2nd-century BC (or Merovingian) man-eating *Tarasque de Noves*, and there is good Renaissance sculpture as well, but the best is in the church of **St-Didier** (1359), just to the north in Place St-Didier – Francesco Laurana's polychrome reredos of Christ bearing the Cross, called Notre-Dame du Spasme for the spasm of pain on Mary's face.

Nearby, at 5 Rue Laboureur, the treasures of a serious art collector named Jean Angladon-Dubrujeaud have been opened as Avignon's newest museum, the **Fondation Angladon-Dubrujeaud** (*open July–Sept Tues–Sun 1–6; Oct–June Wed–Sun 1–6; adm*). It has a fine assortment of modern painting never seen before: works by Modigliani, Picasso, Manet, Degas and Cézanne, as well as the only Van Gogh on display in Provence, called *Les Wagons de chemin de fer*.

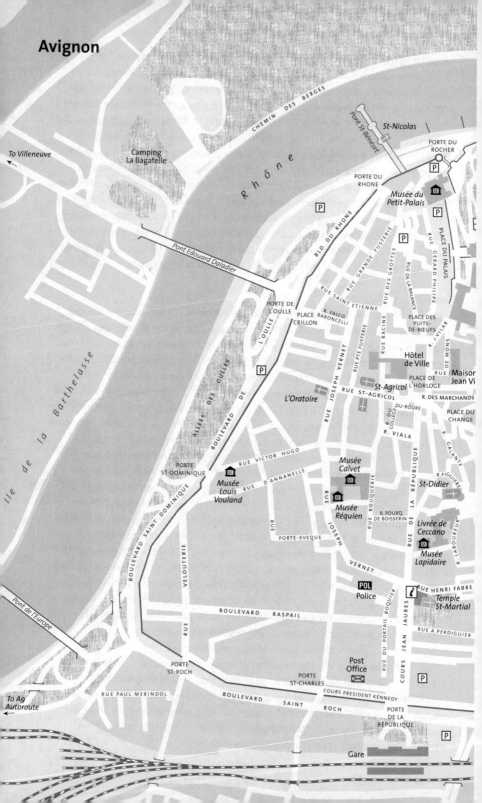

Avignon

To Villeneuve

Camping
La Bagatelle

Rhône

CHEMIN DES BERGES

Pont St-Bénézet

St-Nicolas

PORTE DU
ROCHER

Musée du
Petit-Palais

PORTE DU
RHONE

Pont Edouard Daladier

BLD DU RHONE

PLACE DU PALAIS

RUE GRANDE FUSTERIE

RUE DES GROTTES

RUE DE LA BALANCE

RUE GÉRARD PHILIPE

PORTE DE
L'OULLE
CRILLON

RUE SAINT ETIENNE

PLACE BARONCELLI

R. FALCO

RUE RACINE

PLACE DES
PUITS-
DE-BŒUFS

R. J. VILAR

RUE DE SONS

ALLÉES DES OUILLES

BOULEVARD DE L'OULLE

RUE JOSEPH VERNET

RUE PTE FUSTERIE

Hôtel
de Ville

PLACE DE
L'HORLOGE

Maison
Jean Vi

L'Oratoire

St-Agricol

RUE ST-AGRICOL

R. DU COLLÈGE

R. DU-ROURE

R. DES MARCHANDS

PLACE DU
CHANGE

PORTE
ST-DOMINIQUE

RUE VICTOR HUGO

R. VIALA

Musée
Louis
Vouland

RUE D'ANNANELLE

Musée
Calvet

RUE DE LA RÉPUBLIQUE

R. GALANTE

BOULEVARD SAINT DOMINIQUE

RUE

Musée
Réquien

R. POURQ.
DE BOISSERIN

RUE BOUQUERIE

R. FIGUIÈRE

St-Didier

PORTE-EVEQUE

RUE JOSEPH

Livrée de
Ceccano

R. LABOUREUR

RUE VELOUTERIE

VERNET

Musée
Lapidaire

RUE HENRI FABRE

POL
Police

Temple
St-Martial

BOULEVARD RASPAIL

RUE A PERDIGUIER

RUE

RUE DU PORTAIL BOQUIER

COURS JEAN JAURÈS

Pont de l'Europe

PORTE
ST-ROCH

Post
Office

PORTE
ST-CHARLES

To A9
Autoroute

RUE PAUL MERINDOL

BOULEVARD SAINT ROCH

COURS PRESIDENT KENNEDY

PORTE
DE LA
RÉPUBLIQUE

Gare

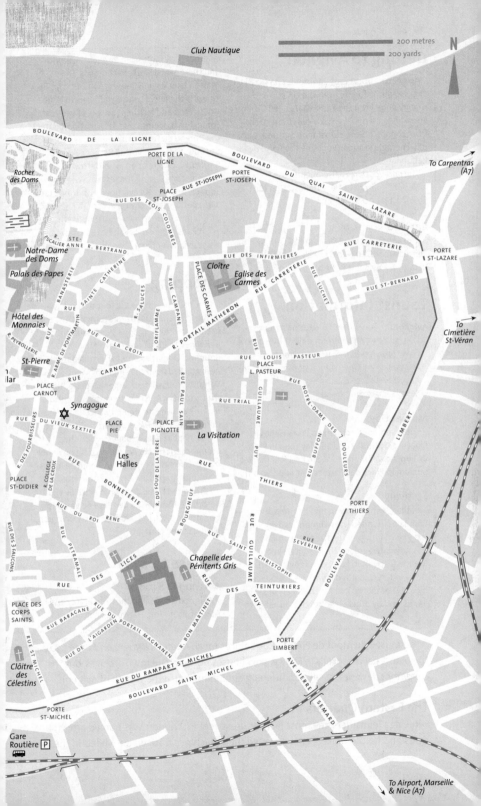

Getting to Avignon

Avignon's **airport** is at Caumont, t 04 90 81 51 51. No direct flights from the UK currently run. Avignon is on the Paris–Marseille TGV line, and has a direct weekly **rail** connection from London on the **Eurostar** on Saturdays, *see* p.11. The **train station** is outside the Porte de la République.

The *gare routière* is also outside the Porte de la République, next to the train station (Bd St-Roch, t 04 90 82 07 35).

Car Hire

Inexpensive car hire firms are **VEO**, 51 Av Pierre Sémard, t 04 90 87 53 43, and **SIXT Locagest**, 3 Av Saint Ruf, t 04 90 86 06 61.

Tourist Information

Avignon: 41 Cours Jean Jaurès, t 04 32 74 32 74, f 04 90 82 95 03, *information@ot-avignon.fr, www.ot-avignon.fr* or *www.avignon-tourisme.com*. Open *April–Oct Mon–Sat 9–6; July Mon–Sat 10–8, Sun 10–5; Nov–Mar Mon–Sat 9–7, Sun 10–12.*

Market Days

Tues–Sun, covered market at **Les Halles** in Place Pie; Saturday and Sunday, food in **Place Crillon**; flower market Sat am and flea market Sun am in **Place des Carmes**; Sat and Sun am.

Festivals

In 1947, Jean Vilar with his Théâtre National Populaire founded the **Avignon Festival**, with the aim of bringing theatre to the masses. It is now rated among the top international theatre festivals in Europe, and Avignon overflows in July and August with performances by the Théâtre National in the Palais des Papes, and by others throughout the city; the cinemas host films from all over the world, and there are concerts in churches. The **Maison Jean Vilar** (8 Rue de Mons, t 04 90 86 59 64) is the nerve centre and hosts exhibitions, films, and lectures the rest of the year. For festival bookings and information, contact the **Bureau du Festival d'Avignon**, Espace St-Louis, 20 Rue du Portail Boquier, Avignon 84000, t 04 90 14 14 69. *www.festival-avignon.com*. During the festival, Avignon's squares and streets overflow with fringe (or 'Off') performers. To receive the Off programme, write to Avignon Public Off., BP5 75521 Paris Cedex 11, or call t 01 48 05 01 19, *www.avignon-off.org*.

Shopping

Chic designer shops are found along Rue St-Agricole and Rue Joseph Vernet. Pâtisseries in this area sell Avignon's gourmand speciality, *papalines*, made of fine chocolate and a liqueur, *d'Origan du Comtat*, distilled from 60 herbs picked from the slopes of Mont Ventoux. You will find regional specialities: *fruits confits d'Apt*, *berlingots de Carpentras*, *melon de Cavaillon*, *nougat de Sault*, *truffe de Carpentras et du Tricastin*, garlic, olives, honey, *pastis*, goat's cheese, *fougasse*, and the omnipresent *herbes de Provence*. If you're not going to Aix, don't fail to buy some delicious, diamond-shaped almond *calissons d'Aix* here.

Behind the Hôtel de Ville, in Place des Puits-de-Bœufs, the **Maison des Pays de Vaucluse**, t 04 90 85 55 24, has a large display of regional products and crafts.

Where to Stay

Avignon ✉ **84000**

Avignon gets full to the brim in July and August, so it's imperative to book ahead.

The **Musée du Mont de Piété**, 6 Rue Saluces (*open Mon–Fri 8.30–12 and 1.30–5.30*), the oldest pawnbroker's in France, now houses not only the town archives, but the *conditions des soies*, or silk-conditioning equipment, once the wealth of Avignon.

The Eastern Quarters

Rue des Teinturiers, the most picturesque street in Avignon, was named after the dyers and textile-makers who powered their machines from water-wheels in the

The Avignon area also has a large number of *gîtes* and rooms in private homes, some on the idyllic Ile de la Barthelasse. For one of these, contact the **CDT Vaucluse**, 21 Rue Collège de la Croix, **t** 04 90 80 47 00, **f** 04 90 86 86 08.

★★★★Hôtel d'Europe, 12 Place Crillon, **t** 04 90 14 76 76, **f** 04 90 14 76 71, *reservations@ hotel-d-europe.fr* (*luxury–expensive*). Classically formal, with Louis XV furnishings, this was built in the 16th century and converted to an inn in the late 18th century.

★★★★Hôtel Clarion Cloître Saint-Louis, 20 Rue du Portail Boquier, **t** 04 90 27 55 55, **f** 04 90 82 24 01, *hotel@cloitre-saint-louis.com* (*expensive*). Built in 1589 as part of a Jesuit school of theology, the beautiful cloister is an island of tranquillity. Rooms have been modernized; meals are served under the portico or by the rooftop swimming pool.

★★★★La Ferme Jamet, Chemin de Rhodes (off Pont Daladier), **t** 04 90 86 88 35, **f** 04 90 86 17 72, *fermja@club-internet.fr* (*expensive*). A 16th-century farmhouse on the Ile de la Barthelasse, this *ferme* has rooms ranging from traditional Provençal in style to a gypsy caravan, around a tennis court and a pool. *Closed Nov–Easter.*

★★Hôtel du Palais des Papes, 3 Place du Palais, **t** 04 90 86 04 13, **f** 04 90 27 91 17 (*expensive–moderate*). Has the best views of the palace; modern soundproof rooms and air-conditioning, and restaurant.

★★Hôtel d'Angleterre, 29 Bd Raspail, **t** 04 90 86 34 31, **f** 04 90 86 86 74, *info@hoteldangle terre.fr* (*inexpensive*). A friendly simple place. *Closed end Dec–Jan.*

★★Saint-Roch, 9 Rue Mérindol, **t** 04 90 16 50 00, **f** 04 90 82 78 30 (*inexpensive*). Quieter, with a delightful garden, just outside the walls of Porte St-Roch.

★Mignon, 12 Rue Joseph Vernet, **t** 04 90 82 17 30, **f** 04 90 85 78 46, *hotel.mignon@ wanadoo.fr* (*inexpensive*). Bright and charming, with small but modern rooms. *Closed Dec.*

Eating Out

Hiély-Lucullus, 5 Rue de la République, **t** 04 90 86 17 07 (*expensive–moderate*). Avignon's gourmet bastion for the past 60 years is a resolutely old-fashioned place with a first-floor dining room. The kitchen never disappoints, with its *tourte* of quail and foie gras and a legendary *cassoulet de moules aux épinards*, accompanied by Châteauneuf-du-Pape or Tavel. *Closed Tues and Wed, and last 2 weeks Jan and last 2 weeks June.*

La Fourchette, 17 Rue Racine, **t** 04 90 85 20 93 (*moderate*). Hiély-Lucullus' less expensive sister restaurant serves just as good food more cheaply. *Closed Sat, Sun end Aug and end Feb.*

Le Bain-Marie, 5 Rue Pétramale, **t** 04 90 85 21 37 (*moderate*). A popular place serving tradi-tional French fare. *Closed Sat lunch, Mon lunch and Sun.*

Entrée des Artistes, Place des Carmes, **t** 04 90 82 46 90 (*moderate*). Located in a quiet square. *Closed Sat and Sun exc in July.*

Rose au Petit Bedon, 70 Rue Joseph Vernet, **t** 04 90 82 33 98 (*moderate*). An Avignon institution for well-prepared dishes seldom found elsewhere, like *lotte au Gigondas*, angler-fish cooked in wine. *Closed Sun and Mon Nov–Mar; Sun and Mon lunch April–Oct.*

Woolloomoolloo, 16 bis Rue des Teinturiers, **t** 04 90 85 28 44 (*moderate*). Go global with a feast of 'world cuisine' and live music.

Terre de Saveur, Rue St-Michel, **t** 04 90 86 68 72 (*cheap*). For lunch try this vegetarian-orientated place, with plenty of omelettes and pasta dishes, many with wild mush-rooms. *Closed Sun, Mon and 15–31 Aug. Open evenings Fri and Sat only.*

Sorgue, two of which survive. Petrarch's Laura, who lived in the area, was buried in the Franciscan church here, although only the Gothic bell tower survived the Revolution. Rue des Teinturiers turns into Rue Bonneterie on its way to Avignon's shopping district. Just beyond Place Carnot, **St-Pierre**'s flamboyant façade boasts a set of beau-tifully carved walnut doors (1551). From Place St-Pierre, Rue Carnot continues to the charming Place des Carmes, dominated by the 14th-century **Eglise des Carmes**, Avignon's biggest church, with a pretty cloister.

Day Trip from Avignon

Villeneuve lez Avignon

The 10th-century abbey of **St-André** above Villeneuve lez Avignon was one of the mightiest monasteries in the south of France, and was soon invaded by cardinals wishing to retreat across the Rhône from the wanton, squalid Avignon of the popes. Though a dormitory suburb these days, Villeneuve still maintains a separate peace, with well-fed cats snoozing in the sun, leisurely afternoons at the *pétanque* court, and some amazing works of art.

In 1307, when Philip the Fair ratified a deal that made Villeneuve royal property, he ordered that a citadel should be built on the approach to Pont St-Bénézet – the bright white **Tour Philippe-le-Bel** (*open Oct–Mar daily 10–12 and 2–5.30; April–Sept daily 10–12.30 and 3–7; closed Mon out of season, and Feb*), with splendid views of Avignon and Mont Ventoux. From here, Montée de la Tour leads up to the 14th-century **Collégiale Notre-Dame**, now Villeneuve's parish church. The church's most famous work, a beaming, swivel-hipped, polychrome ivory statue of the Virgin carved in Paris out of an elephant's tusk (*c.* 1320), has been removed to safer quarters in the nearby **Musée Pierre-de-Luxembourg** (*same hours as Tour Philippe-le-Bel; adm*). The museum's other prize is the masterpiece of the Avignon school – Enguerrand Quarton's 1454 *Couronnement de la Vierge*, one of the greatest works of 15th-century French painting.

In Rue de la République looms what was the largest and wealthiest Charterhouse in France, the **Chartreuse du Val-de-Bénédiction** (*open April–Sept daily 9–6.30; Oct–Mar daily 9.30–5.30; adm*). In 1792, the Revolution forced the monks out, and the charterhouse was sold in 17 lots. Now repurchased and beautifully restored, it hosts seminars, exhibitions and performances, especially during the Avignon festival. Still, the sensation that lingers in the Charterhouse is one of vast silences and austerity. The star attraction is the Tomb of Innocent VI, with its alabaster effigy.

Getting There

Bus no.11 runs to Villeneuve every 30mins from in front of Avignon's post office (buy tickets on board). It takes 15mins.

In July and August, a **Bateau-bus** makes regular trips between Avignon and Villeneuve, starting from the Allées de l'Oulle.

Tourist Information

Villeneuve lez Avignon ✉ 30400: Place Charles-David, t 04 90 25 61 33, f 04 90 25 91 55, *www.villeneuve-lez-avignon.com*, *Tourisme@villeneuve-lez-avignon.com*. Place Charles David is also the best place to **park**. **Note** that everything except the Chartreuse is **closed** on Mondays and in February.

Eating Out

****Le Prieuré, Place du Chapître, t 04 90 15 90 15, f 04 90 25 45 39, *www.leprieure.fr*, *leprieure@relaischateaux.fr* (*expensive*). Exquisite and centrally located, with swimming pool; gardens, tennis and a remarkable restaurant that does delightful things with seafood and truffles. *Closed Nov–mid-Mar.*

Aubertin, 1 Rue de l'Hôpital, t 04 90 25 94 84 (*expensive*). You'll have to book ahead to get a table at this intimate place under the porticoes. *Closed Sun, and Mon lunch in winter.*

La Maison, 1 Rue Montée du Fort St-André, t 04 90 25 20 81 (*moderate*). An old favourite, with a traditional menu and friendly service. *Closed Wed and Aug.*

Touring from Avignon

You'll find that the sights are reliably open 10–12 and 2–5 and charge adm, unless stated.

Day 1: Sources and Fountains

Morning: Start this circle around Avignon on the main road east, the N100 to **L'Isle-sur-la-Sorgue**; the many antique shops here may distract you, but the point is to find the D25 for **Fontaine-de-Vaucluse**, a lovely spot where the source of the Sorgue river comes tumbling out of a cliffside. It's a bit touristy, but the other attractions nearby include interesting museums of speleology and the wartime Résistance.

Lunch: Dine by the riverside, next to an old waterwheel, at the **Hostellerie le Château**, in the old *mairie*, **t** 04 90 20 31 54 (*cheap*). Or for Italian cuisine, try the restaurant in the **Hôtel Le Parc**, Les Bourgades, **t** 04 90 20 31 57 (*inexpensive*). *Closed Nov–mid Feb.*

Afternoon: From Fontaine-de-Vaucluse, back-track on the D25 to the D938 north for **Pernes-les-Fontaines**. This delightful village has no less than 37 fountains, and some of the oldest frescoes in France in the Tour Ferrande. If there's time, take the D25 up to **Venasque** for a drive through the scenic gorges and forests just beyond the village.

Dinner: In Pernes, **Le Palépoli**, Route de Carpentras, **t** 04 90 66 34 00 (*moderate*), serves some of the finest Italian food in Provence. *Closed Sat lunch.* There's an exceptional restaurant in Venasque, the **Auberge de la Fontaine**, Place de la Fontaine, **t** 04 90 66 02 92 (*expensive*), with truffle dishes in season. *Closed mid-Nov–mid-Dec.*

Sleeping: Accommodation in Pernes is simple but pleasant: the two choices are **★★L'Hermitage**, Route de Carpentras, **t** 04 90 66 51 41, **f** 04 90 61 36 41 (*inexpensive*), and the **★★Prato Plage**, **t** 04 90 61 31 72, **f** 04 90 61 33 34 (*inexpensive*). There are also five elegant rooms in the **Auberge de la Fontaine** in Venasque (*see* above).

Day 2: Vaison and the Dentelles

Morning: The D938 will take you north through Carpentras, and then past **Mont Ventoux**, the ancients' holy 'mountain of the winds'. Just beyond it lies **Vaison-la-Romaine**, with acres of ruins from the Roman city to explore (*closed Tues*) and a little occult vortex in its medieval cathedral, where the Devil himself presides over the carvings in the cloister.

Lunch: There's Provençal cooking at its best, in an intimate courtyard, at **Le Brin d'Olivier**, 4 Rue du Ventoux, **t** 04 90 28 74 79 (*moderate*). *Closed Wed and Sat lunch.* For foie gras and hearty country dishes, try **La Fête en Provence**, Place du Vieux Marché, **t** 04 90 36 36 43 (*moderate*). *Closed Wed, and mid-Nov–mid-April.*

Afternoon: You've already seen the lacy peaks of the **Dentelles de Montmirail** on the way to Vaison; now, take the D977 to circle around the other side of this mini-Dolomites, through a little region of gorgeous scenery, sweet *villages perchés* and Côtes-du-Rhône vineyards. Detour off the main road point to **Séguret**, **Sablet** and **Gigondas**, with vineyards for wine-tasting and easy hiking paths up into the Dentelles.

Dinner: For *foie gras*, duck and game dishes try **Le Mas de Bouvau**, Route de Cairanne in Violès, just west of Gigondas, **t** 04 90 70 94 08 (*moderate*). *Closed Sun eve and Mon.* In Gigondas itself, Provençal cooking takes some surprising turns at **L'Oustelet**, Place du Portail, **t** 04 90 65 85 30 (*expensive*). *Closed Sun and Mon.*

Sleeping: Accommodation in Gigondas tends to the simple and rustic, from **★★★Les Florets**, Rte des Dentelles, **t** 04 90 65 85 01, **f** 04 90 65 83 80 (*moderate*), in the middle of the vineyards, to **La Farigoule**, **t** 04 90 70 91 78 (*cheap*), a pleasant bed and breakfast in an old farmhouse. *Closed Nov–Mar.*

Day 3: Orange and the Pont du Gard

Morning: Start back on the D977, south to the end of the road, then take the A7 up to **Orange**, a gritty town, but one that has the best-preserved of all Roman theatres as well as a fine museum and a triumphal arch.

Lunch: Near the theatre, you'll get agreeably stuffed at **Le Parvis**, Cours des Pourtoules, **t** 04 90 34 82 00 (*moderate*). *Closed Mon.* Among the many modest restaurants on Place Sylvian is **Le Yaka**, **t** 04 90 34 70 03 (*inexpensive*). *Closed Tues eve and Wed.*

Afternoon: From Orange, take the A9 south for that marvel of Roman engineering, the **Pont**

du Gard (see p.239). Explore the details at the visitors' centre (open daily June–Aug 9.30am–10pm, Sept–May 8.30–6; adm), or rent a canoe and paddle underneath.

Dinner: Plenty of choices in the villages around the aqueduct: Castillon has two exceptional ones: one in a hotel, **Le Vieux Castillon**, Rue Sabatier, t 04 66 37 61 61 (expensive), famous for truffles, closed Jan and Feb; and **L'Amphitryon**, Place du 8-Mai, t 04 66 37 05 04 (expensive), better known for its seafood. Closed Tues and Wed eve except in summer.

Sleeping: Besides the luxury Relais et Châteaux **★★★★ Le Vieux Castillon** (see above), there are plenty of cheaper options near the Pont,, including **★★Le Béguda St-Pierre**, on the D981 at Vers, t 04 66 63 63 63, f 04 66 22 73 73, with a pool and garden (moderate–inexpensive), and the simple, family-run **★★Le Gardon**, on the river at Collias, t 04 66 22 88 98 (inexpensive). Closed Oct–mid-Mar.

Day 4: Arles and the Camargue

Morning: From Remoulins, the big village near the Pont, the D986 will take you to Beaucaire; follow the signs for Arles from there, down the lonely D15 that follows the Rhône. **Arles** (see pp.240–41) has a lot to see: the Roman theatre and amphitheatre ('Les Arènes), St-Trophime's medieval sculpture, and fine art at the Musée Réattu.

Lunch: Near Arles' famous ancient cemetery, the Alyscamps, **Le Jardin de Manon**, 14 Av des Alyscamps, t 04 90 93 38 68, has local dishes on a pretty terrace (moderate). Vegetarians struggling through a French holiday get a break at **Vitamine**, 16 Rue Dr Fanton, t 04 90 93 77 36 (inexpensive). Closed Sun exc in July.

Afternoon: Arles can keep you busy for longer than a morning, but you might also consider a drive through the wetlands of the **Camargue**, with its famous white horses and flamingos. The best route is the D570 south-west, which passes the Musée de la Camargue (open April–June and Sept 9.15–5.45; July and Aug 9.15–6.45; Oct–Mar 10.15–4.45; closed Tues; adm), with nature trails leading off into the swamps; then a left on the D37 at Albaron, skirting the Etang de Vaccarès where you might see the flamingos nesting.

Dinner: Out in the Camargue, at Albaron on the D570, you can try the speciality bœuf à la gardian at **Le Flamant Rose**, t 04 90 97 10 18 (inexpensive). In Arles, one of the best is **Lou Marquès**, Bd des Lices, t 04 90 93 43 20 (expensive).

Sleeping: In central Arles, and set in an attractive old house, is **★★Hôtel du Musée**, 11 Rue du Grand Prieuré, t 04 90 93 88 88 (moderate). Closed Jan–mid-Feb. Just as good is **★★St Trophime**, 16 Rue de la Calade, t 04 90 96 88 38, f 04 90 96 92 19 (moderate). Closed mid-Nov–Jan.

Day 5: Les Alpilles and St Rémy

Morning: The D17 east from Arles will take you past the medieval **Abbaye de Montmajour**, past Alphonse Daudet's famous windmill at Fontvielle, and into the striking chain of blue-white hills called Les Alpilles. A left on the D78 leads to **Les Baux**, the remarkable ruined town and citadel of the Alpilles' medieval bad-boy counts.

Lunch: Les Baux gets a lot of visitors, and there's plenty of choice, from the refined **Cabro d'Or** on the D27, t 04 90 54 33 21 (expensive), closed Mon and Tues in winter; to the **Hostellerie de la Reine Jeanne**, 3 Rue des Plumelets, t 04 90 54 32 06 (inexpensive), with views over the town. Closed Nov–mid-Dec.

Afternoon: From Les Baux, the scenic D5 descends northwards to **St-Rémy-de-Provence**, an elegant little art town where you can visit Van Gogh's asylum, and see some remarkably preserved Roman monuments called 'Les Antiques' at the ruins of Glanum, St-Rémy's predecessor.

Dinner: In the centre of St-Rémy, dine on the terrace at the **Bistrot des Alpilles**, 15 Bd Mirabeau, t 04 90 92 09 17 (moderate). Closed Sun and Nov. **L'Assiette Marie**, Rue Jaume Roux, t 04 90 92 56 14, has good fresh pasta and vegetarian dishes (moderate). Closed Tues in winter.

Sleeping: An old country mansion under a cedar tree is **★★★Castellet des Alpilles**, 6 Place Mireille, t 04 90 92 45 17 (moderate). Closed Nov–Easter. Out by the ruins, the **★★Villa Glanum**, 46 Av Van Gogh, t 04 90 92 03 59, f 04 90 92 00 08 (inexpensive) has a pool and garden. Closed Nov–Feb.

The Rhône and the Alps

12

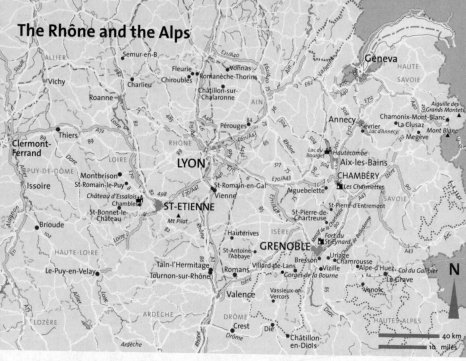

The Rhône and the Alps

The Rhône draws a dramatic squiggly line around the edges of the French Alps. At Lyon, the river, which has been speeding west from Lake Geneva, collides with the Saône, diverting the Rhône southwards. As you'll see when visiting Lyon, though, the Saône fights it out with the more famous Rhône for your attention, and probably wins. Lyon itself fights it out with Marseille these days for the position as second city in France. It's a great, self-confident place, and has been so since Roman times, when the Rhône Valley was one of the major trade routes of antiquity, as nearby towns like Vienne recall. Vines embellish the banks of the Rhône heading south, while by the side of the Saône to the north rise the beloved hills of Beaujolais.

St-Etienne southwest of Lyon is a bit of an unknown quantity, unless you remember its successful football team from the 1970s. It's a former mining town that has gone through bad times since the war, but recently it's been looking up, cleaning itself up. It puts on a good show on the museum front, with an especially surprising modern art collection in its fine-arts centre on the outskirts. And St-Etienne is certainly an excellent starting point for exploring the volcanic landscapes of the Auvergne and the remarkable gorges of the upper Allier and upper Loire – yes, France's longest, greatest Atlantic river starts this close to the Rhône and the Med.

Heading east of the Rhône valley into the French Alps, Chambéry and Grenoble lie in breathtaking locations. Chambéry, former capital of Savoy and holder of one very famous Christian shroud before Turin, has plenty to be proud of. Just escaping the grip of the formidable teeth of the Chartreuse range to the south, it's the ideal starting point for a tour of the most beautiful lakes in France – Lac du Bourget and Lac d'Annecy. Northeast rises Mont Blanc, Europe's highest peak, a vast, otherworldly meringue on the border with Italy and Switzerland.

Grenoble to the south has one of the most sensational mountain settings of any Alpine city, spreading out below the jagged peaks of the Chartreuse, Belledonne and Vercors ranges. People think of this town as uncompromisingly modern; one look at the former capital of the Dauphiné province will put that idea straight. The place is packed with splendid historic monuments, and modern museums explaining them. To the east of Grenoble stand the two greatest French ranges after that of Mont-Blanc, the Vanoise to the north, the Ecrins to the south, their highest peaks also snow-covered all year round.

Lyon

Picture a crate of ripening peaches, with all its variety of hues, and you'll have a notion of Lyon's colours. Traditionally, the Saône has been portrayed as the feminine, graceful half of Lyon's river partnership, the Rhône as the masculine, labouring one. The two unite south of the historic parts of town, at the end of the long, smart central peninsula, the Presqu'île, the heart of the town with all its grand Ancien Régime squares, its great museums, its superb shops and restaurants. On the west bank of the Saône lie the stocky medieval cathedral and the dense network of the finely restored Renaissance quarter below steep Fourvière hillside, dominated by a palatial white church and a copy of the top of the Eiffel tower, but also concealing two Roman theatres and their attendant Roman museum. North above the peninsula, Croix Rousse is the 19th-century weavers' working-class quarter, while in the spacious suburbs east of the Rhône stands the Lumières' house, birthplace of cinema.

The Fourvière Hillside and Gallo-Roman Lyon

Notre-Dame de Fourvière, a pure white sparkling castle of a church, is visible on its hillside from many points in Lyon. Head there for a great view down on to the city and to get your bearings, perhaps taking the cable-car from beside the cathedral to avoid the climb via the steep public gardens. The massive 19th-century basilica was built to Pierre Bossan's design just after the Franco-Prussian War, in gratitude for the city being spared. The outrageously ornate west front hints at the extravaganza that awaits inside. The interior, built on huge Hispano-Moorish-looking arches, feels almost Oriental; mosaics cover the floor and the walls, much of the decoration devoted to the Virgin. Stone-carvings run riot around the place. The large crypt is really a second church, almost on the same scale, in more sober style. The adjoining Musée de l'Œuvre, a museum of religious articles, has recently been modernized.

The basilica occupies the site where the Gallo-Roman forum of Lugdunum (Lyon's mighty predecessor) stood until the 9th century. Down the hillside you can still admire the remnants of two Gallo-Roman theatres (*open 9am–nightfall; adm*) built side by side on their spectacular site (take care not to trip over the rough paving blocks of the ancient paths). The main theatre was built under Augustus, but doubled in size under Hadrian, when it could seat 10,000. The smaller theatre, or *odeon*, was once roofed. Learn more about Lugdunum at the nearby **Musée de la Civilisation**

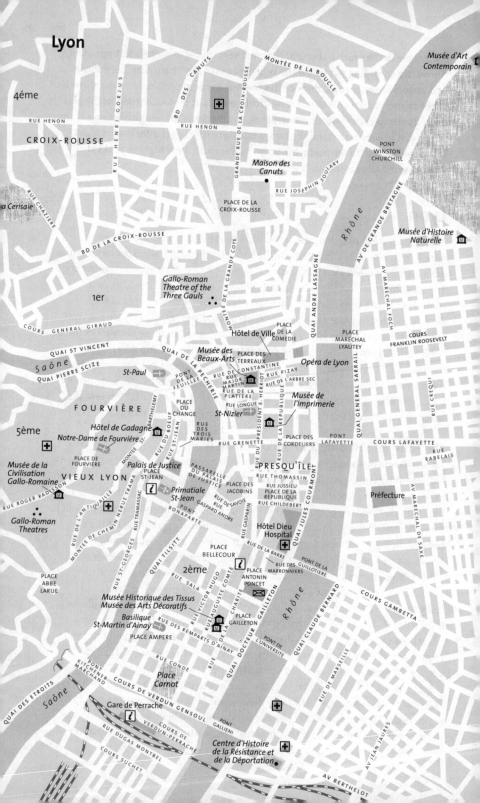

Lyon

4éme

CROIX-ROUSSE

RUE HENON

RUE HENRI GORIUS

BD DES CANUTS

RUE HENON

GRANDE RUE DE LA CROIX-ROUSSE

MONTÉE DE LA BOUCLE

Musée d'Art
Contemporain

Maison des
Canuts

RUE JOSEPHIN SOULARY

PLACE DE LA
CROIX-ROUSSE

PONT
WINSTON
CHURCHILL

a Cerisaie

RUE CHAZIERE

BD DE LA CROIX-ROUSSE

MONTÉE DE LA GRANDE COTE

QUAI ANDRE LASSAGNE

Rhône

AV DE GRANDE BRETAGNE

Musée d'Histoire
Naturelle

AV MARECHAL FOCH

1er

Gallo-Roman
Theatre of the
Three Gauls

COURS GENERAL GIRAUD

Hôtel de Ville

PLACE
DE LA
COMEDIE

PLACE
MARECHAL
LYAUTEY

COURS
FRANKLIN ROOSEVELT

QUAI ST VINCENT

Saône

QUAI PIERRE SCIZE

QUAI DE LA PECHERIE

Musée des
Beaux-Arts

PLACE DES
TERREAUX

Opéra de Lyon

St-Paul

PONT
DE LA
FEUILLEE

RUE DE CONSTANTINE

RUE
MAJOR
MARTIN

RUE PIZAY

RUE DE L'ARBRE SEC

QUAI GENERAL SARRAIL

RUE CREQUI

FOURVIÈRE

PLACE
DU
CHANGE

RUE DE LA
PLATIERE

RUE HERRIOT

RUE DU PRESIDENT E.

Musée de
l'Imprimerie

5ème

Hôtel de Gadagne

Notre-Dame de Fourvière

PLACE DE
FOURVIERE

RUE DU BOEUF

RUE ST-JEAN

RUE
TROIS
MARIES

St-Nizier

RUE LONGUE

RUE GRENETTE

RUE DE LA REPUBLIQUE

PLACE DES
CORDELIERS

PONT
LAFAYETTE

COURS LAFAYETTE

RUE RABELAIS

Musée de la
Civilisation
Gallo-Romaine

RUE BARTHELEMY

MONTÉE

Palais de Justice

PLACE
ST-JEAN

PASSARELLE
DU PALAIS
DE JUSTICE

PRESQU'ÎLE

RUE THOMASSIN

Préfecture

AV MARECHAL DE SAXE

VIEUX LYON

RUE DE L'ANTIQUAILLE

Gallo-Roman
Theatres

RUE ROGER RADISSON

Primatiale
St-Jean

PLACE DES
JACOBINS

RUE
DE SAVOIE

RUE JUSSIEU

PLACE DE LA
REPUBLIQUE

RUE CHILDEBERT

PONT
BONAPARTE

GASPARD ANDRE

RUE GASPARIN

PLACE
ABBE
LARUE

MONTÉE DE CHEMIN NERUE TRAMA

RUE TRAMASSAC

RUE ST-GEORGES

QUAI TILSITT

RUE SALA

RUE VICTOR HUGO

RUE AUGUSTE COMTE

Hôtel Dieu
Hospital

PLACE
BELLECOUR

PLACE
ANTONIN
PONCET

RUE DE LA BARRE

QUAI JULES COURMONT

Rhône

PONT DE LA
GUILLOTIERE

COURS GAMBETTA

2ème

Musée Historique des Tissus
Musée des Arts Décoratifs

Basilique
St-Martin d'Ainay

PLACE AMPERE

RUE DES REMPARTS D'AINAY

CHARITE

PLACE
GAILLETON

RUE DOCTEUR GAILLETON

RUE DE MARSEILLE

PONT DE
L'UNIVERSITE

QUAI DES ETROITS

Saône

PONT
KITCHENER
MARCHAND

RUE CONDE

Place
Carnot

COURS DE VERDUN GENSOUL

PONT
GALLIENI

QUAI CLAUDE BERNARD

Gare de Perrache

RUE DUGAS MONTBEL

COURS SUCHET

COURS
DE VERDUN-PERRACHE

Centre d'Histoire
de la Résistance et
de la Déportation

AV BERTHELOT

AV JEAN JAURES

Gallo-Romaine (*open Wed–Sun 9.30–12 and 2–6; adm*), which also covers earlier periods of civilization across the region, although most of the artefacts explain how Lyon grew so rapidly into such a major Roman political and religious centre. English visitors note that Emperor Claudius, organizer of the successful Roman conquest of England, was born in Lugdunum. Models recreate some of the grand buildings of the Gallo-Roman town. Fabulous finds are still being made under modern Lyon.

Vieux Lyon, Medieval and Renaissance Lyon

Squeezed in between the Saône and Fourvière hillside lie the cramped, lively streets of Vieux Lyon. The most venerable building here is the medieval **Primatiale St-Jean**, the cathedral. Marked by two square towers at either end, it turns its muscular back on the Saône, while its finely chiselled west façade overlooks lovely Place St-Jean. Inside, the tall Gothic nave is soberly grand. By far the most swanky side chapel was decorated with elaborate vaulting for Charles de Bourbon, long-serving archbishop of Lyon in the 15th century. In the squat Romanesque apse and in the transepts, admire some intense 13th-century stained-glass windows. Look out too for a remarkable 14th-century clock, while the separate treasury conceals other marvels.

The clatter of the looms of Lyon's early weavers once rang out in the pleasant St-Georges quarter south of the cathedral. North of it, the well-renovated powdery-coloured façades of mansions built for wealthy residents in the 16th century line up along the tight streets, the area designated a World Heritage Site by UNESCO. Although this is generally known as the Renaissance quarter, a good number of its great houses display late-Gothic features. The main artery, **Rue St-Jean**, rather unappealingly lined with fast-food restaurants and souvenir shops, passes the imposing Palais de Justice, and then continues through a series of sweet little squares. On parallel Rue du Bœuf, No.16 conceals the most famous of Vieux Lyon's many towers, the arch-windowed Tour Rose. One other feature of the area is the secretive but still often dingy covered alleys known as *traboules* (a contraction of the Latin *trans ambulare*, to walk through) which lead from one block of houses to the next.

The **Hôtel de Gadagne**, set in the most rambling Renaissance pile in Vieux Lyon, on Rue du Bœuf, contains two museums. The old-fashioned **Musée Historique de Lyon** (*open Wed, Thurs and Sat–Mon 10.45–6, Fri 10.45–8.30; closed Tues; adm*) displays fabulous Romanesque fragments rescued from a former powerful abbey north of town, and also focuses on dramatic episodes in the city's life, for example how Lyon was violently punished when its leaders resisted the French Revolution. The simpler **Musée International de la Marionnette** (*open same hours*) is devoted to puppets. After the Revolution, a silkweaver-cum-entertainer of Lyon, Laurent Mourguet, created Guignol, Madelon and Gnafron, popular caricatural Lyonnais figures now known across France. Wide-eyed Guignol in his tight black headcap is full of silly banter, but also pokes fun at the authorities. His wife Madelon puts up with him, but grumbles and argues a lot. His great friend Gnafron is a very red-faced Beaujolais drunkard. The museum contains many versions of these figures, but also displays puppets from around the globe.

Getting to Lyon

easyJet (*see* p.6) flies from London Stansted.

Getting from the Airport

Lyon-St-Exupéry **airport, t** 04 72 22 71 27, lies 25km east of the city centre. Satobus **shuttle buses, t** 04 72 68 72 17, *www.satobus.com*, leave every 20mins or so during the day from outside Hall Central Level 1, serving the two central railway stations, for €8. A taxi will cost about €35 in the daytime.

Getting Around

Lyon's two main central **railway stations** are Gare de La Part-Dieu, east of the Rhône, and Gare de Perrache, at the southern end of the Presqu'île. Rail enquiries, **t** 08 36 35 35 35.

For **bus** information, call **t** Allô TCL, **t** 04 78 71 70 00. This number also serves Lyon's *métro* system, with four lines running 5am–11.45pm.

For **taxis**, try Lyon International Taxis, **t** 04 78 88 16 16, or Allô Taxis, **t** 04 78 28 23 23.

Car Hire

There's a choice at the airport: **ADA, t** 04 72 22 74 92; **Avis, t** 04 72 22 75 25; **Budget, t** 04 72 22 74 74; **Europcar, t** 04 72 22 75 28; **Hertz, t** 04 72 22 74 50; **National Citer, t** 04 72 22 72 72. They have offices in the centre too.

Tourist Information

Lyon: Place Bellecour, **t** 04 72 77 69 69, **f** 04 78 42 04 32, *www.lyon-france.com*; *lyoncvb@ lyon-france.com*.

Markets

The **Halles** , or covered market, is at 102 Cours Lafayette, east of Pont Lafayette from the Rhône. Lyon's celebrity chefs come to stock up here at the likes of Mère Richard's cheese boutique, or Colette Sibilia's *charcuterie* shop. Rolle is renowned for delicatessen luxuries. **Quai St-Antoine**, on the Presqu'île side of the Saône, hosts the major outdoor food market, Tues–Sun am. Up on **Boulevard de la Croix Rousse**, the other major outdoor market oper-

ates mornings Tues to Sat, with organic produce on Sat am. **Place Carnot** hosts a market on Wed, with organic produce on sale 4–7pm, and Sun am, the latter with pets. The *bouquinistes* on **Quai de la Pêcherie** (east bank of the Saône) open their bookstalls weekends and hols, 7am–sunset. **Quai Fulchiron**, below the cathedral, displays crafts on Sun am. To enjoy a flea market, head for **Quai Rolland** north of the cathedral on Sun am. On a more serious note, the **Cité des Antiquaires**, 117 Bd de Stalingrad, on the eastern edge of Tête d'Or park, holds the third largest antiques market in Europe (*open Thurs, Sat and Sun 9.30–12.30 and 2.30–7; closed Sun in summer*).

Shopping

The chicest concentration of boutiques is crammed between **Place des Terreaux** and **Place Bellecour**. Look here for clothes, accessories and household goods. The **Rue du Président Herriot**, the main drag, includes Védrenne for fine wines and spirits. The streets just north of **Place Bellecour** are particularly fashionable, Rue Zola including Maison Malleval for alcoholic treats. **Rue de la République** has the Printemps department store. South from immense Place Bellecour, **Rue Victor Hugo** presents other big household-name stores. For very elegant antiques and fine-arts shops try parallel **Rue Auguste Comte**, on which Tousoie presents Lyon silks.

Activities

Bateaux-mouches were invented in Lyon, not Paris, named after the city's La Mouche area. Naviginter, **t** 04 78 42 96 81, **f** 04 78 42 11 09, runs *bateaux-mouches* short trips, plus lunch and dinner cruises, from Quai Claude Bernard in season. It also offers day-trips to Beaujolais, as does Philibert, **t** 04 78 98 56 00, which offers other short cruises.

Where to Stay

Lyon, like Paris, is divided into *arrondissements*, their numbers given in the addresses.

Lyon ✉ **69000**

★★★★La Villa Florentine, 25 Montée St-Barthélémy, 5e, t 04 72 56 56 56, f 04 78 40 90 56, *www.villaflorentine.com* (*luxury*). Exclusive location, high on Fourvière hill, a former convent converted into an Italianate delight. Enjoy the views from the excellent restaurant, Les Terrasses de Lyon.

★★★★La Tour Rose, 22 Rue du Bœuf, 5e, t 04 78 92 69 10, f 04 78 42 26 02, *chavent@asi.fr* (*luxury*). Down in the heart of Renaissance Lyon, set around courtyards with colourful stairtowers. Lyon silks are used in the sumptuous interior decoration, and there is also a superb restaurant.

★★★★Royal, 20 Place Bellecour, 2e, t 04 78 37 57 31, f 04 78 37 01 36 (*luxury–expensive*). The best on the Presqu'île.

★★★Carlton, 4 Rue Jussieu, 2e, t 04 78 42 56 51, f 04 78 42 10 71, *H2950@accor-hotels.com* (*expensive*). Its glamorous dome stands out in the Presqu'île's shopping district.

★★★Globe et Cécil, 21 Rue Gasparin, 2e, t 04 78 42 58 95, f 04 72 41 99 06, *www.globeetcecil-hotel.com* (*expensive*). Also stylish, all rooms with individual touches.

★★★Hôtel des Beaux-Arts, 75 Rue du Prés Herriot, 2e, t 04 78 38 09 50, f 04 78 42 19 19, *H2949@ accor-hotels.com* (*expensive*). Behind the elegant façade, the rooms are more standardized.

★★★Hôtel des Artistes, 8 Rue G. André, 2e, t 04 78 42 04 88, f 04 78 42 93 76, *hartiste@ club-internet.fr* (*moderate*). Simple charm.

★★Hôtel du Théâtre, 10 Rue de Savoie, 2e, t 04 78 42 33 32, f 04 72 40 00 61 (*inexpensive*). Really good value for the peninsula, stylish, some rooms with nice views.

★★L'Elysée, 92 Rue du Président E. Herriot, 2e, t 04 78 42 03 15, f 04 78 37 76 49 (*inexpensive*). Appealing traditional option.

★Hôtel d'Ainay, 14 Rue des Remparts d'Ainay, 2e, t 04 78 42 43 42, f 04 72 77 51 90 (*cheap*). Excellent location for a cheap one-star. Go for the rooms giving on to Place d'Ampère.

Eating Out

Bouchons are typical jovial, cramped Lyonnais family restaurants, serving good-value, hearty fare and wine in pots.

Léon de Lyon, 1 Rue Pléney, 1er, t 04 72 10 11 12 (*luxury*). Superb traditional Lyonnais cuisine. *Closed Sun, Mon and Aug.*

Pierre Orsi, 3 Place Kléber, 6e, t 04 78 89 57 68 (*luxury–expensive*). Another classic luxury Lyon restaurant, just south of the Parc de la Tête d'Or. *Closed Sun and Mon.*

La Tassée, 20 Rue de la Charité, 2e, t 04 72 77 79 00 (*expensive*). Big lively *bouchon* on two levels, but rather classy by *bouchon* standards, especially the upper level with its wall paintings of Beaujolais scenes. *Closed Sun.*

Le Vivarais, 1 Place Gailleton, 2e, t 04 78 37 85 15 (*moderate*). Good Lyonnais pork specialities. *Closed Aug.*

Les Muses de l'Opéra, 7th Floor of the Opera House, 1er, t 04 72 00 45 58 (*moderate*). Extraordinary rooftop location at which to enjoy fine cuisine. *Closed Sun.*

Chabert et Fils, 11 Rue des Marronniers, 2e, t 04 78 37 01 94 (*moderate*). A picturesque, reliably good *bouchon*.

Brasserie Georges 1836, 30 Cours de Verdun-Perrache, 2e, t 04 72 56 54 54 (*moderate*). An enormous, lively Lyonnais culinary institution with outrageous interiors.

Chez Hugon, 12 Rue Pizay, 1er, t 04 78 28 10 94 (*moderate*). A very typical *bouchon*. *Closed Sat, Sun and Aug.*

Café des Fédérations, 10 Rue du Major Martin, 1er, t 04 78 28 26 00 (*moderate*). Another classic *bouchon*. *Closed Sat, Sun and Aug.*

Hôtel de Fourvière, 9 Place Fourvière, 5e, t 04 78 25 21 15 (*moderate–cheap*). Traditional Lyonnais cuisine, accompanied by views.

Les Lyonnais, 1 Rue Tramassac, 5e, t 04 78 37 64 82 (*moderate–cheap*). Really friendly address in Vieux Lyon, smothered with photos. *Closed late July–mid-Aug.*

Entertainment and Nightlife

Lyon has its showy **opera house**, plus two main **theatres**, Célestins and Croix-Rousse. Look out for *Le Petit Bulletin*, a free cultural newspaper. The city has a great selection of cafés and bars, particularly in the 1st *arrondissement*, plus a thriving gay quarter.

Place du Change nearby was where the currency changers set up shop during the Lyon fairs, enormously important European trading events through medieval times, bringing great fortunes to some Lyon merchants. The first exchange in France was built here at the start of the 16th century. The building was redesigned by Soufflot, of Paris Panthéon notoriety, in the middle of the 18th century. He made the place look like an elegant little theatre. Above Place du Change, the medieval **church of St-Paul** looks a bit sorry for itself, while the northern end of Vieux Lyon is still a bit tatty.

The Presqu'île de Lyon

At the northern end of Lyon's glamorous peninsula, on the opposite bank of the Saône from St-Paul, the concave Baroque façade of the church of **St-Vincent** stands out. Just east, the many-fountained **Place des Terreaux** is the big, lively hub of central Lyon, with cafés spilling out around the rearing horses of the main fountain. The massive **town hall** overlooks one side of the square, its elaborate façade designed by Jules Hardouin-Mansart and Robert de Cotte. *Telamones* frame the equestrian statue of King Henri IV, while grizzly lions (a pun on the town's name) rest their paws on globes over the first-floor windows.

The long, subdued classical façade of the **Musée des Beaux-Arts** (*open Wed–Sun 10.30–6; closed Mon, Tues and public hols; adm*) on another side of the square was originally designed as the sober front for a Benedictine convent, the Abbey of Our Ladies of St Peter's, also known as the Palais St-Pierre. After the Revolution it became Lyon's fine-arts museum, wholly refurbished in the 1990s. The first floor has a whole wing devoted to antiquities, another to medieval art and *objets d'art* generally, and a third to the Renaissance. Most of the painting, from the late 15th to the 20th century, is on the second floor. The monumental Egyptian temple doors from Mehamoud, and a figure from the Athens Acropolis, are the highlights of the ancient collections. Vast allegorical dreamscapes typical of Pierre Puvis de Chavannes, a 19th-century artist from Lyon, decorate the staircase leading to the second floor, where famous names from the different schools of European painting are represented: Veronese, Tintoretto and Bassano; El Greco and Zurbaràn; Cranach the Elder, Gérard David, Rembrandt and Rubens; Simon Vouet, Philippe de Champaigne, Boucher and Desportes; Delacroix, Géricault, Daumier, Corot and Courbet, Degas and Gauguin are some of the major names. The abbey's former church now serves as a spacious sculpture gallery.

Behind the town hall rises the brazen **opera house**, its lower parts in classical style, but recently topped by a modern green barrel vault with glass sides, designed by architect Jean Nouvel. Major shopping arteries head south from Place des Terreaux, where you'll find the ornate church of **St-Nizier**, its Gothic forms and gargoyles scrubbed clean. Nearby, the **Musée de l'Imprimerie** (*open Wed–Sun 2–6; adm*) on Rue de la Poulaillerie is a highly regarded print museum set in a lovely Renaissance mansion that once served as Lyon's town hall. In its courtyard, a plaque shows a male and a female pouring water from an urn, symbols of Lyon's two rivers. The museum contains a rare Gutenberg Bible (*c.* 1454), fine prints from the 15th to the 19th centuries, and Doré's famous 19th-century illustrations for Rabelais' *Gargantua*, first published in Lyon.

Place Bellecour, the enormous, rather vacuous centrepiece of the Presqu'île, comes as a bit of a disappointment after the rather glamorous smaller shopping squares to the north. The equestrian statue isolated in the centre represents King Louis XIV, a replacement put up after the Revolution. The still more sterile **Place Antonin Poncet** adjoining Place Bellecour leads to the Rhône, where the massive dome and façade of the **Hôtel-Dieu** make a grand impression. This hospital was long recognized as one of the leading medical centres in Europe, and Rabelais practised here back in the 16th century. The architecture you see now is showy Ancien Régime, designed by Soufflot and his team. You can visit some of the grandiose interiors as well as the **Musée des Hospices Civils de Lyon** (*open Mon–Fri 1.30–5.30; adm*), containing fine decorative features by such accomplished artists as Coysevox and Coustou.

South from Place Bellecour, chic shopping streets lead to two of Lyon's most highly regarded museums, along Rue de la Charité. You'll get a good feeling for grand 18th-century interiors wandering round the sumptuous **Musée des Arts Décoratifs** (*open Tues–Sun 10–12 and 2–5.30; closed Mon and public hols; combined ticket available with Musée Historique des Tissus; adm, free Wed*), devoted to Ancien Régime furnishings, and housed in a huge town house, attributed again to Soufflot. The **Musée Historique des Tissus** (*open Tues–Sun 10–5.30; closed Mon and public hols; adm, free Wed*), in the 18th-century Hôtel de Villeroy, pays homage to textile-making from ancient times to the present. The early sections contain fabulous pieces from around the world, and the Middle East in particular. Lyon has a great silk-weaving tradition; its golden age came in the 18th century, when no one could match the skill of Philippe de Lasalle, whose cameo textile portraits look like the most accomplished paintings.

Place Ampère further south pays its respects to the 18th-century Lyonnais scientist who gave his name to the basic unit of electric current, the amp. To the west, the heavily restored Romanesque **Basilique St-Martin d'Ainay** formed part of a highly influential Benedictine abbey, and retains some engrossing Romanesque decoration.

The Northern and Eastern Quarters: More Silk and Cinema

A short, steep walk north from Place des Terreaux, past the sadly neglected Gallo-Roman theatre of the Three Gauls, you come to the working-class quarter of La Croix Rousse where Lyon's silk-weavers settled after the Revolution. The red cross after which the district was named has long disappeared, as have most of the weavers, but head north from **Place de la Croix-Rousse** up Grande Rue de la Croix-Rousse (*not* the boulevard of the same name) and turn right into Rue d'Ivry to visit the **Maison des Canuts** (*open Mon–Sat 8.30–12 and 2–6.30; closed Sun; adm*) where you can see demonstrations of silk-weaving, watch a video on silk-making, and admire displays of fine silks. In the mid-19th century a staggering 30,000 master-weavers clattered away in this district. Now there are just 12. But you can still buy pieces of fine Lyon silk from the Coopérative des Canuts on the other side of the road. The Chartreux garden on the site of a former monastery has excellent views over the Saône.

It's an awkward climb down from Croix-Rousse to the Rhône. On the opposite bank, across Pont Winston Churchill, lies the large, flat and restful **Tête d'Or park**, named after an extraordinary story which claimed that a golden head of Christ was buried here. The place is now the unlikely home to the new Interpol headquarters, built in 1989, and to the **Musée d'Art Contemporain**, which hosts temporary exhibitions. You can go boating on the park's pleasant lake and wander through its botanical gardens.

Heading south, the chilling **Centre d'Histoire de la Résistance et de la Déportation** (*open Wed–Sun 9–5.30; adm*) on Avenue Berthelot (just east of Pont Gallieni) occupies the buildings where the dreaded Nazi Gestapo had its Lyon headquarters during the Second World War. But the city was one of the most vital centres of the Résistance in France; Jean Moulin, perhaps the greatest of all the French Résistance organizers, did much to bring together the strands of active protest. The place doesn't shy away from the traumatic issue of collaboration. Lyon saw a massive rounding-up of Jews in August 1942, under the Vichy government, and from November 1942 until its liberation the city was at the mercy of notorious Gestapo chief Klaus Barbie. In June 1943, Moulin was captured and tortured to death. Barbie managed to avoid facing trial for decades, but in the 1980s was finally brought back to Lyon and found guilty of dreadful atrocities, which some horrific videos at the centre show all too clearly.

Some way east, discover how cinema came to life at the **Institut Lumière** (*t 04 78 78 18 95, f 04 78 01 36 62; open Tues–Sun 2–6; adm*), on Rue du Premier Film (*métro* station Monplaisir Lumière). Set in a very grand house built for the wealthy Lumière family, this is part (quite technical) museum, part cinema centre, screening films, inviting speakers and encouraging film studies. The first film of all time, shot by Louis Lumière, shows workers emerging from the Lumière factories nearby.

Day Trip from Lyon

Vienne and St-Romain-en-Gal

Lovably tatty old **Vienne** south down the Rhône from Lyon was a very grand town in Gallo-Roman and early Christian times, built on the site of the main settlement of the Celtic Allobroges tribe. It enjoyed a period of immense trading prosperity from the 1st century AD to the 3rd, as did St-Romain-en-Gal just across the river. In fact, to appreciate the magnificence of the ancient legacy in these parts, head first for the excellent modern **Musée et Sites Archéologiques de St-Romain-en-Gal-Vienne** (*open Tues–Sun 10–5; adm*) which presents fabulous Gallo-Roman finds. St-Romain-en-Gal developed into a quarter for wealthy merchants, with fine villas and large warehouses. Marble, ceramics, oil, fish paste, and exotica such as dates and figs were imported to the area. Over 250 mosaic floors have been uncovered in St-Romain-en-Gal and Vienne, making this one of the most prolific areas for such art in the Roman world. The museum displays them beautifully. Some tell stories from Greek mythology, while others feature decorative geometrical motifs. Some are highly coloured, others black and white. The mosaic of the ocean gods, discovered in 1967, has become the symbol of the museum. There are also some outstanding Gallo-Roman mural paintings, models of Vienne and St-Romain-en-Gal in ancient times, and all the other archaeological finds typically associated with Roman towns – amphorae, statues of gods, tools, and so on – creating an evocative picture of Gallo-Roman life in France. Luxurious latrines rescued for posterity are another highlight. Outside, you can wander round the archaeological excavations, with their traces of walls, cramped streets and a market square, as well as the odd part-reconstructed, colonnaded villa.

Heading across to Vienne, the **Roman theatre** (*open April–Aug daily 9.30–1 and 2–6; Sept–Oct Tues–Sun 9.30–1 and 2–6; rest of year Tues–Sat 9.30–12.30 and 2–5, Sun 1.30–5.30; adm*) was fitted snugly into the hillside. Yet with almost 50 tiers of seats, this counts among the largest theatres built in Gaul. A few marble slabs in the stalls show how sumptuous the decorative finish was. Today the place hosts the Vienne summer jazz festival. Remnants from the theatre and other wonderful classical fragments have been moved to the battered church of **St Peter**, now a neglected if fascinating **Musée Lapidaire** (*open April–Oct Tues–Sun 9.30–1 and 2–6; rest of year Tues–Fri 9.30–12.30 and 2–5, weekends 2–6; closed Mon; adm*). Vienne's most extraordinary Roman remains stand in the heart of town, the colonnaded Gallo-Roman **Temple of Augustus and Livia**. Many of its columns are chipped and shoddy, but the building remains extraordinarily evocative of Roman imperial authority.

Vienne was an important Christian centre down the centuries, as its medieval churches attest. The former **Cathédrale St-Maurice** resembles Lyon's cathedral from the front. The three Gothic portals contain some delightful decoration, including adorable musical angels. The scenes in the central doorway illustrate events in Christ's life prefigured in the Old Testament. Inside, Gothic bays were added on to the earlier Romanesque ones down the nave. Some amusing Romanesque carved decoration has survived. Leave by the north door to admire the wonderful stone-carving there. The other main Christian site to visit in the centre is the **Eglise et Cloître St-André-le-Bas** (*open same times as Musée Lapidaire; adm*) its greying Romanesque cloister held up on elegant columns, while historical presentations occupy further spaces. The central **Musée des Beaux-Arts et d'Archéologie** (*open same times as Musée Lapidaire; adm*), looks very old-fashioned and initially off-putting, but, as elsewhere in Vienne, there are amazing discoveries to be made if you're prepared to look beyond the unattractive environment.

In the south of the city, one last Gallo-Roman remain worth going out of your way to see is the monument known as the **Aiguille**, which is claimed, in one of those far-fetched Christian legends, to have been the tomb of Pontius Pilate. In fact the curious arch with its four sides topped by a pyramid probably formed the centrepiece of a Roman circus.

Getting There

Trains from Lyon-Perrache take between 15 and 30mins, with very regular services.

Tourist Information

Vienne ✉ 38200: Cours Brillier, t 04 74 53 80 39, f 04 74 53 80 31, *www.vienne-tourisme.fr*. Big market Sat am taking over town centre, smaller one daily by town hall.

Eating Out

★★★★**La Pyramide**, 14 Bd Fernand Point, t 04 74 53 01 96 (*expensive*). A French temple of haute cuisine. *Closed Tues and Wed.*

Le Bec Fin, 7 Place St-Maurice, t 04 74 85 76 72 (*expensive*). Quality cuisine on the cathedral square. *Closed Mon, and Wed pm.*

Le Cloître, 2 Rue des Cloîtres, t 04 74 31 93 57 (*moderate*). Tasty dishes in this split-level restaurant with a little terrace. *Closed Sun.*

Touring from Lyon

You'll find that the sights are reliably open Easter–Oct 10–12 and 2–5 at least, unless otherwise stated, and charge adm.

Day 1: Beaujolais' Rivers of Wine

Morning: The Lyonnais like to joke that three rivers flow through their city: the Rhône, the Saône, and the Beaujolais. Actually Beaujolais' famous and sometimes infamous vine-slopes rise some way northwest of Lyon. The golden-stoned villages of southern Beaujolais like **Oingt**, **Theizé**, **Ville-sur-Jarnioux**, **Cogny** and **Salles-Arbuissonnas** are perhaps better visited for their gorgeous architecture than their wines.

Lunch: The ****Auberge de Clochemerle** at Vaux, t 04 74 03 20 16 (*expensive*) makes a pleasant stop in a village just west that stars in a French comedy classic. *Closed Tues and Wed.* Odenas and Quincié to the north each have appealing restaurants, as does Beaujeu: ****Anne de Beaujeu**, t 04 74 04 87 58 (*expensive*), serving classic provincial fare. *Closed Sun pm, Mon, and Tues lunch.*

Afternoon: Beaujeu, after which the Beaujolais area is named, has a good historical wine museum (*in Oct, closed Tues*). Beaujolais' wines get better as you go north. The top ten little *appellations* cluster together; try estates in delightful **Chiroubles**, **Fleurie**, or **Juliénas**. For a slick modern museum introduction to Beaujolais wine-making, visit the Hameau du Vin at **Romanèche-Thorins**.

Dinner: Les Platanes de Chénas, t 03 85 36 79 80 (*expensive*) has charm aplenty, along with vineyard views. *Closed Tues and Wed.* The **Auberge du Paradis**, St-Amour-Bellevue, t 03 85 37 10 26 (*moderate*) proves agreeable too. Or try the hotels below. The

Sleeping: For outrageous luxury in a stunning medieval castle, book at ******Château de Bagnols**, Bagnols, t 04 74 71 40 00, f 04 74 71 40 49 (*luxury*). A tempting cheaper option is ****Chez La Rose**, t 04 74 04 41 20, f 04 74 04 49 29 (*moderate*), in Juliénas.

Day 2: Very Well-preserved Pérouges

Morning: Slip into Burgundy to see the beautiful wine route around **Pouilly** and **Fuissé**, while, up **Solutré**'s dramatic hillside, the

museum (*outside June–Sept, closed Tues*) tells a fascinating tale of mass prehistoric horse massacres. Cross the Saône and head for a surprising timberframe display in the delightfully little-known small town of **Châtillon-sur-Chalaronne**. Its church seems to have wandered down from Flanders.

Lunch: Châtillon's *****Hôtel de la Tour**, t 04 74 55 05 12 (*expensive–moderate*) has a tempting restaurant. *Closed Wed, plus Sun pm.* Or travel north to Vonnas, village of local super-chef Georges Blanc. His establishments have taken over the village. For the full extravaganza book at ******Georges Blanc**, t 04 74 50 90 90 (*luxury*); or try the reasonably priced Belle Epoque **Ancienne Auberge**, t 04 74 50 90 50 (*moderate*).

Afternoon: The splendidly preserved hillside village of **Pérouges** stands above the Ain river, south through the flat lakelands of the Dombes, where you might stop at **Villars** for its large ornithological park.

Dinner and sleeping: The beautiful timber-frame and corn-on-the-cob-covered *****Ostellerie du Vieux Pérouges**, t 04 74 61 00 88, f 04 74 34 77 90 (*expensive*) is the most extravagant address at which to stay and eat. The ****Relais de la Tour** is another appealing option on the main square. Or book a B&B place at **Chardon**, t 04 74 61 12 44 (*inexpensive*). *Open May–Sept.*

Day 3: Surprising Vines and Pebbles

Morning: Bypass eastern Lyon for the precariously steep little vineyards rising above the west bank of the Rhône below Vienne. They produce the greatest wines along the Rhône, such as Côte Rôtie and Condrieu, but production is so exclusive that it's hard to buy on the spot. Wandering up and down the slopes and through the wine villages is pleasing enough though. For secretive bucolic peace, head higher above the Rhône valley, for **Mont Pilat park**, with its pine-crested heights, or, at **Ste-Croix-en-Jarez**, a monastery turned village.

Lunch: Sample some of the splendid but elusive local wines on the Rhône's east bank, at ****Domaine de Clairefontaine**, t 04 74 58 81 52 (*luxury–expensive*), in Chonas-l'Amballan. *Closed Mon and Tues.* If you've made it to Ste-Croix, atmospheric

Le Prieuré, t 04 77 20 20 09 (*moderate– cheap*) serves local fare. *Closed Mon.*

Afternoon: Wine-tasting becomes more feasible as you head down along the west bank of the Rhône through the larger *appellation* of **St-Joseph**. Crossing the river, pass via **Tour d'Albon** for **Hauterives**, a village with a very eccentric palace of pebbles built by a local postman called Cheval.

Dinner and sleeping: Traditional **★★Le Relais**, t 04 75 68 81 12, f 04 75 68 92 42 (*inexpensive*), in Hauterives, is a pleasant traditional option. Or seek out sturdy B&B **Les Baumes de Tersanne**, t 04 75 68 90 56 (*inexpensive*), also built from the local pebbles; *table d'hôte* meals are possible if you reserve.

Day 4: Wearing the Shoe Leather

Morning: The major Gothic abbey at **St-Antoine** southeast of Hauterives has retained much of its grandeur, its massive church showing rich decoration, while the museum in further buildings explains the nursing role of the whole medieval Antonin order as well as putting on contemporary art exhibitions. For those of you with an Imelda Marcos shoe complex, **Romans-sur-Isère**, long renowned for stylish footwear, boasts a splendid shoe museum as well as innumerable quality shoe shops.

Lunch: In Romans, **La Cassolette**, 16 Rue Rebatte, t 04 75 02 55 71 (*moderate–cheap*) is an atmospheric place set in a medieval building. *Closed Mon.* A couple of kilometres northwest of town, the **★★Hôtel des Balmes**, t 04 75 02 29 52 (*moderate–cheap*), has a popular restaurant. *Closed Mon.*

Afternoon: Back in Rhône wine territory, practically every centimetre of the hills around **Tain-l'Hermitage** is covered with vines, producing Hermitage and Crozes-Hermitage. Chapoutier is the best-known producer-seller, or try the good Cave Coopérative. On the opposite bank of the Rhône, the pretty historic town of **Tournon-sur-Rhône** calls out for a visit, its hilltop château, gradually being restored, containing a local museum with a splendid Gothic painting, while the Gothic church below contains Gothic frescoes.

Dinner and sleeping: In Tain l'Hermitage, **★★Deux Coteaux**, t 04 75 08 33 01, f 04 75 08 44 20 (*inexpensive*) is pleasantly plain and

has simple rooms, several with views on to the Rhône. **Rive Gauche**, t 04 75 07 05 90 (*expensive*), close by, is an exciting modern restaurant. *Closed Sun pm, Mon, and Wed pm.* Across in Tournon, **★★Les Azalées**, t 04 75 08 05 23 (*inexpensive*) is a decent enough hotel just outside the centre, with reliable restaurant, while **Le Chaudron**, t 04 75 08 17 90 (*moderate*) in the historic part of town offers more traditional surroundings for good French fare. *Closed Thurs pm and Sun.*

Day 5: Heavenly Peace and Pottery

Morning: The ruined medieval **Château de Crussol** curls round the hill opposite Valence like a vast white spiralling fossil. Climb it for dramatic views of the Rhône valley. **St-Péray** below produces a palatable Rhône sparkling wine. Cross the river to reach **Crest**, where the sheer walls of one of the tallest-ever medieval keeps survey the Drôme river.

Lunch: In Crest, at **★Le Kléber**, t 04 75 25 11 69 (*moderate*), fish is the speciality. *Closed Sun pm, Mon, and Tues lunch.* **La Tartine**, t 04 75 25 11 53 (*cheap*) is a friendly address. *Only open Tues–Fri for lunch.*

Afternoon: The Drôme *département* boasts gorgeous peaceful country roads through the foothills of the Alps. Try the divine D538 via **Saou** and **Bourdeaux**. In the little lavender-valley-surrounded town of **Dieulefit** ('God Made It'), talented potters have a go at their own ambitious creations. The **Château de Grignan** still lords it over its pretty servant of a village to the south, even if it had its head chopped off at the Revolution. Mme de Sévigné, supreme 17th-century French correspondent, spent time here with her daughter, as you'll learn on the tour. Don't miss the decadent balustraded terrace, on top of the village church!

Dinner and sleeping: The **★★★★Manoir La Roseraie**, t 04 75 46 58 15, f 04 75 46 58 15 (*expensive*) is the second most exclusive address at which to stay and eat in Grignan. **★★★Le Claire de la Plume**, t 04 75 91 81 30, f 04 75 91 81 31 (*expensive*) makes an utterly charming alternative hotel, while **★★Sévigné**, t 04 75 46 50 97 (*inexpensive*) is friendly. **Le Poème**, t 04 75 91 10 90, is a delightful little address at which to savour local produce.

St-Etienne

St-Etienne may claim to be built on seven hills, but the similarity with Rome ends there. In fact, this surprisingly large city seems to sprawl over far more hills than that, the slag heaps of the former coal mines adding to the confusing geography of the place. St-Etienne may have built up a reputation for economic decline since the Second World War, but apparently it now has one of the most thriving small business sectors in France. That doesn't help turn it into an obvious tourist destination.

History isn't St-Etienne's strong point, but manufacture has been up until recently. The village of St-Etienne-de-Furan grew up by the Cistercian abbey of Valbenoîte in the Middle Ages, but the villagers spurned peaceable activities for the manufacturing of arms – the trade boomed to such an extent down the centuries that at the Revolution the town was briefly renamed Armeville, and it produced a large percentage of the weaponry used in Napoleon's terrible wars. The economic activities diversified through the 19th century. Most people associate St-Etienne with coalmining, though the lot of the workers was a miserable one. On a slightly more cheering note, the town also became a big producer of cycles and ribbons. Nowadays, it hosts a few prestigious higher education establishments, including, not surprisingly, the grand Ecole Nationale Supérieure des Mines.

You can find out more about the city's history at the **Musée du Vieux St-Etienne** (*open Tues–Sat 2.30–6; closed Sun, Mon and public hols; adm*) in the historic quarter.

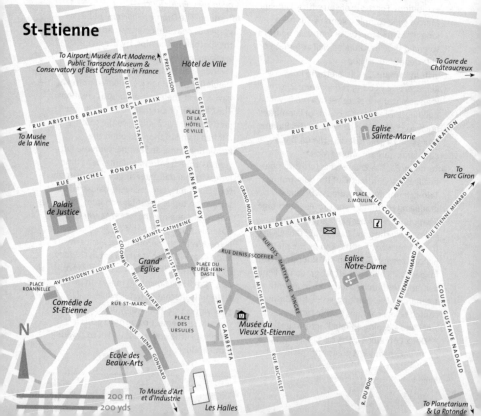

Getting to St-Etienne

Ryanair (*see* p.6) flies from London Stansted.

Getting from the Airport

The **airport** (t 04 77 55 71 71) is a short way north of town, by Andrézieux-Bouthéon. There is a Ryanair shuttle bus, but for central Lyon!

Getting Around

For **taxis** around St-Etienne, call t 04 77 25 42 42, t 04 77 32 37 85/t 04 77 32 57 72.

Tourist Information

St-Etienne: 16 Avenue de la Libération, t 04 77 49 39 00, f 04 77 49 39 03.

Where to Stay

St-Etienne ✉ 42000
★★★**Terminus du Forez**, t 04 77 32 48 47, f 04 77 34 03 30 (*expensive*). By the rail station east of the centre, classic French provincial fare.
★★**Hôtel des Arts**, 11 Rue Gambetta, t 04 77 32 42 11, f 04 77 34 06 72, *www.ArtsHotel.com* (*moderate*). Best option in the centre.

Eating Out

Bistrot de Paris, Place Jean Jaurès, t 04 77 32 21 50 (*moderate*). Best cuisine on the main square. *Closed Sat lunch, Sun and Mon.*
Les Deux Cageots, Place Grenette, t 04 77 32 89 85 (*moderate*). Justly popular bistrot. *Closed Sat lunch, Sun and Mon.*
There's also a good restaurant out at the modern art museum.

But this area, around **Place du Peuple**, only retains a small number of really old houses, built in the peculiarly globular sandstone of the area. A sturdy little selection stands out on one corner of Place du Peuple, and around the appealing, busy little triangular intersection of **Place Neuve**. Trendy bars and clubs and student restaurants fill the streets radiating out from here, making it the place to head to on weekend nights, but not Sundays – St-Etienne sleeps through the Lord's Day, or else the Stéphanois head for the hills. Keen church visitors could make a detour for the **Grand' Eglise** on Place Boivin. The 15th-century façade looks extraordinary; the local stone appears to have melted down like candle wax into intriguing, almost Gaudiesque forms. Note too the modernist-looking carved panels around the main doorway. Inside, the church looks more conventionally Gothic. Nearby stand the Comédie Theatre and the Palais de Justice, as well as the ugly Marché des Ursules, a covered market.

Head north and you enter the grid of shopping streets of central St-Etienne, too tightly packed together to be entirely attractive. A few large, straight-edged squares bring the relief of a bit of space; one extends in front of the dull **Hôtel de Ville**, with plenty of shops around it. **Place Jean Jaurès**, the other side of the town hall, forms the huge hub of the modern centre of St-Etienne; planted with tall plane trees and a big bandstand, it has fountains playing away, and cafés enticing trade on various sides. The grey **cathedral** on one side may be one of the newest in France, but has no significant architectural merit.

For St-Etienne's museums, you'll need to head a bit away from the centre. The town has a substantial mining museum, the **Musée de la Mine** (*open Wed–Mon 10–12.45 and 2–7; closed Tues*), set in a disused mine only just west of the centre, somewhat dismal-looking on the outside but run with plenty of enthusiasm by former miners who help explain what was until recently the main industry of these parts. The renovated **Musée d'Art et d'Industrie** (*open Wed–Mon 10–6; closed Tues*) demonstrates rather sensitively the craftsmanship involved in such industries even as arms-making. It also presents huge collections of cycles and ribbons. Big, broad, tree-lined **Cours Fauriel** makes a grand exit from the centre of St-Etienne, winding up its hillside; along here you'll find the recently renovated **Planétarium** (*check times at tourist office*).

Out of town, on the eastern ring road bypassing St-Etienne, the **Musée d'Art Moderne** (*open Wed–Mon 10–6; closed Tues*), created in the mid-1980s, may look a bit like an enormous bathroom showroom at first sight, but a few outdoor sculptures indicate its true purpose, and this is a seriously good modern-art museum. The superb tubular figures of Fernand Léger seem particularly apt for this industrial city. The central woman in his *Trois Femmes sur fond rouge* has hair which curves like a sheet of black metal, but you'll find tenderness in her ball-bearing eyes. Provocative works by other major 20th-century figures such as Picasso, Dubuffet and Warhol call for attention, while contemporary conceptual artists are afforded generous space.

Day Trip from St-Etienne

Le Puy-en-Velay

Thin fingers of volcanic rock sticking high into the air make the skyline of Le Puy-en-Velay unforgettable. Balanced on top of one finger stands an enormous pink Virgin. On another defiant digit of rock, the precarious-looking chapel of St-Michel d'Aiguilhe counts among the most atmospheric churches in France. A more distant finger is topped by another massive statue, this time of that somewhat sidelined biblical figure, Joseph. But Le-Puy-en-Velay's most dramatic place of worship is its cathedral, entered via a leviathan mouth of a doorway. Le Puy-en-Velay, you'll have gathered, is a very curious religious city indeed. It's certainly no place for those with difficulties negotiating stairs, although the big town museum is down on the flat.

The extraordinary site no doubt encouraged religious veneration in distant, prehistoric times. On one of Le Puy's heights, a stone known as the Feverish Stone, now thought possibly to have formed part of a neolithic dolmen, became a particularly significant place of worship in the city in Gallo-Roman times. At the end of the 4th century, Christianity spread across the Velay area. It was said that the Virgin worked many miracles here, and the first church dedicated to her is thought to have been built in the late 5th century; Le Puy was apparently one of the places where the cult of the Virgin first flourished in France. Moving on, tradition has it that Bishop Gothescalk set out in 950 on the first major pilgrimage from Le Puy to Santiago de Compostela in northern Spain. During the Middle Ages, the place developed into one of the four most important gathering points in France for this hugely popular journey, and a whole administrative city was built to deal with the pilgrims.

Le Puy and the Velay area around it learned to hone other skills beyond administering to the pilgrims' needs. The important tradition of lace-making was probably established in the area around the 15th century. Although the trade was largely

Getting There

Trains from St-Etienne-Châteaucreux take 1hr 20mins, with several choices Mon–Sat, but limited Sunday services.

Tourist Information

Le Puy-en-Velay: Place du Breuil, **t** 04 71 09 38 41, **f** 04 71 05 22 62, *www.ot-lepuyenvelay.fr*.

Where to Stay and Eat

Le Puy-en-Velay ✉ 43000
★★★Régina, 34 Bd Maréchal Fayolle, **t** 04 71 09 14 71, **f** 04 71 09 18 57, *www.hotelrestregina.com* (*moderate–inexpensive*). On one of the busy boulevards encircling the old city, quite stylish, completely modernized, and good value for the standard, which also goes for the cuisine.

★★Le Bristol, 7 Av Maréchal Foch, **t** 04 71 09 13 38, **f** 04 71 09 51 70, *guy.mallet2@wanadoo.fr* (*inexpensive*). Fairly smart, good value again, and with a friendly boss and restaurant.

Eric Tournayre, 12 Rue Chenebouterie, **t** 04 71 09 58 94 (*expensive–moderate*). Swish restaurant in an historic house with vaulted dining room for Auvergnat specialities. *Closed Sun pm, Mon, and Wed pm.*

L'Olympe, 8 Rue du College, **t** 04 71 05 90 59 (*expensive–moderate*). Stylish little restaurant up in a quiet little historic street. *Closed Sat pm, Sun pm, and Mon.*

Le Bateau Ivre, 5 Rue Portail d'Avignon, **t** 04 71 09 67 20 (*moderate*). Cosy restaurant devoted to Auvergnat traditions. *Closed Sun and Mon.*

mechanized in the 19th century, up until the First World War, large numbers of women in the region were still employed producing hand-made *dentelle*. Other specialities cultivated in the Le Puy area are lentils, the first vegetables in France to be granted their *appellation d'origine contrôlée* status to protect their authenticity, and *verveine*, verbena, used in the manufacture of teas and liqueurs.

Up Le Puy's Pinnacles: the Cathedral and the Virgin

One of the most memorable streets in France, steep, many-stepped **Rue des Tables** leads from Place des Tables up to the **cathedral**. Its huge, gaping black porch, like the mouth of a biblical monster, remains wide open below the sheer wall of the late-12th-century façade, embellished with patterns of alternating coloured stones and blind columns, a virtuoso display of Romanesque decoration. Rising to the left of the cathedral façade stand the imposing Hôtel Dieu, or hospital, and a castle-like building concealing the cathedral cloister. The whole complex looks like a very well-defended holy citadel. Enter it via that massive porch, itself the size of a decent church inside. A piece of extraordinarily bold architecture, it was built out from the hilltop to allow the cathedral above to be extended outwards. There are further steps to negotiate to get up into this church. Pilgrims in centuries past would have found themselves popping up out of the floor in the centre of the cathedral's nave; nowadays you have to make your way up via side stairs. The cathedral interior was restored with a disappointingly heavy hand in the 19th and 20th centuries.

Pilgrims would come to venerate the curious Black Virgin standing on the high altar. The original was said to have been brought back from the Orient by a medieval French king, possibly as a gift received from a Middle Eastern ruler. It's now thought that she may have been a representation of the ancient Egyptian goddess Isis. The original was destroyed at the Revolution. The copy shows Jesus popping his head out of his mother's clothing like a baby kangaroo. In the north aisle, an evocative 17th-century painting depicts a procession of the Virgin through the town, in thanks for her intercession during an outbreak of the plague. The sacristy houses a mixed bag of further religious objects associated with the cathedral. The religious authorities miraculously managed to hold on to the splendid illuminated Theodulfe Bible from the Dark Ages, received by the cathedral in the 18th century.

From inside the cathedral, you can enter what is now called the **Chapelle du St-Sacrement**, also known as the chapel of relics, located on the third floor of the crenellated building perpendicular to the cathedral. This long room once served as the library of the school based here. One wall was decorated in the 16th century with marvellous paintings representing the liberal arts as enthroned women in period attire.

A jumbled but atmospheric labyrinth of buildings surrounds the cathedral, some with intriguing features to peer at. You have to pay to visit the **cathedral cloisters** and rooms around it, that house a museum of religious art. Like the cathedral interior, the cloisters with their curious decorative features of stone patterning and of carved beasts have suffered from insensitive restoration. In the chapterhouse, the medieval wall paintings that have survived include a large Crucifixion scene. Among the paintings, carvings and other artefacts in the rooms above, perhaps the most striking object is a 16th-century embroidered coat made for the Black Virgin featuring a splendid Tree of Jesse depicting Christ's lineage.

Gather your energies to mount the enormous sickly pink **Notre-Dame de France** (*open May–Sept daily 9–7; rest of year daily 10–5; adm*) stuck on top of the nearby Rocher Corneille pinnacle in the 19th century. So striking from a distance, this Virgin is a bit of a monstrosity close up. Designed by Jean-Marie Bonnassieux, she measures over 50ft in height and weighs in at over one hundred tons. Once you've made it up to her, you can have the bizarre experience of climbing up inside her, right up to her head. Her innards have been covered head to toe in graffiti.

The Lower Town

Back down at Place des Tables, head along Rue Raphaël. Here, the **Centre d'Enseignement de la Dentelle et du Fuseau** (*open in tourist seasons, Mon–Fri 9.30–12 and 1.30–5.30, Sat 10–5; rest of year Mon–Fri 10–12 and 2–5, Sat 10–12; adm*) presents a video on the history of lace-making in Le Puy-en-Velay, and small exhibitions of pieces; it also offers courses (*t 04 71 02 01 68, f 04 71 02 92 56*).

Little **Rue Rochetaillade** nearby boasts some of the oldest houses in Le Puy. Also take a good look along **Rue Cardinal de Polignac**, lined with fine town houses, one owned by the mighty Polignac clan, one of the greatest historic families from the Auvergne, and one of the most hated at the Revolution. Down below Place de la Platrière, the former Jesuit Eglise du Collège adds a twist of Baroque.

Adjoining **Place du Clauzel** and **Place du Martouret** make up the heart of the old town around the feet of the cathedral. The neoclassical **Hôtel de Ville** was completed in 1766, in time to witness the guillotining of over 40 people, including 18 priests, and the burning in 1794 of the original Black Virgin. An antiques market takes place on Place du Clauzel on Saturday mornings. On the other side of the town hall, **Rue Pannessac**, another of the grandest streets in the old city, curves away from Place du Plot towards the stocky gateway of the Tour Pannessac, a remnant of medieval defences.

Most of these defensive walls came down a long time ago, replaced by boulevards. Just outside these, beyond the town hall, a grandiose area was laid out in the 19th century, stretching from **Place du Breuil** through the shaded *boules-players'* **Vinay gardens** to the substantial **Musée Crozatier** (*open May–Sept Wed–Mon 10–12 and 2–6; rest of year Wed–Mon 10–12 and 2–4; Sun 10–12; closed Tues; adm*), generously paid for by the wealthy sculptor Charles Crozatier. The place is crammed with a confusion of artefacts from down the ages. Regional traditional arts and crafts take up a large number of the cluttered rooms, and there is a good display of lace.

Heading north towards St Michael's needle, you might stop at the recently restored church of **St-Laurent**, by the boulevards just west of the centre, close to the Borne river. Saint Dominic, founder in Toulouse of the Catholic Church's Inquisition, came to Le Puy in the early 13th century and a Dominican monastery was set up here. St-Laurent, one of the few Gothic churches in Le Puy, formed part of it. In the first half of the Hundred Years' War, the fearsome Breton warrior Bertrand du Guesclin became the leader of the French troops waging war against the English across large swathes of France. He died in 1380 besieging Châteauneuf-de-Randon, not far to the south, which explains why his entrails ended up here, and why there is a tomb effigy of this important historical figure, in armour of course.

Up to St-Michel d'Aiguille

Two hundred and sixty steps lead up to the crooked little **Chapelle St-Michel d'Aiguilhe**, isolated high above another atmospheric little corner of town. Before heading up, you might say a quick prayer at the simple **Oratoire St-Grégoire** and visit the **Espace St-Michel**, which briefly explains the geology of the Le Puy basin as well as focusing on the cult of St Michael. It's a fairly sheer climb up to the chapel, but definitely worth the effort. The story goes that Bishop Gothescalk had this extraordinary place built on his return from his pilgrimage to Santiago. The architecture certainly seems to contain several Spanish-Moorish touches, although it may be that these were added in the 11th century. The cramped, contorted shape of the edifice was inevitably dictated by the very narrow peak of rock on which it stands. The interior looks cobbled-together, partly held up on comical little columns with wonderful carved capitals. A few intriguing religious items displayed in the nooks and crannies of the building add to the profound, cave-like atmosphere of this extraordinary chapel perched in such a bizarre spot. An elegant belltower rises from the chapel, similar in shape to the one on the cathedral.

If you've become captivated by the pinnacles of Le Puy, then you may want to head out to **Espahy** to take a closer look at the enormous Joseph, surrounded by more sickly 19th-century religious confections. As with Notre-Dame de France, you can go inside.

Touring from St-Etienne

You'll find that the sights are reliably open Easter–Oct, 10–12 and 2–5 at least, unless otherwise stated, and charge adm.

Day 1: The Upper Loire

Morning: West of St-Etienne, join the spectacular D108 Loire-side road beyond Unieux. Just north, stop at **Chambles** and then the ruined **Château d'Essalois**, in breathtaking locations looking down on the river gorges. Those of you mad about *boules* might make a detour west to **St-Bonnet-le-Château**, with its *boules* museum.

Lunch: Heading north up the Loire, seek out **Les Iris**, t 04 77 36 09 09 (*moderate*) at Andrézieux-Bouthéon, a curious villa of a hotel with elegant dining room. *Closed Sun pm and Mon*. For the finest French cuisine go a bit further north to Montrond-les-Bains for Gilles Etéocle's exquisite cuisine at ★★★**La Poularde**, t 04 77 54 40 06 (*luxury–expensive*). *Closed Mon and Tues lunch.*

Afternoon: The upper Loire plain is littered with little *puys*, worn volcano chimneys. The one sticking up at **St-Romain-le-Puy** south of Montbrison is crowned by a magical, wizened old medieval church. Past the pleasant town of **Montbrison**, the **Château de la Bastie d'Urfé** shows the comical first attempts to import Italian Renaissance fashions into French architecture.

Dinner and sleeping: For a truly unforgettable culinary experience, book at the ★★★★**Troisgros**, t 04 77 71 66 97, f 04 77 70 69 77 (*expensive*), whose renowned restaurant (*luxury*) is the major tourist attraction in dullish Roanne; consider the sister establishment, **Le Central**, for cheaper menus. Or for a memorable B&B evening, book room and *table d'hôte* at the adorable Loire-side **L'Echauguette**, t 04 77 63 15 89 (*inexpensive*), in the quiet old village of St-Maurice-sur-Loire.

Day 2: Romanesque Rock and Roll

Morning: The golden-stoned town of **Charlieu**, north up the Loire from Roanne, has a splendid religious legacy, including several churches worth visiting just for their carvings, like lacework on the ruins of St-Fortunat. The town also has a tradition of silk-making, recalled in the fashion museum.

Lunch: In Charlieu, the **Château de Tigny**, t 04 77 60 09 55 (*moderate*) is an exclusive place for lunch, out in the direction of Roanne. *Closed Mon and Tues*. Closer to the centre, **Le Sornin**, t 04 77 60 03 74 (*moderate*) is a good option. *Closed Mon lunch*.

Afternoon: You'll be spoilt for choice of sweet, rustic villages with delightful Romanesque churches in the golden-stoned Brionnais area north of Charlieu (just in Burgundy). Try **Semur-en-Brionnais**, with a little ruined castle to squeeze round too, **Anzy-le-Duc**, with some of the most weird and wonderful carving, or **Montceaux-l'Etoile**, Christ stepping out like a showbiz queen. **Paray-le-Monial** is a major pilgrimage stop thanks to its Romanesque abbey modelled on nearby Cluny and also to 17th-century Marguerite-Marie Alacoque, who had such a powerful vision of Christ's Sacred Heart that a whole cult developed around it.

Dinner and sleeping: Southern Burgundy is Charolais beef territory. In Paray, try it at the ★★**Grand Hôtel de la Basilique**, t 03 85 81 11 13 (*inexpensive*), a charming hotel favoured by pilgrims. Or have a serious Charolais dinner in Charolles itself, the pleasant town to the east, after which the white cattle are named – the place even has a meat museum. The ★★★**Modern**, t 03 85 24 07 02, f 03 85 24 05 21 (*moderate*) is one good option at which to stay and eat.

Day 3: Testing the Auvergne's Waters

Morning: It's a reasonable drive southwest for **Vichy**, a chic town on the banks of the Allier. There may not be much to do besides tasting the eggy waters or walking in the manicured parks – there's certainly no museum as yet on the collaborationist puppet French government that settled here under the Nazis. But virtually every building in the centre is an intriguing pastiche: mock Gothic, mock Venetian, mock Arabic, etc.

Lunch: Vichy is crammed with hotels and restaurants. The ★★★★**Aletti Palace**, 3 Place Aletti, t 04 70 30 20 20 (*moderate*) is interesting historically, the hotel where the Vichy government set up home; try the extravagant restaurant and cuisine today. The flowery **Hôtel du Rhône**, 8 Rue de Paris,

t 04 70 97 73 00 (*moderate*) has a charming terrace at which to enjoy a fine lunch.

Afternoon: Appealingly dour **Riom** (south towards Clermont-Ferrand) is a historic town of sober mansions that wouldn't look out of place in Scotland. The fine-arts and regional museums (*closed Tues*) and the churches hold several surprises. Adjoining **Mozac** conceals fabulous medieval treasures in its church. Up the hillside, **Volvic**, famed for its waters, has several small tourist curiosities, including its church, the ruined castle of Tournoel, the Maison de la Pierre caverns, and the bottling plant.

Dinner and sleeping: The sleepy spa town of Châtelguyon has a reasonable choice of hotels, like the **★★★Splendid, t** 04 73 86 04 80, **f** 04 73 86 17 56 (*moderate*), the lively place to go, or quieter Belle Epoque **★★Castel Régina, t** 04 73 86 00 15, **f** 04 73 86 19 44 (*inexpensive*).

Day 4: Black Volcanic Clermont

Morning: On a clear day, get up early to beat the crowds up the **Puy de Dôme** (*small fee*), the most majestic (and touristy) of the Monts Dômes volcanic range. Two sharp black spires soar up from the cathedral of **Clermont**, dwarfed by those huge black broken-egg volcano tops of the Monts Dômes. The Maison du Tourisme houses the Espace Art Roman (*closed Sun pm*), a modern introduction to the Romanesque art that flourished in the Auvergne. Seek out the sunken church of Notre-Dame de Bon Port, a mosaic of a building from that period. The Musée Bargoin and Musée du Tapis (*closed Mon*), the twin archaeological and carpet museums, lie by the brightly planted public garden, the Jardin Lecoq.

Lunch: *Le Bougnat, 29 Rue des Chaussetiers, **t** 04 73 36 36 98 (*moderate*) is an atmospheric Auvergnat address on a popular street for restaurants. *Riquier, 11 Rue de l'Etoile, **t** 04 73 36 67 25 (*moderate*) has a delightful terrace as well as a stylish interior for its regional fare.

Afternoon: **Montferrand** was once a quite separate town. It doesn't have the immediate appeal of Clermont, but boasts the excellent fine-arts museum (*closed Mon*) and a grid of restored streets nearby.

South from the joint city, drive up the the high **Plateau de Gergovie,** offering a staggering eagle's-eye view over the Allier valley, plus a cultural centre on the Auvergne's geology and the battle which successfully united the Celts under Vercingétorix against Caesar. Their final defeat came in Burgundy (*see* p.362).

Dinner and sleeping: Make the most of the views over Clermont by eating at splendidly perched **Le Paradis, t** 04 73 35 85 46 (*moderate*) up in Royat, *closed Mon and Tues*, or dine and stay in great 1930s Art Deco style at **★★★Le Radio, t** 04 73 30 87 83, **f** 04 73 36 42 44 (*upper moderate; menus expensive*), high up in neighbouring Chamalières. Down in Clermont, functional **★★Kyriad, t** 04 73 93 59 69 (*moderate*) has rooms with views.

Day 5: Up the Allier

Morning: Children would appreciate the brand new educational volcano theme park of **Vulcania,** 15km west towards Limoges. Or enjoy the glorious upper Allier valley southwards. **Issoire**'s church of St-Austremoine is covered head to toe with Romanesque decoration. The Centre d'Art Roman nearby puts on quite fascinating exhibitions on the theme. The village of **Usson** perches southeast, on a hill of basalt columns like dark organ pipes. **Brioude,** built around another startling Romanesque church, is proud of its lace and salmon-fishing traditions.

Lunch: The village of **Lavaudieu** southeast of Brioude makes a tempting lunchtime halt. Quaint **Auberge de l'Abbaye, t** 04 71 76 44 44 (*moderate*) offers traditional fare. *Closed Mon.* Or likeable **Court La Vigne, t** 04 71 76 45 79 (*moderate*) is good-value, but you have to book in advance. *Closed Tues and Wed.*

Afternoon: **Lavaudieu**'s attractions include the quirky church and cloister, and the stained-glass centre. Franco-American history is well recalled at the Château de Chavaniac-Lafayette, a grand speckled castle, home to that hero of two Revolutions, Marie-Joseph Lafayette, now a museum to his memory. Particularly amazing further volcanic-stone châteaux to visit before Le Puy include **St-Vidal** and **Polignac.**

Dinner and sleeping: Either *see* Le Puy (p 333), or stay just outside.

Chambéry

In Alpine-fresh Chambéry, the long backs of mountains and the odd jagged peak stand out at the end of many a street. It's the former capital of that most mountainous of European kingdoms, Savoy, and the region's flag is posted all over the place, a white cross on a red background, like the Swiss...except that Savoy eventually became attached to Italy, until its Savoyard citizens voted to become French in 1860! Many symbols of Savoy pride stand out around town, though, another common sight being a bellicose heraldic black lion, while various melodramatic monuments pay homage to Savoyard heroes.

Chambéry first acquired some political importance during the 13th century, when it became not just part of Savoy but its capital, after Count Thomas I of Savoy bought the place from a local lord. Incidentally, in the 13th century, Pierre II of Savoy ordered the building of the Savoy palace in London (now site of the famed Savoy Hotel), while his brother Boniface became an archbishop of Canterbury. A line of counts by the name of Amédée saw to the considerable development of the town from the 14th century. For a time, the house of Savoy controlled an Alpine territory and Alpine passes going all the way down from Lake Geneva to the Mediterranean. Amédée VIII acquired Geneva and Piedmont for the family. But then he abdicated and retired to

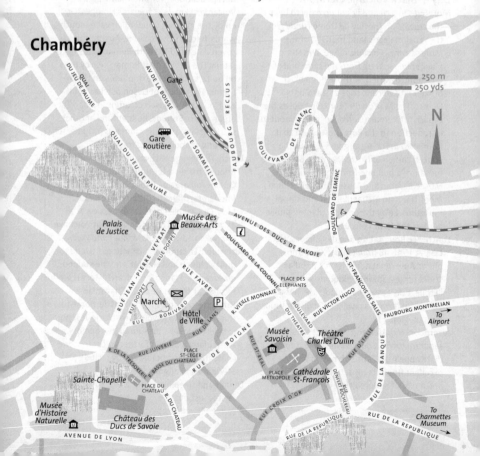

Getting to Chambéry

Buzz (see p.6) flies from London Stansted.

Getting from the Airport

Expect to pay €15 for the quarter-hour taxi drive from Chambéry–Aix-les-Bains **airport** (**t** 04 79 54 49 66. For **taxis**, try Aéroport Taxis Pernet, **t** 04 79 62 66 05/**t** 06 07 22 66 05 or Allô-Taxis, **t** 04 79 69 11 12.

Getting Around

The railway station is close to the compact historic centre.

Car Hire

Avis has an office at the airport, **t** 04 79 33 58 54. **ADA**, **Car'go**, **Europcar**, **Hertz**, **J.M.G**, **Rent a Car** and **Seigle Location** have offices in town.

Tourist Information

Chambéry: **t** 04 79 33 42 47, **f** 04 79 85 71 39, *www.chambery-tourisme.com*.

Shopping

Start at **Place St-Léger**, with chic boutiques for clothes and household goods, plus cafés. The most interesting shopping streets lead off this square. **Rue Juiverie** has an excellent selection of clothes shops, while dark **Rue Ste-Barbe** has a few discreet addresses. Narrow **Rue du Sénat** leads to the exceptionally ugly Halles covered market.

Back with Place St-Léger, stylish, arcaded **Rue de Boigne** cuts across the square, and has a smart array of shops, including perfumeries, a shop selling Lyon silks, and some delectable chocolate shops. **Rue Métropole** is chic too, leading to the cathedral. **Rue Croix d'Or** contains plenty of variety, several shops of particular regional interest, for example La Piste Verte, dealing with mountain matters, or L'Antre des Jeunes, games in wood.

Pause at the cafés in front of the ornate theatre, then there is more shopping along **Rue d'Italie**.

Where to Stay and Eat

Chambéry ⊠ 73000

★★★★**Château de Candie**, Rue du Bois de Candie, **t** 04 79 96 63 00, **f** 04 79 96 63 10, *candie@icor.fr* (*expensive*). Beautifully furnished converted fortress above town. The modern dining room has *trompe-l'œil* decorations and refined cuisine.

★★★**Les Princes**, 4 Rue de Boigne, **t** 04 79 33 45 36, **f** 04 79 70 31 47, *hoteldesprinces@wanadoo.fr* (*moderate*). A reliable, comfortable, very central option. No restaurant.

★★**Le Savoyard**, 35 Place Monge, **t** 04 79 33 36 55, **f** 04 79 85 25 70, *savoyard@noos.fr* (*inexpensive*). Cheerful big-fronted hotel on a main boulevard, with a restaurant serving reliable Savoy classics.

★★**City-Hôtel**, 9 Rue Denfert-Rochereau, **t** 04 79 85 76 79, **f** 04 79 85 86 11 (*inexpensive*). Very central if worn and functional.

★★**Le Revard**, 41 Avenue de la Boisse, **t** 04 79 62 04 64, **f** 04 79 96 37 26 (*inexpensive*). Probably the best of the bunch in the lively quarter opposite the railway station.

★★**Les Pervenches**, Chemin des Charmettes, **t** 04 79 33 34 26, **f** 04 79 60 02 52, *www.pervenches.net* (*inexpensive–cheap*). Lovely location below Rousseau's country house 2km out of town, a simple but very appealing hotel-restaurant.

Hôtel des Voyageurs, 3 Rue Doppet, **t** 04 79 33 57 00 (*cheap*). Very simple, central, fun.

Le Saint Réal, 86 Rue St-Réal, **t** 04 79 70 09 33 (*expensive*). Brilliant restaurant in a 17th-century building in the heart of town, with portraits staring out over you as you eat in its very smart bourgeois décor. *Closed Sun*.

La Maniguette, Rue Juiverie, **t** 04 79 62 25 26 (*moderate*). Trendy restaurant serving a very interesting single menu daily. *Closed Sun, Mon, and Tues pm*.

L'Hypoténuse, Carré Curial, **t** 04 79 85 80 15 (*moderate*). Stylish restaurant in this eccentric cultural quarter. *Closed Sun and Mon*.

Le Tonneau, 4 Rue St-Antoine, **t** 04 79 33 78 26 (*moderate*). Right in the centre, another high-class restaurant.

Le Bistrot, 6 Rue du Théâtre, **t** 04 79 75 10 78 (*moderate–cheap*). Excellent deal for Savoie specialities. *Closed Sun and Mon lunch*.

his castle of a monastery, Ripaille, by Lake Geneva. However, as the Great Papal Schism was creating havoc in the Church, he was elected as anti-pope Felix V at the Council of Basle of 1439, when Pope Eugenius IV was deposed. Felix V resigned nine years later, helping to end the division in the Church of Rome. Most famously, in 1453 the dukes of Savoy came by a shroud said to have covered Christ's dead body; it drew large numbers of pilgrims. But the French monarchy was putting on the pressure. In 1536, King François Ier, head of France's troops, briefly took Chambéry. The then duke fled to Turin. Duke Emmanuel Philibert regained Savoy's independence in 1559, but by 1562, Turin officially became capital of the duchy, and the shroud moved there in 1578. Although the French army continued to be a menace, Chambéry remained an important administrative centre of Savoy, keeping the regional senate and the Chambre des Comptes, effectively the ducal treasury. Many grand houses built by the city's administrators have survived to this day.

Chambéry was repeatedly put upon by French troops, while in the 1740s a Spanish army devastated parts of the town. Victor-Amédée III had much of the castle rebuilt. The French came back during the Revolution and made Chambéry capital of the large *département* of Mont-Blanc. Several colourful Chambériens stand out from this period. Adèle de Bellegarde became quite enthused by the Revolution, and was painted by the major painter of the period, David, in one of his best-known works before she became, much later, in 1977, the face of Marianne, symbol of the French Republic, seen on French postage stamps. In strong contrast, Joseph de Maistre railed against the Revolution in his writings, although his brother Xavier devoted himself to more frivolous literature, including the delightfully titled *Voyage Around My Bedroom*. After Napoleon's defeat, the Savoyards regained control of their territories. Meanwhile, General Benoît de Boigne had avoided the Revolution altogether, fighting in India and making a considerable fortune there, part of which he ploughed back into making civic provisions for Chambéry. But the proud independence of Savoy was reaching its end. First incorporated into the united Italy, the Savoyards then agreed to a political arrangement made by Emperor Napoleon III of France, and voted by a massive majority to become French.

A Tour of the City

The historic kernel of Chambéry is pleasingly compact, encased in broad, busy boulevards. Start a tour by the majestic, white-stoned Gothic **castle of the dukes of Savoy** (*open July and Aug Mon–Sat for tours at 10.30, 2.30, 3.30 and 4.30; Sept daily tour at 2.30 only; adm*) with its imposing machicolated tower. Another striking part of the complex, the aloof-looking **Sainte Chapelle**, is where the Turin shroud once lay. It is heavily restored inside, but some fine 16th-century stained glass has been preserved. The outrageous 19th-century *trompe-l'œil* ceiling is by Vicario. Note that the castle isn't easy to visit as it's now the administrative headquarters of the *département* of Savoie (confusingly, there's also a *département* of Haute-Savoie to the north).

Place du Château below is overseen by a couple of particularly grand mansions facing the castle and the arresting statue of the passionate de Maistre brothers. **Rue de Boigne**, a major arcaded shopping avenue of pink fronts, leads straight as an arrow from this statue to Chambéry's most famous monument, the amusing column of the elephants topped by Benoît de Boigne, some way off.

Picturesque historic streets lead away from Place du Château. Take stocky **Rue Juiverie** or curving **Rue Basse du Château**, the latter lined with boutiques dating back to the 14th century. Their arched fronts are typical of central, historic Chambéry, where arched lanes lead via courtyards from one block to the next and one street to another. Many such passageways lead off **Place St-Léger**, the most vibrant square in the centre, with its pinkish cobbles, its fountains, and its characterful façades, with shutters that seem to have been brought down from Alpine chalets. Explore the maze of alleyways that lead off the square; you may stumble across the odd *trompe l'œil* decoration, a Chambéry speciality. One end of Place St-Léger, **Rue Croix d'Or**, lined with some of the grandest old houses in town, has a fine selection of shops. These continue along **Rue d'Italie** beyond the very fancy 19th-century theatre, which at night, like so much of central Chambéry, is lit up to flattering effect.

In a square tucked away from immediate view between Place St-Léger and Rue Croix d'Or, Chambéry's **cathedral** was originally part of a Franciscan abbey, built in the late-Gothic period in rather sober style, apart from the Flamboyant door. But brace yourself for the dizzying *trompe-l'œil* tracery painted all over the interior, like the campest neo-Gothic wallpaper, the work of Vicario once again. Fragments of some older wall paintings have survived, while the treasury includes a beautiful early-medieval ivory diptych.

The substantial regional museum, the **Musée Savoisien** (*open Wed–Mon 10–12 and 2–6; closed Tues and public hols; adm*), sprawls across the rest of the former Franciscan monastery adjoining the cathedral. It contains displays going back to prehistoric communities that settled by the Lac du Bourget some 3,000 years ago, then suddenly left, perhaps because the waters rose or because the horse-riding Halstatt people drove them out; but pieces of their life have settled here. The Gallo-Roman section contains lots of little finds too. Moving swiftly through the layers of Savoie civilization, one level of corridors and rooms around a cloister is devoted to paintings, many of which have connections with Chambéry and Savoy, the explanations filling in pieces of Savoyard history. A large separate room is devoted to the display of surprising fragments of a 13th-century mural recently rescued from a fort some 30km from Chambéry – such secular as opposed to religious medieval artworks are extremely rare. The figures may look caricatural, but some of the scenes prove powerful, such as that showing an attack on a castle. Further whole sections of the museum are devoted to an interesting ethnographical display on Savoy rural communities and to the effect of the Second World War on the region.

Rue Denfert-Rochereau leads from the theatre out to the recently transformed **Quartier Curial** by the boulevards. Massive buildings devoted to cultural activities vie for attention here. One is a square-sided former barracks, the other a curving, contemporary cultural centre, designed by architect Mario Botta and executed in striking grey and salmon layers of stone.

The wide **Boulevard du Théâtre** behind the Musée Savoisien leads to the **De Boigne column**, where you can admire the elephants close up. They look rather serious and dignified, although jokes are often made about the fact that the Chambéry pachyderms lack posteriors. Some stylish modernist blocks have been built around here. Boulevard de la Colonne leads on to several grandiose buildings, including that holding the **Musée des Beaux-Arts** (*open Wed–Mon 10–12 and 2–6; closed Tues and public hols; adm*), opposite the law courts. Its Italian collections are particularly rich, a strong reminder of Savoy's connections across the Alps. Gothic highlights include an enchanting retable of St Christopher carrying Jesus by Bartolo di Fredi, and a stunning profile portrait of a young man, attributed to Paolo Uccello. Titian and Giordano also feature, as well as some notable Flemish names. A few well-known French artists do get a look in, such as Georges de La Tour.

Maison des Charmettes

Open Wed–Mon 10–12 and 2–6; Oct–Mar 10–12 and 2–4.30; closed Tues and public hols; adm.

The most famous resident of Chambéry from the 18th century was the young Jean-Jacques Rousseau. He's remembered at the Maison des Charmettes, a steep but pleasant two-mile walk from the centre into still-idyllic countryside, little sloping orchards allowing open views of the mountains. The house is dedicated to Rousseau and Madame de Warens. The young Jean-Jacques had run away from an unhappy situation in Geneva at the age of 16 and was taken into the bosom of this immensely influential figure in his life, also his first lover. They lived in Chambéry from 1731 until 1736, Rousseau teaching music to the bourgeoisie, then moved to Les Charmettes, where he developed his *magasin d'idées* through his voracious studies. The simple interiors and garden somehow reflect Rousseau's simplistic idealizing works.

Day Trip or Overnighter from Chambéry

Aix-les-Bains and the Lac du Bourget

Framed by steep mountains, the Lac du Bourget is the largest natural lake in France, a long expanse of water left over from the last ice age. Sloping quite elegantly down its eastern bank, Aix-les-Bains is the main resort. In the 19th century it was renowned as one of the most fashionable spas in Europe. Way back before that, its hot sulphurous waters had been celebrated by the Celtic Allobroges tribe, and in Gallo-Roman times it boasted splendid baths. Spas then went out of fashion for a long, long time. A medieval settlement here was fortified; and the remnants of a Gothic-to-Renaissance 16th-century château have been turned into the town hall.

In the early 1600s King Henri IV of France enjoyed cavorting here, while in the 18th century Duke Amédée III of Savoy ordered new spa buildings, making provision for the poor as well as for the aristocracy. Napoleon's family took the waters, but the best-remembered French visitor was the sickly young Romantic poet Lamartine, who came in October 1816. He was introduced to Julie Charles, a young married woman suffering from tuberculosis, with whom he fell madly in love. They spent passionate times together that year, and promised to meet up again the following season, but Julie

Getting There

Aix-les-Bains is just 10mins by **train** from Chambéry. Or you could go straight to Aix from the airport.

Tourist Information

Aix-les-Bains: Rue Jean Monard, **t** 04 79 35 15 35, **f** 04 79 88 88 01.

For trips on the Lac du Bourget, contact the **Bateaux du Lac du Bourget et du Haut-Rhône**, **t** 04 79 88 92 09, **f** 04 79 63 45 00, *www.gwel.com*.

Where to Stay and Eat

Aix-les-Bains ✉ **73100**

★★★Le Manoir, 37 Rue Georges 1er, **t** 04 79 61 44 00, **f** 04 79 35 67 67 (*expensive*). Close to the Thermes Nationaux, a calm, green retreat with stylish restaurant.

★★★Astoria, 7 Place des Thermes, **t** 04 79 35 12 28, **f** 04 79 35 11 05 (*moderate*). There's a great Belle Epoque feel to this central hotel, with just one menu.

★★Au Petit Vatel, 11 Rue du Temple, **t** 04 79 35 04 80, **f** 04 79 34 01 51 (*inexpensive*). Old-style charm, right by the Anglican church where Queen Victoria is said to have worshipped when she was in town. Menus *moderate*.

★★Davat, 21 Chemin des Bateliers, Le Grand Port, **t** 04 79 63 40 40, **f** 04 79 54 35 68 (*inexpensive*). Pleasant traditional hotel by the lake, meals served in the garden in season.

Le Chalet du Coucou, 1 Bd Charcot, **t** 04 79 88 00 01. Generous traditional food (*moderate*) at this spot opposite the public beach.

---

was too ill by then and died before the end of 1817. The forlorn Lamartine immortalized her in his poems, notably 'Le Lac', under the name of Elvire.

The most famous British visitor to Aix-les-Bains came on several occasions from 1885 on, using the subtle pseudonym of the 'Countess of Balmoral'. She was none other than Queen Victoria. It came to be said that Aix was 'queen of spas and the queen of spas'. A whole English colony followed in Victoria's wake. At the end of the century extravagant, Belle Epoque villas were built on the slopes above the town.

Although Aix-les-Bains is something of an architectural jumble now, it retains a certain style and flair, and that curious spa mixture of sickness and jollity, both among the visitors and the architecture. Outside the rather grim main treatment centre, the **Thermes Nationaux**, stand the remnants of two Gallo-Roman monuments, the **Arch of Campanus** and the **Temple of Diana**. On the guided tour of the town you're taken into the Thermes Nationaux, which specialize in treatments for rheumatism, to peer at the dark remnants of the Gallo-Roman **baths** beneath. At the start of the new millennium, the swanky modern **Thermes Chevalley** opened above the old thermal centre, catering in part for those in search of luxury treatments. On the opposite side of the town hall from the Thermes Nationaux, try to find an excuse to go and have a look inside the **Grand Casino** (not to be confused with the Nouveau Casino). Some of the original mosaics and stained glass are still in place in this outrageous extravaganza of an entertainment hall, which was the first place in France to witness Wagner's *Tristan and Isolde*, in 1897. The **Musée Faure** (*open 6 Jan–19 Dec daily 10–12 and 1.30–6; closed Tues and public hols; adm*) north of the Thermes Nationaux contains Impressionist works and sculptures by the likes of Rodin.

It's some way down to the lakeshore, where you'll find the ports for lake cruising, a beach, a freshwater aquarium, and the rather vacuous lake-side promenade.

Touring from Chambéry

You'll find that the sights are reliably open Easter–Oct, 10–12 and 2–5, unless otherwise stated, and charge adm.

Day 1: Around Lac du Bourget

Morning: Admire the dramatic scenery of lake and mountains travelling up the western side of the Lac du Bourget. The main sight is the **Abbaye de Hautecombe** (*closed Tues*). A Cistercian monastery was founded here in the 12th century. Two of its 13th-century abbots became short-lived popes. Then in the 14th century this became the resting place of the lords of Savoy. Abandoned from the 16th century, it was revived in the 19th century in neo-Gothic style by the house of Savoy. The last king of Italy, Humbert II of Savoy, was buried here in 1983.

Lunch: *See* Aix-les-Bains, p.343.

Afternoon: Take a boat tour on the Lac du Bourget from Aix's port. Then drive up the **Mont Revard** to the east, the first defence in the **Bauges range**, now a regional nature park; its valleys produce Tomme cheese.

Dinner and sleeping: Press on to Annecy. The **★★★★Imperial Palace**, 32 Av d'Albigny, t 04 50 09 30 00, f 04 50 09 33 33, is the luxury option by the lake. **★★★Les Trésoms**, 3 Bd de la Corniche, t 04 50 51 43 84, f 04 50 45 56 49 (*expensive*) has certain rooms with lake views, and a smart restaurant. **★★Palais de l'Isle**, 13 Rue Perrière, t 04 50 45 86 87, f 04 50 51 87 15 (*moderate*), is the best-located two-star, in the heart of town (no restaurant).

Day 2: Annecy

Morning: Comparisons with Venice are always absurd, but **Annecy** probably equals any place in France for sheer watery romanticism. The old streets around the town's few canals are utterly captivating, the odd church façade in white stone rising above the houses. Start a tour of town at the Thiou bridge, with its famed view onto the prow of the Palais de l'Isle, a wonderful boat of a fortified building moored in the middle of the river and holding the cramped maze of Annecy's Musée d'Histoire (*closed Tues outside June–Sept*). Historically, Annecy is closely linked with Geneva, but when that Swiss city became the centre of the Reformation in the 16th century, the Catholic institutions based there moved to Annecy. The town even became the seat of the bishopric of Geneva, its most famous incumbent the gently persuasive 17th-century François de Sales, who set up the Order of the Visitation, an important charitable order, with Jeanne de Chantal. The 17th-century scrolled church of St-François de Sales makes quite an impression. Also pay your respects at the nearby churches of St-Maurice, a big Gothic barn of a building endowed with fine works of art, the cathedral of St Peter, an embellished Franciscan establishment, and Notre-Dame de Liesse.

Lunch: Among the many touristy restaurants in the centre of Annecy, **★Le Petit Zinc**, 11 Rue du Pont Morens, t 04 50 51 12 93 (*moderate*) is a warm little Savoyard restaurant. South on the heights above town, **Le Belvédère**, t 04 50 45 04 90 (*expensive*) is a reputed restaurant with splendid views. *Closed Wed.*

Afternoon: A boat trip around the lake is a must. Also consider visiting the impressive but disparate buildings of Annecy castle (*closed Tues outside June–Sept*) on the hill above the town centre. They contain a large, rambling regional museum, and a more focused museum on the region's lakes.

Dinner and sleeping: If you're comfortable in Annecy, consider staying another night. Or book in one of the exquisite hotels on the eastern side of the lake at very upmarket Talloires. For an outrageous treat, try the **★★★★Auberge du Père Bise**, t 04 50 60 72 01, f 04 50 60 73 05 (*luxury*), one of the greatest hotel-restaurants in southeastern France. The three-stars are spectacular too, with good restaurants, such as **★★★L'Abbaye**, t 04 50 60 77 33, f 04 50 60 78 81 (*expensive*), and **★★★Villa des Fleurs**, t 04 50 60 71 14, f 04 50 60 74 06 (*expensive–moderate*).

Day 3: Romance Around Lac d'Annecy

Morning: The drive around the lake is stunning. The resorts down the eastern side look particularly splendid, **Menthon St-Bernard** standing out for its restored medieval castle, possibly the birthplace of the saint after whom a couple of the most famous Alpine passes are named. On the western side, **Duingt** is overseen by a grand château, **St-Jorioz** has a quite good expanse of beach, and **Sévrier** has a bell museum (*outside summer, closed Sun and Mon*).

Lunch: For Talloires, *see* choices above. On the western side, Duingt's **★★★Hôtel du Lac**, t 04 50 68 90 90 (*moderate*) makes a bright stop for lunch. At Sévrier, the **Auberge du Bessard**, t 04 50 52 40 45 (*moderate*) offers a great lake-side seat.

Afternoon: The lakeside resorts offer all sorts of **watersports** opportunities. West from Annecy, medieval hilltop **Château de Montrottier** (*outside June–mid-Sept, closed Tues*) has disparate collections and spectacular views. Exploring the dramatic nearby **Gorges du Fier** is not for those who suffer from vertigo or claustrophobia.

Dinner and sleeping: You might spend another night by Lac d'Annecy. Or move northeast to Aviernoz. Here, the most welcoming British couple, passionate about their adoptive region, run the warm, simple village hotel , the **★★★Auberge Camelia**, t 04 50 22 44 24, f 04 50 22 43 25 (*moderate*).

Day 4: To Mont Blanc

Morning: If staying at Aviernoz, head up past the **Château de Thorens** (*open daily July–Aug*) with many mementos of the de Sales family (*see* Annecy), to the well-hidden **Plateau de Glières** to discover a secretive spot and its Résistance past. For the most picturesque route from Annecy, head east via the D909 for **La Clusaz**, an unusually picturesque modern ski resort full of chalets. Continue to ultra-chic Megève via the cute chapel at **Col des Avaris**.

Lunch: Megève has some very classy restaurants, like that of the **★Chalet du Mont d'Arbois**, t 04 50 21 25 03 (*expensive*).

Afternoon: Attractive walks head up the slopes from central **Megève**, for example to the calvary. For the first unimpeded views of Mont Blanc, head on to Cordon and Combloux – the vast mountain filling the end of Arve valley makes a memorable sight.

Dinner and sleeping: Book early for these parts. Combloux's **★★★Idéal-Mont-Blanc**, 419

Route du Feug, t 04 50 58 60 54, f 04 50 58 64 50 (*moderate*) is a chalet with splendid views of the big one, a nice restaurant and extras such as a covered heated pool. Much simpler, in sensationally located Servoz, the **Gîte de l'Alpe**, t 04 50 47 22 66 (*inexpensive*) is one of a handful of old-fashioned chalets with simple accommodation in this sprawling village.

Day 5: Up Europe's Biggest Meringue

Morning: Three stages of swaying cable-cars take you up from Chamonix to the **Aiguille du Midi**, the highest point you can get to near the peak of Mont Blanc without climbing all the way on foot. For even greater exhilaration, take the Hellbronner cable-car from level 2 (*book tickets in advance*, t 04 50 53 40 00). If you're scared of cable-cars, take the train up to the less dramatic **Mer de Glace** glacier, which you can walk inside.

Lunch: Chamonix's **★★★Le Labrador**, 101 Route du Golf, just outside town at Les Praz, t 04 50 55 90 09, f 04 50 53 15 85 (*menus expensive–moderate*), stands by the golf course, a reminder that Chamonix has summer as well as winter attractions.

Afternoon: If you're obsessed by going up high even in summer, take the cable-car north of Chamonix up to Argentière's **Aiguille des Grands Montets** (*book tickets on* t 04 50 54 00 71),set among huge glaciers. Or go walking up among the high lakes west of Chamonix. In bad weather, visit the town's mountaineering museum.

Dinner and sleeping: **★★★★Le Hameau Albert 1er**, t 04 50 53 05 09, f 04 50 55 95 48 (*luxury–expensive*) is the best-known high-quality hotel-restaurant in the centre of the resort, with excellent facilities and restaurant, although in a not very inspiring corner. **★★★La Savoyarde**, 28 Route des Moussoux, t 04 50 53 00 77, f 04 50 55 86 82 (*expensive*), by contrast, is in a much better location, a quaint chalet above the town, with a great view of the Aiguille du Midi. **★★Le Montagny**, 490 Le Pont, at Les Houches, t 04 50 54 57 37, f 04 50 54 52 97 (*moderate*) is an exclusive little chalet (without restaurant) at a reasonable price.

Grenoble

With valleys leading off towards Savoy and Switzerland to the north, Provence and Italy to the south, and the Rhône Valley to the west, Grenoble was an obvious location for the commercial, cultural and intellectual capital of the Dauphiné region. Tarnished by a reputation for being uncompromisingly modern and industrial, it turns out to have a fascinating history, and as many museums as there are months of the year.

Grenoble's Gallo-Roman predecessor was insignificant compared to magnificent Vienne on the Rhône (see p.326), under whose authority it lay, but by the 3rd century it was surrounded by substantial oval walls. Christianity got an early footing here, as you can still see at the church of St-Laurent. In the early medieval period, the bishops battled with local lords to rule the city. The mighty counts of Albon took control of Grenoble, ruling lands from the Rhône to Savoy. One of their number, Guiges IV, was given the name of Dauphin (Dolphin), which was adopted by his descendants, the region they ruled becoming known as the Dauphiné. One Dauphin, Humbert II, established his council and treasury at Grenoble. Humbert III, however, wasted the family fortune and was forced to sell the region. So the French crown bought the Dauphiné, given to the then king's eldest son. From that time on, the heir to the French throne would be known as the Dauphin. Only one of their number, the future King Louis XI, actually ruled the region before becoming monarch; it was he who created the Parlement or law courts of the region in 1453.

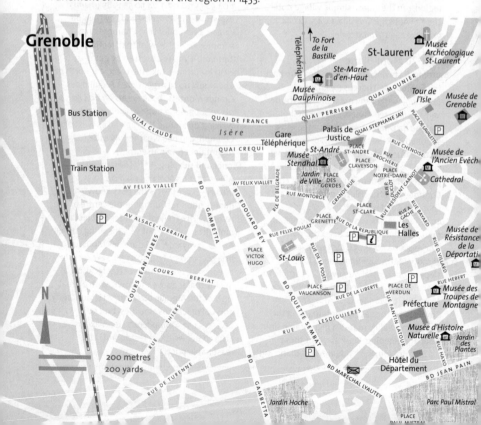

The 16th-century Wars of Religion caused bitter fighting in the Dauphiné, the fanatical Catholic Baron des Adrets wreaking devastation. But the leading Protestant Lesdiguières put his stamp firmly on Grenoble, extending the ramparts, ruling the

Getting to Grenoble

Buzz (*see* p.6) flies from London Stansted.

Getting from the Airport

Grenoble St-Geoirs **airport** (**t** 04 76 65 48 48), 41km northwest of the city, is in fact almost as close to Lyon as to Grenoble. A **shuttle bus** service operates to and from the centre of Grenoble. For return flights, it leaves Grenobles *gare routière* (bus station) 2hrs before departures, but always double-check.

Getting Around

The **train station** is west of the centre along Av Félix Viallet. The **bus station** is next door. Allô Tag, **t** 04 76 20 66 66, operates bus services. Among **taxi** companies operating 24hr services, try Taxis Grenoblois, **t** 04 76 54 42 54.

Car Hire

Most of the major names in car hire have offices in Place de la Gare.

Tourist Information

Grenoble: 14 Rue de la République, **t** 04 76 42 41 41, **f** 04 76 00 18 98, *www.grenoble-isere-tourisme.com*.

Shopping

The central shopping quarter stretches out from around the Jardin de Ville. **Place Grenette** is the major shopping hub, with cafés. On the square, La Noix de Grenoble sells culinary specialities such as walnuts and Chartreuse liqueur. **Grande Rue** and **Rue de Bonne** are the major shopping arteries off Place Grenette. A bit east, in the 19th-century **Halles Ste-Claire** you'll find fresh local produce, cheeses, and some Italian specialities too. **Rue Gaché** has a couple of épiceries offering local specialities, e.g. Jean-Pierre Bresson and La Feuille de Chêne. On **Rue Bayard**, Laiterie Bayard sells fine wines as well as all manner of cheeses.

Where to Stay and Eat

Grenoble ✉ 38000
The choice of decent hotels is limited.
****Park Hôtel**, 10 Place Paul Mistral, **t** 04 76 85 81 23, **f** 04 76 46 49 88, *www.park-hotel-grenoble.fr* (*expensive*). Looking out on to the picturesque Paul Mistral park, the luxury option in central Grenoble, with restaurant.
***Hôtel d'Angleterre**, 5 Place Victor Hugo, **t** 04 76 87 37 21, **f** 04 76 50 94 10, *www.hotel-angleterre.fr* (*expensive*). Pleasant and central. No restaurant.
Splendid, 22 Rue Thiers, **t** 04 76 46 33 12 (*moderate–inexpensive*). Heading southwest of the centre.
Acacia, 13 Rue de Belgrade, **t** 04 76 87 29 90 (*inexpensive*). Central, on the western side of the Jardin de Ville.
L'Europe, 22 Place Grenette, **t/f** 04 76 46 16 94 (*inexpensive–cheap*). Central, in a Hausmannian-style block with wrought-iron decoration but modern rooms.

Standard hotels cluster round the station.
L'Escalier, 6 Place Lavalette, **t** 04 76 54 66 16 (*expensive*). Excellent restaurant close to the art museum, serving classic French cuisine. *Closed Sat lunch, Sun, and Mon lunch.*
Auberge Napoléon, 7 Rue Montorge, **t** 04 76 87 53 64 (*expensive*). Stylish, excellent little restaurant by the central garden. *Closed lunch Mon–Wed, and all Sun.*
L'Arche, 4 Rue Pierre Duclot, **t** 04 76 44 22 62 (*moderate*). Fine regional cuisine at a reasonable price, plus a terrace. *Closed Sun.*
Le Chasse-Spleen, 6 Place de Lavalette, **t** 04 38 37 03 52 (*moderate*). Fish is the speciality in this restaurant on the same street by the museum; you'll find other good choices here, like the **Caffé Forte**. *Closed weekends.*
Chez le Pèr'Gras, **t** 04 76 42 09 47 (*moderate*). For a meal with a great view head up to this restaurant at La Tronche (La Bastille) by cable-car over the Isère. *Closed Sun pm.* **Le Petit Montorge**, 15 Rue Montorge, **t** 04 76 46 06 04 (*inexpensive–cheap*). Actually larger than the above, and with bargain deals for good quality cooking. *Closed Sun.*

city with firmness and defending the Dauphiné against Savoy. Despite its image of aristocratic elegance, as the Ancien Régime cracked up, Grenoble became a hotbed of sedition. The celebrated Journée des Tuiles, a riot in town brought about by the monarchy's attempt to close France's regional Parlements which were proving too awkward, has been seen as a warning rumble before the Revolution. The rioters threw roof-tiles down on the royal troops sent to quell the unrest, while the three Estates of the Dauphiné gathered to call for a national meeting of the French Estates.

In the event, the Revolutionary period passed off relatively peacefully in Grenoble, but through the 19th century the place was massively fortified, notably with the building of the Fort de la Bastille high above the Isère. Industrialization and working-class struggles came early. And so did skiing. The first attempts to introduce the sport in France took place at Chamrousse east of town. A major centre for the production of arms in the First World War, Grenoble's chemical industries developed enormously through the 20th century. Nowadays, the place has gained an international reputation for its centre for nuclear particle research. It also hosted the Winter Olympics in 1968 and is now a gateway to France's greatest concentration of ski resorts, around the Ecrins range to the east. All told, this is a cosmopolitan place today.

On a tour of Grenoble, head first for the grand **Place Notre-Dame**, in the quarter where the bishops of Grenoble held sway in medieval times. The **cathedral** looks as if it's had to jostle to stay on the square, with town houses shouldering in beside it. The stocky front is topped by a mighty, square brick bell tower which went up in the early 13th century. From inside the edifice you can visit the adjoining church of **St-Hugues**, a grim and messy early-Gothic building.

While a new tramway was being built around here in the 1980s, vestiges were unearthed of earlier episcopal buildings (including a rare 5th-century baptistry), plus Gallo-Roman walls, all now well housed in the splendidly presented **Musée de l'Ancien Evêché** (*open Thurs–Mon 10–7, Wed 10am–10pm; closed Tues; adm*). In fact, all the different eras in Dauphiné civilization are covered in this museum, starting with prehistoric hunter-gatherers. The section on the Dark Ages boasts the rare Vézeronce helmet, also known as Clodomir's helmet, after a Frankish prince who was killed at the Battle of Vézeronce near the Rhône in 524. With its superb frieze decorated with tiny grapes and birds, it may have been made in Byzantium, and was probably purely ceremonial. You can then follow the history of the medieval lords of the Dauphiné, and the foundation of three religious orders here in the 11th century – the Antonine, the Chalais (absorbed by the Cistercian), and the Chartreuse or Carthusian, the last founded by St Bruno in the Chartreuse range just north of Grenoble, hence the name.

The even swisher modern **Musée de Grenoble** (*open Thurs–Mon 10–7, Wed 10–10; closed Tues; adm*), built in the 1990s, is Grenoble's fine-arts museum, standing on the eastern edge of the historic centre, near the river. The city's connection with Champollion, who was educated here and went on to make the ground-breaking discovery of how to decipher hieroglyphics, explains the fine Egyptian works. Paintings, however, form the bulk of the collection. Among the highlights are Perugino's *St Sebastian*, Giuseppe Cesari's *Portrait of an Architect*, Rubens' *Pope Gregory surrounded by saints*, and French works by Philippe de Champaigne, Vouet and Claude Lorrain, plus an extraordinary series of New Testament scenes by Zurbarán. David's 1780 *Tête de femme* looks like a precursor of Lucien Freud. Henri Fanti-Latour, an accomplished 19th-century from Grenoble, has his own space. The museum also boasts one of the finest modern art collections in France outside Paris: there are good Fauvist and Cubist pieces, a few wonderful Matisses, and canvases by the likes of Léger and Modigliani. The 14th-century Tour de l'Isle nearby, originally built as the seat of the consuls of Grenoble, has been converted to display drawings, while major sculptors feature outside in the sculpture garden.

West of the Musée de Grenoble lie the liveliest, most atmospheric streets of the city. Sumptuous residences built for members of the Parlement stand along Rue Chenoise and Rue Brocherie, which lead to the city's prettiest square, **Place St-André**, overseen by the former **Parlement du Dauphiné**, by the church of **St-André**. You could pause to watch the world go by from the terrace of the Café de la Table Ronde, which claims to be the second-oldest café in France. The adjoining **Place des Gordes** leads to the **Jardin de Ville**, a leafy garden created for Lesdiguières. The **Musée Stendhal** (*open Tues–Sun 2–6; adm*) occupies part of Lesdiguières' town-house; the **Maison Stendhal** (*open Tues–Sun 9–12; adm*), in a house once owned by the writer's grandfather, lies nearby, off the Grande Rue. Both museums prove disappointingly dreary for such a passionate if ironic Romantic, Grenoble's most famous son and author of *Le Rouge et le Noir* and *La Chartreuse de Parme*, two of the greatest French 19th-century novels.

Moving to the heights above town, bubble cars will take you over the metallic grey-green waters of the Isère up to the **Fort de la Bastille**, which guards the city from the north. From here you'll see how Grenoble sprawls in its flat valleys, and how dramatically it's surrounded by high peaks. On clear days you're supposed to see Mont Blanc; nearer giants include Taillefer and Obiou.

Down the slopes below the fort, Grenoble's oldest church has been converted into the **Musée Archéologique St-Laurent** (*open Wed–Mon 9–12 and 2–6; adm*). So many layers of Christian buildings have been discovered one on top of another that the place is deeply confusing. In the 4th century, a Christian necropolis was established here, just outside the city, protected from the floods of the Isère. At the end of the 5th century a rectangular chapel went up. A rare little funerary church in the shape of a cross, with trefoil ends to each arm, was then built on the site in the 6th century. This was transformed in the 8th and 9th centuries, each arm converted into a crypt, with a new church built on top. Following all this, in the 11th and 12th centuries the church was transformed as part of a Benedictine priory. Confused? Through its now floorless nave, amid a jumble of gaping tombs, you can start identifying the different periods, including the rounded ends of the 6th-century Merovingian church. Alarming swastikas feature among the early-20th century decorations on the ceiling; when they were painted in 1910 they were merely taken as solar symbols. In the maze of corners you can then visit in this museum, don't miss the crypt of St-Oyand, named after a monk from the Jura. Wolfish monsters and birds feature among the foliage of the beautiful Carolingian carved capitals. Outside, the narrow **St-Laurent quarter**, with its massive 14th-century gateway, its 19th-century fortified terraces and its ethnic restaurants, is more laid-back than central Grenoble on the opposite bank.

A steep walk back up the hill takes you to the **Musée Dauphinois** (*open 2 May–Oct Wed–Mon 10–7; rest of year Wed–Mon 10–6; closed Tues; adm*), in a former convent, Ste-Marie-d'en-Haut, built in its prominent site during the Counter-Reformation by François de Sales' and Jeanne de Chantal's Order of the Visitation. Its nuns came from wealthy families, and the architecture has a spacious air, although the interiors have been much transformed, having served since the Revolution as prison, school, barracks and housing centre. However, the Baroque chapel has survived intact, covered head to toe with paintings depicting the life of François de Sales (*see* Annecy, p.344). The outrageous gilded retable with twisted columns is topped by a figure of God looking like a wild-eyed preacher. The museum has two permanent collections, one on Alpine village life, the other devoted to the history of skiing, while temporary exhibitions on aspects of the Dauphiné are mounted in the other spaces.

Day Trip from Grenoble

Château de Vizille

Open April–Oct Wed–Mon 10–6; rest of year Wed–Mon 10–5; closed Tues and public hols; grounds free; adm for château.

Set in gorgeous grounds, with their backdrop of sharp mountains, the massive Château de Vizille was built from 1600 to 1619 for Lesdiguières (*see* p.347), and houses an engrossing, huge **Museum of the French Revolution**. The reason for the puzzling phenomenon of such a grand castle's being devoted to the Revolution is that it hosted the celebrated meeting of the representatives of the three estates of the Dauphiné on 21 July 1788, in a ground-breaking act of independent cooperation between the nobles, the Church and the bourgeoisie. The entrance hall contains a useful time-chart of Revolutionary events, while throughout the rooms, fascinating and enlightening paintings, objects and models are cleverly fused with text to illustrate the unfolding stages of the Revolution. In the splendid, spacious gardens you'll find plenty to occupy children, such as the zoo, the little train, or the pony rides.

Getting There

VFD **buses, t** 0820 833 833, run to Vizille from Grenoble bus station.

Tourist Information

Vizille: Place du Château, **t** 04 76 68 15 16, **f** 04 76 78 94 49, *www.ot-vizille.com*.

Eating Out

Le Relais du Château, Place du Château, **t** 04 76 68 03 10 (*moderate–cheap*). On the square outside the entrance to the castle, a pleasant place for lunch.

L'Aventure, 50 Rue de la République, **t** 04 76 78 81 10 (*cheap*). This restaurant advertizes itself as a pizzeria, but it also does good traditional French food. It's by Place du Château, on the street parallel to the main shopping artery, Rue du Général de Gaulle. *Closed Mon.*

★★★Château de Cornage, **t** 04 76 68 28 00 (*moderate*). A healthy walk (15mins) will take you up to this *grand bourgeois* house in the Cornage hillside zone to the north, where you'll be rewarded by the finest cuisine in Vizille.

Touring from Grenoble

You'll find that the sights are reliably open Easter–Oct 10–12 and 2–5, unless otherwise stated, and charge adm.

Day 1: Up to the Chartreuse Range

Morning: Take the steep road north via Corenc to **Fort du St-Eynard** with its vertiginous views over Grenoble. Head north again for **St-Hugues-de-Chartreuse**, contented in its broad valley, its church containing an intriguing cycle of contemporary paintings and decoration by the artist Arcabas.

Lunch: Nearby touristy St-Pierre-de-Chartreuse in a bowl of mountains has a pleasant choice of restaurants, including that at ★★★**Beau Site, t** 04 76 88 61 34 (*moderate*). *Closed Mon.* ★**Le Beauregard, t** 04 76 88 60 12 (*moderate–cheap*) is in a great location too. *Closed Wed.*

Afternoon: The Couvent de la Grande Chartreuse, headquarters of the punishing Charterhouse order of monasteries, is out of bounds, but the Musée de la Grande Chartreuse in lovely buildings at **La Correrie** west of St-Pierre gives you an excellent picture of the order's history and rigorous monastic life, plus plenty on the green liqueur. Explore dramatic mountain roads either on a loop round the **Guiers gorges**, or heading up to the **Col du Granier**.

Dinner and sleeping: The **Auberge du Cucheron, t** 04 76 88 62 06 (*cheap*), 3km north of St-Pierre, has grandiose views, plenty of atmosphere, and nice menus (*moderate*). South towards Grenoble, the very appealing chalet-hotel ★★**Hôtel des Skieurs**, Le Sappey-en-Chartreuse, **t** 04 76 88 82 76, **f** 04 76 88 85 76 (*inexpensive*) has bright rooms and a restaurant with terrace.

Day 2: Up to the Belledonne Range

Morning: The massive **Château de Vizille** and its splendid grounds are covered opposite. For a heady morning, take the tortuous mountain loop round via **Chamrousse**, where French skiing was born, to and from the spa resort of **Uriage**. Alternatively, enjoy a pampering at Uriage's Institut d'Hydrothérapie Thermale, **t** 04 76 89 29 00.

Lunch: In Uriage, treat yourself to a fabulous meal in the palatial Second Empire ★★★**Grand Hôtel, t** 04 76 89 10 80 (*expensive*). Or *see* dinner options below.

Afternoon: Follow the D280 from Uriage up to Allevard, along the road known as the **Route des Balcons**. From **Allevard**, a 19th-century spa resort, head into the heart of the range along the (dead-end) **Bréda valley** with its pleasant Alpine villages.

Dinner and sleeping: In Allevard, ★**La Bonne Auberge, t** 04 76 97 53 04 (*cheap*), is a friendly simple option. Back down on the southern outskirts of Grenoble are two very stylish places, ★★★★**Chavant**, at Bresson, **t** 04 76 25 25 38, **f** 04 76 62 06 55 (*expensive*), with a highly regarded restaurant, although the ★★★**Château de la Commanderie**, at Eybens, **t** 04 76 25 34 58, **f** 04 76 24 07 31 (*expensive*) is more spacious and historic, set in lovely grounds, also with an excellent restaurant. For a cheaper option, return to Grenoble centre (*see* p.347).

Day 3: The Ecrins Range

Morning: The **Romanche valley** east of Grenoble takes you to this stupendous range. Up the north side of the valley, the modern resort of **L'Alpe d'Huez** has sensational views and is in an area with some surprising history. Take the breathtaking **Route Pastorale** back down into the valley. The modern resort of **Les Deux-Alpes** high above the south side of the valley is the foremost summer skiing destination in France, but with many other sports on offer through the year. Between the two, a delightful traditional Alpine route up the **Vénéon valley** into the heart of the Ecrins passes **Venosc**, selling woodwork and pottery.

Lunch: At Venosc, ★**Les Amis de la Montagne, t** 04 76 11 10 00 (*moderate*) has just the mountain atmosphere you want. Or west up at La Danchère, **Le Lauvitel, t** 04 76 80 06 77 (*moderate*) has splendid views to accompany quite inventive menus. (*These addresses are closed several months of the year, so always book in advance*). Or head east to more touristy La Grave.

Afternoon: La Grave faces the highest peaks of Les Ecrins, reaching almost 4,000m. Take a fabulous cable-car ride up monumental

La Meije. At **Col du Lautaret** to the east, the Jardin Alpin actually features plants from around the globe. **Col du Galibier** nearby links the southern and northern French Alps and has some of the finest views of the range – when it's open.

Dinner and sleeping: La Grave has a choice of reasonable *inexpensive* hotel-restaurants including **★★La Meijette**, t 04 76 79 90 34, **★★L'Edelweiss**, t 04 76 79 90 93, and **★★Le Castillan**, t 04 76 79 90 04. Or just east, Monêtier-les-Bains (alias ski resort Serre Chevalier 1500) has good choices such as characterful **★★★Auberge du Choucas**, t 04 92 24 42 73, f 04 92 24 51 60 (*expensive*).

Day 4: The Vercors Range

Morning: Southwest of Grenoble, the Vercors mountains may be much shorter than other surrounding ranges, but peaks don't come much more savagely picturesque, while the frightening roads up the Vercors' steep sides and gorges aren't for faint-hearted drivers. Set off early from the Ecrins to reach the pleasant little ski resort of **Villard-de-Lans**.

Lunch: At Villard, **★★★Le Christiana**, t 04 76 95 12 51 (*moderate*), is a big modern chalet with a gastronomic restaurant. **★★A La Ferme du Bois Barbu**, 3km away, t 04 76 95 13 09 (*moderate*) makes a good mountain halt on the edge of its forest. *Closed Wed.*

Afternoon: To the west, the gaping **Gorges de la Bourne** lead to the **Grottes de Choranche**, perched high on a steep mountainside, the caves decorated with natural filaments. Then take the spectacularly narrow and unforgettable **Goulet gorge** for **Vassieux-en-Vercors**, with two Résistance war museums, the first an old-fashioned one in the valley, set up by a Résistance veteran, the other high up above the plateau and a slick modern affair.

Dinner and sleeping: A staggering series of hairpin bends takes you down to Die and the Diois. South of Die, the historic inn at Luc-en-Diois, **★★Hôtel du Levant**, t 04 75 21 33 30, f 04 75 21 31 42 (*inexpensive*), has some brilliant views and a warm, old-fashioned restaurant. A cheap rustic alternative is L'Aubergerie at Barnave (midway between Die and Luc), t 04 75 21 82 13 (*inexpensive*). West of Die at picturesque riverside Pontaix,

L'Eau Vive, t 04 75 21 22 40 (*cheap*) is a basic bargain.

Day 5: The Quietly Dramatic Drôme

Morning: Explore **Die**, a tiny cathedral city with a surprise Romanesque mosaic. Then explore the local countryside, for example around picturesque **Châtillon-en-Diois** (east of town) trying the simple local sparkling wine, Clairette de Die.

Lunch: In a great location above Châtillon, **★★Le Mont Barral**, t 04 75 21 12 21 (*moderate–cheap*) is a very traditional French country hotel where you can go for a good solid meal. *Closed Wed out of season.* Along Die's main street, **★★Le St-Domingue**, t 04 75 22 03 08 (*moderate–cheap*) has a friendly old-style restaurant. *Closed Mon.*

Afternoon: The southern Drôme is a kind of pre-Provençal paradise, semi-ruined villages clinging to the sides of unlikely-shaped little mountains. You might branch off the D93 just north of Luc-en-Diois to take the D61 south, making detours to typical villages like **Chalancon** or, south past the Col de Soubeyrand, **Le Poet Sigillat**. This stands above the gorgeous great basin of **Ste-Jalle**. Follow the goats of the area, and go walking on these magnificent slopes. Head west towards the Rhône along the D64 Ennuye valley and then the D94 Aigues valley. Or press on to the happy market town of **Nyons**, at the exit of the Aigues river's mountain gorges. The lower slopes of the surrounding mountains are covered with olive groves, for which the place is famous, as well as with divine fruit orchards.

Dinner and sleeping: The wonderfully secretive **★★★Hameau de Valouse**, t 04 75 27 72 05, f 04 75 27 75 61 (*moderate*), more a little village of a hotel-restaurant than a hamlet, is actually quite well signposted off the D70 after St-Ferréol-Trente-Pas. A reliably good place to eat in the area, **La Charrette Bleue**, t 04 75 27 72 33 (*moderate*) lies right by the D94 at Les Pilles. *Closed Sun pm, Tues pm and Wed pm.* In Nyons, long-fronted **★★★Le Colombet**, Place de la Libération, t 04 75 26 03 66, f 04 75 26 42 37 (*moderate*) stands at the heart of the action, and has a restaurant.

Northeast France: Burgundy and Alsace

13

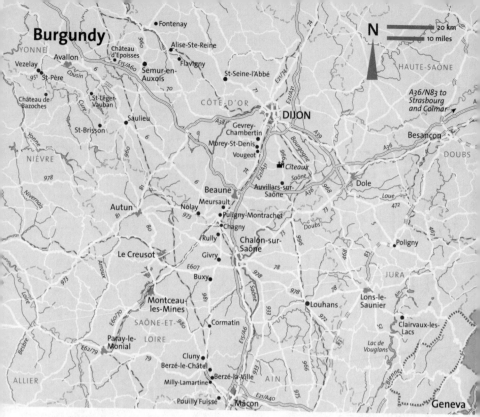

Mustard is the taste most people will have had of Dijon before visiting the capital of Burgundy. They may also associate the name with the finest wines of Bourgogne (the French name for the region), as the fabled Côte d'Or wine route runs south from the city. They'll probably be familiar with the intense blackcurrant liqueur produced locally, Crème de Cassis, often mixed with white wine to make the drink nicknamed Kir, after a one-time mayor of Dijon. But first-time visitors may be thrilled to see that the culinary even extends to the architecture in this splendid Burgundian town. One of its greatest attractions is its façades weighed down with fruit garlands, in stone. They adorn courtyards still crying out for the gilded carriage to come back into fashion, not cheap air flights. The sumptuous Ancien Régime mansions of Dijon play as much of a starring role in the old city as its major medieval monuments, its churches and its museums. These museums cover not just Dijonnais but also Burgundian archaeology and history, fine arts and popular traditions...and of course Flemish art, as Flanders belonged to the Burgundian Valois dukes.

In the 14th and 15th centuries, these formidably powerful men, difficult and dangerous cousins of the kings of France, grabbed hold of Flanders and Holland, as well as portions of northern France. The ultra-ambitious ducal line began with Philippe le Hardi (the Bold, 1342–1404), fourth son of King Jean II of France, who married Marguerite of Flanders in 1369 and so inherited lucrative Flemish domains. He was followed by Jean sans Peur (the Fearless, 1371–1419), who infamously opposed mad King Charles VI's brother, Louis d'Orléans, eventually having him assassinated, only to be murdered in his turn. Then came Philippe le Bon (the Good, 1396–1467), the badly named, as he proved a ruthless ruler and endlessly switched sides between the English and the French in the Hundred Years' War. He acquired Holland, becoming one of the richest and most powerful rulers in western Europe. His son, Charles le Téméraire (the Bold, 1433–1477), brought the line to an end with his vain ambitions to recreate the greater Burgundy of the Dark Ages, stretching from the North Sea to the Mediterranean; he was killed fighting over the region of Lorraine.

As well as wine, little present-day Burgundy is renowned for its extraordinary religious legacy. The region became the powerhouse of medieval monasticism – Cluny, with the largest church in Europe until St Peter's in Rome was built, Cîteaux, headquarters of the sober Cistercians, and pilgrimage Vézelay, built on the supposed bones of Mary Magdalene, were of major significance in European medieval history. In parts, it seems every Burgundian wooded hill is topped by a church; a few also have a château. Then there are Burgundy's great Roman remains, including Alésia, where, as *Astérix* readers may recall, the Gauls were crushed once and for all by Caesar.

Northeast of Burgundy, the red sandstone range of the Vosges mountains divides Alsace from Lorraine, and from the rest of France. Utterly cute, this tiny region is quite unlike any other in France, sweeping down from the Vosges to the Rhine, looking across to Germany's Black Forest mountains. So well-ordered, so full of big cakes, coffee houses and *choucroute*, Alsace feels very Germanic, but the Alsatians don't wish to be considered German, despite the ring of their names and the old German dialect. Goethe, that great symbol of German culture, studied for a time in Strasbourg, the gorgeous red-stoned and timberframe capital, not just of Alsace nowadays – the place is also joint-capital of the European Union today. But the EU parliament building doesn't stand in the centre, which is dominated by the vast red cathedral, one of the most staggering examples of Gothic architecture and a landmark in central Alsace. Even the huge Ancien Régime palace of the decadently *bon vivant* cardinals of Rohan is quite dwarfed by the medieval giant. The irresistible old city spreads out across the rest of the island on the Ill river at the heart of Strasbourg. The town has one of the largest ports in France, by the Rhine, but the historic centre is so packed with riches, including splendid art museums, that visitors rarely notice.

Dijon

Some books claim that Dijon was a place of only minor significance until medieval times. However, the tentative roots go far back, with a Gallo-Roman centre called Divio, and early Christian activity traced to a semi-legendary martyr called Bénigne, who died pierced by a multitude of sharp weapons. Dijon features in some high drama in Gregory of Tours' 6th-century *The History of the Franks*, described as a place with no less than 33 towers, and watermills outside with wheels turning at wondrous speed – he also noted that the place produced excellent wine even back then.

Late in the 10th century, the brilliant Italian William of Volpiano was sent to Dijon to reform the abbey of St-Bénigne. Then came the period when Burgundy was ruled by

Capetian Burgundian dukes, but they preferred Beaune as their capital. The Valois who followed turned the centre of Dijon into a spectacular place. But much of the architectural legacy you see today dates from after their time, when Dijon became the seat of one of the Ancien Régime's regional Parlements, or law courts. The town only became a city with a bishop in the 18th century. Then the construction of the railways in the mid-19th century encouraged industries to grow in the outskirts. But we ignore them here; Dijon has too many artistic and culinary distractions at its heart.

Place St-Bénigne and Around

The imposing medieval church dedicated to St Bénigne has been a cathedral only since 1731. Virtually nothing remains of the 11th-century original, except the **crypt** (*small fee*) which is damp and badly restored, but still in some ways more atmospheric than the building above. Among the maze of underground chapels stands the base of a rotunda, said originally to have had three storeys. Some of the capitals show bizarre to barbaric primitive Carolingian figures. The vast Gothic building above was begun around 1280. After the typically colourful Burgundian tiled roofs outside, the wide interior looks extremely sober, although the shift from the pink-tinged stone of the nave to the golden-orange stone of the choir is striking. A few Ancien Régime embellishments add visual interest, including statues on the columns, some elaborate tombs in the side aisles, and a wild baptismal font.

Housed in an impressive wing of the medieval abbey next to the cathedral is Dijon's **archeological museum** (*open June–Sept daily exc Tues 10–8; rest of year daily exc Tues 9–12 and 2–6; adm*). The prehistoric finds include glittering pieces of jewellery, most spectacularly the Blanot treasure, very flashy Bronze Age high-fashion belly jewellery.

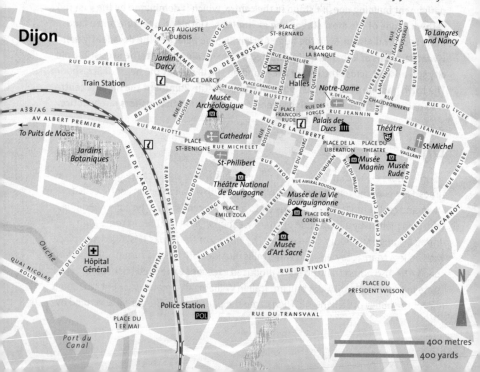

The Gallo-Roman collections feature votive offerings to Sequana, goddess of the Seine, whose source rises in northern Burgundy. The medieval pieces prove the most beautiful of all, with agonizing representations of St Bénigne in particular.

The Palais des Ducs and Around

The **Palais des Ducs**, with its copies of classical arms on top, looks more than a little pompous. The bulk of what you see was in fact built long after the Valois dukes had disappeared. But the tall watchtower looming over the palace is a remnant from the time of Philippe le Bon. With Burgundy's absorption into the French kingdom under Louis XI at the end of the 15th century, the palace became the Logis du Roi. It was reshaped in the late 17th century by Jules Hardouin-Mansart and Martin de Joinville. It now holds the **town hall** and the enormous **Musée des Beaux-Arts** (*open daily exc Tues 10–6; adm*). Before the art, look inside the ducal kitchen, its six monumental fire-places giving an indication of the scale of catering demanded. The ducal chapel has vanished, but the chapterhouse has survived, and contains fabulous Burgundian statuary and religious items, including the filigree crozier for Robert de Molesmes, founder of the Cistercian order, and ascetic St Bernard's shockingly silver-gilded porringer, plus Philippe le Hardi's gorgeous funerary crown.

The museum's most famous pieces lie in the **Salle des Gardes**: the brilliantly carved tombs of the dukes of Burgundy, especially Claus Sluter of Haarlem's magnificent one for Philippe le Hardi. One of the finest of all medieval sculptors, Sluter also trained his brilliant nephew Claus de Werve. The master carved most of the mourning monks, known as *pleurants*, around the base of the tomb; his pupil completed the collection. The tomb of Jean sans Peur and his wife Marguerite of Bavaria by Spaniard Juan de la Huerta and Antoine Le Moiturier of Avignon copied the style of the first tomb. Stupendous retables made for the ducal charterhouse by the Flemish artists Melchior Broederlam of Ypres and Jacques de Baerze decorate the walls, along with tapestries, one depicting an infamous siege of Dijon in 1513, and the town's Virgin protectoress.

Among the museums's other delights is a room devoted to Flemish painters, with a famed Nativity scene by Robert Campin or the Master of Flémalle. The riches continue in the Dutch, German, Swiss, Italian and French late-Gothic and Ancien Régime collections, but the 19th- and 20th-century collections prove a bit disappointing apart from some Delacroix drawings. Local artists feature around the museum. Look out for pieces by the sculptors Sambin and Dubois, and the artists Quantin, Gilles and Dubois in the Ancien Régime collections. A few pieces by the monumental 19th-century Dijonnais sculptor François Rude stand out here and there, while the smooth Burgundian animal sculptor Pompon is awarded a room of his own.

Dijon's grand quarter just north of the Palais des Ducs contains truly spectacular mansions. **Rue des Forges** boasts some of the very finest. The **Maison Maillard**, built from the second half of the 16th century for one of Dijon's mayors, wins the prize for most overdressed house, the façade groaning under a bumper crop of garlands. Nearby, three rows of hefty gargoyles, with floral decoration stuffed between their contorted figures, decorate the spectacular Gothic church of **Notre-Dame**, which more than holds its own among all the neighbourhood's excesses. The portal

Getting to Dijon

Buzz (*see* p.6) flies from London Stansted.

Getting from the Airport

Dijon-Bourgogne **airport** (**t** 03 80 67 67 67, **f** 03 80 63 02 99, *www.dijon.cci.fr*) is 6km southeast of town at Longvic. A **shuttle bus** serves Buzz flights. For a **taxi** (should cost under €20), **t** 03 80 41 41 12, **f** 03 80 30 93 39.

Getting Around

Car Hire

Ask the companies in central Dijon if they can organize a car at the airport: **Avis, t** 03 80 42 05 90; **Budget, t** 03 80 43 86 49; **Europcar, t** 08 03 02 14 03; **Hertz, t** 03 80 53 14 00.

Tourist Information

Dijon: 34 Rue des Forges, **t** 03 80 44 11 44, **f** 03 80 30 90 02, *www.ot-dijon.fr*, *infotourisme@ot-dijon.fr*. There's also a branch on Place Darcy, open through lunch. You can buy a 24hr, 48hr or 72hr '*Dijon à la Carte*' card, which gives you savings if you visit many sites and use local town buses.

Market Day

Place du Marché: Tues am, Fri am and Sat am.

Shopping

Rue de la Liberté is the main shopping street in the centre. As well as shops selling clothes and household items, look out for Pâtisserie Vannier, one of the very finest in town, and Maille, a household name in France for mustard, here with varieties flavoured with Burgundy wine, marc, or even cassis. Boutiques spread into the streets off Rue de la Liberté. **Place de la Libération** has upmarket food and wine stores. See also **Les Halles** covered market for culinary specialities. For antiques look at **Rue Verrerie** and **Rue Comte**.

Where to Stay and Eat

Dijon ✉ 21000

The hotels often have the best restaurants. ★★★★**Hostellerie du Chapeau Rouge**, 5 Rue Michelet, **t** 03 80 50 88 88, **f** 03 80 50 88 89, *www.bourgogne.net/chapeaurouge* (*expensive*). Good hotel with old stone façade on the edge of the historic heart of Dijon, with exquisite cuisine (*expensive*).

---

sculptures were unfortunately hacked to bits, but the plethora of stone carvings above remain. Green *jacquemarts*, or bell-strikers, add a carnival touch to the bell tower. Inside, the church has been greyly restored, but seek out vestiges of frescoes and medieval glass.

The streets north and east of Notre-Dame have more fabulous town houses; along Rue de la Chouette, the **Hôtel de Vogüé** vies with the Maison Maillard for the accolade of finest in town. It exudes refinement, its pink-stoned arch leading into an exquisite courtyard embellished with enchanting carvings. Rue Jeannin, Rue Verrerie, Rue Chaudronnerie, Rue Lamannoye, Rue Jean-Jacques Rousseau and Rue Vannerie contain more wonderful buildings.

To the south of the Palais des Ducs, the charming semicircular **Place de la Libération** is the most elegant place to shop. Hidden just off it down Rue des Bons Enfants, the **Musée Magnin** (*open daily Tues–Sun 10–12 and 2–6; adm*) lets you enter one of Dijon's great houses without an invitation to dinner. It's crammed full of minor works of art, a curious mixture of the religious, the homely and the erotic, collected in the late 19th century and early 20th century by Maurice Magnin and his sister Jeanne.

★★★★**Sofitel La Cloche**, 14 Place Darcy, **t** 03 80 30 12 32, **f** 03 80 30 04 15, *www.hotel-lacloche.com* (*expensive*). Fine hotel with excellent restaurant (*open pm; moderate*).

★★★**Hôtel Wilson**, 1 Rue de Longvic, **t** 03 80 66 82 50, **f** 03 80 36 41 54, *hotelwilson@wanadoo.fr* (*moderate*). Comfortable rooms set around a charming little courtyard, part of a 17th-century posting inn. No restaurant.

★★★**Hôtel du Nord**, Place Darcy, **t** 03 80 50 80 50, **f** 03 80 50 80 51, *www.bourgogne.net/hotelnord* (*moderate*). Central, a bit dull on the outside, but with well-equipped rooms, a fine restaurant, La Porte Guillaume (*moderate*), and a cellar for Burgundy wine-tastings.

★★★**Philippe Le Bon**, 18 Rue Ste-Anne, **t** 03 80 30 73 52, **f** 03 80 30 95 51 (*moderate*). Doesn't quite make the grade of a charming hotel, but not bad, and the restaurant with outdoor summer space serves good food.

★★**Ibis Central**, 3 Place Grangier, **t** 03 80 30 44 00, **f** 03 80 41 69 48 (*inexpensive*). Pretty good standard, and the Rôtisserie restaurant is appreciated by Dijonnais. *Closed Sun.*

★★**Le Jacquemart**, 32 Rue Verrerie, **t** 03 80 60 09 60, **f** 03 80 60 09 69 (*inexpensive*). Utterly delightful, well-run, old-style but stylish hotel in the centre of town.

★★**Le Sauvage**, 64 Rue Monge, **t** 03 80 41 31 21, **f** 03 80 42 06 07, *hotel-le-sauvage.com* (*inexpensive*). Lovely former posting inn, with timberframe walls and courtyard; practical for parking.

★★**Hôtel du Palais**, 23 Rue du Palais, **t** 03 80 67 16 26, **f** 03 80 65 12 16 (*inexpensive*). Lovely hotel in an 18th-century limestone building, well located in the centre of the city.

★★**Le Chambellan**, 92 Rue de la Vannerie, **t** 03 80 67 12 67, **f** 03 80 38 00 39 (*inexpensive*). Hotel in another historic house close to the theatre.

Hôtel Lamartine, 12 Rue Jules Mercier, **t** 03 80 30 37 47, **f** 03 80 30 04 43 (*inexpensive*). Well located but basic.

Le Pré aux Clercs, 13 Place de la Libération, **t** 03 80 38 05 05 (*expensive*). Splendid restaurant in excellent location. *Closed Sun pm, Mon.*

Stéphane Derbord, 10 Place Wilson, **t** 03 80 67 74 64, **f** 03 80 63 87 72 (*expensive–moderate*). Top class Burgundian cuisine and wines. *Closed Sun pm, Mon lunch and Tues lunch.*

Au Moulin à Vent, 8 Place François Rude, **t** 03 80 30 81 43 (*moderate*). Typical Burgundian cuisine served in fine timber-frame house, in friendly, lively atmosphere. *Closed Sun pm and Mon.*

Coum'Chez Eux, 68 Rue Jean-Jacques Rousseau, **t** 03 80 73 56 87, **f** 03 80 73 34 45 (*moderate*). Specialities from Burgundy's central Morvan hills in this rustic restaurant. *Closed Sun.*

Just to the east, the 19th-century sculptor François Rude has been given his own museum, the **Musée Rude** (*open June–Sept Wed–Mon 10–12 and 2–5.45; closed Tues; adm*), in the converted church of St-Etienne. Highlight of the collection is the lifesize plaster of this melodramatic sculptor's celebrated work for Paris' Arc de Triomphe, depicting the bellicose Revolutionary volunteers heading off to battle. On the same square stands the classical **theatre**. Beyond, the virtuoso façade of the church of **St-Michel** makes a grand Renaissance song and dance at the end of Rue Vaillant. In the centre, the Christ of the Last Judgement appears like an over-enthusiastic conductor who has turned up for a last night of the Proms in a toga.

Two lesser-known museums stand next to each other down Rue Ste-Anne. The **Musée d'Art Sacré** (*open Wed–Mon 9–12 and 2–6; closed Tues; adm*) occupies the domed circular church of the Bernardines, a dramatic setting for a whole mix of absorbing religious works. The **Musée de la Vie Bourguignonne** (*open Wed–Mon 9–12 and 2–6; closed Tues; adm*) has taken over other buildings of the former convent, set around a rose-clad classical cloister. The rambling collection includes 19th-century Burgundian costumes and interiors, recreated old shops and rather lifeless if worthy displays on local artists, crafts and produce.

The Valois dukes' burial charterhouse was built west of the city. The sorry remnants stand among the sprawling buildings of a **psychiatric hospital** (1km west of Place Darcy) but they include some of the finest statues to be have survived from Gothic Europe, adorning the so-called **Puits de Moïse** (or Moses Well), in fact a calvary. These astonishingly forceful figures of Old Testament prophets were once again the work of that genius Claus Sluter. Also out on the western side of town, the **Musée Amora** or **Musée de la Moutarde**, 48 Quai Nicolas Rolin (*guided tours mid-June–mid-Sept daily exc Sun at 3pm only; adm*) gives you the story of mustard-making in Dijon, the recipe apparently invented by the son of a Roman prefect of Gaul back in the 4th century.

Day Trip from Dijon

Beaune

Crammed with wine cellars and wine-lovers, Beaune looks as if it has sold its soul to Bacchus. It is the main centre for marketing the great wines of Burgundy. These have benefited from rich foreign buyers who have pushed the prices to obscene levels. But Beaune also has the celebrated and secretive charitable foundation, the **Hospices de Beaune** (*open late Mar–late Nov daily 9–6.30; rest of year daily 9–11.30 and 2–5.30; adm*), proprietor of a large number of the best vineyards, their produce auctioned off at vast prices each November for the benefit of many of the town's inhabitants.

The original hospices buildings were commissioned by the massively wealthy Nicolas Rolin and his wife after the local population had suffered poverty, famine and disease in the wake of the Hundred Years' War. It was meant initially to accommodate the poor, to be cared for by religious sisters. Begun in 1443, it was probably designed by a Flemish architect, Jehan Wiescrère. Its reputation grew rapidly so that merchants and nobles also came to be treated here. It served as a hospital right up until 1971, when it was turned into a museum, devoted mainly to hospitals in medieval times – these were involved as much with treating the soul as the body. Typically, wondrous works of art were commissioned for the place.

Inside the courtyard, the building is highly decorated: the famed coloured tiles form complex diamond patterns on the roofs; ornate pinnacles rise from the dormers; carved angels glide down from the gables, their feet hanging comically in the air. Inside, the enormous paupers' ward looks extremely impressive with its neat, crimson-covered beds. The carvings on the ceiling may represent leading figures in 15th-century Beaune. The chapel at one end was always an integral part of the paupers' ward, where **Van der Weyden's polyptych** originally stood. This sublime work now takes pride of place in a separate room. On the outer panels the donors look deeply miserable; Nicolas Rolin holds his helmet, a red-faced angel blowing its trumpet by his side. An Annunciation scene is depicted above, the text of the Virgin's book beautifully illustrated – just one example of the artist's amazing attention to detail. The breathtaking main scene depicts the Christ of the Last Judgement sitting on a rainbow, like a poised gymnast, holding the lily, symbol of purity, and the sword, symbol of punishment. Magnificent purple-clad angels blow their trumpets to either

Getting There

Dijon has regular **train** services to Beaune.

Tourist Information

Beaune ✉ **21200**: 1 Rue de l'Hôtel Dieu, **t** 03 80 26 21 30, **f** 03 80 26 21 39, *www.ot-beaune.fr*. **Safari-Tours**, run via the Beaune tourist office, offer a good if pricey introduction (in English) to selected vineyards.

Market Day

Halles de Beaune: Wed am and Sat am.

Shopping

There are numerous specialized wine merchants' houses or *négociants* you can visit, for a small fee. They invariably have impressive cellars.
Caves Patriache Père et Fils, 7 Rue du Collège, **t** 03 80 24 53 78. Boasts the largest medieval cellars in town.

For a more exclusive tasting, ask at the tourist office about fixing a visit to a small-scale merchant house, which will expect you to be serious about buying.
Maison Champy, 5 Rue du Grenier à Sel, **t** 03 80 24 97 30. Claims to be the oldest of the great Burgundy wine companies, founded back in 1720. It has recently been taken over by a dynamic new team of experts.
Denis Perret, on Place Carnot. An excellent wine shop representing some of the really top-class Burgundy *négociants* at quite competitive prices.

Le Tast' Fromage. Sells superlative Burgundian cheeses, including Epoisses, Chambertin, Cîteaux, and more.

Eating Out

★★★★Le Cep, 27 Rue Maufoux, **t** 03 80 22 35 48, **f** 03 80 22 76 80 (*expensive*). A Renaissance town house in an arcaded courtyard. Attached to it, **Bernard Morillon**, **t** 03 80 24 12 06, has a splendid old dining room for classic Burgundian cuisine. *Closed Mon and Tues lunch.*
★★★Central, 2 Victor Millot, **t** 03 80 24 77 24, **f** 03 80 22 30 40 (*moderate*). A satisfying address, both for its central location, its good-value, comfortable rooms and its original cuisine in the **Cheval Blanc**, **t** 03 80 24 69 70.
★★★Grillon, 21 Rte de Seurre, **t** 03 80 22 44 25, **f** 03 80 24 94 89 (*inexpensive*). In a substantial town house, charming and reasonably priced. In the garden, a striking building houses **Le Verger**, a lovingly run restaurant. *Closed Tues, and Wed lunch.*
La Ciboulette, 69 Rue Lorraine, **t** 03 80 24 70 72 (*inexpensive*). The décor may be basic, but the food is satisfyingly tasty and not overpriced by Burgundy standards.
Ma Cuisine, Passage Ste-Hélène, **t** 03 80 22 30 22 (*moderate–cheap*). A husband and wife team run this bright little restaurant. From your table you may be able see the wife preparing Burgundy favourites with great dexterity in the kitchen. *Closed Sat and Sun.*

side. Below, the androgynous St Michael with his piercing gaze and brilliant peacock-coloured wings weighs souls. To the left, the Virgin, apostles and saints pray to Christ. To the right John the Baptist is accompanied by further apostles and female saints.

Elsewhere in Beaune, the Romanesque **Notre-Dame** contains some great late-Gothic art treasures including a series of tapestries depicting the life of the Virgin. The **Musée des Beaux-Arts** (*open April–Oct daily 2–6; adm*) presents lesser Flemish works of art and scenes by the local 19th-century painter Félix Ziem. The rather wooden **Musée du Vin de Bourgogne** (*open daily 9.30–6; Dec–Mar closed Tues; adm*) occupies a property once owned by the dukes of Burgundy. Even better, go tasting in one of the fabulous cellars in the underground city below Beaune's streets.

Touring from Dijon

You'll find that the sights are reliably open Easter–Oct 10–12 and 2–5 at least, unless otherwise stated, and charge adm.

Day 1: To the Sources of Gaul

Morning: Head northwest from Dijon for **St-Seine-l'Abbaye**. The source of the Seine rises to the north. This tranquil wooded corner, owned by the city of Paris, was turned into a curiously urban-looking park in the mid-19th century, with a sizeable statue of the river goddess Sequana. Fortified hilltop **Flavigny** nearby starred in the film of the bestseller *Chocolat*, but the air is actually scented with aniseed, from the sweets made here in the abbey of St-Pierre.

Lunch: Just west, along Alise-Ste-Reine's challengingly narrow main street, the **Auberge du Cheval Blanc**, t 03 80 96 01 55 (*moderate*) offers refined Burgundian cuisine. *Closed Mon*. **Hôtel Alésia**, t 03 80 96 19 67 (*cheap*) proposes simpler regional fare, plus oriental dishes outside the main summer season.

Afternoon: Unfussily quaint, **Alise-Ste-Reine** clings to the side of Mont Auxois, the hill where the Gauls, under their dashing commander Vercingétorix, were defeated once and for all by Caesar. There's a small museum in the village and an archaeological site above. Nearby, at the **Château de Bussy-Rabutin**, witty guides lead you round this exquisitely acerbic castle, decorated for a charismatic 17th-century court rake.

Dinner and sleeping: West, in historic Semuren-Auxois, there's 18th-century **Les Cymaises**, 7 Rue de Renaudot, t 03 80 97 21 44, f 03 80 97 18 23 (*moderate*), or the former coaching inn **La Côte d'Or**, 3 Place Gaveau, t 03 80 97 03 13, f 03 80 97 29 83 (*moderate*). Rustic restaurant **Le Calibressan**, t 03 80 97 32 40 (*moderate*) is a curiosity, with Madame's Californian roots adding original touches to the chef's fine French credentials.

Day 2: Pilgrimage to Vezelay

Morning: **Fontenay**, one of the best-preserved abbeys of the sober, hard-working, hard-praying Cistercian monks, stands pretty well complete, if empty, outside Montbard, north of Semur. The abbey has been declared a UNESCO World Heritage Site.

Lunch: Head on west to Avallon. In the centre, the excellently renovated 18th-century posting inn ★★★★**Hostellerie de la Poste**, t 03 86 34 16 16 (*expensive*) has a swish restaurant. *Closed Sun pm and Mon*. **Le Relais des Gourmets**, t 03 86 34 18 90 (*expensive–moderate*) features fish dishes as well as Burgundian specialities.

Afternoon: The small ramparted hilltop town of **Avallon** has charm and monuments aplenty, but is rather eclipsed by its smaller hilltop neighbour **Vézelay**. The supposed relics of Mary Magdalene made Vézelay into one of the greatest pilgrimage stops in medieval Europe. The enormous church crowning the hilltop was one of the very finest Romanesque buildings ever conceived. Infamously, that fanatical 12th-century Christian fanatic, St Bernard, set the western world alight here preaching for the disastrous Second Crusade in 1146.

Dinner and sleeping: At St-Père-sous-Vézelay, swanky ★★★**L'Espérance**, t 03 86 33 39 10, f 03 86 33 26 15 (*luxury–expensive*) is a Mecca for food-lovers, but you'll have to pay a high price for your gluttony. It has posh rooms too. Up in the heart of Vézelay, ★★★**Le Pontot**, Place du Pontot, t 03 86 33 24 40, f 03 86 33 30 05 (*expensive*) exudes charm from every stone, but is pricey and oversubscribed. Lower down, at the busy village entrance, ★★★**La Poste**, t 03 86 33 21 23, f 03 86 32 30 92 (*moderate*) and ★★**Le Relais du Morvan**, t 03 86 33 25 33, f 03 86 33 36 98 (*inexpensive*) are comfortable, if crowded, and have restaurants.

Day 3: The Morvan Hills

Morning: The splendidly restored medieval **Château de Bazoches** surveys Vézelay from the northern slopes of the **Morvan hills**. This great castle preserves the memory of the 17th-century military genius and local boy Vauban, who acquired it from the reward Louis XIV gave to him for his successful siege of Maastricht in 1672. Take a country route east, for example via **Quarve-les-Tombes**, **St-Léger-Vauban** and the **Lac de St-Aignan**, through the Morvan to reach **Saulieu**.

Lunch: Saulieu is best known for celebrity chef Bernard Loiseau's melodramatic ★★★★**La Côte d'Or**, 2 Rue d'Argentine, t 03 80 90 53 53,

f 03 80 64 08 92 (*expensive*). There are several more affordable options along this busy road; you might try the menus at ★★★**La Poste**, **t** 03 80 64 05 67 (*moderate*).

Afternoon: Saulieu's medieval Basilique St-Andoche contains some memorable animal imagery, as does the Musée Pompon, whose ultra-polished creatures are a far cry from the works of his teacher, Rodin. A short way west of Saulieu, the Maison du Parc at **St-Brisson** (*open June–mid-Sept daily exc Fri; rest of period Easter–early Oct weekends and public hols only*) offers ideas for pottering in the Morvan.

Dinner and sleeping: Head east for dinner and a hotel on the Burgundy wine route. Gevrey-Chambertin boasts legendary *luxury* restaurants like **Les Millésimes**, 25 Rue de l'Eglise, **t** 03 80 51 84 24, or the **Rôtisserie du Chambertin**, Rue du Chambertin, **t** 03 80 34 33 20. ★★**Aux Vendanges de Bourgogne**, Rte des Grands Crus, **t** 03 80 34 30 24, **f** 03 80 58 55 44 (*expensive*) has a down-to-earth restaurant offering well-chosen wines. For better accommodation try either arty ★★★**Arts et Terroirs**, 28 Route de Dijon, **t** 03 80 34 30 76, **f** 03 80 34 11 79 (*moderate*), or ★★★**Les Grands Crus**, Route des Grands Crus, **t** 03 80 34 34 15, **f** 03 80 51 89 07 (*moderate*), modern but very comfortable, set among the vineyards.

Day 4: Côte de Nuits Wine Route

Morning: Discover the delightful string of wine villages south of Dijon. Wine-making was really developed in these parts by medieval monks, as you'll discover on a tour of the magnificent **Château du Clos-Vougeot**. If you're in search of a more spiritual experience, visit the vestiges of the once mighty **Abbaye de Cîteaux** (*open mid-May–mid-Oct daily exc Tues*), headquarters of the strict Cistercian monastic order, on the flat across the Saône from Nuits-St-George.

Lunch: At Morey-St-Denis (north of Vougeot) the walled manor of ★★★**Castel de Très Girard**, **t** 03 80 34 33 09 (*expensive*) offers a calm retreat among the vines – the wines are very pricey. *Closed Sat lunch.* South of Cîteaux at Auvillars, the **Auberge de l'Abbaye**, **t** 03 80 26 97 37 (*moderate*) provides good fare in an appealing setting. *Closed Wed lunch.*

Afternoon: Wine-crazed **Beaune** is covered on pp.360–61. To the south of it lie some of the most superlative wine-making villages in France. For those needing a break from wine, visit down-at-heel but colourfully tiled **Château de Rochepot** (*closed Tues*), standing out on its hillside, or the slightly tatty but appealing village of **Nolay**.

Dinner and sleeping: At the celebrated wine village of Meursault south of Beaune, sample well-prepared Burgundian classics at **Le Relais de la Diligence**, **t** 03 80 21 21 32, then stay in the lovely manor of **Les Magnolias**, **t** 03 80 21 23 23, **f** 03 80 21 29 10 (*expensive–moderate*). Or, south at Puligny-Montrachet, ★★★**Le Montrachet**, **t** 03 80 21 30 06, **f** 03 80 21 39 06 (*expensive*) may have unexciting rooms, but the restaurant is very special. For cheaper options in Nolay, contact the tourist office, **t/f** 03 80 21 80 73.

Day 5: Mixing Châteaux with Wine

Morning: Follow the D981 south from Chagny to the Côte Chalonnaise wine towns of **Rully**, **Mercurey** and **Givry**, where standards are high but prices lower than the Côte d'Or.

Lunch: The town of Buxy has the tempting **Aux Années Vin**, **t** 03 85 92 15 76 (*inexpensive*), which doubles as a wine shop. *Closed Tues and Wed.* In Chalon-sur-Saône, stop at the bargain ★★★**St-Georges**, 32 Av Jean Jaurès, **t** 03 85 90 80 50 (*moderate*), which has a highly reputed restaurant plus a cheaper brasserie. *Closed Sat lunch.*

Afternoon: Further south along the D981 are the glittering chambers of playful **Château de Cormatin** and the remains of the important abbey of **Cluny**. Gorgeous villages lie off the N79: choose from **Berzé-le-Châtel**, **Milly** and **Pierreclos**.

Dinner and sleeping: Go back to medieval times at the ★★★★**Château d'Igé** east of Cluny, **t** 03 85 33 33 99, **f** 03 85 33 41 41 (*expensive*). Some rooms are vaulted. Cheaper delights include ★★**Le Relais du Mâconnais**, La Croix Blanche, 2km from Berzé-la-Ville, **t** 03 85 36 60 72 (*inexpensive*) with charming rooms and a sensational restaurant (*expensive*). Cluny also has a wide selection of hotels and restaurants – check with the tourist office on **t** 03 85 54 05 34.

Strasbourg

Strasbourg is Alsace's answer to Paris, with its gorgeous historic centre set on an island on the Ill, and its cathedral one of the glories of European Gothic. Strasbourg of course also has its own little parliament, that of the European Union; when the EU parliament is sitting, members move into town with their retinues, adding to the flocks of businessmen, students and tourists.

Strasbourg grew up as a port on the west bank of the Rhine, and was also a place where culture and intellectual advances often thrived. A lot is made of Gutenberg's years here working on the invention of the printing press, and the city attracted some of the major figures of the Reformation: von Kaysersberg, Bucer and Calvin. The university opened in 1566; one of its most famous students was Goethe, who studied here from 1770 to 1771. In the late 17th century, Strasbourg became part of France along with the rest of Alsace, and it was an aristocratic French family, the Rohans, who most left their mark on the city in the 18th century. Once France had lost the Franco-Prussian War Strasbourg became capital of the annexed territory of Elsass-Lothringen, and only reverted to France at the end of the First World War.

The Cathedral and Around

What an overwhelming skyscraper of a medieval building Strasbourg's **cathedral** is! It was built mainly in the 13th and 14th centuries; the massive Romanesque choir went up first, followed in the mid-13th century by the Gothic nave. The soaring 466ft spire, one of the landmarks of the Rhine Valley, was completed in 1439. The fabulous west façade, designed by Erwin de Steinbach, is one of the greatest in the world. Work began around 1280 but it was not completed until well into the middle of the 14th century, after Erwin's death. The tiny-looking green wings of a row of high-perched angels stand out against the almost uniformly red sandstone façade; the central rose windows are stunning; the gabled doorways are filled with sculpture. Prophets feature in the arches of the central door, with Christ's life told in the tympanum. The right-hand portal contrasts the wise and the foolish virgins above signs of the zodiac. The women of the left-hand portal, representations of the virtues, lance the vices at their feet. Those cavaliers much higher up represent Merovingian, Carolingian and later kings. Apostles stand even higher above the rose window. Climb up to the spire to admire views of Strasbourg's roofs and the Rhine valley.

Inside, splendid stained-glass windows spread their mysterious light down the long nave. In contrast, the choir is lit by a single, small central opening. A startling nest of an organ loft, elaborately gilded, hangs precariously in the nave, while the pulpit is richly carved. The Chapelle Ste-Catherine is lit by gem-like 14th-century glass. The transept beyond is held up by a fabulous central pillar known as the Angels' Pillar or Pillar of the Last Judgement, an exceptional piece of Gothic art with expressive figures of the Evangelists, musical angels, and the Christ of the Last Judgement, his foot on a globe.

Strasbourg

To European Parliament and Parc de l'Orangerie (1km)

N

250 mètres
250 yards

BD DE LA VICTOIRE

QUAI DES PÊCHEURS

RUE DE LA KRUTENAU

RUE DE ZURICH

RUE DU JEU-DE-PAUME

AV DE LA LIBERTÉ

AV DE LA MARSEILLAISE

QUAI ST-ÉTIENNE

RUE DE ZURICH

PLACE DE ZURICH

RUE DES ORPHELINS

PLACE DE LA RÉPUBLIQUE

Église St-Étienne

PLACE ST-ÉTIENNE

RUE DE LA CROIX

RUE DES SOEURS

RUE DES BATELIERS

RUE DE LA 1ÈRE ARMÉE

RUE DES JUIFS

PLACE DU MARCHÉ GUYOT

RUE DES ÉCRIVAINS

QUAI DES BATELIERS

PLACE D'AUSTERLITZ

Hôtel de Ville

RUE DES FRÈRES

RUE BRÛLÉE

RUE DU MAROQUIN

PLACE DU CORBEAU

RUE D'AUSTERLITZ

QUAI STURM

PLACE BROGLIE

Cathedral

Palais Rohan

Musée de l'Oeuvre Notre-Dame

RUE DES BOUCHERS

RUE DU DÔME

RUE DU CHÂTEAU

PLACE DU CHÂTEAU

Musée Alsacien

RUE DE LA FONDERIE

RUE DU TEMPLE NEUF

RUE DU SANGLIER

RUE DE LA OUTRE

RUE DES ORFÈVRES

RUE DU VIEUX MARCHÉ AUX POISSONS

Palais de Justice

QUAI FINKMATT

RUE DE LA NUÉE BLEUE

PLACE GUTENBERG

RUE DU FAUBOURG DE PIERRE

QUAI KELLERMANN

Église St-Pierre-le-Jeune

PLACE DE L'HOMME-DE-FER

RUE DES ARCADES

RUE DES FRANCS-BOURGEOIS

RUE DE LA DIVISION LECLERC

Église St-Thomas

PLACE ST-THOMAS

Église St-Louis

PLACE KLÉBER

RUE STE-HÉLÈNE

RUE DU BOUCLIER

RUE DE LA MONNAIE

FOSSÉ DES TANNEURS

RUE DES DENTELLES

QUAI FINKWILLER

Hôpital Civil

RUE DE SÉBASTOPOL

GRAND RUE

PETITE FRANCE

RUE HUMANN

Les Halles

QUAI KLÉBER

QUAI DE PARIS

RUE DU 22 NOVEMBRE

RUE STE-MARGUERITE

QUAI PETITE FRANCE

RUE DE WASSELONNE

PONTS COUVERTS

Barrage Vauban

Hôtel du Département

RUE DU FAUBOURG DE SAVERNE

BD DU PRÉSIDENT WILSON

QUAI ST-JEAN

QUAI DE TURKEIM

QUAI ALTORFFER

Église St-Pierre-le-Vieux

RUE DU MAIRE-KUSS

RUE DU FAUBOURG NATIONAL

Musée d'Art Moderne et Contemporain

RUE DE MOLSHEIM

Train Station

PLACE DE LA GARE

BD DE METZ

Across the square, the **Musée de l'Œuvre Notre-Dame** (*open Tues–Sat 10–12 and 1.30–6; Sun 10–5; closed Mon; adm*) has dozens of rooms devoted to medieval and Renaissance art – religious art in particular – and lays claim to the oldest known piece of figurative stained glass, the Wissembourg head of Christ, dated to around 1070.

Getting to Strasbourg

Ryanair (*see* p.6) flies from London Stansted.

Getting from the Airport

Strasbourg-Entzheim **airport** (**t** 03 88 64 67 67) lies 15km southwest of the city centre; the airport **shuttle bus** runs to the train station every 15mins Mon–Fri, Sat am and Sun pm, and every 30mins Sat pm/Sun am and costs €4.57. **Taxis** into the centre cost €20–30.

Getting Around

The **train station** is west of the city centre on Place de la Gare. For local **taxis**, call Taxi 13, **t** 03 88 36 13 13.

Car Hire

Avis, Pl de la Gare, **t** 03 88 32 30 44.
Budget, 14 Rue Déserte, **t** 03 88 52 87 52.
Citer, 200 Av Colmar, **t** 03 88 65 87 88.
Hertz, airport and 10 Bd Matz, **t** 03 88 32 57 62.

Tourist Information

Strasbourg: 17 Pl de la Cathédrale, **t** 03 88 52 28 28, **f** 03 88 52 28 29, *www.strasbourg.com*, *info@ot-strasbourg.fr*. There are also offices at Place de la Gare, **t** 03 88 32 51 49, and Pont de l'Europe, **t** 03 88 61 39 23, both closed Sun. You can take a relaxing *vedette* or riverboat cruise around central Strasbourg from the terraces on the riverside of the Palais Rohan.

Market Days

Place Broglie: Wed and Fri 9–5.
Bd de la Marne: food market, Tues/Sat am.
Rue du Vieux-Hôpital: flea market, Wed/Sat.

Shopping

The major shopping streets lie on the **central island**, west of the cathedral quarter, around **Place des Halles**, **Place Gutenberg**, **Rue des Arcades** and **Place Kléber**. The Bookworm, 3 Rue de Pâques, is an English-language bookshop, and Christian Maître Chocolat, 12 Rue de l'Outre, sells traditional-style chocolates, such as pralines, liqueur chocolates, truffles and the Alsatian speciality, chocolate 'chestnuts'.

Where to Stay

Strasbourg ✉ 67000

You should book well ahead if you want to stay in Strasbourg, which is packed out when the European Union Parliament is sitting.

****Régent Contades, 8 Av de la Liberté, **t** 03 88 15 05 05, **f** 03 88 15 05 15, *www.regent-hotels.com* (*luxury–expensive*). Spacious, luxurious hotel with old-fashioned style in an imposing building in the Prussian quarter just east of the central island. No restaurant.

****Régent Petite France, 5 Rue des Moulins, **t** 03 88 76 43 43, **f** 03 88 76 43 76, *www.regent-hotels.com* (*luxury–expensive*). Sister hotel with a contemporary feel in big converted old buildings in the delightful Petite France district. Dull exterior but exciting interior, even more outrageously expensive than its older relative. This one has a restaurant.

***Maison Kammerzell, 16 Place de la Cathédrale, **t** 03 88 32 42 14, **f** 03 88 23 03 92, *www.maison-kammerzell.com* (*expensive*). Near the cathedral, a fabulous many-storeyed timberframe house built in the 15th and 16th centuries, with sumptuous interior decoration. A small number of lovely rooms, but known above all for its restaurant and the *choucroute Baumann*, named after the proud proprietor. *Closed Feb hols*.

***Beaucour, 5 Rue des Bouchers, **t** 03 88 76 72 00, **f** 03 88 76 72 60, *www.hotel-beaucour.com* (*expensive*). Appealing group of timberframe façades just on the south side of the Ill close to the Pont du Corbeau, also owned by Baumann. A bit overdone for

Also in Place du Château, the outrageous bishops' residence, the **Palais Rohan**, was badly damaged in 1944, and the restoration of the ground-floor apartments was only completed in 1980. A trio of major museums is housed within (*all open Wed–Mon 10–12 and 1.30–6; Sun 10–5; closed Tues; adm*). The **Musée Archéologique** down in the

some tastes and very pricey, but the rooms are really luxurious.

★★★**Hôtel Cardinal de Rohans**, 17–19 Rue du Maroquin, **t** 03 88 32 85 11, **f** 03 88 75 65 37, *info@hotel-rohan.com* (*expensive*). Charming, comfortable hotel close to the cathedral. No restaurant,

★★★**Maison Rouge**, 4 Rue des Francs-Bourgeois, **t** 03 88 32 08 60, **f** 03 88 22 43 73, *www.maison-rouge.com*, *Maison.Rouge@wanadoo.fr* (*expensive*). Large, but the rooms have individual style.

★★**Hôtel Suisse**, 24 Rue de la Râpe, **t** 03 88 35 22 11, **f** 03 88 25 74 23, *www.hotel-suisse.com* (*moderate*). Excellent location opposite the cathedral, with a stylish blue façade behind the pavement terraces.

★★**Hôtel de l'Ill**, 8 Rue des Bateliers, **t** 03 88 36 20 01, **f** 03 88 35 30 03 (*inexpensive*). In a great location just south of the main island, close to the church of Ste-Madeleine.

★★**Couvent du Franciscain**, 18 Rue du Faubourg de Pierre, **t** 03 88 32 93 93, **f** 03 88 75 68 46, *www.hotel-franciscain.com* (*inexpensive*). Just north of the main island, good value and reasonable rooms.

Eating Out

Buerehiesel, 4 Parc de l'Orangerie, **t** 03 88 45 56 65, **f** 03 88 61 32 00, *www.buerehiesel.fr* (*luxury*). Absolutely fabulous cuisine in a ridiculously pretty old Alsatian house. *Closed Tues, Wed, Jan and Aug.*

Au Crocodile, 10 Rue de l'Outre, **t** 03 88 32 13 02, **f** 03 88 75 72 01, *www.au-crocodile.com* (*luxury–expensive*). Another starry reputation for superlative light but classic cuisine. *Closed Sun, Mon, July, Xmas and New Year.*

L'Ami Schutz, 1 Ponts-Couverts, **t** 03 88 32 76 98, **f** 03 88 32 38 40 (*expensive*). Strasbourg institution in a medieval setting in Petite France, with a well-located terrace and Alsatian specialities.

Chez Yvonne, 10 Rue du Sanglier, **t** 03 88 32 84 15 (*moderate*). Famous *winstub* near the

cathedral, where regional fare is prepared with perfection. Book. *Closed Sun.*

La Choucrouterie, 20 Rue St-Louis (just south of the main island, opposite the church of St-Thomas), **t** 03 88 36 52 87, *www.choucrouterie.com* (*moderate–cheap*). An extremely popular and lively place to try *choucroute*, in a converted 18th-century posting inn. Musical evenings, especially gypsy bands. *Open till 1am; closed Sun eve and last 3 weeks Aug.*

Le Festin de Lucullus, 18 Rue Ste-Hélène, **t** 03 88 22 40 78 (*moderate–cheap*). Fine fresh cooking near the centre of the main island. *Closed Aug; Sun and Mon.*

Le Café du TNS, 1 Av de la Marseillaise (*cheap*). The National Theatre of Strasbourg café with a striped ceiling and stylish designer furniture, all black and white. Brunch-type breakfasts, fresh sandwiches and exquisite regional dishes. *Open daily 11am–12.30am.*

Opéra Café, Place Broglie, **t** 03 88 22 98 51 (*cheap*). Attractive baroque-style café in the beautiful opera house. Attracts a fashionable, arty crowd. Limited menu available at lunch time. *Open 11am–3am, Sun 2–8pm.*

Entertainment and Nightlife

There are often free concerts in Parc des Contades and Parc de l'Orangerie.

Le Bateau Ivre, Quai des Alpes, **t** 03 88 61 27 17. A spacious, elegant boat, moored on the quay near the city centre, a popular spot for the trendy and fashionable. *Open Thurs–Sun 11pm–4am.*

Café P'ti Max, 4 Place de l'Homme de Fer, **t** 03 88 23 05 00 (*moderate*). A pillar of Strasbourg nightlife, with singers and dinner concerts. *Open 11.30pm–1.30am.*

Les Aviateurs, 12 Rue des Sœurs, **t** 03 88 36 52 69. Stronghold of the eternally attractive Michèle Noth, Strasbourg's night queen. *Open daily 6pm–4am.*

basement covers Alsace culture from 600,000 BC to AD 800. On the ground floor the formal apartments of the **Musée des Art Décoratifs** count among the most ostentatious anywhere, with gilded, stuccoed ceilings and painted allegories. The Salon des Evêques, decorated with images of the virtues, was the games room under the Rohans. The Chambre du Roi, exquisitely gilded, is where Louis XV stayed in 1744, and Marie-Antoinette in 1770. Copies of works by Raphael adorn this room and the Salon d'Assemblée. A whole series of rooms display Strasbourg ceramics. The **Musée des Beaux-Arts** is one of France's great provincial museums. The major European schools are covered, with a wealth of Italian, Flemish and 17th-century French paintings. One of the oldest works is a small Giotto Crucifixion. Botticelli, Piero di Cosimo, Del Sarto and Correggio are all here, but look out too for lesser-known artists such as Barocci and Negretti, and Flemish masterpieces including Rubens' *Resurrected Christ*.

Elsewhere around Strasbourg

The **Musée Alsacien** (*open Wed–Mon 10–12 and 1.30–6; closed Tues; adm*) lies on the southern quay of the Ill. Three substantial houses have been knocked into one to make a rambling museum of popular arts and crafts, a good introduction to traditional life in Alsace. Don't miss the fantastical prophylactic masks.

In the centre of **Place Gutenberg**, the green statue, a 19th-century work by David d'Angers, honours the inventor of the printing press. The Rue des Arcades leads up to **Place Kléber**, which commemorates a more controversial figure. Born in Strasbourg, Jean-Baptiste Kléber is remembered above all as a ruthlessly determined general who fought for the Revolution and then for Napoleon, notably in Egypt, where he was eventually assassinated.

Tourists flock to the line of smaller islands, and the *quartier* which goes by the curious title of **Petite France**. The waterways here reflect some splendid timberframe houses, where millers, tanners and fishermen once lived. The **Barrage Vauban** is a covered walkway, a remnant of the fortifications Vauban planned for the city. From its roof there are great views over Petite France to the cathedral. On the opposite side you also get an excellent view of Strasbourg's slick new modern art museum, a sculpture of a horse calmly perched on its roof. This **Musée d'Art Moderne et Contemporain** (*open Mon and Wed–Sat 10–12 and 1.30–6; Sun 10–5; closed Tues; adm*), opened in November 1998 as the focal point of a whole new quarter. The collection starts in the last decades of the 19th century: there are paintings by Monet, Renoir, Boudin, Emile Bernard, Burne-Jones and Klimt, followed by Vlaminck, Gris and Picasso. A special place is reserved for Jean Arp, born in Strasbourg and a founding figure of the Dada movement. There's space too for contemporary installations and exhibitions.

East and north of the cathedral, **Place du Marché Gayot** is a popular haven of restaurants and cafés. Cross the northern branch of water embracing Strasbourg's central island and the **Place de la République** is dominated by the imposingly pompous German structures of the late 19th century. The Prussian architecture extends outwards to the university and the Orangerie, a park originally designed by Le Nôtre at the end of the 17th century.

The **new European Union Parliament building** was opened in 1999, and has been something of an architectural fiasco. Many important features of the state-of-the-art building would not function at the inauguration, and the colours inside were considered so repellent by those who were going to work there that a great deal of the interior has had to be redecorated. Check with the tourist office if you want to visit the parliament building and see the latest colour scheme.

Day Trip from Strasbourg

Colmar

For the very best timberframe show in Alsace, head for Colmar, Strasbourg's rival as tourist capital of the region. Red-tinged Gothic churches and stupendous Gothic paintings are the main attractions, the Musée d'Unterlinden famously housing Grünewald's harrowing Issenheim altarpiece. One museum is devoted to Bartholdi, the creator of the Statue of Liberty.

Set in the Rhine plain by the Lauch river, Colmar grew up around a Carolingian villa which Charlemagne and his sons visited several times. The prosperous place became a free imperial city in 1226. In the mid-15th century the emperor's representative in Alsace, the Archduke Sigismond, temporarily gave up part of his province to Charles the Bold of Burgundy in exchange for much needed funds. The Burgundian appointed Pierre de Hagenbach to rule Colmar; his cruelty towards the locals was eventually repaid when he had his head chopped off.

Getting There

Colmar is on the frequent **train** line through Alsace from Strasbourg to Mulhouse and Basle. The journey takes c. 30mins.

Tourist Information

Colmar ✉ 68000: 4 Rue des Unterlinden, **t** 03 89 20 68 92, *www.ot-colmar.fr*.

Eating Out

Au Fer Rouge, 52 Grand'Rue, **t** 03 89 41 37 24, **f** 03 89 23 82 24. The finest address for classic regional cuisine (*luxury–expensive*). *Closed Mon, Sun also in Nov, and last 3 weeks Jan.*

****Les Têtes, 19 Rue des Têtes, **t** 03 89 24 43 43, **f** 03 89 24 58 34, *info@la-maison-des-tetes.com* (*expensive*). An unforgettable hotel in an unmissable 17th-century house covered in little figures in the busy centre of town; once a wine exchange. The restaurant (*expensive*) is luxurious. *Restaurant closed Sun eve, Mon, and Tues lunch, and Feb.*

****Romantik Hôtel Le Maréchal, 5 Place des Six-Montagnes-Noires, **t** 03 89 41 60 32, **f** 03 89 24 59 40, *www.hotel-le-marechal.com* (*expensive*). A fabulous timberframe hotel in the Little Venice district. The restaurant (*expensive–moderate*) with its dining room overlooking the water serves exciting regional cuisine.

Le Caveau St-Pierre, 24 Rue de la Herse, **t** 03 89 41 99 33 (*moderate*). Characterful Little Venice restaurant with a terrace by the water, serving good-value Alsatian dishes. *Closed Fri lunch, Sun lunch and Mon.*

Les Tanneurs, 12 Rue des Tanneurs, **t** 03 89 23 72 12 (*moderate*). In the same area, also with a terrace; try trout in riesling sauce. *Closed Wed and Thurs.*

A la Ville de Paris, 4 Place Jeanne d'Arc, **t** 03 89 24 53 15, **f** 03 89 23 65 24 (*moderate*). In a house with a typical timberframe façade. *Closed Mon eve and Tues.*

As you wander round the **Musée d'Unterlinden** (*open April–Oct daily 9–6; rest of year daily Wed–Mon 10–5, closed Tues; adm*) the fountain splashes in the the unkempt cloister garden. The convent was founded in the 13th century and until the Revolution was renowned for its strict rule and a strain of Christian mysticism. It now contains one of the finest collections of Rhenish art in the world.

It is impossible to avoid being shocked into reflection by the greatest piece in the museum, Grünewald's **Issenheim altarpiece**, a complex work, brilliantly displayed in the former convent church. A model shows how the layers of panels were meant to be put together. The outer panels depict a gruesome crucifixion scene. Christ's body is covered with gaping, bleeding sores, his fingers are contorted, rigid with suffering, while a disturbing growth emerges from one of his feet. He wears a heavy crown of thorns and hangs, mutilated and dead, against a black backdrop. The figure of St Sebastian is reckoned by some to be a portrait of the artist. The second layer of painted panels depicts the Annunciation to the Virgin and the resurrected Christ. The temptations of St Anthony, the most disturbing scenes of all, are saved until last.

The **Eglise des Dominicains** (*small fee*), topped by a patterned roof of green diamond tiles, is home to the most famous Virgin in Alsace, Schongauer's *Virgin in the Rose Bower*, with Mary and Jesus against a background trellis of roses teeming with birds. But the painting is utterly dwarfed by the vast Gothic edifice: the church is held up by some of the tallest Gothic columns in France, soaring uninterrupted by capitals to pointed vaults. The first stone was laid in 1283, but the building is essentially 14th- and 15th-century.

Don't miss the concentration of superlative historic houses along the **Rue des Marands** just off the Place de la Cathédrale, especially where it meets Rue Mercière and Rue Schongauer. The **Maison Pfister** boasts wonderful wooden galleries with Renaissance paintings below Old Testament figures, evangelists and symbols of Christian virtues.

The beautiful naked buttocks of Patriotism may entice you into the courtyard of the **Musée Bartholdi** (*open Mar–Nov Wed–Mon 10–12 and 2–6; closed Tues; adm*) at 30 Rue des Marands. This museum occupies the opulent 18th-century house where the sculptor was born in 1834. Many of his works celebrated leading lights in the history of Colmar and Alsace, including General Rapp, a firm-headed Colmarien who served as aide-de-camp to Napoleon. Bartholdi is particularly known as the sculptor of the Statue of Liberty, and the second floor concentrates on its creation. A room on the ground floor is devoted to Jewish history in Colmar.

In **Place de l'Ancienne Douane**, the imposing **Koifhus** was Colmar's late 15th-century customs house and warehouse. The delightful **Place du Marché aux Fruits** is overlooked on one side by the 18th-century **Palais de Justice**. The enormous Gothic **St-Mathieu**, now Protestant, originally served a Franciscan monastery.

South of the Place du Marché aux Fruits, the stunning timberframe houses lead you to the ravishing waterways of Colmar's **Petite Venise**. Take a punt out on the water and watch the tourists peeping between the railings and the façades decorated with colourful hanging baskets.

Language

Everywhere in France the same level of politeness expected: use *monsieur, madame* or *mademoiselle* when speaking to everyone (and never *garçon* in restaurants!), from your first *bonjour* to your last *au revoir*.
For food vocabulary, *see* pp.23–6.

Pronunciation

Vowels
a/à/â between *a* in 'bat' and 'part'
é/er/ez at end of word as *a* in 'plate' but a
   bit shorter
e/è/ê as *e* in 'bet'
e at end of word not pronounced
e at end of syllable or in one-syllable word
   pronounced weakly, like *er* in 'mother'
i as *ee* in 'bee'
o as *o* in 'pot'
ô as *o* in 'go'
u/û between *oo* in 'boot' and *ee* in 'bee'

Vowel Combinations
ai as *a* in 'plate'
aî as *e* in 'bet'
ail as *i* in 'kite'
au/eau as *o* in 'go'
ei as *e* in 'bet'
eu/œu as *er* in 'mother'
oi between *wa* in 'swam' and *wu* in 'swum'
oy as 'why'
ui as *wee* in 'twee'

Nasal Vowels
Vowels followed by an **n** or **m** have a
nasal sound.
an/en as *o* in 'pot' + nasal sound
ain/ein/in as *a* in 'bat' + nasal sound
on as *aw* in 'paw' + nasal sound
un as *u* in 'nut' + nasal sound

Consonants
Many French consonants are pronounced as in English, but there are some exceptions:
c followed by *e, i* or *y*, and *ç* as *s* in 'sit'
c followed by *a, o, u* as *c* in 'cat'
g followed by *e, i* or *y* as *s* in 'pleasure'
g followed by *a, o, u* as *g* in 'good'
gn as *ni* in 'opinion'
j as *s* in 'pleasure'
ll as *y* in 'yes'
qu as *k* in 'kite'
s between vowels as *z* in 'zebra'
s otherwise as *s* in 'sit'
w except in English words as *v* in 'vest'
x at end of word as *s* in 'sit'
x otherwise as *x* in 'six'

Stress
The stress usually falls on the last syllable except when the word ends with an unaccented **e**.

Useful Phrases

hello *bonjour*
good evening *bonsoir*
good night *bonne nuit*
goodbye *au revoir*
please *s'il vous plaît*
thank you (very much) *merci (beaucoup)*
yes *oui*
no *non*
good *bon* (*bonne*)
bad *mauvais*
excuse me *pardon, excusez-moi*
Can you help me? *Pourriez-vous m'aider?*
My name is... *Je m'appelle...*
What is your name? *Comment t'appelles-tu?*
   (informal), *Comment vous appelez-vous?*
   (formal)
How are you? *Comment allez-vous?*
Fine *Ça va bien*
I don't understand *Je ne comprends pas*

I don't know *Je ne sais pas*
Speak more slowly *Pourriez-vous parler plus lentement?*
How do you say ... in French? *Comment dit-on ... en français?*
Help! *Au secours!*

WC *les toilettes*
men *hommes*
ladies *dames* or *femmes*

doctor *le médecin*
hospital *un hôpital*
emergency room *la salle des urgences*
police station *le commissariat de police*

No smoking *Défense de fumer*

Shopping and Sightseeing

Do you have...? *Est-ce que vous avez...?*
I would like... *J'aimerais...*
Where is/are...? *Où est/sont...*
How much is it? *C'est combien?*
It's too expensive *C'est trop cher*

entrance *l'entrée*
exit *la sortie*
open *ouvert*
closed *fermé*
push *poussez*
pull *tirez*

bank *une banque*
money *l'argent*
traveller's cheque *un chèque de voyage*
post office *la poste*
stamp *un timbre*
phone card *une télécarte*
postcard *une carte postale*
public phone *une cabine téléphonique*
Do you have any change? *Avez-vous de la monnaie?*

shop *un magasin*
central food market *les halles*
tobacconist *un tabac*
pharmacy *la pharmacie*
aspirin *l'aspirine*
condoms *les préservatifs*
insect repellent *un produit inséctifuge*
sun cream *la crème solaire*

tampons *les tampons hygiéniques*

beach *la plage*
booking/box office *le bureau de location*
church *l'église*
museum *le musée*
sea *la mer*
theatre *le théâtre*

Accommodation

Do you have a room? *Avez-vous une chambre?*
Can I look at the room? *Puis-je voir la chambre?*
How much is the room per day/week? *C'est combien la chambre par jour/semaine?*
single room *une chambre pour une personne*
twin room *une chambre à deux lits*
double room *une chambre pour deux personnes*
... with a shower/bath *... avec douche/salle de bains*
... for one night/one week *... pour une nuit/une semaine*

bed *un lit*
blanket *une couverture*
cot (child's bed) *un lit d'enfant*
pillow *un oreiller*
soap *du savon*
towel *une serviette*

Transport

I want to go to... *Je voudrais aller à...*
How can I get to...? *Comment puis-je aller à..?*
When is the next...? *Quel est le prochain...?*
What time does it leave (arrive)? *A quelle heure part-il (arrive-t-il)?*
From where does it leave? *D'où part-il?*
Do you stop at...? *Passez-vous par...?*
How long does the trip take? *Combien de temps dure le voyage?*
A (single/return) ticket to... *un aller* or *aller simple/aller et retour) pour...*
How much is the fare? *Combien coûte le billet?*
Have a good trip! *Bon voyage!*

airport *l'aéroport*
aeroplane *l'avion*
berth *la couchette*
bicycle *la bicyclette/le vélo*

mountain bike *le vélo tout terrain, VTT*
bus *l'autobus*
bus stop *l'arrêt d'autobus*
car *la voiture*
coach *l'autocar*
coach station *la gare routière*
flight *le vol*
on foot *à pied*
port *le port*
railway station *la gare*
ship *le bateau*
subway *le métro*
taxi *le taxi*
train *le train*

delayed *en retard*
on time *à l'heure*
platform *le quai*
date-stamp machine *le composteur*
timetable *l'horaire*
left-luggage locker *la consigne automatique*
ticket office *le guichet*
ticket *le billet*
customs *la douane*
seat *la place*

Directions

Where is...? *Où se trouve...?*
left *à gauche*
right *à droite*
straight on *tout droit*
here *ici*
there *là*
close *proche*
far *loin*
forwards *en avant*
backwards *en arrière*
up *en haut*
down *en bas*
corner *le coin*
square *la place*
street *la rue*

Driving

breakdown *la panne*
car *la voiture*
danger *le danger*
driver *le chauffeur*
entrance *l'entrée*
exit *la sortie*

give way/yield *céder le passage*
hire *louer*
(international) driving licence *un permis de conduire (international)*

motorbike/moped *la moto/le vélomoteur*
no parking *stationnement interdit*
petrol (unleaded) *l'essence (sans plomb)*
road *la route*
road works *les travaux*

This doesn't work *Ça ne marche pas*
Is the road good? *Est-ce que la route est bonne?*

Numbers

one *un*
two *deux*
three *trois*
four *quatre*
five *cinq*
six *six*
seven *sept*
eight *huit*
nine *neuf*
ten *dix*
eleven *onze*
twelve *douze*
thirteen *treize*
fourteen *quatorze*
fifteen *quinze*
sixteen *seize*
seventeen *dix-sept*
eighteen *dix-huit*
nineteen *dix-neuf*
twenty *vingt*
twenty-one *vingt et un*
twenty-two *vingt-deux*
thirty *trente*
forty *quarante*
fifty *cinquante*
sixty *soixante*
seventy *soixante-dix*
seventy-one *soixante et onze*
eighty *quatre-vingts*
eighty-one *quatre-vingt-un*
ninety *quatre-vingt-dix*
one hundred *cent*
two hundred *deux cents*
one thousand *mille*

Months

January *janvier*
February *février*
March *mars*
April *avril*
May *mai*
June *juin*
July *juillet*
August *août*
September *septembre*
October *octobre*
November *novembre*
December *décembre*

Days

Monday *lundi*
Tuesday *mardi*
Wednesday *mercredi*
Thursday *jeudi*
Friday *vendredi*
Saturday *samedi*
Sunday *dimanche*

Time

What time is it? *Quelle heure est-il?*
It's 2 o'clock (am/pm) *Il est deux heures (du matin/de l'après-midi)*
... half past 2 *...deux heures et demie*
... a quarter past 2 *...deux heures et quart*
... a quarter to 3 *...trois heures moins le quart*
it is early *il est tôt*
it is late *il est tard*

month *un mois*
week *une semaine*
day *un jour/une journée*
morning *le matin*
afternoon *l'après-midi*
evening *le soir*
night *la nuit*
today *aujourd'hui*
yesterday *hier*
tomorrow *demain*
day before yesterday *avant-hier*
day after tomorrow *après-demain*
soon *bientôt*

Index

Main page references are in **bold**. Page references to maps are in *italics*.